Lecture Notes in Computer Science 4801

Commenced Publication in 1973
Founding and Former Series Editors:
Gerhard Goos, Juris Hartmanis, and Jan van Leeuwen

T0180892

Christine Parent   Klaus-Dieter Schewe
Veda C. Storey   Bernhard Thalheim (Eds.)

Conceptual Modeling – ER 2007

26th International Conference on Conceptual Modeling
Auckland, New Zealand, November 5-9, 2007
Proceedings

 Springer

Volume Editors

Christine Parent
University of Lausanne
1015 Lausanne, Switzerland
E-mail: christine.parent@unil.ch

Klaus-Dieter Schewe
Massey University
Private Bag 11 222, Palmerston North 5301, New Zealand
E-mail: k.d.schewe@massey.ac.nz

Veda C. Storey
Georgia State University
Box 4015, Atlanta, GA 30302, USA
E-mail: vstorey@gsu.edu

Bernhard Thalheim
Christian Albrechts University Kiel
Olshausenstr. 40, 24098 Kiel, Germany
E-mail: thalheim@is.informatik.uni-kiel.de

Library of Congress Control Number: Applied for

CR Subject Classification (1998): H.2, H.4, F.4.1, I.2.4, H.1, J.1, D.2, C.2

LNCS Sublibrary: SL 3 – Information Systems and Application, incl. Internet/Web and HCI

ISSN   0302-9743
ISBN-10   3-540-75562-4 Springer Berlin Heidelberg New York
ISBN-13   978-3-540-75562-3 Springer Berlin Heidelberg New York

Springer is a part of Springer Science+Business Media

springer.com

© Springer-Verlag Berlin Heidelberg 2007
Printed in Germany

Typesetting: Camera-ready by author, data conversion by Scientific Publishing Services, Chennai, India
Printed on acid-free paper   SPIN: 12172535   06/3180   5 4 3 2 1 0

Preface

Conceptual modeling is fundamental to the development of complex systems, because it provides the key communication means between systems developers, end-users and customers. Conceptual modeling provides languages, methods and tools to understand and represent the application domain; to elicitate, conceptualize and formalize system requirements and user needs; to communicate systems designs to all stakeholders; to formally verify and validate system designs on high levels of abstractions; and to minimize ambiguities in system development. Initially, conceptual modeling mainly addressed data-intensive information systems and contributed to data modeling and database application engineering. The area of conceptual modeling has now matured to encompass all kinds of application areas such as e-applications (including e-business and e-learning), web-based systems (including the semantic web and ubiquitous systems), life science and geographic applications.

The annual International Conference on Conceptual Modeling serves as the premiere forum for presenting and discussing research and applications in all areas associated with conceptual modeling. This year, the Call for Papers solicited contributions dealing with logical and philosophical foundations of conceptual modeling, information modeling concepts including ontologies, correctness in modeling, web-based and mobile information systems, semi-structured data and XML, information and database integration, information retrieval, organization and evaluation, design methodologies and tools, reuse, re-engineering and reverse engineering, quality assurance in conceptual modeling, conceptual change and evolution, data warehousing and data mining, spatial and temporal modeling, business process and workflow modeling, knowledge management, requirements elicitation, and advanced applications.

This Call for Papers attracted 167 submissions from authors from 28 countries. Each paper was carefully reviewed by at least three members of the program committee. Finally, the program committee accepted 37 research papers, giving an acceptance rate of 22.2%. This volume contains these papers, presented at the 26th International Conference on Conceptual Modeling (ER 2007), which was held in Auckland, New Zealand, on November 5–8, 2007.

In addition, following a separate Call for Workshops, six workshops were selected as co-located ER-workshops. A total of 43 research papers, including three invited papers, were presented at the workshops. The average acceptance rate for the co-located workshops was 33.3%. The workshop papers have been published in a separate LNCS volume: LNCS 4802. Furthermore, the conference program included 4 systems demonstrations, 1 panel, 6 tutorials, 32 poster presentations, and 3 keynotes.

We are very happy that Profs. Egon Börger from the University of Pisa, Enrico Franconi from the Free University of Bolzano-Bozen, and Peter Hunter from the University of Auckland accepted our invitations to present keynotes to this year's conference.

Prof. Börger gave a presentation on *The Abstract State Machine System Design and Analysis Method: An Illustration by Modeling Workflow Patterns from First Principles*, in which he first surveyed the basic ingredients of the Abstract State Machine method and its applications for the design and the validation of complex computer-based systems, and then illustrated the method by the definition of a small set of parameterized abstract models for workflow patterns.

Prof. Franconi gave a presentation on *Conceptual Schemas and Ontologies for Database Access: Myths and Challenges*, in which he argued that well-founded conceptual modeling and ontology design is required to support intelligent information access, and then demonstrated which are the technical consequences of such choices, and the foundational and computational problems to be faced.

Prof. Hunter gave a presentation on *Heart Modeling, Computational Physiology and the IUPS Physiome Project*, in which he outlined the major goal of the Physiome project to use computational modeling to analyze integrative biological function in terms of underlying structure and molecular mechanisms. He argued for the need to develop supporting XML markup languages (CellML & FieldML) for encoding models, and software tools for creating, visualizing and executing these models, focusing in particular on the development of the Auckland heart model.

Many people contributed to the success of ER 2007. We are most grateful to all keynote speakers, authors of submitted papers, posters, tutorials and panels, and members of the program committees of the main ER conference and its associated workshops. Thanks are due to the chairs of the workshops, tutorials, panels, and posters and demonstrations, and the industry chair: Jean-Luc Hainaut, Elke Rundensteiner, Sven Hartmann, Alberto Laender, John Roddick, Leszek Maciaszek, and John Grundy, whose efforts contributed to the creation of an attractive program at a very high quality level. We would like to express our thanks to the local organizers Gill Dobbie and Patricia Rood and their collaborators, without whom this conference would not have come to life. Thanks are also due to Tok Wang Ling and Steve Liddle, who supported the conference from the steering committee. Finally, we offer our special thanks to our publicity chair and webmaster Markus Kirchberg, who maintained the conference website and the conference reviewing system, took care of all communication with the public, the program committee members and authors, and finally composed this proceedings volume as well as all other documentation associated with the conference.

November 2007

Christine Parent
Klaus-Dieter Schewe
Veda Storey
Bernhard Thalheim

Conference Organization

General Chair

Bernhard Thalheim (Christian-Albrechts-University Kiel, Germany)

Program Committee Co-chairs

Christine Parent (University of Lausanne, Switzerland)
Klaus-Dieter Schewe (Massey University, New Zealand)
Veda C. Storey (Georgia State University, USA)

Organization Chair

Gillian Dobbie (University of Auckland, New Zealand)

Steering Committee Liaison

Tok Wang Ling (National University of Singapore, Singapore)

Publicity Chair

Markus Kirchberg (Massey University, New Zealand)

Workshop Co-chairs

Jean-Luc Hainaut (University of Namur, Belgium)
Elke A. Rundensteiner (Worcester Polytechnic Institute, USA)

Tutorial Co-chairs

Sven Hartmann (Massey University, New Zealand)
Alberto H.F. Laender (UFMG, Brazil)

Panel Chair

John F. Roddick (Flinders University, Australia)

Industrial Chair

John Grundy (University of Auckland, New Zealand)

Demonstration and Poster Chair

Leszek Maciaszek (Macquarie University, Australia)

Treasurers

Patricia Rood (University of Auckland, New Zealand)
Stephen W. Liddle (Brigham Young University, USA)

Workshops

Conceptual Modelling for Life Sciences Applications (CMLSA)
Yi-Ping Phoebe Chen, Deakin University, Australia
Sven Hartmann, Massey University, New Zealand

Foundations and Practices of UML (FP-UML)
Juan Trujillo, University of Alicante, Spain
Jeffrey Parsons, Memorial University of Newfoundland, Canada

Ontologies and Information Systems for the Semantic Web (ONISW)
Mathias Brochhausen, IFOMIS, Germany
Martin Doerr, FORTH, Greece
Hyoil Han, Drexel University, USA

Quality of Information Systems (QoIS)
Samira Si-Saïd Cherfi, CEDRIC-CNAM, France
Geert Poels, University of Ghent, Belgium

Requirements, Intentions and Goals in Conceptual Modelling (RIGiM)
Colette Rolland, Université Paris 1 Panthéon Sorbonne, France
Eric Yu, University of Toronto, Canada

Semantic and Conceptual Issues in Geographic Information Systems (SeCoGIS)
Esteban Zimanyi, Université Libre de Bruxelles, Belgium
Michela Bertolotto, University College Dublin, Ireland

Tutorials

Agent-Oriented Modelling of Distributed Systems by Leon Sterling and Kuldar Taveter (University of Melbourne, Australia)

Conceptual Modeling for Virtual Reality by Olga De Troyer, Frederic Kleinermann, and Bram Pellens (Vrije Universiteit Brussel, Belgium)

Know your Limits: Enhanced XML Modeling with Cardinality Constraints by Sebastian Link and Thu Trinh (Massey University, New Zealand)

Modeling and Engineering Adaptive Complex Systems by Leszek A. Maciaszek (Macquarie University, Australia)

Selfish-brain Theory: Challenges in the Top-down Analysis of Metabolic Supply Chains by Dirk Langemann (University of Lübeck, Germany)

The CIDOC Conceptual Reference Model – A New Standard for Knowledge Sharing by Martin Doerr (FORTH, Greece)

Program Committee

Witold Abramowicz, Poland
Sabah Saleh Al-Fedaghi, Kuwait
Valeria de Antonellis, Italy
Catriel Beeri, Israel
Boualem Benatallah, Australia
Sonia Bergamaschi, Italy
Leopoldo Bertossi, Canada
Mokrane Bouzeghoub, France
Kankana Chakrabarty, Australia
Roger Chiang, USA
Isabelle Comyn-Wattiau, France
Lois M.L. Delcambre, USA
Debabrata Dey, USA
Gillian Dobbie, New Zealand
Martin Doerr, Greece
Dov Dori, Israel
Dirk Draheim, Germany
Daniela Durakova, Czech Republic
Antje Düsterhöft, Germany
Hans-Dieter Ehrich, Germany
Ramez Elmasri, USA
David W. Embley, USA
Vadim Ermolayev, Ukraine
Ulrich Frank, Germany
Andrew Gemino, Canada
Aditya K. Ghose, Australia
Paulo Goes, USA
Angela Eck Soong Goh, Singapore
Hele-Mai Haav, Estonia
Jean-Luc Hainaut, Belgium
Sven Hartmann, New Zealand
Roland Hausser, Germany
Stephen J. Hegner, Sweden
Brian Henderson-Sellers, Australia
Carlos A. Heuser, Brazil
Annika Hinze, New Zealand
Carlos Hurtado, Chile
Sushil Jajodia, USA

Wolfgang H. Janko, Austria
Christian S. Jensen, Denmark
Manfred A. Jeusfeld, Netherlands
Paul Johannesson, Sweden
Gerti Kappel, Austria
Kamalakar Karlapalem, India
Yasushi Kiyoki, Japan
Tosiyasu Laurence Kunii, Japan
Alberto H.F. Laender, Brazil
Chiang Lee, Taiwan
Maurizio Lenzerini, Italy
Qing Li, China
Stephen W. Liddle, USA
Tok Wang Ling, Singapore
Oscar Pastor López, Spain
Pericles Loucopoulos, UK
Johann A. Makowsky, Israel
Salvatore T. March, USA
Heinrich C. Mayr, Austria
Pavle Mogin, New Zealand
Mukesh K. Mohania, India
Renate Motschnig-Pitrik, Austria
Moira Norrie, Switzerland
Jyrki Nummenmaa, Finland
Andreas Oberweis, Germany
Antoni Olivé, Spain
Christine Parent, Switzerland
Jeffrey Parsons, Canada
Zhiyong Peng, China
Barbara Pernici, Italy
Jaroslav Pokorný, Czech Republic
Alexandra Poulovassilis, UK
Sandeep Purao, USA
Martin Purvis, New Zealand
P. Radhakrishna, India
Sudha Ram, USA
John F. Roddick, Australia
Colette Rolland, France

Gustavo H. Rossi, Argentina
Matti Rossi, Finland
Klaus-Dieter Schewe, New Zealand
Arne Sølvberg, Norway
Il-Yeol Song, USA
Stefano Spaccapietra, Switzerland
Srinath Srinivasa, India
Veda C. Storey, USA
Markus Stumptner, Australia
Vijayan Sugumaran, USA
Yuzuru Tanaka, Japan
Dimitri Theodoratos, USA

Alexei Tretiakov, New Zealand
Olga De Troyer, Belgium
Juan Trujillo, Spain
X. Sean Wang, USA
Roel J. Wieringa, Netherlands
Mary-Anne Williams, Australia
Jeffrey Xu Yu, China
Eric Yu, Canada
Yanchun Zhang, Australia
Shuigeng Zhou, China
Esteban Zimanyi, Belgium

External Referees

Birger Andersson, Sweden
Danilo Ardagna, Italy
Guilherme Tavares de Assis, Brazil
Cecilia Bastarrica, Chile
Dizza Beimel, Israel
Domenico Beneventano, Italy
Maria Bergholtz, Sweden
Devis Bianchini, Italy
Flavio Bonfatti, Italy
Serge Boucher, Switzerland
Cinzia Cappiello, Italy
Eugenio Capra, Italy
Moisés Gomes de Carvalho, Brazil
Bo Chen, Singapore
Chi-Wei Chen, Taiwan
Xing Chen, Japan
Samira Si-Saïd Cherfi, France
Yu-Chi Chung, Taiwan
Shalom Cohen, Israel
Cesar Collazos, Chile
Theodore Dalamagas, Greece
Clodoveu A. Davis Jr., Brazil
Marie Duzi, Czech Republic
Eyas El-Qawasmeh, Jordan
Petr Gajdoš, Czech Republic
Yunjun Gao, China
Françoise Gire, France
Shantanu Godbole, India
Cesar Gonzalez-Perez, Spain
Jaap Gordijn, Netherlands

Georg Grossmann, Australia
Michael Grossniklaus, Switzerland
Francesco Guerra, Italy
Hakim Hacid, France
Yanan Hao, Australia
John Horner, USA
Siv Hilde Houmb, Netherlands
Yuan-Ko Huang, Taiwan
Weng Jianshu, Singapore
Jürgen Jung, Germany
Hima Prasad Karanam, India
Horst Kargl, Austria
Roland Kaschek, New Zealand
Zoubida Kedad, France
Ritu Khare, USA
Markus Kirchberg, New Zealand
George Koliadis, Australia
Woralak Kongdenfha, Australia
Subodha Kumar, USA
Peep Küngas, Estonia
Nadira Lammari, France
Ki Jung Lee, USA
Chien-han Liao, Taiwan
Baoping Lin, China
Hai Liu, China
Jiangang Ma, Australia
Federica Mandreoli, Italy
Da Chung Mao, Taiwan
Riccardo Martoglia, Italy
Michele Melchiori, Italy

Organized by

Massey University, New Zealand
The University of Auckland, New Zealand

Sponsored by

The ER Institute

In Cooperation with

ACM SIGMIS
ACM SIGMOD

Table of Contents

Keynotes

Data Warehousing and Data Mining

Design Methodologies and Tools

Information and Database Integration

Information Modelling Concepts and Ontologies

Integrity Constraints

Logical Foundations of Conceptual Modelling

Patterns and Conceptual Meta-modelling

Requirements Elicitation

Reuse and Reengineering

Semi-structured Data and XML

Web Information Systems and XML

Modeling Workflow Patterns from First Principles

Egon Börger

Università di Pisa, Dipartimento di Informatica, I-56125 Pisa, Italy
boerger@di.unipi.it

Abstract. We propose a small set of parameterized abstract models for workflow patterns, starting from first principles for sequential and distributed control. Appropriate instantiations yield the 43 workflow patterns that have been listed recently by the Business Process Modeling Center. The resulting structural classification of those patterns into eight basic categories, four for sequential and four for parallel workflows, provides a semantical foundation for a rational evaluation of workflow patterns.

1 Introduction

In [3] we have provided Abstract State Machine (ASM) models for the 43 workflow pattern descriptions that have been presented recently in [8] by the Business Process Modeling Center. Our goal there was to make the underlying relevant questions and implicit parameters explicit and to turn the patterns into a precise and truly abstract form. To easen the validation of these ASM ground models, in the sense defined in [1], we esssentially followed the order of presentation adopted in [8] and only hinted at the most obvious streamlining the ASM models offer for the classification presented in [8].

In this paper we revisit those workflow pattern ASMs and define eight basic workflow patterns, four for sequential and four for distributed control, from which all the other patterns can be derived by parameter instantiation.[1] This provides a conceptual basis for a rational workflow pattern classification that can replace the partly repetitive listing presented in [8].

We use again the ASM method to provide a high-level, both state-based and process-oriented view of workflow patterns. This provides a solid semantic foundation for reasoning about workflow functionality. In the ASM models the behavioral interface is defined through actions performed with the help of submachines that remain largely abstract. The parameterization exploits the possibility the ASM method offers the specifier to build 'models with holes', that is to leave

---

[1] We omit here the four so-called State-Based Patterns in [10], which concern "business scenarios where an explicit notion of state is required" and are only loosely connected to workFLOW. Exploiting the most general character of the ASM notion of state, these four state-based patterns can be expressed by rather simple ASMs.

C. Parent et al. (Eds.): ER 2007, LNCS 4801, pp. 1–20, 2007.

parts of the specification either as completely abstract parameters or to accompany them by assumptions or informal explanations, which are named, but verified respectively detailed only at later refinement stages. The parameterization allows one in particular to leave the design space open for further refinements to concrete pattern instantiations.

Most of what we use below to model workflow patterns by ASMs is self-explanatory, given the semantically well-founded pseudo-code character of ASMs, an extension of Finite State Machines (FSMs) by a general notion of state. For a recent tutorial introduction into the ASM method for high-level system design and analysis see [2], for a textbook presentation, which includes a formalized version of the definition of the semantics of ASMs, see the Asm-Book [6]. For sequential patterns we use mono-agent (so-called sequential) ASMs, for patterns of distributed nature multiple-agent asynchronous (also called distributed) ASMs.

We make no attempt here to provide a detailed analysis of the basic concepts of *activity, process, thread*, of their being *active, enabled, completed* etc., which are used in [8] without further explanations. It seems to suffice for the present purpose to consider an activity or process as some form of high-level executable program, which we represent here as ASMs. Threads are considered as agents that execute activities. An *active activity*, for example, is one whose executing agent is active, etc. The quotes below are taken from [8] or its predecessor [10].

We start with the more interesting case of parallel control flow patterns, followed by the more traditional patterns for sequential control flow known from programmming.

2   Parallel Control Flow Patterns

The patterns related to parallel control flow can be conceptually categorized into four types: *splitting* one flow into multiple flows, *merging* multiple flows into one flow, forms of *interleaving* and *trigger* variations. As Andreas Prinz has pointed out, there are good reasons to use instead a classification into splitting and merging only. Interleaving appears then as parameter for different instances of splitting, whereas triggering is considered as belonging to start patterns in the context of distributed (not mono-agent sequential) computations. We do not claim to have a unique answer to the classification problem. What we believe is important is to start with a small number of basic patterns out of which more complex patterns can be obtained by composition and refinement.

2.1   Parallel Split Patterns

We quote the description of the parallel split pattern:

> A point in the workflow process where a single thread of control splits into multiple threads of control which can be executed in parallel, thus allowing activities to be executed simultaneously or in any order.

This description contains two not furthermore specified parameters, which we represent by two sets *Activity* and *Thread* capturing the underlying activities and the threads executing them. It is left open whether *Activity* is declared as static or as dynamic, thus providing for static instantiations and for dynamic ones, whether as known at design time or as known only at the moment of executing the parallel split. In contrast the set *Thread* has to be declared as dynamic, since multiple threads of control have to be created without committing to the precise nature of the underlying parallelism, which is left unspecified in the above pattern description.

The parallelism may be further specified as an interleaving execution, using one of the interleaving patterns of Sect. 2.3, or as a simultaneous synchronous or as asynchronous execution. The latter two cases can be expressed using synchronous respectively asynchronous (also called distributed) ASMs. The particular choice can be left open if we create for each $a \in$ *Activity* a new thread to execute a. For this purpose we use a function *new* that is assumed to provide a fresh element each time it is applied to a set. To provide a handle for expressing the possible independence of the execution mechanisms for different threads, we explicitly name a third parameter, namely a machine that triggers the execution of an activity by a thread. For the representation of such a mechanism we avoid committing to a particular framework, e.g. Petri nets where triggering is traditionally represented by placing tokens that enable a transition. This is the reason why we introduce an abstract machine TRIGGEREXEC(t, a). It is not furthermore specified except for requiring that its call triggers enables the execution of activity a by thread t.

PARALLELSPLIT(*Activity*, *Thread*, TRIGGEREXEC) =
    forall $a \in$ *Activity*   **let** $t = new($*Thread*$)$ **in**   TRIGGEREXEC(t, a)

This pattern is widely used in various forms. A well-known one is represented by the Occam instruction [7] to spawn finitely many parallel subprocesses of a given process p, which matches this pattern exactly. See the OCCAMPARSPAWN-rule in [6, p.43], where TRIGGEREXEC(t, a) describes the initialization of a by linking it to the triggering process p as its parent process, copying from there the current environment, setting a to run and p to wait (for all the spawned subprocesses to terminate). This instance of PARALLELSPLIT uses as underlying parallelism the concept of asynchronous ASMs.

An instance with synchronous parallelism takes the following form, where all the activities in question are executed simultaneously, e.g. as action of one agent. This is already captured by the default parallelism of basic non-distributed ASMs so that it suffices to instantiate TRIGGEREXEC as not depending on the thread parameter (whereby the creation of new threads can simply be deleted):

SYNCPARSPLIT(*Activity*, TRIGGEREXEC) = **forall** $a \in$ *Activity* TRIGGEREXEC(a)

In [8] other parallel split patterns are discussed for multiple instances of one activity. One of the descriptions runs as follows.

Within the context of a single case (i.e., workflow instance) multiple instances of an activity can be created, i.e. there is a facility to spawn off new threads of control. Each of these threads of control is independent of other threads.

This so-called *Multiple Instances Without Synchronization* pattern, which apparently comes with an asynchronous understanding of the underlying parallelism, is an instance of PARALLELSPLIT where *Activity* is further specified to be a multiset of multiple instances of one activity *act*. Formally *Activity* = *MultiSet(act, Mult)* where *Mult* denotes the number of occurrences of *act* in the multiset and determines the multitude with which new threads for the execution of instances of *act* are to be created and triggered to execute *act*.

MULTINSTWITHOUTSYNC(*act*, *Mult*, *Thread*, TRIGGEREXEC) =
    PARALLELSPLIT(*MultiSet(act, Mult)*, *Thread*, TRIGGEREXEC)

In [10] some variations of this pattern appear, which essentially differ by their interpretations on the static or dynamic character of the *Mult*itude parameter. In the ASM framework this is merely a matter of how the parameter is declared. Since in the formulation of these pattern variants some additional conditions appear that have to do with synchronization features, we postpone their discussion to Sect. 2.2 where combinations of split and join patterns are discussed.

2.2   Merge Patterns

The following characterization seems to capture what is common to all the synchronization and merge patterns in [8]:

A point in the workflow process where multiple parallel subprocesses/ activities converge into one single thread of control ... once ... completed some other activity needs to be started.

The general scheme appears to be that one has to perform a specific convergence action that characterizes the start of the merge phase, namely when a *MergeEv*ent occurs, and then to complete the merge by some further actions. To represent these two successive and possibly durative aspects of a merge we use separate abstract machines STARTMERGE and COMPLETEMERGE. To capture that multiple actions may be involved to complete a merge cycle, we formalize the above description by the following control state ASM MERGE, i.e. an ASM all of whose rules have the form pictorially depicted in Fig. 1. Here $i, j_1, \ldots, j_n$ denote the control states corresponding to the internal states of an FSM (Finite State Machine), *cond*$_\nu$ (for $1 \leq \nu \leq n$) the guards and *rule*$_\nu$ the rule actions.

The control state ASM MERGE switches between two modes *mergeStart*, *MergeCompl* and takes the merge event predicate and the two submachines for starting and completing the merge as not furthermore specified abstract parameters.

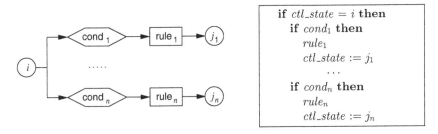

Fig. 1. Control state (FSM like) ASM rules

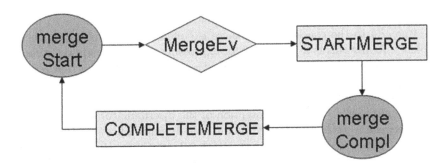

Fig. 2. General Merge Pattern ASM MERGE

In accordance with the understanding of activities as executed by agents representing threads, we name explicitly also these underlying agents since they are the ones to be merged (not really the activities). We use for this a parameter $exec$ denoting for every $a \in Activity$ the agent $exec(a)$ executing a, if there is one. It typically serves as parameter for defining the merge event $MergeEv$.

MERGE($Activity$, $exec$, $MergeEv$, STARTMERGE, COMPLETEMERGE) =
 if $ctl\_state = mergeStart$ **and** $MergeEv(exec)$ **then**
  STARTMERGE
  $ctl\_state := mergeCompl$
 if $ctl\_state = mergeCompl$ **then**
  COMPLETEMERGE
  $ctl\_state := mergeStart$

Various forms of synchronizing merge patterns, whether with or without synchronization, can be described as instances of the general merge pattern ASM MERGE. We illustrate this here by deriving the various merge patterns that appear in [8].

Discriminators. One class of patterns in [8] that represent instances of the two-phase merge pattern MERGE are the so-called Discriminator patterns. They present the durative character of a merging phase together with two additional basic merge features, namely merging with or merging without synchronization. The so-called *Structured Discriminator* pattern is described as follows:

> The discriminator is a point in a workflow process that waits for one of the incoming branches to complete before activating the subsequent activity. From that moment on it waits for all remaining branches to complete and "ignores" them. Once all incoming branches have been triggered, it resets itself so that it can be triggered again...

To view this pattern as an instance of MERGE, essentially we have to instantiate *MergeEv* to the check whether there is "one of the incoming branches to complete". Really this is a shorthand for expressing that a thread executing the activity a associated to a branch has reached a completion point for that activity, formally whether $Completed(a, exec(a))$.

As a cosmetic adaptation one may rename the control states *mergeStart* and *mergeCompl* to reflect the basic intention of the discriminator pattern as alternation between a *waitingToProceed* mode, namely until a first incoming branch completes, and a *reset* mode, during which all remaining branches will complete "without synchronization". Similarly one may rename STARTMERGE and COMPLETEMERGE to PROCEED respectivelyRESET.

Speaking about waiting "for one of the incoming branches to complete" leaves the case open where more activities complete simultaneously. We formalize the pattern so that this latter more general case is contemplated, where multiple activities that complete together may be synchronized. In doing this we foresee that the way to PROCEED may be parameterized by the set of incoming branches whose activities have been the first to be simultaneously completed. Note that this formalization allows one to refine the 'synchronization' to choosing one among the simultaneously completed activities. This leads to the following instantiation of MERGE by Fig. 3.

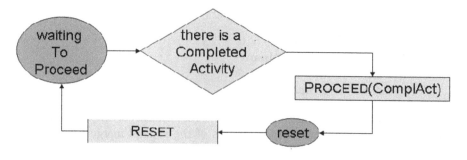

Fig. 3. Discriminator control-state ASM

DISCRIMINATOR($Activity, exec, Completed,$ PROCEED, RESET) =
   MERGE($Activity, exec, MergeEv,$ PROCEED($ComplAct$), RESET)
where
   $MergeEv =\mid ComplAct \mid \geq 1$
   $ComplAct = \{a \in Activity \mid Completed(a, exec(a))\}$

The variant *Structured N-out-of-M Join* discussed in [8] is the very same DISCRIMINATOR machine, replacing the cardinality threshold 1 by N and letting $M =\mid Activity \mid^2$. The pattern discussed in [8] under the name *Generalized AND-Join* is the same as Structured N-out-of-M Join with additionally $N = M$.

RESET appears in the above quoted description of the structured discriminator as a durative action of waiting for other activities to complete. It suffices to refine RESET to the following machine STRUCTURED DISCRIMINATOR RESET. To check whether "all incoming branches have been triggered", one has to distinguish the activities which have not yet been detected as completed. Thus one needs a *NotYetDetected* test predicate, which initially is satisfied by every element of the set *Activity* and is updated until it becomes empty. In the description below *init, exit* denote the initial respectively final control state of the refined machine. As Fig. 4 shows, for the replacement of RESET by STRUCTURED DISCRIMINATOR RESET we identify *init* with the *reset* mode, in which it is called by DISCRIMINATOR, and *exit* with the initial mode *waitingToProceed*.

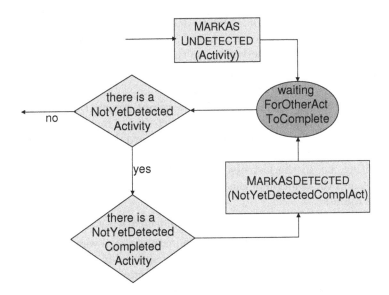

Fig. 4. STRUCTURED DISCRIMINATOR RESET

---

[2] $\mid A \mid$ denotes the cardinality of set A.

STRUCTUREDDISCRIMINATORRESET =
   if $mode = init$ **then**
      MARKASUNDETECTED($Activity$)
      $mode := waitingForOtherActToComplete$
   if $mode = waitingForOtherActToComplete$ **then**
      if $NotYetDetected \neq \emptyset$ **then let** $A = ComplAct \cap NotYetDetected$
         if $A \neq \emptyset$ **then** MARKASDETECTED(A)
      else $mode := exit$
  where
     MARKASDETECTED(A) = (**forall** $a \in A$ $NotYetDetected(a) := false$)
     MARKASUNDETECTED(A) = (**forall** $a \in A$ $NotYetDetected(a) := true$)
     $ComplAct = \{a \in Activity \mid Completed(a, exec(a))\}$

The variations called *Cancelling Discriminator* and *Cancelling N-out-of-M Join* are described in [8] by the additional requirement that "Triggering the discriminator (join) also cancels the execution of all of the other incoming branches and resets the construct". This comes up to define the following instances of RESET:

CANCELLINGDISCRIMINATORRESET =
  forall $a \in Activity \setminus ComplAct$ CANCEL($exec(a)$)

In [8] some more variations, coming under the names *Blocking Discriminator* and *Blocking N-out-of-M Join*, are described by the additional requirement that "Subsequent enablements of incoming branches are blocked until the discriminator (join) has reset." It comes up to declare *Completed* as a set of queues *Completed(a)* of completion events (read: announcing the completion of some thread's execution) for each activity a, so that in each discriminator round only the first element *fstout* to leave a queue is considered and blocks the others. This leads to the following refinement step:

- refine the abstract completion predicate to **not** $Empty(Completed(a))$,
- refine the updates of $NotYetDetected(a)$ by replacing a by $fstout(Completed(a))$ (under the additional guard that $fstout(Completed(a))$ is defined),
- for exiting, i.e. in the last **else** branch of STRUCTUREDDISCRIMINATOR − RESET, add the deletion of the completion events that have been considered in this round:

    forall $a \in Activity$ DELETE($fstout(Completed(a))$, $Completed(a)$)

In [8] also variations of the preceding discriminator pattern versions are presented that work in concurrent environments. This is captured in our model by the fact that we have parameterized it among others by *Activity* and *Completed*, so that it can execute in an asynchronous manner simultaneously for different instances of these parameters.

Synchronizing Merge. This pattern too presents two merge components, one with and one without synchronization. It is described in [8] as follows:

A point in the workflow process where multiple paths converge into one single thread. If more than one path is taken, synchronization of the active threads needs to take place. If only one path is taken, the alternative branches should reconverge without synchronization. It is an assumption of this pattern that a branch that has already been activated, cannot be activated again while the merge is still waiting for other branches to complete. ... the thread of control is passed to the subsequent branch when each active incoming branch has been enabled.

This is a merge pattern instance where the threads, which execute the activities associated to branches and are described as *Active*, have to be synchronized, whereas the remaining threads have to "reconverge without synchronization". The synchronization event denotes the crucial pattern parameter "to decide when to synchronize and when to merge" and to determine the branches "the merge is still waiting for ... to complete". Nevertheless no definition of threads being *Active*, *Activated* or *Enabled* is given, so that in particular it is unclear whether by interpreting enabledness as completion this pattern reduces to the structured discriminator pattern. Since a decision is needed, we choose to formalize the synchronization event in terms of enabledness of active branch activities by instantiating the *MergeEv*ent in MERGE correspondingly. As a cosmetic change we rename STARTMERGE and COMPLETEMERGE to CONVERGE respectively RECONVERGE. The iterative nature of the not furthermore specified RECONVERGE machine can be formalized by a structured version, as done for the discriminator RESET submachine. In this case the description of this pattern in fact is just another wording for the structured version of the discriminator.

SYNCHRONIZINGMERGE(*Activity*, *exec*, *Active*, *SyncEnabled*, CONVERGE, RECONVERGE) =
    MERGE(*Activity*, *exec*, *MergeEv*, CONVERGE(*Active*), RECONVERGE(*Activity* \ *Active*))
where
    MergeEv =**forall** $a \in$ *Activity* **if** *Active*(*exec*(a)) **then** *SynEnabled*(*exec*(a))

The assumption "that each incoming branch of a synchronizer is executed only once" relates each $a \in$ *Activity* to a unique executing thread *exec*(a). It is natural to assume that at the beginning of the execution of a, *SyncEnabled*(*exec*(a)) is false and that after having become true during this execution, it is reset to false by CONVERGE respectively RECONVERGE, thus resetting SYNCHRONIZINGMERGE for the next synchronization round.

The machine SYNCHRONIZINGMERGE has been further simplified in [8] to a pattern called SYNCHRONIZER. This can be defined as an instantiation of SYNCHRONIZINGMERGE by declaring all activities to be active (i.e. *Active*(*exec*(a)) holds for each $a \in$ *Activity* when the pattern is used) and reconverging to be empty (RECONVERGE = **skip**).

The Acyclic Synchronizing Merge pattern presented in [8] is another variation described by the following additional requirement:

Determination of how many branches require synchronization is made on the basis of information locally available to the merge construct. This may be communicated directly to the merge by the preceding diverging construct or alternatively it can be determined on the basis of local data such as the threads of control arriving at the merge.

This variation is easily captured by refining the *MergeEv*ent predicate to check whether the necessary *synchNumber* of to be synchronized enabled and active branches has been reached:

ACYCLSYNCHRMERGE = SYNCHRONIZINGMERGE **where**
  MergeEv= | {$a{\in}Activity$ | $Active(exec(a))$ **and** $SyncEnabled(exec(a))$} |$\geq$
  synchNumber

Another variation called *General Synchronizing Merge* is described in [8] by relaxing the firing condition from "when each active incoming branch has been enabled" through the alternative "or it is not possible that the branch will be enabled at any future time". To reflect this restriction it suffices to relax $SyncEnabled(exec(a))$ in *MergeEv* by the disjunct "**or** *NeverMoreEnabled(exec(a))*)", but obviously the crux is to compute such a predicate. It "requires a (computationally expensive) evaluation of possible future states for the current process instance" [8, pg.71].

Simple and Thread Merge. The *Simple Merge* pattern described in [10] is an example of merging without synchronization. Its description runs as follows.

A point in the workflow process where two or more alternative branches come together without synchronization. It is an assumption of this pattern that none of the alternative branches is ever executed in parallel.

This is an instance SIMPLE MERGE of the MERGE ASM where the two control states are identified and we set COMPLETEMERGE = **skip**. In [8] the description is weakened as follows, withdrawing the uniqueness condition.

The convergence of two or more branches into a single subsequent branch. Each enablement of an incoming branch results in the thread of control being passed to the subsequent branch.

This weakening can be made explicit by incorporating into the STARTMERGE submachine of SIMPLEMERGE a choice among two or more branches that try to converge simultaneously, using one of the selection patterns discussed in Sect. 3.4. In [8] two more variations are discussed under the names *Thread Merge with Design/Run-Time Knowledge*, where a merge number *MergeNo* appears explicitly:

At a given point in a process, a ... number of execution threads in a single branch of the same process instance should be merged together into a single thread of execution

This number is furthermore specified to be either "nominated" or "not known until run-time", which is a question of how the number is declared. As to the definition of THREADMERGE, it can be obtained as follows, reusing the instantiation of MERGE to SIMPLE MERGE and refining the *MergeEv* further by an analogous condition as the one used for ACYCLSYNCHMERGE above:

THREADMERGE(*Activity, exec, MergeEnabled*, PROCEED, *MergeNo*) =
   MERGE(*Activity, exec, MergeEv*, PROCEED, **skip**)
where
   MergeEv = (| {*a* ∈ *Activity* **and** *MergeEnabled*(*exec*(*a*))} |= *MergeNo*)
   mergeStart = *mergeCompl*

Thus SIMPLEMERGE appears as THREADMERGE with *MergeNo* = 1 under the mutual-exclusion hypothesis.

RELAXSIMPLEMERGE is the variant of THREADMERGE with cardinality check | *A* |≥ 1 and PROCEED refined to **forall** *a* ∈ *A* PROCEED(*a*).[3] At a later point in [10] this pattern is called Multi-Merge and described as follows: "A point in the workflow process where two or more branches reconverge without synchronization. If more than one branch gets activated, possibly concurrently, the activity following the merge is started *for every activation of every incoming branch*."[4]

To capture the two Thread Merge variants it suffices to instantiate *Activity* to the set of execution threads in the considered single branch of a process and to declare *MergeNo* as static respectively dynamic. It is unclear whether there is a difference worth the two namings between the SYNCHRONIZER and the THREADMERGE pattern besides considering in the latter only the "execution threads in a single branch of the same process instance".

Coupled Split and Join Patterns. For the instantiation of PARALLELSPLIT to the pattern MULTINSTWITHOUTSYNC for multiple instances without synchronization (see Sect. 2.1) three variations appear in [10]. They derive from different interpretations of the static or dynamic nature of the *Multi*tude parameter and from adding a join component to the split feature.

For the *Multiple Instances With a Priori Design Time Knowledge* pattern the set *Mult* is declared to be known a priori at design time. In addition the following is required:

---

[3] It comes natural to assume here that when PROCEED(*a*) is called, *MergeEnabled*(*exec*(*a*)) changes to false and *exec*(*a*) to *undefined*. This guarantees that each completed activity triggers "the subsequent branch" once per activity completion. One way to realize this assumption is to require such an update to be part of PROCEED(*a*); another possibility would be to add it as update to go in parallel with PROCEED(*a*).

[4] It is possible that the relaxed form of Simple Merge was intended not to allow multiple merge-enabled branches to proceed simultaneously, in which case it either implies a further selection of one *a* ∈ *A* to PROCEED(*a*) as proxy for the others or a sequentialization of PROCEED(*a*) for all *a* ∈ *A*.

... once all instances are completed some other activity needs to be started.

These two requirements can be captured by using the two phases of the MERGE machine, one for the (unconditioned)[5] splitting action and one to PROCEED upon the completion event, when all newly created agents have *Completed* their run of the underlying activity. Since in [8] also a variation is considered under the name *Static N-out-of-M Join for Multiple Instances*, where to PROCEED only N out of $Mult = M$ activity instances need to have completed, we make here the cardinality parameter explicit. It can then be specialized to $N =\mid Agent(act) \mid$. The variation *Static Cancelling N-out-of-M Join for Multiple Instances* in [8] can be obtained by adding a cancelling submachine.

MULTINSTNMJOIN(act, $Mult$, $Thread$, $Completed$, TRIGGEREXEC, PROCEED, N) =
  MERGE(*MultiSet*(act, $Mult$), $-$, $true$,
    MULTINSTWITHOUTSYNC(act, $Mult$, $Thread$, TRIGGEREXEC),
    if *CompletionEv* **then** PROCEED)
  where
    CompletionEv = $(\mid \{t \in Thread \mid Completed(t, act)\} \mid \geq N)$

MULTINSTAPRIORIDESIGNKNOWL
  (act, $Mult$, $Thread$, $Completed$, TRIGGEREXEC, PROCEED) =
    MULTINSTNMJOIN
      (act, $Mult$, $Thread$, $Completed$, TRIGGEREXEC, PROCEED, $\mid Thread(act) \mid$)

The pattern *Multiple Instances With a Priori Run Time Knowledge* is the same except that the *Mult*itude "of instances of a given activity for a given case varies and may depend on characteristics of the case or availability of resources, but is known at some stage during runtime, before the instances of that activity have to be created." This can be expressed by declaring *Mult* for MULTINSTAPRIORIRUNKNOWL as a dynamic set.

The *Multiple Instances Without a Priori Run Time Knowledge* pattern is the same as *Multiple Instances With a Priori Run Time Knowledge* except that for *Mult*itude it is declared that "the number of instances of a given activity for a given case is not known during desing time, nor is it known at any stage during runtime, before the instances of that activity have to be created", so that "at any time, whilst instances are running, it is possible for additional instances to be initiated" [8, pg.31]. This means that as part of the execution of a RUN(a, act), it is allowed that the set *Agent*(act) may grow by new agents a' to RUN(a', act), all of which however will be synchronized when *Completed*. Analogously the pattern *Dynamic N-out-of-M Join for Multiple Instances* discussed in [8] is a variation of Static N-out-of-M Join for Multiple Instances.

The *Complete Multiple Instance Activity* pattern in [8] is yet another variation: "... It is necessary to synchronize the instances at completion before any subsequent activities can be triggered. During the course of execution, it is possible that the activity needs to be forcibly completed such that any remaining

---

[5] As a consequence the parameter *exec* plays no role here.

instances are withdrawn and the thread of control is passed to subsequent activities."

To reflect this additional requirement it suffices to add the following machine to the second submachine of MULTINSTAPRIORIDESIGNKNOWL:

if *Event*(*ForcedCompletion*) **then**
  forall $a \in (Thread(act) \setminus Completed)$ **do** CANCEL(a)
  PROCEED

2.3 Interleaving Patterns

As observed by Andreas Prinz and mentioned above, interleaving should perhaps be considered as parameter for different forms of parallelism and not as pattern. Interleaving is described in [8] as follows:

> A set of activities is executed in an arbitrary order: Each activity in the set is executed, the order is decided at run-time, and no two activities are executed at the same moment (i.e. no two activities are active for the same workflow at the same time).

We illustrate some among the numerous ways to make this description rigorous, depending on the degree of detail with which one wants to describe the interleaving scheme. A rather liberal way is to execute the underlying activities one after another until *Activity* has become empty, in an arbitrary order, left completely unspecified:

INTERLEAVEDPAR(*Activity*) = **choose** $act \in Activity$
  act
  DELETE(*act, Activity*)

A more detailed scheme forsees the possibility to impose a certain scheduling algorithm for updating the currently executed activity *curract*. The function *schedule* used for the selection of the next not-yet-completed activity comes with a name and thus may be specified explicitly elsewhere. For example, to capture the generalization of this pattern in [8, pg.34], where the activities are partially ordered and the interleaving is required to respect this order, *schedule* can simply be specified as choosing a minimal element among the not-yet-completed activities.

SCHEDULEDINTERLEAVING(*Activity, Completed, schedule*) =
  if *Completed*(*curract*) **then**   *curract* := *schedule*({$a \in Activity$ | **not** *Completed*(a)})

A more sophisticated interleaving scheme could permit that the execution of activities can be suspended and resumed later. A characteristic example appears in [9, Fig.1.3] to describe the definition of the multiple-thread Java interpreter using a single-thread Java interpreter. It can be paraphrased for the workflow context as follows, assuming an appropriate specification of what it means to SUSPEND and to RESUME an activity and using an abstract predicate *ExecutableRunnable* that filters the currently executable and runnable activities from *Activity*.

INTERLEAVEWITHSUSPENSION
   (*Activity, ExecutableRunnable*, EXECUTE, SUSPEND, RESUME) =
     choose $a \in ExecutableRunnable(Activity)$ **if** $a = curract$ **then** EXECUTE($curract$)
     else
       SUSPEND($curract$)
       RESUME(a)

The generalization from atomic activities to critical sections, proposed in [8] as separate pattern *Critical Section*, is a straightforward refinement of the elements of *Activity* to denote "whole sets of activities". Also the variation, called *Interleaved Routing*, where "once all of the activities have completed, the next activity in the process can be initiated" is simply a sequential composition of Interleaved Parallel Routing with NextActivity.

There is a large variety of other realistic interpretations of Interleaved Parallel Routing, yielding pairwise different semantic effects. The informal requirement description in [10,8] does not suffice to discriminate between such differences.

2.4 Trigger Patterns

Two basic forms of trigger patterns are discussed in [8], called *Transient Trigger* and *Persistent Trigger*. The description of Transient Trigger reads as follows:

> The ability for an activity to be triggered by a signal from another part of the process or from the external environment. These triggers are transient in nature and are lost if not acted on immediately by the receiving activity.

Two variants of this pattern are considered. In the so-called 'safe' variant, only one instance of an activity 'can wait on a trigger at any given time'. In the unsafe variant multiple instances of an activity 'can remain waiting for a trigger to be received'.[6]
The description of the Persistent Trigger goes as follows:

> ... These triggers are persistent in form and are retained by the workflow until they can be acted on by the receiving activity.

Again two variants are considered. In the first one 'a trigger is buffered until control-flow passes to the activity to which the trigger is directed', in the second one 'the trigger can initiate an activity (or the beginning of a thread of execution) that is not contingent on the completion of any preceding activities'.

We see these patterns and the proposed variants as particular instantiations of one Trigger pattern, dealing with monitored events to trigger a process and

---

[6] Note that this safety notion is motivated by the Petri net framework underlying the analysis in [8].

instantiated depending on a) whether at a given moment multiple processes wait for a trigger and on b) the time that may elapse between the trigger event and the reaction to it. We add to this the possibility that in a distributed environment, at a given moment multiple trigger events may yield a simultaneous reaction of multiple ready processes. We leave the submachines for BUFFERing and UNBUFFERing abstract and only require that as result of an execution of BUFFER(a) the predicate $Buffered(a)$ becomes true. For notational reasons we consider monitored events as consumed by the execution of a rule.[7]

TRIGGER =
  TRIGGEREVENT
  TRIGGERREACTION
where
  TRIGGEREVENT = **if** $Event(Trigger(a))$ **then** BUFFER(a)
  TRIGGERREACTION =
    if not $Empty(Buffered \cap Ready)$ **then**
      choose $A \subseteq Buffered \cap Ready$ **forall** $a \in A$ **do**
        a
        UNBUFFER(a)

The two variants considered for the Persistent Trigger differ from each other only by the definition of $Ready(a)$, meaning in the first case $WaitingFor(Trigger(a))$ and in the second case $curract = a$ ('process has reached the point to execute a'), where $curract$ is the activity counter pointing to the currently to be executed activity.

For the Transient Trigger it suffices to stipulate that there is no buffering, so that $Buffered$ coincides with the happening of a triggering event. Upon the arrival of an event, TRIGGEREVENT and TRIGGERREACTION are executed simultaneously if the event concerns a $Ready(a)$, in which case (and only in this case) it triggers this activity.

TRANSIENTTRIGGER = TRIGGER **where**
  BUFFER = UNBUFFER = **skip**
  $Buffered(a) = Event(Trigger(a))$

The difference between the safe and unsafe version is in the assumption on how many activity (instances) may be ready for a trigger event at a given moment in time, at most one (the safe case) or many, in which case a singleton set A is required to be chosen in TRIGGERREACTION.

3   Sequential Control Flow Patterns

The patterns related to sequential control flow can be conceptually categorized into four types: *sequencing* of multiple flows, *iteration* of a flow,

---

[7] This convention allows us to suppress the explicit deletion of an event from the set of active events.

begin/termination of a flow and *choice* among (also called sequential split into) multiple flows. These patterns capture aspects of process control that are well known from sequential programming.

3.1 Sequence Patterns

We find the following description for this well-known control-flow feature:

"An activity in a workflow is enabled after the completion of another activity in the same process".

One among many ways to formalize this is to use control-state ASMs, which offer through final and initial states a natural way to reflect the completion and the beginning of an activity. If one wants to hide those initial and final control states, one can use the **seq**-operator defined in [5] for composing an ASM A_1 **seq** A_2 out of component ASMs A_i $(i = 1, 2)$.

SEQUENCE(A_1, A_2) = A_1 **seq** A_2

A related pattern is described as follows under the name *Milestone*:

The enabling of an activity depends on the case being in a specified state, i.e. the activity is only enabled if a certain milestone has been reached which did not expire yet.

This rather loose specification can be translated as follows:

MILESTONE(*milestone, Reached, Expired, act*) =
    if *Reached*(*milestone*) **and not** *Expired*(*milestone*) **then** *act*

3.2 Iteration Patterns

For arbitrary cycles the following rather loose description is given:

A point in a workflow process where one or more activities can be done repeatedly.

For the elements of *Activity* to be repeatedly executed, it seems that a *StopCriterion* is needed to express the point where the execution of one instance terminates and the next one starts. The additional stipulation in the revised description in [8] that the cycles may "have more than one entry or exit point" is a matter of further specifying the starting points and the *StopCriterion* for activities, e.g. exploiting initial and final control states of control-state ASMs. The ITERATE construct defined for ASMs in [5] yields a direct formalization of this pattern that hides the explicit mentioning of entry and exit points.

ARBITRARYCYCLES(*Activity, StopCriterion*) =
    forall $a \in Activity$ ITERATE(a) **until** *StopCriterion*(a)

In [8] two further 'special constructs for structured loops' are introduced, called Structured Loop and Recursion. The formalization of STRUCTUREDLOOP comes up to the constructs **while** *Cond* **do** *M* respectively **do** *M* **until** *Cond*, defined for ASMs in [5]. For an ASM formalization of RECURSION we refer to [4] and skip further discussion of these well known programming constructs.

3.3 Begin/Termination Patterns

In [10] the following *Implicit Termination* pattern is described.

> A given subprocess should be terminated when there is nothing else to be done. In other words, there are no active activities in the workflow and no other activity can be made active (and at the same time the workflow is not in deadlock).

The point of this patterns seems to be to make it explicit that a subprocess should TERMINATE depending on a typically dynamic *StopCriterion*. This varies from case to case. It may depend upon the subprocess structure. It may also include global features like that "there are no active activities in the workflow and no other activity can be made active"; another example is the projection of the run up-to-now into the future, namely by stipulating that the process should terminate "when there are no remaining work items that are able to be done either now or at any time in the future" [8, pg.25]. Such an abstract scheme is easily formulated as an ASM. It is harder to define reasonable instances of such a general scheme, which have to refine the *StopCriterion* in terms of (im)possible future extensions of given runs.

TERMINATION(P, *StopCriterion*, TERMINATE) =
   if *StopCriterion*(P, *Activity*) **then** TERMINATE(P)

In [8] the following variation called *Explicit Termination* is discussed.

> A given process (or sub-process) instance should terminate when it reaches a nominated state. Typically this is denoted by a specific end node. When this end node is reached, any remaining work in the process instances is cancelled and the overall process instance is recorded as having completed successfully.

It is nothing else than the instantiation of TERMINATION by refining a) the *StopCriterion* to *currstate* = *exit*, expressing that the current state has reached the end state, and b) TERMINATE(P) to include CANCEL(P) and marking the overall process *parent*(P) as *CompletedSuc*cessfully.

Related to termination patterns are the so-called cancellation patterns. The *Cancel Activity* pattern is described as follows:

> An enabled activity is disabled, i.e. a thread waiting for the execution of an activity is removed.

Using an association *agent*(*act*) of threads to activities allows one to delete the executing agent, but not the activity, from the set *Agent* of currently active agents:

CANCELACT(*act*, *Agent*, *exec*) =
  let *a* = *exec*(*act*) **in if** *Enabled*(*a*) **then** DELETE(*a*, *Agent*)

The *Cancel Case* pattern is described as follows: "A case, i.e. workflow instance, is removed completely (i.e., even if parts of the process are instantiated multiple times, all descendants are removed)."

If we interpret 'removing a workflow instance' as deleting its executing agent,[8] this pattern appears to be an application of CANCELACT to all the *Descendants* of an *activity* (which we assume to be executed by agents), where for simplicity of exposition we assume *Descendant* to include *act*.

CANCELCASE(*act*, *Agent*, *exec*, *Descendant*) =
  forall *d* ∈ *Descendant*(*act*) CANCELACT(*d*, *Agent*, *exec*)

For the *Cancel Region* pattern we find the following description in [8]: "The ability to disable a set of activities in a process instance. If any of the activities are already executing, then they are withdrawn. The activities need not be a connected subset of the overall process model."

CANCELREGION is a straightforward variation of CANCELCASE where *Descendant*(*p*) is defined as the set of activities one wants to cancel in the process instance *p*. Whether this set includes *p* itself or not is a matter of how the set is declared. The additional requirement that already executing activities are to be withdrawn is easily satisfied by refining the predicate *Enabled*(*a*) to include executing activities *a*. The question discussed in [8] whether the deletion may involve a bypass or not is an implementation relevant issue, suggested by the Petri net representation of the pattern.

An analogous variation yields an ASM for the *Cancel Multiple Instance Activity* pattern, for which we find the following description in [8]: "Within a given process instance, multiple instances of an activity can be created. The required number of instances is known at design time. These instances are independent of each other and run concurrently. At any time, the multiple instance activity can be cancelled and any instances which have not completed are withdrawn. This does not affect activity instances that have already completed." Here it suffices to define *Descendant*(*p*) in CANCELCASE as the set of multiple instances of an activity one wants to cancel and to include 'activity instances which have not yet completed' into the *Enabled* predicate of CANCELACT.

3.4   Selection Patterns

A general workflow selection pattern named *Multichoice* is described in [8] as follows:

> A point in the workflow process where, based on a decision or workflow control data, a number of branches are chosen.

---

[8] To delete the activity and not only its executing agent would imply a slight variation in the ASM below.

Besides the parameter for the set *Activity* of subprocesses among which to choose, we see here as second parameter a *ChoiceCriterion*,[9] used to "choose multiple alternatives from a given set of alternatives" that have to be executed together. It may take workflow control data as arguments. Using the non deterministic **choose** construct for ASMs yields the following formalization:

MULTICHOICE(*Activity, ChoiceCriterion*) =
   choose $A \subseteq Activity \cap ChoiceCriterion$
     forall $act \in A$
      act

An equivalent wording for this machine explicitly names a choice function, say *select*, which applied to *Activity* $\cap$ *ChoiceCriterion* yields a subset of activities chosen for execution:

CHOICE(*Activity, ChoiceCriterion, select*) =
   forall $act \in select(Activity \cap ChoiceCriterion)$
     act

The *Exclusive Choice* pattern is described in [8] as follows, where the additional assumption is that each time an exclusive choice point is reached (read: EXCLCHOICE is executed), the decision criterion yields exactly one $a \in Activity$ that fulfills it:

> A point in the workflow process where, based on a decision or workflow control data, one of several branches is chosen.

This is a specialization of CHOICE where the range of the *select* function is requested to consist of singleton sets.

We also find the following description of a *Deferred Choice*:

> A point in the workflow process where one of several branches is chosen. In contrast to the XOR-split, the choice is not made explicitly (e.g. based on data or a decision) but several alternatives are offered to the environment. However, in contrast to the AND-split, only one of the alternatives is executed ... It is important to note that the choice is delayed until the processing in one of the alternative branches is actually started, i.e. the moment of choice is as late as possible.

This is captured by an instance of EXCLCHOICE ASM where the *ChoiceCriterion* is declared to be a monitored predicate because the decision for the choice may depend on runtime data.

---

[9] The revised version of the multi-choice pattern in [8, pg.15] describes the selection as "based on the outcome of distinct logical expressions associated with each of the branches". This can be reflected by the parameterization of *ChoiceCriterion* with the set *Activity*, e.g. to represent a disjunction over the "distinct logical expressions associated with each of the (activity) branches".

4 Conclusion and Outlook

We have identified a few elementary workflow patterns that help to structure the variety of individually named workflow patterns collected in [10,8]. We hope that this provides a basis for an accurate analysis and evaluation of practically relevant control-flow patterns, in particular in connection with business processes and web services, preventing the pattern variety to grow without rational guideline.

Acknowledgement. We thank Andreas Prinz and three anonymous referees for valuable criticism of previous versions of this paper.

References

1. Börger, E.: The ASM ground model method as a foundation of requirements engineering. In: Dershowitz, N. (ed.) Verification: Theory and Practice. LNCS, vol. 2772, pp. 145–160. Springer, Heidelberg (2003)
2. Börger, E.: The ASM method for system design and analysis. A tutorial introduction. In: Gramlich, B. (ed.) Frontiers of Combining Systems. LNCS (LNAI), vol. 3717, pp. 264–283. Springer, Heidelberg (2005)
3. Börger, E.: A critical analysis of workflow patterns. In: Prinz, A. (ed.) ASM 2007, Grimstadt (Norway) (June 2007), Agder University College (2007)
4. Börger, E., Bolognesi, T.: Remarks on turbo ASMs for computing functional equations and recursion schemes. In: Börger, E., Gargantini, A., Riccobene, E. (eds.) ASM 2003. LNCS, vol. 2589, pp. 218–228. Springer, Heidelberg (2003)
5. Börger, E., Schmid, J.: Composition and submachine concepts for sequential ASMs. In: Clote, P.G., Schwichtenberg, H. (eds.) CSL 2000. LNCS, vol. 1862, pp. 41–60. Springer, Heidelberg (2000)
6. Börger, E., Stärk, R.F.: Abstract State Machines. A Method for High-Level System Design and Analysis. Springer, Heidelberg (2003)
7. INMOS. Transputer Implementation of Occam – Communication Process Architecture. Prentice-Hall, Englewood Cliffs, NJ (1989)
8. Russel, N., ter Hofstede, A., van der Aalst, W.M.P., Mulyar, N.: Workflow control-flow patterns. A revised view. BPM-06-22 (July 2006), at http://is.tm.tue.nl/staff/wvdaalst/BPMcenter/
9. Stärk, R.F., Schmid, J., Börger, E.: Java and the Java Virtual Machine: Definition, Verification, Validation. Springer, Heidelberg (2001)
10. van der Aalst, W.M., ter Hofstede, A., Kiepuszewski, B., Barros, A.: Workflow patterns. Distributed and Parallel Databases 14(3), 5–51 (2003)

Heart Modeling, Computational Physiology and the IUPS Physiome Project

Peter J. Hunter

Auckland Bioengineering Institute (ABI), University of Auckland, New Zealand
p.hunter@auckland.ac.nz

Abstract. The Physiome Project of the International Union of Physiological Sciences (IUPS) is attempting to provide a comprehensive framework for modelling the human body using computational methods which can incorporate the biochemistry, biophysics and anatomy of cells, tissues and organs. A major goal of the project is to use computational modelling to analyse integrative biological function in terms of underlying structure and molecular mechanisms. To support that goal the project is developing XML markup languages (CellML & FieldML) for encoding models, and software tools for creating, visualizing and executing these models. It is also establishing web-accessible physiological databases dealing with model-related data at the cell, tissue, organ and organ system levels. Two major developments in current medicine are, on the one hand, the much publicised genomics (and soon proteomics) revolution and, on the other, the revolution in medical imaging in which the physiological function of the human body can be studied with a plethora of imaging devices such as MRI, CT, PET, ultrasound, electrical mapping, etc. The challenge for the Physiome Project is to link these two developments for an individual - to use complementary genomic and medical imaging data, together with computational modelling tailored to the anatomy, physiology and genetics of that individual, for patient-specific diagnosis and treatment.

References

[1] Hunter, P.J., Borg, T.K.: Integration from proteins to organs: The Physiome Project. Nature Reviews Molecular and Cell Biology 4, 237–243 (2003)

[2] Crampin, E.J., Halstead, M., Hunter, P.J., Nielsen, P.M.F., Noble, D., Smith, N.P., Tawhai, M.: Computational physiology and the Physiome Project. Exp. Physiol. 89, 1–26 (2004)

[3] Hunter, P.J., Nielsen, P.M.F.: A strategy for integrative computational physiology. Physiology 20, 316–325 (2005)

[4] Hunter, P.J.: Modeling living systems: the IUPS/EMBS Physiome Project. Proceedings of the IEEE 94, 678–691 (2006)

[5] http://www.cellml.org

C. Parent et al. (Eds.): ER 2007, LNCS 4801, p. 21, 2007.
© Springer-Verlag Berlin Heidelberg 2007

Conceptual Schemas and Ontologies for Database Access: Myths and Challenges

Enrico Franconi

Faculty of Computer Science, Free University of Bozen-Bolzano,
Piazza Domenicani 3, I-39100 Bozen-Bolzano BZ, Italy
franconi@inf.unibz.it

Abstract. First, I will argue that well-founded conceptual modelling and ontology design is required to support intelligent information access. Then, I will show which are the technical consequences of such choices, and how the foundational and computational problems to be faced are non-trivial. The arguments are based on the use of classical logics and description logics as a formal tools for the framework, and I will make use of languages and examples taken from the Entity-Relationship arena.

C. Parent et al. (Eds.): ER 2007, LNCS 4801, p. 22, 2007.

Multidimensional Data Modeling for Business Process Analysis

Svetlana Mansmann[1], Thomas Neumuth[2], and Marc H. Scholl[1]

[1] University of Konstanz, P.O.Box D188, 78457 Konstanz, Germany
{Svetlana.Mansmann,Marc.Scholl}@uni-konstanz.de
[2] University of Leipzig, Innovation Center Computer Assisted Surgery (ICCAS),
Philipp-Rosenthal-Str. 55, 04103 Leipzig, Germany
Thomas.Neumuth@medizin.uni-leipzig.de

Abstract. The emerging area of business process intelligence attempts to enhance the analytical capabilities of business process management systems by employing data warehousing and mining technologies. This paper presents an approach to re-engineering the business process modeling in conformity with the multidimensional data model. Since the business process and the multidimensional model are driven by rather different objectives and assumptions, there is no straightforward solution to converging these models.

Our case study is concerned with Surgical Process Modeling which is a new and promising subdomain of business process modeling. We formulate the requirements of an adequate multidimensional presentation of process data, introduce the necessary model extensions and propose the structure of the data cubes resulting from applying vertical decomposition into flow objects, such as events and activities, and from the dimensional decomposition according to the factual perspectives, such as function, organization, and operation. The feasibility of the presented approach is exemplified by demonstrating how the resulting multidimensional views of surgical workflows enable various perspectives on the data and build a basis for supporting a wide range of analytical queries of virtually arbitrary complexity.

1 Introduction

Conventional business process management systems, focused on operational design and performance optimization, display rather limited analysis capabilities to quantify performance against specific metrics [1]. Deficiencies of business process modeling (BPM) approaches in terms of supporting comprehensive analysis and exploration of process data have been recognized by researchers and practitioners [1,2]. The new field of *Business Process Intelligence* (BPI), defined as the application of performance-driven management techniques from Business Intelligence (BI) to business processes, claims that the developing convergence of BI and BPM technologies will create value beyond the sum of their parts [3]. However, no straightforward guidelines for converging the flow-oriented process specification and the snapshot-based multidimensional design are in existence.

C. Parent et al. (Eds.): ER 2007, LNCS 4801, pp. 23–38, 2007.

To be admitted into an OLAP (On-line Analytical Processing) system, the descriptions of the business processes have to undergo the transformation imposed by the underlying multidimensional data model. However, the source and the target models are driven by rather conflicting and partially incompatible objectives: business process modeling is concerned with operational efficiency and workflow behavior, whereas OLAP enables aggregation over accumulated numerical data modeled as a set of uniformly structures fact entries.

In medical engineering "the term *Surgical Workflows* refers to the general methodological concept of the acquisition of process descriptions from surgical interventions, the clinical and technical analysis of them" [4]. One of the major challenges is the acquisition of accurate and meaningful Surgical Process Models (SPM). Surgical Process Models are "simplified pattern of a surgical procedure that reflect a predefined subset of interest of the real intervention in a formal or semi-formal representation"[5]. Formalization of the SPM recording scheme is required to support both, manual and automatic data acquisition, and to apply state-of-the-art analysis and visualization techniques for gaining insight into the data.

Use cases of Surgical Workflows are manifold, ranging from supporting the preoperative planning by retrieving similar precedent cases to the postoperative exploration of surgical data, from analyzing the optimization potential with respect to instruments and systems involved to verifying medical hypotheses, for education purposes, answering qualitative and quantitative queries, etc. Whatever abstraction approach is adopted, there is a need for an unambiguous description of concepts that characterize a surgical process in a way adequate for modeling a wide range of different workflow types and surgical disciplines.

The prevailing process modeling standards, such as Business Process Modeling Notation (BPMN) [6] and the reference model of Workflow Management Coalition (WfMC) [7], are too general to address the domain-specific requirements adequately. Multidimensional modeling seems a promising solution as it allows to view data from different perspectives and at different granularity and define various measures of interest. To identify the major design challenges, we proceed by inspecting the fundamentals of the involved modeling techniques.

1.1 Multidimensional Data Model

Multidimensional data model emerged as an alternative to the relational data model optimized for quantitative data analysis. This model categorizes the data as *facts* with associated numerical *measures* and descriptive *dimensions* characterizing the facts [8]. Facts can thus be viewed as if shaped into a multidimensional cube with dimensions as axes and measure values as the cube cells. For instance, a surgical process can be modeled as a fact entry SURGERY characterized by dimensions Location, Surgeon, Patient, and Discipline. Members of a dimension are typically organized in a containment type hierarchy (e.g., location ↗ hospital ↗ city) to support multiple granularities.

Relational OLAP structures the data cubes according to the *star* or *snowflake* schema [9]. Both schemas are composed of a *fact table* and the associated *dimension tables.* In the star schema, for each dimension, its whole hierarchy is placed into a single table, whereas the snowflake schema extracts each hierarchy level into a separate table and uses foreign keys for mapping child-parent relationships between the members. Within a dimension, the attributes that form the hierarchy are called *dimension levels*, or *categories*. Other descriptive attributes belonging to a particular category are *property attributes*. For instance, hospital and city are categories of the dimension location, whereas hospital name and city code are property attributes of the respective categories. Dimension levels along with parent-child relationships between them are referred to as the *intension*, or *schema*, of a dimension whereas the hierarchy of its members, i.e., the actual data tree, forms its *extension*.

1.2   Business Process Modeling and Workflow Management

BPM and Workflow Management (WfM) foster a process-oriented perspective on organizations that comprises *activities* and their *relationships* within and beyond an organization context. Relationships may be specified using control flow (consecutive, parallel, or alternative execution) and/or hierarchical decomposition; the organizational context comprises organizational units and resources [10]. The differentiation in the definition of business processes vs. workflows lies in the levels of abstraction: while business processes are mostly modeled in a high-level and informal way, workflow specifications serve as a basis for the largely automated execution and are derived by refining the business process specification [11]. A workflow is specified in terms of work steps, denoted *activities*, which are either automated or include a human part. The latter type is assigned roles filled by human actors at runtime. The role of the WfM system is to determine the (partial) invocation order of activities. Therefore, a formal specification of *control flow* and *data flow* is required.

Coexistence of different workflow specification methods is common in practice. We restrain ourselves to naming a few techniques applicable in the context of Surgical Workflows and refer the interested reader to [12] for a detailed overview. *Net-based*, or *graph-based*, methods enjoy great popularity due to their ability to visualize processes in a way understandable even for non-expert users. Especially the *activity and state charts* are frequently used to specify a process as an oriented graph with nodes representing the activities and arcs defining the ordering in which these are performed. *Logic-based* methods use temporal logic to capture the dynamics of the system. Finally, *Event-Condition-Action* rules are used for specifying the control flow between activities in the conditional form.

Surgical Process Modeling, classified as a specific domain of BPM [4], adopts the concepts from both WfM and BPM. The WfM approach of decomposing a workflow into activities is useful for providing a task-oriented surgery perspective. However, since surgical work steps are predominantly manual and involve extensive organizational context, such as participants, their roles, patients and treated structures, instruments, devices and other resources, etc., high-level BPM abstractions enable modeling such domain-specific elements.

2 Related Work

Relevant work can be subdivided into the following categories: 1) enhancing business process analysis by employing the data warehousing approach, 2) extending the OLAP technology to support complex scenarios, and 3) approaches to surgical workflow analysis.

Grigori et al. present a BPI tool suite built on top of the HP Process Manager (HPPM) and based on a data warehouse approach [2]. The process data is modeled according to the star schema, with process, service, and node state changes as facts and the related definitions as well as temporal and behavioral characteristics as dimensions. While this approach focuses on the analysis of process execution and state evolution, we pursue the task-driven decomposition into logical work steps, in which horizontal characteristics, or the factual perspectives[13], extended by means of domain-specific taxonomies serve as dimensions.

An approach to visual analysis of business process performance metrics, called impact factors, is given in [14]. The proposed visualization interface *VisImpact* is especially suitable for aggregating over large amounts of process-related data and is based on analyzing the process schema and instances to identify business metrics. The selected impact factors and the corresponding process instances are presented using a symmetric circular graph to display the relationships and the details of the process flows.

Pedersen et al. have made remarkable contributions in the field of multidimensional modeling for non-standard application domains. In [15], a medical cases study concerned with patient diagnosis is used to demonstrate the analysis requirements not supported by traditional OLAP systems. The proposed model extensions aim at supporting non-summarizable hierarchies, symmetric treatment of dimensions and measures, and correct aggregation over imprecise or incomplete data. In [16], Jensen et al. present the guidelines for designing complex dimensions in the context of spatial data such as mobile, location-based services.

In a previous work [17] we analyzed the limitations of conventional OLAP systems and the underlying data model in handling complex dimension hierarchies and proposed model extensions at the conceptual level and their relational mapping as well their implementation in a prototype frontend tool. A comprehensive classification of dimensional hierarchies, including those not addressed by current OLAP systems, formalized at both the conceptual model and the logical level, may be found in [18].

Interdisciplinary research in the field of surgical workflow modeling, analysis and visualization is carried out at the Innovation Center Computer Assisted Surgery (ICCAS) located in Leipzig, Germany. Recent results and findings of the ongoing projects may be found in [4,5].

3 Case Study: Surgical Workflows

Surgeons, medical researchers and engineers work jointly on obtaining a well-defined formal Surgical Process Model that would enable managing huge volumes

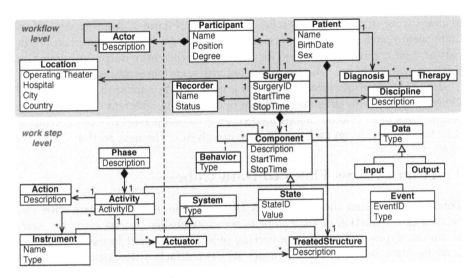

Fig. 1. Recording scheme of a surgical process model as a UML class diagram

of intervention models in a single data warehouse in a uniform manner and querying that data for analytical purposes. A basic recording scheme of a surgery in UML class notation is shown in Figure 1. The diagram denotes a further stage of the scheme presented by Neumuth et al. in [4]. The use of UML offers an implementation-independent view of the process scheme and is a widely accepted specification standard for both BPM [19] and data warehouse design [20]. The upper part of the diagram contains the characteristics describing the surgery as a whole and corresponding to the dimensions of analysis for aggregating across multiple surgical interventions (for instance, to query the number of patients treated by a particular surgeon). Classes in the lower part of the diagram belong to the intra-surgical level, i.e., they represent elements constituting a surgical procedure.

To obtain the structure of a workflow recording scheme whilst avoiding the information overload, we employ vertical and horizontal process decomposition.

Vertical decomposition corresponds to identifying core elements of a process. Here, we account for two complementary data acquisition practices in the field of SPM, namely a task-driven, or temporal, and an system-based structuring. *Activities* represent surgical tasks, or work steps, similarly to the corresponding WfM concept. Examples of activities are "irrigation of a vessel with a coagulator" or "cutting at the skin with a scalpel". Sequential ordering of activities symbolizes the acquired surgical intervention [4]. System-based structuring uses the concepts of *System, State,* and *Event* to capture the state evolution of involved systems and events that trigger state transitions. The concept of a system is very generic and may refer to a participant or his/her body part, a patient or a treated structure, an instrument or a device, etc. For instance, the gaze direction of surgeon's eyes can be modeled as states, while surgeon's instructions may be captured as events. To reflect the heterogeneous nature of the notion *system*, we modeled it as an abstract superclass as shown in Figure 1. Another superclass Component enables uniform treatment of the two data acquisition practices in part of their common properties, e.g., to retrieve the entire output generated in the coarse of a surgery, whether by its activities, system states or events.

Horizontal decomposition of a process is conceptually similar to identifying the dimensions of a data cube and is drawn by recognizing different complementary perspectives in a workflow model, following the factual perspective categorization [13]. Further details on each perspective are given in the next section.

4   From Process Flows to Data Cubes

Transformation from the semantically rich BPM notation into a data cube can be seen as a reduction of the complete set of extensible process elements, such as various types of flow and connecting objects, to a rigid format that forces decomposition into a set of uniformly structured facts with associated dimensions. We proceed in three steps: 1) identify the main objectives of the business process analysis, 2) provide the overall mapping of generic BPM concepts, such as activity, object, resource, event etc. into the multidimensional data model, and 3) transfer the application-specific characteristics into the target model.

Subjects, or focal points, of the analysis are mapped to facts. In business process analysis, the major subjects of the analysis are the process itself (process level) as well as its components (intra-process level). Process level analysis is concerned with analyzing the characteristics of the process as a whole and aggregating over multiple process instances. Back to our case study, sample analytical tasks at this level are the utilization of hospital locations, surgery distribution by discipline, surgeon ranking, etc. At the intra-process level, occurrence, behavior and characteristics of process components, such as activities, actors, and resources are analyzed. Examples from the surgical field are the usage of instrument and devices, work step duration, occurrence of alarm states, etc.

4.1   Handling Generic BPM Constructs

The conceptual design of a data warehouse evolves in modeling the structure of business facts and their associate dimensions. Once major fact types have been defined, aggregation hierarchies are imposed upon dimensions to enable additional granularities. In what follows we present a stepwise acquisition of the multidimensional perspective of a process.

Determining the Facts. As the fact entries within a data cube are required to be homogeneous, i.e., drawn from the same set of dimensions, applications dealing with multiple heterogeneous process types have to place each type into a separate cube. In our scenario, surgery is the only process type, but if we had to add a different type, e.g., a routine examination of a patient, the corresponding fact entries would be stored separately from surgical facts.

At the process element level, we suggest modeling work steps, or activities, as facts while other components, such as resources and actors, are treated as dimensional characteristics of those facts. However, in many contexts, process activities may be rather heterogeneous in terms of their attributes. To preserve homogeneity within the fact type, we propose to extract each homogeneous group of activity types into a separate fact type. To account for common characteristics of all activity types, generalization into a common superclass is used.

Determining the Dimensions. Dimensions of a fact are a set of attributes determining the measure value of each fact entry. These attributes are obtained via a horizontal decomposition along the factual perspective categories of workflow modeling defined in [13]. Availability and contents of particular perspective categories as well as their number depend on the type of process at hand. Our approach to transforming the fundamental factual perspectives into dimensions is as follows:

1. The *function* perspective describes recursive decomposition of process into subprocesses and tasks. This composition hierarchy is mapped into a dimension of Activity, such as Phase in our case study.
2. The *operation* perspective describes which operations are supported by a task and which applications implement these operations. In case of a surgical work step, operations are mapped to the dimension Action (e.g., "cut", "suction", "stitch up", etc.) and the applications are represented by Instrument.
3. The *behavior* perspective defines the execution order within the process. Behavior can be subdivided into temporal (along the timeline), logical (parallelism, synchronization, looping) and causal. Temporal characteristics, such as StartTime and StopTime, are used as time dimensions. Relationships between pairs of components (a reflexive association of Component with Behavior in Figure 1) are more complex and will be discussed in the next section.
4. The *information* perspective handles the data consumed and produced by the workflow components. These resources can be mapped to (Input) and (Output) dimensions.
5. The *organization* perspective specifies which resource is responsible which task. Organization dimensions may involve human actors, systems, and devices. Back to the surgical activity case, an example of such resource is Participant (e.g., "surgeon", "assistant", etc.).

5   Challenges of the Multidimensional Modeling

Apart from the standard OLAP constraints, such as normalization of the dimension hierarchies and avoidance of NULL values in the facts, the following domain-specific requirements have been identified:

- *Many-to-many relationships between facts and dimensions* are very common. For instance, during a single surgery, multiple surgical instruments are used by multiple participants.
- *Heterogeneity of fact entries.* Treating Component elements as the same fact type would disallow capturing of subclass specific properties, while modeling

each subclass as a separate fact type would disable treating heterogeneous elements as the same class for querying their common characteristics.

- *Interchangeability of measure and dimension roles.* In a classical OLAP scenario the measures of interest are known at design time. However, "raw" business process data may contain no explicit quantitative characteristics. The measure of interest varies from one query to another. Therefore, it is crucial to enable the runtime measure specification from virtually any attribute. For instance, a query may investigate the number of surgeries per surgeon or retrieve the distribution of surgeons by discipline.
- *Interchangeability of fact and dimension roles.* Surgery has dimensional characteristics of its own (location, patient, etc.) and therefore, deserves to be treated as a fact type. However, with respect to single work steps, Surgery clearly plays the role of a dimension (e.g., events may be rolled-up to surgery).

5.1   Terminology

In this work, we adopt the notation proposed by Pedersen et al. [15] by simplifying and extending it to account for BPM particularities.

An *n-dimensional fact schema* is a pair $\mathcal{S} = (\mathcal{F}, \{\mathcal{D}_i, i = 1, \ldots, n\})$, with $\mathcal{F}$ as the fact schema and $\{\mathcal{D}_i\}$ as the set of corresponding dimension schemata.

A *dimension schema* is a four-tuple $\mathcal{D} = (\{\mathcal{C}_j, j = 1, \ldots, m\}, \sqsubseteq_{\mathcal{D}}, \top_{\mathcal{D}}, \bot_{\mathcal{D}})$, where $\{\mathcal{C}_j\}$ are the categories, or aggregation levels, in $\mathcal{D}$, with the distinguished top and bottom category denoted $\top_{\mathcal{D}}$ and $\bot_{\mathcal{D}}$, respectively, and $\sqsubseteq_{\mathcal{D}}$ being the partial order on the $\mathcal{C}_j$s.

The top category of a dimension corresponds to an abstract root node of the data hierarchy and has a single value referred to as ALL (i.e., $\top_{\mathcal{D}} = \{\text{ALL}\}$).

A non-top *dimension category* is a pair $\mathcal{C} = (\{\mathcal{A}_k, k = 1, \ldots, p\}, \bar{\mathcal{A}}_{\mathcal{C}})$ where $\bar{\mathcal{A}}_{\mathcal{C}}$ is the distinguished *hierarchy attribute*, i.e., whose values represent a level in the dimension hierarchy, whereas $\{\mathcal{A}_k\}$ is a set of *property attributes* functionally dependent on $\bar{\mathcal{A}}_{\mathcal{C}}$, i.e., $\forall \mathcal{A}_k \in \mathcal{C} : \mathcal{A}_k = f(\bar{\mathcal{A}}_{\mathcal{C}})$.

A *fact schema* is a triple $\mathcal{F} = (\{\bar{\mathcal{A}}_{\bot}\}_{\mathcal{F}}, \{\mathcal{M}_q, q = 1, \ldots, t\}, \bar{\mathcal{A}}_{\mathcal{F}})$, where $\{\bar{\mathcal{A}}_{\bot}\}$ is a set of bottom-level hierarchy attributes in the corresponding dimension schema $\{\mathcal{D}_i\}$ (i.e., $\forall \mathcal{C} = \bot_{\mathcal{D}_i} : \bar{\mathcal{A}}_{\mathcal{C}} \in \{\bar{\mathcal{A}}_{\bot}\}_{\mathcal{F}})$, $\{\mathcal{M}_q\}$ is a set of *measure attributes*, defined by its associated dimensions, such that $\forall \mathcal{M}_q \in \mathcal{F} : \mathcal{M}_q = f(\{\bar{\mathcal{A}}_{\bot}\}_{\mathcal{F}})$, and $\bar{\mathcal{A}}_{\mathcal{F}}$ is an optional *fact identifier attribute*.

We allow the set of measure attributes to be empty ($\{\mathcal{M}_q\} = \emptyset$), in which case the resulting fact schema is called *factless* [9] and the measures need to be defined dynamically by applying the desired aggregation function to any category in $\{\mathcal{D}_i\}$. The fact identifier attribute plays the role of a single-valued primary key, useful for specifying the relationship between different fact schemata.

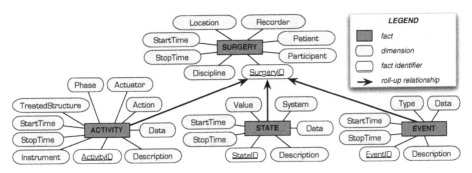

Fig. 2. Vertical decomposition of the surgical workflow into a fact hierarchy

5.2 Fact Constellation vs. Fact Hierarchy and Fact Generalization

In our usage scenario, fact table modeling is an iterative process starting with a coarse definition of the basic fact types with their subsequent refinement under the imposed constraints. Vertical decomposition of a surgical process results in two granularity levels of the facts, as depicted in Figure 2:

— Surgery. Each surgical case along with its attributes and dimensional characteristics represents the top-level fact type.
— Activity, State, and Event. The three types of workflow components have their specific sets of dimensions and are thus treated as distinct fact types.

At this initial stage, we disregarded existence of many-to-many relationships between facts and dimensions. However, disallowance of such relationships is crucial in the relational context as each fact entry is stored as a single data tuple with one single-valued attribute per dimension. Consider the problem of modeling Participant as a dimension of Surgery: most surgeries involve multiple participants, hence, it is impossible to store the latter as a single-valued attribute.

Our solution is based on a popular relational implementation of a non-strict dimension hierarchy by means of *bridge tables* [9]. A bridge table captures a non-strict ordering between any two categories by storing each parent-child pair. Back to our example, a many-to-many relationship between Surgery and Participant as well as that between Surgery and Discipline are extracted each into a separate table, as shown in Figure 3. We denote such extracted fact-dimensional fragments *satellite facts* to stress their dependent nature. Availability of the fact identifier attribute SurgeryID facilitates the connection of the satellite fact to its base fact

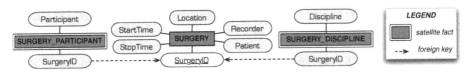

Fig. 3. Extracting many-to-many relationships into "satellite" facts

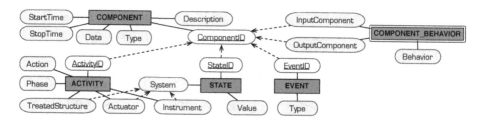

Fig. 4. Using generalization (dashed lines) for unifying heterogeneous categories

table; a natural join between the two fact tables is necessary in order to obtain the entire multidimensional view of Surgery.

Another phenomenon worthwhile consideration is the presence of parent-child relationships between fact types, such as the hierarchy Activity ∕ Surgery. Similar to a hierarchical dimension, Activity records can be rolled-up to Surgery.

A *fact hierarchy* relationship between $\mathcal{F}_j$ and $\mathcal{F}_i$, denoted $\mathcal{F}_j \nearrow \mathcal{F}_i$, is a special case of the fact constellation in which the fact schema $\mathcal{F}_i$ appears to serve as a dimension in $\mathcal{F}_j$, such that $\mathcal{A}_{\mathcal{F}_i} \in \{\bar{\mathcal{A}}_\perp\}_{\mathcal{F}_j}$.

So far, the three workflow component types have been modeled as separate fact types Activity, State, and Event. However, these heterogeneous classes have a subset of common characteristics that qualify them to be generalized into superclass fact type Component, resulting in a *fact generalization* depicted in Figure 4. A simple relational implementation of Component can be realized by defining a corresponding view as a union of all subclass projections onto the common subset of schema attributes.

$\mathcal{F}_j$ is a *fact generalization* of $\mathcal{F}_i$, denoted $\mathcal{F}_j \subset \mathcal{F}_i$, if the dimension and measure sets of $\mathcal{F}_j$ are a subset of the respective sets in $\mathcal{F}_i$:
$$\{\bar{\mathcal{A}}_\perp\}_{\mathcal{F}_j} \subset \{\bar{\mathcal{A}}_\perp\}_{\mathcal{F}_i} \wedge (\forall \mathcal{M}_q \in \mathcal{F}_j : \mathcal{M}_q \in \mathcal{F}_i).$$

An obvious advantage of the generalization is the ability to treat heterogeneous classes uniformly in part of their common characteristics. A further advantage is the ability to model the behavior of components with respect to each other (see Behavior class in Figure 1) in form of a satellite fact table Component_Behavior depicted in Figure 4.

5.3   Modeling Dimension Hierarchies

A key strategy in designing dimension hierarchies for OLAP is that of *summarizability*, i.e., the ability of a simple aggregate query to correctly compute a higher-level cube view from a set of precomputed views defined at lower aggregation levels. Summarizability is equivalent to ensuring that 1) facts map directly to the lowest-level dimension values and to only one value per dimension, and 2) dimensional hierarchies are balanced trees [21]. Originally motivated by performance considerations, the summarizability has regained importance in the

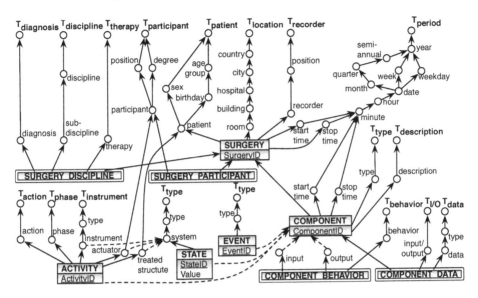

Fig. 5. A (simplified) Dimensional Fact Model of a surgical workflow scheme

context of visual OLAP as it ensures the generation of a proper browser-like navigation for visual exploration of multidimensional cubes [17].

The resulting structure of the entire surgery scheme (with some simplifications) in terms of facts, dimension hierarchies, and the relationships between them is presented in Figure 5 in the notation similar to the Dimensional Fact Model [22]. Solid arrows show the roll-up relationships while dashed arrows express the "is a" relationships, namely the identity in case of a satellite fact and the generalization in case of a fact hierarchy. The chosen notation is helpful for explicitly presenting all shared categories, and therefore, all connections and valid aggregation paths in the entire model.

We limit ourselves to naming a few non-trivial cases of dimensional modeling.

Multiple alternative hierarchies. The time hierarchy in the dimension Period is a classical example of alternative aggregation paths, such as date ↗ month and date ↗ week. These paths are mutually exclusive, i.e., within the same query, the aggregates may be computed only along one of the alternative paths.

Parallel hierarchies in a dimension account for different analysis criteria, for example, the member values of Patient can be analyzed by age or by sex criteria. Apparently, such hierarchies are mutually non-exclusive, i.e., it is possible to compute the aggregates grouped by age and then by sex, or vice versa.

Generalization hierarchies are used to combine heterogeneous categories into a single dimension. System is an example of a superclass, which allows to model the belonging of the categories Instrument, TreatedStructure, and Actuator to the dimension System of the fact type STATE, as shown in Figure 4.

Fact as dimension. In the case of a fact hierarchy or a satellite fact, the whole n-dimensional fact schema $\mathcal{S}$ of the basis fact is included as a hierarchical dimension into its dependent fact. For instance, COMPONENT treats SURGERY as its dimension, while the dimensions Patient, Location, etc. of the latter are treated as parallel hierarchies [18] within the same dimension.

Dimension inclusion is a special case of shared dimensions, in which dimension $\mathcal{D}_j$ represents a finer granularity of dimension $\mathcal{D}_i$, or formally, $\mathcal{D}_i \subset \mathcal{D}_j$ if $\exists \mathcal{C}_k \in \mathcal{D}_j : \mathcal{C}_k \sqsubseteq \bot_{\mathcal{D}_i}$. For example, TreatedStructure in ACTIVITY rolls up to Patient in SURGERY. Dimension inclusion implies that all categories in $\mathcal{D}_i$ become valid aggregation levels of $\mathcal{D}_j$.

The guidelines for modeling complex dimensions are provided in [15,18,17].

5.4   Runtime Measure Specification

Compulsory elements of any aggregate query are 1) a measure specified as an aggregate function (e.g., sum, average, maximum etc.) and its input attribute, and 2) a set of dimension categories to use as the granularity of the aggregation. Conventional OLAP tools require the set of the available measures within a cube to be pre-configured at the metadata level. It is also common to provide a wizard for defining a new measure, however, limiting the selection of qualifying attributes to the

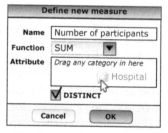

Fig. 6. Defining a measure

set $\mathcal{M}_q$ of fact schema $\mathcal{F}$, i.e., to the actual measure attributes encountered in the fact table. In our scenario, the measure definition routine needs to be modified to account for the following phenomena:

– The fact schema is factless, i.e., $\{\mathcal{M}_q\} = \emptyset$.
– Each non-satellite fact schema disposes of a fact identifier attribute $\bar{\mathcal{A}}_{\mathcal{F}}$ belonging neither to the measure nor to the dimension set of $\mathcal{F}$.
– Any attribute of a data cube, whether of the fact table itself or of any of its dimensions, can be chosen as an input for a measure. Examples of commonly queried measures are the total number of patients operated, average number of surgeries in a hospital, most frequent diagnoses, number of distinct instruments per surgery, etc.

In accordance with the above requirements, we propose to enable runtime measure specification by the analyst as a 3-step process, depicted in Figure 6:

1. Selecting an aggregate function from the function list;
2. Specifying the measure attribute: in a visual interface, this can be done via a "drag&drop" of a category from the navigation, as shown in Figure 6, where Hospital category is being dragged into the measure window;
3. Specifying whether the duplicates should be eliminated from the aggregation by activating the DISTINCT option.

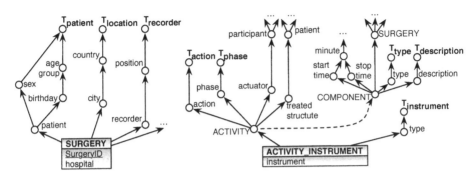

Fig. 7. Changes in the conceptual schema caused by deriving a measure from a dimension category: (*left*) number of hospitals, (*right*) number of instruments

Optionally, the newly defined measure may be supplied with a user-friendly name. As long as no user-defined measure is specified, the default setting of COUNT(*), i.e., simple counting of the qualifying fact entries, is used. In terms of the conceptual model, derivation of a measure from virtually any element of the n-dimensional fact schema is equivalent to re-designing the entire schema.

Let us consider an example of analyzing the number of hospitals, i.e., using category Hospital from dimension Location as the measure attribute. Obviously, to support this measure, SURGERY facts need to be aggregated to the Hospital level, Hospital turns into a measure attribute within SURGERY and the bottom granularity of Location changes from Room to City. The resulting data schema is shown in Figure 7 (left). Location granularities below Hospital simply become invalid in the defined query context.

A more complicated example of selecting the number of instruments to serve as a measure is presented in Figure 7 (right). Instrument category is turned into a measure attribute of the fact table ACTIVITY_INSTRUMENT. From this perspective, all upper-level facts, such as ACTIVITY and SURGERY, are treated as dimension categories. Thus, the analyst may pursue any aggregation path valid in the context of the chosen measure. For example the number of instruments can be rolled-up to SURGERY, Action, Phase, etc.

In practice, the schemata of the designed data cubes remains unchanged and only a virtual view corresponding to the adjusted schema is generated to support querying user-defined measures. For frequently used measures, materialization of the respective view may improve the performance.

6   Results

The feasibility of our model can be shown by implementing it into a relational OLAP system and running domain-specific queries against the accumulated data. We present an application case of analyzing the use of instruments in the surgical intervention type discectomy. The goal of a discectomy is partial

Dimensions	Measures							
	COUNT(ActivityID)				AVG(StopTime − StartTime)			
	SurgeryID				SurgeryID			
Instrument	A	B	C	D	A	B	C	D
coaugulator	7	17	4	8	00:00:31	00:00:23	00:00:34	00:00:27
dissector	3	3	14	4	00:00:56	00:00:16	00:00:25	00:00:45
forceps	12	3	7	10	00:01:50	00:00:32	00:00:54	00:01:51
hook	15	7	7	12	00:01:14	00:01:01	00:00:31	00:00:47
punch	9	22	10	9	00:02:38	00:00:35	00:00:46	00:01:27
scalpel	2	3	2	2	00:00:53	00:01:23	00:00:22	00:01:09
suction tube	6	26	2	2	00:14:42	00:00:12	00:16:29	00:11:21
Total	54	81	46	47	00:03:15	00:00:37	00:02:52	00:02:32

Fig. 8. Results of sample aggregate queries 1 und 2 as a pivot table

removal of the herniated intervertebral disc. Typical expert queries in this scenario focus on the occurrence of particular instruments, frequency of their usage throughout the surgery, and duration of usage periods. Figure 8 shows a pivot table with the results of the following two queries:

Query 1. *For each of the interventions of type discectomy, find the instruments used by the surgeon and the frequency of their occurrence (i.e., the number of activities in which that instrument is used).*

The measure of this query, i.e., the number of activities (COUNT(DISTINCT ActivityID)), is rolled-up by SurgeryID and Instrument with a selection condition along Discipline. The input data cube is obtained by joining the fact tables SURGERY and ACTIVITY with their respective satellites SURGERY_DISCIPLINE and ACTIVITY_INSTRUMENT and joining the former two with each other via COMPONENT. The left-hand half of the table in Figure 8 contains the computed occurrence aggregates, with Instrument mapped to the table rows and SurgeryID as well as the measure COUNT(DISTINCT ActivityID) in the columns.

Query 2. *For each of the interventions of type discectomy, calculate the mean usage times of each instrument used by the surgeon (i.e., the average duration of the respective activities).*

The duration of a step corresponds to the time elapsed between its start and end, so that the measure can be specified as (AVG(StopTime-StartTime)). The rollup and the filtering conditions are identical to the previous query. The resulting aggregates are contained in the right-hand half of the pivot table.

Other examples of surgical queries supported by our proposed multidimensional design for Surgical Workflows are 'How much time does the surgeon spend on action X?', 'At which anatomical structures has instrument Y been used?', or 'Which input is needed to execute a particular work step?'.

7   Conclusion

In this work we applied the data warehousing approach to business process analysis. Conventional BPMS are rather limited in the types of supported analysis tasks, whereas data warehousing appears more suitable when it comes to managing large amounts of data, defining various business metrics, and running complex queries. The case study presented in this work is concerned with designing a recording scheme for acquiring process descriptions from surgical interventions for their subsequent analysis and exploration.

As the business process model and the multidimensional model are based on different concepts, it is crucial to find a common abstraction for their convergence. We propose to map the vertical decomposition of a process into temporal or logical components to fact entries at two granularity levels, namely, at the process and at the work step level. Horizontal decomposition according to the factual perspectives, such as function, organization, operation, etc., is used to identify dimensional characteristics of the facts.

We evaluated the relational OLAP approach against the requirements of our case study and proposed an extended data model that addresses such challenges as non-quantitative and heterogeneous facts, many-to-many relationships between facts and dimensions, runtime definition of measures, interchangeability of fact and dimension roles, etc. The proposed model extensions can be easily implemented using current OLAP tools, with facts and dimensions stored in relational tables and queried with standard SQL. We presented a prototype of a visual interface for the runtime measure definition and concluded the work by producing the results of sample analytical queries formulated by the domain experts and run against the modeled surgical process data warehouse.

Acknowledgement

We would like to thank Oliver Burgert from ICCAS at the University of Leipzig as well as Christos Trantakis and Jürgen Meixensberger from the Neurosurgery Department at the University Hospital of Leipzig for their expert support.

References

1. Dayal, U., Hsu, M., Ladin, R.: Business process coordination: State of the art, trends, and open issues. In: VLDB 2001: Proc. 27th Int.Conf. on Very Large Data Bases, pp. 3–13 (2001)
2. Grigori, D., Casati, F., Castellanos, M., Dayal, U., Sayal, M., Shan, M.-C.: Business process intelligence. Computers in Industry 53(3), 321–343 (2004)
3. Smith, M.: Business process intelligence. Intelligent Enterprise, Online (December 2002), http://www.intelligententerprise.com/021205/601feat2_1.jhtml
4. Neumuth, T., Strauß, G., Meixensberger, J., Lemke, H.U., Burgert, O.: Acquisition of process descriptions from surgical interventions. In: Bressan, S., Küng, J., Wagner, R. (eds.) DEXA 2006. LNCS, vol. 4080, pp. 602–611. Springer, Heidelberg (2006)

5. Neumuth, T., Trantakis, C., Eckhardt, F., Dengl, M.: Supporting the analysis of intervention courses with surgical process models on the example of fourteen microsurgical lumbar discectomies. International Journal of Computer Assisted Radiology and Surgery 2(1), 436–438 (2007)
6. OMG (Object Management Group): BPMN (Business Process Modeling Notation) 1.0: OMG Final Adopted Specification, Online (February 2006), http://www.bpmn.org
7. WfMC (Workflow Management Coalition): WfMC Standards: The Workflow Reference Model, Version 1.1, Online (January 1995), http://www.wfmc.org/standards/docs/tc003v11.pdf
8. Pedersen, T.B., Jensen, C.S.: Multidimensional database technology. IEEE Computer 34(12), 40–46 (2001)
9. Kimball, R., Reeves, L., Ross, M., Thornthwaite, W.: The Data Warehouse Lifecycle Toolkit. John Wiley & Sons, Inc., New York (1998)
10. Jung, J.: Meta-modelling support for a general process modelling tool. In: DSM 2005: Proc. 5th OOPSLA Workshop on Domain-Specific Modeling, pp. 602–611 (2005)
11. Muth, P., Wodtke, D., Weißenfels, J., Weikum, G., Kotz-Dittrich, A.: Enterprise-wide workflow management based on state and activity charts. In: Proc. NATO Advanced Study Institute on Workflow Management Systems and Interoperability, pp. 281–303 (1997)
12. Matousek, P.: Verification of Business Process Models. PhD thesis, Technical University of Ostrava (2003)
13. Jablonski, S., Bussler, C.: Workflow Management. Modeling Concepts, Architecture and Implementation. International Thomson Computer Press (1996)
14. Hao, M.C, Keim, D.A, Dayal, U.: Business process impact visualization and anomaly detection. Information Visualization 5, 15–27 (2006)
15. Pedersen, T.B., Jensen, C.S., Dyreson, C.E.: A foundation for capturing and querying complex multidimensional data. Information Systems 26(5), 383–423 (2001)
16. Jensen, C.S., Kligys, A., Pedersen, T.B., Timko, I.: Multidimensional data modeling for location-based services. The VLDB Journal 13(1), 1–21 (2004)
17. Mansmann, S., Scholl, M.H.: Empowering the OLAP technology to support complex dimension hierarchies. International Journal of Data Warehousing and Mining 3(4), 31–50 (2007)
18. Malinowski, E., Zimányi, E.: Hierarchies in a multidimensional model: From conceptual modeling to logical representation. Data & Knowledge Engineering 59(2), 348–377 (2006)
19. Hruby, P.: Structuring specification of business systems with UML (with an emphasis on workflow management systems). In: Proc. OOPSLA'98 Business Object Workshop IV, Springer, Heidelberg (1998)
20. Luján-Mora, S., Trujillo, J., Vassiliadis, P.: Advantages of uml for multidimensional modeling. In: ICEIS 2004: Proc. 6th Int. Conf. on Enterprise Information Systems, pp. 298–305 (2004)
21. Lenz, H.-J., Shoshani, A.: Summarizability in OLAP and statistical data bases. In: SSDBM 1997: Proc. of 9th Int. Conf. on Scientific and Statistical Database Management, pp. 132–143 (1997)
22. Golfarelli, M., Maio, D., Rizzi, S.: The dimensional fact model: A conceptual model for data warehouses. International Journal of Cooperative Information Systems 7(2-3), 215–247 (1998)

Mining Hesitation Information by Vague Association Rules

An Lu and Wilfred Ng

Department of Computer Science and Engineering
The Hong Kong University of Science and Technology
Hong Kong, China
{anlu,wilfred}@cse.ust.hk

Abstract. In many online shopping applications, such as Amazon and eBay, traditional Association Rule (AR) mining has limitations as it only deals with the items that are sold but ignores the items that are *almost sold* (for example, those items that are put into the basket but not checked out). We say that those *almost sold* items carry *hesitation information*, since customers are hesitating to buy them. The hesitation information of items is valuable knowledge for the design of good selling strategies. However, there is no conceptual model that is able to capture different statuses of hesitation information. Herein, we apply and extend vague set theory in the context of AR mining. We define the concepts of attractiveness and hesitation of an item, which represent the overall information of a customer's intent on an item. Based on the two concepts, we propose the notion of Vague Association Rules (VARs). We devise an efficient algorithm to mine the VARs. Our experiments show that our algorithm is efficient and the VARs capture more specific and richer information than do the traditional ARs.

1 Introduction

Association Rule (AR) mining [1] is one of the most important data mining tasks. Consider the classical market basket case, in which AR mining is conducted on transactions that consist of items bought by customers. There are many items that are not bought but customers may have considered to buy them. We call such information on a customer's consideration to buy an item the *hesitation* information of the item, since the customer hesitates to buy it. The hesitation information of an item is useful knowledge for boosting the sales of the item. However, such information has not been considered in traditional AR mining due to the difficulty to collect the relevant data in the past. Nevertheless, with the advance in technology of data dissemination, it is now much easier for such data collection. A typical example is an online shopping scenario, such as "Amazon.com", which we are able to collect huge amount of data from the Web log that can be modelled as hesitation information. From Web logs, we can infer a customer's browsing pattern in a trail, say how many times and how much time s/he spends on a Web page, at which steps s/he quits the browsing, what and how many items are put in the basket when a trail ends, and so on. Therefore, we can further identify and categorize different browsing patterns into different hesitation information with respect to different applications.

There are many statuses of a piece of hesitation information (called *hesitation status (HS)*). Let us consider a motivating example of an online shopping scenario that

C. Parent et al. (Eds.): ER 2007, LNCS 4801, pp. 39–55, 2007.

involves various statuses: (s_1) HS of the items that the customer browsed only once and left; (s_2) HS of the items that are browsed in detail (e.g., the figures and all specifications) but not put into their online shopping carts; (s_3) HS of the items that customers put into carts and were checked out eventually. All of the above-mentioned HSs are the hesitation information of those items. Some of the HSs are comparable based on some criterion, which means we can define an order on these HSs. For example, given a criterion as the possibility that the customer buys an item, we have $s_1 \leq s_2 \leq s_3$. The hesitation information can then be used to design and implement selling strategies that can potentially turn those "interesting" items into "under consideration" items and "under consideration" items into "sold" items.

Our modelling technique of HSs of an item rests on a solid foundation of *vague set theory* [2,3,4]. The main benefit of this approach is that the theory addresses the drawback of a single membership value in *fuzzy set theory* [5] by using interval-based membership that captures three types of evidence with respect to an object in a universe of discourse: *support*, *against* and *hesitation*. Thus, we naturally model the hesitation information of an item in the mining context as the evidence of hesitation with respect to an item. The information of the "sold" items and the "not sold" items (without any hesitation information) in the traditional setting of AR mining correspond to the evidence of support and against with respect to the item. For example, if a customer bought an item 5 times, hesitated to buy (when different HSs are not distinguished) it 2 times, and did not browse it 3 times (in 10 visits), then we can obtain a vague membership value, $[0.5, 0.7]$ (where $0.7 = 1 - 3/10$), for the item. When we distinguish different HSs, say the customer hesitated to buy the item 2 times in HSs s_1 once and s_2 once, where $s_1 \leq s_2 \leq s_3$. Then the vague membership value for s_1 is $[0.5, 0.6]$ and that for s_2 is $[0.6, 0.7]$. As for s_3, since there is no hesitation evidence for it, and $s_2 \leq s_3$, its vague membership value is a single point, $[0.7, 0.7]$.

To study the relationship between the support evidence and the hesitation evidence with respect to an item, we propose *attractiveness* and *hesitation* of an item, which are derived from the vague membership in vague sets. An item with high attractiveness means that the item is well sold and has a high possibility to be sold again next time. An item with high hesitation means that the customer is always hesitating to buy the item due to some reason (e.g., the customer is waiting for price reduction) but has a high possibility to buy it next time if the reason is identified and resolved (e.g., some promotion on the item is provided). For example, given the vague membership value, $[0.5, 0.7]$, of an item, the attractiveness is 0.6 (the median of 0.5 and 0.7) and the hesitation is 0.2 (the difference between 0.7 and 0.5), which implies that the customer may buy the item next time with a possibility of 60% and hesitate to buy the item with a possibility of 20%.

Using the attractiveness and hesitation of items, we model a database with hesitation information as an AH-pair database that consists of AH-pair transactions, where A stands for attractiveness and H stands for hesitation. Based on the AH-pair database, we then propose the notion of *Vague Association Rules* (*VARs*), which capture four types of relationships between two sets of items: the implication of the attractiveness/hesitation of one set of items on the attractiveness/hesitation of the other set of items. For example, if we find an AH-rule like "People always buy quilts and pillows(A) but quit the process of buying beds at the step of choosing delivery method(H)". Thus, there might be something wrong with the delivery method for beds (for example, no home delivery service provided) which causes people hesitate to buy beds. To evaluate the quality of the different types of VARs, four types of support and confidence are defined. We also investigate the properties of the support and confidence of VARs, which can be used to speed up the mining process.

Our experiments on both real and synthetic datasets verify that our algorithm to mine the VARs is efficient. Compared with the traditional ARs mined from transactional databases, the VARs mined from the AH-pair databases are more specific and are able to capture richer information. Most importantly, we find that, by aggregating more transactions into an AH-pair transaction, our algorithm is significantly more efficient while still obtaining almost the same set of VARs. The concept of VARs is not limited to the online shopping scenario. In our experiments, we demonstrate that VARs are applied to mine Web log data.

Organization. This paper is organized as follows. Section 2 gives some preliminaries on vague sets and ARs. Section 3 introduces VARs and presents the related concepts. Section 4 discusses the algorithm that mines VARs. Section 5 reports the experimental results. Section 6 discusses the related work and Section 7 concludes the paper.

2   Preliminaries

2.1   Vague Sets

Let I be a classical set of objects, called the universe of discourse, where an element of I is denoted by x.

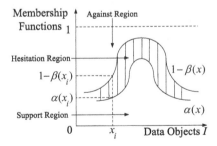

Fig. 1. The True (α) and False (β) Membership Functions of a Vague Set

Definition 1 (Vague Set). *A vague set V in a universe of discourse I is characterized by a true membership function, α_V, and a false membership function, β_V, as follows: $\alpha_V : I \rightarrow [0,1]$, $\beta_V : I \rightarrow [0,1]$, where $\alpha_V(x) + \beta_V(x) \leq 1$, $\alpha_V(x)$ is a lower bound on the grade of membership of x derived from the evidence for x, and $\beta_V(x)$ is a lower bound on the grade of membership of the negation of x derived from the evidence* against x. Suppose $I = \{x_1, x_2, \ldots, x_n\}$. *A vague set V of the universe of discourse I is represented by* $V = \sum_{i=1}^{n} [\alpha(x_i), 1 - \beta(x_i)]/x_i$, *where* $0 \leq \alpha(x_i) \leq (1 - \beta(x_i)) \leq 1$. □

The grade of membership of x is bounded to $[\alpha_V(x), 1 - \beta_V(x)]$, which is a subinterval of $[0, 1]$ as depicted in Fig. 1. For brevity, we omit the subscript V from α_V and β_V.

We say that $[\alpha(x), 1 - \beta(x)]/x$ is a *vague element* and the interval $[\alpha(x), 1 - \beta(x)]$ is the *vague value* of the object x. For example, $[\alpha(x), 1 - \beta(x)] = [0.5, 0.7]$ is interpreted as "the degree that the object x belongs to the vague set V is 0.5 (i.e. $\alpha(x)$) and the degree that x does not belong to V is 0.3 (i.e. $\beta(x)$)." For instance, in a voting process, the vague value $[0.5, 0.7]$ can be interpreted as "50% of the votes support the motion, 30% are against, while 20% are neutral (abstentions)."

2.2 Median Memberships and Imprecision Memberships

In order to compare vague values, we introduce two derived memberships: median membership and imprecision membership [4]. Note that given a vague value $[\alpha(x), 1 - \beta(x)]$, we have unique median membership $M_m(x)$ and imprecision membership $M_i(x)$, and vice versa.

Median membership is defined as $M_m = \frac{1}{2}(\alpha + (1 - \beta))$, which represents the overall evidence contained in a vague value. It can be checked that $0 \leq M_m \leq 1$. Obviously, the vague value $[1, 1]$ has the highest M_m, which means the corresponding object definitely belongs to the vague set (i.e., a crisp value). While the vague value $[0, 0]$ has the lowest M_m, which means that the corresponding object definitely does not belong to the vague set.

Imprecision membership is defined as $M_i = ((1 - \beta) - \alpha)$, which represents the overall imprecision of a vague value. It can be checked that $0 \leq M_i \leq 1$. The vague value $[a, a](a \in [0, 1])$ has the lowest M_i which means that the membership of the corresponding object is exact (i.e., a fuzzy value). While the vague value $[0, 1]$ has the highest M_i which means that we do not have any information about the membership of the corresponding object.

The median membership and the imprecision membership are employed in this paper to measure the attractiveness and the hesitation of an item with respect to a customer.

2.3 Association Rules

Let $I = \{x_1, x_2, \ldots, x_n\}$ be a set of items [1]. An *itemset* is a subset of I. A *transaction* is an itemset. We say that a transaction Y *supports* an itemset X if $Y \supseteq X$. For brevity, we write an itemset $X = \{x_{k_1}, x_{k_2}, \ldots, x_{k_m}\}$ as $x_{k_1} x_{k_2} \ldots x_{k_m}$.

Let D be a database of transactions. The *frequency* of an itemset X, denoted as $freq(X)$, is the number of transactions in D that support X. The *support* of X, denoted as $supp(X)$, is defined as $\frac{freq(X)}{|D|}$, where $|D|$ is the number of transactions in D. X is a *Frequent Itemset (FI)* if $supp(X) \geq \sigma$, where σ ($0 \leq \sigma \leq 1$) is a user-specified *minimum support threshold*.

Given the set of all FIs, the set of ARs is obtained as follows: for each FI Y and for each non-empty subset X of Y, we generate an AR, r, of the form $X \Rightarrow Y - X$.

---

[1] We refer to the terms *item* and *object* interchangeably in this paper.

The *support* of r, denoted as $supp(r)$, is defined as $supp(Y)$ and the *confidence* of r, denoted as $conf(r)$, is defined as $\frac{supp(Y)}{supp(X)}$. We say that r is a *valid AR* if $conf(r) \geq c$, where c $(0 \leq c \leq 1)$ is a user-specified *minimum confidence threshold*.

3 Vague Association Rules

In this section, we first propose the concept of Hesitation Statuses (*HSs*) of an item and discuss how to model HSs. Then we introduce the notion of *Vague Association Rules* (*VARs*) and four types of support and confidence used in order to fully evaluate their quality. Some properties of VARs that are useful to improve the efficiency of mining VARs are presented.

3.1 Hesitation Information Modeling

A *Hesitation Status (HS)* is a specific state between two certain situations of "buying" and "not buying" in the process of a purchase transaction.

Here we use a more detailed example of placing an order with "Amazon.com" [6] to illustrate the idea of HS. There are following nine steps, which forms a queue, to place an order: (s_1) Find the items you want; (s_2) Add the items to your shopping cart; (s_3) Proceed to checkout; (s_4) Sign in; (s_5) Enter a shipping address; (s_6) Choose a shipping method; (s_7) Provide a password and payment information; (s_8) Review and submit your order; (s_9) Check your order status.

A customer may quit the ordering process at any step for some reason, for example, forgetting the sign name or password. Therefore, the HSs with respect to different quitting steps are different, since the more steps a customer goes, the higher possibility the customer buys the item.

However, some HSs are incomparable. For example, a customer may put an item into the wishing list if the item is out of stock. The HS in this case is incomparable to the HS of the item with respect to quitting order at step 6, since we lack evidence to support any ordered relationship between these two HSs.

We now formally model the hesitation information of an item as follows.

Definition 2 (Hesitation and Overall Hesitation). *Given an item $x \in I$ and a set of HSs $S = \{s_1, s_2, \ldots, s_w\}$ with a partial order $\leq$. The hesitation of x with respect to an HS $s_i \in S$ is a function $h_i(x) : I \to [0, 1]$, such that $\alpha(x) + \beta(x) + \sum_{i=1}^{w} h_i(x) = 1$, where $h_i(x)$ represents the evidence for the HS s_i of x. The overall hesitation of x with respect to S is given by $H(x) = \sum_{i=1}^{w} h_i(x)$.* □

It can be easily checked from the above definition that $H(x) = 1 - \alpha(x) - \beta(x)$. S can also be represented by a Hasse Diagram whose vertices are elements in S and the edges correspond to $\leq$. All components in S can be partitioned into two groups of HSs: a Chain Group (*CG*) consists of connected components that are chains (including the case of a singleton HS node), and a Non-Chain Group (*NCG*) consists of components that are non-chains (not chains).

In order to capture the hesitation evidence and the hesitation order $\leq$, a subinterval of $[\alpha(x), 1 - \beta(x)]$ is used to represent the customer's *intent* of each item with respect to different HSs. To obtain the intent value, the idea of linear extensions of a partial order is used. However, computing the number of extensions is a #P-complete problem [7]. An algorithm that generates all of the linear extensions of a partially ordered set in constant amortized time is given in [8]. In real applications, say the online-shopping scenario, we can simplify $\leq$ in order to reduce the computation complexity. From now on, we assume that a component G in the NCG is a chain of *Incomparable Chain Sets* (ICSs), $\{ICS_1 \leq ICS_2 \leq \cdots \leq ICS_l\}$, where $ICS_i \in G$ is a set of chains satisfying the following condition: the parent (child) HSs of the top (bottom) elements in all chains, if any, are in the same ICS.

Note that this condition implies that the parent (child) HS of a chain in the top (bottom) ICS is an empty set.

We now present an algorithm that partitions a component G in NCG into different ICSs in Algorithm 1.

Algorithm 1. PartitionNCG(G)

---

1. $i := 1$;
2. **while** $G \neq \emptyset$
3.   Let ICS_i be the set of all minimal HS $s \in G$;
4.   **forall** $s \in ICS_i$ **do**
5.   Search the longest chain segment of s such that each HS (excluding s itself) in it has a unique child, and the child has a unique parent;
6.   Put all HSs of the chain segment in ICS_i if any;
7. $G := G - ICS_i; i := i + 1$;
8. **return** the result $\{ICS_1 \leq ICS_2 \leq \cdots \leq ICS_i\}$.

Example 1. Let $S = \{s_1, \ldots, s_{17}\}$, and its Hasse diagram consists of four components as shown in Fig. 2. We see that the component g_2 is in CG, since it is a chain, and the components g_1, g_3, and g_4 are in NCG, where different ICSs are represented by the dashed ellipses. Consider the component g_1, s_1 is the only element in ICS_1, since it has more than one parent (i.e. s_2 and s_3) and the longest chain segment of s_1 (according to Line 5 of Algorithm 1) contains itself only, while s_2 and s_3 are in ICS_2, since they are the top HSs and have no parents. Thus, we partition g_1 into the chain of ICSs as

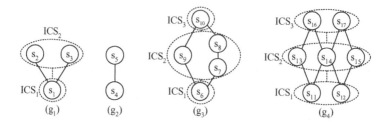

Fig. 2. The Hasse Diagram of the Ordered Set of HSs

$ICS_1 \leq ICS_2$. Consider the component g_3, s_6 is the only element in ICS_1. s_9 and s_7 are the minimal HSs in ICS_2. s_8 is also in ICS_2, since it has a unique child s_7 and s_7 has a unique parent s_8. s_{10} is not in ICS_2, since it has two children (i.e. s_8 and s_9). Consider the component g_4, s_{11} and s_{12} are in ICS_1, since they both have more than one parents. s_{13}, s_{14} and s_{15} are in ICS_2 and finally, the top HSs s_{16} and s_{17} form ICS_3.   □

Given a set of purchase transactions, we can aggregate the transactions to obtain the *intent* of each item with respect to different HSs. Although aggregating the transactions may lose some exact information of the items for customers, in many cases the overall knowledge is more useful than the details of every transaction. For example, in our online shopping scenario, by aggregating the data we alleviate the problem of high cost of mining on huge log data sets.

Definition 3 (Intent and Overall Intent). *Given a set of HSs, $(S, \leq)$, the* intent *of an item x with respect to an HS $s_i \in S$, denoted as $int(x, s_i)$, is a vague value $[\alpha_i(x), 1 - \beta_i(x)]$ which is a subinterval of $[\alpha(x), 1 - \beta(x)]$ and satisfies the following conditions:*

1. $(1 - \beta_i(x)) = \alpha_i(x) + h_i(x)$.
2. For each ICS_j in the chain $ICS_1 \leq ICS_2 \leq \cdots \leq ICS_j \leq \cdots \leq ICS_l$, of an NCG component G, we assume a linear extension of G ($s_1 \leq s_2 \leq \cdots \leq s_m$) such that there exists a segment ($s_{p+1} \leq \cdots \leq s_{p+q}$) consistent with all the chains in ICS_j, where $1 \leq p+1$ and $p + q \leq m$. The intent for ICS_j, denoted as $[\alpha_{ICS_j}(x), 1 - \beta_{ICS_j}(x)]$, is given by $\alpha_{ICS_j}(x) = \frac{\alpha(x) + (1 - \beta(x))}{2} - \frac{1}{2} \sum_{k=1}^{m} h_k(x) + \sum_{k=1}^{p} h_k(x)$, $1 - \beta_{ICS_j}(x) = \alpha_{ICS_j}(x) + \sum_{k=p+1}^{p+q} h_k(x)$.
3. – If s_i is in a chain of the CG, $s_1 \leq s_2 \leq \cdots \leq s_i \leq \cdots \leq s_n$, then for $1 \leq i \leq n$, we define
$$\alpha_i(x) = \frac{\alpha(x) + (1 - \beta(x))}{2} - \frac{1}{2} \sum_{k=1}^{n} h_k(x) + \sum_{k=1}^{i-1} h_k(x).$$
   – If s_i is in a chain of ICS_j, $s_g \leq s_{g+1} \leq \cdots \leq s_i \leq \cdots \leq s_v$, where $((p + 1) \leq g \leq v \leq (p + q))$, then for $g \leq i \leq v$, we define
$$\alpha_i(x) = \frac{\alpha_{ICS_j}(x) + (1 - \beta_{ICS_j}(x))}{2} - \frac{1}{2} \sum_{k=g}^{v} h_k(x) + \sum_{k=g}^{i-1} h_k(x).$$
The overall intent *of x, denoted as $INT(x)$, is the interval $[\alpha(x), 1 - \beta(x)]$.*   □

Condition 1 shows the relationship among $(1 - \beta_i(x))$, $\alpha_i(x)$ and $h_i(x)$. Together with condition 3, we can determine the intent $[\alpha_i(x), 1 - \beta_i(x)]$, since $h_i(x)$, $\alpha(x)$ and $(1 - \beta(x))$ are given parameters.

The formulas in condition condition 3 are similar, which are defined to ensure that the numerical order of median membership of the HSs is consistent with the order of HSs. This also fits for the cases in most real life applications.

Example 2. Table 1 shows the transactions of a single customer derived from an online shopping system, where we use 1 and 0 to represent that an item is bought and not bought (without any hesitation information), as in the traditional AR mining setting. The set of HSs is given by $S = \{s_1 \leq s_2, s_1 \leq s_3, s_4 \leq s_5\}$, that is, the graphs g_1 and g_2 in Fig. 2.

In Table 1, given 10 transactions, we have 7 *buy* and 1 *not buy* and 2 HSs (s_1 and s_3) for an item A. Consider $g_1 = \{s_1 \leq s_2, s_1 \leq s_3\}$, we have one of its linear extension

Table 1. Ten Transactions of a Customer

TID	A	B	C	D
1	1	s_4	s_4	s_1
2	1	0	s_1	0
3	1	1	s_1	s_3
4	0	s_5	s_3	s_3
5	s_1	1	s_2	s_2
6	1	0	s_5	s_3
7	s_1	s_5	s_3	s_3
8	1	0	s_4	s_5
9	s_3	0	0	0
10	1	s_5	1	s_5

Table 2. An Intent Database for Different HSs

H	A	B	C	D
$h_1(x)$	[0.6,0.8]	[0.4,0.4]	[0.25,0.45]	[0.1,0.2]
$h_2(x)$	[0.85,0.85]	[0.4,0.4]	[0.55,0.65]	[0.4,0.5]
$h_3(x)$	[0.8,0.9]	[0.4,0.4]	[0.5,0.7]	[0.25,0.65]
$h_4(x)$	[0.75,0.75]	[0.2,0.3]	[0.35,0.55]	[0.3,0.3]
$h_5(x)$	[0.75,0.75]	[0.3,0.6]	[0.55,0.65]	[0.3,0.5]
$H(x)$	[0.6,0.9]	[0.2,0.6]	[0.1,0.9]	[0,0.8]

Table 3. An *AH*-pair Database for Different HSs

H	A	B	C	D
$h_1(x)$	<0.7,0.2>	<0.4,0>	<0.35,0.2>	<0.15,0.1>
$h_2(x)$	<0.85,0>	<0.4,0>	<0.6,0.1>	<0.45,0.1>
$h_3(x)$	<0.85,0.1>	<0.4,0>	<0.6,0.2>	<0.45,0.4>
$h_4(x)$	<0.75,0>	<0.25,0.1>	<0.45,0.2>	<0.3,0>
$h_5(x)$	<0.75,0>	<0.45,0.3>	<0.6,0.1>	<0.4,0.2>
$H(x)$	<0.75,0.3>	<0.4,0.4>	<0.5,0.8>	<0.4,0.8>

$s_1 \leq s_2 \leq s_3$. Since $ICS_1 = \{s_1\}$ and $ICS_2 = \{s_2, s_3\}$, we have $int(A, s_1) = [0.6, 0.8]$, $int(A, s_2) = [0.85, 0.85]$ and $int(A, s_3) = [0.8, 0.9]$, according to Definition 3. As s_4 and s_5 is a chain in CG, we then obtain $int(A, s_4) = int(A, s_5) = [0.75, 0.75]$. Thus, we obtain all the intent of A for the HSs in S as shown in the first column of Table 2 and in Fig. 3. It can be checked that s_2, s_4 and s_5 are single points, since the hesitation evidence is zero for them. The intent database of all items (A, B, C, D) for different HSs ($s_1, \ldots, s_5$) can be similarly determined, which is shown in Table 2 and also illustrated by Fig. 3. Note that the values in the last row of the table are $[\alpha(x), 1 - \beta(x)]$, indicating the overall hesitation $H(x)$.   □

Given the intent of an item for an HS, we further define the attractiveness of the item which represents the overall evidence for it with respect to an HS.

Definition 4 (Attractiveness and Overall Attractiveness). *The* attractiveness *of x with respect to an HS s_i, denoted as $att(x, s_i)$, is defined as the median membership of x with respect to s_i, that is, $\frac{1}{2}(\alpha_i(x) + (1 - \beta_i(x)))$. The* overall attractiveness *of x is a function $ATT(x) : I \to [0, 1]$, such that $ATT(x) = \frac{1}{2}(\alpha(x) + (1 - \beta(x)))$.*   □

Given the intent $[\alpha_i(x), 1 - \beta_i(x)]$ of an item x for an HS s_i, we have a one-one corresponding pair of the attractiveness and hesitation of x, called the *AH*-pair, denoted as $\langle att(x, s_i), h_i(x) \rangle$. Attractiveness and hesitation are two important concepts, since people may have special interest in finding ARs with items of high attractiveness (sold well) or high hesitation (almost sold).

We now define an *AH*-pair transaction and an *AH*-pair database.

Definition 5 (*AH*-Pair Transaction and Database). *An* AH-pair transaction *T is a tuple $<v_1, v_2, \ldots, v_m>$ on an itemset $I_T = \{x_1, x_2, \ldots, x_m\}$, where $I_T \subseteq I$ and*

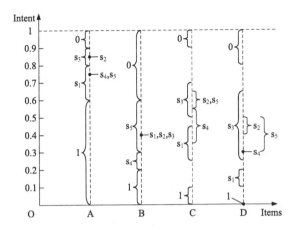

Fig. 3. Intent for Different HSs of Items

$v_j = \langle M_A(x_j), M_H(x_j) \rangle$ *is an AH-pair of the item* x_j *with respect to a given HS or the overall hesitation, for* $1 \leq j \leq m$. *An* AH-*pair database is a sequence of AH-pair transactions.* □

We can transform the intent database shown in Table 2 to its equivalent *AH*-pair database shown in Table 3 without losing any information and present the attractiveness and hesitation of the items directly.

We can further calculate *AH*-pairs directly without calculating the intent first, and the calculation process can be simplified. Since $att(x, s_i) = \alpha_i(x) + \frac{1}{2}h_i(x)$, and $h_i(x)$ is known, the three conditions in Definition 3 can be replaced by three equivalent conditions. Formally, we give the method of calculating *AH*-pairs as follows.

The *AH*-pair of an item x with respect to an HS s_i, $\langle att(x, s_i), h_i(x) \rangle$, satisfies the following conditions:

1. Assume the same setting as stated as condition 2 of Definition 3.
   The attractiveness for ICS_j, denoted as $att(x, ICS_j)$, is given as follows.
   $att(x, ICS_j) = ATT(x) - \frac{1}{2}\sum_{k=1}^{m} h_k(x) + \sum_{k=1}^{p} h_k(x) + \frac{1}{2}\sum_{k=p+1}^{p+q} h_k(x)$,
2. If s_i is in a chain of the CG, $s_1 \leq s_2 \leq \cdots \leq s_i \leq \cdots \leq s_n$, for $1 \leq i \leq n$, we define $att(x, s_i) = ATT(x) - \frac{1}{2}\sum_{k=1}^{n} h_k(x) + \sum_{k=1}^{i-1} h_k(x) + \frac{1}{2}h_i(x)$.
3. If s_i is in a chain of ICS_j, $s_g \leq s_{g+1} \leq \cdots \leq s_i \leq \cdots \leq s_v$, where $((p+1) \leq g \leq v \leq (p+q))$, for $g \leq i \leq v$, we define $att(x, s_i) = att(x, ICS_j) - \frac{1}{2}\sum_{k=g}^{v} h_k(x) + \sum_{k=g}^{i-1} h_k(x) + \frac{1}{2}h_i(x)$. □

The following proposition states the relationship between the hesitation order of two HSs and the attractiveness for them of an item.

Proposition 1. *If* $s_i \leq s_j$, *then* $att(x, s_i) \leq att(x, s_j)$.

Proof. It follows directly from the method of calculating *AH*-pairs above. □

The following proposition states the relationship between the overall attractiveness and hesitation, and the attractiveness and hesitation for different HSs.

Proposition 2. *Given* $S = \{s_1, s_2, \ldots, s_w\}$, $ATT(x)H(x) = \sum_{i=1}^{w} att(x, s_i)h_i(x)$.

Proof Sketch. We first prove the case that S contains CG components only, where condition 2 in the method of calculating AH-pairs above applies to all chains in S. Then we extend the proof to the case that S includes both CG and NCG components, where condition 3 applies for the chains of ICSs in NCG. When S contains CG components only, for any chain, $(s_1 \leq \cdots \leq s_i \leq \cdots \leq s_n)$, in S, we have $ATT(x) - att(x, s_i) = \frac{1}{2}\sum_{k=1}^{n} h_k(x) - \sum_{k=1}^{i-1} h_k(x) - \frac{1}{2}h_i(x) = \frac{1}{2}(h_{i+1}(x) + h_{i+2}(x) \cdots + h_n(x) - h_1(x) - h_2(x) - \cdots - h_{i-1}(x))$. It can be checked that $\sum_{i=1}^{n}(ATT(x) - att(x, s_i))h_i(x) = 0$. Then we extend this conclusion to the whole S, since any chains in S satisfies this conclusion, that is to say, we have $\sum_{i=1}^{w}(ATT(x) - att(x, s_i))h_i(x) = 0$. Thus, $ATT(x)H(x) = \sum_{i=1}^{w} att(x, s_i)h_i(x)$. When S contains both CG and NCG components, since each ICS_j of NCG in condition 3 can be regarded as the case of CG in condition 2, in a similar way, we can check that the conclusion also holds for the case including NCG components. $\qquad\square$

Proposition 2 indicates that the sum of the product of attractiveness and hesitation with respect to all HSs preserves the product of overall attractiveness and hesitation.

3.2   Vague Association Rules and Their Support and Confidence

We now present the notion of VARs and define the support and confidence of a VAR.

Definition 6 (Vague Association Rule). *A Vague Association Rule (VAR), $r = (X \Rightarrow Y)$, is an association rule obtained from an AH-pair database.* $\qquad\square$

Based on the attractiveness and hesitation of an item with respect to an HS, we can define different types of support and confidence of a VAR. For example, if we have special interest in the association between well-sold items (high attractiveness) and almost-sold items (high hesitation). Then, with some analysis between the former and the latter, we may make some improvements to boost the sales of the latter. For this purpose, we define *Attractiveness-Hesitation* (AH) support and AH confidence of a VAR to evaluate the VAR. Similarly, we can obtain the association between an itemset with high hesitation and another itemset with high attractiveness, between two itemsets with high attractiveness, and between two itemsets with high hesitation for different purposes. Accordingly, we define four types of support and confidence to evaluate the VARs as follows.

Note that here A (or H) can refer to either the overall attractiveness (or hesitation), or the attractiveness (or hesitation) of a given HS.

Definition 7 (Support). *Given an AH-pair database, D, we define four types of support for an itemset Z or a VAR $X \Rightarrow Y$, where $X \cup Y = Z$, as follows.*

1. *The A-support of Z, denoted as $Asupp(Z)$, is defined as* $\dfrac{\sum_{T \in D} \prod_{z \in Z} M_A(z)}{|D|}$.
2. *The H-support of Z, denoted as $Hsupp(Z)$, is defined as* $\dfrac{\sum_{T \in D} \prod_{z \in Z} M_H(z)}{|D|}$.

3. *The AH-support of Z, denoted as AHsupp(Z), is defined as* $\frac{\sum_{T \in D} \prod_{x \in X, y \in Y} M_A(x) M_H(y)}{|D|}$.

4. *The HA-support of Z, denoted as HAsupp(Z), is defined as* $\frac{\sum_{T \in D} \prod_{x \in X, y \in Y} M_H(x) M_A(y)}{|D|}$.

Z is an A (or H or AH or HA) FI if the A- (or H- or AH- or HA-) support of Z is no less than the (respective A or H or AH or HA) minimum support threshold σ. □

Definition 8 (Confidence). *Given an AH-pair database, D, we define the confidence of a VAR, $r = (X \Rightarrow Y)$, where $X \cup Y = Z$, as follows.*

1. *If both X and Y are A FIs, then the confidence of r, called the A-confidence of r and denoted as Aconf(r), is defined as* $\frac{Asupp(Z)}{Asupp(X)}$.
2. *If both X and Y are H FIs, then the confidence of r, called the H-confidence of r and denoted as Hconf(r), is defined as* $\frac{Hsupp(Z)}{Hsupp(X)}$.
3. *If X is an A FI and Y is an H FI, then the confidence of r, called the AH-confidence of r and denoted as AHconf(r), is defined as* $\frac{AHsupp(Z)}{Asupp(X)}$.
4. *If X is an H FI and Y is an A FI, then the confidence of r, called the HA-confidence of r and denoted as HAconf(r), is defined as* $\frac{HAsupp(Z)}{Hsupp(X)}$. □

Table 4. An AH-pair database on items with respect to s_1

CID	A	B	C	D
1	<0.7,0.2>	<0.4,0>	<0.35,0.2>	<0.15,0.1>
2	<0.9,0.2>	<0.7,0.2>	<0.6,0.8>	<0.5,0.8>
3	<0.7,0.1>	<0.8,0.4>	<0.4,0.7>	<0.5,0.9>
4	<0.8,0>	<0.9,0>	<0.5,0.9>	<0.4,0.7>
5	<1,0>	<0.9,0.1>	<0.4,0.8>	<0.6,0.8>

Table 5. The Four Types of Support and Confidence of $A \Rightarrow B$

	A	H	AH	HA
supp	0.618	0.016	0.112	0.06
conf	0.754	0.16	0.137	0.6

Example 3. Given the AH-pair database in Table 4 with respect to a given HS s_1 for customers with different CID, let $\sigma = 0.5$ and $c = 0.5$. Note that the first line in Table 4 is from the first line in Table 3, which represents the AH-pairs of different items for HS s_1 with respect to the customer with CID 1. Then, $Asupp(A) = (0.7 + 0.9 + 0.7 + 0.8 + 1)/5 = 0.82$, $AHsupp(A \Rightarrow D) = (0.7 \times 0.1 + 0.9 \times 0.8 + 0.7 \times 0.9 + 0.8 \times 0.7 + 1 \times 0.8)/5 = 0.556$, $AHconf(A \Rightarrow D) = \frac{0.556}{0.82} = 0.678$. Similarly, we calculate $AHsupp(A \Rightarrow B) = 0.112 \leq \sigma$, $AHconf(A \Rightarrow B) = 0.137 \leq c$. Thus, $A \Rightarrow D$ is a valid VAR with respect to AH-support and AH-confidence, but $A \Rightarrow B$ is not. □

We also compute all the four types of support and confidence of $A \Rightarrow B$ as shown in Table 5. It shows that $A \Rightarrow B$ is a valid VAR with respect to A-support and A-confidence, but not a valid VAR with respect to other types of support and confidence.

Problem Description. Given an AH-pair database D with respect to an HS s_i or the overall hesitation, σ and c, the problem of VAR mining is to find all VARs r such that $supp(r) \geq \sigma$ and $conf(r) \geq c$, where $supp$ and $conf$ are one of the A-, H-, AH-, and HA- support and confidence. □

Note that the thresholds σ and c can be different for different types of VARs. Hereafter, we just set them to be the same for different types of VARs, and this can be easily generalized to the case of different thresholds.

We give some properties of VARs which can be used to design an efficient algorithm for mining VARs. The following proposition states that the support defined for a certain itemset with respect to HSs has the anti-monotone property.

Proposition 3. *Given two different HSs s_i and s_j, let $supp_i$ ($conf_i$) and $supp_j$ ($conf_j$) be the corresponding support (confidence) with respect to different HSs. The following statements are true.*

1. *If $s_i \leq s_j$, then $Asupp_i(Z) \leq Asupp_j(Z)$.*
2. *If $s_i \leq s_j$ and $\forall y \in Y$, $h_i(y) \leq h_j(y)$, then $AHsupp_i(Z) \leq AHsupp_j(Z)$.*
3. *If $\forall x \in X$, $h_i(x) \leq h_j(x)$ and $s_i \leq s_j$, then $HAsupp_i(Z) \leq HAsupp_j(Z)$.*
4. *If $\forall z \in Z$, $h_i(z) \leq h_j(z)$, then $Hsupp_i(Z) \leq Hsupp_j(Z)$.*

Proof. It follows from Definition 7 and Proposition 1. $\qquad\square$

According to Proposition 3, when we find the support of an itemset with respect to an HS to be less than σ, we can prune the same itemset in the mining search space. The pruning applies to all the HSs less than or equal to, or in the same ICS with the original HS.

The following proposition states that the support defined for an itemset in an *AH*-pair database with respect to a certain HS has the anti-monotone property.

Proposition 4. *If $X \subseteq X'$, then $Asupp(X') \leq Asupp(X)$ and $Hsupp(X') \leq Hsupp(X)$.*

Proof. Since $X \subseteq X'$ and $0 \leq M_A(x) \leq 1$ ($x \in X'$), we have $\prod_{x \in X'} M_A(x) \leq$ $\prod_{x \in X} M_A(x)$. Thus $Asupp(X') = \dfrac{\sum_{T \in D} \prod_{x \in X'} M_A(x)}{|D|} \leq \dfrac{\sum_{T \in D} \prod_{x \in X} M_A(x)}{|D|} = Asupp(X)$.
And we also have $AHsupp(X') \leq AHsupp(X)$, since $AHsupp(X') = Asupp(X')$ and $AHsupp(X) = Asupp(X)$. Similarly, we can prove the cases of $Hsupp$ and $HAsupp$. $\qquad\square$

According to Proposition 4, when we find the support of an itemset to be less than σ, we can prune all its supersets in the mining search space. We can obtain greater pruning by the following two propositions.

Proposition 5. *Given an item x, $\dfrac{M_H(x)}{2} \leq M_A(x) \leq 1 - \dfrac{M_H(x)}{2}$.*

Proof. Since $\alpha(x) \geq 0$, $\dfrac{M_H(x)}{2} = \dfrac{(1-\beta(x))-\alpha(x)}{2} \leq \dfrac{(1-\beta(x))+\alpha(x)}{2} = M_A(x)$. Since $\beta(x) \geq 0$, $M_A(x) = \dfrac{\alpha(x)+(1-\beta(x))}{2} \leq \dfrac{\alpha(x)+(1+\beta(x))}{2} = 1 - \dfrac{(1-\beta(x))-\alpha(x)}{2} = 1 - \dfrac{M_H(x)}{2}$.

Proposition 6. *Given a VAR, $r = (X \Rightarrow Y)$, where $|X| = m$ and $|Y| = n$, we have*

1. $(\frac{1}{2})^m Hsupp(r) \leq AHsupp(r) \leq 2^n Asupp(r)$;
2. $(\frac{1}{2})^n Hsupp(r) \leq HAsupp(r) \leq 2^m Asupp(r)$;
3. $AHconf(r) \leq 2^n Aconf(r)$;
4. $(\frac{1}{2})^n Hconf(r) \leq HAconf(r)$.

Proof Sketch. The proof follows from Proposition 5. $\qquad\square$

By Proposition 6, we can prune VARs according to the relationship among different support and confidence. For example, if we have $2^n Asupp(r) < \sigma$, then $AHsupp(r) \leq 2^n Asupp(r) < \sigma$; thus, we can prune r directly without computing $AHsupp(r)$.

4   Mining Vague Association Rules

In this section, we present an algorithm to mine the VARs. We first mine the set of all A, H, AH and HA FIs from the input AH-pair database with respect to a certain HS or the overall hesitation. Then, we generate the VARs from the set of FIs.

Let A_i and H_i be the set of A FIs and H FIs containing i items, respectively. Let $A_i H_j$ be the set of AH FIs containing i items with A values and j items with H values. Note that $A_i H_j$ is equivalent to $H_j A_i$. Let C_W be the set of *candidate FIs*, from which the set of FIs W is to be generated, where W is A_i, H_i, or $A_i H_j$.

Algorithm 2.   MineVFI(D, σ)

---

1. Mine A_1 and H_1 from D;
2. Generate C_{A_2} from A_1, $C_{A_1 H_1}$ from A_1 and H_1, and C_{H_2} from H_1;
3. Verify the candidate FIs in C_{A_2}, $C_{A_1 H_1}$ and C_{H_2} to give A_2, $A_1 H_1$ and H_2, respectively;
4. **for each** $k = 3, 4, \ldots$, where $k = i + j$, **do**
5.   Generate C_{A_k} from A_{i-1} and C_{H_k} from H_{i-1}, for $i = k$;
6.   Generate $C_{A_i H_j}$ from $A_{i-1} H_j$, for $2 \leq i < k$, and from $A_1 H_{j-1}$, for $i = 1$;
7.   Verify the candidate FIs in C_{A_k}, C_{H_k}, and $C_{A_i H_j}$ to give A_k, H_k, and $A_i H_j$;
8. **return** all A_i, H_j, and $A_i H_j$ mined;

The algorithm to compute the FIs is shown in Algorithm 2. We first mine the set of frequent items A_1 and H_1 from the input AH-pair database D. Next, we generate the candidate FIs that consists of two items (Line 2) and compute the FIs from the candidate FIs (Line 3). Then, we use the FIs containing $(k - 1)$ items to generate the candidate FIs containing k items, for $k \geq 3$, which is described as follows.

For each pair of FIs, $x_1 \cdots x_{k-2} y$ and $x_1 \cdots x_{k-2} z$ in A_{k-1} or H_{k-1}, we generate the itemset $x_1 \cdots x_{k-2} yz$ into C_{A_k} or C_{H_k}. For each pair of FIs, $x_1 \cdots x_{i-2} u y_1 \cdots y_j$ and $x_1 \cdots x_{i-2} v y_1 \cdots y_j$ in $A_{i-1} H_j$, or $x_1 y_1 \cdots y_{j-2} u$ and $x_1 y_1 \cdots y_{j-2} v$ in $A_1 H_{j-1}$, we generate the itemset $x_1 \cdots x_{i-2} uv y_1 \cdots y_j$ or $x_1 y_1 \cdots y_{j-2} uv$ into $C_{A_i H_j}$.

After generating the candidate FIs, we obtain the FIs as follows. For each $Z \in C_{A_k}$ (or $Z \in C_{H_k}$), if $\exists X \subset Z$, where X contains $(k-1)$ items, $X \notin A_{k-1}$ (or $X \notin H_{k-1}$), then we remove Z from C_{A_k} (or C_{H_k}). For each $Z = x_1 \cdots x_i y_1 \cdots y_j \in C_{A_i H_j}$, if $\exists i'$, where $1 \leq i' \leq i$, $(Z - \{x_{i'}\}) \notin A_{i-1} H_j$; or $\exists j'$, where $1 \leq j' \leq j$, $(Z - \{y_{j'}\}) \notin A_i H_{j-1}$, then we remove Z from $C_{A_i H_j}$. Here, the *anti-monotone property* [1] of support is applied to prune Z if any of Z's subsets is not an FI. After that, the support of the candidate FIs is computed and only those with support at least σ are retained as FIs.

Finally, the algorithm terminates when no candidate FIs are generated and returns all FIs.

After we mine the set of all FIs, we generate the VARs from the FIs. There are four types of VARs. First, for each A or H FI Z, we can generate the VARs $X \Rightarrow Y, \forall X, Y$ where $X \cup Y = Z$, using the classical AR generation algorithm [1]. Then, for each AH (or HA) FI $Z = (X \cup Y)$, where X is an A FI and Y is an H FI, we generate two VARs $X \Rightarrow Y$ and $Y \Rightarrow X$. The confidence of the VARs can be computed by Definition 8.

After we generate all the VARs with respect to the given HS or overall hesitation, we can repeat our algorithm on the mi-pair database of different HS. Properties in Proposition 3 can be used to prune itemsets if the current HS has the relationships indicated in Proposition 3 with the original HS.

5 Experiments

In this section, we use both real and synthetic datasets to evaluate the efficiency of the VAR mining algorithm and the usefulness of the VARs. All experiments are conducted on a Linux machine with an Intel Pentium IV 3.2GHz CPU and 1GB RAM. Due to space limitation, the experimental results are related to the overall hesitation.

5.1 Experiments on Real Datasets

For the first set of experiments, we use the Web log data from IRCache [9], which is the NLANR Web Caching project.

We first preprocess the Web log and identify the browsing trails of each user. Then, we define the weight, W_{wp}, of a Web page, wp, in a trail as the product of the time spent on wp and the position of wp in the trail. If wp appears more than once in the trail, we sum up its weights. Finally, we normalize the weights of the Web pages within a trail. Thus, W_{wp} measures the degree that wp satisfies the user. Given two thresholds H_L and H_U ($0 \le H_L \le H_U \le 1$), we can classify Web pages into three categories: *target* (if $W_{wp} \ge H_U$), *non-target* (if $W_{wp} \le H_L$), and *transition* (if $H_L < W_{wp} < H_U$). The three categories correspond to the three statuses of items, i.e., 1, 0 and h (overall hesitation), respectively.

Since the Web log data contain a huge number of different Web sites, we only report the result on the Web log of a single Web site (www.google.com) from all nine IRCache servers on a single day (Aug. 29, 2006). We identify 6066 trails and aggregate them by the user ID (the remote host). The corresponding AH-pair database consists of 263 AH-pair transactions and 260 items (i.e., Web pages). Here we set H_L to be 0.01 and H_U to be 0.7.

When $\sigma = 0.001$ and $c = 0.9$, we obtain only one VAR: *http://gmail.google.com/*, *http://gmail.google.com/mail/* $\Rightarrow$ *http://mail.google.com/mail/*, with HA-support of 0.003 and HA-confidence of 0.99. This VAR shows that *http://gmail. google.com/* and *http://gmail.google.com/mail/* always play the role of transition pages to the target page *http://mail.google.com/mail/*. As a possible application, we can add a direct link from the transition pages (*http://gmail.google.com/* or *http://gmail.google.com /mail/*) to the target page (*http://mail.google.com/mail/*) to facilitate the user traversal of the Web site.

Actually, by typing either the URL of the two transition pages in a Web browser, it is redirected to the URL of the target page, where the redirect mechanism serves as a special kind of direct link.

If we set c to be 0.7, we obtain more VARs as follows:

1. $H_1 A_1$: *http://google.com/* $\Rightarrow$ *http://www.google.com/* (0.001, 0.77)
2. $H_1 A_1$: *http://gmail.google.com/* $\Rightarrow$ *http://mail.google.com/mail/* (0.004, 0.86)
3. $A_2 H_1$: *http://mail.google.com/mail/, http://gmail.google.com/mail/*
   $\Rightarrow$ *http://gmail.google.com/* (0.001, 0.77)
4. $A_2 H_1$: *http://mail.google.com/mail/, http://gmail.google.com/*
   $\Rightarrow$ *http://gmail.google.com/mail/* (0.001, 0.84)
5. $H_1 H_1$: *http://gmail.google.com/* $\Rightarrow$ *http://gmail.google.com/mail/* (0.003, 0.75)

In each VAR, the number in the bracket shows the support and confidence of the VAR. We find that, in the first two $H_1 A_1$ rules, the transition page is redirected to the target page. The next two $A_2 H_1$ rules show that *http://gmail.google.com/mail/* and *http://gmail.google.com/* can both play the role of transition or target pages, while *http://mail.google.com/mail/* is always the target page with high confidence (above 0.7). The last $H_1 H_1$ rule shows that both of the two pages are transition pages. We may combine them together or delete one of them to make the website more concise.

In order to compare with the traditional ARs, we also test on the database that contains all the trails without distinguishing the Web pages by their weights and aggregating the pages by user. At $\sigma = 0.0008$ and $c = 1$, 70 ARs are returned. Among them, 59 ARs (84%) contain the entrance page (www.google.com), which is not that interesting. Among the remaining ARs, the following rule is found:
http://mail.google.com/, http://gmail.google.com/, http://gmail.google.com/mail/
$\Rightarrow$ *http://mail.google.com/mail/* with support 0.001 and confidence 1, which is similar to one of the VARs we find.

The above results show the effectiveness of mining VARs, since the traditional AR mining approach returns many ARs but it is hard for the user to tell which ARs are more important for practical uses, while mining VARs can find more specific rules directly.

5.2   Experiments on Synthetic Datasets

We test on the synthetic datasets to evaluate the efficiency and the scalability of our algorithm. We modify the IBM synthetic data generator [10] by adding "hesitation" items. The ID and the number of "hesitation" items in each transaction are generated according to the same distributions as those for the original items. We generate a dataset with 100000 transactions and 100 items. We use a parameter *Step* to represent the number of transactions which are aggregated to give an AH-pair transaction.

We first test the algorithm under different values of *Step*. Fig. 4 and Fig. 5 report the running time and the number of FIs. From Fig. 4, the running time increases with the decrease in the value of σ due to the larger number of FIs generated. We also find that, for the same value of σ, the running time decreases significantly with the increase in the value of *Step*. This is because we aggregate more transactions to a single AH-pair transaction and hence the number of AH-pair transactions is smaller in the database. However, Fig. 5 shows that the number of FIs for the different *Step* values varies only

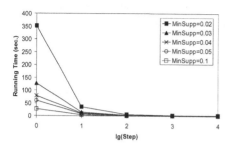

Fig. 4. Running Time

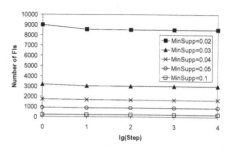

Fig. 5. Number of FIs

slightly (note that all the five lines are nearly horizontal in Fig. 5). This result shows that we can actually aggregate more transactions to give the AH-pair transactions so that we can improve the efficiency of the mining operation but still obtain the same set of FIs and hence the VARs.

6 Related Work

We are aware of a number of studies that extend the traditional AR mining for uncertain data in different applications, such as mining fuzzy ARs. However, there is no modelling of hesitation information in an application [11,12,13]. Fuzzy ARs are proposed to handle quantitative items in the form "X is A" $\Rightarrow$ "Y is B", where X, Y are the set of items and A, B are fuzzy concepts represented by fuzzy sets. For example, "position is senior" $\Rightarrow$ "salary is high".

Although the formulas of different kinds of support and confidence in VARs seem to relate to their counterparts in fuzzy ARs, VARs and fuzzy ARs are fundamentally different. VARs focus on the associations between crisp itemsets based on the attractiveness and hesitation of items, while fuzzy ARs do not consider hesitation information and focus on the associations between fuzzy concepts.

In our previous works, we extend the concepts of Functional Dependency (FD), Chase procedure [14], SQL and AR in standard relational databases by applying vague set theory in order to handle the widely existent vague information, and propose VFD [3], VChase [15], VSQL [4] and VAR [16], respectively. In [16], a basic approach to incorporate the hesitation information into the ARs is given. However, the modelling of hesitation information with respect to different HSs is newly developed in this paper.

7 Conclusion

We model hesitation information by vague set theory in order to address a limitation in traditional AR mining problem, which ignores the hesitation information of items in transactions. We propose the notion of VARs that incorporates the hesitation information of items into ARs. We define two important concepts, attractiveness and hesitation, of an item with respect to different HSs, which reflect the overall information of a customer's intent on the item. We also define different types of support and confidence for VARs in order to evaluate the quality of the VARs for different purposes. An efficient algorithm is proposed to mine the VARs, while the effectiveness of VARs is also revealed by experiments on real datasets. As for future work, mining VARs in different applications is an interesting topic that deserves further study. For example, different ranking scores together with clickthrough data of a search result can be modelled as an object having different HSs. In this case VARs can be minded to reflect different users' preferences.

Acknowledgements. We would like to thank Yiping Ke and James Cheng for their valuable comments on this topic.

References

1. Agrawal, R., Imielinski, T., Swami, A.N.: Mining association rules between sets of items in large databases. In: SIGMOD Conference, pp. 207–216 (1993)
2. Gau, W.-L., Buehrer, D.J.: Vague sets. IEEE Transactions on Systems, Man, and Cybernetics 23(2), 610–614 (1993)
3. Lu, A., Ng, W.: Managing merged data by vague functional dependencies. In: Atzeni, P., Chu, W., Lu, H., Zhou, S., Ling, T.-W. (eds.) ER 2004. LNCS, vol. 3288, pp. 259–272. Springer, Heidelberg (2004)
4. Lu, A., Ng, W.: Vague sets or intuitionistic fuzzy sets for handling vague data: Which one is better? In: Delcambre, L.M.L., Kop, C., Mayr, H.C., Mylopoulos, J., Pastor, Ó. (eds.) ER 2005. LNCS, vol. 3716, pp. 401–416. Springer, Heidelberg (2005)
5. Zadeh, L.A.: Fuzzy sets. Information and Control 8, 338–353 (1965)
6. Amazon.com Help, http://www.amazon.com/gp/help/customer/display.html?nodeId=524700
7. Brightwell, G., Winkler, P.: Counting linear extensions. Order 8, 225–242 (1991)
8. Pruesse, G., Ruskey, F.: Generating linear extensions fast. SIAM J. Comput. 23, 373–386 (1994)
9. NLANR, http://www.ircache.net/
10. Data Mining Project. The Quest retail transaction data generator (1996), http://www.almaden.ibm.com/software/quest/
11. Kuok, C.M., Fu, A.W., Wong, M.H.: Mining fuzzy association rules in databases. SIGMOD Record 27, 41–46 (1998)
12. Au, W., Chan, K.C.C.: Mining fuzzy association rules in a bank-account database. IEEE Trans. Fuzzy Systems 11, 238–248 (2003)
13. Chen, G., Wei, Q.: Fuzzy association rules and the extended mining algorithms. Inf. Sci. 147, 201–228 (2002)
14. Levene, M., Loizou, G.: A Guided Tour of Relational Databases and Beyond. Springer, Heidelberg (1999)
15. Lu, A., Ng, W.: Handling inconsistency of vague relations with functional dependencies. In: ER (2007)
16. Lu, A., Ke, Y., Cheng, J., Ng, W.: Mining vague association rules. In: DASFAA, pp. 891–897 (2007)

A Model Driven Modernization Approach for Automatically Deriving Multidimensional Models in Data Warehouses

Jose-Norberto Mazón and Juan Trujillo

Dept. of Software and Computing Systems
University of Alicante, Spain
{jnmazon,jtrujillo}@dlsi.ua.es

Abstract. Data warehouses integrate several operational sources to provide a multidimensional (MD) analysis of data. Therefore, the development of a data warehouse claims for an in-depth analysis of these data sources. Several approaches have been presented to obtain multidimensional structures from data sources in order to guide this development. However, these approaches assume that a wide documentation of the data sources is available and only provide informal guidelines to support the discovery of MD elements. Therefore, this task may become highly difficult for complex and large data sources (e.g. legacy systems). To overcome these problems, we consider the development of the data warehouse as a modernization scenario that addresses the analysis of the available data sources, thus discovering MD structures to either derive a data-driven conceptual MD model or reconcile a requirement-driven conceptual MD model with data sources. Specifically, we use concepts from Architecture Driven Modernization (ADM) in order to automatically perform the following tasks: (i) obtain a logical representation of data sources (ii) mark this logical representation with MD concepts, and (iii) derive a conceptual MD model from the marked model. Finally, we have provided a case study based on a real world project in order to exemplify the application of our approach.

1 Introduction

Data warehouses (DW) integrate heterogeneous data sources in multidimensional (MD) structures (i.e. facts and dimensions) in support of the decision-making process [1,2]. Importantly, current approaches for developing DWs claim for an in-depth analysis of these data sources in order to discover MD structures for (i) directly deriving a conceptual MD model from data sources [3,4], or (ii) reconciling data sources with a conceptual MD model previously defined from information requirements [5,6,7].

However, any kind of data sources (including data legacy systems) normally present two main problems in real world DW projects: they are too large and complex, and not enough documentation is provided. Due to this fact, the analysis of these data sources is not only a tedious and time-consuming task for designers, but also it may become unattainable in large DW projects.

C. Parent et al. (Eds.): ER 2007, LNCS 4801, pp. 56–71, 2007.

Considering these problems, analyzing data sources to discover MD elements is not a trivial task in DW projects and several ad-hoc mechanisms that ease the designer labour have been developed up to now (see Section 2). Unfortunately, they only provide informal guidelines to support the discovery of MD elements from well-documented data sources, which prevents their automatization. Hence, current approaches may be difficult to use for non-expert designers in the application domain of the DW project, especially in advanced information systems[1]. Furthermore, although these approaches suggest the development of a data-driven conceptual MD model from the analysis of data sources, they do not take into account this data analysis as a fundamental component of a wider development framework in order to reconcile these sources with user requirements.

On the other hand, software modernization is described as the process of understanding and evolving existing software assets for several purposes, such as software improvement or migration to a new platform or technology [9]. Modernization facilitates the analysis, redesign and redeployment of existing information systems when (i) it does not deliver the expected support to achieve business goals, (ii) the required changes are not as simple as a maintenance task, and (iii) not enough documentation is available. Therefore, software modernization requires an initial reverse engineering stage in which the elements of the existing information system and their relationships are captured in a conceptual model which guides the development of the new software system [10]. Lately, the Model Driven Architecture (MDA) [11] has been proven useful for reverse engineering, since it allows developers to manage models at different levels of abstraction in an easy and structured way with a high degree of automatization. Specifically, an arising standard named Architecture Driven Modernization (ADM) [12] aims at the integration of MDA and reverse engineering.

In order to solve the above-mentioned problems, we propose a modernization approach for the development of DWs based on ADM. The shaded area of Fig. 1 summarizes this approach, which comprises several tasks. The first step is to analyze the existing data sources to obtain their logical representation. Afterwards, the discovery of MD elements in this logical representation must be performed, thus deriving a logical model whose elements are related to MD concepts by means of a marked model. Then, we can either directly obtain a conceptual MD model or use the marked model to reconcile data sources with a previously defined conceptual MD model from information requirements, thus obtaining a mixed model [6,7]. It is worth noting that our modernization approach is part of an overall MDA framework for the development of DWs [13,14,15]. Within this framework (see Fig. 1), the conceptual MD model drives the following design stages (i.e. logical and physical) in order to implement the DW.

---

[1] Advanced information systems play a crucial role in the new generation of DWs [8]. This new generation of systems requires a high degree of expertise and experience in DW developers to analyze data sources, since they involve new and more complex data types than the traditional and simple alphanumerical data, such as specialized data structures used in GIS (Geographic Information Systems) or data streams related to Business Process Monitoring (BPM).

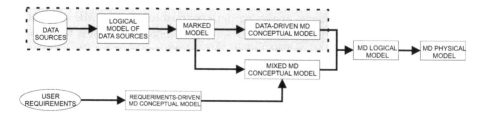

Fig. 1. Our modernization approach for DW development

The motivation of our modernization approach is twofold. On one hand, we propose how to directly obtain a conceptual MD model from existing data sources. On the other hand, the logical model marked with the discovered MD elements can be used to reconcile data sources with a conceptual MD model specified from user requirements, which completes our previous work [6,7], where we assumed that the data sources had been manually marked with MD concepts.

The remainder of this paper is structured as follows. Section 2 briefly describes current approaches for discovering MD elements from operational data sources. Section 2 also describes relations between ADM and the development of DWs. Section 3 describes our approach for using modernization in DW development. Finally, we point out our conclusions and sketch some future work in Section 4.

2   Related Work

There are several approaches that propose discovering MD elements from the analysis of data sources in order to derive a conceptual MD model. Most of them [3,4,16,17] suggest mechanisms, as algorithms or guidelines, to specify a conceptual MD model starting from an operational database described by an Entity-Relationship (ER) model. However, these mechanisms have to be manually applied to discover certain MD elements (such as facts), and only the discovery of strict hierarchies are done automatically (by navigating through the ER model along many-to-one relationships), thus resulting costly to apply when the designer is not an expert in DW development. Furthermore, they make a number of assumptions on the initial ER schema that limit their applicability to certain MD structures. For example, these approaches only take into account the definition of strict hierarchies, but they do not consider other important kind of hierarchies, such as non-strict or generalized hierarchies.

Only in the algorithm proposed in [18], the level of automation to discover MD elements in an ER model has been increased. Unfortunately, the output of this algorithm is not a conceptual MD model, but a set of candidate models, and although a complete set of steps is described to choose the most appropriate model, the success in choosing the right model highly depends on designer's expertise in the application domain.

Apart from the level of automatization, every of these current approaches presents a major drawback: it is assumed that well-documented ER diagrams are available. Unfortunately, the operational data sources are usually real legacy systems and the documentation is not generally available or it can not be obtained [19]. Moreover, if the data sources are complex, although the documentation exists it may be not easily understandable. Therefore, the application of these approaches is unfeasible if data sources are too large and complex, even though if expert designers in the application domain take part in the development process.

To the best of our knowledge, the only attempt to ameliorate the above-presented problems has been proposed in [20] where a set of algorithms is presented to automatically discover MD structures in the data sources. Furthermore, this approach suggests a "metadata obtainer" as a reverse engineering stage in which relational metadata is obtained from data sources. However, this approach is based on analyzing data instances, which could be unsuitable for large data sources or advanced information systems due to the huge amount and complexity of data. Finally, this approach is not based on standard techniques to specify the different models, so it could be difficult to apply.

To overcome all these problems, in this paper we propose the use of ADM in the development of DWs. ADM suggests several scenarios in which it could be successfully applied. Interestingly, ADM suggests a scenario for DW development in which the main task is the identification of relevant data that needs to be analyzed, reconciled, validated and loaded into the DW. However, it only focuses on the integration of data and it does not provide mechanisms to specify a conceptual MD model that drives the implementation of the envisaged DW. Due to this fact, we deeply believe that a scenario for applying ADM to DWs should aim at analyzing existing data sources to obtain a more reliable and adaptable logical representation. From this representation, a conceptual MD model can be then easily obtained by increasing the level of abstraction. Therefore, we propose that ADM be used for (i) describing a data reverse engineering stage for DWs that only takes into account the data schema and some useful measures (instead of considering all data instances) in order to obtain a logical representation of data sources, (ii) defining a set of formal transformations that are automatically applied to mark the logical representation of data sources with MD concepts as a previous step for deriving a conceptual MD model, and (iii) allowing the designer the possibility of applying a mixed approach in order to reconcile user requirements and data sources.

3   A Modernization Approach for Data Warehouses

The development of a DW starts when the information needs of decision makers are not properly delivered by available operational data sources. Then, this development can be described as a modernization scenario in which a DW is designed from existing data sources in support of the decision making process.

The most challenging task of this modernization scenario is related to data reverse engineering. This task addresses the analysis of the available data sources, thus discovering MD structures to either directly deriving a conceptual MD model from data sources or reconciling data sources with a conceptual MD model previously defined from requirements[2]. In our modernization approach, ADM [12] is used to accomplish this data reverse engineering task.

ADM is an OMG (Object Management Group) standard which addresses the integration of MDA and reverse engineering [21]. MDA is useful for reverse engineering because it provides mechanisms to establish different models at different levels of abstraction in order to focus on particular concerns within the system. Specifically, MDA encourages defining a Platform Independent Model (PIM) which contains no specific information about the platform or the technology that is used to implement the system. Then, this PIM can be transformed into a Platform Specific Model (PSM) in order to include information about a specific technology or platform. Afterwards, each PSM is transformed into code to obtain the final implementation. The transformations between these models are performed in an automatic way by means of a transformation language such as Query/View/Transformation (QVT) [22]. Therefore, ADM advocates the use of MDA concepts (such as PIM, PSM and transformations between them) to facilitate the automatic analysis of existing software systems in order to obtain their corresponding conceptual models (i.e. obtaining a PIM from a PSM that has been previously obtained from the implementation of an information system).

In our modernization approach, the following tasks are performed (see Fig. 2): first data sources are analyzed and their logical representations are specified in a PSM. Before deriving the conceptual MD model in a PIM, the PSM is marked with MD concepts in order to associate every element with their corresponding MD element. A set of QVT relations has been developed for both marking the PSM and obtaining the PIM in an automatic way.

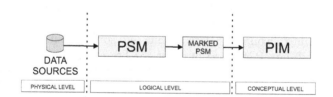

Fig. 2. Obtaining a conceptual MD model from data sources

3.1   Obtaining a PSM

In this section, we describe how to obtain a PSM from existing operational data sources. In common scenarios, data sources can be implemented according to a plethora of techniques, such as relational databases, XML files or even text files. For the sake of clarity, we assume a specific scenario in which a relational database has been implemented in the Oracle DataBase Management System

---

[2] In this paper, we focus on deriving a conceptual MD model from data sources, since the reconciliation process has been already covered in [6,7].

(DBMS). Within a relational DBMS, all the information about data structures is stored in a data dictionary, so a relational model of the implemented database can be specified from such data dictionary. Then, our PSM is based on a relational approach and it is specified by using CWM (Common Warehouse Metamodel) [23].

In addition, several measures are obtained from the database schema. These measures will be later considered in a set of defined QVT relations to properly discover MD elements.

Data Dictionary. A data dictionary is a repository of all the relevant metadata of the elements stored in a database. Each DBMS has its own way of storing definitions and representations of data elements, but they contain information about integrity constraints, space allocation or general database structures. Although we focus on the Oracle data dictionary, any other data dictionary could be used, since (i) a CWM representation of the data sources could be obtained and (ii) the proposed measures could be calculated.

Oracle data dictionary consists of a set of tables in which metadata is stored in two levels: the internal level that contains the data dictionary tables themselves and the external level that provides several views of the internal level tables, thus allowing us to access metadata. Then, the required metadata for deriving a relational PSM can be extracted from the data dictionary by querying the following views: USER_TABLES (data about tables), USER_TAB_COLUMNS (data about columns in each table), USER_CONSTRAINTS (data about constraints in a table), USER_CONS_COLUMNS (data about constraints defined on columns).

We assume that the existing database was developed taking into account the definition of every required constraint (such as primary or foreign keys) in order to implement a schema in third normal form. This can be assumed since these constraints can be easily discovered [24].

Relational PSM. The relational metamodel of CWM is a standard to represent the structure of a relational database, thus allowing us to model tables, columns, primary keys, foreign keys, and so on. An excerpt of the relational metamodel is shown in Fig. 3.

This metamodel is used to specify a relational representation of the data sources from the Oracle data dictionary in a PSM. Furthermore, a set of three measures is obtained from the data dictionary. Specifically, these measures are used in the QVT relations in order to know which elements of the data sources represent facts. The following measures are obtained:

- Number of instances per table (NIT). It is the amount of rows in a table.
- Insert frequency of each table (IFT). It is the average of inserts in a table.
- Number of measures of each table (NMT). It is the quantity of numerical columns of a table.

From the Data Dictionary to the PSM. The process of obtaining a relational PSM from the Oracle data dictionary has been implemented by using

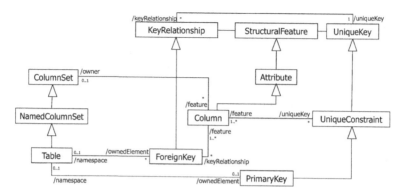

Fig. 3. Part of the relational CWM metamodel

Java in the Eclipse framework. Within this process, the `java.sql.Connection` interface is used to connect with the Oracle database and execute the required SQL statements in order to obtain metadata from the data dictionary. From this metadata, the corresponding PSM is obtained by using a developed CWM plugin for Eclipse within Borland Together Architect (BTA) CASE tool.

To illustrate our approach, an excerpt from a real DW project is considered. This project is related to the information system of a hotel. We focus on the operational data sources that support the booking business process. Within this process a customer books a room in the hotel for a certain date. These bookings contain the following data: number of nights, price per night, discount and total cost of the booking. Regarding the customer, the database contains data about identification number, name, gender, data of birth, city and country. It is interesting to know the name and the population of the city and the name of the country. Finally, a hotel room is in certain floor of the building and it has an area. A room belongs to one certain type: single or double. For a single room the size of the bed is stored, while for a double room, the possibility of having an extra bed is stored.

The Oracle data dictionary is queried to obtain the metadata of the data sources that support this booking business process. After obtaining all the required metadata, the corresponding PSM is derived by using Eclipse facilities and a CWM plugin within BTA. Figure 4 shows the PSM (already marked) deriving from the hotel information system in BTA. A more detailed model is shown in Fig. 5.

3.2   Obtaining a PIM

Once a relational PSM of data sources and the corresponding set of measures have been obtained, a conceptual MD representation has to be derived in a PIM. This derivation process is composed of two tasks: marking the PSM and deriving a conceptual MD model from the marked PSM. In the former task, every element of the PSM is marked as a certain MD element to ease the development of the

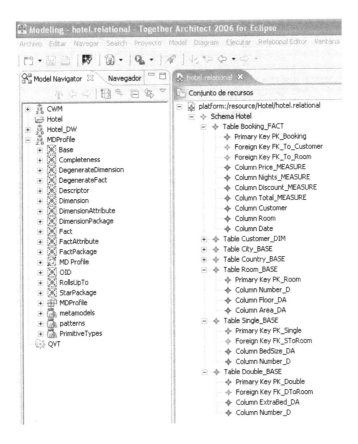

Fig. 4. Part of the marked PSM obtained from operational sources in BTA

latter task. QVT transformations have been defined to automatically perform both tasks. As final step, since a DW stores historical data, it is recommended to add a temporal dimension in the conceptual MD model of the DW [2].

MD Profile. The PIM is based on our UML (Unified Modeling Language) [25] profile for conceptual MD modeling presented in [26]. This profile contains the necessary stereotypes in order to elegantly represent main MD properties at the conceptual level by means of a UML class diagram in which the information is clearly organized into facts and dimensions. These facts and dimensions are represented by *Fact* (represented as ▦) and *Dimension* classes (represented as ◳), respectively. *Fact* classes are defined as composite classes in shared aggregation relationships of n *Dimension* classes. The minimum cardinality in the role of the *Dimension* classes is *1* to indicate that every fact must be always related to all the dimensions. However, the *many-to-many* relationships between a fact and a specific dimension can be specified by means of the cardinality *1...n* in the role of the corresponding *Dimension* class.

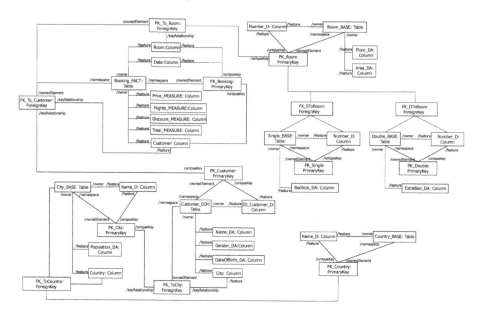

Fig. 5. Marked PSM derived from operational data sources

A fact is composed of measures or fact attributes (*FactAttribute* stereotype, **FA**). Furthermore, derived measures (and their derivation rules) can also be explicitly represented as tagged values of a *FactAttribute*.

With respect to dimensions, each level of a classification hierarchy is specified by a *Base* class (**B**). Every *Base* class can contain several dimension attributes (*DimensionAttribute* stereotype, **DA**) and must also contain a *Descriptor* attribute (*D* stereotype, **D**). An association with a *Rolls-UpTo* stereotype (<<Rolls-UpTo>>) between *Base* classes specifies the relationship between two levels of a classification hierarchy. Within this association, role *R* represents the direction in which the hierarchy rolls up, whereas role *D* represents the direction in which the hierarchy drills down. Due to flexibility of UML, we can also consider non-strict hierarchies (an object at a hierarchy's lower level belongs to more than one higher-level object) and generalized hierarchies (a hierarchy's level has subtypes to model additional features). These characteristics are specified, respectively, by means of the cardinality of the roles of the associations and by means of the generalization/specialization relationships of UML.

Although in this section we focus on describing a subset of this UML profile (see Fig. 6), the whole profile is defined in [26].

QVT Relations to Obtain a Marked PSM. To ameliorate the complexity of obtaining a conceptual MD model as a PIM, a previous step is needed to relate every element in the relational PSM to MD concepts. This step is achieved by marking every element of the PSM as MD elements. Marking models is a technique that provides mechanisms to extend elements of the models in order

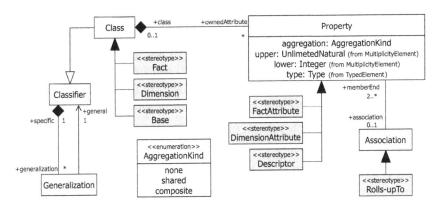

Fig. 6. Extension of the UML with the stereotypes used in this paper

to capture additional information [11]. Marks are widely used in MDA to prepare a model in order to guide a transformation.

A mark represents a concept from one model, which can be applied to an element of other different model. Our marks then indicate how every element of the relational PSM must be matched with certain MD element. Later, this marking will allow us to properly specify the PIM by easily discovering different complex MD structures in the PSM, such as different kind of hierarchies. In our approach, the PSM is marked by appending a suffix to the name of each element according to the conceptual MD elements of the above-described profile. Table 1 shows how the relational model of data sources must be marked. A QVT transformation has been developed to properly identify the MD elements in the PSM and perform the marking. This transformation includes several heuristics that make use of the measures defined in Section 3.1 in order to automatically mark every relational element in a reliable way.

Table 1. Marks applied to the relational PSM

Mark	PSM element	PIM element
_FACT	Table	Fact
_DIM	Table	Dimension
_BASE	Table	Base
_MEASURE	Column	FactAttribute
_DA	Column	DimensionAttribute
_D	Column	Descriptor

We would like to recall that this marked model can also be used to reconciliate data sources with a conceptual MD model specified from user requirements, as considered in our previous works [6,7], where the models of the data sources were supposed to be manually marked.

Next, the discovery of the different MD elements in the PSM is described: first facts must be discovered (and their respective fact attributes), then dimensions and hierarchy levels (and their respective descriptors and dimension attributes). To this aim, a set of QVT relations has been developed. However, due to space constraints, only one sample QVT relation is shown: `DiscoverFacts`. The resulting marked PSM for our case study is shown in Fig. 4 and Fig. 5.

Discovering Facts. A fact is related to a business process that is typically supported by operational data sources [2]. These data sources store measures of the business process that are useful for supporting the decision making process. A fact then contains all the numerical measures from the data sources related to a business process in order to support their analysis. Therefore, a table in the PSM is marked as a fact according to the following heuristics that are based on the measures described in Section 3.1:

- A table is much larger than other tables, because it stores data about operational activities of a business process. This heuristic is applied by using the NIT measure.
- A table is frequently updated to reflect that it stores data related to dynamic events of a business process. This heuristic is applied by using the IFT measure.
- A table stores measures related to the business process. This heuristic is applied by using the NMT measure.

These heuristics are included in the `DiscoverFacts` relation as functions in the *when* clause. This relation (shown in Fig. 7) marks tables of the PSM as facts provided that the heuristics are true. Once this relation holds, fact attributes and dimensions have to be discovered according to the statements in the *where* clause.

In our example, once this QVT relation is applied, the *Booking* table is marked as a fact (see Fig. 4 and Fig. 5).

Discovering Fact Attributes. When a table corresponds to a fact, their columns are either foreign keys that reference to a table (which corresponds to a dimension) or fact attributes. These fact attributes are measures whose values are

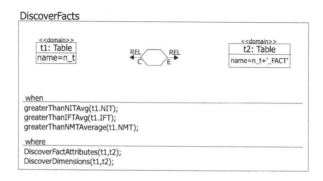

Fig. 7. QVT relation that marks tables as facts

analyzed to support the decision making process. Therefore, a column that belongs to a table marked as a fact is marked as a fact attribute provided that (i) its type is numerical and (ii) it is not a foreign key.

Discovering Dimensions. A dimension represents the context for analyzing a fact. Actually, the set of dimensions related to a fact determines every measure of the fact. Therefore, a table is marked as a dimension if a table marked as a fact has a column that, at the same time, takes part in a primary key and is a foreign key to the table marked as a dimension.

Discovering Bases. Every table that has not been marked as a fact or dimension should be marked as base. Later, when the PIM is defined, the relations between the tables marked as bases will be useful to model the required kind of hierarchy.

Discovering Dimension Attributes and Descriptors. The columns of each table marked as a dimension or as a base can be considered either as dimension attributes or descriptors. A column is marked as a descriptor if it is a primary key. Otherwise, it is marked as a dimension attribute.

QVT Relations to Obtain a PIM. Once the marked PSM is obtained, a set of QVT relations can be applied to derive a PIM for MD modeling. These QVT relations allow us to obtain different MD structures as facts and their relations with dimensions or different kind of hierarchies. After applying these QVT relations to the marked PSM by using BTA, the conceptual MD model of Fig. 8 has been derived. Nevertheless, for the sake of clarity, a complete representation of this PIM is also shown in Fig. 9.

Obtaining Facts and Dimensions. From the marked PSM, the fact and dimension classes (according to our UML profile for conceptual MD modeling) are easily obtained. Moreover, the cardinality between every discovered fact and a specific dimension must also be considered, since two possibilities arise:

- *Many-to-one*: the minimum cardinality in the role of a dimension class is *1* to indicate that every fact must always be related to one dimension. This cardinality appears in the marked PSM when a table marked as a fact has a foreign key to a table marked as a dimension.
- *Many-to-many*: it can be specified by means of the cardinality *1...n* in the role of the corresponding dimension. This cardinality appears in the marked PSM when a table marked as a fact has two foreign keys: one that refers to a table marked as a dimension and other that refers to a table marked as a fact. The columns that take part in the foreign key form a primary key for the table, thus representing a bridge table [2].

Obtaining Hierarchies. Preliminarily, we recall that within a conceptual MD model the terminal dimension levels of a fact are those that are immediately attached to the dimensions, i.e. those bases that provide the finest level of detail within each dimension. Then, the first step for obtaining a hierarchy is to create

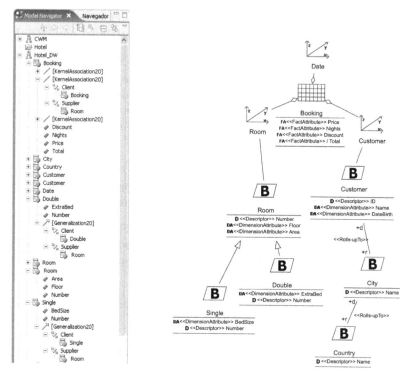

Fig. 8. PIM in BTA   **Fig. 9.** PIM obtained from the marked PSM

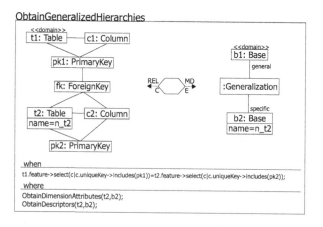

Fig. 10. QVT relation that obtains generalized hierarchies

a base class that is associated to its corresponding dimension class. This base class is the terminal dimension level and it stores every element that belongs to the table marked as a dimension.

Then, starting from a dimension already discovered, we can discover several levels of the hierarchy by following the foreign keys. Different QVT relations have been developed for deriving every kind of hierarchy (non-strict, generalized, etc.). Due to space constraints, we focus on defining how to model generalized hierarchies. These hierarchies are described in the marked model by making the primary key of the supertype a foreign key in the tables representing the subtypes as shown in the relation ObtainGeneralizedHierarchies in Fig. 10.

In our example, once this QVT relation is applied, the generalized hierarchy related to the *Room* dimension is created (see Fig. 8 and Fig. 9), since in the marked PSM (see Fig. 4 and Fig. 5) the primary key of the *Room* table (supertype) is referenced by tables *Double* and *Single* (subtypes).

4 Conclusions and Future Work

In this paper, we have presented a modernization approach for the development of DWs. Our approach is based on ADM (Architecture Driven Modernization) in order to analyze the operational data sources and obtain a PSM whose elements are marked with MD concepts. This marked model can be used either for directly deriving a PIM (i.e. a conceptual MD model) from data sources or for reconciling data sources with a previously defined PIM from decision makers' requirements. Within our modernization approach, we focus on the following tasks: (i) data sources are analyzed and their logical representation is specified in a PSM, (ii) the PSM is marked with MD concepts, and finally (iii) a PIM is derived from the marked PSM. Several metamodels (such as UML or CWM) have been used to define the required models and a set of QVT relations has been developed for both marking the PSM and obtaining the PIM, thus performing this data reverse engineering task in an automatic way.

The final objective of ADM is to define a set of interoperability metamodels that facilitate the analysis and transformation of existing information systems. This standard plans to incorporate new metamodels to facilitate the analysis, identification and measurement of relevant data. Our intention is using these metamodels together with the current used MDA concepts (i.e. PIM, PSM and transformation between them) and standards (i.e. CWM, UML and QVT).

On the other hand, in the present work we focus on obtaining a relational PSM of a data dictionary. However, other kind of data sources can be taken into account according to different platforms or technologies, thus taking advantage of ADM. For example, COBOL files should be considered [27] since a lot of information systems still store data in these kinds of files.

Acknowledgements

This work has been partially supported by the METASIGN (TIN2004-00779) project from the Spanish Ministry of Education and Science, and by the DADS (PBC-05-012-2) project from the Castilla-La Mancha Ministry of Education and

Science (Spain). Jose-Norberto Mazón is funded by the Spanish Ministry of Education and Science under a FPU grant (AP2005-1360).

References

1. Inmon, W.: Building the Data Warehouse. Wiley & Sons, Chichester (2002)
2. Kimball, R., Ross, M.: The Data Warehouse Toolkit. Wiley & Sons, Chichester (2002)
3. Golfarelli, M., Maio, D., Rizzi, S.: The Dimensional Fact Model: A conceptual model for data warehouses. Int. J. Cooperative Inf. Syst. 7(2-3), 215–247 (1998)
4. Hüsemann, B., Lechtenbörger, J., Vossen, G.: Conceptual data warehouse modeling. In: 2nd Int. Workshop on Design and Management of Data Warehouses, DMDW 2000
5. Giorgini, P., Rizzi, S., Garzetti, M.: Goal-oriented requirement analysis for data warehouse design. 8th Int. Workshop on Data Warehousing and OLAP, DOLAP, 47–56 (2005)
6. Mazón, J.N., Trujillo, J., Lechtenbörger, J.: A set of QVT relations to assure the correctness of data warehouses by using multidimensional normal forms. In: Embley, D.W., Olivé, A., Ram, S. (eds.) ER 2006. LNCS, vol. 4215, pp. 385–398. Springer, Heidelberg (2006)
7. Mazón, J.N., Trujillo, J., Lechtenbörger, J.: Reconciling requirement-driven data warehouses with data sources via multidimensional normal forms. Data & Knowledge Engineering (doi:10.1016/ j.datak.2007.04.004)
8. Rizzi, S., Abelló, A., Lechtenbörger, J., Trujillo, J.: Research in data warehouse modeling and design: dead or alive? In: 9th Int. Workshop on Data Warehousing and OLAP, DOLAP, pp. 3–10 (2006)
9. Seacord, R., Plakosh, D., Lewis, G.: Modernizing Legacy Systems: Software Technologies, Engineering Processes and Business Practices. Addison-Wesley, London, UK (2003)
10. Olivé, A.: Conceptual schema-centric development: A grand challenge for information systems research. In: Pastor, Ó., Falcão e Cunha, J. (eds.) CAiSE 2005. LNCS, vol. 3520, pp. 1–15. Springer, Heidelberg (2005)
11. OMG.: MDA Guide, 1.0.1., http://www.omg.org/cgi-bin/doc?omg/03-06-01
12. OMG: Architecture Driven Modernization (ADM) http://adm.omg.org/
13. Mazón, J.N., Trujillo, J., Serrano, M., Piattini, M.: Applying MDA to the development of data warehouses. In: 8th Int. Workshop on Data Warehousing and OLAP, DOLAP, pp. 57–66 (2005)
14. Mazón, J.N., Pardillo, J., Trujillo, J.: Applying transformations to model driven data warehouses. DaWaK 2006. LNCS, vol. 4081, pp. 13–22. Springer, Heidelberg (2006)
15. Mazón, J.N., Trujillo, J.: An MDA approach for the development of data warehouses. Decision Support Systems (doi:10.1016 /j.dss.2006.12.003)
16. Böhnlein, M., vom Ende, A.U.: Deriving initial data warehouse structures from the conceptual data models of the underlying operational information systems. In: 2nd Int. Workshop on Data Warehousing and OLAP, DOLAP, pp. 15–21 (1999)
17. Moody, D.L., Kortink, M.A.R.: From enterprise models to dimensional models: a methodology for data warehouse and data mart design. In: 2nd Int. Workshop on Design and Management of Data Warehouses, DMDW (2000)

18. Phipps, C., Davis, K.C.: Automating data warehouse conceptual schema design and evaluation. In: 4th Int. Workshop on Design and Management of Data Warehouses, DMDW 2000, pp. 23–32 (2000)
19. Alhajj, R.: Extracting the extended entity-relationship model from a legacy relational database. Inf. Syst. 28(6), 597–618 (2003)
20. Jensen, M.R., Holmgren, T., Pedersen, T.B.: Discovering multidimensional structure in relational data. In: Kambayashi, Y., Mohania, M.K., Wöß, W. (eds.) DaWaK 2004. LNCS, vol. 3181, pp. 138–148. Springer, Heidelberg (2004)
21. van den Heuvel, W.J.: Matching and adaptation: Core techniques for MDA-(ADM)-driven integration of new business applications with wrapped legacy systems. Workshop on Model-Driven Evolution of Legacy Systems (2004)
22. OMG: MOF 2.0 Query/View/Transformation. (2005), `http://www.omg.org/cgi-bin/doc?ptc/2005-11-01`
23. OMG: Common Warehouse Metamodel Specification 1.1, `http://www.omg.org/cgi-bin/doc?formal/03-03-02`
24. Soutou, C.: Relational database reverse engineering: Algorithms to extract cardinality constraints. Data Knowl. Eng. 28(2), 161–207 (1998)
25. OMG: Unified Modeling Language Specification 2.0, `http://www.omg.org/cgi-bin/doc?formal/05-07-04`
26. Luján-Mora, S., Trujillo, J., Song, I.Y.: A UML profile for multidimensional modeling in data warehouses. Data Knowl. Eng. 59(3), 725–769 (2006)
27. Hick, J.M., Hainaut, J.L.: Strategy for database application evolution: The DB-MAIN approach. In: Song, I.-Y., Liddle, S.W., Ling, T.-W., Scheuermann, P. (eds.) ER 2003. LNCS, vol. 2813, pp. 291–306. Springer, Heidelberg (2003)

Cost-Based Fragmentation for Distributed Complex Value Databases

Hui Ma and Markus Kirchberg

Information Science Research Centre, Massey University,
Private Bag 11 222, Palmerston North, New Zealand
{h.ma,m.kirchberg}@massey.ac.nz

Abstract. The major purpose of the design of distributed databases is to improve system performance and to increase system reliability. Fragmentation and allocation play important roles in the development of a cost-efficient system. This paper addresses the problem of fragmentation in the context of complex value databases, which cover the common aspects of object-oriented databases, object-relational databases and XML. In this paper, we present a cost-based approach for horizontal and vertical fragmentation. Our approach is based on a cost model that takes the structure of complex value databases into account.

1 Introduction

Fragmentation and allocation are the main techniques used in the design of distributed databases. The research problems for fragmentation and allocation have been investigated in the context of the relational model and object-oriented model. With the current popularity of web information systems that often support web-based database application, including object-oriented databases, object-relational databases and databases based on the eXtensible Markup Language (XML), it is desired to have efficient and effective database design techniques that take into account the common aspects of these complex data models.

In the literature, fragmentation and allocation have been studied since the 1970s. They are often dealt with independently disregarding the fact that both design procedures rely on similar input information to achieve the same objectives, i.e. improve system performance and increase system reliability. Horizontal fragmentation is either performed with a set of minterm predicates [3, 8, 21] or with a set of predicates grouped according predicate affinities [1, 4, 22]. Horizontal fragmentation with minterm predicates often results in a big number of fragments, which will later be allocated to a small number of network nodes. Thus, fragment recombination is needed to match the required number of horizontal fragments, which is less or equal to the number of network nodes. Affinity-based horizontal fragmentation approaches cannot guarantee an optimal system performance as data locality information is lost while computing predicate affinities. In fact, neither of two approaches include local data availability as an objective of fragmentation.

C. Parent et al. (Eds.): ER 2007, LNCS 4801, pp. 72–86, 2007.

For vertical fragmentation, algorithms proposed in the literature are either cost-driven or affinity-based. In the context of the relational model, cost-driven approaches are based on cost models, which measure the total number of disk accesses to the database [5, 7]. Affinity-based approaches group attributes according to attribute affinities [11, 17, 19, 20, 21]. Navathe *et al* [18] propose mixed fragmentation, which also uses affinities as the main parameters for both horizontal and vertical fragmentation. In the context of object-oriented data models, fragmentation is mainly affinity-based and different affinities, e.g. method affinities, attribute affinities or instance variable affinities [2, 9, 12], are used as parameters. Attribute affinities only reflect the togetherness of attributes accessed by applications. Vertical fragmentation based on affinities may reduce the number of disk accesses, but has never been proven to increase system performance. For distributed databases, transportation costs dominate the total query costs. This means that improving local data availability, which in turn reduces data transportation requirements, plays an important role towards improving system performance.

It is our aim to overcome the shortcomings of exiting approaches for both horizontal and vertical fragmentation. In this paper, we discuss both types of fragmentation in the context of complex value databases and present corresponding cost-based approaches. Thus, we extend earlier work as presented in [14, 16]. In short, we will incorporate all query information and also including site information by using a simplified cost model for fragmentation. This way, we can perform fragmentation and fragment allocation simultaneously. Properties of our approach include a low computational complexity and increased system performance.

The remainder of this paper is organised as follows: In Section 1, we briefly introduce a complex value data model. In Section 2, we define fragmentation techniques for the complex value data model. In Section 3, we present a cost model for complex value databases. In Section 4, we propose a cost-based design approach for horizontal and vertical fragmentation. We conclude with a short summary in Section 5.

1.1   Complex Value Databases

We define complex values on the basis of a type system. Using abstract syntax, types can be defined by

$$t = b \mid \mathbb{1} \mid (a_1 : t_1, \ldots, a_n : t_n) \mid a : \{t\} \mid a : [t] \tag{1}$$

with pairwise different labels $a_1, \ldots, a_n$. Here b represents a not further specified collection of base types, which may include *BOOL, CARD, INTEGER, DECIMAL, DATE*, etc. Furthermore, $(\cdot)$ is a record type constructor, $\{\cdot\}$ a set type constructor, $[\cdot]$ a list type constructor and $\mathbb{1}$ is a trivial type.

Each type t defines a set of values, its *domain $dom(t)$*, as follows:

- The domain $dom(b_i)$ of a base type b_i is some not further specified set V_i, e.g. $dom(BOOL) = \{\mathbf{T}, \mathbf{F}\}$, $dom(CARD) = \{0, 1, 2, \ldots\}$, etc.
- We have $dom(\mathbb{1}) = \{\top\}$.

- We have $dom((a_1 : t_1, \ldots, a_n : t_n)) = \{(a_1 : v_1, \ldots, a_n : v_n) \mid v_i \in dom(t_i)\}$ for record types.
- For set types we have $dom(a : \{t\}) = \{a : \{v_1, \ldots, v_k\} \mid v_i \in dom(t)\}$.
- For list types we have $dom(a : [t]) = \{a : [v_1, \ldots, v_k] \mid v_i \in dom(t)\}$, i.e. elements may appear more than once and are ordered.

In the following, we use the term *atomic attribute* to refer to an attribute with a base type as domain, and the term *complex attribute* to denote an attribute with a domain of a record type, set type or list type.

On the basis of this type system, we can define database schemata, which are sets of database types. A *database type of level k* has a name E and consists of a set $comp(E) = \{r_1 : E_1, \ldots, r_n : E_n\}$ of components with pairwise different role names r_i and database types E_i on levels lower than k with at least one database type of level exactly $k - 1$, a set $attr(E) = \{a_1, \ldots, a_m\}$ of attributes, each associated with a data type $dom(a_i)$ as its domain, and a key $id(E) \subseteq comp(E) \cup attr(E)$. We shall write $E = (comp(E), attr(E), id(E))$. A *database schema* is a finite set $\mathcal{S}$ of database types such that for all $E \in \mathcal{S}$ and all $r_i : E_i \in comp(E)$ we also have $E_i \in \mathcal{S}$. That is, schemata are closed under component references.

Given a database schema $\mathcal{S}$, we associate two types $t(E)$ and $k(E)$, called *representation type* and *key type*, respectively, with each $E = (\{r_1 : E_1, \ldots, r_n : E_n\}, \{a_1, \ldots, a_k\}, \{r_{i_1} : E_{i_1}, \ldots, r_{i_m} : E_{i_m}, a_{j_1}, \ldots, a_{j_\ell}\}) \in \mathcal{S}$:

- The representation type of E is the tuple type $t(E) = (r_1 : k(E_1), \ldots, r_n : k(E_n), a_1 : dom(a_1), \ldots, a_k : dom(a_k))$.
- The key type of E is the tuple type $k(E) = (r_{i_1} : k(E_{i_1}), \ldots, r_{i_m} : k(E_{i_m}), a_{j_1} : dom(a_{j_1}), \ldots, a_{j_\ell} : dom(a_{j_\ell}))$.

Finally, a *database db* over a schema $\mathcal{S}$ is an $\mathcal{S}$-indexed family $\{db(E)\}_{E \in \mathcal{S}}$ such that each $db(E)$ is a finite set of values of type $t(E)$ satisfying two conditions, with one as that whenever $t_1, t_2 \in db(E)$ coincide on their projection to $id(E)$, they are already equal; while the other one is that for each $t \in db(E)$ and each $r_i : E_i \in comp(E)$ there is some $t_i \in db(E_i)$ such that the projection of t onto r_i is t_i.

Example 1. The following is the complex value database schema for a simple university application:

DEPARTMENT = $(\emptyset, \{dname, homepage, contacts\}, \{dname\})$
LECTURER = $(\{in: DEPARTMENT\}, \{id, name, email, phone, homepage\}, \{id\})$
PAPER = $(\emptyset, \{no, ptitle, level, points\}, \{no\})$
LECTURE = $(\{paper: PAPER\}, \{semester, schedule\}, \{paper: PAPER, semester\})$

with $dom(schedule) = \{slot : (time: TIME, day: STRING, room: STRING)\}$ in the database type LECTURE. All other domains have been omitted.

The corresponding representation types for the university database schema are as follows:

$t(\text{DEPARTMENT}) = $ (dname: *STRING*, homepage: *URI*, contacts: {contact: (location: *STRING*, phone: *CARD*)})

$t(\text{LECTURER}) = $ (in: (dname: $STRING$), id: $STRING$, name: (fname: $STRING$,
  lname: $STRING$, titles: {title: $STRING$}), email: $EMAIL$,
  phone:(areacode: $CARD$, number: $CARD$) homepage: URI)
$t(\text{PAPER}) = $ (no: $CARD$, ptitle: $STRING$, level: $CARD$, points: $CARD$)
$t(\text{LECTURE}) = $ (paper: (no: $CARD$), semester: $STRING$, schedule: {slot:
  (time: $TIME$, day: $STRING$, room: $STRING$)})

1.2   A Query Algebra and Heuristic Query Optimisation

For complex value databases, to describe fragmentation and its effect on query optimisation, we need a query algebra. It is sufficient to take the recursive algebra for nested relations discussed in [6], because it allows to access data values at any level of complex values without any special navigational operation or flattening the complex values. Also, most of the query optimisation techniques developed for the relational algebra can be applied to queries expressed in the recursive algebra.

   In the recursive algebra, the selection operation $\sigma_{path_i=c}(db(E))$ allows to define selection conditions on an attribute at any level using a path expression. The project operation $\pi_{path_i}(db(E))$ permits projections on attributes at all levels without restructuring. The join operation $db(E_1) \bowtie_{path_i} db(E_2)$ allows two instances to be joined on any attribute level defined by the path $path_i$. $path_i$ is a list of attribute names starting from a top attribute name or reference name of a representation type, e.g. a_i, $a_i.a_{ij}$ or $r_i.a_i$.

2   Schema Fragmentation

Let us now introduce operations for fragmentation. Similar to the relational approach to horizontal fragmentation, we utilise the fact that each database type E defines a set $db(E)$ in a database db. Thus it can be partitioned into disjoint subsets.

2.1   Horizontal Fragmentation

As in any database db, the database type E is associated with a finite set $db(E)$. We obtain an easy generalisation of relational horizontal fragmentation. For this let E be some database type. Take boolean-valued functions φ_i $(i = 1, \ldots, n)$ such that for each database db we obtain

$$db(F_i) = \bigcup_{i=1}^{n} \sigma_{\varphi_i}(db(E))$$

with disjoint sets $\sigma_{\varphi_i}(db(E))$. We then replace E in the schema by n new database types F_i, all with the same definition as E.

Example 2. Let us consider an instance $db(\text{DEPARTMENT})$ (as outlined in Table 1) of database type DEPARTMENT from Example 1. Horizontal fragmentation with two predicates $\varphi_1 \equiv$ contacts.contact.location = 'Turitea' and $\varphi_2 \equiv$ contacts.contact.location $\neq$ 'Turitea' results in two fragments $db(\text{TURITEA\_DEPARTMENT})$ and $db(\text{NO\_TURITEA\_DEPARTMENT})$ as outlined in Table 1.

Table 1. HORIZONTAL FRAGMENTATION OF db(DEPARTMENT)

db(DEPARTMENT)			
dname	homepage	contacts	
		location	phone
Information	is.massey.ac.nz	Turitea	063566199
		Wellington	045763112
Computer	cs.massey.ac.nz	Turitea	063563188
		Albany	098132699
Education	ed.massey.ac.nz	Napier	068355202
		Albany	094437900

db(TURITEA_DEPARTMENT)			
dname	homepage	contacts	
		location	phone
Information	is.massey.ac.nz	Turitea	063566199
Computer	cs.massey.ac.nz	Turitea	063563188

db(NO_TURITEA_DEPARTMENT)			
dname	homepage	contacts	
		location	phone
Information	is.massey.ac.nz	Wellington	045763112
Computer	cs.massey.ac.nz	Albany	098132699
Education	ed.massey.ac.nz	Napier	068355202
		Albany	094437900

2.2 Vertical Fragmentation

Taking a database type $E = (\{r_1 : E_1, \ldots, r_n : E_n\}, \{a_1, \ldots, a_k\}, \{r_{i_1} : E_{i_1}, \ldots, r_{i_m} : E_{i_m}, a_{j_1}, \ldots, a_{j_\ell}\})$, vertical fragmentation on E replaces E with a set of new types $F_1, \ldots, F_m$ with $F_j = (\{r_1^j : E_1^j, \ldots, r_n^j : E_n^j\}, \{a_1^j, \ldots, a_k^j\}, \{r_{i_1}^j : E_{i_1}^j, \ldots, r_{i_m}^j : E_{i_m}^j, a_{j_1}^j, \ldots, a_{j_\ell}^j\})$ such that:

- the components and attributes will be distributed:

$$\{E_1, \ldots, E_n\} = \bigcup_{j=1}^{m} \{E_1^j, \ldots, E_{n_i}^j\}, \{a_1, \ldots, a_k\} = \bigcup_{j=1}^{m} \{a_1^j, \ldots, a_{n_i}^j\},$$

- $db(E)$ is split into $db(F_1), \ldots, db(F_m)$ such that $db(E)$ could be reconstructed by using the join operation on all the instances:

$$db(E) = db(F_1) \bowtie \ldots \bowtie db(F_m).$$

Using the query algebra, vertical fragmentation could be written as $db(F_j) = \pi_{F_j}(db(E))$ for all $j \in \{1, \ldots, m\}$. To meet the criteria of reconstructivity, it is

Table 2. An Instance of LECTURE

db(LECTURE)				
paper	semester	schedule		
no		time	day	room
157111	0702	10am	Monday	SSLB1
		1pm	Wednesday	SSLB5
157221	0701	9am	Tuesday	AH1
		10am	Friday	AH2
157331	0701	1pm	Tuesday	SSLB3
		3pm	Thursday	SSLB2

db(LECTURE_TIME)				
paper	semester	schedule		
no		I	time	day
157111	0702	1	10am	Monday
		2	1pm	Wednesday
157221	0701	1	9am	Tuesday
		2	10am	Friday
157331	0701	1	1pm	Tuesday
		2	3pm	Thursday

db(LECTURE_VENUE)			
paper	semester	schedule	
no		I	room
157111	0702	1	SSLB1
		2	SSLB5
157221	0701	1	AH1
		2	AH2
157331	0701	1	SSLB3
		2	SSLB2

required that the key type $k(E)$ is part of all types F_j. In addition, when projection is applied on attributes of a tuple type within a set type, e.g. $\{(a_{i1}, \ldots, a_{in})\}$, an index I should be inserted as an arrogate attribute in the set constructor before fragmentation. This index should later be attached to each of the vertical fragments to ensure the reconstructivity.

Example 3. Let us consider the database type LECTURE from Example 1 and alter the representation type t_{LECTURE} to $t_{\text{LECTURE}'}$ by attaching an index attribute as a subattribute of attribute 'slot'. Assume that we are given two subtypes $t_{\text{LECTURE\_TIME}}$ and $t_{\text{LECTURE\_VENUE}}$, each containing a subset of the attributes from t_{LECTURE}:

$t_{\text{LECTURE}'}$ = (paper: (no: *CARD*), semester: *STRING*, schedule: {slot: (*I*: *CARD*,
time *TIME*, day: *STRING*, room: *STRING*)});

$t_{\text{LECTURE\_VENUE}}$ = (paper: (no: *CARD*), semester: *STRING*, schedule: {slot:
(*I*:*CARD*, room: *STRING*)});

$t_{\text{LECTURE\_TIME}}$ = (paper: (no : *CARD*), semester: *STRING*, schedule: {slot: (*I*:
CARD, time: *TIME*, day: *STRING*)}).

Accordingly, we get the two vertical fragments that result from project operations:

$db(\text{LECTURE\_TIME}) = \pi_{t_{\text{LECTURE\_TIME}}}(db(\text{LECTURE}))$ and
$db(\text{LECTURE\_VENUE}) = \pi_{t_{\text{LECTURE\_VENUE}}}(db(\text{LECTURE}))$.

Analogously, the instances of type LECTURE and the resulting fragments are shown in Table 2.

3   A Cost Model

In order to measure system performance, we need a cost model to compute total query costs for the queries represented by query trees. In this section, we first present formulae for estimating the sizes of intermediate results for all intermediate nodes in the query tree. These sizes determine the costs for retrieving data for the next step, i.e. the operation associated with the predecessor in the query tree, and the costs for the transportation of data between nodes. Afterwards, we present a cost model for measuring system performance.

3.1   Size Estimation

In order to estimate the size of leaf nodes and intermediate nodes that are of complex values, we first look at types t, and estimate the size $s(t)$ of a value of type t, which depends on the context. Then, the size of an instance $db(E)$ is $n_E \cdot s(t(E))$, where n_E is the average number of elements in $db(E)$.

Let s_i be the average size of elements for a base type b_i. This can be used to determine the size $s(t)$ of an arbitrary type t, i.e. the average space needed for it on storage. We obtain:

$$s(t) = \begin{cases} s_i & \text{if } t = b_i \\ \sum_{i=1}^{n} s(t_i) & \text{if } t = (a : t_1, \ldots, a_n : t_n) \\ r \cdot s(t') & \text{if } t = \{t'\} \text{ or } t = [t']. \end{cases}$$

In the last of these cases, r is the average number of elements in sets, $t = [t']$ or $t = \langle t' \rangle$, respectively, within a value of type t.

Then, for $E = (\{r_1 : E_1, \ldots, r_n : E_n\}, \{a_1, \ldots, a_k\}, id(E))$ we obtain:

$$s(t(E)) = \sum_{i=1}^{n} s(t(E_i)) + \sum_{j=1}^{k} s(a_i).$$

The calculation of sizes of database instances applies also to the intermediate results of all queries. However, we can restrict our attention to the nodes of selection and projection, as the other nodes in the query tree will not be affected by fragmentation and subsequent heuristic query optimisation [16].

- The size of a selection node σ_φ is $p \cdot s$, where s is the size of the successor node and p is the probability that a tuple in the successor will satisfy φ.
- The size of a projection node π_X is $(1 - c) \cdot s \cdot \dfrac{s(t_X)}{s(t)}$ where t is the representation type of a complex value database type associated with the successor node, and t_X is the representation type associated with the projection node.

For sizes of results for other algebra operations, refer to the work in [13].

3.2   Query Processing Costs

Taking the cost model in [15], we now analyse the query costs in the case of fragmentation. For the convenience of discussion, we briefly present the cost model first. The major objective is to base the fragmentation decision on the efficiency of the most frequent queries.

Fragmentation results in a set of fragments $\{F_1, \ldots, F_n\}$ of average sizes $s_1, \ldots, s_n$. If the network has a set of nodes $N = N_1, \ldots, N_k$ we have to allocate these fragments to one of the nodes, which gives rise to a mapping $\lambda : \{1, \ldots, n\} \to \{1, \ldots, k\}$, which we call a *location assignment*. This decides the allocation of leaves of query trees, which are fragments. For each intermediate node v in each relevant query tree, we must also associate a node $\lambda(v)$. $\lambda(v)$ indicates the node in the network that the intermediate query result, which corresponds to v, will be stored at.

Given a location assignment λ, we can compute the total costs of query processing. Let the set of queries be $Q^m = \{Q_1, \ldots, Q_m\}$, each of which is executed with a frequency f_j. The total costs of all the queries in Q^m are the sum of the costs of each query multiplied by its frequency. The cost of each query are composed of two parts, the storage costs and transportation costs. Storage costs measure the costs of retrieving the data back from secondary storage. Those costs depend on the size of the intermediate results and on the assigned locations, which determine the storage cost factors. The transportation costs provide a measure for data transmission between two nodes of the network. Such transportation costs depend on the sizes of the involved sets and on the assigned locations, which determine the transport cost factor between every pair of sites.

$$Costs_\lambda(Q^m) = \sum_{j=1}^{m} (stor_\lambda(Q_j) + trans_\lambda(Q_j)) \cdot f_j$$

$$= \sum_{j=1}^{m} (\sum_h s(h) \cdot d_{\lambda(h)} + \sum_h \sum_{h'} c_{\lambda(h')\lambda(h)} \cdot s(h')) \cdot f_j$$

where h ranges over the nodes of the query tree for Q_j, $s(h)$ are the sizes of the involved sets, and d_i indicates the storage cost factor for node N_i $(i = 1, \ldots, k)$, h' runs over the predecessors of h in the query tree, and c_{ij} is the transportation cost factor for data transport from node N_i to node N_j $(i, j \in \{1, \ldots, k\})$.

Because transportation costs dominate the total query costs, we can develop cost minimisation heuristics by considering query frequencies, transportation cost factors and the size of data that need to be transfered between network sites. As discussed in [16, 14, 15], the allocation of fragments to sites according to cost minimisation heuristics already determines the location assignment provided that an optimal location assignment is given prior to the fragmentation.

4   A Cost-Based Methodology for Fragmentation

In this section, we present a cost-based approach for horizontal and vertical fragmentation. In each of the following sections, we first define some terms to facilitate the discussion of fragmentation. Then, we present algorithms for fragmentation based on the analysis on the cost model in Section 3. In the following, we assume a database instance $db(E)$ with a representation type $t(E)$ being accessed by a set of the most frequent queries $Q^m = \{Q_1, \ldots, Q_j, \ldots, Q_m\}$, with frequencies $f_1, \ldots, f_m$, respectively.

4.1   A Cost-Based Approach for Horizontal Fragmentation

Given a list of sorted queries, which access the instance of a given database type, by decreasing frequency $Q = [Q_1, \ldots, Q_j, \ldots, Q_m]$, we obtain a set of simple predicates needed for horizontal fragmentation using *Num_Simple_Predicates* [15]. Let $\Phi^m = \{\varphi_1, \ldots, \varphi_m\}$ be the chosen set of simple predicates defined on a database type E. Then, the set of *normal predicates* $\mathcal{N}^m = \{\mathcal{N}_1, \ldots, \mathcal{N}_n\}$ on relation schema E is the set of all satisfiable predicates of the form $\mathcal{N}_j \equiv \varphi_1^* \wedge \cdots \wedge \varphi_m^*$, where φ_i^* is either φ_i or $\neg \varphi_i$. Normal predicates can be represented in the following form:

$$\mathcal{N}_j = \bigwedge_{i \in J} \varphi_i \wedge \bigwedge_{i \notin J} \neg \varphi_i.$$

with $J \subseteq \{1, \ldots, m\}$ as a set of indices of a subset of all simple predicates. Let f_i be the frequency of predicate φ_i, $J_\theta = \{i | i \in J \wedge \varphi_i$ executed at site $\theta\}$ be a subset of indices of all simple predicates, executed at site N_θ. We define the following terms:

Definition 1. An *atomic horizontal fragment* F_j is a fragment that is defined by a normal predicate:

$$F_j = \sigma_{\mathcal{N}_j}(E).$$

Definition 2. The *request* of an atomic fragment at site θ is the sum of frequencies of predicates issued at site θ:

$$request_\theta(F_j) = \sum_{j=1, j \in J_\theta}^{k} f_j.$$

Definition 3. The *pay* of allocating an atomic horizontal fragment at a site θ is the costs of accessing the atomic horizontal fragment by all queries from sites other than θ:

$$pay_\theta(F_j) = \sum_{\theta'=1, \theta' \neq \theta}^{k} request_{\theta'}(F_j) \cdot c_{\theta \theta'}.$$

With the terms defined above, we now present an algorithm of horizontal fragmentation as shown in Table 3. The algorithm first finds the site that has the biggest value of *pay* of each atomic fragment and then allocates the atomic fragment to the site. A fragmentation schema and fragment allocation schema can be obtained simultaneously.

An evaluation has been conduced with satisfiable results. For detailed discussion of horizontal fragmentation refer to [15].

Table 3. Algorithm for Horizontal Fragmentation

Input:	$\Phi^y = \{\varphi_1, \ldots, \varphi_y\}$ /* a set of simple predicates a set of network nodes $N = \{1, \ldots, k\}$ with cost factors c_{ij}
Output:	Horizontal fragmentation and allocation schema $\{F_{H1}, \ldots, F_{Hk}\}$
| Method: | ```
for each θ ∈ {1, ..., k}
    F_Hθ = ∅
endfor
define a set of normal predicates N^y using Φ^y
define a set of atomic horizontal fragments F^y using N^y
for each atomic fragment F_j ∈ F^y, 1 ≤ i ≤ 2^y do
    for each node θ ∈ {1, ..., k} do
        calculate request_θ(F_j)
        calculate pay_θ(F_j)
    endfor
    choose w such that pay_w(F_j) = min(pay_1(F_j), ..., pay_k(F_j))
                        /* find the minimum value
    λ(F_j) = N_w   /* allocate F_j to the site of the smallest pay
    define F_Hθ with F_Hθ = ∪{F_j : λ(F_j) = N_θ}
endfor
``` |

4.2 A Cost-Based Approach for Vertical Fragmentation

In this section, we adapt the cost-efficient vertical fragmentation approach from [10, 14] to complex value databases. We start with some terminology, continue to present a vertical fragmentation design methodology and, finally, illustrate it with an example.

If $db(E)$ is vertically fragmented into a set of fragments $\{F_{V1}, \ldots, F_{Vu}, \ldots, F_{Vk_i}\}$, each of the fragments will be allocated to one of the network nodes $N_1, \ldots, N_\theta, \ldots, N_k$. Note that the maximum number of fragments is k, i.e. $k_i \leq k$. Let $\lambda(Q_j)$ indicate the site issuing query Q_j, $atomic(E) = \{a_1, \ldots, a_n\}$ indicate the set of atomic attributes of E, f_{ji} be the frequency of the query Q_j accessing a_i. Here, $f_{ji} = f_j$ if the attribute a_i is accessed by Q_j. Otherwise, $f_{ji} = 0$.

Definition 4. The *request* of an attribute at a site θ is the sum of frequencies of all queries at the site accessing the attribute:

$$request_\theta(a_i) = \sum_{j=1, \lambda(Q_j)=\theta}^{m} f_{ji}.$$

Definition 5. The *pay* of allocating an attribute a_i to a site θ measures the costs of accessing attribute a_i by all queries from sites θ' other than site θ:

$$pay_\theta(a_i) = \sum_{\theta'=1, \theta \neq \theta'}^{k} \sum_{j=1, \lambda(Q_j)=\theta}^{m} f_{ji} \cdot c_{\theta\theta'}.$$
```

Table 4. Algorithm for Vertical Fragmentation

Input:	the $AUFM$ of E
	$atomic(E) = \{a_1, \ldots, a_n\}$ /* a set of atomic attribute
	$PATH(E) = \{path_i, \ldots, path_n\}$ /* a set of path of all atomic attributes
	a set of network nodes $N = \{1, \ldots, k\}$ with cost factors c_{ij}
Output:	vertical fragmentation and fragment allocation schema $\{F_{V1}, \ldots, F_{Vk}\}$
Method:	**for each** $\theta \in \{1, \ldots, k\}$ let $atomic(F_{V\theta}) = k(E)$ **endfor**
	for each attribute $a_i \in atomic(E), 1 \le i \le n$ **do**
	for each node $\theta \in \{1, \ldots, k\}$
	do calculate $request_\theta(a_i)$
	endfor
	for each node $\theta \in \{1, \ldots, k\}$
	do calculate $pay_\theta(a_i)$
	endfor
	choose w such that $pay_w(a_i) = \min_{\theta=1}^{k} pay_\theta(a_i)$
	$atomic(F_{Vw}) = atomic(F_{Vw}) \cup \{a_i\}$ /* add a_i to F_{Vw}
	$PATH(F_{Vw}) = PATH(F_{Vw}) \cup \{path_i\}$ /* add $path_i$ to $PATH(F_{Vw})$
	endfor
	for each $\theta \in \{1, \ldots, k\}, F_{Vw} = \pi_{PATH(F_{Vw})}(db(E))$ **endfor**

In order to record query information, we use an *Attribute Usage Frequency Matrix* (AUFM), which records frequencies of queries, the set of atomic attributes accessed by the queries and the sites that issue the queries. Each row in the AUFM represents one query Q_j; the head of each column contains the set of attributes of a given representation type $t(E)$, the site issuing the queries and the frequency of the queries. Here, we do not distinguish between references and attributes, but record them in the same matrix. The values on a column indicate the frequencies f_{ji} of the queries Q_j that use the corresponding atomic attribute a_i grouped by the site that issues the queries. Note that we treat any two queries issued at different sites as different queries, even if the queries themselves are the same. The AUFM is constructed according to optimised queries in order to record all the attribute requirements returned by queries as well as all the attributes used in some join predicates. If a query returns all the information of an attribute then all its sub-attributes are accessed by the query.

With the *AUFM* as an input, we now present a vertical fragmentation algorithm as described in Table 4. For each atomic attribute at each site, the algorithm first calculates the *request* and then calculates the *pay*. At last, all atomic attributes are clustered to the site that has the lowest value of the *pay*. Correspondingly, a set of path expressions for each vertical fragment are obtained. Vertical fragmentation is performed by using the sets of paths. A vertical fragmentation and an allocation schema are obtained simultaneously.

Using the algorithm in 4 we can always guarantee that the resulting vertical fragmentation schema meet the criteria of correctness rules. Disjointness and completeness are satisfied because all atomic attributes occur and only occur in one of the fragments. Reconstruction is guaranteed because all fragments are composed of key attributes. In addition, if an attribute with a domain of a type

Table 5. Attribute *Usage* Frequency Matrix

site	query	frequency	in	id	name			email	phone		homepage
			dname		fname	lname	titles		areacode	number	
							title				
length			20	20	20·8	20·8	2·15·8	30·8	10	20	50·8
1	Q_1	20	20	20	20	20	20	20	20	20	20
	Q_4	50	0	0	50	0	0	50	0	0	0
2	Q_2	30	0	0	0	30	30	0	0	0	30
	Q_5	70	0	0	0	0	70	0	70	0	0
3	Q_3	100	0	0	0	100	0	0	100	100	0

Table 6. Attribute *Request* Matrix

request	in	id	name			email	phone		homepage
	dname		fname	lname	titles		areacode	number	
					title				
$request_1(a_i)$	20	20	70	20	20	70	20	20	20
$request_2(a_i)$	0	0	0	30	100	0	70	0	30
$request_3(a_i)$	0	0	0	100	0	0	100	100	0

inside a set type is decomposed, an index is attached to the attribute before vertical fragmentation, which will then be attached to each of fragments.

Example 4. We now illustrate the algorithm using an example. Assume there are five queries that constitute the 20% most frequently executed queries, which access an instance of database type LECTURER from three different sites:

- Query 1 $\pi_{\text{LECTURER}}(\sigma_{\text{name.titles}\ni\text{'Professor'}}(\text{LECTURER}))$ issued at site 1 with $f_1 = 20$,
- Query 2 $\pi_{\text{titles, homepage}}(\text{LECTURER})$ issued at site 2 with $f_2 = 30$,
- Query 3 $\pi_{\text{name.lname, phone}}(\text{LECTURER})$ issued at site 3 with $f_3 = 100$,
- Query 4 $\pi_{\text{fname, email}}(\text{LECTURER})$ issued at site 1 with $f_4 = 50$, and
- Query 5 $\pi_{\text{titles, areacode}}(\text{LECTURER})$ issued at site 2 with $f_5 = 70$.

In order to perform vertical fragmentation using the design procedure as introduced in Section 4.2, we first construct an Attribute *Usage* Frequency Matrix as shown in Table 5. Secondly, we compute the *request* for each attribute at each site, the results of which are shown in the Attribute *Request* Matrix in Table 6. Thirdly, assuming the values of transportation cost factors are: $c_{12} = c_{21} = 10$, $c_{13} = c_{31} = 25$, $c_{23} = c_{32} = 20$, we can now calculate the *pay* for each attribute at each site using the values of the *request* from Table 6. The results are shown in an Attribute *Request* Matrix in Table 6 and an Attribute *Pay* Matrix in Table 7.

Table 7. Attribute *Pay* Matrix

pay	in	id	name			email	phone		homepage
	dname		fname	lname	titles		areacode	number	
					title				
$pay_1(a_i)$	0	0	0	2800	1000	0	3200	2500	300
$pay_2(a_i)$	200	200	700	2200	200	700	2200	2200	200
$pay_3(a_i)$	500	500	1750	1100	2500	1750	1900	500	1100
site	1	1,2,3	1	3	2	1	3	3	2

Once atomic attributes are grouped and allocated to sites, we get a set of paths for each site to be used for vertical fragmentation:

- $db(F_{V1}) = \pi_{\text{id, in.dname, name.fname, email}}(db(\text{LECTURE}))$,
- $db(F_{V2}) = \pi_{\text{id, name.titles.title, homepage}}(db(\text{LECTURE}))$ and
- $db(F_{V3}) = \pi_{\text{id, name.lname, phone}}(db(\text{LECTURE}))$

We now look at how the system performance is changed due to the outlined fragmentation by using the cost model presented above. Assume that the average number of lecturers is 20 and the average number of titles for each lecturer is 2. With the average length of each attribute given in Table 5, we can compute the total query costs. Assume that distributed query processing and optimisation are supported, then, selection and projection should be processed first locally to reduce the size of data transported among different sites. In this case, the optimised allocation of $db(\text{LECTURERS})$ is site 2, which leads to total query costs of 16,680,000 while the total query costs after the vertical fragmentation and allocation are 4,754,000, which is about one fourth of the costs before the fragmentation. This shows that vertical fragmentation can indeed improve system performance.

4.3   Discussion

In order to obtain optimised fragmentation and allocation schemata for complex value databases, a cost model should be involved to evaluate the system performance. However, due to the complexity of fragmentation and allocation it is practically impossible to achieve an optimal fragmentation and allocation schema by exhaustively comparing different fragmentation schemata and allocation schemata using the cost model. However, from the cost model above, we observe that the less the value of the pay of allocating an attribute or an atomic fragment to a site the less the total costs will be to access it [14]. This explains that the proposed cost-based fragmentation approach above can at least determine a semi-optimal vertical fragmentation schema.

5   Conclusion

In this paper, we presented a cost-driven approach for fragmentation in complex value databases. This approach takes into consideration the structure of complex value databases. Furthermore, algorithms are presented for each of the fragmentation techniques used in distribution design to obtain fragmentation schemata, which can indeed improve the system performance.

A related problem left for future work is a design methodology to integrate the use horizontal and vertical fragmentation techniques in design distributed databases.

References

[1] Bellatreche, L., Karlapalem, K., Simonet, A.: Algorithms and support for horizontal class partitioning in object-oriented databases. Distributed and Parallel Databases 8(2), 155–179 (2000)

[2] Bellatreche, L., Simonet, A., Simonet, M.: Vertical fragmentation in distributed object database systems with complex attributes and methods. In: Thoma, H., Wagner, R.R. (eds.) DEXA 1996. LNCS, vol. 1134, pp. 15–21. Springer, Heidelberg (1996)

[3] Ceri, S., Negri, M., Pelagatti, G.: Horizontal data pertitioing in database design. In: Proc. the ACM SIGMOD International Conference on Management of Data, pp. 128–136. ACM Press, New York (1982)

[4] Cheng, C.-H., Lee, W.-K., Wong, K.-F.: A genetic algorithm-based clustering approach for database partitioning. IEEE Transactions on Systems, Man, and Cybernetics, Part C 32(3), 215–230 (2002)

[5] Chu, P.-C.: A transaction oriented approach to attribute partitioning. Information Systems 17(4), 329–342 (1992)

[6] Colby, L.S.: A recursive algebra and query optimization for nested relations. In: SIGMOD '89: Proceedings of the 1989 ACM SIGMOD international conference on Management of data, Portland, Oregon, United States, pp. 273–283. ACM Press, New York, NY, USA (1989)

[7] Cornell, D., Yu, P.: A vertical partitioning algorithm for relational databases. In: International Conference on Data Engineering, Los Angeles, California, pp. 30–35 (1987)

[8] Ezeife, C.I., Barker, K.: A comprehensive approach to horizontal class fragmentation in a distributed object based system. Distributed and Parallel Databases 3(3), 247–272 (1995)

[9] Ezeife, C.I., Barker, K.: Vertical fragmentation for advanced object models in a distributed object based system. In: Proceedings of the 7th International Conference on Computing and Information, pp. 613–632. IEEE Computer Society Press, Los Alamitos (1995)

[10] Hartmann, S., Ma, H., Schewe, K.-D.: Cost-based vertical fragmentation for xml. In: DBMAN 2007, Springer, Heidelberg (to appear 2007)

[11] Hoffer, J.A., Severance, D.G.: The use of cluster analysis in physical database design. In: Proceedings of the First International Conference on Very Large Data Bases, Framingham, MA (Septemper 1975)

[12] Karlapalem, K., Navathe, S.B., Morsi, M.M.A.: Issues in distribution design of object-oriented databases. In: IWDOM, pp. 148–164 (1992)

[13] Ma, H.: Distribution design in object oriented databases. Master's thesis, Massey University (2003)

[14] Ma, H., Schewe, K.-D., Kirchberg, M.: A heuristic approach to vertical fragmentation incorporating query information. In: Vasilecas, O., Eder, J., Caplinskas, A. (eds.) Proceedings of the 7th International Baltic Conference on Databases and Information Systems, pp. 69–76. IEEE Computer Society Press, Los Alamitos (2006)

[15] Ma, H., Schewe, K.-D., Wang, Q.: A heuristic approach to cost-efficient fragmentation and allocation of complex value databases. In: Bailey, G.D.J. (ed.) Proceedings of the 17th Australian Database Conference, Hobart, Australia. CRPIT 49, pp. 119–128 (2006)

[16] Ma, H., Schewe, K.-D., Wang, Q.: Distribution design for higher-order data models. Data and Knowledge Engineering (to appear 2007)

[17] Muthuraj, J., Chakravarthy, S., Varadarajan, R., Navathe, S.B.: A formal approach to the vertical partitioning problem in distributed database design. In: Proceedings of the Second International Conference on Parallel and Distributed Information Systems, San Diego, CA, USA, January 1993, pp. 26–34 (1993)

[18] Navathe, S., Karlapalem, K., Ra, M.: A mixed fragmentation methodology for initial distributed database design. Journal of Computer and Software Engineering 3(4) (1995)

[19] Navathe, S.B., Ceri, S., Wiederhold, G., Dour, J.: Vertical partitioning algorithms for database design. ACM TODS 9(4), 680–710 (1984)

[20] Navathe, S.B., Ra, M.: Vertical partitioning for database design: A graphical algorithm. SIGMOD Record 14(4), 440–450 (1989)

[21] Özsu, M.T., Valduriez, P.: Principles of Distributed Database Systems. Alan Apt, New Jersey (1999)

[22] Zhang, Y.: On horizontal fragmentation of distributed database design. In: Orlowska, M., Papazoglou, M. (eds.) Advances in Database Research, pp. 121–130. World Scientific Publishing, Singapore (1993)

From Business Models to Service-Oriented Design: A Reference Catalog Approach

Amy Lo[1] and Eric Yu[2]

[1] Department of Computer Science, University of Toronto,
Toronto, Canada
ayylo@cs.utoronto.ca
[2] Faculty of Information Studies, University of Toronto,
Toronto, Canada
yu@fis.utoronto.ca

Abstract. Service-oriented architecture (SOA) is rapidly becoming the dominant paradigm for next generation information systems. It has been recognized, however, that the full benefits of SOA would not be realized unless its capabilities are exploited at the business level. In the business arena, innovations in e-business have led to the identification and classification of business models and analysis of their properties. To ease the transition from business design to service-oriented system design, we propose a reference catalog approach. Recurring business designs are collected, pre-analyzed, and documented as a set of reference business models, following a standardized template. Each reference business model is realized through a set of service-oriented design patterns. The *i** framework is the basis for modeling and analysis at both the business and service design level, taking advantage of its agent orientation for modeling service relationships, and its goal orientation to facilitate adaptation from generic patterns to specific needs.

Keywords: Service-oriented design, business models, business modeling techniques, agent and goal-oriented conceptual modeling.

1 Introduction

As the Internet gives rise to many new business opportunities and dramatically changes the traditional ways of conducting business, the concept of business models has become a tool of interest in the e-business world to capture new ways of doing business [2]. As we expect the concept of SOA will further revolutionize how enterprises use the Internet for business interaction and integration, new types of business models will emerge and have great impact on the underlying IT infrastructure. Consequently, design options will multiply rapidly, and technical system design will need to interact more closely with business design to explore and select among various alternatives, creating the need of conceptual modeling techniques to assist in capturing the design properties and bridging the gap between the two different levels of concepts.

In recent years, the Information Systems (IS) community recognized the demand for business models and started to develop modeling techniques for this purpose

C. Parent et al. (Eds.): ER 2007, LNCS 4801, pp. 87–101, 2007.
© Springer-Verlag Berlin Heidelberg 2007

[7, 16, 17]. However, our research on existing literature indicates that the idea of business models has not yet had widespread impact on IS modeling, and the following question remains unclear: How can business model reasoning be used more effectively and efficiently in guiding the design process of an SOA implementation?

Although the value of business model design and analysis has been gradually realized, business design knowledge is often underused in existing modeling approaches. However, to improve the design and analysis process over time, it is important to capture repeatable solutions and be able to apply them to similar problems in the future. Our approach is to express and capture recurring business models and patterns in an expandable reference catalog, which consists of two parts: a set of reference business models and a set of business service patterns.

This paper first identifies the importance of business models and the use of business modeling techniques, and explains the relevance of the $i*$ modeling framework [25] in this context. Then, it proposes a business model driven SOA system design methodology, which is an application of the $i*$ framework to business modeling and SOA design. Its main idea is to maintain a set of reference business models in a reference catalog, so that common design knowledge in recurring business models can be reused to solve similar business problems and help define the technical specifications.

2   Business Models and Business Modeling

The concept of business models became popular in the late 1990's, and has been considered to be central in the discussion of e-business, as the success or failure of a firm is often attributed to the viability of its business model. Despite its popular usage, there is no agreement on what the term should precisely encompass [18]. In the business literature, business models refer to the actual design of business, such as a method of doing business [19] or a company's business architecture [22]. On the other hand, business models in the IS engineering literature are *representation* of business concepts in the real world, often with the aid of some graphical notation and business modeling techniques. The notion of business modeling, as discussed in this paper, refers to the analysis and design process of business level concepts using business models in the IS engineering sense.

So far, the study on business models in the business literature has focused on descriptive aspects, such as what concepts can be expressed in them and how business practices from the real world can be captured as types of business models with a name and textual descriptions. Thus, its focus is less on the design and analytical powers of business modeling. On the other hand, the notion of business models in the IS engineering community is a tool for representing the business concepts, such that they can be properly expressed, designed and analyzed using various conceptual modeling techniques. Thus, the soundness of a business model in this sense would relate to how accurately it reflects the reality; whereas the soundness of a business model in the business community would be measured by how well it helps a company to successfully conduct its business.

3 *i* for Business Modeling*

A number of existing business modeling techniques has been studied in [12], including an extended version of Unified Modeling Language (UML) [5], the Business Model Ontology (BMO) [16, 17], the Business Modeling Method (BMM) [14], the e³value framework [7], and a value network approach [1]. The result of the study shows that business goals and strategic interactions between business actors are often missing or underused in the design and analysis process of business models. However, as discussed in the business model literature such as [2], [6] and [13], a sound business model should effectively express and deliver the vision and objectives of the business, as well as model actor relationships and interactivity, because in the real world, consumers and other partners are actively co-producing values with the organization through various interactions.

Therefore, we turn to the *i** modeling framework [25], because it offers a set of agent and goal-oriented notation and analysis techniques that are highly relevant for modeling and analyzing business concepts, which are not offered by the other approaches mentioned above. Its notation, as shown in Fig. 1, captures business objectives and goals in terms of softgoals and goals, and models strategic relationships among business actors as dependencies, which can be in terms of a goal, resource, task, or softgoal. Using this framework also adds value to the model design process because it provides techniques to explore unmet goals, establish alignment between objectives and activities, and perform alternative exploration and evaluation. These are advantages for designing and analyzing business models using the proposed reference catalog, because usually reference models do not fit exactly to specific cases and need adaptation. Therefore, the *i** goal models provide analysis and reasoning behind the model design, thus facilitating the adaptation from generic business models to specific business cases. In addition, the Tropos design process [3, 23], which extends the i* framework, offers an integrated set of technical system design models that can be systematically derived from *i** models, further aids the alignment of business level concepts and technical design models.

Furthermore, we adapted the notation of *i** to include the modeling of business services, as shown in the legend of Fig. 2, because both the business and IT communities have proposed to analyze and design business operations as a set of discrete processes and services, which leverages the principles of SOA to achieve flexibility, agility and responsiveness to changing business needs [4, 8].

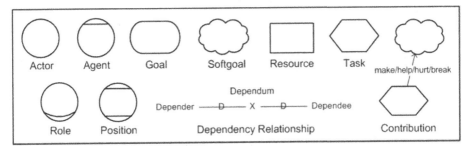

Fig. 1. Major modeling concepts in the *i** framework

4 The Reference Catalog Approach

The proposed approach consists of a set of pre-analyzed, reusable, structured and connected model components that will be provided in a reference catalog, as described in the following sections.

4.1 Reference Business Models

A reference business model, as defined in [2], is a model that provides a generalized representation of a business model. It can be referenced or used as a basis for adaptation to the business of a specific company.

A sample set of reference business models for the reference catalog includes: *Direct-to-Consumer, Full-Service Provider, Intermediary, Shared Infrastructure* and *Value Chain Integrator*. Each of these represents a particular way of conducting

Table 1. The set of components in a reference business model

No.	Component Name	Component Description
1	Name	A unique name to identify the model in the reference catalog.
2	Summary	A brief description of the reference business model.
3	Key business drivers	The major issues that motivate the use of this model.
4	Solution	Description of how this model solves the issues listed as the key business drivers.
5	Potential advantages	A list of potential advantages that this model targets to deliver.
6	Challenges and limitations	A list of challenges and limitations that might be caused by the implementation of this model.
7	Key business actors	A list of key business actors that are involved in this model, and their roles.
8	Strategic dependencies	Strategic dependencies between the different business partners.
9	Revenue model	A description of how business participants can generate revenue by participating in this model.
10	Related models	Other reference business models that are similar to this model.
11	Sources	The source where this model is defined or proposed.
12	Examples	Examples of model usage in the real world.
13	*i** Strategic Dependency (SD) business model	A graphical representation of the reference business model, indicating the business actors, business goal dependencies, business collaborations and value exchanges.
14	*i** Strategic Rationale (SR) Business Model	A more comprehensive graphical representation of the reference business model, indicating the internal business objectives and activities of business actors.
15	Business Services	The business services that are identified from the *i** SR business model.
16	Extended Actor Diagram	A diagram that shows the architectural structure of the set of IT services and other subsystems.

business, thus companies wishing to implement a particular business model similar to one expressed in the catalog can retrieve the reusable model components from it to aid its business and technical system design process. These models are adapted from the set of e-business models proposed in [20] and [24]. A sample reference catalog containing details can be found in the appendix of [12]. The *Value Chain Integrator* business model is extracted from this catalog and used here as an example.

4.2   Reference Model Template

In the reference catalog, each reference business model is defined using a standardized template, which consists of the set of components listed in Table 1. The first 12 are general descriptions that help users to find a reference business model from the catalog that best fit their purpose, and the rest are pre-analyzed and generic models created using the *i** framework, which are effective tools for the representation and analysis of business concepts. In the following sections, we will describe in more detail each type of these model components.

The *i** Strategic Dependency (SD) Business Model. The *i** SD business model provides a graphical representation of the reference business model, indicating the business actors, business goal dependencies, business collaborations and value exchanges. The SD model provides a high level of abstraction showing only external relationships among actors, suitable for browsing and selecting from the catalog.

The *i** Strategic Rationale (SR) Business Model. The *i** SR business model provides a more comprehensive graphical representation of the reference business model, indicating the internal business objectives and activities of business actors. The SR model contains the details needed by business model designers to adapt the reference model to a particular business under question, by modifying goals, tasks and dependency relationships, and analyze it using *i** techniques to explore and evaluate various design options. For completeness, the SR model includes all relationships with external actors, which allows the SD model to be generated from the SR simply by hiding the internal elements of each business actor. An example SR model for the *Value Chain Integrator* reference business model is shown in Fig. 2.

Business Services. Each reference business model also comes with a set of business services, which are identified from the SR business model. They are organized in a table (exemplified in Table 2), in which each row links to a business service pattern in the second part of the catalog. The purpose of this separation between reference business models and business service patterns is that business service patterns often recur in business models, such as the *Place Order* service in the *Value Chain Integrator* example, hence referring to patterns in a separate section will avoid duplicate entries and increase reusability of model components.

Then, for each business service that is identified from the SR models, model designers may use the corresponding business service pattern and associated collaboration diagrams to further analyze and design how their specific service can be carried out, while guided by design options and rationales that are collected from previous experience or other experts.

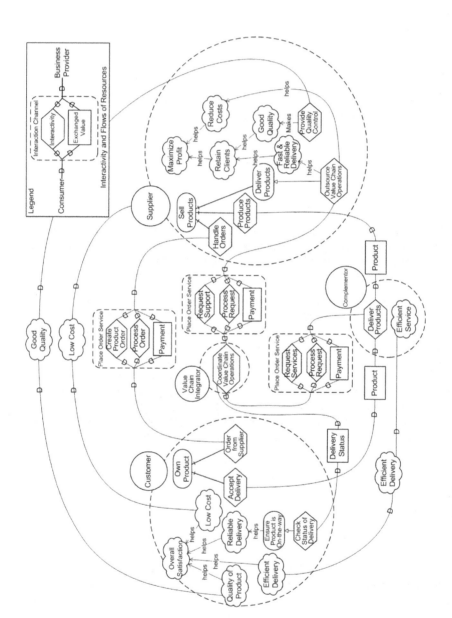

Fig. 2. An example *i** SR model for the *Value Chain Integrator* reference model

Table 2. Business Services used in the *Value Chain Integrator* business model

Service in SR model			Business Service Pattern
	Requester	Provider	
Place (Product) Order	Customer	Supplier	Place Order Service
Place (Service) Order	Supplier	Value Chain Integrator	Place Order Service
Place (Service) Order	Value Chain Integrator	Complementor	Place Order Service
Request Status	Customer	Value Chain Integrator	Obtain Data Service

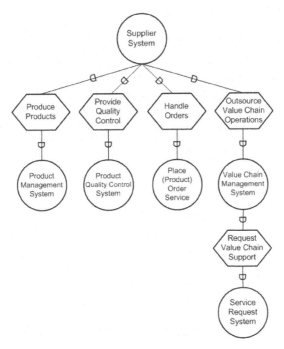

Fig. 3. An extended actor diagram for the *Supplier* actor

Extended Actor Diagrams. We then use an extended actor diagram to illustrate the IT services or subsystems that each business actor needs for the business model to work. This diagram can be generated using the Tropos methodology as described in [11], where each of the actor's tasks is modeled in a task dependency, of which the fulfillment is dependent on a subsystem within the actor. As shown in Fig. 3 below, the actor diagram illustrates the architectural structure of the technical system that needs to be implemented by the business actor *Supplier*. It also guides the identification of IT services that the actor should provide, e.g., the *Place (Product) Order* service that will be used by its customers.

4.3 Business Service Patterns

The second part of the reference catalog contains a set of business service patterns. Each business service pattern consists of the following components:

- A diagram illustrating the recurring business service
- Design rationales, if any
- One or more derived business collaboration diagrams
- Optional business process models corresponding to each business collaboration diagram.

These components capture common patterns of dependencies and collaborations between business partners, as well as provide design alternatives and reasoning to help analysts design strategic business services that will benefit them in their specific case. They are further explained in the following sections using the *Value Chain Integrator* example. Additional diagrams and details of the example may be found in [12], but are not included here due to space limitations.

Business Service Pattern Diagram. When a recurring business service is found in the *i** business models, it is captured and added to the reference catalog as a business service pattern in terms of generic business actors, such as service consumer and provider, and generic dependency relationships. For instance, the *Place Order* service occurred several times in the *Value Chain Integrator* model, and therefore is specified as a service pattern in the catalog with the diagram in the Fig. 4 below.

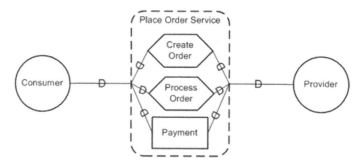

Fig. 4. The recurring *Place Order* service pattern

Design Rationales. Design options and the reasoning behind each business service may also be recorded in the design rationale section under each service pattern, because they will be helpful when designing the same or a similar business service again in the future. For instance, the *Place Order* service pattern can support various payment options, and they are recorded in Table 3.

Table 3. Payment options for the *Place Order* service.

No.	Design Options	Description, Intentions or Concerns
1	Pay-per-use (immediate payment)	Fees are incurred according to usage rates, and payment must be made at the time of usage.
2	Pay-per-use (periodic invoice)	Fees are incurred according to the usage rates, and fee statements are sent to the user periodically.
3	Subscription-based	Users of the service are charged periodically, such as daily, monthly or annually, and the subscription fees are incurred irrespective of actual usage rates.

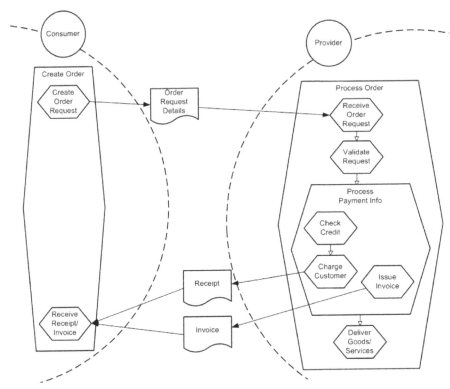

Fig. 5. The business collaboration diagram for the *Place Order* service pattern that supports both the *immediate online payment* and *periodic invoice* payment options

Business Collaboration Diagrams. There is at least one business collaboration diagram for each business service pattern to illustrate the sequence of business activities and resource exchanges involved in the service. Each one of them can be generated based on the method described in [10], where the task originating or receiving the service request is decomposed into more specific tasks performed in sequential order, and the interactions between business partners are shown as information or resources being transferred between them. An example is shown in Fig. 5.

Business Process Models. Business process models are optional, but in cases where a business service can be automated by IT services, a business process model can be used for generating process definitions that can be implemented and executed via IT service orchestration engines. For instance, some collaboration activities, such as the delivery of products, can only be done manually; whereas a *Place Order* service can be done electronically and be automated. There are various options for constructing a business process model, such as using the Unified Modeling Language (UML).

5 Guided Design Via Reference Model

The agent- and goal-orientation of *i** modeling provides support during the adaptation of a reference business model (taken from the reference catalog) to a specific case.

Fig. 6 outlines the procedure for this adaptation process. The process begins by selecting a reference business model from the reference catalog based on business drivers that relate to the company's specific needs. Then, to decide whether a reference

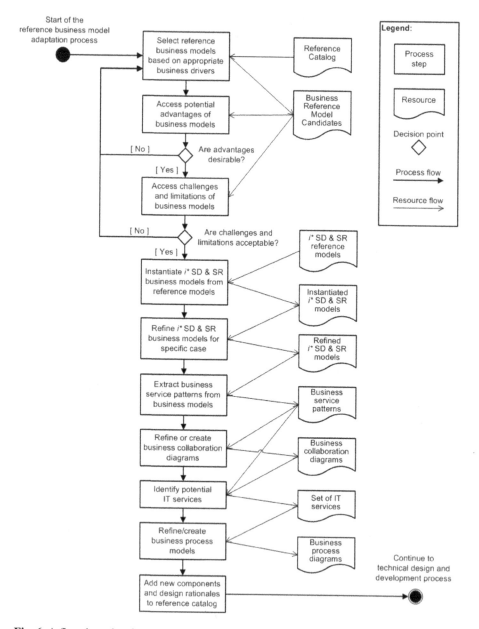

Fig. 6. A flowchart showing the procedure to adapt reference business model components to a specific case

business model is an appropriate one to start with, we assess the potential advantages of implementing the model as well as the challenges and limitations it may bring. Once a reference business model is selected, we instantiate $i*$ SD and SR models from the reference models, and refine them based on the company's characteristics and design decisions. The refinement process can be guided by design rationales recorded in the reference catalog from previous cases, as well as the $i*$ techniques that are described in the next section. Next, business service patterns are extracted from the $i*$ models, and are further analyzed and designed using business collaboration diagrams, either to be created or derived from the existing ones in the reference catalog. Then, potential IT services are identified from the set of business services, and for each of them, business process models are derived. The set of IT services, described in an extended actor diagram, along with the corresponding business process models will then be passed to the technical design and development process. Lastly, new model components and design rationales generated during the process will be added back to the catalog for future reference. In [12], the adaptation process is illustrated with a real world case study from the literature.

5.1 Business Model Instantiation

As explained earlier, the proposed approach begins with the selection of a reference business model that is similar to the business model to be implemented by the company under study. Then, the next step is to instantiate and refine the $i*$ SD and SR business models for this specific case by adding in the case's specific properties and by applying the $i*$ analysis and reasoning techniques. A refined $i*$ SR model is shown in Fig. 7, which analyzes and designs a supplier's product shipping process using its specific organizational structure, such as its extra business roles as sales/shipping agent, warehouse and loading dock; while keeping the goals of improving efficiency and reliability in mind. The refinement process using the $i*$ analysis and reasoning techniques are described in the following sections.

Goal Analysis. This involves the addition of missing business goals that are relevant to the specific case, as well as the removal of goals that are irrelevant but given in the original model. Once the high-level goals are determined, they can be decomposed into more specific sub-goals as appropriate. The *supplier* in the example has the same high-level goals as in the reference business models, therefore no changes are needed.

Task Decomposition and Means-Ends Reasoning. Tasks in the original models are examined to see whether they are relevant to the business goals of our specific case. Irrelevant tasks are removed, and new tasks are added for goals that have not been addressed. Also, given more details in the company's scenario, some tasks can be decomposed into more specific subtasks. For instance, the *outsource shipping* task of the *supplier* in our example can be delegated to different roles in the company, i.e. the *shipping agent* is responsible for requesting shipping support from the *transport consolidator*, whereas the *loading dock* confirms the pickup of products. This helps the business analyst to analyze the business processes, as well as to check that all complicated tasks can be fulfilled.

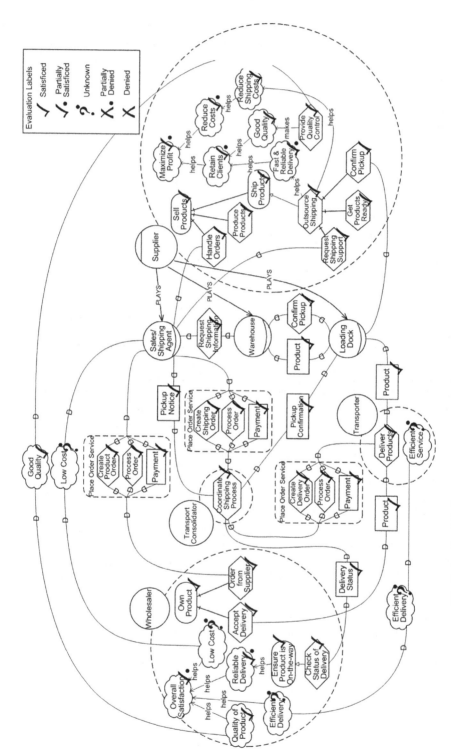

Fig. 7. A refined i* SR model with qualitative evaluation labels for a specific business case

Alternative Exploration and Evaluation. The *i** framework supports the exploration and evaluation of various design alternatives in achieving the same set of business goals by evaluating the contributions of business activities to goals. For example, *outsource shipping* is one of many options to fulfill the *ship product* task. Therefore, the business analyst can later replace this by another alternative, such as *handle shipping internally*, and see how this option contributes to the company's business objectives. The contribution links from options to goals will provide a qualitative evaluation for each alternative.

Feasibility Analysis. To verify that the instantiated business models are feasible, the refined SR model can be analyzed using the evaluation propagation rules defined in [9]. The evaluation labels, such as the ones shown in fig. 7, provide the results of the evaluation process and indicate any unachievable tasks or unfulfilled business goals. Initial label values are assigned to elements that involve design decisions, and then they are propagated to other elements via contribution or dependency links. For example, since it is the supplier's decision to outsource its shipping process, the *outsource shipping* task should have initial value 'satisfied'. To see the effect of this decision, the propagation rules are applied to label its neighboring elements, including the business goals that it affects. According to the resulting model, outsourcing should help the supplier to satisfy its need to *ship products*, as well as partially fulfilling its needs to *reduce shipping cost* and provide *fast and reliable delivery*.

This analysis process not only helps to check for capability issues, semantic errors or inconsistencies, but also allows the designer to discover any unintentional omissions or misrepresentations of important business concepts after refining the business models.

5.2 Service Identification and Design

After the business models are analyzed and refined, the next step is to use these models to guide service identification and design. Service patterns, design rationales, business collaboration diagrams and business process models are all captured in the reference catalog to aid the analysis. Although there are a number of business services identified in the business models, not all of them can be implemented by IT services. For instance, the delivery of products in the case study cannot be automated but must be done manually; whereas interaction between the supplier and transport consolidator can be automated, because shipping request can be stored and sent electronically, and its design and implementation can be guided by the *Place Order* service model components provided in the reference catalog.

6   Conclusions and Future Work

This paper discussed the importance of business modeling in the context of both business and service-oriented design, and adopted the agent and goal-oriented *i** framework as the conceptual modeling framework in this context. It also proposed a reference catalog approach that offers guidance and reusable knowledge to bridge the gap between the business and service design processes. This approach provides a set of pre-analyzed, reusable, structured and connected model components, and illustrated how the *i** modeling techniques are useful in the analysis and reasoning process for business modeling, helping business and system designers to adapt reference business models to specific cases. A number of other approaches, including an extended version of Unified Modeling Language (UML) [5], the Business Model Ontology (BMO) [16, 17], the Business Modeling Method (BMM) [14], and the *e³value* framework [7] also intended to support the business modeling process. However, these existing approaches are not agent and goal-oriented, and lack the modeling and analysis techniques that are needed for pre-analyzing reference business models and adapting them to specific business cases.

Future works for this research include a more in-depth evaluation of the *i** business modeling techniques and the proposed adaptation process, and to validate it in practice. Also, tool support will be needed to help constructing, analyzing and refining business and service model components, as well as storing and accessing reference business models in the proposed catalog. Possible tools that can be extended for these purposes include OpenOME [15] and TAOM4E [21], which are existing tools developed for constructing *i** models.

Lastly, the sample set of reference business models mentioned in this paper is expected to be preliminary and incomplete. To maintain an ongoing expansion of the reference catalog, experts can be invited to join the effort in refining and adding new models and components to the catalog as the business models and strategies evolve in the real world. Therefore, workable solutions to recurring business problems and best practices can be shared among members in the community.

Acknowledgments. Financial support from the Natural Sciences and Engineering Research Council of Canada (NSERC) and Bell University Laboratories is gratefully acknowledged.

References

1. Allee, V. A Value Network Approach for Modeling and Measuring Intangibles. Presented at Transparent Enterprise, Madrid. Available at http://www.vernaallee.com. November 2002.
2. Alt, R., Zimmermann, H.D. Preface: Introduction to Special Edition - Business Models. In Journal on Electronic Markets - Anniversary Edition: Business Models, Vol 11(1), 2001.
3. Bresciani, P., Giorgini, P., Giunchiglia, F., Mylopoulos, J., Perini, A. TROPOS: An Agent-Oriented Software Development Methodology. In Journal of Autonomous Agents and Multi-Agent Systems, Kluwer Academic Publishers, May 2004.
4. Brown, J.S., Hagel III, J. Flexible IT, Better Strategy. In McKinsey Quarterly, McKinsey & Group, No. 4, pp.50-59, 2003.
5. Eriksson, H.E., Penker, M. Business modeling with UML: Business Patterns at Work. Wiley Interscience - John Wiley & Sons, 2000.
6. Essler, U., Whitaker, R. Rethinking E-commerce Business Modelling in Terms of Interactivity. In Journal on Electronic Markets, Vol 11(1):10-16, 2001.
7. Gordijn, J., Akkermans, J.M. Value-based Requirements Engineering: Exploring Innovative e-Commerce Ideas. In Requirements Engineering, vol. 8(2), pp. 114-134, July 2003.

8. Hagel III, J., Brown, J.S. Your Next IT Strategy. Harvard Business Review, Volume 79, Issue 9, October 2001.
9. Horkoff, J. Using *i** Models for Evaluation. Master's Thesis, Department of Computer Science, University of Toronto, 2006.
10. Kazhamiakin, R., Pistore, M., Roveri, M. A Framework for Integrating Business Processes and Business Requirements. In Enterprise Distributed Object Computing Conference, Eighth IEEE International (EDOC'04), Monterey, California, pp. 9-20, September 20-24, 2004.
11. Lau, D., Mylopoulos, J. Designing Web Services with Tropos. In Proceedings of the 2004 IEEE International Conference on Web Services, San Diego, California, USA, July 6-9, 2004.
12. Lo, A. From Business Models to Service-Oriented Design: A Reference Catalog Approach. Master's Thesis, Department of Computer Science, University of Toronto, October 2006.
13. Magretta, J. Why Business Models Matter. In Harvard Business Review, Vol. 80, Issue 5, p86, 7p, 1c, May 2002.
14. Montilva, J.C., Barrios, J.A. BMM: A Business Modeling Method for Information Systems Development. In the Clei Electronic Journal, Vol. 7, No. 2, Paper 3, December 2004.
15. OpenOME - an Open-Source Requirements Engineering Tool. Available at http://www.cs.toronto.edu/km/openome/.
16. Osterwalder, A. The Business Model Ontology: A Proposition in a Design Science Approach. PhD thesis, University of Lausanne - HEC, Lausanne, Switzerland, 2004.
17. Osterwalder, A., Pigneur, Y. An Ontology for e-Business Models. Chapter in Value Creation from E-Business Models, W. Currie (Ed), Butterworth-Heinemann, 2004.
18. Osterwalder, A., Pigneur, Y., Tucci, C.L. Clarifying Business Models: Origins, Present, and Future of the Concept. In Communications of the AIS, Vol. 15, Article, May 2005.
19. Rappa, M. Business Models on the Web. Available at Managing the Digital Enterprise website: http://digitalenterprise.org/, May 2003.
20. Straub, D. Business Models and Strategic Planning For NE. In Chapter 8 of Foundations of Net-Enhanced Organizations, the Wiley Series on Net-Enhanced Organizations, 2004.
21. TAOM4E – a Tool for Agent Oriented Visual Modeling for the Eclipse Platform. Available at: http://sra.itc.it/tools/taom4e/.
22. Timmers, P. Electronic Commerce: Strategies and Models for Business-to-Business Trading. Wiley Interscience, New York, 1999.
23. Tropos - a Requirements-Driven Development Methodology for Agent Software. Available at: http://www.troposproject.org/.
24. Weill, P., Vitale, M. R. Place to Space: Migrating to e-Business Models. Harvard Business School Press, 2001.
25. Yu, E.S.K. Towards modeling and reasoning support for early-phase requirements engineering. In Proceedings of the 3rd IEEE International Symposium on Requirements Engineering (RE'97), Annapolis, USA, pp. 226 -235, IEEE Computer Society Press, 1997.

Teaching a Schema Translator to Produce O/R Views

Peter Mork[1], Philip A. Bernstein[2], and Sergey Melnik[2]

[1] The MITRE Corporation and
[2] Microsoft Research
pmork@mitre.org, {philbe,melnik}@microsoft.com

Abstract. This paper describes a rule-based algorithm to derive a relational schema from an extended entity-relationship model. Our work is based on an approach by Atzeni and Torlone in which the source EER model is imported into a universal metamodel, a series of transformations are performed to eliminate constructs not appearing in the relational metamodel, and the result is exported. Our algorithm includes novel features that are needed for practical object to relational mapping systems: First, it generates forward- and reverse-views that transform instances of the source model into instances of the target and back again. These views automate the object-to-relational (O/R) mapping. Second, it supports a flexible mapping of inheritance hierarchies to flat relations that subsumes and extends prior approaches. Third, it propagates incremental updates of the source model into incremental updates of the target. We prove the algorithm's correctness and demonstrate its practicality in an implementation.

1 Introduction

Object-to-relational (O/R) mapping systems are now mainstream technology. The Java Data Objects (JDO) specification is supported by many vendors of Enterprise Java Beans [20]. The Hibernate system is in widespread use [17]. Ruby on Rails includes the Active Record package [29]. And Microsoft recently released an ER-to-relational mapper in the next version of ADO.NET [1].

Developers often start building new applications by designing a conceptual model E of the application and translating it into a relational schema R to persist the data. In JDO and Hibernate, E is expressed as a set of Java classes. In ADO.NET, E is expressed in the Entity Data Model (EDM), a variant of the extended entity-relationship (EER) model [6]. Thus, the object-oriented (OO) constructs in E can include inheritance, associations, complex types, and nested collections, all of which have to be mapped to relational structures.

The problem of translating schemas between metamodels, or schema definition languages, has received attention in [2][3][9][16][23][25][26]. However, published approaches lack solutions to several issues that are required for practical applications: bidirectional semantic mappings, flexible translation of inheritance hierarchies, and incremental schema modification. These problems are non-trivial. They require architectural and algorithmic advances, which are the main subject of this paper. A preliminary, short description of the work reported here appears in [5].

C. Parent et al. (Eds.): ER 2007, LNCS 4801, pp. 102–119, 2007.

Our basic strategy follows the rule-based approach of Atzeni and Torlone in [2]. Using this approach, we define a universal metamodel that has all of the main modeling constructs in the metamodels of interest, in our case EER and relational. New constructs can be added to the universal metamodel to support a new metamodel or extend an existing one. We then define a collection of transformation rules. For example, one simple rule transforms an entity type into a complex type (e.g., a relation). The goal is to execute a series of transformation rules whose composition eliminates from the source model all modeling constructs absent in the target metamodel. The result of this *translation step* is exported into the desired syntax.

Our first contribution is the generation of instance-level transformations between the source schema and generated target schema. While there are solutions to this problem (e.g., [3][25][26]), they require passing the instances through an intermediate generic representation. This is impractical for large databases and does not generate the view definitions that are required to drive EER-to-relational mapping systems. We take a different approach. We augment each transformation rule applied in the translation step to generate not only target schema elements but also forward- and reverse-views that describe how each eliminated construct of the source model is represented in the target. We have proved that these views are correct, i.e., do not lose information, and give one example proof in this paper.

The series of transformation rules executed in the translation step produces a series of elementary views. These views are composed via view unfolding to generate the final forward- and reverse-views between the source and target schemas. The correctness of the composition is ensured by the correctness of the elementary views. The composed views are expressed in terms of the universal metamodel. They are fed into a component that translates them into the native mapping language.

Our second contribution is a rich set of transformations for inheritance mapping. It allows the data architect to decide on the number of relations used for representing a sub-class hierarchy and to assign each direct or inherited property of a class independently to any relation. These transformations allow a per-class choice of inheritance mapping strategy. They subsume all inheritance mapping strategies we know of, including horizontal and vertical partitioning [22], their combinations, and many new strategies. The transformations are driven by a data structure called a mapping matrix. We present algorithms for populating mapping matrices from per-class annotations of the inheritance hierarchy and generating provably correct elementary views. The complexity of inheritance mapping is encapsulated in a single transformation rule. Since the final views are obtained by composition, inheritance mappings do not interfere with mapping strategies for other EER constructs.

Our third contribution is a technique for propagating incremental updates of the source model into incremental updates of the target. To do this, we ensure that an unchanged target object has the same id each time it is generated, so we can reuse the previous version instead of creating a new one. This avoids losing a user's customizations of the target and makes incremental updating fast. This practical requirement arises when the schema translation process is interactive. A data architect analyzes different translation choices, switching back and forth between the source and target schemas, which may be large and thus require careful on-screen layout. Since it is unacceptable to regenerate the target schema and discard the layout information after changes in the schema translation, incremental update propagation is required.

Finally, we discuss the implementation of our O/R translation algorithm. We developed an extensible, rule-driven core that can be customized to specific model-translation tasks with moderate effort. To support efficient rule execution, we wrap the native meta-model APIs so that the rules directly manipulate the objects representing the model elements, avoiding the conversion penalty often incurred by using rule-based systems.

The rest of this paper is structured as follows. Section 2 describes our universal metamodel. Section 3 specifies our syntax for transformations and gives an example correctness proof for one of them. Section 4 describes how we support multiple strategies for mapping inheritance hierarchies into relations. Section 5 explains how we do incremental updating. Section 6 discusses our implementation. Section 7 discusses related work and Section 8 is the conclusion.

2 Metamodel

Before we can define any transformation rules, we need to describe the universal metamodel in which they are expressed. The universal metamodel we use in this paper, called $\mathcal{U}$, is similar to the universal metamodel in [21]. $\mathcal{U}$ supports most of the standard constructs found in popular metamodels, enough to illustrate our techniques. It is not intended to be complete, i.e., capture all of the features of rich metamodels such as XSD or SQL with complex constraints and triggers, but it can easily be extended to incorporate additional features.

Table 1 lists the basic constructs of $\mathcal{U}$ and examples of their use in popular metamodels. We base our discussion of the semantics of $\mathcal{U}$ on its relational schema shown in Fig. 1. A detailed description and formal semantics for $\mathcal{U}$ appear in [24].

In $\mathcal{U}$ there are three simple types: Atomic types are called *lexicals*, which we assume to be uniform across all metamodels. The remaining simple types are collections, either *lists* or *sets* of some base type. For example, in SQL, apart from lexicals, the only simple type is a set whose base type is a tuple.

Complex types are either *structured* types (e.g., relations) or *abstract* types (e.g., entities). Complex types are related to other types via *attributes* and *containment*. For an attribute A The domain of A is the complex type on which A is defined, and the range of A is the type associated with A. An attribute can have minimum and maximum cardinality constraints. For example, in SQL every attribute's domain must be a structured type and its maximum cardinality must be one. A containment is similar to an attribute; it establishes a (named) structural relationship between the parent type and the child type such that each such instance of the child type is nested within an instance of the parent type.

The constraints supported by $\mathcal{U}$ include key constraints, inclusion dependencies and generalizations. Each *key constraint* consists of a set of attributes that uniquely identify instances of some complex type. Multiple candidate keys can be defined for a complex type, but at most one primary key can be defined. An *inclusion dependency* establishes a relationship between a key and another complex type. For each attribute in an inclusion dependency there is a corresponding attribute in the related key. For any instance of a model containing an inclusion dependency, the projection of the

Table 1. Relationships among common metamodels

Construct	SQL	EER	Java	XSD
Lexical Type	int, varchar	scalar	int, string	integer, string
Structured Type	tuple			element
Abstract Type		entity	class	complex type
List Type			array	list
Set Type	table			
Attribute	column	attribute, relationship	field	attribute
Containment		aggregation		nesting

Simple types include lexicals and collections:
LexicalType(TypeID, TypeName)
ListType(TypeID, TypeName, BaseType)
SetType(TypeID, TypeName, BaseType)

Complex types can be structured or abstract:
  StructuredType(TypeID, TypeName)
  AbstractType(TypeID, TypeName)
Complex types have *attributes* and can be nested:
  Attribute(AttrID, AttrName, Domain, Range, MinCard, MaxCard)
  Containment(ConID, AttrName, Parent, Child, MinCard, MaxCard)
  Domain/Parent must be a complex type.
  Range/Child can be any type.
  Min/MaxCard are Zero, One or N and apply to the range/child.

A *key* indicates a set of attributes that identify a complex object:
  KeyConstraint(KeyID, TypeID, IsPrimary)
  TypeID references the type for which this is a key.
  Primary indicates if this is the primary key for the type.
  KeyAttribute(KeyAttrID, KeyID, AttrID)
  KeyID references the key for which this is an attribute.
  AttrID references an attribute of the associated type.

An *inclusion dependency* establishes a subset relationship:
  InclusionDependency(InclD, TypeID, KeyID)
  TypeID references the type for which this dependency holds.
  KeyID references the associated key.
  InclusionAttribute(IncAttrID, InclD, AttrID, KeyAttrID)
  InclD references the inclusion for which this is an attribute.
  AttrID references an attribute of the associated type.
  KeyAttrID: references a key attribute of the key of the superset type.

Generalization is used to extend a type or construct a union:
  Generalization(GenID, TypeID, IsDisjoint, IsTotal)
A type can serve as the parent for multiple generalizations.
Disjoint and Total tells whether children are disjoint and cover the parent.
  Specialization(SpecID, GenID, TypeID)
  GenID references the parent generalization.
  TypeID references the associated specialized type.

Fig. 1. Relational schema for universal metamodel $\mathcal{U}$

inclusion attributes must be a subset of the projection of the key attributes. Finally, a *generalization* establishes a relationship between a complex type (the supertype) and a set of more specialized subtypes. Each subtype inherits any attributes or containment relationships associated with the supertype.

3 Transformations

Using the Atzeni-Torlone approach, schema translation has four steps: (1) manually or automatically generate a valid transformation plan consisting of a sequence of transformations (2) import the source model (3) [translation step] execute the transformations in the plan, and (4) export the result. In this section and the next, we explain step (3), the transformations, which is the core of the algorithm and where most of our innovations lie. Due to lack of space, we omit a description of step (1), our A*-based algorithm for automatic generation of a transformation plan; it appears in [24]. We briefly discuss steps (2) and (4) in Section 6 on Implementation.

3.1 Defining a Transformation

Each step of a transformation plan is a transformation that removes certain constructs from the model and generates other constructs plus view definitions. A *transformation* is a triple of the form $<D, F, R>$ where D is a set of rules that expresses a model transformation, F is a rule that produces an elementary forward view that expresses the target model as a view over the source, and R is a rule that produces an elementary reverse view that expresses the source as a view over the target.

Rules in D contain predicates, each of which is a construct in $\mathcal{U}$. Each rule is of the form "<body> $\Rightarrow$ <head>", where <body> and <head> are conjunctions of predicates. For example, the following is a simplified version of the rule that replaces an abstract type, such as a class definition, by a structured type, such as relation definition:

AbstractType(*id*, *name*) $\Rightarrow$ **StructuredType**(newAS(*id*), *name*)

AbstractType and **StructuredType** are predicates from Fig. 1, and *id* and *name* are variables. The Skolem function newAS(*id*) generates a new type ID for the structured type definition based on the abstract type's *id*. Skolem function names are prefixed by "new" to aid readability.

The semantics of a rule in D with body b and n terms in the head is defined by a Datalog program with n rules, each with one term in the head implied by b. For example, A(x, y) $\Rightarrow$ B(x), C(f(y)) is equivalent to the Datalog program B(x) :- A(x, y) and C(f(y)) :- A(x, y). We chose our rule syntax because it is less verbose than Datalog when many rules have the same body, which arises often in our transformations. In essence, each rule is a tuple-generating dependency [11] or a second-order dependency without equalities [12], if the Skolem functions are considered existentially quantified.

For some rules, expressing them in logic is impractical, because they are too verbose or hard to understand. Such rules can be implemented in an imperative language. But for succinctness and clarity, we use only the logic notation in this section.

Some of the rules in each model transformation D also populate a binary predicate Map, whose transitive closure identifies all of the elements derived from a given source element. For example, adding Map to the rule that replaces an abstract type by a structured type, we get:

AbstractType(id, $name$) $\Rightarrow$ StructuredType(newAS(id), $name$), Map(id, newAS(id))

Map(id, newAS(id)) says that the element identified by id is mapped to a new element identified by newAS(id).

After executing all of the transformations, we can extract from the transitive closure of Map those tuples that relate source elements to target elements. Tools that display the source and target models can use this mapping to offer various user-oriented features, such as the ability to navigate back and forth between corresponding elements or to copy annotations such as layout hints or comments.

Rules add tuples to the head predicates but never delete them. Since we need to delete tuples that correspond to constructs being replaced in a model, we use a unary predicate Delete that identifies elements to delete. After all rules of a transformation are executed, a non-rule-based post-processing step deletes the elements identified in Delete predicates. For example, in the rule that replaces an abstract type by a structured type, the predicate Delete removes the abstract type being replaced, as follows:

AbstractType(id, $name$) $\Rightarrow$ StructuredType(newAS(id), $name$), Map(id, newAS(id)), Delete(id)

The rules in a model transformation D are schema-level mappings. Forward- and reverse-views are instance-level mappings. The predicates and variables in a view are variables in the rules of D. For example, a simplified version of the forward-view for replacing an abstract type by a structured type is "$id(x) \Rightarrow$ newAS[id](x)". This rule says that if x is the identifier of an instance (i.e., an object) of the abstract type identified by id, then it is also the identifier of an instance (i.e., a tuple) of the structured type identified by newAS[id]. Notice that we use the same identifier to denote two different types of items, namely objects and tuples, which enables us to express instance-level mappings between them.

To generate such views in rules, we can define predicates that create their components, such as the following:

ViewHead(newRule(newAS(id)), newPredicate(id, "x"))
ViewBody(newRule(newAS(id)), newPredicate(newAS(id), "x"))

We can then conjoin these to the head of the rule that replaces an abstract type by a structured type. However, in this paper we will use the simpler and more readable notation "$id(x) \Rightarrow$ newAS[id](x)".

We represent a model before and after a transformation as a *model graph*. Its nodes correspond to simple and complex types. Its edges correspond to attributes. For example, on the left side of Fig. 2, R is a structured type with attributes k and a. The value of k is a lexical type and the value of a is a structured type S with attributes b and c. An instance of a model graph is an *instance graph*, which is comprised of a set of values for each node and a set of value pairs for each edge. A view defines how to populate the nodes and edges of one instance graph from those of another.

A transformation is *correct* if the forward-view converts every instance I_S of the source schema into a valid instance I_T of the target schema, and the reverse-view converts I_T back into I_S without loss of information. That is, the composition of the forward- and reverse-views is the identity. Unlike [9][13], we do not require the converse; there may be instances of the target model that cannot be converted into instances of the source. Our definition of correctness is more stringent than [26], which requires only that the forward view generates a valid instance of the target.

Sections 3.2–3.3 define two of the main transformations to convert from EER to SQL. For each transformation, we give its model transformation and its forward-/reverse-views. We write the views as instance transformations and omit the verbose rule predicates that would generate them. Since the forward- and reverse-views for the first transformation are inverses of each other, correctness is immediately apparent. We give a detailed correctness argument for the transformation of Section 3.3.

3.2 Convert Abstract to Structured Type

This transformation replaces each abstract type with a structured type. To preserve object identity, a new oid attribute is added to the structured type, unless the abstract type already included a primary key. The model transformation rules are as follows:

AbstractType(*id*, *name*)
⇒ **StructuredType**(newAS(*id*), *name*), Map(*id*, newAS(*id*)), Delete(*id*)

AbstractType(*id*, *name*), ¬**KeyConstraint**(_, *id*, "True")
⇒ **Attribute**(newOID(*id*), "oid", newAS(*id*), "Int", "1", "1"),
KeyConstraint(newASKey(*id*), newAS(*id*), "True"),
KeyAttribute(newASKeyAttr(*id*), newASKey(*id*), newOID(*id*))

We are careful in our use of negation, as in ¬**KeyConstraint** above, to ensure that stratification is possible.

The forward view is: *id*(*x*) ⇒ newAS[*id*](*x*), newOID[*id*](*x*, newID(*x*)). The last predicate says that newOID[*id*] is an attribute whose value for the tuple *x* is newID(*x*).

The reverse view is: newAS[*id*](*x*) ⇒ *id*(*x*). Notice that we do not need to map back the new oid attribute of the structured type, since it is not needed for information preservation of the source abstract type. It is immediately apparent that the forward- and reverse-views are inverses of each other and hence are correct.

3.3 Remove Structured Attribute

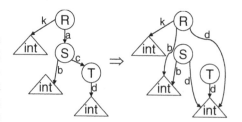

This transformation replaces an attribute *a* that references a structured type *S* all of whose attributes are lexicals. It replaces *a* by lexical attributes that uniquely identify a tuple of *S*. If *S* has a primary key, then *a* is replaced by the key attributes of *S* and there is an inclusion dependency from the new attributes

Fig. 2. Removing structured attributes

to that key. Otherwise, *a* is replaced by all of *S*'s attributes. (If the latter is desired even if *S* has a primary key, then a user-defined tag on *a* can be used to ask that the latter rule be applied.) The transformation is applied iteratively to eliminate nested types.

For example, consider three structured types: R, S and T (see Fig. 2). R references S using attribute a and has primary key k (an Int). S has no primary key, but it has two attributes b (an Int) and c (which references T). T has a primary key attribute d (an Int). Applying the transformation to $S.c$ replaces that attribute by $S.d$ and adds an inclusion dependency from $S.d$ to $T.d$. Now all attributes of S are lexicals. So we can apply the transformation again to replace $R.a$ by $R.b$ and $R.d$.

The model transformation rules are as follows (we use an underscore in a slot for an existential variable that appears only once in the rule, to avoid useless variables):

StructuredType(*domain, name*),
Attribute(*id, _, domain, range, _,* "One"), ¬ **LexicalType**(*range, _*)
⟹ **MixedTypeHelper**(*domain, name*)

Attribute(*id, name1, domain, range1, min1,* "One"),
StructuredType(*range1, name*), ¬MixedTypeHelper(*range1, name*),
Attribute(*attr, name2, range1, range2, min2,* "One"), Min(*min1, min2, min*)
⟹ **Attribute**(newSA(*id, attr*), newName(*name1, name2*), *domain, range2, min,* "One") ,
  Map(*id,* newSA(*id, attr*)), Delete(*id*)

Attribute(*id, _, _, range, _,* "One"), **KeyAttribute**(*keyAttr, key, id*), **StructuredType**(*range, _*),
Attribute(*attr, _, range, _, _,* "One")
⟹ **KeyAttribute**(newSAKeyAttr(*keyAttr, attr*), key, newSA(*id, attr*)),
  Map(keyAttr, newSAKeyAttr(*keyAttr, attr*)), Delete(*keyAttr*)

The first rule identifies all "mixed" structured types—those types that reference another complex (i.e., non-lexical) type. In Fig. 2 S is a mixed type, but T is a "leaf" type. The second rule replaces an attribute (id) that references a leaf type (such as c) with the attributes (newSA($id, attr$)) of the leaf type (in this case d). The third rule updates any key constraints that referenced the old attribute to reference the new attribute. After the first iteration, S becomes a leaf type, and attributes that reference it (such as a) are replaced by attributes of S. Thus, a is replaced with attributes b and d.

For each id and $attr_i$ that satisfy the second model transformation rule, there is a forward view:

$$id[x, z], attr_i[z, y] \Rightarrow newSA(id, attr_i)[x, y]$$

In the following reverse view, either $attr_1 \ldots attr_k$ are the attributes in the key of structured type $range1$, or $range1$ has no key and k attributes in total:

$$newSA(id, attr_1)[x, t_1], attr_1(s, t_1), ..., newSA(id, attr_k)[x, t_k], attr_k(s, t_k) \Rightarrow attr[x, s]$$

To explain the above view definitions and argue their correctness, we simplify the notation by replacing the terms id, $attr_i$, and newSA($id, attr_i$) in the view definitions by the symbols a, b_i, and ab_i, yielding the following:

$a(r, s), b_i(s, t) \Rightarrow ab_i(r, t)$	// forward views
$ab_1(r, t_1), b_1(s, t_1), ... ab_k(r, t_k), b_k(s, t_k) \Rightarrow a(r, s)$	// reverse view

Structure S has n attributes, k of which are key attributes (if there is a key). The attribute $R.a$ that refers to the structure S is replaced by new attributes that correspond one-to-one with the attributes of S. To show that the forward- and reverse-views are correct, we need to show that their composition is the identity. We form the composition by substituting the forward view for each ab$_i$ in the reverse view, yielding:

$$a(r, s_1), b_1(s_1, t_1), b_1(s, t_1), ..., a(r, s_k), b_k(s_k, t_k), b_k(s, t_k) \Rightarrow a(r, s)$$

Since a is a function, $a(r, s_i)=a(r, s_j)$ for all i,j. So $s_1 = s_2 = ... = s_k$. Replacing the s_i's by s_1 we get:

$$a(r, s_1), b_1(s_1, t_1), b_1(s, t_1), ..., a(r, s_1), b_k(s_1, t_k), b_k(s, t_k) \Rightarrow a(r, s)$$

Since $b_1, ... b_k$ is either a key or comprises all the attributes of s, we have $s = s_1$. Replacing the s_1's by s we get:

$$a(r, s), b_1(s, t_1), ..., b_k(s, t_k) \Rightarrow a(r, s)$$

Since there must exist values for $t_1, ..., t_k$ in s, the above rule reduces to a(r, s) :- a(r, s), which is the identity.

3.4   Additional Transformations

In addition to the transformations in Sections 3.2-3.3, we have a transformation to replace a multi-valued attribute by a join relation and another to eliminate containments. They are quite simple, like converting an abstract type to a structured type, and are described in detail in [24]. We also implemented transformations to address more target metamodels. We provide a brief summary of some of them:

Convert structured types to abstract types. This transformation is the inverse of the one presented in Section 3.2.

Replace an attribute with a maximum cardinality of N by a new attribute with a maximum cardinality of One. If the range of the old attribute was T, the range of the new attribute is a set of T. The difference between the old and new attributes is evident when the attribute participates in a key constraint. A multi-valued attribute provides multiple unique key values, one for each value of the attribute; a set-valued attribute provides a single key value, namely, the set itself.

Replace a list of T with a set of indexed structures. The new structured type has two attributes, Index and Value. The range of the former is Integer and the latter is T. This transformation creates an explicit association between values and their original positions in the list.

Stratify sets. This transformation takes a set of sets and converts it into a set of indexed structures; each nested set is assigned a unique identifier, which is associated with the values in that set. This transformation is needed to support the nested relational model.

Remove multiple-containment. If type T is contained in multiple parent types, then create a new specialization of T. Each old containment relationship is transformed into a new containment that references exactly one of the new specializations of T. For example, if type A is contained in both B and C, then create types B-A and C-A, which are contained in B and C, respectively.

3.5   Composing Transformations

The execution of a transformation plan is a sequence of n transformations. The first transformation takes the initial model m_0 as input and the last transformation produces the final model m_n as output. Our goal is to generate a forward view V_F that defines m_n

as a function of m_0 and a reverse view V_R that defines m_0 as a function of m_n. Given the forward- and reverse-views, this can be done incrementally. The initial transformation from m_0 to m_1 defines the initial views V_F and V_R. Suppose we have forward- and reverse-views V_F and V_R for the first i-1 transformations. For the ith transformation, its forward view v_f and reverse view v_r are composed with V_F and V_R, i.e., $V_F \circ v_f$ and $V_R \circ v_r$, using ordinary view unfolding, thereby generating V_F and V_R.

4 Inheritance Mappings

So far, we have assumed that all instances of a given source model construct are transformed using the same transformation rule. We now consider a more general strategy for mapping inheritance hierarchies of abstract types into structured types that allows the user to customize the transformation. Since this is the familiar object-to-relational mapping problem, we use the terms class and relation instead of abstract type and structured type.

Several strategies for mapping classes to relations exist. For example, consider the inheritance hierarchy in Fig. 3. Typical strategies for mapping these classes to flat relations include the following [17]: relation per concrete class (a.k.a. horizontal partitioning), in which each relation contains one column for every attribute, inherited or otherwise; relation per subclass (a.k.a. vertical partitioning), in which each relation contains a column only for the class' directly defined attributes; and relation per hierarchy, in which one relation stores all classes with a discriminator column to indicate which rows are in which concrete classes.

These simple strategies reflect only a few of the storage possibilities. For example, in Fig. 3, the designer has indicated that the system should partition Person (and its

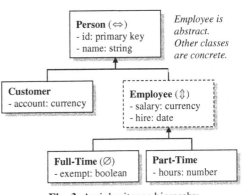

Fig. 3. An inheritance hierarchy

subclasses) using a horizontal strategy ($\Leftrightarrow$). However, Employee (and its subclasses) should be partitioned vertically ($\updownarrow$), except for Full-Time whose attributes should be stored with those of the base class ($\varnothing$).

Based on these declarations, we automatically generate the inheritance mapping shown in Table 2. Each column of this table corresponds to a class. Each of the first 4 rows corresponds to a database relation. (The rows *rel* and *attr** are discussed below.) Reading down a column, we can easily verify that every concrete class' (non-key) attributes are stored in some relation. Reading across a row, we can determine the relational structure. For example, because of horizontal partitioning, relation C contains all attributes (direct and inherited) of Customer. Similarly, vertical partitioning is used for Employee, so E is the only relation to contain salary and hire information.

Table 2. A mapping matrix from classes to relations

	Person	Customer	Full-Time	Part-Time
P	id, name		id, name	id, name
C		id, name, account		
E			id, salary, hire, exempt	id, salary, hire
PT				id, hours
rel	{P}	{C}	{P, E}	{P, E, PT}
attr*	id, name	id, name, account	id, name, salary, hire, exempt	id, name, salary, hire, hours

For a given hierarchy, let C be the set of all classes in the (source) hierarchy and let R be the set of target relations. The predicate $c(x)$ indicates that x is a direct instance of $c \in C$. Similarly, $r(x)$ indicates that x is a tuple of $r \in R$.

A mapping matrix M describes how to map the attributes of classes to attributes of relations. The mapping matrix contains one column for each concrete $c \in C$ and one row for each $r \in R$. Each cell $M[r, c]$ of the mapping matrix indicates which attributes of c appear in r. For example, to map a class's direct and inherited attributes to one relation (a.k.a., horizontal partitioning), all of the attributes of c appear in a single cell of M. To flatten a hierarchy, R contains a single relation, so M has just one row.

To explain the construction of view definitions from M, we need some additional notation: $PK(c)$ returns the primary key of c, $attr*(c)$ returns the direct and indirect attributes of c, $rel(c)$ returns the relations used to store instances of c (the non-empty cells of column c), and $r.a$ refers to attribute a of relation r. *Flagged* is the set of all relations that contain a *flag* attribute, the values of which are type identifiers. The type identifier of c is $TypeID(c)$.

The forward-view for this transformation can be directly inferred from M. For each attribute a in a cell $M[r, c]$ the forward-view is: $c(x), a(x, y) \Rightarrow r(x), r.a(x, y)$. The reverse-view is more complex and is based on the following constraints on M.

a) $\bigcup_{r \in R} M[r,c] = attr*(c)$

b) $r \in rel(c) \rightarrow PK(c) \subseteq M[r,c]$

c) $rel(c_1) = rel(c_2) \rightarrow c_1 = c_2 \vee rel(c_1) \subseteq Flagged$

Constraint (a) says that every attribute of c must appear in some relation. Constraint (b) guarantees that an instance of c stored in multiple relations can be reconstructed using its primary key, which we assume can be used to uniquely identify instances. Constraint (c) says that if two distinct classes have the same $rel(c)$ value, then each of them is distinguished by a type id in *Flagged*.

To test these constraints in our example, consider the last two rows of Table 2. Constraint (a) holds since every attribute in the bottom row appears in the corresponding column of M. Constraint (b) holds because *id* appears in every non-empty cell. Constraint (c) holds because no two classes have the same signature.

Constraint (c) guarantees that the mapping is invertible, so there exists a correct reverse-view for the mapping. There are two cases: For a given $c \in C$, either there is another class c' with $rel(c') = rel(c)$, or not. If so, then there exists $r \in (rel(c) \cap Flagged)$, so we can use $r.flag$ to identify instances of c:

$r(x), r.flag(x, TypeID(c)) \Rightarrow c(x)$

Otherwise, $rel(c)$ is unique, so the instances of c are those that are in all $rel(c)$ relations and in no other relation, that is:

$$\bigwedge_{r\in rel(c)} r(x) \bigwedge_{r\notin rel(c)} \neg r(x) \Rightarrow c(x)$$

In relational algebra, this is the join of all $r\in rel(c)$ composed with the anti-semijoin of $r\notin rel(c)$, which can be further simplified exploiting the inclusion dependencies between the relations in $rel(c)$. In both cases, the reverse view is an inverse of the forward view. The reverse-view for a given attribute is read directly from the mapping matrix. It is simply the union of its appearances in M:

$$\{ r.a(x, y) \Rightarrow c.a(x, y) \mid c\in C, r\in R, a\in M[c,r] \}$$

The mapping matrix M is very general, but can be hard to populate to satisfy the required constraints (a)-(c) above. So instead of asking users to populate M, we offer them easy-to-understand class annotations from which M is populated automatically.

Each class can be annotated by one of three strategies: $\updownarrow$, $\Leftrightarrow$, or $\varnothing$. Strategy $\updownarrow$ does vertical partitioning, the default strategy: each inherited property is stored in the relation associated with the ancestor class that defines it. Strategy $\Leftrightarrow$ yields horizontal partitioning: the direct instances of the class are stored in one relation, which contains all of its inherited properties. Strategy $\varnothing$ means that no relation is created: the data is stored in the relation for the parent class. The strategy selection propagates down the inheritance hierarchy, unless overridden by another strategy in descendant classes. These annotations exploit the flexibility of the inheritance mapping matrices only partially, but are easy to communicate to schema designers.

procedure PopulateMappingMatrix(c: class, r: target relation)

if (strategy(c) $\in$ {$\updownarrow$, $\Leftrightarrow$}) **then** r = ⟨new relation⟩ **end if**   // 1
if (c is concrete) **then**
    M[r, c] = M[r, c] ∪ ⟨key attributes of c⟩   // 2

    if (strategy(c) = $\Leftrightarrow$)
    then M[r, c] = M[r, c] ∪ ⟨declared and inherited attributes of c⟩   // 3
    else
        toPlace = attrs = ⟨declared and inherited non-key attributes of c⟩   // 4
        for each relation r_p created for ancestor class of c, traversing bottom-up
            for each cell M[r_p, p] **do**
                M[r_p, c] = M[r_p, c] ∪ (M[r_p, p] ∩ toPlace)   // 5
                toPlace = toPlace − M[r_p, p]
            end for
        end for
        M[r, c] = M[r, c] ∪ toPlace   // 6
    end if
end if
for each child c´of c **do** PopulateMappingMatrix(c´, r) **end for**   // 7
return

Fig. 4. PopulateMappingMatrix generates a mapping matrix from an annotated schema

Let strategy(c) be the strategy choice for class c. For a given annotated schema, the mapping matrix is generated by the procedure PopulateMappingMatrix in Fig. 4 (for brevity, we focus on strategy annotations for classes only, omitting attributes).

The root classes must be annotated as $\updownarrow$ or $\Leftrightarrow$. For every root class c, PopulateMappingMatrix(c, undefined) should be called. After that, for each two equal columns of the matrix (if such exist), the first relation from the top of the matrix that has a non-empty cell in those columns is added to Flagged.

The steps of the algorithm are as follows:

1. Each class labeled horizontal or vertical requires its own relation
2. A relation that contains concrete class c must include c's key so that c can be reassembled from all relations that store its attributes.
3. This is the definition of horizontal partitioning
4. These are the attributes of c that need to be assigned to some relation
5. These attributes have already been assigned to a relation r_p, so use that relation.
6. The remaining attributes of c are assigned to c's target relation
7. Now populate the matrix for c's children

5 Incremental Updating

Translating a model between metamodels can be an interactive process, where the user incrementally revises the source model and/or various mapping options, such as the strategy for mapping inheritance. Typically, a user wants to immediately view how design choices affect the generated result. The system could simply regenerate the target model from the revised input. However, this regeneration loses any customization the user performed on the target, such as changing the layout of a diagrammatic view of the model or adding comments. We can improve the user's experience in such scenarios by translating models in a stateful fashion: the target model is updated incrementally instead of being re-created from scratch by each modification. This incremental updating also improves performance. For example, our implementation uses a main memory object-oriented database system, in which a full regeneration of the target schema from a large source model can take a minute or so.

Let m_0 be a source model and $m_1, \ldots, m_n$ be a series of target model snapshots obtained by an application of successive transformations (i.e., a transformation plan). Each transformation is a function that may add or delete schema elements. Let f_i be a function that returns new elements in m_{i+1} given the old ones in m_i. Since f_i uses Skolem functions to generate new elements, whenever it receives the same elements as input, it produces the same outputs. Clearly, invoking a series of such functions f_1, $\ldots, f_n$ preserves this property. That is, re-running the entire series of transformations on m_0 yields precisely the same m_n as the previous run, as the functions in effect cache all generated schema elements.

Now suppose the user modifies m_0 producing m_0'. When m_0' is translated into a target model, the same sequence of transformations is executed as before. In this way, no new objects in the target model are created for the unchanged objects in the source model. Previously-created objects are re-used; only their properties are updated. For example, renaming an attribute in the source model causes renaming of some target model elements (e.g., attribute or type names), but no new target objects are created.

The mechanism above covers incremental updates to m_0. Deletion is addressed as follows. Let m_n be the schema generated from m_0. Before applying the transformations to m_0', a shallow copy m_{copy} of m_n is created which identifies all of the objects in m_n. All transformations are re-run on m_0' to produce m_n'. If an element is deleted from m_0 when creating m_0', then some elements previously present in m_{copy} might not appear in m_n'. These target elements can be identified by comparing m_{copy} to m_n'. They are marked as "deleted," but are not physically disposed of. If they appear in m_n at some later run, the elements are resurrected by removing the "deleted" marker. Thus, the properties of generated objects are preserved upon deletion and resurrection. In our implementation, for small changes to the source model, this incremental regeneration of the target takes a fraction of a second.

6 Implementation

Our implementation runs inside an integrated development environment. It has a graphical model editor and an in-memory object-oriented database system (OODB) that simplifies data sharing between tools and supports undo/redo and transactions.

The EER model and schemas are stored as objects in the OODB. We wrote relational wrappers that expose an updateable view of the objects. The wrappers are generic code that use reflection and on-the-fly generated intermediate language code. We then wrote rules that translate between those wrappers and the relational representation of $\mathcal{U}$. As others have noted [2][23][25], this translation is very straightforward; since there is a 1:1 mapping between constructs of the source and target metamodels and universal metamodel (i.e., $\mathcal{U}$), the translation rules are trivial.

We wrote our own rules engine, partly because of limitations on the functionality of Datalog engines that were available to us and partly because we wanted native support for rules with compound heads (see Section 3). It supports Skolem functions and user-defined functions. We used the latter to generate forward- and reverse-views.

The size of our implementation is summarized in Fig. 5 (viewed best in the electronic version in color). The rule engine is more than half of our code. It includes the calculus representation, in-memory processing, view unfolding, and parser. The main routines include the rules and plan generator (described in [24]). We coded a few rules in C#, such as the rule to remove structured attributes since the recursion was

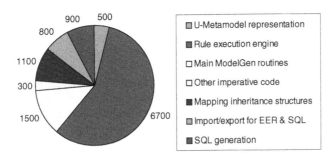

Fig. 5. Code size (in lines of code)

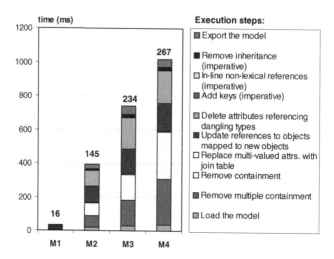

Fig. 6. Execution times in milliseconds

hard to understand. The logic for mapping inheritance structures into relations includes populating the mapping matrix from class annotations and generating reverse-views with negation when necessary. The import/export routines include 120 lines of rules; the rest is in C#.

Our implementation is relatively fast. Execution times for four models are shown in Fig. 6. These models use a custom EER model—a rather rich one. For example, it permits a class to contain multiple classes, requiring us to use our transformation that eliminates multiple containment. The number of elements in each model is shown above each bar. The execution time was measured in milliseconds and averaged over 30 runs on a 1.5 GHz machine. The largest model, M4, generates 32 relations—not a huge model, but the result fills many screens.

7 Related Work

The problem of translating data between metamodels goes back to the 1970's. Early systems required users to specify a schema-specific mapping between a given source and target schema (e.g., EXPRESS [30]). Later, Rosenthal and Reiner described schema translation as one use of their database design workbench [28]. It is generic but manual (the user selects the transformations), its universal metamodel is less expressive (no inheritance, attributed relationships, or collections), and mappings are not automatically generated.

Atzeni and Torlone [2] showed how to automatically generate the target schema. They introduced the idea of a repertoire of transformations over models expressed in a universal metamodel (abbr. UMM), where each transformation replaces one construct by others. They used a UMM based on one proposed by Hull and King in [19]. They represented transformation signatures as graphs but transformation semantics was hidden in imperative procedures. They did not generate instance-level transformations, or even schema-level mappings between source and target models, which are main contributions of our work.

Two recent projects have extended Atzeni and Torlone's work. In [25], Papotti and Torlone generate instance translations via three data-copy steps: (1) copy the source data into XML, in a format that expresses their UMM; (2) use XQuery to reshape the XML expressed in the source model into XML expressed in the target model; and (3) copy the reshaped data into the target system. Like [2], transformations are imperative programs. In [3], Atzeni et al. use a similar 3-step technique, except transformations are Datalog rules: (1) copy the source database into their relational data dictionary; (2) reshape the data using SQL queries that express the rules; and (3) copy it to the target.

In contrast to the above two approaches, we generate view definitions that *directly* map the source and target models in both directions and could drive a data transformation runtime such as [1][17]. The views provide access to the source data using the target model, or vice versa, without copying any data at all. If they were executed as data transfer programs, they would move data from source to target in just one copy step, not three. This is more time efficient and avoids the use of a staging area, which is twice the size of the database itself to accommodate the second step of reshaping the data. Moreover, neither of the above projects offer flexible mapping of inheritance hierarchies or incremental updating of models, which are major features our solution.

Transformation strategies from inheritance hierarchies to relations, such as horizontal and vertical partitioning, are well known [15][22]. However, as far as we know, no published strategies allow arbitrary combinations of vertical and horizontal partitioning at each node of an inheritance hierarchy, like the one we proposed here.

Hull's notion of information capacity [18] is commonly used for judging the information preservation of schema transformations. In [18] a source and target schema are equivalent if there exists an invertible mapping between their instances. Our forward- and reverse-views are examples of such mappings.

Using a UMM called GER, Hainaut has explored schema transformations for EER and relational schemas in a sequence of papers spanning two decades. He presented EER and relational transformations in [13]. Although instance transformations were mentioned, the focus was on schema transformations. Instance mappings for two transformations are presented in [14] as algebraic expressions. In this line of work, instance transformations are mainly used for generating wrappers in evolution and migration scenarios. An updated and more complete description of the framework is in [16].

Poulovasilis and McBrien [27] introduce a universal metamodel, based on a hypergraph. They describe schema transformation steps that have associated instance transformations. Boyd and McBrien [9] apply and enrich these transformations for ModelGen. Although they do give a precise semantics for the transformations, it is quite low-level (e.g., add a node, delete an edge). They do not explain how to abstract them to a practical query language, nor do they describe an implementation.

Another rule-based approach was proposed by Bowers and Delcambre [7][8]. They focus on the power and convenience of their UMM, Uni-Level Descriptions, which they use to define model and instance structures. They suggest using Datalog to query the set of stored models and to test the conformance of models to constraints.

Barsalou and Gagopadhyay [4] give a language (i.e., UMM) to express multiple metamodels. They use it to produce query schemas and views for heterogeneous database integration. Issues of automated schema translation between metamodels and generation of inheritance mappings are not covered.

Claypool and Rundensteiner [10] describe operators to transform schema structures expressed in a graph metamodel. They say the operators can be used to transform instance data, but give no details.

8   Conclusion

In this paper, we described a rule-driven platform that can translate an EER model into a relational schema. The main innovations are the ability to (i) generate provably-correct forward and reverse view definitions between the source and target models, (ii) map inheritance hierarchies to flat structures in a more flexible way, and (iii) incrementally generate changes to the target model based on incremental changes to the source model. We implemented the algorithm and demonstrated that it is fast enough for interactive editing and generation of models. We embedded it in a tool for designing object to relational mappings. Commercial deployment is now underway.

References

[1] ADO.NET, http://msdn.microsoft.com/data/ref/adonetnext/
[2] Atzeni, P., Torlone, R.: Management of Multiple Models in an Extensible Database Design Tool. In: Apers, P.M.G., Bouzeghoub, M., Gardarin, G. (eds.) EDBT 1996. LNCS, vol. 1057, pp. 79–95. Springer, Heidelberg (1996)
[3] Atzeni, P., Cappellari, P., Bernstein, P.: ModelGen: Model Independent Schema Translation. In: Ioannidis, Y., Scholl, M.H., Schmidt, J.W., Matthes, F., Hatzopoulos, M., Boehm, K., Kemper, A., Grust, T., Boehm, C. (eds.) EDBT 2006. LNCS, vol. 3896, pp. 368–385. Springer, Heidelberg (2006)
[4] Barsalou, T., Gangopadhyay, D.: M(DM): An Open Framework for Interoperation of Multimodel Multidatabase Systems. ICDE, 218–227 (1992)
[5] Bernstein, P., Melnik, S., Mork, P.: Interactive Schema Translation with Instance-Level Mappings (demo), VLDB, pp. 1283–1286 (2005)
[6] Blakeley, J., Muralidhar, S., Nori, A.: The ADO.NET Entity Framework: Making the Conceptual Level Real. In: Embley, D.W., Olivé, A., Ram, S. (eds.) ER 2006. LNCS, vol. 4215, pp. 552–565. Springer, Heidelberg (2006)
[7] Bowers, S., Delcambre, L.M.L.: On Modeling Conformance for Flexible Transformation over Data Models, Knowl. Transformation for the Semantic Web (at 15th ECAI), pp. 19–26.
[8] Bowers, S., Delcambr, L.M.L.: The Uni-Level Description: A Uniform Framework for Representing Information in Multiple Data Models. In: Song, I.-Y., Liddle, S.W., Ling, T.-W., Scheuermann, P. (eds.) ER 2003. LNCS, vol. 2813, pp. 45–58. Springer, Heidelberg (2003)
[9] Boyd, M., McBrien, P.: Comparing and Transforming Between Data Models Via an Intermediate Hypergraph Data Model. J. Data Semantics IV, 69–109 (2005)
[10] Claypool, K.T., Rundensteiner, E.A.: Sangam: A Transformation Modeling Framework. DASFAA, pp. 47–54 (2003)
[11] Fagin, R.: Multivalued Dependencies and a New Normal Form for Relational Databases. ACM TODS 2(3), 262–278 (1977)

[12] Fagin, R., Kolaitis, P.G., Popa, L., Tan, W.C.: Composing Schema Mappings: Second-Order Dependencies to the Rescue. ACM TODS 30(4), 994–1055 (2005)

[13] Hainaut, J.-L.: Entity-Generating Schema Transformations for Entity-Relationship Models. ER, 643–670 (1991)

[14] Hainaut, J.-L.: Specification preservation in schema transformations-Application to semantics and statistics. Data Knowl. Eng. 16(1), 99–134 (1996)

[15] Hainaut, J.-L., Hick, J.-M., Englebert, V., Henrard, J., Roland, D.: Understanding the Implementation of IS-A Relations. In: Thalheim, B. (ed.) ER 1996. LNCS, vol. 1157, pp. 42–57. Springer, Heidelberg (1996)

[16] Hainaut, J.-L.: The Transformational Approach to Database Engineering. In: Lämmel, R., Saraiva, J., Visser, J. (eds.) GTTSE 2005. LNCS, vol. 4143, pp. 89–138. Springer, Heidelberg (2006)

[17] Hibernate, http://www.hibernate.org/

[18] Hull, R.: Relative Information Capacity of Simple Relational Database Schemata. SIAM J. Comput. 15(3), 856–886 (1986)

[19] Hull, R., King, R.: Semantic Database Modeling: Survey, Applications and Research Issues. ACM Comp. Surveys 19(3), 201–260 (1987)

[20] Java Data Objects, http://java.sun.com/products/jdo

[21] Jeusfeld, M.A., Johnen, U.A.: An Executable Meta Model for Re-Engineering of Database Schemas. Int. J. Cooperative Inf. Syst. 4(2-3), 237–258 (1995)

[22] Keller, A.M., Jensen, R., Agrawal, S.: Persistence Software: Bridging Object-Oriented Programming and Relational Databases. SIGMOD, 523–528 (1993)

[23] Kensche, D., Quix, C., Chatti, M.A., Jarke, M.: GeRoMe. A Generic Role Based Metamodel for Model Management. In: Meersman, R., Tari, Z. (eds.). OTM 2005. LNCS, vol. 3781, pp. 1206–1224. Springer, Heidelberg (2005)

[24] Mork, P., Bernstein, P.A., Melnik, S.: A Schema Translator that Produces Object-to-Relational Views. Technical Report MSR-TR-36. (2007), http://research.microsoft.com

[25] Papotti, P., Torlone, R.: An Approach to Heterogeneous Data Translation based on XML Conversion. CAiSE Workshops 1, 7–19 (2004)

[26] Papotti, P., Torlone, R.: Heterogeneous Data Translation through XML Conversion. J. of Web Eng 4(3), 189–204 (2005)

[27] Poulovassilis, A., McBrien, P.A.: General Formal Framework for Schema Transformation. Data Knowl. Eng. 28(1), 47–71 (1998)

[28] Rosenthal, A., Reiner, D.: Tools and Transformations? Rigorous and Otherwise? for Practical Database Design. ACM TODS 19(2), 167–211 (1994)

[29] Ruby on Rails, http://api.rubyonrails.org/

[30] Shu, N.C., Housel, B., Taylor, R., Ghosh, S., Lum, V.: EXPRESS: A Data EXtraction, Processing, and REStructuring System. ACM TODS 2(2), 134–174 (1977)

Building a Tool for Cost-Based Design of Object-Oriented Database Schemas

Joachim Biskup and Ralf Menzel

Universität Dortmund, 44221 Dortmund, Germany
{biskup,menzel}@ls6.cs.uni-dortmund.de

Abstract. In the traditional waterfall approach for building a software application, the phases of requirements analysis, design, implementation, testing, and maintenance follow one another. Aiming at the efficiency of a database application, we see that the outcome of the implementation phase decisively determines how much time the execution of queries and updates requires and how much space is needed to store the application data. But, these costs of the application result from decisions made not only in the implementation phase but also before that during the design phase. In this paper, we describe a tool to support the cost-based design of database applications. Based on earlier research where we designed a cost-model for an abstract object-oriented database machine, the tool shall provide its user with cost estimates during the design phase. We discuss which modifications and additions to our cost-model we use to build the tool. Specifically, we portray how we adapt the tool to a concrete DBMS. After picturing a design process that employs our tool, we conclude by assessing the achievements of the present work and how we benefited from our earlier underlying research.

1 Introduction

For any database application, following the ideal waterfall model of software engineering [10, 11], a conceptual design resulting in a conceptual schema should strictly precede the implementation in terms of classes (relations), access structures (sortings, search trees, ...), storage management (realms, disks, ...), and further low-level features. Besides the general reasons, there are more specific justifications as well: (1) In general, a well "normalized" conceptual schema already exhibits good overall efficiency since its instances will never contain redundant data and thus avoid "anomalies" [6, 8, 14]. (2) Usually, a database application supports many different and diverse clients, some of them even still unknown at design time, and the conceptual design should be "neutral", giving all of them a uniform and firm basis [13].

In practice, however, often a spiral model turns out to be more appropriate, permitting to reinspect and revise the decisions taken in previous steps. Again, there are general justifications for deviating from the ideal, mainly accepting the common failure to correctly and completely specify all requirements in advance. In fact, one may argue that a full specification is never achievable due

C. Parent et al. (Eds.): ER 2007, LNCS 4801, pp. 120–131, 2007.

to the overall complexity. Besides such general justifications, there might also be more specific arguments regarding database applications: (1) For a specific situation, the stated efficiency claim on "normalized schema" might not be valid. (2) For a specific application, some clients might be discretionarily favoured over others.

Now, accepting that conceptual design and implementation might be intertwined, the database administrator needs a design tool to analyse the requirements and options on both layers, their mutual interactions, and the potential trade-offs [12]. Unfortunately, traditional database design tools [1, 7, 15] do not satisfy this urgent need. Though this shortcoming might purposely originate from the waterfall paradigm, a deeper fundamental problem appears as an obstacle as well. The vocabulary of conceptual schema design languages does not provide the needed expressiveness for dealing with the items on the implementation layer and their analysis in terms of actual execution costs of queries and updates, not to mention for considering the impact of an optimiser on these costs.

Our preparatory research [2, 3, 4] aimed at providing means to resolve the fundamental problem. The work reported in this paper directly addresses the administrator's need. More specifically, previously we designed the following:

- a unifying vocabulary for both layers, enabling to relate concepts of object-oriented database schemas with an abstract database machine for operations on instances [2];
- a cost model for the abstract database machine, offering to predict the expected performance of operations on instances in term of consumption of abstract time and abstract space [3];
- a framework for determining and comparing the expected costs before and after a schema transformation, e.g., for a normalization step, in terms of the costs of the operations on instances of the two schemas involved [4].

Currently, we are building an experimental design tool of the needed kind, called CBOODT (for Cost-Based Object-Oriented Design Tool). More specifically, in this paper we deal with the following issues:

- We outline the architecture of CBOODT, and explain the basic design decisions (Sect. 2).
- We reflect the actual achievements of our preparatory research and, where needed, suggest appropriate adjustments for the sake of the overall usefulness of CBOODT (Sect. 3).
- We show how we adapt CBOODT to a concrete DBMS by instantiating the system dependent cost parameters of our cost model (Sect. 4).
- We develop a high-level guideline for an administrator to employ CBOODT, describing a typical workflow (Sect. 5).
- We critically validate our approach, in particular, reinspecting the abstract database machine, the cost model, the cost framework for schema transformations as well as the new schema design tool (Sect. 6).

2   Architecture of CBOODT

A simple conceptual object-oriented schema design tool allows its user to define classes, their attributes and types. Tools that are more elaborate often support the application of schema transformations. Besides such ordinary schema design tasks, we want our tool to support additional functions that enable the user to base design decisions on expected query time costs of a later implementation. In particular the user of the tool shall be able to exercise cost estimates to guide the application of schema transformations.

The time cost estimates build on our cost model [3]. This cost model allows us to calculate cost estimates for a machine program. For this calculation several cost parameters are used as input.

As an exemplary schema transformation we will work with pivoting [5] for our experimental design tool. In our implementation, we use an extended version of the schema transformation that not only transforms a schema consisting of classes, their attributes and types but also transforms access structures, queries, and cost parameters that depend on the schema.

Taking the theoretical results of our earlier research, we face two main problems in their practical implementation.

First, there exists a multitude of cost parameters. We would like to spare the user the trouble of providing many cost parameters that might not be decisive for a cost evaluation under consideration. We achieve this by providing default values for all cost parameters (even if these defaults can sometimes only be wild guesses). But we annotate cost estimates when default values are used. This enables the user to provide proper values and re-evaluate the costs.

Second, the cost model operates on machine programs. It is cumbersome for the user to express them. When he is working at the conceptual layer, he surely prefers to use high-level queries to represent the behaviour of the modelled application. Therefore the user of CBOODT can input (restricted) high-level queries. The tool translates them into machine programs. For this we need a (simple) query optimiser.

Figure 1 shows the architecture of CBOODT. It consists of three components. In its centre is the schema design component that contains several packages. The schema package and its sub-packages model the data structures that represent schemas and all things that can be part of a schema: classes, indexes, queries, machine programs, and (application dependent) cost parameters. The cost estimation package contains the algorithms of our cost model to calculate cost statements for machine programs. The query optimiser package enlists the cost estimation package to translate high-level queries into machine programs. The schema transformation package contains the routines to do pivoting.

The user interface component provides the facilities to control the design components. It allows the user to define classes, indexes, and queries; export and import schemas; provide cost parameters; and activate schema transformations. The user is shown a graphical representation of the schema. The queries and their costs are listed. The user can select a schema transformation for consideration. Early versions of CBOODT will then display the costs after the transformation

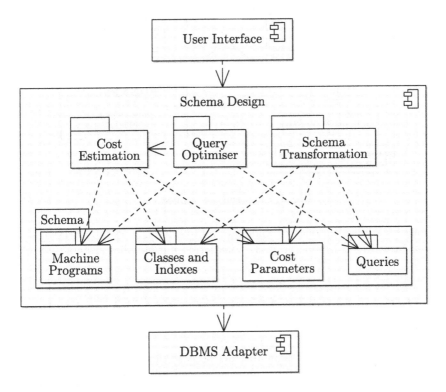

Fig. 1. CBOODT architecture

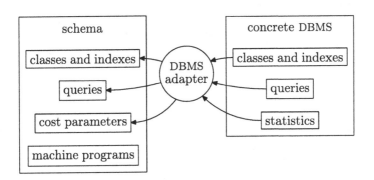

Fig. 2. Importing an existing concrete DBMS application

for all the queries. Given this information, the user can decide to apply a transformation. Later versions of the tool can improve user support by proposing profitable transformations or even sequences of transformtions.

The DBMS adapter component allows to connect to a specific DBMS and an existing database application. It allows to import schemas and statistics, i.e., application dependent cost parameters (Fig. 2). In addition, it allows to export

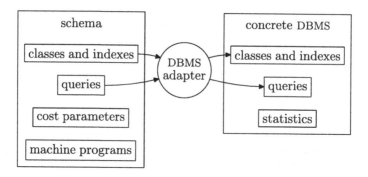

Fig. 3. Exporting an application

schemas by translating classes, indexes and queries into DDL and DML statements of the DBMS system (Fig. 3). Furthermore it supplies system dependent
cost parameters.

3   Abstract Database Machine, Cost Model, and Schema Transformations Revisited

The basis of our cost model is an abstract object-oriented database machine [2].
The type system of the machine is inductively defined. Depending on the domain
used there are some scalar types, e.g., string, integer, boolean. For the application
we can define object types by providing attribute type assignments. An attribute
type assignment specifies the value types for all attributes of the object type. A
value type is either a scalar type, an object identifier type, or a set type. For
every object type there is a corresponding object identifier type, while set types
are available for every scalar type and every object identifier type.

In our theoretical research we assumed that types are given implicitly, i.e.,
that types have value semantics. But, using object types and object identifier
types the type system allows for cyclic type structures. For practical purposes,
it is difficult to set up such cyclic structures when the identity of an object type
is defined by how it assigns value types for its attributes. Therefore in our tool
we use names to identify object types, independent of possible changes to their
attribute type assignments.

The operations of our abstract object-oriented database machine work on
streams. A stream is a sequence of lists of values. A machine program is a
sequence of machine program steps. Each step performs one machine operation.
The input and output streams of steps are held in channels, which are stream-
typed variables. The cost model uses its cost functions and cost parameters to
annotate the channels and steps of a machine program with cost statements.
The sum of all step cost statements is the total cost statement for the machine
program.

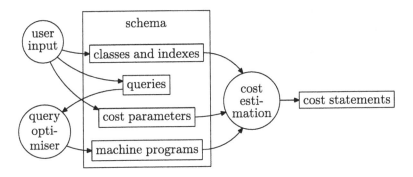

Fig. 4. Cost estimation

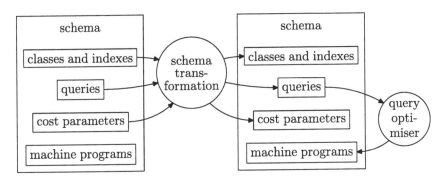

Fig. 5. Transformation

In CBOODT we want to enable the user to provide high-level queries instead of machine programs. A query optimiser is used to translate the high-level queries into the machine-programs that the cost estimation needs to do its work (Fig. 4).

For the implementation of CBOODT, we made the following adjustments to our cost model.

As mentioned in Sect. 2 we want the tool to provide default cost parameters. To facilitate this the tool manages the *confidence level* for each cost parameter value. Between "specified by user" and "default" there can be further levels like "derived from other parameters", "used type-based parameter in place of class-based parameter" or, "produced by transformation".

To work with confidence levels for cost parameters we enrich the cost statements. To the cost estimate we add which cost parameters were used to calculate the cost estimate and with which confidence level these parameters were available.

Our model provides the stream type for every channel. In CBOODT we additionally carry along in the channel cost statement the information from which classes and attributes the stream originated. With this information available, we can improve the quality of cost parameters by using more specific class-based and attribute-based parameters instead of just type-based parameters.

In CBOODT we implement pivoting as schema transformation. Formerly we specified how pivoting acts on classes. In our tool a schema contains classes, indexes, queries, cost parameters and machine programs. To transform a complete schema, we extend pivoting to handle indexes, queries and cost parameters as well. The machine programs of the transformed schema can be produced by the use of the query optimiser (Fig. 5).

4   Adapting CBOODT to a Concrete DBMS

The design of our abstract cost model contains cost parameters that allow to characterise the database application and the concrete DBMS. The parameters that describe the database application are managed by our tool as the cost parameters in the schema. The parameters that describe the concrete DBMS are managed by the DBMS adapter. Tables 1 and 2 show these cost parameters as given by our previous work.

The cost parameters in Table 2 are type-based. As we said above, in CBOODT, we have class and attribute information available in our channel cost statements and can therefore use class-based and attribute-based parameters instead. In particular, we can derive them by introducing simpler parameters for sizes in bytes of all scalar types and for the size of an OID, and a parameter that gives the bytes per block. When we need to know the size of a set we can refer to the application dependent cost parameter that gives the average multiplicity for the attribute involved.

Furthermore we introduce two cost parameters to convert the abstract time estimates into real time estimates: one parameter, T_b, that gives the time required for a block access and one parameter, T_v, for the time required per value access. Table 3 summarises all new parameters.

In our first version of CBOODT that doesn't estimate space costs, we don't need a value for n_a. But we must provide the values for the following parameters:

Table 1. System dependent cost parameters

parameter	description	relevant for
n_a:	fraction of a block that is needed for the non-data part of an access structure per element of the stored set.	*space*
n_{OID}:	number of object identifiers that fit into one block.	scan, *space*
n_{mem}:	size of memory that is reserved for sorting and similar operations.	sort, product, join$_0$
n_{files}:	maximum number of open files for sorting.	sort
$\eta(n)$:	number of block accesses required to locate an element using an access structure for a set with n elements.	write, delete, access

Table 2. Cost parameters derivable from domain dependent parameters

parameter	description	relevant for
n_t:	average number of blocks for an object of type t.	activate, write, delete, access, *space*
$n_{(t_1,\ldots,t_n)}$:	average number of blocks for a value list of type $(t_1,\ldots,t_n)$.	duplicate, sort, product, $join_0$

Table 3. CBOODT's new system and domain dependent cost parameters

parameter	description
b_{t_s}:	average number of bytes for a value of the scalar type t_s.
b_{OID}:	average number of bytes for an object identifier.
b_{block}:	number of bytes of a block.
T_b:	average number of seconds per block access.
T_v:	average number of seconds per value access.

n_{OID}, n_{mem}, n_{files}, $\eta(n)$, b_{t_s}, b_{OID}, b_{block}, T_b, T_v. For most of them we can find the values in the documentation or the data dictionary of the concrete DBMS. When this is not the case, we can derive the values from time measurements for queries and updates on test data. This is most likely necessary for the parameters n_{files}, $\eta(n)$, T_b, and T_v.

Our design tool contains an DBMS adapter for the object-relational DBMS Oracle. When we import and export schemas, we must take care to translate between the object-relational model of Oracle and the object model of our tool. In the first version of CBOODT we will only use a subset of the modelling possibilities provided by Oracle. Especially when we import an existing Oracle application we map relations into suitable classes. For this we provide the possibility to mark classes as relationship classes. This causes them to be exported as relations. But there is the restriction that it is not possible to use OIDs to refer to objects of relationship classes.

5   An Administrator's Workflow

Figure 6 depicts the way that a database designer should leverage CBOODT. Based on the requirements analysis, he designs the application schema by specifying classes and queries. Then he provides the first application dependent cost parameters. We recommend to provide the sizes for all class extensions. After that he can use CBOODT to evaluate cost estimates for all specified queries. When the cost estimates are based on too many default values for cost parameters he should consider providing additional cost parameters and then

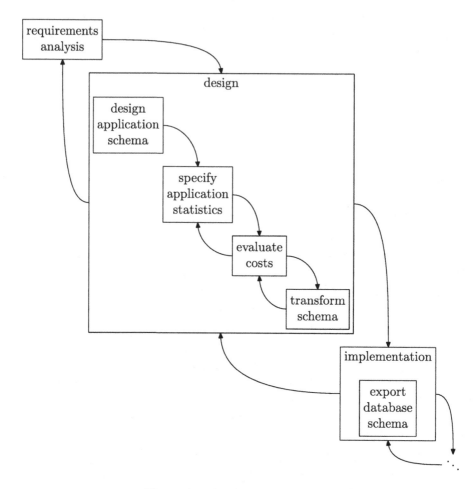

Fig. 6. An administrator's workflow

reevaluate the cost estimates. Typically, the database designer will want to re-place defaults for parameters that describe multiplicities of associations. Most other parameters only have to be provided when the need for fine-tuning arises.

The cost estimates can give different kinds of hints how to improve the schema. First, some queries could profit from adding an index to the schema. Second, some queries could profit from transforming the schema.

After the database designer decides to change the schema as suggested by the cost evaluation, he should reevaluate the cost estimates, which, in turn, might induce him to provide further application statistics.

For an existing database application, the DBMS adapter component can be used to import a database schema and its statistics. In this way, the adapter supports the application schema design and application statistics specification sub-steps of the design step. Furthermore, the DBMS adapter can translate the classes, indexes and queries of the conceptual design schema into DML and DDL statements of a database system. In this way it supports the database schema export sub-step of the implementation step.

6   Validation and Conclusions

In this paper we presented a cost-based object-oriented design tool CBOODT. The tool is based on earlier work where we developed an abstract object-oriented database machine and a cost model for the database machine. For the practical implementation we made some adjustments to the theoretical preparations. In particular, we added or changed the following:

- We introduced default values and confidence levels for cost parameter values. This enables the user of the tool to provide parameter values only when it is necessary.
- In our original object model the object types have a value semantic, i.e., the identity of an object type is defined by how it assigns value types to attributes. For the practical purpose of the implementation of CBOODT, we gave identifying names to object types. This makes it possible to easily specify cyclic type structures. And in cases where we have differently named types with identical attribute type assignments, we get distinct cost parameters and thus improved expressiveness.
- Besides this, we increased the expressiveness of cost parameters by enriching channel cost statements with the information from which classes and attributes the values in the channels originate. This way we can supply the cost functions with class and attribute specific parameters where we formerly used type specific parameters.
- A major change to our cost estimation framework was the addition of a query optimiser. This enables the user to specify high-level queries instead of machine programs and thus greatly enhances the attractiveness for the user. In addition, we can improve on the differential cost statements from earlier research [4] where we worked without an optimiser. In the next version of CBOODT, we plan to enhance the optimiser to support not only queries but also updates.

In all, our earlier theoretical research proved to be a solid foundation for the implementation of CBOODT. More than this, we judge that our abstract database machine and its cost model are fit to support future enhancements of CBOODT, as outlined in the following.

In general, we expect that the cost parameters of our generic cost functions give us enough latitude to appropriately model the cost characteristics of a concrete DBMS. When this should not suffice for a particular concrete DBMS, our cost model allows to replace the generic cost functions with DBMS specific cost functions. In a similar way we could extend our database machine with further machine operations that, e.g., represent different (join) algorithms available to the concrete DBMS. We consider to add appropriate extensions to a future version of CBOODT.

A further possibility to adapt our cost model that we plan for a future version of CBOODT is to parameterise the behaviour of the optimiser. On the one hand, we could restrict the acceptable machine programs to trees instead of the more general directed acyclic graphs. Or we could restrict the use of operations. For instance, when we want to model a system that allows to store only one intermediate result, we can restrict the use of the duplicate operation so that a machine program can contain more than one duplicate operation only if all outputs of earlier duplicate operations are used before a new one can appear. On the other hand we can fine tune the adaption to a concrete DBMS by adding system specific compound operations (e.g., for semi-join) and appropriate cost functions.

We even assess that our cost model is flexible enough that it is possible to change the underlying abstract object-oriented database machine and its type system. For a DBMS like Oracle, we can extend our object model to get an object-relational model. This would require an appropriate extension of the type system and the addition of operations to manipulate relations. Altogether we would need about four new operations for reading a relation, writing a relation, deleting from a relation, and accessing a relation through an index. For each new operation we would need new cost functions and probably some new cost parameters.

References

[1] Agrawal, S., Chaudhuri, S., Kollár, L., Marathe, A.P., Narasayya, V.R., Syamala, M.: Database Tuning Advisor for Microsoft SQL Server 2005. In: Nascimento, M.A., et al. (eds.) [9], pp. 1110–1121 (2005)

[2] Biskup, J., Menzel, R.: An abstract database machine for cost driven design of object-oriented database schemas. In: Caplinskas, A., Eder, J. (eds.) ADBIS 2001. LNCS, vol. 2151, pp. 25–28. Springer, Heidelberg (2001)

[3] Biskup, J., Menzel, R.: A flexible cost model for abstract object-oriented database schemas. In: Spaccapietra, S., March, S.T., Kambayashi, Y. (eds.) ER 2002. LNCS, vol. 2503, pp. 444–462. Springer, Heidelberg (2002)

[4] Biskup, J., Menzel, R.: Optimising abstract object-oriented database schemas. In: Embley, D.W., Olivé, A., Ram, S. (eds.) ER 2006. LNCS, vol. 4215, pp. 528–543. Springer, Heidelberg (2006)

[5] Biskup, J., Menzel, R., Polle, T., Sagiv, Y.: Decomposition of relationships through pivoting. In: Thalheim, B. (ed.) ER 1996. LNCS, vol. 1157, pp. 28–41. Springer, Heidelberg (1996)

[6] Cerpa, N.: Pre-physical data base design heuristics. Information and Management 28(6), 351–359 (1995)

[7] Dageville, B., Das, D., Dias, K., Yagoub, K., Zaït, M., Ziauddin, M.: Automatic SQL tuning in Oracle 10g. In: Nascimento, M.A., et al. (eds.) [9], pp. 1098–1109.

[8] Lee, H.: Justifying database normalization: a cost/benefit model. Information Processing & Management: an International Journal 31(1), 59–67 (1995)

[9] Nascimento, M.A., Özsu, M.T., Kossmann, D., Miller, R.J., Blakeley, J.A., Schiefer, K.B. (eds.): Proceedings of the 30th International Conference on Very Large Data Bases, Toronto, Canada, August 27–September 3. Morgan Kaufmann, San Francisco (2004)

[10] Parnas, D.L., Clements, P.C.: A rational design process: How and why to fake it. IEEE Transactions on Software Engineering 12(2), 251–257 (1986)

[11] Royce, W.W.: Managing the development of large software systems. In: Proceedings, IEEE WESCON, pp. 1–9. The Institute of Electrical and Electronics Engineers, Inc. (August 1970)

[12] Martin Steeg. RADD/raddstar: A Rule-based Database Schema Compiler, Evaluator, and Optimizer. PhD thesis, Fakultät Mathematik, Naturwissenschaften und Informatik der Brandenburgischen Technischen Universität Cottbus (2000)

[13] Tsichritzis, D., Klug, A.C.: The ANSI/X3/SPARC DBMS framework report of the study group on database management systems. Information Systems 3(3), 173–191 (1978)

[14] Tupper, C.: The physics of logical modeling. Database Programming & Design 11(9) (September 1998)

[15] Zilio, D.C., Rao, J., Lightstone, S., Lohman, G., Storm, A., Garcia-Arellano, C., Fadden, S.: DB2 Design Advisor: Integrated automatic physical database design. In: Nascimento, M.A., et al. (eds.) [9], pp. 1087–1097

Generic Schema Mappings

David Kensche, Christoph Quix, Yong Li, and Matthias Jarke

RWTH Aachen University, Informatik 5 (Information Systems), 52056 Aachen, Germany
{kensche,quix,liyong,jarke}@i5.informatik.rwth-aachen.de

Abstract. Schema mappings come in different flavors: simple correspondences are produced by schema matchers, intensional mappings are used for schema integration. However, the execution of mappings requires a formalization based on the extensional semantics of models. This problem is aggravated if multiple metamodels are involved. In this paper we present extensional mappings, that are based on second order tuple generating dependencies, between models in our Generic Role-based Metamodel *GeRoMe*. By using a generic metamodel, our mappings support data translation between heterogeneous metamodels. Our mapping representation provides grouping functionalities that allow for complete restructuring of data, which is necessary for handling nested data structures such as XML and object oriented models. Furthermore, we present an algorithm for mapping composition and optimization of the composition result. To verify the genericness, correctness, and composability of our approach we implemented a data translation tool and mapping export for several data manipulation languages.

1 Introduction

Information systems often contain components that are based on different models or schemas of the same or intersecting domains of discourse. These different models of related domains are described in modeling languages (or metamodels) that fit certain requirements of the components such as representation power or tractability. For instance, a database may use SQL or an object oriented modeling language. A web service described in XML Schema may be enriched with semantics by employing an ontology of the domain. All these different types of models have to be connected by mappings stating how the data represented in one model is related to the data represented in another model. Integrating these heterogeneous models requires different means of manipulation for models and mappings which is the goal of a *Model Management* system. [3]. It should provide operators such as Match that computes a mapping between two models [17], ModelGen that transforms models between modeling languages [1], or Merge that integrates two models based on a mapping in between [16].

An important issue in a model management system is the representation of mappings which can be categorized as *intensional* and *extensional* mappings. Intensional mappings deal with the intended semantics of a model and are used, for example, in schema integration [16]. If the task is data translation or data integration, extensional mappings have to be used [9]. In this paper, we will deal only with extensional mappings as our goal is to have a generic representation for executable mappings.

An extensional mapping can be represented as two queries which are related by some operator (such as equivalent or subset) [9]. As the query language depends on

C. Parent et al. (Eds.): ER 2007, LNCS 4801, pp. 132–148, 2007.

the modeling language being used, the question of mapping representation is tightly connected to the question how models are represented. In schema matching systems, which often represent the models as directed labeled graphs, mappings are represented as pairs of model elements with a confidence value which indicates their similarity [17]. Such mappings can be extended to path morphisms on tree schemas which can be translated into an executable form but have limited expressivity [12]. Other existing mapping representation rely on the relational model, e.g. tuple generating dependencies (tgds), GLAV mappings [11] or second order tgds [4]. For a nested relational model, a nested mapping language has been proposed [5].

Each mapping representation has its strengths and weaknesses regarding the requirements for a mapping language [3]: (i) mappings should be able to connect models of different modeling languages; (ii) the mapping language should support complex expressions between sets of model elements (m:n mappings); (iii) support for the nesting of mappings (to avoid redundant mapping specificiations) and nested data structures should be provided; (iv) mappings should have a rich expressiveness while being generic across modeling languages; (v) mappings should support the data translation between the instances of the connected models. While the mapping representations mentioned above fulfill these requirements for the (nested) relational model, they fail at being generic as they do not take into account other modeling languages. The goal of this paper is to define a mapping representation which is generic across several modeling languages and still fulfills the requirements regarding expressiveness and executability. This allows for a generic implementation of model management operators which deal with these mappings. Furthermore, each mapping language has its own characteristics regarding questions such as composability, invertability, decidability, and ability to be executed. Using a generic mapping representation, such questions can be addressed *once* for the generic mapping representation and do not have to be reconsidered for each combination mapping and modeling language.

A prerequisite for a generic representation of mappings is a generic representation of models. We developed the role based generic metamodel *GeRoMe* [7]. It provides a generic, but yet detailed representation of data models originally represented in different metamodels and is the basis for our model management system *GeRoMeSuite* [8]. *GeRoMeSuite* provides a framework for *holistic* generic model management; unlike other model management systems it is neither limited by nature to certain modeling languages nor to certain model management operators. The generic mapping language shown here is the basis for the data translation component of *GeRoMeSuite* and can be translated into a specific data manipulation language such as SQL.

The main contributions of our work define also the structure of the paper. After reviewing related work in section 2, we will define in section 3 a *generic mapping representation* based on the semantics of *GeRoMe*. We adapt second order tuple generating dependencies (SO tgds, [4]) originally defined for relational models to mappings between *GeRoMe* models which also allow for complex grouping and nesting of data. To show the usefulness and applicability of our mapping representation, we will present in section 4 an *algorithm for mapping composition*, and, in section 5, algorithms to translate our generic mapping representation into *executable mappings*. The *evaluation* of our approach with several examples of the recent literature is shown in section 6.

2 Background

Mappings: Extensional mappings are defined as local-as-view (LAV), global-as-view (GAV), source-to-target tuple generating dependencies (s-t tgds) [9,12], second order tuple generating dependencies (SO tgds) [4], or similar formalisms.

Clio [6] defines mappings over a nested relational model to support mappings between relational databases and XML data. However, it would still be difficult to extend this mapping representation to express a mapping between other models, such as UML models, because there is simply no appropriate query language. On the other hand, it is always possible to compose these mappings, because the composition of such mappings is equivalent to the composition of queries [14].

Besides being not generic, another drawback of these *basic mappings* is pointed out: they do not reflect the nested structure of the data [5]. This leads to an inefficient execution of the mappings and redundant mapping specifications as parts of the mapping have to be repeated for different nesting levels. Furthermore, the desired grouping of the target data cannot be specified using basic mappings which leads to redundant data in the target. Fuxman et al. [5] proposed a nested mapping language which addresses these problems. The desired nesting and grouping of data can be expressed in the mapping specification. Another form of basic mappings based on a Prolog-like representation is used by Atzeni et al. [1]. These mappings are generic as they are based on a generic metamodel, but they require the data to be imported to the generic representation as well. This leads to an additional overhead during execution of the mappings.

Mapping Composition: In general, the problem of composing mappings has the following formulation: given a mapping M_{12} from model S_1 to model S_2, and a mapping M_{23} from model S_2 to model S_3, derive a mapping M_{13} from model S_1 to model S_3 that is equivalent to the successive application of M_{12} and M_{23} [4].

Mapping composition has been studied only for mappings which use the Relational Data Model as basis. Fagin et al. [4] proposed a semantics of the Compose operator that is defined over instance spaces of schema mappings. To this effect, M_{13} is the composition of M_{12} and M_{23} means that the instance space of M_{13} is the set-theoretical composition of the instance spaces of M_{12} and M_{23}. Under this semantics, which we will also adopt in this paper, the mapping composition M_{13} is unique up to logical equivalence. Fagin et al. also explored the properties of the composition of schema mappings specified by a finite set of s-t tgds. They proved that the language of s-t tgds is not closed under composition. To ameliorate the problem, they introduced the class of SO tgds and proved that (i) SO tgds are closed under composition by showing a mapping composition algorithm; (ii) SO tgds form the smallest class of formulas (up to logical equivalence) for composing schema mappings given by finite sets of s-t tgds; and (iii) given a mapping M and an instance I over the source schema, it takes polynomial time to calculate the solution J which is an instance over the target schema and which satisfies M. Thus, SO tgds are a good formalization of mappings.

Another approach for mapping composition uses expressions of the relational algebra as mappings [2]. The approach uses an incremental algorithm which tries to replace as many symbols as possible from the "intermediate" model. As the result of mapping composition cannot be always expressed as relational algebra expressions, the algorithm may fail under certain conditions which is inline with the results of [4].

Executable Mappings: Executable mappings are necessary in many meta-data intensive applications, such as database wrapper generation, message translation and data transformation [12]. While many model management systems were used to generate mappings that drive the above applications, few of them were implemented using executable mappings. Because executable mappings usually drive the transformation of instances of models, Melnik et al. [12] specified a semantics of each operator by relating the instances of the operator's input and output models. They also implemented two model management system prototypes to study two approaches to specifying and manipulating executable mappings. In the first implementation, they modified *Rondo*'s [13] language to define path morphisms and showed that it is possible to generate executable mappings in a form of relational algebra expressions. On the positive side, this system works correctly whenever the input is specified using path morphisms, and the input is also closed under operators which return a single mapping. However, the expressiveness of path morphisms is very limited. To overcome this limitation, they developed a new prototype called Moda [12] in which mappings are specified using embedded dependencies. The expressiveness is improved in the second implementation, but it suffers from the problem that embedded dependencies are not closed under composition. Because of this problem, the output of the Compose operator may not be representable as an embedded dependency and thus a sequence of model management operators may not be executable in the system. Although they further developed a script rewriting procedure to ameliorate this problem, it has not been completely solved.

3   Mapping Representation

Before we define the representation of mappings for *GeRoMe* models, we first present the main concepts of *GeRoMe* using an example (section 3.1). As mappings relate instances of models, we have to define how instances of a *GeRoMe* model can be represented, i.e. defining a formal semantics for *GeRoMe* as described in section 3.2. This representation forms the basis for our mapping representation presented in section 3.3.

3.1   The Generic Metamodel *GeRoMe*

Our representation of mappings is based on the generic role based metamodel *GeRoMe* [7], which we will introduce briefly here. *GeRoMe* provides a generic but detailed representation of models originally expressed in different modeling languages. In *GeRoMe* each model element of a native model (e.g. an XML schema or a relational schema) is represented as an object that plays a set of roles which decorate it with features and act as interfaces to the model element. Fig. 1 shows an example of a *GeRoMe* model representing an XML schema.

The grey boxes in fig. 1 denote model elements, the attached white boxes represent the roles played by the model elements. XML Schema is in several aspects different from "traditional" modeling languages such as EER or the Relational Metamodel. The main concept of XML Schema "element" represents actually an association between the

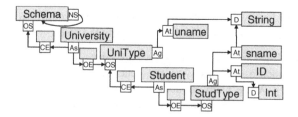

Fig. 1. *GeRoMe* representation of an XML schema

nesting and the nested complex type. This is true for all elements except those which are allowed as root element of a document. In the *GeRoMe* representation of an XML schema, the root element is an association between the schema node and the top-level complex type, as there is no complex type in which the root element is nested. In the example of fig. 1 [1], the element University is an association between the model element Schema and the complex type UniType. The fact that the University element is an association is described by the *Association* (As) role which connects the *ObjectSet* (OS) roles of Schema and UniType via two anonymous model elements playing a *CompositionEnd* (CE) and an *ObjectAssociationEnd* (OE) role, respectively. The same structure is used for the element Student which is an association between the complex types UniType and StudType. The two complex types have also attributes; therefore, they play also the *Aggregate* (Ag) role which links these model elements to their attributes. The model elements representing attributes play an *Attribute* (At) role which refers also to the type of the attributes which are, in this example, simple domains denoted by the *Domain* (D) role.

It is important to emphasize that this representation is not to be used by end users. Instead, it is a representation employed internally by model management applications, with the goal to generically provide more information to model management operators than a simple graph based model.

3.2   *GeRoMe* Semantics: Instances of a *GeRoMe* Model

Before we can formally define *GeRoMe* mappings, we first need to define the formal semantics of *GeRoMe* instances. Our mappings are second-order tuple generating dependencies (SO tgds) which requires that the instances are represented as a set of logical facts. In addition, the semantics should also capture all the structural information that is necessary to reflect the semantics of the model. To fulfill both requirements, the semantics should contain facts that record literal values of an instance of a model and also facts that describe the structure of that instance. To record the literal values of an instance, *value* predicates are used to associate literal values with objects. To describe the structure of an instance, we identify *Attribute* and *Association* as the roles which essentially express the structure of instances.

---

[1] XML documents may have only one root element. Thus, the schema needs to have another element "Universities" to allow for a list of universities in the XML document. For reasons of simplicity, we omitted this extra element in our example and assume that XML documents may have multiple elements at the top-level.

```
                              inst(#0, Schema),
                              inst(#1, UniType), av(#1, uname, 'RWTH'),
<University uname="RWTH">      inst(#2, StudType),
  <Student sname="John"       av(#2, sname, 'John'), av(#2, ID, 123),
          ID="123"/>          inst(#3, University), inst(#4, Student),
</University>                 part(#3, parent_U, #0), part(#3, child_U, #1),
                              part(#4, parent_S, #1), part(#4, child_S, #2)
```

Fig. 2. XML document and its representation as *GeRoMe* instance

Definition 1 (Interpretation of a *GeRoMe* model). *Let M be a* GeRoMe *model with $\mathcal{A}$ being the set of all literal values, and $\mathcal{T}$ the set of all abstract identifiers $\{id_1, \ldots, id_n\}$. An interpretation $\mathcal{I}$ of M is a set of facts $\mathcal{D}_M$, where:*

- *$\forall$ objects (represented by the abstract identifier id_i) which are an instance of model element m: $inst(id_i, m) \in \mathcal{D}_M$,*
- *$\forall$ elements m playing a Domain role and $\forall$ values v in this domain: $\{value(id_i, v), inst(id_i, m)\} \subseteq \mathcal{D}_M$ (id_i is an abstract ID of an object representing the value v).*
- *$\forall$ elements m playing an Aggregate role and having the attribute a, and the instance id_i has the value v for that attribute: $\{attr(id_i, a, id_v), value(id_v, v)\} \subseteq \mathcal{D}_M$.*
- *$\forall$ model elements m playing an Association role in which the object with identifier o participates for the association end ae: $part(id_i, ae, o) \in \mathcal{D}_M$.*

Thus, each "feature" of an instance object is represented by a separate fact. The abstract IDs connect these features so that the complete object can be reconstructed. For the example from fig. 1, an instance containing a university and a student is defined as show in fig. 2. As the predicates $attr$ and $value$ often occur in combination, we use the predicate av as a simplification: $av(id_1, a, v) \Leftrightarrow \exists id_2 attr(id_1, a, id_2) \wedge value(id_2, v)$. In addition, we labeled the association ends with "parent" and "child" to make clear which association end is referred to. The first $inst$-predicate defines an instance of the schema element which represents the XML document itself. Then, two instances of the complex types and their attributes are defined. The last three lines define the associations and the relationships between the objects defined before.

As the example shows, association roles and attribute roles are not only able to define flat structures, e.g. tables in relational schemas, but also hierarchical structures, e.g. element hierarchies in XML schemas. Compared to the original definition of SO tgds, which were only used to represent tuples of relational tables, our extension to the original SO tgds significantly improves the expressiveness of SO tgds.

3.3 Formal Definition of GeRoMe Mappings

Based on the formal definition of *GeRoMe* instances, the definition of *GeRoMe* mappings as SO tgds is straightforward. We extend the definition of a mapping between two relational schemas in [4] to the definition of a mapping between two *GeRoMe* models:

Definition 2 (*GeRoMe* Mapping). *A* GeRoMe *model mapping is a triple $\mathcal{M} = (\mathbf{S}, \mathbf{T}, \Sigma)$, where $\mathbf{S}$ and $\mathbf{T}$ are the source model and the target model respectively, and where Σ is a set of formulas of the form: $\exists \mathbf{f}((\forall \mathbf{x_1}(\varphi_1 \rightarrow \psi_1)) \wedge \ldots \wedge (\forall \mathbf{x_n}(\varphi_n \rightarrow \psi_n)))$*

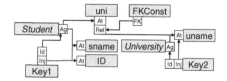

Fig. 3. *GeRoMe* representation of a relational schema

$\exists f, g \quad \forall o_0, o_1, o_2, o_3, o_4, u, s, i$
$inst(o_1, \texttt{University}) \wedge part(o_1, \texttt{parent}_U, o_0) \wedge part(o_1, \texttt{child}_U, o_2) \wedge$
$inst(o_3, \texttt{Student}) \wedge part(o_3, \texttt{parent}_S, o_2) \wedge part(o_3, \texttt{child}_S, o_4) \wedge$
$av(o_2, \texttt{uname}, u) \wedge av(o_4, \texttt{sname}, s) \wedge av(o_4, \texttt{ID}, i) \rightarrow$
$\qquad inst(f(u), \texttt{University}) \wedge inst(g(i), \texttt{Student}),$
$\qquad av(f(u), \texttt{uname}, u) \wedge av(g(i), \texttt{sname}, s) \wedge av(g(i), \texttt{ID}, i) \wedge av(g(i), \texttt{uni}, u)$

Fig. 4. Mapping between XML and relational schema

where **f** *is a collection of function symbols, and where each* φ_i *is a conjunction of atomic predicates and/or equalities over constants defined in* **S** *and variables, and* ψ_i *is a conjunction of atomic predicates over constants defined on* **T**, *variables, and function symbols. Valid atomic predicates are those defined in def. 1. Furthermore, we require that every element name in these atomic predicates is a constant, i.e. the second arguments of inst, attr and part predicates are constants.*

To show an example of a mapping between models originally represented in two different modeling languages, we define in fig. 3 a *GeRoMe* model representing a relational schema that corresponds to the XML schema in fig. 1. The schema contains two relations University(uname) and Student(id, sname, uni). The keys uname and id are defined in *GeRoMe* using separate model elements representing the key constraint. These model elements play an *Injective* (Inj) role to indicate that an attribute is unique, and an *Identifier* (Id) role to specify the aggregate for which the attribute is the key. The foreign key constraint between Student and University is also represented by a separate model element which plays a *Foreign Key* (FK) role. The FK role points to a *Reference* (Ref) role which is played by the attribute that references the key of the other relation.

Now, we can define a mapping using the XML schema as source and the relational schema as target (cf. fig. 4). The predicates in the conditional part of the rule correspond to the instance predicates shown in fig. 2, now just with variables instead of constants. A remark has to be made about the variables o_0 to o_4: these variables represent abstract identifiers (to be named *abstract variables* in the following), their main function is to describe (implicitly) the structure of the source data; in the example we can see, that the student element o_3 is nested under the university element o_1. In other approaches for mapping representation (e.g. [5]), this is done by nesting different sub-expressions of a query. Although nested mappings are easier to understand, they are less expressive than SO tgds [5]. In addition, several tasks dealing with mappings such as composition, inverting, optimization, and reasoning have to be reconsidered for nested mappings (e.g. it is not clear how to compose nested mappings and whether the result composing two nested mappings can be expressed as a nested mapping). As our approach is based on SO tgds, we can leverage the results for SO tgds for our generic mapping representation.

Similarly to the abstract variables on the source side, the functions f and g represent abstract identifiers on the target side and therefore describe the structure of the generated data in the target. We will call such functions (which generate abstract identifiers) in the following *abstract functions*. Abstract functions can be understood as Skolem functions which do not have an explicit semantics; they are interpreted by syntactical representation as term. Please note that abstract variables and abstract functions just specify the structure of data, there will be no values assigned to abstract variables or evaluation of abstract functions during the execution of a mapping. Instead, as we will present in section 5, abstract identifiers and functions determine the structure of the generated code to query the source and to insert the data in the target.

To describe the structure of the target data, it is important to know which values are used to identify an object. According to the definition of the relational schema, universities are identified by their name (u) and students by their ID (i); that is why we use u and i as arguments of the abstract functions f and g. We will explain below that for nested data these functions will usually have more than one argument.

In addition to abstract functions, a mapping can also contain "normal" functions for value conversions or some other kind of data transformation (e.g. concatenation of first and last name). While executing a mapping, these functions must be actually evaluated to get the value which has to be inserted into the target.

The example shows also that only variables representing values occur on both sides of the implication. Abstract variables will be used only on the source side of a mapping as they refer only to source objects, abstract functions will appear only on the target side as they refer only to objects in the target. This implies that for the execution of the mapping, we need to maintain a table with the values extracted from the source, and then generate the target data using these values according to the mapping.

Grouping and Nesting: The generation of complex data structures which can be arbitrarily nested is an important requirement for a mapping representation. In order to show that our mapping language is able to express complex restructuring operations in a data transformation, we use an example that transforms relational data into XML. The relational schema is as in fig. 3 with the exception that we now assume that students may study at multiple universities. To have a schema in 3NF, we add a relation Studies with two foreign keys uni and id. The foreign key from the Student relation is removed. On the target side, the data should be organized with students at the top level, and the list of universities nested under each student. The mapping between the updated relational and XML schemas is shown in fig. 5.

The source side is almost identical with the target side of the previous mapping: the abstract functions f and g have been replaced with the abstract variables o_1 and o_2; a variable o_3 for the Studies relation and the corresponding av predicates have been added. On the target side, we first generate an instance of the Student element; as students are identified by their ID, the abstract function f has only i as argument. $f'(i)$

$\exists f, f', g, g', d \quad \forall o_1, o_2, o_3, u, s, i$
$inst(o_1, \texttt{University}) \wedge inst(o_2, \texttt{Student}), inst(o_3, \texttt{Studies})$
$av(o_1, \texttt{uname}, u) \wedge av(o_2, \texttt{sname}, s) \wedge av(o_2, \texttt{ID}, i) \wedge av(o_3, \texttt{uni}, u) \wedge av(o_3, \texttt{id}, i) \rightarrow$
$\qquad inst(f(i), \texttt{Student}) \wedge part(f(i), \texttt{parent}_S, d()) \wedge part(f(i), \texttt{child}_S, f'(i)) \wedge$
$\qquad av(f'(i), \texttt{sname}, s) \wedge av(f'(i), \texttt{ID}, i) \wedge$
$\qquad inst(g(i, u), \texttt{University}) \wedge part(g(i, u), \texttt{parent}_U, f'(i)) \wedge$
$\qquad part(g(i, u), \texttt{child}_U, g'(i, u)) \wedge av(g'(i, u), \texttt{uname}, u)$

Fig. 5. Mapping from relational data to XML

represents an instance of StudType[2] for which we also define the attribute values of sname and ID. Thus, if a student studies at more than one university and therefore occurs multiple times in the result set of the source, only one element will be created for that student and all universities will be correctly grouped under the Student element.

On the other hand, we must make sure that there is more than one University element for each university, as the universities have to be repeated for each student. This is guaranteed by using both identifiers (of the nesting element Student and the nested element University, i and u) as arguments of the abstract function g. Finally, we assign a value to the attribute uname of the instance $g'(i, u)$ of UniType, similarly as before for the instance of StudType.

Constructing Mappings: Our mappings have a rich expressivity, but are hard to understand in their formal representation, even for an information system developer who is used to working with modeling and query languages. As mentioned above, *GeRoMe* should not replace existing modeling languages, users will still use the modeling language that fits best their needs. *GeRoMe* is intended as an internal metamodel for model management applications. This applies also to the *GeRoMe* mappings, users will not define mappings using the SO tgds as defined above, rather they will use a user interface in which they can define the mappings graphically.

As part of our model management system *GeRoMeSuite* [8], we are currently developing mapping editors for the various forms of mappings. In these mapping editors, the models are visualized as trees (based on the hierarchy of associations and aggregations), and the mapping can be defined by connecting elements of the trees. However, such a visualization of models and mappings has limited expressivity (it roughly corresponds to the path morphisms and tree schemas used in Rondo [13]) as not every model can be easily visualized as a tree. Even an XML schema can break up the tree structure by having references between complex types.

Our current design for an editor for extensional mappings also visualizes models as trees. In addition, mappings as nested structures to represent their possibly complex grouping and nesting conditions. Still, an appropriate representation of complex mappings is an active research area [18], and we have to evaluate whether our design will be accepted by users.

---

[2] The *inst* predicate has been omitted as it is redundant: $f'(i)$ is declared as child of a Student element; thus, it is an instance of StudType according to the schema definition.

4 Mapping Composition

Composition of mappings is required for many model management tasks [2]. In a data integration system using the global-as-view (GAV) approach, a query posed to the integrated schema is rewritten by composing it with the mapping from the sources to the integrated schema. Schema evolution is another application scenario: if a schema evolves, the mappings to the schema can be maintained by composing them with an "evolution" mapping between the old and the new schema.

According to [4], the composition of two mappings expressed as SO tgds can be also expressed as SO tgd. In addition, the algorithm proposed in [4] guarantees, that predicates in the composed SO tgd must appear in the two composing mappings. Thus, the composition of two *GeRoMe* mappings is always definable by a *GeRoMe* mapping. It is important that *GeRoMe* mappings are closed under composition, because otherwise the **Compose** operator may not return a valid *GeRoMe* mapping.

In the following, we will first show the adaptation of the algorithm of [4] to *GeRoMe*, which enables mappings between heterogeneous metamodels. In the second part of this section, we address an inherent problem of the composition algorithm, namely that the size of the composed mapping is exponential in the size of the input mappings. We have developed some optimization techniques which reduce the size of the composed mapping using the semantic information given in the mapping or model.

Composition Algorithm: The composition algorithm shown in fig. 6 takes two *GeRoMe* mappings $\mathcal{M}_{12}$ and $\mathcal{M}_{23}$ as input. The aim is to replace predicates on the left hand side (lhs) of Σ_{23}, which refer to elements in $\mathbf{S}_2$, with predicates of the lhs of Σ_{12}, which refer only to elements in $\mathbf{S}_1$. As the first step, we rename the predicates in such a way that the second argument (which is always a constant) becomes part of the

---

Input: Two *GeRoMe* mappings $\mathcal{M}_{12} = (\mathbf{S}_1, \mathbf{S}_2, \Sigma_{12})$ and $\mathcal{M}_{23} = (\mathbf{S}_2, \mathbf{S}_3, \Sigma_{23})$
Output: A *GeRoMe* mapping $\mathcal{M}_{13} = (\mathbf{S}_1, \mathbf{S}_3, \Sigma_{13})$

Initialization: Initialize $\mathcal{S}_{12}$ and $\mathcal{S}_{23}$ to be empty sets.
Normalization: Replace in Σ_{12} and Σ_{23} predicates $P(x, c, y)$ (or $P(x, c)$) where $P \in \{inst, attr, av, part\}$ with $P.c(x, y)$ (or $P.c(x)$); replace implications in Σ_{12} of the form $\phi \rightarrow p_1 \wedge \ldots \wedge p_n$ with a set of implications $\phi \rightarrow p_1, \ldots, \phi \rightarrow p_n$. Put the resulting implications into $\mathcal{S}_{12}$ and $\mathcal{S}_{23}$, respectively.
Composition: Repeat until all predicates on the lhs of implications in $\mathcal{S}_{23}$ do not refer to $\mathbf{S}_2$:
  Let χ be an implication of the form $\psi \rightarrow \phi \in \mathcal{S}_{23}$ with a predicate $P.c(\mathbf{y})$ in ψ and $\phi_1(\mathbf{x}_1) \rightarrow P.c(\mathbf{t}_1), \ldots, \phi_n(\mathbf{x}_n) \rightarrow P.c(\mathbf{t}_n)$ be all the implications in $\mathcal{S}_{12}$ with predicate $P.c$ on the rhs ($\mathbf{x}$, $\mathbf{y}$ and $\mathbf{t}_i$ being vectors of variables and terms, respectively). If there is no such implication, remove χ from $\mathcal{S}_{23}$ and consider the next predicate. Remove χ from $\mathcal{S}_{23}$. For each implication $\phi_i(\mathbf{x}_i) \rightarrow P.c(\mathbf{t}_i)$, create a copy of this implication using new variable names, and replace $P.c(\mathbf{y})$ in ψ with $\phi_i(\mathbf{x}_i) \wedge \theta_i$ where θ_i are the component-wise equalities of $\mathbf{y}$ and $\mathbf{t}_i$ and add the new implication to $\mathcal{S}_{23}$.
Remove Variables: Repeat until all variables originally from Σ_{23} are removed: For each implication χ in $\mathcal{S}_{23}$, select an equality $y = t$ introduced in the previous step and replace all occurences of y in χ by t.
Create Result: Let $\mathcal{S}_{23} = \{\chi_1, \ldots, \chi_r\}$. Replace the predicates with their original form (e.g. $P.c(x, y)$ with $P(x, c, y)$). Then, $\Sigma_{13} = \exists \mathbf{g}(\forall \mathbf{z}_1 \chi_1 \wedge \ldots \wedge \forall \mathbf{z}_r \chi_r)$ with $\mathbf{g}$ being the set of function symbols appearing in $\mathcal{S}_{23}$ and $\mathbf{z}_i$ being all the variables appearing in χ_i.

Fig. 6. Algorithm **Compose**

predicate name. This lets us avoid considering the constant arguments of a predicate when we are looking for a "matching" predicate, we can just focus on the predicate name. Then, we replace each implication in Σ_{12} with a set of implications which just have one predicate on the right hand side (rhs). We put the normalized implications from Σ_{12} with the updated predicate names into $\mathcal{S}_{12}$. For the implications in Σ_{23}, we just need to change the predicate names, and then we insert them into $\mathcal{S}_{23}$.

The next step performs the actual composition of the mappings. As long as we have an implication in $\mathcal{S}_{23}$ with a predicate $P.c(\mathbf{y})$ in the lhs that refers to $\mathbf{S}_2$, we replace it with every lhs of a matching implication from $\mathcal{S}_{12}$. Moreover, we have to add a set of equalities which reflect the unification of the predicates $P.c(\mathbf{y})$ and $P.c(\mathbf{t}_i)$.

During the composition step, the size of the resulting mapping may grow exponentially. As a first step towards a simpler result, we remove in the next step the variables which were originally in $\mathcal{M}_{23}$. This reduces the number of equalities in the mapping. The final step creates the composed mapping as one formula from the set of implications $\mathcal{S}_{23}$. The following theorem states that the algorithm produces actually a correct result. Due to space restrictions, we cannot show the proof of the theorem (the full proof is given in [10]), it is based on the correctness of the composition algorithm in [4].

Theorem 3. *Let* $\mathcal{M}_{12} = (\mathbf{S}_1, \mathbf{S}_2, \Sigma_{12})$ *and* $\mathcal{M}_{23} = (\mathbf{S}_2, \mathbf{S}_3, \Sigma_{23})$ *be two GeRoMe mappings. Then the algorithm Compose($\mathcal{M}_{12}$, $\mathcal{M}_{23}$) returns a GeRoMe mapping* $\mathcal{M}_{13} = (\mathbf{S}_1, \mathbf{S}_3, \Sigma_{13})$ *such that* $\mathcal{M}_{13} = \mathcal{M}_{12} \circ \mathcal{M}_{23}$.

Semantic Optimization of the Composition Result: We realized that the composed mapping has on the lhs many similar sets of predicates. The reason for this is that we replace a predicate in $\mathcal{S}_{23}$ with a conjunction of predicates in $\mathcal{S}_{12}$ and the same set of predicates in $\mathcal{S}_{12}$ may appear multiple times. Although the result is logically correct, the predicates on the lhs of the composition seems to be duplicated. We show in the following that both undesired implications and duplicated predicates can be removed.

A detailed inspection of our mapping definition reveals that only variables representing values correspond to values in an instance of the underlying model. All other arguments are either constants which correspond to names in a model or terms which correspond to abstract identifiers that identify *GeRoMe* objects. These abstract identifiers and the functions that return an abstract identifier are interpreted only syntactically. Thus, we are able to formulate the following conditions for *abstract functions*:

$$\forall f \forall g \forall \mathbf{x} \forall \mathbf{y} (f \neq g) \to f(\mathbf{x}) \neq g(\mathbf{y}), \; f, g \text{ are abstract functions}$$
$$\forall \mathbf{x} \forall \mathbf{y} (f(\mathbf{x}) = f(\mathbf{y}) \to \mathbf{x} = \mathbf{y}), \; f \text{ is an abstract function}$$

The first statement says that different abstract functions have different ranges. Using this statement, we can remove implications which have equalities of the form $f(\mathbf{x}) = g(\mathbf{y})$ on the lhs, because they never can become true. The second statement says that an abstract function is a bijection, i.e. whenever two results of an abstract function are equal, then the inputs are equal, too. This statement can be used to reduce the number of predicates in the composed mapping, e.g. if $f(o) = f(p)$ is contained in the lhs of an implication, then we can infer that $o = p$ and therefore replace all occurences of o with p (or vice versa). This will produce identical predicates in the conjunction, duplicates can then be removed without changing the logical meaning of the formula. Other optimizations use the constraint information of the model to reduce the complexity of the composed mapping, e.g. keys or cardinality constraints.

5 Mapping Execution

In this section we first describe the architecture of our data translation tool before we explain how we generate queries from a set of generic mappings and how we use these queries to produce target data from source data.

Fig. 7 shows the architecture of our data translation tool. Given the mapping and the source model as input, the code generator produces queries against the source schema. An implementation of this component must be chosen, so that it produces queries in the desired data manipulation language. In the same way, the target model code generator produces updates from the mapping and the target *GeRoMe* model.

Given the generated queries and updates the query executor produces variable assignments from the evaluation of the queries against the source data. The update executor then receives these generic variable assignments as input and produces the target data. Hence, components related to source and target respectively are only loosely coupled to each other by the variable assignments whereas the query/update generator and the executor components have to fit to each other.

Our query generation is based on the model transformations between native metamodels and *GeRoMe*. We now exemplarily introduce our algorithm for generating XQueries from our generic mappings (cf. fig. 8). However, our tool transforms data arbitrarily between relational and XML schemas; these generation and execution components can also be replaced by components that handle other metamodels (e.g. OWL or UML).

The element hierarchy T describes the structure that is queried for, the condition set P contains select and join conditions and the return set R assigns XQuery variables for values of attributes and simple typed elements in the source side of the mapping. The last step uses the computed data to produce the actual XQuery where _fname will be replaced with the actual XML file name when the query is executed.

We now generate an XQuery from the mapping in fig. 4 that can be used to query the document in fig. 2. In fig. 4, we omitted the term specifying the document element for

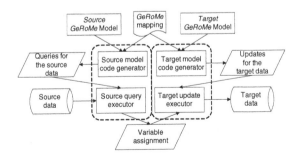

Fig. 7. The architecture of the data translation tool

Input: An implication χ in an SO tgd Σ with source schema σ
Output: A set of XQuery queries over σ.

Initialization: $T = Open = Close = R = \emptyset$
Find document variable: This is the only variable symbol S that occurs in a term of the form $inst(S, \texttt{Schema})$ on the lhs of χ where $\texttt{Schema}$ is the name of the schema element. Add $(S, \text{``/''})$ as the root to T and add it to $Open$.
Construct element hierarchy T: Repeat the following until $Open = \emptyset$. Let $(X, path) \in Open$. For each subformula $inst(Id, name) \wedge part(Id, ae_1, X) \wedge part(Id, ae_2, Y)$ on the lhs of χ where $Id, X,$ and Y are variable symbols, $name, ae_1$ and ae_2 are *GeRoMe* element names, and there is no $path'$ with $(Y, path') \in Close$, add $(Y, path/name)$ to $Open$ and add it as a child to $(X, path)$ in T with label $name$. Finally, remove $(X, path)$ from $Open$ and add it to $Close$.
Construct return set R: For each term $av(X, a, V)$ on the lhs of χ, where X, V are variable symbols, a is a constant name of an attribute, and $(X, path) \in T$, add $(V, \text{``\$X/@a''})$ to $R$. For each term $value(X, V)$ on the lhs of $\chi$, where $X, V$ are variable symbols and $(X, path) \in T$, add $(V, \text{``\$X/text()''})$ to R.
Construct condition set P: $V_1 = V_2$ on the lhs of χ with $(V_1, path_1) \in R \wedge (V_2, path_2) \in R$ specifies an explicit join condition. Add "$path_1$ **eq** $path_2$" to P. If $(V, path_1) \in R \wedge (V, path_2) \in R$ this specifies an implicit join condition. Add "$path_1$ **eq** $path_2$" to P. For each term $value(V, c)$ on the lhs of χ, where c is a constant, add "V **eq** c" to P.
Produce XQuery: Let $T = (doc, \text{``/''})[(e_{1,1}, p_{1,1}, l_{1,1})][(e_{2,1}, p_{2,1}, l_{2,1})[\ldots], \ldots, (e_{2,k_2}, p_{2,k_2}, l_{2,k_2})]]$ be the computed element tree, where $(e, p, l)[\ldots, (e', p', l'), \ldots]$ means (e', p') is a child of (e, p) with label l' in T. Let $(v_1, path_1), (v_2, path_2), \ldots, (v_n, path_n) \in R$, and $p_{1,1}, p_2, \ldots, p_n \in P$. The XQuery query for χ is:

for $\$e_{1,1}$ **in** fn:doc(_fname)/l_1
   for $\$e_{2,1}$ **in** $\$e_{1,1}/l_{2,1}$ ...
   for $\$e_{2,k_2}$ **in** $\$e_{1,1}/l_{2,k_2}$
      for $\$e_{3,1}$ **in** $\$e_{2,i_{3,1}}/l_{3,1}$ ...
where p_1 **and** p_2 **and** ... **and** p_n
return \<result\> $< v_1 >path_1</v_1 > \ldots < v_n >path_n</v_n >$ \</result\>

Fig. 8. Algorithm **XQueryGen**

brevity and simplicity. Assume the lhs of the mapping contains a term $inst(o_0, \texttt{Schema})$. Then o_0 is the variable referencing the document element. Therefore, we put $(o_0, /)$ as the root into T and also into $Open$.

Now, we construct the element hierarchy T. For $(o_0, /)$ in $Open$ the required pattern is satisfied by the subformula $inst(o_1, \texttt{University}) \wedge part(o_1, \texttt{parent}_U, o_0) \wedge part(o_1, \texttt{child}_U, o_2)$ We add $(o_2, /\texttt{University})$ to $Open$ and also add it to T as a child of $(o_0, /)$ with label $\texttt{University}$. As no other subformula satisfies the pattern, we remove $(o_0, /)$ from $Open$ and add it to $Close$. We get $Open = \{(o_2, /\texttt{University})\}$, $T = (o_0, /)[(o_2, /\texttt{University}, \texttt{University})]$ and $Close = \{(o_0, /)\}$. We repeat the step for $(o_2, /\texttt{University})$. The result for T after this step is $(o_0, /)[(o_2, /\texttt{University}, \texttt{University})[(o_4, /\texttt{University}/\texttt{Student}, \texttt{Student})]]$. The last iteration does not add any elements.

Three variables on the lhs of χ are assigned by the query, u, s and i. According to the rules described in the algorithm, we add $(u, /\texttt{University}/\texttt{@uname})$, $(s, /\texttt{University}/\texttt{Student}/\texttt{@sname})$ and $(i, /\texttt{University}/\texttt{Student}/\texttt{@ID})$ to the return set R. There are no join or select conditions in the mapping, therefore, the condition set for this mapping remains empty. The assignments to the variables u,

s and i that are returned by the query are used as input when executing the rhs of the mapping. The XQuery generated from χ is:

```
for     $o₂ in  fn:doc(_fname)/University
            for $o₄ in  $o₂/Student
return <result>
            <u>$o₂/@uname</u> <s>$o₄/@sname</s> <i>$o₄/@ID</i>
            </result>
```

6 Evaluation

Correctness and Performance: To evaluate mapping composition we used nine composition problems drawn from recent literature [4,12,14]. The original mappings had to be translated manually into our representation before composing. The results of composition were logically equivalent to the documented results. The same set of problems had been used to evaluate the performance of our implementation. As was proven in [4] the computation time of composition may be exponential in the size of the input mappings. Fig. 9 displays the time performance of our composition implementation.

NI12	MP23	IC	TT(ms)
3	3	2	200
6	4	3	420
6	4	4	605
3	3	1	372
5	5	1	391
5	5	1	453
7	7	4	1324
15	6	99	16122
15	9	288	100170

Note: *NI12*: the number of implications in the normalized S_{12}

MP23: the maximum number of predicates in each implication in Σ_{23}

IC: the number of implications in the un-optimized composition

TT: the total run time of running the composition algorithm 200 times.

Fig. 9. Time performance of the composition algorithm

The upper bound of the number of implications in the non-optimized composition is $O(\sum_i(I^{P_i}))$, where I is the number of implications in the normalized Σ_{12} and P_i is the number of source predicates in each implication in Σ_{23}. In the second step of our composition algorithm, a predicate on the left hand side of χ can have at most I matched implications in S_{23}. Since only one implication is generated for each matched implication, after replacing the predicate, the number of implications in S_{23} will increase at most at the factor of I. Repeat the same reasoning for every source predicate in Σ_{23} will lead to the stated upper bound. In table 9, we listed, for each test case, the I, the maximum of P_i, the size of the un-optimized composition and its running time. It can be seen that the execution time may indeed be exponential in the size of input mappings. Even though composing mappings may be expensive, the performance is still reasonable. It takes about 80 milliseconds to run a test that generates in total 99 implications and about half a second for a test which generates 288 implications.

To evaluate mapping execution we defined seven test cases between relational data-bases and XML documents. The performance was linear in the size of the output and thus, our framework does not impose a significant overhead to data exchange tasks. These tests included also executing the composition of two mappings from a relational to an XML Schema and back. The result was an identity mapping and execution of the optimized result was about twice as fast as subsequent execution of the mappings. Our tests showed that our mapping execution yields the desired results satisfying both, the logical formalisms and the grouping semantics specified in the mappings. All tests were run on a Windows XP machine with a P4 2.4GHz CPU and 512MB memory.

Comparison with Other Mapping Representations: Source-to-target tuple-generating-dependencies (s-t tgds) and GLAV assertions are used to specify mappings between relational schemas. They are strict subsets of our adaptation of SO tgds. Every s-t tgd has a corresponding *GeRoMe* mapping but not vice versa. *GeRoMe* mappings can express nested data structures, e.g. XML data, while s-t tgds can not.

Path-conjunctive constraints [15] are an extension of s-t tdgs for dealing with nested schemas. However, they may suffer from several problems [5]. First, the same set of paths may be duplicated in many formulas which induces an extra overhead on map-ping execution. Second, grouping conditions cannot be specified, leading to incorrect grouping of data. Nested mappings [5] extend path-conjunctive constraints to address the above problems. Nested mappings merge formulas sharing the same set of high level paths into one formula, which causes mapping execution to generate less redundancy in the target. In addition, nested mappings provide a syntax to specify grouping conditions. Compared to nested mappings, *GeRoMe* mappings are also able to handle nested data and specify arbitrary grouping conditions for elements. Furthermore, the language of SO tgds is a superset of the language of nested mappings [5]. Since every SO tgd speci-fied for relational schemas can be transformed into a corresponding *GeRoMe* mapping, our mapping language is more expressive than the nested mapping language.

Like path-conjunctive constraints, a *GeRoMe* mapping cannot be nested into another *GeRoMe* mapping. Therefore, a common high-level context has to be repeated in dif-ferent formulas of a *GeRoMe* mapping. Again, this leads to less efficient execution. However, duplication in target data is overcome by grouping conditions. We may also borrow from the syntax of nested mappings to allow nested mapping definitions.

7   Conclusion

In this paper we introduced a rich mapping representation for mappings between models given in our Generic Role-based Metamodel *GeRoMe* [7]. Our mapping language is closed under composition as it is based on second order tuple-generating dependencies [4]. The mapping language is generic as it can be used to specify mappings between any two models represented in our generic metamodel. Moreover, mappings can be formulated between semistructured models such as XML schemas and are not restricted to flat models like relational schemas. Another feature of the proposed language is that it allows for grouping conditions that enable intensive restructuring of data, a feature also supported by nested mappings [5] which are not as expressive as SO tgds.

To verify the correctness and usefulness of our mapping representation we implemented an adapted version of the composition algorithm for second order tuple-generating dependencies [4]. Furthermore, we developed a tool that exports our mappings to queries and updates in the required data manipulation language and then uses them for data translation. As an example, we showed an algorithm that translates the lhs of a generic mapping to a query in XQuery. The components for mapping export and execution can be arbitrarily replaced by implementations for the required metamodel. The evaluation showed that both, mapping composition and mapping execution, yield the desired results with a reasonable time performance.

In the future we will develop techniques for visualizing our mappings with the goal to implement a graphical editor for generic, composable, structured extensional mappings. This editor will be integrated into our holistic model management system *GeRoMeSuite* [8]. We will also investigate the relationship between our extensional mappings and intensional mappings that are used for schema integration [16].

Acknowledgements. The work is supported by the Research Cluster on Ultra High-Speed Mobile Information and Communcation UMIC (www.umic.rwth-aachen.de).

References

1. Atzeni, P., Cappellari, P., Bernstein, P.A.: Model-independent schema and data translation. In *EDBT*. In: Ioannidis, Y., Scholl, M.H., Schmidt, J.W., Matthes, F., Hatzopoulos, M., Boehm, K., Kemper, A., Grust, T., Boehm, C. (eds.) EDBT 2006. LNCS, vol. 3896, pp. 368–385. Springer, Heidelberg (2006)
2. Bernstein, P.A., Green, T.J., Melnik, S., Nash, A.: Implementing mapping composition. In: Proc. VLDB 2006, Seoul, pp. 55–66 (2006)
3. Bernstein, P.A., Halevy, A.Y., Pottinger, R.: A vision for management of complex models. SIGMOD Record 29(4), 55–63 (2000)
4. Fagin, R., Kolaitis, P.G., Popa, L., Tan, W.C.: Composing schema mappings: Second-order dependencies to the rescue. ACM Trans. Database Syst. 30(4), 994–1055 (2005)
5. Fuxman, A., Hernández, M.A., Ho, C.T.H., Miller, R.J., Papotti, P., Popa, L.: Nested mappings: Schema mapping reloaded. In: Proc. VLDB 2006, Seoul, pp. 67–78 (2006)
6. Hernández, M.A., Miller, R.J., Haas, L.M.: Clio: A semi-automatic tool for schema mapping. In: Proc. ACM SIGMOD, p. 607. ACM Press, New York (2001)
7. Kensche, D., Quix, C., Chatti, M.A., Jarke, M.: GeRoMe: A generic role based metamodel for model management. Journal on Data Semantics VIII, 82–117 (2007)
8. Kensche, D., Quix, C., Li, X., Li, Y.: GeRoMeSuite: A system for holistic generic model management. In: Proc. 33rd Int. Conf. on Very Large Data Bases (to appear 2007)
9. Lenzerini, M.: Data integration: A theoretical perspective. In: PODS, pp. 233–246 (2002)
10. Li, Y.: Composition of mappings for a generic meta model. Master's thesis, RWTH Aachen University (2007)
11. Madhavan, J., Halevy, A.Y.: Composing mappings among data sources. In: Proc. VLDB, pp. 572–583. Morgan Kaufmann, San Francisco (2003)
12. Melnik, S., Bernstein, P.A., Halevy, A.Y., Rahm, E.: Supporting executable mappings in model management. In: Proc. SIGMOD Conf, pp. 167–178. ACM Press, New York (2005)
13. Melnik, S., Rahm, E., Bernstein, P.A.: Rondo: A programming platform for generic model management. In: Proc. SIGMOD, pp. 193–204. ACM Press, New York (2003)

14. Nash, A., Bernstein, P.A., Melnik, S.: Composition of mappings given by embedded dependencies. In: Li, C. (ed.) PODS, pp. 172–183. ACM Press, New York (2005)
15. Popa, L., Tannen, V.: An equational chase for path-conjunctive queries, constraints, and views. In: Beeri, C., Bruneman, P. (eds.) ICDT 1999. LNCS, vol. 1540, pp. 39–57. Springer, Heidelberg (1998)
16. Quix, C., Kensche, D., Li, X.: Generic schema merging. In: Krogstie, J., Opdahl, A., Sindre, G. (eds.) CAiSE 2007. LNCS, pp. 127–141. Springer, Heidelberg (2007)
17. Rahm, E., Bernstein, P.A.: A survey of approaches to automatic schema matching. VLDB Journal 10(4), 334–350 (2001)
18. Robertson, G.G., Czerwinski, M.P., Churchill, J.E.: Visualization of mappings between schemas. In: Proc. SIGCHI, pp. 431–439 (2005)

Relational Data Tailoring Through View Composition[*]

Cristiana Bolchini, Elisa Quintarelli, and Rosalba Rossato

Dipartimento di Elettronica e Informazione – Politecnico di Milano
Piazza Leonardo da Vinci, 32 – 20133 Milano, Italy
{bolchini,quintare,rossato}@elet.polimi.it

Abstract. This paper presents a methodology to derive views over a relational database by applying a sequence of appropriately defined operations to the global schema. Such *tailoring* and *composition* process aims at offering personalized views over the database schema, so as to improve its ability to support the new needs of customers, support evolutionary software development, and fix existing legacy database design problems. The process is driven by the designer's knowledge of the possible operational contexts, in terms of the various dimensions that contribute to determine which portions of the global schema are relevant with respect to the different actors and situations. We formally introduce some operators, defined on sets of relations, which tailor the schema and combine the intermediate views to derive different final views, suitable for the different envisioned situations. The application to a case study is also presented, to better clarify the proposed approach.

1 Introduction

The development of complex systems dealing with huge amounts of information requires a careful design phase, where all actors need be identified together with all the elements that may determine what portion of the entire data they should have access to in the various situations. Actually, this is not so much a matter of privacy and security, as of efficiency and usability, when too much information may cause confusion rather than knowledge.

In the relational scenario, the above problem consists in designing appropriate views to provide different, selected data access to portions of the entire data schema. Yet, if the number of elements, or *dimensions*, determining the subset of data interesting for each given *context*, is high, the designer's task may be quite complex, since all possible contexts for a target scenario have to be examined and, for each one of them, the associated view has to be defined.

The aim of our proposal is the definition of a systematic methodology that first supports the designer in identifying, for a given application scenario, the dimensions for characterizing the context and their possible values, and then, once the designer has identified *partial views* with respect to such context dimensions, combines them to produce the final views, one for each possible context. We refer to this view production process as *schema tailoring*, since it amounts to *cutting out* the appropriate data portion which fits each possible context.

---

[*] This research is partially supported by the MIUR projects ESTEEM and ARTDECO.

C. Parent et al. (Eds.): ER 2007, LNCS 4801, pp. 149–164, 2007.

Our claim is that, even for small application scenarios (such as the running example introduced below), where the number of dimensions driving the tailoring of the schema is quite small, the resulting number of possible contexts is rather high: as a consequence, the adoption of the proposed approach not only helps the designer consider all possible situations, with no omission, but also automatically performs the (computationally significant) view generation task.

The rest of this paper is organized as follows. Section 2 presents the overall scenario, together with the motivations of our work and its contribution with respect to related studies. Section 3 introduces the view definition methodology and the necessary operators supporting view composition. The application to a real example is discussed in order to validate the approach and its feasibility. Future work and concluding remarks are reported in the last section.

2   Background, Motivations and Rationale

The proposed methodology aims at providing the database designer with a systematic approach to view design, in a scenario where different database users, situations and other elements (altogether called dimensions) affect the choice of the subset of data to be considered interesting and made available to such actors.

In order to define the methodology, three elements are necessary:

a) a model expressing the dimensions, and their values, driving schema tailoring. The model should be able to capture the dimensions as well as all the possible contexts deriving from their instantiations;

b) a strategy for identifying for each dimension, independently of the others, a relevant portion of data on the entire schema – the so-called *partial views*; and

c) a set of operators for combining the partial views to derive the final view(s) associated with each context.

In previous work [2,4], we have presented a context model, called *Context Dimension Tree*, which takes care of point (a), whereas in this paper we focus on the last two points, where the Context Dimension Tree is used to create and compose views for data tailoring purposes.

Let us consider the case of a real estate agency storing data related to its agents, estates and owners and wanting to support the agents in their work (in office and also on-site, when they take prospective clients to visit the properties), and to promote its business on the Web. The agency database stores also information on the closed contracts (rents and sales), to provide the supervisor with an overview of the situation. The scenario, although simple, has four different actors: supervisors, agents, buyers and sellers. Supervisors must have a global view of the business, in terms of the estates the agency deals with, and of the agents' work. Agents are in charge of the visits and of acquiring new estates for the agency portfolio. The corporate database is also the source for a Web site to promote business, and views need be designed to provide all and only the necessary data. In this paper we base our considerations on the relational data model, thus the real estate database is composed by the tables reported in Fig. 1.

OWNER(<u>IdOwner</u>, Name, Surname, Type, Address,City, PhoneNumber)
ESTATE(<u>IdEstate</u>, IdOwner, Category, Area, City, Province, RoomsNumber,
           Bedrooms, Garage, SquareMeters, Sheet, CadastralMap)
CUSTOMER(<u>IdCustomer</u>, Name, Surname, Type, Budget, Address, City, PhoneNum)
AGENT(<u>IdAgent</u>, Name, Surname, Office, Address,City,Phone)
AGENDA(<u>IdAgent, Data, Hour</u>, IdEstate, ClientName)
VISIT(<u>IdEstate, IdAgent, IdCustomer, Date</u>, ViewDuration)
SALE(<u>IdEstate, IdAgent, IdCustomer, Date</u>, AgreePrice, Status)
RENT(<u>IdEstate, IdAgent, IdCustomer, Date</u>, RatePrice, Status, Duration)
PICTURE(<u>IdPicture</u>, IdEstate, Date, Description, FileName)

Fig. 1. The database schema

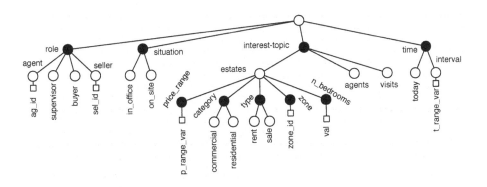

Fig. 2. The Context Dimension Tree

The first step of our approach consists in specifying the context dimensions characterizing the possible contexts in this application scenario, also listing the expected values, according to the methodology presented in [4]. More precisely, our context model,
the Context Dimension Tree, is an extension of the context model presented in [6], and
is used to systematically describe the user needs, and to capture the context the user is
acting in. It plays a fundamental role in tailoring the target application data according to
the user information needs. Once the possible contexts have been designed, each must
be connected with the corresponding view definition. In this way, when the context becomes current, the view is computed and delivered to the user. The various ways to
operate such design-time connection are the subject of this paper.

Fig. 2 shows the Context Dimension Tree we have elaborated for our real estate
agency, better explained below.

2.1 Background

The Context Dimension Tree is a tree $\mathcal{T} = \langle N, E, r \rangle$, whose nodes are the context dimensions and their values. The set of nodes N is partitioned into the subsets N_D, N_C and
N_A. The two main types of nodes are: *dimension nodes*, N_D, black, and *concept nodes*,
N_C, white. N_A is the set of *attributes*, whose explanation we postpone for the moment.

The root's children are the *top dimensions*, which capture the different characteristics of the users and of the context they are acting in; in our example, the top dimensions are the database user's *role*, his or her *situation*, the current *interest topic* and the *time span* of interest. A dimension value can be further analyzed with respect to different viewpoints (sub-dimensions), generating a subtree in its turn. For example, the interest topic "estates" can be analyzed w.r.t. the price range, the category, the business type, the zone and the number of bedrooms.

The root r of the tree is a concept node: it models all the possible contexts, thus represents the entire dataset, before tailoring.

The edge set E is partitioned into the two subsets E_R and E_A: E_R contains *sub-element of* arcs, whereas E_A contains *attribute of* arcs.

Coherently with the meaning of dimension and concept nodes, each "generation" contains nodes of the same color, and colors are alternated while descending the tree: $\forall e = \langle n,m \rangle \in E_R$, either $n \in N_D \wedge m \in N_C$ or $n \in N_C \wedge m \in N_D$; i.e., a dimension node has concept nodes as children and a concept node has dimension nodes as children.

We consider now *attribute nodes*: $\forall n \in N_A, \forall e = \langle m,n \rangle \in E_A$, $m \in N_D \cup N_C$; i.e., the parent of an attribute node is either a dimension node or a concept node. In the first case, the attribute represents a *parameter*, while in the second case it represents a *variable*. Consider the sub-dimensions of estates: while category and type have white children (i.e., their values), price_range only features a small square, an em attribute node; this attribute is a selection parameter whose instances represent the possible values of the price_range dimension, e.g., a price interval. Thus, dimension branching can be represented in both ways: either by explicitly drawing the values as white nodes, or by indicating a parameter whose instances are the dimension values. This does not modify the expressive power of the model: rather, it makes it more readable, and more usable for the designer.

Also white nodes may feature a variable indicating how to select a specific set of data instances. As an example, consider the ag_id variable associated with the agent role: it is an identifier used, at run-time, to select the data related to a specific agent.

Attribute nodes are *leaves*, i.e., $\forall n \in N_A, \neg \exists m \; s.t. \langle n,m \rangle \in E$. Moreover, according to the meaning of attribute nodes, each attribute node is *an only child*: $\forall n \in N_A, \forall e = \langle m,n \rangle \in E_A$, if $\exists e_1 = \langle m,n_1 \rangle \in E$ then $n = n_1$.

Dimension nodes without concept children *must have an attribute child*, i.e., $\forall n \in N_D$ such that $\neg \exists e = \langle n,m \rangle \in E_R$ then $\exists e_1 = \langle n,m_1 \rangle \in E_A$. Indeed, black nodes must necessarily feature either white children or the parameter node, whose values are those of the corresponding subdimension. Thus, leaf nodes can only be either attribute nodes or white nodes.

Finally, in order to simplify the discussion, we also introduce, although redundant, two more sets: $\overline{N_D}$, which identifies dimension nodes that have an attribute child (i.e., $\overline{N_D} = \{n \in N_D | \; \not\exists e = \langle n,m \rangle \in E_R\}$); *context elements* c are in $N_C \cup \overline{N_D}$, which identifies either a concept node (white node), such as the supervisor, or a dimension node (black node) with a parameter (such as price_range(p_range_var)).

The tree is formalized in [2], and can be specified in several ways; in particular we propose an ontological representation in the OWL language [12], and an XML representation based on a DTD [5].

The complex structure originating from the composition of the context elements of a Context Dimension Tree is called a *context* or *configuration*, and determines a portion of the entire data set, i.e., a *chunk*, specified at design-time, to be selected later, at run-time, when the corresponding context becomes active. A *context* is expressed as a tuple of context elements, each of them described with the form

$$\text{dim\_name} : \text{value}$$

where dim_name is the name of a (sub-)dimension, and value is a value for that dimension. The values for each context element may be at any level in the tree, thus allowing for different levels of granularity. Note that sibling white nodes are *mutually exclusive* since they represent orthogonal concepts, while sibling black nodes represent the different (sub-)dimensions which define a concept. Therefore, when building a configuration, for each top dimension, at each level, only one white node among each set of siblings, and any number of black siblings may be included.

Note that a context can lack some dimension value(s): this means that those dimensions are not taken into account to tailor data, i.e., the view corresponding to that configuration does not filter the data for these dimension(s).

Let us consider the situation of an agent ($ag_id="XYZ") ready to take prospective buyer clients to visit the residential estates properties located in the "Piola" area ($zone_id="Piola"). The current context (or configuration) C is composed by the nodes

$$\langle\ \text{role} : \text{agent("XYZ")},$$
$$\text{category} : \text{residential},$$
$$\text{type} : \text{sale},$$
$$\text{zone} : \text{zone("Piola")},$$
$$\text{situation} : \text{on\_site},$$
$$\text{time} : \text{today(getdate())}\rangle$$

wherefrom we have to derive the specification of the information related to the interesting properties.

Such configuration must be associated at design time with the (definition of the) piece of data which must become available when C occurs, and the same must be done for each possible (and reasonable) configuration. Note that the instantiation of the zone is based on the value "Piola", appropriately fed to the system at run time: this is an example of use of a *variable*, to be suitably used by the run-time system.

The designer can also express constraints or preferences on the possible combinations of the context elements; in fact, not all of them make sense for a given scenario, thus, if we combinatorially generate the complete set, many configurations must be discarded. Hence, the tree model is enriched by introducing *forbid constraints*: they allow the context designer to specify configurations that are not significant, thus discarding those that would represent semantically meaningless context situations or would be irrelevant for the application. For example, such a constraint can be established to forbid that the buyer role's context contains interest topics related to the agents' administrative data.

The introduction of these constraints, not further discussed here, allows the designer to represent with the Context Dimension Tree all and only the significant contexts for the given application scenario.

2.2 Goal and Contributions

Once the Context Dimension Tree has been designed, the subsequent work of the designer can take two different directions, one more time-consuming but allowing for a more precise view definition, the second one more automatic but more prone to possible errors, thus to be verified a-posteriori.

When the first strategy is adopted, once the configurations are combinatorially derived the designer associates each of them with the corresponding portion of the information domain schema. This is called *configuration-based mapping*, and can be done by directly writing a query in the language supported by the underlying database, or by selecting these portions by means of a graphical interface which will derive the corresponding view. This process is already supported by a tool we have developed [3]; however, as it can be expected, even after excluding the meaningless configurations by means of the appropriate constraints, a medium-size Context Dimension Tree originates a huge number of configurations (e.g., in our running example there are 816 significant contexts), thus the task of associating each significant context with its view is unpractical. Moreover, if the context model changes, e.g., if a new concept is inserted, a high number of new configurations will have to be generated from its combination with the other concepts, and the designer will have to redefine all the mappings for these. Similarly, also a change in the underlying database schema will require a complete revision of all derived views.

To overcome the limitations of this first approach, in this work we formalize a compositional strategy, called *node-based mapping*, whereby the designer selects the schema portion to be associated *with each context element* and then the system will combine them within the configurations. In this paper we first define the possible policies to associate schema portions with context elements, then introduce the appropriate logical operators to derive the view associated with a configuration. Different combination policies will also be presented, involving the use of proper operators, such as intersection or union of schemata and instances, to produce the final result.

The proposed approach to relational data tailoring taking into account all these aspects has been implemented in another tool we developed, supporting the user in all steps of the methodology.

2.3 Related Work

In the past years, the view definition process has been exhaustively investigated in the database literature; the first models and view-design methodologies were for relational databases [8].

When focusing on the relational model of data, a few solutions have been presented to introduce the notion of context in the data being modeled, by means of additional attributes explicitly defining the context (e.g., space and time characteristics) the data belongs to.

In [15] the authors present a Context Relational Model as an extension of the relational one: the notion of context is treated as a first-class citizen that must be modeled and can be queried by using standard SQL expressions. A lot of attention is devoted to the investigation of instance changes on the basis of context dimension values. This is a significant difference with respect to our approach, where the context model is aimed at data tailoring, that is the extraction of the relevant portion of a relational schema for a given context.

In [16] the authors introduce a context-aware system that uses context, described as a finite set of context parameters, to provide relevant information and/or services to its users. The proposed system supports preference queries whose results depend on context. Users express their basic preferences by associating a degree of interest between attribute values and instances of a context parameter; basic preferences are combined to compute aggregate preferences, that reflect the users' selection with respect to a more complex notion of context. The approach is more focused on personalization of query answering, however, the context-dependent view definition process is not performed at design time, but is guided by the available user's preferences.

The success of XML has motivated, in the recent years, the necessity of proposals that are independent of the underlying data model: the problem of view definition for XML has been formalized in [1,7], and some other works in the XML area are [10,20]. Some other view models based on ontologies have been proposed in [17,18] in the Semantic Web Area.

All the above cited models follow the classical notion of view extraction process; thus, the state-of-the-art in view design needs to be extended to consider also user's activity, tasks, and intentions: the user's context.

In [9,13,14,19] the authors propose formal frameworks for specifically addressing the problem of view design for XML and ontological data sources, guided by a notion of context; in [14] some conceptual operators are formalized for constructing conceptual context dependent views on XML data; the notion of context is related to facts of data warehouses and the operators extract information related to a single specific fact, without combining different views. In our opinion, the notion of context we use in this paper is much more articulated (mutual exclusive and orthogonal dimensions are modeled) and thus, we need to define operators both to extract and to combine partial views; the composition step is required to obtain views suitable to represent the relevant portion of data for a notion of context that depends on more than one perspective.

3   View Definition

In this section we describe the way to derive a view for each possible context, by starting from the representation of the application context by means of a Context Dimension Tree and by adopting a *node-based mapping* strategy. The process is composed by two main steps, detailed in the rest of the section:

– *Relevant area assignment*: a partial view, expressed as a set of relational algebra expressions, is associated with each context element;
– *View composition by algebraic operators*: the previously defined partial views, associated with the context elements in a configuration, are properly combined to automatically obtain a final view defining all the information relevant for that configuration.

3.1 Relevant Area Assignment

In this section we formalize the way to associate a partial view with each context element c ($c \in N_C \cup \overline{N_D}$). In this step, the designer annotates the Context Dimension Tree by labeling each context element with the partial view assigned to it via the mapping

$$\mathcal{R}el : N_C \cup \overline{N_D} \rightarrow \wp(\mathcal{V}) \tag{1}$$

where $\mathcal{V}$ is the set of views on the global database, and each partial view $V \in \wp(\mathcal{V})$ is a *set of relational algebra expressions* e_i, each one of them recursively defined as follows:

$$e_i \stackrel{\text{def}}{=} R_j | \pi_{att}(e_i) | \sigma_\theta(e_i) | e_i \times_\theta e_j | e_i \bowtie_\theta e_j \tag{2}$$

where R_j is a relation belonging to the global schema, and *att* and θ are shorthands to denote a set of attributes and a boolean condition, respectively.

Relevant Area Policies

When tailoring the relevant area (partial view) for a given context element c, two policies have been identified:

a) **Maximal relevant area:** the partial view V for c contains all the schema portions that *might be related* to that element. For example, the maximal relevant area for the `estate` would be

   $$\mathcal{R}el(\texttt{estate}) = \{\text{ESTATE, OWNER, VISIT, SALES, RENT, AGENDA, PICTURE}\}$$

   thus, the partial view associated with the `estate` element includes all the information that is related, in some way, to estates; that is, besides the ESTATE and PICTURE tables, which contain all and only information on the estates, the view also contains all the further information related to properties, including the OWNER, VISIT, SALES, RENT, and AGENDA tables.

b) **Minimal relevant area:** the partial view V of a given context element c contains only the portions of the global schema that *are strictly related* to c.
   For example, for the `estate` interest topic, the minimal relevant area would be

   $$\mathcal{R}el(\texttt{estate}) = \{\text{ESTATE, PICTURE}\}$$

   which only includes tables ESTATE and PICTURE.

Independently of the adopted policy, an important consideration on the relationships among partial views associated with context elements must be highlighted. More precisely, the hierarchical structure of the Context Dimension Tree has been designed with the aim of increasing the detail level adopted to select data while descending the subtree related to each context dimension. Indeed, while descending a sub-tree rooted in a dimension, we add details in specifying how to use that dimension to tailor data. Thus, in our opinion it is desirable that the partial view for a node n contain the partial view of each descendant m of n. We say that a node n is more abstract than m, and write $n \prec m$, if and only if $m \in Descendant(n)$.

Notation. Given a generic relation R, we denote with $\text{Sch}(R)$ its schema, i.e., its name and the set of its attributes. Moreover, given two relations R_i and R_j, we say that $\text{Sch}(R_i)$ is a sub-schema of $\text{Sch}(R_j)$, and write $\text{Sch}(R_i) \subseteq \text{Sch}(R_j)$, if and only if the attributes of R_i are a (sub-)set of the attributes of R_j.

The *containment relationship* between partial views is defined as follows:

Definition 1. *Let w and k be context elements and $\mathcal{R}el(w)$, $\mathcal{R}el(k)$ the corresponding partial views. $\mathcal{R}el(w) \subseteq \mathcal{R}el(k)$ if and only if:*

$$\forall R_i \in \mathcal{R}el(w) \exists R_j \in \mathcal{R}el(k) \ s.t. \ \text{Sch}(R_i) \subseteq \text{Sch}(R_j) \tag{3}$$

Based on the philosophy of the Context Dimension Tree and its hierarchical structure to support a refinement of the tailoring criteria as the depth of the tree increases, we introduce the following assumption, used throughout this paper.

Assumption 1. *For each pair of context elements n and m in a Context Dimension Tree, if $n \prec m$ then $\mathcal{R}el(n) \supseteq \mathcal{R}el(m)$.*

To satisfy Assumption 1, given two context elements n and m in a Context Dimension Tree such that $n \prec m$, and supposing the designer has set $\mathcal{R}el(n) = \{R_1, \ldots, R_k\}$, then each relation S_i in $\mathcal{R}el(m) = \{S_1, \ldots, S_t\}$, with $t \leq k$, is recursively defined as follows:

$$S_i \stackrel{\text{def}}{=} R_j | \pi_{att}(S_i) | \sigma_\theta S_i | S_i \bowtie_\theta S_j | S_i \bowtie_\theta R \tag{4}$$

where $R_j \in \mathcal{R}el(n)$, and R is a relation of the global database.

Example 1. Let us now explain our assumption about containment of partial views related to two context elements, one element a descendant of the other. The partial view for the `estate` *interest-topic* is a view containing all the information available in the database regarding properties and related information. Formally, using the maximal area policy, we have:

$$\mathcal{R}el(\texttt{estate}) = \{\text{ESTATE}, \text{OWNER}, \text{VISIT}, \text{SALES}, \text{RENT}, \text{AGENDA}, \text{PICTURE}\}$$

The partial view for the `residential` *category* is a set of views further restricting $\mathcal{R}el(\texttt{estate})$ only to information about the residential estates:

$\mathcal{R}el(\texttt{residential}) = \{\sigma_{Category="Residential"}\text{ESTATE}, \text{OWNER} \bowtie (\sigma_{Category="Residential"}\text{ESTATE}),$

$\quad \text{VISIT} \bowtie (\sigma_{Category="Residential"}\text{ESTATE}), \text{SALE} \bowtie (\sigma_{Category="Residential"}\text{ESTATE}),$

$\quad \text{RENT} \bowtie (\sigma_{Category="Residential"}\text{ESTATE}), \text{AGENDA} \bowtie (\sigma_{Category="Residential"}\text{ESTATE}),$

$\quad \text{PICTURE} \bowtie (\sigma_{Category="Residential"}\text{ESTATE})\}$ ◆

Context Dimension Tree Traversal During Relevant Area Assignment

In our opinion and experience, the maximal area policy is intended to assign the widest possible view for each context element of the Context Dimension Tree; consequently, it is more natural for the designer, once this policy is selected, to perform the relevant area assignment phase by navigating the Context Dimension Tree *top-down* (from the root to the leaves). This actually means that the view for the root node is the entire database, and the partial view for a node *m* is defined by restricting the partial view of its nearest white ancestor. Thus, this phase is performed by navigating the Context Dimension Tree top-down and by specifying for each node *m* a view ($\mathcal{R}el(m)$) on the (previously defined) view ($\mathcal{R}el(n)$) of its parent *n*, according to the recursive definition reported in Equation 4.

On the contrary, the minimal area policy should be used when the designer prefers to specify more detailed views, i.e., the minimal partial view, for each context element of the Context Dimension Tree; thus, when this policy has been chosen, in order to be adherent with the spirit of the Context Dimension Tree, it is recommended to perform the relevant area assignment phase by navigating the Context Dimension Tree *bottom-up*. This means that the partial views are defined by starting from the leaf context elements and the view of a non-leaf node can be obtained by composing the partial views associated with its children.

The composition is obtained by using the double-union operator (introduced later in the paper) and possibly including additional portions of the global database that the designer considers useful for the more general (non-leaf) context element. For example, when using the minimal policy, $\mathcal{R}el(\texttt{estates})$ can be obtained by combining $\mathcal{R}el(\texttt{price\_range})$, $\mathcal{R}el(\texttt{zone})$, $\mathcal{R}el(\texttt{category})$, $\mathcal{R}el(\texttt{type})$, and $\mathcal{R}el(\texttt{n\_bedrooms})$.

In the *node-based mapping* approach, whose dynamics is shown in Fig. 3, once each context element has an associated partial view (Relevant Area Assignment Phase of Fig. 3), the next step consists in automatically composing for each configuration its final

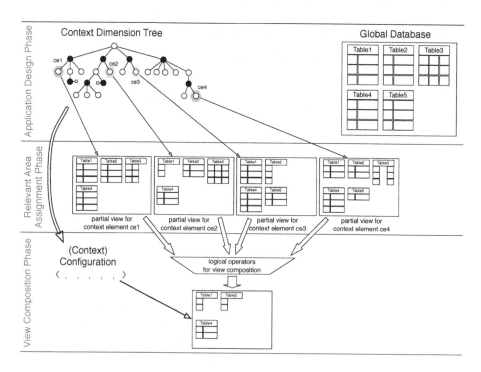

Fig. 3. The node-based mapping strategy

view, computed as a combination of the partial views corresponding to each context element in the configuration (View Composition Phase of Fig. 3). The combination is performed by means of opportunely defined operators acting on sets of views.

This *node-based mapping* approach is more efficient than the *configuration-based mapping* previously developed, yet it is less precise in the definition of the final view associated with a configuration. Thus, we also consider, although not further discussed here, the possibility to integrate additional information in the resulting view, should the designer deem the automatic procedure to have excluded some relevant information.

Example 2. Let us assume the designer has mapped the buyer *role* to a view describing both commercial and residential flats and houses, that is, the ESTATE table deprived of the *IdOwner* and *CadastralMap* attributes. Formally:

$$\mathcal{R}el(\text{buyer}) = \{\Pi_Z \text{ESTATE}, \text{PICTURE}\}$$

where

$$Z = \{IdEstate, Category, Area, City, Province, RoomsNumber, Bedrooms, Garage, SquareMeters\}.$$

The residential *category* has a partial view describing residential flats and houses, that is:

$$\mathcal{R}el(\text{residential}) = \{\sigma_{Category="Residential"}\text{ESTATE}, \text{PICTURE} \bowtie (\sigma_{Category="Residential"}\text{ESTATE})\}$$

The view for the configuration $C = \langle \text{role} : \text{buyer}, \text{category} : \text{residential} \rangle$ is obtained by applying a suitable operator for view composition between $\mathcal{R}el(\text{buyer})$ and $\mathcal{R}el(\text{residential})$. ◆

We have defined two possible operators for view composition, based on the union and the intersection relational algebra operators, discussed in the next section.

3.2   Logical Operators for View Composition

The context-defined views on a relational database may be written by using relational algebra or, equivalently, in SQL. In order to compose different partial views, and automatically gather all and only the information of interest with respect to a specific context, we need to introduce a suite of new algebraic operators which work on *sets of relations*. These operators combine tuples of relations selected by the designer during the partial views definition; therefore, in order to maintain the identity of each tuple during manipulation, we include for each relation in a partial view, its primary key attribute(s). Let $\mathcal{A}$ and $\mathcal{B}$ be two sets of relations, and $\mathcal{S}_\mathcal{A}$ and $\mathcal{S}_\mathcal{B}$ the corresponding sets of relational schemata.

Double Union Operator: The double union $\mathcal{A} \uplus \mathcal{B}$ between two set of relations $\mathcal{A}$ and $\mathcal{B}$ returns the union of (1) the set of all relations R_i whose schema is in $(\mathcal{S}_\mathcal{A} - \mathcal{S}_\mathcal{B}) \bigcup (\mathcal{S}_\mathcal{B} - \mathcal{S}_\mathcal{A})$ and (2) a sort of intersection between R_A and R_B for each pair of relations $R_A \in \mathcal{A}$ and $R_B \in \mathcal{B}$, having a common sub-schema. In this way we preserve selection conditions which have possibly been applied on the same tables in the definition phase of both $\mathcal{A}$ and $\mathcal{B}$, as we will prove in Theorem 1. Formally:

Definition 2. *Let $\mathcal{A}$ and $\mathcal{B}$ be sets of relations.*

$$\mathcal{A} \uplus \mathcal{B} = \left\{ R \left| \begin{array}{l} (R \in \mathcal{A} \wedge \neg \exists R' \in \mathcal{B}, \mathrm{Sch}(R) \cap \mathrm{Sch}(R') \neq \emptyset) \vee \\ (R \in \mathcal{B} \wedge \neg \exists R' \in \mathcal{A}, \mathrm{Sch}(R) \cap \mathrm{Sch}(R') \neq \emptyset) \vee \\ (R = \pi_S(R_A) \cap \pi_S(R_B), R_A \in \mathcal{A}, R_B \in \mathcal{B}, S = \mathrm{Sch}(R_A) \cap \mathrm{Sch}(R_B) \neq \emptyset) \end{array} \right. \right\}$$

According to its formal definition, the Double Union Operator is *commutative* and *associative*.

Property 1. *Let $\mathcal{A}$ and $\mathcal{B}$ be two sets of relations. For each pair of relations $R_A \in \mathcal{A}$ and $R_B \in \mathcal{B}$ such that $R_A = \Pi_{Z_A}(\sigma_{\theta_A}(R))$ and $R_B = \Pi_{Z_B}(\sigma_{\theta_B}(R))$, with R a relation obtained from the global database, $Z_A \subseteq \mathrm{Sch}(R)$, $Z_B \subseteq \mathrm{Sch}(R)$, the selection conditions θ_A and θ_B are preserved by the application of $\mathcal{A} \uplus \mathcal{B}$.*

Proof. R_A and R_B are obtained by considering only those tuples of R that satisfy the selection conditions θ_A and θ_B, restricted on the sub-schemata Z_A and Z_B, respectively. Let $Z = Z_A \cap Z_B$ be the (possibly empty) common sub-schema of R_A and R_B; then, according to the definition of $\uplus$, the relation Y, defined as follows, belongs to $\mathcal{A} \uplus \mathcal{B}$:

$$Y = \pi_Z(R_A) \cap \pi_Z(R_B)$$
$$= \pi_Z(\pi_{Z_A}(\sigma_{\theta_A}(R))) \cap \pi_Z(\pi_{Z_B}(\sigma_{\theta_B}(R)))$$

By starting from the fact that $Z \subseteq Z_A$, $Z \subseteq Z_B$ and according to the known equivalence transformation between relational algebra expressions, we can conclude that

$$Y = \pi_Z(\sigma_{\theta_A \wedge \theta_B}(R)) \in \mathcal{A} \uplus \mathcal{B}$$

that is, both conditions θ_A and θ_B are preserved in the resulting relation included in $\mathcal{A} \uplus \mathcal{B}$.   □

Example 3. Assume the partial views of the `residential` *category* and the `buyer` *role* reported in Example 2 (minimal area policy). The view associated with the configuration $C = \langle$`role : buyer, category : residential`$\rangle$ obtained by applying the Double Union operator between $\mathcal{R}el(\mathtt{buyer})$ and $\mathcal{R}el(\mathtt{residential})$ is the following:

$\mathcal{R}el(\mathtt{C}) = \mathcal{R}el(\mathtt{buyer}) \uplus \mathcal{R}el(\mathtt{residential})$

$\quad = \{\sigma_{Category=\text{"Residential"}}(\Pi_Z(\mathrm{ESTATE})), (\mathrm{PICTURE}) \bowtie \sigma_{Category=\text{"Residential"}}((\mathrm{ESTATE}))\}$

where $Z = \{IdEstate, Category, Area, City, Province, RoomsNumber, Bedrooms, Garage, SquareMeters\}$.   ◆

Example 4. Assume the relevant area for the `residential` *category* as in Example 3, and for the `agent` *role* the minimal relevant area containing his/her data and agenda:

$\mathcal{R}el(\mathtt{agent(\$ag\_id)}) = \{\sigma_{IdAgent=\$ag\_id}(\mathrm{AGENT}), \sigma_{IdAgent=\$ag\_id}(\mathrm{AGENDA})\}$

The view associated with $C = \langle$`role : agent($ag_id), category : residential`$\rangle$ obtained by applying the Double Union operator between $\mathcal{R}el(\mathtt{agent(\$ag\_id)})$ and $\mathcal{R}el(\mathtt{residential})$ is:

$\mathcal{R}el(\mathtt{C}) = \mathcal{R}el(\mathtt{agent(\$ag\_id)}) \uplus \mathcal{R}el(\mathtt{residential})$

$\quad = \{\sigma_{IdAgent=\$ag\_id}(\mathrm{AGENT}), \sigma_{IdAgent=\$ag\_id}(\mathrm{AGENDA}),$

$\qquad \sigma_{Category=\text{"Residential"}}(\mathrm{ESTATE}), (\mathrm{PICTURE}) \bowtie \sigma_{Category=\text{"Residential"}}((\mathrm{ESTATE}))\}$ ◆

Double Intersection Operator: The double intersection $\mathcal{A} \cap\!\!\!\cap \mathcal{B}$ between two sets of relations $\mathcal{A}$ and $\mathcal{B}$, applies the intersection operator $\cap$ of relational algebra to the maximal common sub-schemata of the pairs of relations R_A and R_B, belonging to $\mathcal{A}$ and $\mathcal{B}$, respectively, where either $\text{Sch}(R_A) \subseteq \text{Sch}(R_B)$ or viceversa.

On the result produced by the application of such intersections, the union operator $\cup$ is iteratively applied to pairs of the obtained relations having the same schema, since the Double Intersection can generate more than a single relation with the same schema; this final step aims at removing such duplicates.

Definition 3. *Let $\mathcal{A}$ and $\mathcal{B}$ be sets of relations.*

a) Let S be computed as follows:

$$S = \{X \mid X = \pi_S(X_A) \cap \pi_S(X_B) \text{ s.t. } X_A \in \mathcal{A}, \, X_B \in \mathcal{B}, S = \text{Sch}(X_A) \cap \text{Sch}(X_B) \neq \emptyset)\}$$

b) $\mathcal{A} \cap\!\!\!\cap \mathcal{B}$ is recursively obtained as follows:

$$\mathcal{A} \cap\!\!\!\cap \mathcal{B} = \left\{ R \, \middle| \, \begin{matrix} (R = R_1 \cup R_2, \, \forall R_1, R_2 \in S \text{ s.t. } \text{Sch}(R_1) = \text{Sch}(R_2)) \vee \\ (R \in S \wedge \, \nexists R' \in S \text{ s.t. } \text{Sch}(R) = \text{Sch}(R')) \end{matrix} \right\}$$

According to its formal definition, the Double Intersection Operator is *commutative* and *associative* too.

Example 5. The partial view associated with the agent *role* in case of maximal area policy is

$$\mathcal{R}el(\texttt{agent(\$ag\_id)}) = \{\sigma_{IdAgent=\$ag\_id}\text{AGENT}, \sigma_{IdAgent=\$ag\_id}\text{AGENDA},$$
$$\text{VISIT, SALES, RENT, OWNER, CUSTOMER, ESTATE, PICTURE}\}$$

Consider now the context of an agent $\texttt{\$ag\_id}$ specified by the configuration $C = \langle \texttt{role}:$ $\texttt{agent(\$ag\_id)}, \texttt{category}: \texttt{residential}\rangle$. The view obtained by applying the Double Intersection operator between $\mathcal{R}el(\texttt{agent(\$ag\_id)})$ and $\mathcal{R}el(\texttt{residential})$, whose partial view is that reported in Example 1, is the following:

$$\mathcal{R}el(C) = \mathcal{R}el(\texttt{agent(\$ag\_id)}) \cap\!\!\!\cap \mathcal{R}el(\texttt{residential})$$
$$= \{\sigma_{Category=\text{"Residential"}}\text{ESTATE}, \text{OWNER} \ltimes (\sigma_{Category=\text{"Residential"}}\text{ESTATE}),$$
$$\text{VISIT} \ltimes (\sigma_{Category=\text{"Residential"}}\text{ESTATE}), \text{SALES} \ltimes (\sigma_{Category=\text{"Residential"}}\text{ESTATE}),$$
$$\text{RENT} \ltimes (\sigma_{Category=\text{"Residential"}}\text{ESTATE}), \text{PICTURE} \ltimes (\sigma_{Category=\text{"Residential"}}\text{ESTATE}),$$
$$(\sigma_{IdAgent=\$ag\_id}(\text{AGENDA})) \ltimes (\sigma_{Category=\text{"Residential"}}\text{ESTATE})\} \qquad \blacklozenge$$

For the sake of clarity, in the examples we have used configurations with two context elements only, yet the *commutative* and *associative* properties of the introduced Double Union and Double Intersection operators allow their application to configurations C with any number of context elements.

These logical operators have been defined to support our methodology for view composition, a problem deeply formalized from a theoretical point of view in [11]; nevertheless they are general-purpose integration operators, appropriate for any schema and instance integration over relational schemata. Within our context-driven methodology, a few properties useful for the final view composition phase can be derived.

View Composition Properties

The mapping and the compositional operators used to obtain a context-dependent view allows us to prove the following properties. The next two theorems show how, given the view for a configuration C related to a context described by k context elements (i.e. $C = \langle V_1, \ldots, V_k \rangle$), we can obtain the view for a configuration with an additional context element w.r.t. C (i.e. $C' = \langle V_1, \ldots, V_k, V_{k+1} \rangle$), by simply composing (by Double Union or Double Intersection) the partial view of V_{k+1} with $\mathcal{R}el(C)$.

Property 2. *Let $\mathcal{R}el(\langle V_1, \ldots, V_k \rangle)$ be the partial view defined for the configuration $C = \langle V_1, \ldots, V_k \rangle$ w.r.t. the maximal area policy. Then:*

$$\mathcal{R}el(\langle V_1, \ldots, V_k, V_{k+1} \rangle) = \mathcal{R}el(\langle V_1, \ldots, V_k \rangle) \cap \mathcal{R}el(V_{k+1})$$

Proof. Starting from the fact that $\cap$ is a commutative and associative operator, by applying its definition to a set of $k + 1$ operands we obtain:

$$\begin{aligned}
\mathcal{R}el(\langle V_1, \ldots, V_k, V_{k+1} \rangle) &= \mathcal{R}el(V_1) \cap \ldots \cap \mathcal{R}el(V_k) \cap \mathcal{R}el(V_{k+1}) \\
&= (\mathcal{R}el(V_1) \cap \cdots \cap \mathcal{R}el(V_k)) \cap \mathcal{R}el(V_{k+1}) \\
&= \mathcal{R}el(\langle V_1, \ldots, V_k \rangle) \cap \mathcal{R}el(V_{k+1})
\end{aligned}$$

$\square$

Property 3. *Let $\mathcal{R}el(\langle V_1, \ldots, V_k \rangle)$ be the partial view defined for the configuration $C = \langle V_1, \ldots, V_k \rangle$ w.r.t. the minimal area policy. Then:*

$$\mathcal{R}el(\langle V_1, \ldots, V_k, V_{k+1} \rangle) = \mathcal{R}el(\langle V_1, \ldots, V_k \rangle) \cup \mathcal{R}el(V_{k+1})$$

Proof. The proof is the same of Theorem 2 where the operator $\cap$ is replaced with $\cup$. $\square$

The next theorem extends the containment relationships between partial views of CDT context elements (see Assumption 1) to views.

Property 4. *Let $C = \langle V_1, \ldots, V, \ldots, V_k \rangle$ be a configuration and V, W two context elements such that $V \prec W$. Then:*

$$\mathcal{R}el(\langle V_1, \ldots, V, \ldots, V_k \rangle) \supseteq \mathcal{R}el(\langle V_1, \ldots, W, \ldots, V_k \rangle)$$

Proof. This result is independent of the operator used to compose partial views. Let us now consider the case of composition by means of the Double Intersection operator. According with Assumption 1, since $V \prec W$, then $\mathcal{R}el(V) \supseteq \mathcal{R}el(W)$. Hence:

$$\begin{aligned}
\mathcal{R}el(\langle V_1, \ldots, V, \ldots, V_k \rangle) &= \mathcal{R}el(V_1) \cap \ldots \cap \mathcal{R}el(V) \cap \mathcal{R}el(V_k) \\
&\supseteq \mathcal{R}el(V_1) \cap \cdots \cap \mathcal{R}el(W) \cap \mathcal{R}el(V_k) \\
&= \mathcal{R}el(\langle V_1, \ldots, W, \ldots, V_k \rangle)
\end{aligned}$$

$\square$

The view associated with a specific context can include or not some portions of the global database on the basis of (i) the width of the partial views specified during the tailoring process for each context element and (ii) the operator used to combine partial views.

The different policies that can be adopted to identify the relevant area associated with a context element impose the use of different operators for combining such partial views to obtain the final ones. These operators can be applied for two purposes: (i) to derive the view associated with a configuration, starting from the partial views, and (ii) to define the partial view associated with non-leaf nodes, as discussed for the bottom-up navigation of the Context Dimension Tree during the relevant area assignment phase.

4   Closing Remarks and Future Work

The approach presented in this paper aims at providing a semi-automatic support to view definition in a relational database scenario, taking into account various possible users, situations and interests that lead to the selection of different portions of the global schema and data. To this end, we have formally introduced a group of logical operators which allow the combination of partial views incrementally derived on the global schema.

A prototype tool has been developed to support the designer in all the phases of the methodology, from the design of the Context Dimension Tree and the *Relevant Area Assignment* to the automatic *View Composition* phase. The designer can then review the obtained views associated with the significant configurations corresponding to the application contexts, and eventually introduce modifications to fulfill her/his needs.

These operators and their application have been here presented within the relational framework; current research is focused on the extension of this methodology to other scenarios, characterized by semi-structured sources, to cope with nowadays variety of information representations.

Acknowledgements. The authors wish to thank Prof. Letizia Tanca for the helpful discussions.

References

1. Abiteboul, S.: On Views and XML. In: Proc. 18th ACM SIGACT-SIGMOD-SIGART Symp. on Principles of Database Systems, pp. 1–9. ACM Press, New York (1999)
2. Bolchini, C., Curino, C., Quintarelli, E., Schreiber, F.A., Tanca, L.: Context information for knowledge reshaping. Int. Journal on Web Engineering and Technology (to appear 2007)
3. Bolchini, C., Curino, C.A., Orsi, G., Quintarelli, E., Schreiber, F.A., Tanca, L.: CADD: a tool for context modeling and data tailoring. In: Proc. IEEE/ACM Int. Conf. on Mobile Data Management - Demo Session, May 7-11, ACM Press, New York (2007)
4. Bolchini, C., Quintarelli, E.: Filtering mobile data by means of context: a methodology. In: Meersman, R., Tari, Z., Herrero, P. (eds.). OTM 2006 Workshops. LNCS, vol. 4278, pp. 1986–1995. Springer, Heidelberg (2006)
5. Bolchini, C., Quintarelli, E.: Filtering mobile data by means of context: a methodology. In: Proc. 2nd Int. Workshop on Context Representation and Reasoning, pp. 13–18 (2006)
6. Bolchini, C., Schreiber, F.A., Tanca, L.: A methodology for very small database design. Information Systems 32(1), 61–82 (2007)
7. Cluet, S., Veltri, P., Vodislav, D.: Views in a large scale of XML repository. In: Proc. 27th Int. Conf. on Very Large Data Bases, pp. 271–289 (2001)
8. Elmasri, R., Navathe, S.: Fundamentals of database systems, 4th edn. Pearson/Addison Wesley (2004)
9. Ghidini, C., Giunchiglia, F.: Local Models Semantics, or contextual reasoning=locality+compatibility. Artificial Intellicence 127(2), 221–259 (2001)
10. Liefke, H., Davidson, S.B.: View maintenance for hierarchical semistructured data. In: Kambayashi, Y., Mohania, M.K., Tjoa, A.M. (eds.) DaWaK 2000. LNCS, vol. 1874, pp. 114–125. Springer, Heidelberg (2000)
11. Madhavan, J., Halevy, A.Y.: Composing mappings among data sources. In: Aberer, K., Koubarakis, M., Kalogeraki, V. (eds.) Databases, Information Systems, and Peer-to-Peer Computing. LNCS, vol. 2944, pp. 572–583. Springer, Heidelberg (2004)

12. McGuinness, D.L., van Harmelen, F.: OWL Web Ontology Language Overview, W3C Recommendation (2004)
13. Rajugan, R., Chang, E., Dillon, T.S.: Ontology views: A theoretical perspective. In: Meersman, R., Tari, Z., Herrero, P. (eds.). OTM 2006 Workshops. LNCS, vol. 4278, pp. 1814–1824. Springer, Heidelberg (2006)
14. Rajugan, R., Dillon, T.S., Chang, E., Feng, L.: A Layered View Model for XML Repositories and XML Data Warehouses. In: Proc. IEEE 5th Int. Conf. on Computer and Information Technology, pp. 206–215. IEEE Computer Society Press, Los Alamitos (2005)
15. Roussos, Y., Stavrakas, Y., Pavlaki, V.: Towards a context-aware relational model. In: Proc. Context Representation and Reasoning - CRR'05, pp. 7.1–7.12 (2005)
16. Stefanidis, K., Pitoura, E., Vassiliadis, P.: Modeling and storing context-aware preferences. In: Manolopoulos, Y., Pokorný, J., Sellis, T. (eds.) ADBIS 2006. LNCS, vol. 4152, pp. 124–140. Springer, Heidelberg (2006)
17. Volz, R., Oberle, D., Studer, R.: Implementing views for light-weight web ontologies. In: Proc. IEEE 7th Int. Database Engineering and Applications Symp., pp. 160–169. IEEE Computer Society Press, Los Alamitos (2003)
18. Volz, R., Oberle, D., Studer, R., Staab, S.: Views for light-weight web ontologies. In: Proc. ACM Symp. on Applied Computing, pp. 1168–1173. ACM Press, New York (2003)
19. Wouters, C., Rajugan, R., Dillon, T.S., Rahayu, J.W.R.: Ontology extraction using views for semantic web. In: Web Semantics and Ontology, pp. 1–40. Idea Group Pub., USA (2005)
20. Zhuge, Y., Garcia-Molina, H.: Graph structured views and their incremental maintenance. In: Proc. IEEE 14th Int. Conf. on Data Engineering, pp. 116–125. IEEE Computer Society Press, Los Alamitos (1998)

On the Discovery of Preferred Work Practice Through Business Process Variants

Ruopeng Lu and Shazia Sadiq

School of Information Technology and Electrical Engineering,
The University of Queensland, Brisbane, Australia
{ruopeng,shazia}@itee.uq.edu.au

Abstract. Variance in business process execution can be the result of several situations, such as disconnection between documented models and business operations, workarounds in spite of process execution engines, dynamic change and exception handling, flexible and ad-hoc approaches, and collaborative and/or knowledge intensive work. It is imperative that effective support for managing process variance be extended to organizations mature in their BPM (Business Process Management) uptake so that they can ensure organization wide consistency, promote reuse and capitalize on their BPM investments. Process variants are complex objects that contain features of different dimensions, such as variant design or variant execution data. This paper provides a technique for effective utilization of the adaptations manifested in process variants. In particular, we will present a facility for discovery of preferred variants through effective search and retrieval based on the notion of process similarity, where multiple aspects of the process variants are compared according to specific query requirements. The major advantage of this approach is the ability to provide a quantitative measure for the similarity between process variants, which further facilitates various BPM activities such as process reuse, analysis and discovery.

Keywords: Business process variants, business process similarity, process discovery, flexible workflows, business process analysis.

1 Introduction

In recent years, there have been many efforts towards providing agile business process management (BPM) support [4, 9, 11]. Business process management systems (BPMS) have been recognized as a substantial extension to the legacy of workflow management systems (WFMS). While a typical WFMS supports process design, deployment and enactment, BPMS extend WFMS functionality by facilitating *process diagnosis* activities. Process diagnosis refers to BPM activities including business process analysis (BPA) and process discovery [2]. These post-executional activities are intended to identify and resolve operational process problems, discover preferred work practices, and provide business intelligence. Furthermore, new requirements emerging from the flexibility and dynamism of business processes require support for *instance adaptation* [11], which further impacts on the design,

C. Parent et al. (Eds.): ER 2007, LNCS 4801, pp. 165–180, 2007.

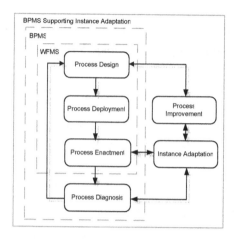

Fig. 1. The extended BPMS lifecycle supporting instance adaptation and process improvement

execution and especially the diagnosis activities of BPM, and eventually will contribute to process evolution/improvement (*cf.* Fig. 1).

Instance adaptation is an emerging paradigm due to various reasons such as the frequent change in underlying business objectives and operational constraints, and the emergence of unexpected events that cannot be handled by predefined exception handling policies [9, 11]. Consequently, the execution of process instances needs to be changed at runtime causing different instances of the same business process to be handled differently according to instance specific conditions.

The typical consequence of instance adaptation is the production of a large number of *process variants* [6, 11]. An executed process instance reflects a variant of realization of process constraints, and provides valuable knowledge of organization at the operational level. There is evidence that work practices at the operational level are often diverse, incorporating the creativity and individualism of knowledge workers and potentially contributing to the organization's competitive advantage [5]. Such resources can provide valuable insight into work practice, help externalize previously tacit knowledge, and provide valuable feedback on subsequent process design, improvement, and evolution.

Nevertheless, the way that domain experts reason about the situation during instance adaptation cannot be truly reconstructed using computational techniques. Building a repository to systematically capture, structure and subsequently deliberate on the decisions that led to a particular design is a more pragmatic way to approach the problem. We observe that a process variant at least contains information from the following dimensions:

– *Structural* dimension contains the process model based on which the process instance is executed. For a given process variant, the instance-specific process model is adapted from the design time model during instance adaptation.
– *Behavioral* dimension contains executional information such as the set of tasks involved in the process execution (may differ from structural dimension due to choice constructs), the exact sequence of task execution, the performers and their

roles in executing these tasks, the process-relevant data, execution duration of the process instance and constituent tasks.

– *Contextual* dimension contains descriptive information (annotations) from the process modeler about the reasoning behind the design of a particular process variant.

In the meantime, there are various occasions in the BPM lifecycle when precedents of process variants need to be retrieved. This is due to two main reasons. Firstly is to assist instance adaptation, *i.e.*, retrieve and reuse precedent process variants according to current runtime conditions such that the knowledge from the past under similar situation is utilized to provide reference to current process instance adaptation [5]. Secondly is to support process analysis and diagnosis, typically analyzing deviations from process models, and generalization of general process model from process variants [2]. Using appropriate analysis techniques, a collection of sufficiently similar process variants could be generalized as the preferred/successful work practice, and consequently contribute to the design of a given instance and may lead to process improvement/evolution.

In our previous work, we have developed a reference architecture for managing such process variants for effective retrieval [6, 7]. The contribution of this paper is on the approach for utilizing the retained process variants, based on a practical measure for process variant similarity. In particular, we propose a query formalization technique where the properties of process variants to be retrieved can be structurally specified. We also present a progressive refinement technique for processing the retrieval query.

An essential concept in this regard is the definition of *similarity* between process variants in terms of their features in various dimensions. In other words, how to characterize the degree of match between similar process variants. This is a hard problem in general due to the informal nature of commonly adopted process description languages, and more so due to the subjectivity in process model conceptualization. For example, questions such as how to measure the similarity between two process variants having different process models but same sequence of task execution can come forth. From the behavioral perspective two variants are equivalent since the have the same execution behavior, while are dissimilar from the structural perspective. Thus variants can share features in one dimension but be dissimilar in another dimension, making an objective evaluation of similarity rather difficult. At the same time, it is desirable that the similarity between the variants can be quantified, *i.e.*, to be able to define a metric space to indicate the degree of similarity or dissimilarity.

The rest of the paper is organized as follows. Section 2 will provide background concepts for the process variant repository (PVR). In section 3, we define the schema for process variants, based on which various types of queries and their formalization are discussed in section 4. In section 5, we propose a quantitative measure for defining process variants similarity, covering structural, behavioral and contextual dimensions. The progressive-refinement technique for query processing is discussed in section 6. Related work is presented in section 7, followed by the conclusion and future work in section 8.

2 Reference Architecture for Process Variant Repository

Process Variant Repository (PVR) provides a well-formed structure to store past process designs, as well as an instrument to utilize process variants as an information resource. The capture of executed process variants in the repository and the subsequent retrieval of preferred process variants are the two major functions of PVR.

Fig. 2 presents an overview of the PVR reference architecture. In *Step1-2* as annotated in Fig. 2, the properties of an executed process variant is retained in the repository according to the schema provided by PVR. Later, a query is formulated to specify variant retrieval requirements (*Step3*). The query requirement is formulated with the help of the query processing component. In *Step4*, variants are searched to find matching variants according to query requirements. The goal of this step is to retrieve a set of sufficiently similar process variants. In *Step5*, the best matches are selected from the set of initial matches according to the degree of similarity compared to the query. The further selection process involves a ranking process. *Step 4-5* will be repeated if a progressive refinement approach is taken, where the initial query definition is refined in order to obtain a more restrictive set of results.

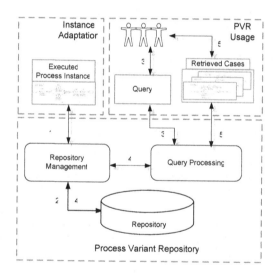

Fig. 2. Reference architecture of PVR

3 Schema of Process Variants

We consider a process variant an instance level adaptation of a business process. The creation of instance level adaptations is facilitated by flexible process execution environments [11]. In this paper, we do not focus on the flexible process management system, except to assume that each process variant in PVR could be represented by a potentially unique process model. The particular design of a variant is reflective of a knowledge worker's preferred work practice. However, (given groups of) variants are derived from a common design time process model and hence can have a significant overlap as well. In the rest of this paper, we refer to the process model as the runtime model adapted for a particular process variant. Before we present the schema of process variant, we first define two important concepts, including process model and execution sequence.

Definition 1 (Process Model). A process model *W* is a pair (*N, E*), which is defined through a directed graph consisting a finite set of nodes *N*, and a finite set of flow relations (edges) *E⊆N×N*. Nodes are classified into tasks *T* and coordinators *C*, where *N=C∪T*, and *C∩T=∅*. *Task* is the set of tasks in *W*, and *C* contains coordinators of the type {*Begin, End, Fork, Synchronizer, Choice, Merge*}, which have typical workflow semantics [13].

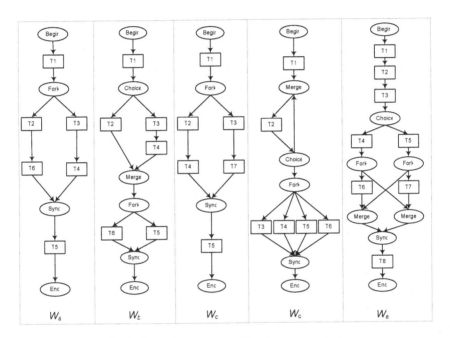

Fig. 3. Example process models of process variants

Fig. 3 presents example process models of different process variants. Suppose these process variants belong to a network diagnosis process in a Telco company, and tasks *T1,…,T8* correspond to a list of network testing activities. For example, T1 represents "*Send Test Message*", T2 represents "*Test Hub201*", and T3 "*Test ExchangeA30*" etc. In the rest of this paper, we omit the full task names for clarity. Given a process model *W* and a task *Ti∈T, Trigger(W, Ti)* denotes the set of tasks that can be triggered by task *Ti* in *W* as the result of execution. E.g., *Trigger(We, T1)={T2}*. For tasks followed by a *Fork* (*AND-SPLIT*) or a *Choice* (*XOR-SPLIT*) coordinator, we consider that all subsequent tasks after the coordinator can be triggered. E.g., *Trigger(Wa, T1)=Trigger(Wb, T1)={T2, T3}*. *Disable(W, Ti)* denotes the set of tasks disabled as the consequence of executing *Ti*, which is defined to realize the semantics of the *Choice* coordinator. For example, $Disable(W_b, T2)=\{T3\}$ and $Disable(W_b, T3)=\{T2\}$, which means either $T2$ or $T3$ is executed but not both.

The process models shown in Fig. 3 are derived from the common design time process model during instance adaptation, and hence sharing some properties in common. $E.g.$ activities consisting the process models are chosen from a fixed set of tasks $\{T1, ..., T8\}$, $T1$ is always the first task, and $T5$ is always executed after $T2$, to name a few. At the same time many differences exist as can be observed in the figure.

An $execution\ sequence$ of a process variant is referred to as the trace of execution in a process model, which reflects the actual order of task executions at runtime. Typically, a process model with parallel ($Fork$) or alternative branches ($Choice$) contains more than one possible execution sequences. For example, sequences $<T1, T2, T6, T5>$, $<T1, T2, T5, T6>$, $<T1, T3, T4, T6, T5>$ and $<T1, T3, T4, T5, T6>$ are four possible execution sequences in W_b ($cf.$ Fig. 3), since $T2$ and $<T3, T4>$ are in alternative branches, and $T5, T6$ in parallel branches. Note however that for a given process instance, there is exactly one execution sequence resulting from execution.

We follow the general mathematical definition to define an execution sequence: A finite sequence $s=\{s_1, s_2, ..., s_n\}$ is a function with the domain $\{1, 2,..., n\}$, for some positive integer n. The i-th element of s is denoted by s_i.

Definition 2 (Execution Sequence). An execution sequence s^W of a process model W is a finite sequence of tasks $T' \subseteq T$ in W, which is defined by the sequence $<T_1, T_2, ..., T_n>$, $n \geq 1$.

Note that the subscripts i of T in s^W are task identifiers, which do not indicate the order of sequence elements. Thus, we use the angle brackets "$<$" and "$>$" to denote the order in an execution sequence. For example, given $s^W=<T1, T3, T2>$, $s_1^W=T1$, $s_2^W=T3$, and $s_3^W= T2$. Note that in some process model W, it is possible that $n \geq |s^W|$, for some execution sequence $s^W=<T_1, T_2, ... , T_n>$. E.g., in W_d, a possible execution sequence is $<T1, T2, T2, T3, T4, T5, T6>$, where $T2$ has been executed twice due to the loop structure. The superscript ^{W} of an execution sequence s^W for a process model W can be omitted if no ambiguity is caused.

Besides the process model and execution sequence, the schema of a process variant should define a list of runtime properties.

Definition 3 (Process Variant). A process variant V is defined by $(id, W, s^W, R, D, T, C, M)$, where

- id is the identifier for the process variant;
- W is the process model (N, E) for V defined on the task set $T \subseteq N$;
- s^W is the execution sequence of tasks T in V based on W;
- $R=\{R_1, ..., R_m\}$ is a finite set of resource instances allocated to V;
- $D=\{D_1, ..., D_k\}$ is a finite set of process-relevant data items related to V;
- $T=\{T_1, ..., T_n\}$ is the set of tasks in V. $\forall T_i \in T$, $T_i=<n_i, r_i, T_i^-, T_i^+>$, where n_i is the identifier of T_i. $r_i \in R$ is the resource instance allocated to task T_i. T_i^- and T_i^+ are the time stamps when task T_i commenced and completed execution;
- C is an annotation that textually describes the design of the variant;
- M is the set of modeler(s) who participated in the instance adaptation for V.

The schema for process variants contains *instance level* (*id*, *W*, s^W, *R*, *D*, *C*, *M*) and *task level* features (*T*). The *id* can be combined with the variant symbol *V*, i.e., V_{10} denotes variant *V* with the feature (*id*, 10). Occasionally we omit the subscript *i* for *V* when there is no ambiguity. Each element in *V* is referred to as a *feature* of *V*. In this way, the schema of process variant is defined by a list of features from structural, behavioral and contextual dimensions. The process variant repository is the set of all collected process variants, that is $PVR=\{V_1, ..., V_n\}$.

PVR is expected to contain a large numbers of process variants. Table 1 shows some example process variants in PVR based on the graphical process models presented in Fig. 3. Only the variant *id*, process model *W* and execution sequence *s* is shown for simplicity. It is likely that many process variants can have the same process model (if the design time process model is adapted in the same way), while the execution sequences are different. For example, V_1 and V_8 have the same process model W_a, while due to instance-specific runtime conditions, the execution sequences are different. However, V_1 and V_5 have the same execution sequence although their process models differ. This observation leads to an interesting problem when defining similarity of process variants regarding *W* and *s*, which will be discussed in section 5.

Table 1. Tabular view of a typical PVR showing the first three features

id	*W*	s^W	...
V_1	W_a	$<T_1, T_2, T_3, T_6, T_4, T_5>$	
V_2	W_c	$<T_1, T_3, T_2, T_4, T_7, T_5>$	
V_3	W_d	$<T_1, T_2, T_2, T_3, T_4, T_5, T_6>$	
V_4	W_b	$<T_1, T_2, T_5, T_6>$	
V_5	W_d	$<T_1, T_2, T_3, T_6, T_4, T_5>$	
V_6	W_e	$<T_1, T_2, T_3, T_4, T_6, T_8>$	
V_7	W_e	$<T_1, T_2, T_3, T_5, T_7, T_8>$	
V_8	W_a	$<T_1, T_3, T_4, T_2, T_6, T_5>$	
...	...	...	...

4   Query Formulation

A *query* is a structural expression of search criteria representing partial or complete description for a process variant, or multiple process variants sharing similar features. Based on different retrieval requirements, a query may contain a single feature, or multiple features from the same or different dimension. For example, a multi-feature query can be to find all process variants in which *execution duration is less than 3 hours*, or *any performers of role senior engineer were involved*. Such queries can be expressed by a typical structural query language, and can mostly be satisfied using well established techniques.

Unlike traditional query systems however, the search criteria for process variants may also include reference to complex structural features. *e.g.*, task *Test Hub201 (T2) and Test ExchangeA30 (T3) were executed immediately after Send Test Message (T1), and Test Hub430 (T4) was performed in parallel with Test ServerII (T7) etc.* (cf. W_c in Fig. 3), or simply *having the same process model as given in the query*. Queries containing multi-dimension features can be *e.g.*, tasks *T1, T2 and T3 were performed* *by a senior engineer in sequence, and finished execution within 1 day (cf. W_e in Fig. 3), or having execution sequence <T1, T3, T4, T5, T6> and tasks T5 and T6 were in parallel branches in the process model (cf. W_b in Fig. 3).* We are specifically interested in providing a facility to find process variants for queries that provide complex criteria, as in the above examples.

We propose that the structural query requirement be expressed in a way that is in like with the query-by-example (QBE) paradigm, where a process model W^Q is presented in the query containing the desired structural features, and the objective is to retrieve all process variants with a process model W similar to W^Q. W^Q can resemble a *complete* process model (cf. W_a^Q in Fig. 4), which specifies the exact structure required for the process variants to be retrieved; or a *partial* process model (cf. W_b^Q in Fig. 4), which contains a fragment of the process model characterizing the desired structural features to be retrieved. Based on the above discussion, we define the schema for a query as follows:

Definition 4 (Query). Let F be the set of all features in *PVR*. A query Q is defined by the set of query features $\{F_1^Q, ..., F_k^Q\}$, where $\forall F_i^Q \in F$, F_i^Q corresponds to a feature defined in the schema of V. The function *Type* maps a query feature into one of the process variant features, *i.e.*, $Type:F \rightarrow TYPE$, where $TYPE=\{id, W, s, R, D, T, C, M\}$.

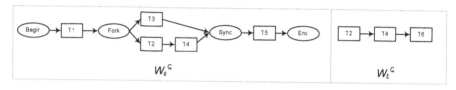

Fig. 4. Example of structural query features, W_a^Q as a complete process model and W_b^Q as a partial process model

5   Similarity of Process Variants

In order to determine the degree of match between the desired and actual process variants, the *similarity measure* is defined.

5.1   Overall Similarity

It is desirable that given a query Q with one or more query features $\{F_1^Q, ..., F_k^Q\}$, and a process variant V described by the list of features $\{F_1^V, ..., F_k^V\}$ according to the variant schema (Def. 3), applying a similarity function $Sim(V, Q)$ yields a *quantitative* figure that indicates the degree of match between V and Q. Nevertheless, each different type of feature has specific semantics, *e.g.*, the similarity measure for execution sequence and allocated resources should be different. For each different feature F_i, a similarity function $sim(F_i^V, F_i^Q)$ should be defined according to the specific semantics of F_i. The overall similarity score $Sim(V, Q)$ is the sum of the similarity score for each pair of *comparable features* (F_i^V, F_i^Q), *i.e.*, $F_i^V, F_i^Q \in F$ and $Type(F_i^V)=Type(F_i^Q)$.

We define the metric space for process variant similarity (and for each similarity function *sim*) in the interval of real numbers between 0 and 1, where 0 indicates complete dissimilarity, 1 indicates *complete* matching, and a number between 0 and 1 indicates *partial* matching. For all similarity functions *sim* defined in PVR, the following properties [15] should hold:

- *Non-negativity, i.e.,* $\forall F_i, F_j \in F, sim(F_i, F_j) \geq 0$
- *Symmetry, i.e.,* $\forall F_i, F_j \in F, sim(F_i, F_j) = sim(F_j, F_i)$
- *Reflexivity, i.e.,* $\forall F_i \in F, sim(F_i, F_i) = 1$
- *Triangle Inequality, i.e.,* $\forall F_i, F_j, F_k \in F, sim(F_i, F_k) \leq sim(F_i, F_j) + sim(F_j, F_k)$

In order to distinguish different similarity functions, we append the feature type to the function symbol *sim*, e.g., sim_F_1 denotes the similarity function defined for feature F_1.

Definition 5 (Overall Similarity). Let $Q = \{F_1^Q, ..., F_k^Q\}$, $k \geq 1$ be a query, $V = (W, s, R, D, T, C, M)$ be a process variant described by the list of feature $\{F_1^V, ..., F_k^V\}$. Let $sim\_F_i: F^V \times F^Q \rightarrow \{0, ..., 1\}$ be a similarity function for a feature type in *TYPE*. Then the overall similarity (*Sim*) between the process variant V and the query Q is given as:

$$Sim(V, Q) = \frac{1}{|Q|} \sum_{i=1}^{k} sim\_F_i \ (F_i^V, F_i^Q) \tag{1}$$

whereby (F_i^V, F_i^Q) is a pair of comparable features.

For features in behavioral and contextual dimension (including s, R D, T, C and M), the similarity function can be defined based on known techniques. For example, simple set membership can be used to compare resources specified in the query to resources utilized in the variant. Similarly, Euclidean distance can be used to define similarity between execution sequences [14]. The matching for these features is referred to as *simple matching*. Implementation detail for the similarity measure of these features is outside the scope of this paper.

5.2 Structural Similarity

As mentioned in section 4, structural feature of process variants is described by a complete or partial process model. Structural aspect is arguably the most important aspect of a process variant. Defining the similarity based on the metric space is useful for quantifying the degree of match for structural features, especially for ranking partial matching process models. At the same time, there have been several proposals [1, 14] for graph similarity matching that satisfy our metric space requirements.

Nevertheless, we argue that graph-based similarity measure alone is inadequate for determining *complex matching* involving structural features in PVR. This is primarily due to the specialized structural relationships within process graphs, *i.e.* graphs may be structurally different but semantically similar. It is desirable that the similarity of process models can be quantified to some extent, such that when the closeness of the query process model and process variant model cannot be visually observed, partial matching variants can be presented using a ranking function to produce a similarity score base on the metric space.

Furthermore, as we have discovered in section 3, it is often the case that exact matching execution sequences may result from completely different process models. While from the same process model, different execution sequences can be derived. There has been study towards the interplay between the similarity of design time process models and actual execution sequences, which advocates defining structural similarity according to typical execution behaviors as reflected by a chosen set of execution sequences [1]. According to the typical behaviors, the more 'useful' fragments of the process model are assigned more weight towards the overall structural similarity score.

Based on this observation, we propose to define the structural similarity according to both the structural and the execution behavior of the process model, *i.e.*, the execution sequence. Given the structural feature (as described by a process model) W^Q of a query Q, to retrieve all process variants V in which its process model W is similar to W^Q. Our approach is to first qualify the initial structural matches between a particular W and W^Q, based on three structural relationships, where complete and (near perfect) partial matches can be visually identified. We then apply a ranking algorithm (similarity function) for the (not so perfect) partial matching process models and produce a similarity score between each such model and W^Q (presented in section 6). As for the first step, we utilize three structural relationships [12] between W and W^Q.

Definition 6 (Structural Similarity). Let $W=(N, E)$ be the process model of a process variant V, and $W^Q=(N^Q, E^Q)$ be a query process model. W is said to be structurally *equivalent* to W^Q if $N=N^Q$ and $E=E^Q$. W is said to structurally *subsume* W^Q if $N^Q \subseteq N$, and W^Q preserves the structural constraints between nodes N^Q as specified in W. W is said to structurally *imply* W^Q if $N^Q=N$, and W^Q preserves the structural constraints between nodes N^Q as specified in W.

Additionally, if W and W^Q conform to equivalent relationship, then they also conform to subsume and imply relationship. Given a query process model W^Q, a variant process model variant W is said to be a *complete match* to W^Q if equivalent or subsume relationship holds between W and W^Q. (Imply relationship holds means near prefect partial matches.) The technique to determine complete match is by SELECTIVE_REDUCE [6], which applies graph reduction techniques to determine the match between W and W^Q. The algorithm is to *reduce* a variant W that holds the equivalent or subsume relationship with W_Q, into a structurally identical (not empty) graph as the W_Q. The rationale of the technique is to firstly eliminate from N all task nodes that are not contained in N^Q, and secondly to reduce redundant flow relations in E^Q using reduction rules. Due to the space limit, the algorithm is not elaborated further. Please refer to [6] for detailed description.

Fig. 5 shows the results of applying SELECTIVE_REDUCE to process variant models W_a to W_e (*cf.* Fig. 3) against structural query model W_a^Q (*cf.* Fig. 4). In Fig. 5, the reduced process model RW_c from W_c is structurally equivalent to W_a^Q, which is considered as a complete match.

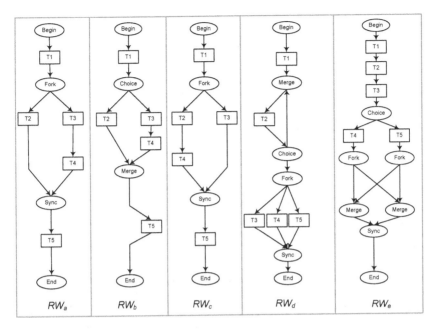

Fig. 5. Reduced process models against query feature W^Q from process variants W_a, W_b, W_c, W_d and W_e after applying SELECTIVE_REDUCE. The reduced process models consist of only tasks $\{T1, T2, T3, T4, T5\}$ as in W^Q.

6   Process Variant Retrieval

In this section, the progressive refinement approach for query execution including the ranking technique for partial matches is presented. A detail example is provided for illustrating the retrieval process for queries inclusive of all three dimensions.

6.1   Process Variant Retrieval Based on Progressive-Refinement

In the query processing approach, given a query $Q=\{F_1^Q, \ldots, F_k^Q\}$, a candidate set of process variants $CV^Q=\{V_1, V_2, \ldots, V_m\}$ is first chosen from PVR, where each $V_i \in CV^Q$ is described by a set of corresponding features $\{F_1^{Vi}, \ldots, F_k^{Vi}\}$. When a query feature $F_j^Q \in Q$ is to be compared, all $V_i \in CV^Q$ are collected according to the value of feature F_j^{Vi} which is comparable to F_j^Q. Each different F_j^{Vi} is then compared with F_j^Q. For all V_i where F_j^{Vi} is a complete match to F_j^Q, V_i will remain in the candidate set CV^Q. While for those containing partial matching features can be ranked according to the similarity score of $sim\_F_j(F_j^{Vi}, F_j^Q)$. The process variants with "the most similar" partial matching feature can also remain in CV^Q. The process variants not "similar enough" are removed from CV^Q. This process is repeated until all $F_j^Q \in Q$ have been compared, or the ideal result set is obtained. The overall similarity score can be calculated for each process variant V_i in the result set by applying $Sim(V_i, Q)$. Fig. 7 provides an illustration for this approach.

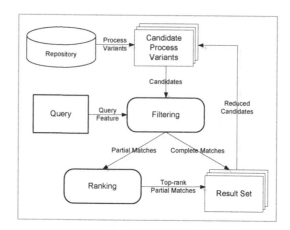

Fig. 6. Progressive-refinement query processing approach

For simple matching features, we can apply similarity function *sim* to produce a ranking for partial matches. The filtering step for complex matching involving structural features however, is to apply SELECTIVE_REDUCE, which qualifies the structural relationship between the *reduced* process variant models and the query process model, when complete matches (*equivalent* or *subsume*) and near perfect partial matches (*imply*) can be identified. The ranking step is to provide measurable result that fits in the metric space for ranking partial matches.

We have adapted the so-called *behavioral precision and recall* approach from [1] for ranking partial structural matches. The rationale of the ranking technique called RANK_STRUCTURAL, is to calculate the structural similarity between a reduced variant process model RW and the query process model W^Q with reference to the collection of all execution sequences S from partial matching variants. The two models are compared according to how well each different execution sequence fits in both models. In this way, applying RANK_STRUCTURAL for W and W^Q produces a relative similarity score with regard to rest of reduced variant models W in CV^Q.

Given the candidate set of process variants CV^Q containing *reduced* partial matching models RW and the set of all execution sequences S from CV^Q, each sequence s in S is associated with the number of appearance *count(s)* in CV^Q, and is denoted by Δ (*cf.* Table 2). The algorithm takes as inputs a reduced process variant model RW, the query process model W^Q, and Δ, and produces a similarity score *sim* between RW and W^Q with reference to Δ. Functions *Trigger* and *Disable* given in Def. 1 are utilized. The RANK_STRUCTURAL procedure is shown in Fig. 7.

TW and TQ is given the current set of triggered tasks as the result of executing task T_j in RW and W^Q respectively in step 5 and 6. For each task T_j in a sequence s, step 7 accumulates the proportion of tasks in W^Q triggered by T_j which are also triggered by T_j in RW. Step 8 accumulates the similarity score (resulting from step 7) for RW and W^Q in each sequence s, which is weighted by the number of appearance of s in CV^Q divided by the length of s. After all different sequences in Δ have been accounted for, the final similarity score is scaled according to the total number of sequences in Δ and

---

Procedure RANK_STRUCTURAL

Input RW, W_a^Q, Δ

Output sim

1. sim, $counter \leftarrow 0$

2. TW, $TQ \leftarrow \emptyset$

3. For each different sequence s in Δ

4.   For each task T_j in s, $j \leftarrow 0, \ldots, |s\text{-}1|$

5. $TW = (TW - \{T_j\} - Disable(RW, T_j)) \cup Trigger(RW, T_j)$

6. $TQ = (TQ - \{Tj\} - Disable(W_a^Q, T_j)) \cup Trigger(W_a^Q, T_j)$

7. $counter \leftarrow counter + \left(\dfrac{|TW \cap TQ|}{|TQ|} \right)$

8. $sim \leftarrow sim + \dfrac{count(s)}{|s|} \times counter$

9. $counter \leftarrow 0$

10. Return $\dfrac{1}{|\sum count(s)|} \times sim$

Fig. 7. Algorithm RANK_STRUCTURAL

returned (step 10). Note that $|TQ|$ may evaluate to 0. We postulate in such case $0/0=0$, and $1/0=0$.

The output of RANK_STRUCTURAL satisfies our metric space requirements (section 5). The complexity of the algorithm is bound by the number of tasks in W_a^Q and the number of different sequences in Δ.

6.2 Example

Suppose it is required to retrieve process variants that *any performer of role senior engineer was involved in executing a process model similar to* W_a^Q, *and its execution duration is less than 3 hours*. A query $Q=\{F_1^Q, F_2^Q, F_3^Q\}$ containing multi-dimension features is formulated. $F_1^Q=\{senior\ engineer\}$ is the resource feature. $F_2^Q=\{<3\ hours\}$ is the temporal feature derived from the task level features in T. Lastly, $F_3^Q=W_a^Q$ is the structural feature of Q, as defined by the query user.

The initial candidate set $CV^Q=\{V_1, V_2, \ldots, V_m\}$ is first chosen from PVR. $\forall V_i \in CV^Q$, $V_i=\{F_1^{Vi}, F_2^{Vi}, F_3^{Vi}\}$, where $F_1^{Vi}=role(V_i)$, $F_2^{Vi}=duration(V_i)$, and $F_3^{Vi}=W_i$. *role* is a function defined to extract the roles of performers in R for a given V. *duration* is a function giving the execution duration of V. These functions can be defined in an application-specific way, *e.g.*, $duration(V)=|T_n^+-T_1^-|$, where T_n^+ is the completion time stamp of the last task executed in W of V and T_1^- is the start time stamp of the first task in its execution sequence. We can start filtering process variants in CV^Q by F_1^{Vi}. Applying $sim\_F_1(F_1^{Vi}, F_1^Q)$ for each $V_i \in CV^Q$ the set of complete matching variants can be identified, *i.e.*, $sim\_F_1(F_1^{Vi}, F_1^Q)=1$ if $F_1^{Vi}=F_1^Q=\{senior\ engineer\}$. As we are only interested in exact matches in F_1^Q and F_2^Q, CV^Q is updated with the set of process variants having complete matching feature F_1^{Vi} (when all partial matching variants are removed from CV^Q). Similarly, CV^Q is further filtered by applying

$sim\_F_2(F_2^{Vi}, F_2^Q)$ for each remaining $V_i \in CV^Q$. Suppose $|CV^Q|{=}150$ after filtering by F_1^Q and F_2^Q, and for all F_3^{Vi} in CV^Q there are 5 common process models $\{W_a, W_b, W_c, W_d, W_e\}$ as shown in Fig. 3.

For filtering by the structural feature F_3^Q, we first aggregate all V_i in CV^Q according to F_3^{Vi}, *i.e.*, W_i (*cf.* the first two columns in Table 3). Then we apply SELECTIVE_REDUCE to each different W_i, yields reduced variant models $\{RW_a, RW_b, RW_c, RW_d, RW_e\}$ (*cf.* Fig. 5). The *equivalent* relationship between RW_c and W_a^Q is identified. As a result, for all $V_i \in CV^Q$ where $F_3^{Vi}{=}W_c$ are complete matches to F_3^Q, and the rest are partial matches. We apply RANK_STRUCTURAL to the partial matches against W_a^Q to provide the similarity ranking. The collection of execution sequences and counters Δ from all W_i in CV^Q is generated as shown in Table 2.

Table 2. The list of all execution sequences S and their counters from reduced partial matching process models which forms Δ. In this case S contains 7 different execution sequences, from 150 process variants.

s	$count(s)$
$<T_1, T_2, T_2, T_3, T_4, T_5>$	5
$<T_1, T_2, T_3, T_4, T_5>$	30
$<T_1, T_3, T_2, T_4, T_5>$	25
$<T_1, T_3, T_4, T_2, T_5>$	45
$<T_1, T_2, T_3, T_4>$	15
$<T_1, T_2, T_3, T_5>$	10
$<T_1, T_2, T_5>$	20

Table 3 shows the ranked result of applying RANK_STRUCTURAL to the each partial matches Wi against W_a^Q. A pre-defined similarity threshold[1] (*e.g.*, $sim{\geq}0.72$) may be set to define the minimal matching score. In this case, for all $V_i \in CV^Q$ where $F_3^{Vi} \in \{W_c, W_a, W_d\}$, *e.g.*, $\{V_2, V_1, V_8, V_3, V_5, \ldots\}$ remain in the final result set CV^Q.

Table 3. Similarity ranking details for reduced partial matching process models against W_a^Q

W	Variants V	structural similarity
W_c	$\{V_2, \ldots\}$	1.00
W_a	$\{V_1, V_8, \ldots\}$	0.90
W_d	$\{V_3, V_5, \ldots\}$	0.73
W_b	$\{V_4, \ldots\}$	0.71
W_e	$\{V_6, V_7, \ldots\}$	0.67

7 Related Work

The issue of managing business processes as an information resource was first brought into attention in [5], which points out that process models containing

---

[1] The similarity threshold can be determined at runtime with respect to the distribution of partial similarity ranking, or pre-determined through a variety of statistical analysis techniques from historical matching results.

constraints, procedures and heuristics of cooperate knowledge should be regarded as intellectual assets of enterprises. It is quite often nowadays that a large amount of variances are produced during business process execution. Managing such process variants and subsequently reusing the knowledge from the variants needs to be supported explicitly. In many cases, the source of these variants is the system execution log that stores event-based data for traces of different process executions. As a result, various *process mining* techniques [3] have been proposed, aiming at reconstructing meaningful process models from executional data. The reconstructed process models can then be used to facilitate a range of process redesign and auditing activities such as to compare with the design models such that the runtime behaviors such as exception handlings and derivations can be discovered and diagnosed. In addition, more specific techniques have been proposed to represent and utilize *change logs* [10] which specifically capture the events and conditions of changes and trace of modification to the process model.

The proposed approach sets apart from the process mining approach, with the emphasis on supporting knowledge acquisition and process discovery. In particular, it supports the reuse of past instances of process execution to achieve new operational goals in similar situations. Compared to a typical process execution log, the repository in PVR has a richer schema defined to provide an appropriate characterization to describe the preferred work practices represented through process variants, and subsequently facilitate processing queries with complex requirements for process variants retrieval. An essential concept in process retrieval is the definition of process equivalence, particularly regarding the structural similarity between two given process models. There have been many proposals for defining process equivalence based on single aspect, such as structural similarity [8], or (execution sequence as) behavioral similarity [14]. It has been shown that the similarity definition in structural and behavioral aspect should be combined to be a more practical approach [1]. The key distinction of our approach is to formally address the issue of process similarity with regard to process variant properties in multiple dimensions (multi-modality).

8 Conclusion and Future Work

Variations in work practice often represent the competitive differentiation within enterprise operations. In this paper we have argued for the value of variants in business process management platforms. We have focused on the process similarity concept in the scenario of managing process variants as an information resource. In particular, the presented methods provide effective means of searching and matching process variants against a given query from simple to complex aspects, and generate result sets that can be conveniently ranked, thereby empowering process designers to tap into effective precedents. The main contribution of this paper is to lay a theoretical foundation for query specification and processing for effective search and retrieval of process variants. The proposed approach is intended, but not limited to assist in dynamic instance adaptation and process discovery. In a border scope, the process variant repository (PVR) and its retrieval techniques provides reference for implementing similar functionalities in process aware information systems (PAIS).

As the foremost step in future work we plan to implement the query processing approach such that empirical evaluation for the effectiveness of the algorithm can be performed and scalability and complexity analysis can be rigorously conducted.

References

1. van der Aalst, W.M.P., de Medeiros, A.K., Alves Weijters, A.J.M.M.: Process Equivalence: Comparing Two Process Models Based on Observed Behavior. In: Dustdar, S., Fiadeiro, J.L., Sheth, A.P. (eds.) Proc. of 4th International Conference on Business Process Management (2006)
2. van der Aalst, W.M.P., ter Hofstede, A.H.M., Weske, M.: Business Process Management: A Survey. In: van der Aalst, W.M.P., H. M. ter Hofstede, A., Weske, M. (eds.) Proc. of International Conference on Business Process Management (2003)
3. van der Aalst, W.M.P., van Dongen, B.F., Herbst, J., Maruster, L., Schimm, G., Weijters, A.J.M.M.: Workflow Mining: A Survey of Issues and Approaches. Data & Knowledge Engineering 47, 237–267 (2003)
4. van der Aalst, W.M.P., Weske, M.: Case handling: a new paradigm for business process support. Data & Knowledge Engineering 53(2), 129–162 (2005)
5. Leymann, F., Altenhuber, W.: Managing Business Processes as an Information Resource. IBM Systems Journal 33(2) (1994)
6. Lu, R., Sadiq, S.: On Managing Process Variants as an Information Resource. Technical Report, No.464. School of Information Technology and Electrical Engineering, University of Queensland (2006)
7. Lu, R., Sadiq, S.: A Reference Architecture for Managing Business Process Variants. In: Proc. of 9th International Conference on Enterprise Information Systems (2007)
8. Madhusudan, T., Zhao, L., Marshall, B.: A Case-Based Reasoning Framework for Workflow Model Management. Data Knowledge Engineering 50(1), 87–115 (2004)
9. Rinderle, S., Reichert, M.: Data-Driven Process Control and Exception Handling in Process Management Systems. In: Proc. 18th International Conference on Advanced Information Systems Engineering (2006)
10. Rinderle, S., Reichert, M., Jurisch, M., Kreher, U.: On Representing, Purging, and Utilizing Change Logs in Process Management Systems. In: Dustdar, S., Fiadeiro, J.L., Sheth, A.P. (eds.) Proc. of 4th International Conference on Business Process Management (2006)
11. Sadiq, S., Sadiq, W., Orlowska, M.: A Framework for Constraint Specification and Validation in Flexible Workflows. Information Systems 30(5) (2005)
12. Sadiq, W., Orlowska, M.E.: On Business Process Model Transformations. In: Laender, A., Liddle, S., Storey, V. (eds.) Proc. of 19th International Conference on Conceptual Modeling (2000)
13. WFMC. Workflow management coalition terminology & glossary. Technical Report WFMC-TC-1011, Workflow Management Coalition (1999)
14. Wombacher, A., Rozie, M.: Evaluation of Workflow Similarity Measures in Service Discovery. In: Schoop, M., Huemer, C., Rebstock, M., Bichler, M. (eds.) Service Oriented Electronic Commerce. LNI, vol. 80, GI (2006)
15. Zezula, P., Amato, G., Dohnal, V., Batko, M.: Similarity Search - The Metric Space Approach. Springer, Heidelberg (2006)

Towards Automated Reasoning on ORM Schemes

Mapping ORM into the $\mathcal{DLR}_{idf}$ Description Logic

Mustafa Jarrar*

STARLab, Vrije Universiteit Brussels, Belgium
Department of Computer Science, University of Cyprus

Abstract. The goal of this article is to formalize Object Role Modeling (ORM) using the $\mathcal{DLR}$ description logic. This would enable automated reasoning on the formal properties of ORM diagrams, such as detecting constraint contradictions and implications. In addition, the expressive, methodological, and graphical capabilities of ORM make it a good candidate for use as a graphical notation for most description logic languages. In this way, industrial experts who are not IT savvy will still be able to build and view axiomatized theories (such as ontologies, business rules, etc.) without needing to know the logic or reasoning foundations underpinning them. Our formalization in this paper is structured as 29 formalization rules, that map all ORM primitives and constraints into $\mathcal{DLR}$, and 2 exceptions of complex cases. To this end, we illustrate the implementation of our formalization as an extension to DogmaModeler, which automatically maps ORM into DIG and uses Racer as a background reasoning engine to reason about ORM diagrams.

1 Motivation and Background

This article proposes to formalize ORM (Object Role Modeling [8]) using the $\mathcal{DLR}$ description logic. This would enable automated reasoning to be carried out on the formal properties of ORM diagrams, such as detecting constraint contradictions and implications. In addition, the expressive, methodological, and graphical power of ORM make it a good candidate for use as a graphical notation for most description logic languages. With this, non-IT trained industrial experts will be able to build axiomatized theories (such as ontologies, business rules, etc.) in a graphical manner, without having to know the underpinning logic or foundations.

ORM is a conceptual modeling method that allows the semantics of a universe of discourse to be modeled at a highly conceptual level and in a graphical manner. ORM has been used commercially for more than 30 years as a database modeling methodology, and has recently becoming popular not only for ontology engineering but also as a graphical notation in other areas such as the modeling of business rules, XML-Schemes, data warehouses, requirements engineering, web forms, etc[1].

---

* The author is currently moving from Brussels to Nicosia and soon will be affiliated only with the university of Cyprus.

[1] Many commercial and academic tools that support ORM solutions are available, including the ORM solution within Microsoft's Visio for Enterprise Architects, VisioModeler, NORMA, CaseTalk, Infagon, and DogmaModeler. DogmaModeler and its support for ontology engineering will be presented later in this paper.

C. Parent et al. (Eds.): ER 2007, LNCS 4801, pp. 181–197, 2007.

ORM has an expressive and stable graphical notation. It supports not only n-ary relations and reification, but as will be shown in this article it supports a fairly comprehensive treatment of many "practical" and "standard" business rules and constraint types. Furthermore, compared with, for example, EER or UML, ORM's graphical notation is more stable since it is attribute-free; in other words, object types and value types are both treated as concepts. This makes ORM immune to changes that cause attributes to be remodeled as object types or relationships.

ORM diagrams can be automatically verbalized into pseudo natural language sentences. In other words, all rules in a given ORM diagram can be translated into fixed-syntax sentences. For example, the mandatory constraint in section 2.3 is verbalized as: "*Each Professor must WorksFor at least one University*". The subset constraint in section 2.8 is verbalized as: "*If a Person Drives a Car then this Person must be AuthorizedWith a DrivingLicense*". Additional explanation can be found in [21] and [11], which provide sophisticated and multilingual verbalization templates. From a methodological viewpoint, this verbalization capability simplifies communication with non-IT domain experts and allows them to better understand, validate, or build ORM diagrams. It is worthwhile to note that ORM is the historical successor of NIAM (Natural Language Information Analysis Method), which was explicitly designed (in the early 70's) to play the role of a stepwise methodology, that is, to arrive at the "semantics" of a business application's data based on natural language communication.

Indeed, the graphical expressiveness and the methodological and verbalization capabilities of ORM makes it a good candidate for a graphical notation for modeling and representing ontologies and their underpinning logic.

ORM's formal specification and semantics are well-defined (see e.g. [7][26][27][5]). The most comprehensive formalization in first-order logic (FOL) was carried out by Halpin in [7]. Later on, some specific portions of this formalization were reexamined, such as subtypes[12], uniqueness[9], objectification[10], and ring constraints [8]. Since reasoning on first order logic is far complex, namely undecidable[1], the above formalizations do not enable automated reasoning on ORM diagrams, which comprises e.g. detection of constraint contradictions, implications, and inference.

In [19] and [20], we presented a reasoning approach based on heuristics (called pattern-based reasoning) for detecting the common constraint contradictions in ORM. This approach was designed to be user friendly and easy to apply in interactive modeling. It indicates not only constraint contradictions, but also a clear explanation about the detected contradictions, the causes, and suggestions on how to resolve these contradictions. Although this reasoning approach is easy to apply specially by non-IT domain experts, in comparison with DL-based reasoning, but it cannot be complete. In other words, there is no guarantee that by passing the predefined patterns, that the ORM schema is satisfiable. Please refer to [20] for more details on this approach and for a comparison (and a synergy) between the pattern-based and the DL-based reasoning mechanisms.

Enable automated and complete reasoning can only be done in description logic. This papers maps all ORM primitives and constraints into the $\mathcal{DLR}_{ifd}$ Description Logic, which is an expressive and decidable fragment of first-order logic. Our mapping is based on the ORM syntax and semantics specified in [7] and [8].

The remainder of the paper is organized as follows. In the following section, we give a quick overview about the $\mathcal{DLR}$ description logic. Section 2 presents the complete formalization of ORM using $\mathcal{DLR}$. In section 3, we illustrate the implementation of this formalization as an extension to DogmaModeler and present some related work. Finally, the conclusions and directions for future work are presented in section 4.

Remark: In this paper, we focus only on the *logical* aspects of reusing ORM for ontology modeling. The conceptual aspects (i.e. ontology modeling versus data modeling) are discussed in [15] [17] [22] [16], while a case study that uses the ORM notation can be found in [23].

The $\mathcal{DLR}$ Description Logic

Description logics are a family of logics concerned with knowledge representation. A description logic is a decidable fragment of first-order logic, associated with a set of automatic reasoning procedures. The basic constructs for a description logic are the notion of a concept and the notion of a relationship. Complex concept and relationship expressions can be constructed from atomic concepts and relationships with suitable constructs between them. The expressiveness of a description logic is characterized by the constructs it offers. The simplest description logic is called $\mathcal{FL}^-$[1], which offers only the intersection of concepts, value restrictions, and a simple form of existential quantification. In other words, a *TBox* in $\mathcal{FL}^-$ is built as a set of inclusion assertions of the following forms: $C, D \rightarrow A \mid C \sqcap D \mid \forall R.C \mid \exists R$.

In this paper, we use the $\mathcal{DLR}_{ifd}$ description logic[3], which is an extension to $\mathcal{DLR}$. $\mathcal{DLR}_{ifd}$ is an expressive description logic, and allows the majority of the primitives and constraints used in data modeling to be represented [1], including n-ary relations, identification, and functional dependencies. The basic constructs of $\mathcal{DLR}$ are concepts and n-ary relations ($n \geq 2$). Let A denote an atomic concept, and P an atomic n-ary relation. Arbitrary concepts, denoted by C in $\mathcal{DLR}$ and arbitrary relations denoted by R, can be built according to the following syntax respectively:
$$C ::= \top_1 \mid A \mid \neg C \mid C_1 \sqcap C_2 \mid (\leq k[i]R), \text{and } R ::= \top_n \mid P \mid (i/n : C) \mid \neg R \mid R_1 \sqcap R_2,$$
where n denotes the arity of the relations P, R, R_1 and R_2, i denotes a component of a relationship, and k denotes a non-negative integer. Relations in $\mathcal{DLR}$ are *well-typed*, which means that only relations of the same arity n can be used in expressions like $R_1 \sqcap R_2$ and $i \leq n$ whenever i denotes a component of a relation of arity n. The following are abbreviations: $\bot$ for $\neg \top_1$; $C_1 \sqcup C_2$ for $\neg(\neg C_1 \sqcap \neg C_2)$; $C_1 \Rightarrow C_2$ for $\neg C_1 \sqcup C_2$; $(\leq k[i]R)$ for $\neg(\leq k - 1 \ [i]R)$; $\exists[i]R$ for $(\geq 1[i]R)$; $\forall[i]R$ for $\neg\exists[i]\neg R$; and $(i : C)$ for $(i/n : C)$ if n is clear from the context.

The semantics of $\mathcal{DLR}$ is specified as follows. An *interpretation* I is constituted by an interpretation domain $\triangle^I$, and an interpretation function $.^I$ that assigns to each concept C a subset C^I of $\triangle^I$ and to each R of arity n a subset R^I of $(\triangle^I)^n$. $t[i]$ denotes the i-th component of tuple t.

$$
\begin{array}{ll}
\top_n^I \subseteq (\triangle^I)^n & \top_1^I = \triangle^I \\
P^I \subseteq \top_n^I & A^I \subseteq \triangle^I \\
(i/n : C)^I = \{t \in \top_n^I \mid t[i] \in C^I\} & (\neg C)^I = \triangle^I \backslash C^I \\
(\neg R)^I = \top_n^I \backslash R^I & (C_1 \sqcap C_2)^I = C_1^I \cap C_2^I \\
(R_1 \sqcap R_2)^I = R_1^I \cap R_2^I & (\leq k[i]R)^I = \{a \in \triangle^I \mid \sharp\{t \in R^I \mid t[i] = a\} \leq k\}
\end{array}
$$

A $\mathcal{DLR}$ *TBox* is constituted by a finite set of inclusion assertions, where each assertion has the form: $C_1 \sqsubseteq C_2$ or $R_1 \sqsubseteq R_2$, with R_1 and R_2 of the same arity. Beside these inclusion assertions in $\mathcal{DLR}$, $\mathcal{DLR}_{ifd}$ allows identification id and functional dependencies fd assertions to be expressed, which have the following form: (**id** C $[r_1]R_1, ..., [r_n]R_n$) and (**fd** R $r_1, ..., r_h \rightarrow r_j$). Furthermore, another useful extension that has been recently included in $\mathcal{DLR}$-*Lite* [2] which we shall use in this paper, is inclusion between projections of relations, which has the following form: $R_2[r_{j_1}, ..., r_{j_k}] \sqsubseteq R_1[r_{i_1}, ..., r_{i_k}]$. Inclusion, identification id and functional dependencies fd shall be explained later in this paper.

2   The Formalization of ORM Using $\mathcal{DLR}_{ifd}$

2.1   Object-Types

ORM allows a domain to be modelled by using object-types that play certain roles. There are two kinds of object-types in ORM: Non-Lexical Object-Types (NOLOT) and Lexical Object-Types (LOT). Both object-types are depicted as ellipses in ORM's notation. a LOT is depicted as a dotted-line ellipse and a NOLOT is a solid-line ellipse[2]. We represent both NOLOTs and LOTs as classes in $\mathcal{DLR}$. To distinguish between NOLOT and LOT in a $\mathcal{DLR}$ knowledge base, we introduce four classes: LEXICAL, STRING, NUMBER, and BOOLEAN. The class LEXICAL is considered to be a super-type of the other three classes, while the other three classes are considered to be disjoint. Unless specified, each LOT is mapped by default into the class STRING. We shall return to this issue later in the paper.

2.2   Roles and Relationships

ORM supports n-ary relationships, where $n \geq 1$. Each argument of a relationship in ORM is called a *role*. The examples below show binary and ternary relationships. For example, the binary relationship has two roles, $WorksFor$ and $Employs$. The formalization of the general case of an ORM n-ary relationship[7] is: $\forall x_1...x_n(R(x_1...x_n) \rightarrow A_1(x_1) \wedge ... \wedge A_n(x_n))$. $\mathcal{DLR}$ supports n-ary relationships, where $n \geq 2$. Each argument of a relationship in $\mathcal{DLR}$ is called a *component* [1]. As shown in the examples below, we represent a relationship in ORM as a relationship in $\mathcal{DLR}$; thus, a role in ORM is seen as a component of a relationship in $\mathcal{DLR}$.

For people who are familiar with ORM, the formalization of ORM roles and relationships shown in the examples seems to be trivial. However, people who are familiar with description logics may not find it intuitive. This is because, unlike ORM, the components of relationships in description logics are typically not used and do not have linguistic labels. For example, one expects to see the binary relationship in the example below represented in description logic as, $Person \sqsubseteq \forall WorksFor.University$, and $University \sqsubseteq \forall Employs.Person$. In this case, both $WorksFor$ and $Employs$

---

[2] Although they are not exactly similar, the notions of LOT and NOLOT in ORM can be, for the sake of simplicity, compared to the concepts of 'Attribute' and 'Class' in UML.

are two different relationships. This formalization requires an additional axiom to state that both relations are inverse to each other: $WorksFor \sqsubseteq Employs^-$. ORM schemes formalized in this way are not only lengthy, but also become more complex when relationships other than binary are introduced. As will be shown later, our method of formalizing ORM roles and relationships will make the formalization of the ORM constraints intuitive and more elegant. Rule-1 formalizes ORM n-ary relations, where $n \geq 2$.

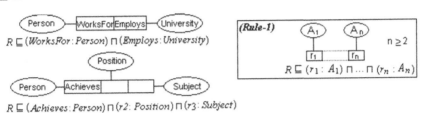

$R \sqsubseteq (WorksFor : Person) \sqcap (Employs : University)$

$R \sqsubseteq (Achieves : Person) \sqcap (r_2 : Position) \sqcap (r_3 : Subject)$

Remark: When mapping an ORM schema into a $\mathcal{DLR}$ knowledge base: Each role in the ORM schema should have a unique label within its relationship. In case a role label is null, an automatic label is assigned, such as r_1, r_2, etc. In case of a relationship having the same labels of its roles, such as $ColleagueOf/ColleagueOf$, new labels are assigned to these roles, such as: $ColleagueOf - r_1$, $ColleagueOf - r_2$. Usually, ORM relationships do not have labels; thus, a unique label is automatically assigned, such as: R_1, R_2, etc.

ORM unary roles. Unlike $\mathcal{DLR}$, ORM allows the representation of unary relations. The relationship in the example below means that a person may smoke. The population of this role is either true or false. In first-order logic, this fact can be formalized [7] as: $\forall x (Smokes(x) \rightarrow Person(x))$. To formalize ORM unary roles in $\mathcal{DLR}$, we introduce a new class called BOOLEAN, which can take one of two values: either TRUE or FALSE. Each ORM unary fact is seen as a binary relationship in $\mathcal{DLR}$, where the second concept is BOOLEAN. Rule-2 presents the general case formalization of ORM unary fact types.

$R \sqsubseteq (Smokes : Person) \sqcap (r_2 : BOOLEAN)$

2.3 Mandatory Constraints

There are two kinds of mandatory constraints in ORM: roles and disjunctive.

Role Mandatory. The role mandatory constraint in ORM is depicted as a dot on the line connecting a role with an object type. The example below indicates that, in every interpretation of this schema, each instance of the object-type Professor must work for at least one University. Rule-3 presents the general case formalization of the role mandatory constraint.

Disjunctive Mandatory. The disjunctive mandatory constraint is used to constrain a set of two or more roles connected to the same object type. It means that each instance of the object type's population must play at least one of the constrained roles. For example, the disjunctive mandatory in the example below means that each account must be owned by at least a person, a company, or both. Rule-4 presents the general case formalization of a disjunctive mandatory constraint.

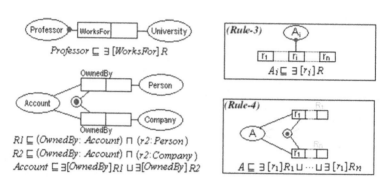

2.4   Uniqueness Constraints

We distinguish between three types of uniqueness constraints in ORM: role uniqueness, predicate uniqueness, and external uniqueness.

Role Uniqueness. Role uniqueness is represented by an arrow spanning a single role in a binary relationship. As shown in the example below, the uniqueness constraint states that, in every interpretation of this schema, each instance of a Professor must work for at most one University, i.e. each occurrence is unique. Rule-5 presents the general case formalization of the role uniqueness constraint.

Predicate Uniqueness. An arrow spanning more than a role in a relationship of arity n represents *predicate uniqueness*. As shown in the example below, the uniqueness constraint states that, in any population of this relationship, the person and subject pair must be unique together. The general case of this constraint is formalized in FOL[7] as: $\forall x_1, .., x_i, .., x_n, y (R(x_1, .., x_i, .., x_n) \wedge R(x_1, .., y, x_{i+1}, .., x_n) \rightarrow x_i = y)$. We formalize this uniqueness constraint using the notion of *functional dependency* **fd** in $\mathcal{DLR}_{ifd}$ [3], which has the form: (**fd** $R\ r_1, ..., r_h \rightarrow r_j$); where R is a relation, and $r_1, ..., r_h, r_j$ denote roles in R. The notion of functional dependency requires two tuples of a relationship that agree on the constrained components $r_1, ..., r_h$ to also agree on the un-constrained component r_j. The set of the constrained roles (on the the left-side of the **fd** assertion) uniquely determines the un-constrained role (which is on the the right side of the assertion).

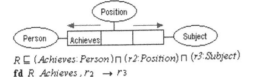

$R \sqsubseteq (Achieves: Person) \sqcap (r2: Position) \sqcap (r3: Subject)$
fd R $Achieves, r_2 \rightarrow r_3$

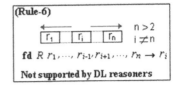

(Rule-6)

$n > 2$
$i \neq n$

fd R $r_1, ..., r_{i-1}, r_{i+1}, ..., r_n \rightarrow r_i$

Not supported by DL reasoners

Notice that our formalization excludes the following cases:

- Role uniqueness in a binary relationship: Although it is theoretically possible to use the above formalization in case of a binary relationship, we keep the formalization of this case separate (see rule-5) for implementation reasons. This is because: 1) rule-5 is supported in most description logic reasoners while rule-6 is not implemented in any reasoner yet, and 2) reasoning on functional dependencies cannot be performed on TBox only. In other words, as functional dependencies in $\mathcal{DLR}_{ifd}$ are seen as extra assertions (i.e. outside the TBox), the reasoning process to check whether the **fd** assertions are violated is reduced to ABox satisfiability. If there is no ABox, one cannot reason over the **fd** assertions.
- A single role uniqueness in an $n-$ary relationship where $(n > 2)$, since it is always a non-elementary fact type. This case is considered an illegal constraint in ORM (see [8], chapter 4), with [3] proving that it leads to undecidability in reasoning. Therefore, this case is ruled out in our formalization.

External Uniqueness. External uniqueness constraints (denoted by "U") apply to roles from different relationships. The roles that participate in such a uniqueness constraint uniquely refer to an object type. As shown in the example below, the combination of (Author, Title, Edition) must be unique. In other words, different values of (Author, Title, Edition) refer to different Books. Formalizing this constraint in description logic is possible using the notion of identity **id** in $\mathcal{DLR}_{ifd}$ [3]. In case the external uniqueness is defined on binary relationships and the common concept to be constrained is directly connected to these relations, the formalization is direct. In other cases, the formalization becomes more complex. We shall try to simplify and explain this complexity in the following.

The notion of identity **id** in $\mathcal{DLR}_{ifd}$ has the form: (**id** C $[r_1]R_1, ..., [r_n]R_n$), where C is a concept, each R_i is a relation, and each r_i is a role in R_i that is connected to C. The identity **id** in $\mathcal{DLR}_{ifd}$ states that two instances of the concept C cannot agree on the participation in $R_1, ..., R_n$ via their roles $r_1, ..., r_n$, respectively. See [3] for more details on this. In ORM, the intuition of external uniqueness is that the combination of $r_1, ..., r_n$ in $R_1, ..., R_n$ respectively must be unique. The formalization of the general case [7] of this constraint (see the figure in rule-7) is: $\forall x_1, x_2, y_1..y_n (R_1(x_1, y_1) \wedge ... \wedge R_n(x_1, y_n) \wedge (R_1(x_2, y_1) \wedge ... \wedge R_n(x_2, y_n) \rightarrow x_1 = x_2)$.

This allows one to define uniqueness on roles that are not directly connected to a *common concept*. For example, although the external uniqueness in the second example below means that the combination of {CountryCode, CityCode} must be unique, it does not tell us that the combination is unique for which concept. In other words, the notion of "common concept" is not explicitly regarded, neither in the ORM graphical notation nor in its underlying semantics [7] [9] [26]. To interpret the external uniqueness (i.e. the semantics) in this example, a join path should be performed on $R4 - R1$ and $R5 - R2$. In other words, although the notion of "common concept" does not exist in ORM, it is assumed that there must be a join path between the constrained roles. If this path cannot be constructed, then the external uniqueness is considered illegal [9], i.e. an error in the ORM schema. The construction of such join paths becomes more complex (even for human eyes) in large schemes or when objectified (i.e. reified) predicates are involved. [27] shows many cases of complex external uniqueness.

We formalize the general case of external uniqueness using the notion of **id** in $\mathcal{DLR}_{ifd}$, but we use the concept Top as the common concept C (see rule-7). As shown in the examples, the formalization (using Top) means that *any* two individuals must agree on their participation in roles: [WrittenBy]R1, [Has]R2 and [Has]R3. Although the use of the Top concept yields a simple and elegant formalization, intensive ABox reasoning may be required. In practice, we recommend using the Uniquest algorithm [27]. This algorithm is designed to compute the shortest join path connecting the constrained roles for an external uniqueness constraint, no matter what its level of complexity is. The result is a *derived relation*, which represents the shortest join path. This derived relation can then be used instead of the concept Top in rule-7.

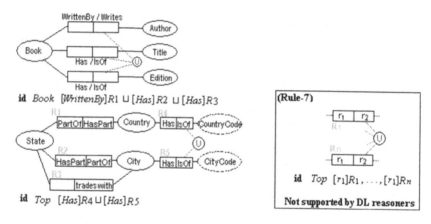

2.5 Frequency Constraints

In the following we formalize the Frequency Constraints. We distinguish between frequency constraints that span 1) a single role, which we call "role frequency" constraints, and 2) multiple roles, which we call "multiple-role frequency" constraints.

Role Frequency Constraints. A frequency constraint $(min - max)$ on a role is used to specify the number of occurrences that this role can be played by its object-type. A frequency constraint on the ith role of an n-ary relation is formalized [7] as: $\forall x[x \in R.i \rightarrow \exists^{n,m}z(R(z) \wedge z_i = x)]$. For example, the frequency constraint in the example below indicates that *if* a car has wheels, then it must have at least 3 and at most 4 wheels. We formalize this constraint by conjugating $\perp$ to the $(min - max)$ cardinality, i.e. either there is no occurrence, or it must be within the $(min - max)$ range, which is the exact meaning in ORM. Rule-8 presents the general case mapping rule of a role frequency constraint.

Multiple-role Frequency Constraints. A multiple-role frequency constraint spans more than one role (see the second example). This constrain means that, in the population of this relationship, A and C must occur together (i.e. as a tuple) at least 3 times and at most 6 times. Up to our knowledge, such a cardinality constraint cannot be formalized in description logic. However, this constraint is extremely rare in practice, [8] presents an example of this constraint and shows that it can be remodeled and achieved by a combination of uniqueness and single-role frequency constraints, which are indeed cheaper to compute and reason about. *Exception-1* presents the general case of a multiple-role frequency constraint and its formalization in first order logic [7].

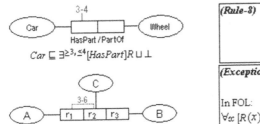

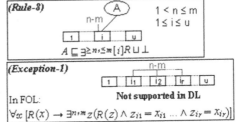

2.6 Subtypes

Subtypes in ORM are proper subtypes. For example, we say that B is a proper subtype of A if and only if the population of B is always a subset of the population of A, and $A \neq B$. This implies that the subtype relationship is acyclic; hence, loops are illegal in ORM. To formalize this relationship in $\mathcal{DLR}$, we introduce an additional negation axiom for each subtype relation. For example, (Man Is-A Person) in ORM is formalized as: $(Man \sqsubseteq Person) \sqcap (Person \not\sqsubseteq Man)$. Rule-9 presents the general case formalization of ORM subtypes. Notice that "$\not\sqsubseteq$" is not part of the $\mathcal{DLR}$ syntax. However, it can be implemented by reasoning on the ABox to make sure that the population of A and the population B are not equal.

Remark: Subtypes in ORM should be *well-defined*, which means that users should introduce some rules explicitly to define a subtype. Such definitions are not part of the graphical notation and are typically written in the FORMAL language [7]. The idea of the ORM FORMAL language is similar to the idea the OCL language for UML. For example: if one states that (Man Is-A Person), then a textual rule on Man is defined e.g. *"who has Gender='Male'"*. Since such rules are not part of the graphical notation, we do not include them in our formalization. We assume that textual rules that are not part of the ORM graphical notation are written in $\mathcal{DLR}$ directly.

Total Constraint. The total constraint ($\odot$) between subtypes means that the population of the supertype is exactly the union of the population of these subtypes (see rule-10).

Exclusive Constraint. The exclusive constraint ($\otimes$) between subtypes means the population of these subtypes is pairwise distinct, i.e. the intersection of the population of each pair of the subtypes must be empty (see Rule-11).

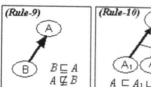
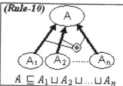
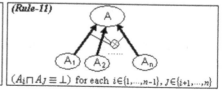

2.7 Value Constraints

The value constraint in ORM indicates the possible values (i.e. instances) for an object type. A value constraint on an object type A is denoted as a set of values $\{s_1, ..., s_n\}$ depicted near an object type, which indicate that $(\forall x[A(x) \equiv x \in \{s_1, ..., s_n\}])$ [7]. Value constraints can be declared only on lexical object types LOT, and values should be well-typed, i.e. its datatype should be either a string such as $\{'be', '39', 'it', '32'\}$ or a number such as $\{1, 2, 3\}$. Notice that quotes are used to distinguish string values from number values. As discussed earlier, if a LOT has no value constraint on it, then it is, by default, seen as a subtype of LEXICAL. If it has a value constraint, it must be a subtype of either the STRING or the NUMBER classes.

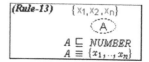

Outlook: We plan to extend our formalization of the ORM value constraint to include other data types, such as real, integer, and boolean, which are not discussed in this paper.

2.8 Subset Constraint

The subset constraint ($\rightarrow$) between roles (or sequences of roles) is used to restrict the population of these role(s), since one is a subset of the other. See the examples below. The first example indicates that each person who drives a car must be authorized by a driving license: $\forall x(x \in R2.Drives \rightarrow x \in R1.AuthorizedWith)$ [7]. If an instance plays the subsuming role, then this instance must also play the subsumed role. Rule-14 formalizes a subset constraint between two roles. A subset constraint that is declared between all roles in a relationship and all roles in another relationship implies that the set of tuples of the subsuming relation is a subset of the tuples of the subsumed relation. See the second example below. Rule-15 formalizes of a subset constraint between two relations. ORM also allows subset constraints between tuples of (not necessarily contiguous) roles as shown in rule-16, where each ith and j^{th} roles must have the same type. The population of the set of the jth roles is a subset of the population of the set of the ith roles. The FOL formalization of the general case of this constraint [7] is :
$\forall x_1...x_k[\exists y(R_2(y) \wedge x_1 = y_{i_1} \wedge ... \wedge x_k = y_{i_k}) \rightarrow \exists z(R_1(z) \wedge x_1 = z_{j_1} \wedge ... \wedge x_k = z_{j_k})]$.

To formalize this constraint in description logic, we use the recent extension to *DLR-Lite* [2] that allows inclusion assertions between *projections* of relations of the forms: $R_2[r_{j_1}, ..., r_{j_k}] \sqsubseteq R_1[r_{i_1}, ..., r_{i_k}]$, where R_1 is an n-ary relation, $r_{i_1}, ..., r_{i_k} \in \{r_1, ..., r_n\}$, and $r_{i_p} \neq r_{i_q}$ if $r_p \neq r_q$; R_2 is an m-ary relation, $r_{j_1}, ..., r_{j_k} \in \{r_1, ..., r_m\}$, and $r_{j_p} \neq r_{j_q}$ if $r_p \neq r_q$. Using this extension, any ORM set-comparison constraint formalized hereafter between two sets of (not contiguous) roles becomes direct. Rule-16 shows the subset general case.

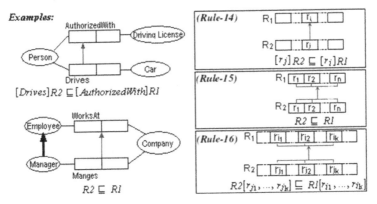

2.9   Equality Constraint

Similar to the subset constraint, the equality constraint ($\leftrightarrow$) between roles, relations, or sequences of roles is formalized in the following rules.

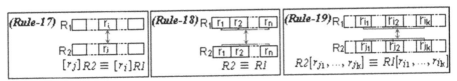

2.10   Exclusion Constraint

Similar to the subset and quality constraints, the exclusion constraint ($\otimes$) between roles, relations, or sequences of roles is formalized in the following rules.

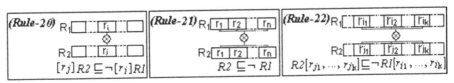

2.11   Ring Constraint

In the following we formalize the Ring Constraints. ORM allows ring constraints to be applied to a pair of roles (i.e. on binary relations) that are connected directly to the same object-type, or indirectly via supertypes. Six types of ring constraints are supported by ORM: symmetric (sym), asymmetric (as), antisymmetric (ans), acyclic (ac), irreflexive (ir), and intransitive (it).

Symmetric Ring Constraint (sym). The symmetric constraint states that if a relation holds in one direction, it should also hold on the other direction, such as "colleague of" and "partner of". R is symmetric over its population *iff* $\forall x, y[R(x, y) \longrightarrow R(y, x)]$. The example shown in rule-23 illustrates the symmetric constraint and its general case formalization in $\mathcal{DLR}$.

Asymmetric Ring Constraint (as). The asymmetric constraint is the opposite of the symmetric constraint. If a relation holds in one direction, it cannot hold on the other; an example would be "wife of" and "parent of". R is asymmetric over its population *iff* $\forall xy, R(x, y) \longrightarrow \neg R(y, x)$ The example shown in rule-24 illustrates the asymmetric constraint and its general case formalization in $\mathcal{DLR}$.

Antisymmetric Ring Constraint (ans). The antisymmetric constraint is also an opposite to the symmetric constraint, but not exactly the same as asymmetric; the difference is that all asymmetric relations must be irreflexive, which is not the case for antisymmetric. R is antisymmetric over its population *iff* $\forall xy, x \neq y \wedge R(x, y) \longrightarrow \neg R(y, x)$ (see the example in rule-25). To formalize this constraint (and some other constraints below) in description logic, we use the concept $(\exists R.Self)$ that has been introduced recently to the $\mathcal{SROIQ}$ description logic and $\mathcal{RIQ}$ [13]. The semantics of this concept simply is: $(\exists R.Self)^I = \{x \mid < x, x >\in R^I\}$. Notice that this concept is not *yet* included in the $\mathcal{DLR}$ description logic that we use in this paper. However, as [13] shows, this concept can be added without causing difficulties in reasoning. Rule-25 illustrates the antisymmetric constraint and its general case formalization.

Irreflexive Ring Constraint (ac). The irreflexive constraint on a relation states that an object cannot participate in this relation with himself. For example, a person cannot be the "parent of" or "sister of" himself. R is Irreflexive over its population *iff* $\forall x, \neg SisterOf(x, x)$. As discussed above, formalizing this constraint in description logic is also possible using the concept $\exists R.Self$. Rule-26 illustrates the irreflexive constraint and its general case formalization in description logic.

Acyclic Ring Constraint (ac). The acyclic constraint is a special case of the irreflexive constraint; for example, a Person cannot be directly (or indirectly through a chain) ParentOf himself. R is acyclic over its population *iff* $\forall x[\neg Path(x, x)]$. In ORM, this constraint is preserved as a difficult constraint. "Because of their recursive nature, acyclic constraints maybe expensive or even impossible to enforce in some database systems."[8]. Indeed, even some highly expressive description logics support notions such as n-tuples and recursive fixed-point structures, from which one can build simple lists, trees, etc. However, to our knowledge, acyclicity with any depth on binary relations cannot be represented.

Intransitive Ring Constraint (ac). A relation R is intransitive over its population *iff* $\forall x, y, z[R(x, y) \wedge R(y, z) \longrightarrow \neg R(x, z)]$. If Person X is FatherOf Person Y, and Y is FatherOf Z, then it cannot be that X is FatherOf Z. We formalize this constraint using the notion of *role-composition* in description logic. The composition of the two relations R and S (written as $R \circ S$) is a relation, such that: $R^I \circ S^I = \{(a,c)|\exists b.(a,b) \in R^I \wedge (b,c) \in S^I\}$. Hence, any composition with R itself ($R \circ R$) should not imply R, see rule-28.

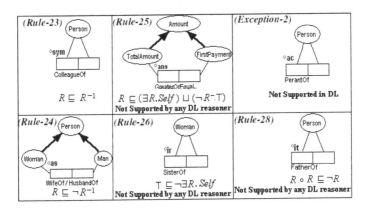

2.12   Objectified Relations

An objectified relation in ORM is a relation that is regarded as an object type, receives a new object type name, and is depicted as a rectangle around the relation. To help explain predicate objects in ORM, we use a familiar example (see figure 26 [8]). In this example, each (Person, Subject) enrollment is treated as an object that scores a rating. Predicate objects in ORM are also called objectified relationship types or nested fact types. The general case of predicate objects in ORM is formalized in [7] as: $\forall x[A(x) \equiv \exists x_1, ..., x_n(R(x_1, ..., x_n) \wedge x = (x_1, ..., x_n))]$ In addition to this axiom, it is assumed that there must be a uniqueness constraint spanning all roles of the objectified relation, although it is not explicitly stated in the diagram. This is to indicate that e.g. each person may enroll in many subjects, and the same subject may be enrolled by many persons; see [8] or the recent [10] for more details.

Predicate objects in ORM can be formalized using the notion of *reification* in $\mathcal{DLR}_{ifd}$. Reifying an n-ary relationship into a $\mathcal{DLR}_{ifd}$ concept is done by representing this concept with n binary relations, with one relationship for each role[4]. To understand this reification, one can imagine the "Enrollment" example by remodeled into two binary relations, one for the role "Enrolls" and one for the role "EnrolledBy". The new concept "Enrollment" is defined in the example below. In this definition: ($[\$1]Enrolls$ and $[\$1]EnrolledBy$) specify that the concept "Enrollment" must have all roles "Enrolls" and "EnrolledBy" of the relationship, ($\leq 1[\$1]Enrolls$ and $\leq 1[\$1]EnrolledBy$) specify that each of these roles is single-valued, and ($\forall[\$1](Enrolls \Rightarrow \$2 : Student)$ and $\forall[\$1]((EnrolledBy \Rightarrow \$2 : Subject)$) specify the object type each role belong to. The last identity **id** assertion is to specify a uniqueness constraint spanning all roles (i.e. "Enrolls" and "EnrolledBy"). Rule-29 presents the general case formalization of the objectified predicates in $\mathcal{DLR}_{ifd}$.

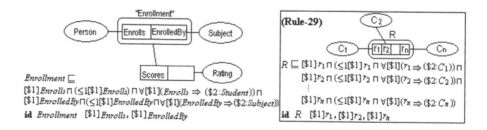

3   Implementation and Related Work

In this section, we illustrate the implementation of the formalization presented in this paper. The formalization is implemented as an extension to the DogmaModeler [15]. DogmaModeler is an ontology modeling tool based on ORM. In DogmaModeler, ORM diagrams are mapped automatically into DIG, which is a description logic interface (XML-based language) that most reasoners (such as Racer, FaCT++, etc) support. DogmaModeler is integrated with the Racer description logic reasoning server which acts as a background reasoning engine. See a screen shot of DogmaModeler below. The first window shows an ORM diagram, while the second window shows the reasoning results on this digram. The results indicate that the role "Person Reviews Book" cannot be satisfied. DogmaModeler currently implements three types of reasoning services: schema satisfiability, concept satisfiability, and role satisfiability. The other types of reasoning services that are being implemented or are scheduled to be implemented include constraint implications, inference, and subsumption. Please refer to [18] for the technical details of DogmaModeler's mapping into DIG.

The main problem we faced during the implementation is that several ORM constraints cannot be mapped into DIG; that is, these constraints were not yet supported by any description logic reasoner. Each formalization rule that could not be implemented is marked by *"Not supported by any DL reasoner yet"* in the previous section.

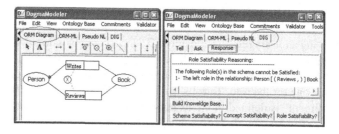

One may notice that, in the first place, we did not map ORM into OWL, the standard web ontology language. The reason is that OWL is based on a description logic called $\mathcal{SHOIN}$ [14], rather than the $\mathcal{DLR}_{ifd}$ that we use in this paper. Compared with $\mathcal{DLR}_{ifd}$, $\mathcal{SHOIN}$ does not support n-ary relations, identification, functional dependencies, and projection of relations, among other things. This implies that several ORM constraints cannot be formalized in $\mathcal{SHOIN}$, and thus cannot be supported in OWL. These constraints are: predicate uniqueness, external uniqueness, set-comparison constraints (subset, equality, and exclusion) between single roles and between not contiguous roles, objectification, as well as n-ary relationships.

Notice that without these constraints, mapping ORM into OWL becomes direct, based on our formalization. In other words, formalizing ORM using $\mathcal{SHOIN}$/OWL can be seen as a subset of the formalization presented in this paper. All formalization rules can hold for $\mathcal{SHOIN}$/OWL except {rules-6,7,14,16,17,19,20,22, and 29}. The syntax of some rules need to be modified such as Rule-1: $A1 \sqsubseteq \forall R.A2$, Rule-2: $A \sqsubseteq \forall R.BOOLEAN$, Rule-4: $A \sqsubseteq \exists R_1.C_1 \sqcup .... \sqcup \exists R_n.C_n$, etc. Actually, what DogmaModeler currently maps into DIG is what can be mapped into OWL. A DogmaModeler functionality to export OWL in this way (i.e. as a subset of ORM) will be released in the near future.

3.1 Related Work

Similar to our work, there have been several efforts to reuse the graphical notation of UML and EER for ontology modeling. Some approaches, such as [24], considered this to be a visualization issue and did not consider the underpinning semantics. Others (e.g. [25]) are motivated only to detect consistency problems in conceptual diagrams. We have found the most decent work in formalizing UML in [4], and in [1] for EER. These two formalization efforts have studied the FOL semantics of UML and EER and mapped it into the $\mathcal{DLR}_{ifd}$ description logic, which we use in this paper. It is also worth noting that the ICOM tool was one of the first tools to enable automated reasoning with conceptual modeling. ICOM [6] supports ontology modeling using a graphical notation that is a mix of the UML and the EER notations. ICOM is fully integrated with the FaCT description logic reasoning server, which acts as a background inference engine.

4 Conclusion and Future Work

In this paper, we have formalized ORM using the $\mathcal{DLR}_{ifd}$ description logic. Our formalization is structured into 29 formalization rules which map all ORM primitives and constraints, except for two complex cases (see exception 1 and 2). We have shown which formalization rules can be implemented by current description logic reasoning engines, and which can be mapped into $\mathcal{SHOIN}$/OWL. We have illustrated the implementation of our formalization as an extension to the DogmaModeler. Hence, we have explained how ORM can be used as as a graphical notation for ontology modeling with the reasoning being carried out by a background reasoning engine.

Various issues remain to be addressed. These include extending our formalization to cover more datatypes besides the String, Number, and Boolean types; implementing additional types of reasoning services, specifically constraint implications and inferencing; developing a functionality in DogmaModeler to export OWL; studying the computational complexity of ORM constraints; and last but least, is to extend the ORM graphical notation to include some description of logical notions, such as the composition of relations and intersection and union between relations.

Acknowledgment. This research was initiated during my visit to Enrico Franconi at the Free University of Bozen-Bolzano, which was funded by the Knowledge Web project

(FP6-507482). I am indebted to Enrico for his very valuable suggestions, contributions, and encouragement. I am also indebted to Sergio Tessaris, Terry Halpin, and Rob Shearer for their valuable comments and feedback on the final version of this paper. I wish to thank Diego Calvanese, Maurizio Lenzerini, Stijn Heymans, Robert Meersman, Ian Horrocks, Alessandro Artale, Erik Proper, Marijke Keet, and Jeff Pan for their comments and suggestions during this research. This research is partially funded by the SEARCHiN project (FP6-042467, Marie Curie Actions).

References

1. Baader, F., Calvanese, D., McGuinness, D., Patel-Schneider, D.N.P.: The Description Logic Handbook: Theory, Implementation and Applications. Cambridge University Press, Cambridge (2003)
2. Calvanese, D., De Giacomo, G., Lembo, D., Lenzerini, M., Rosati, R.: Data complexity of query answering in description logics. In: Doherty, P., Mylopoulos, J., Welty, C. (eds.) Proceedings of the 10th International Conference on Principles of KnowledgeRepresentation and Reasoning (KR2006), Menlo Park, California, pp. 178–218. AAAI Press, Stanford, California, USA (2006)
3. Calvanese, D., De Giacomo, G., Lenzerini, M.: Identification constraints and functional dependencies in description logics. In: Proceedings of the 17th Int. Joint Conf. on Artificial Intelligence (IJCAI2001), pp. 155–160 (2001)
4. Berardi, D., Calvanese, D., Giacomo, G.D.: Reasoning on uml class diagrams. Artificial Intelligence 168(1), 70–118 (2005)
5. de Troyer, O.: A formalization of the binary object-role model based on logic. Data and Knowledge Engineering 19, 1–37 (1996)
6. Franconi, E., Ng, G.: The i.com tool for intelligent conceptual modelling. In: 7th Int. WS on Knowledge Representation meets Databases(KRDB'00), Springer, Heidelberg (2000)
7. Halpin, T.: A logical analysis of information systems: static aspects of the data-oriented perspective. PhD thesis, University of Queensland, Brisbane, Australia (1989)
8. Halpin, T.: Information Modeling and Relational Databases. Morgan Kaufmann, San Francisco (2001)
9. Halpin, T.: Join constraints. In: Halpin, T., Siau, K., Krogstie, J. (eds.) Proceedings of the 7th International IFIP WG8.1 Workshop on Evaluation ofModeling Methods in Systems Analysis and Design (EMMSAD'02) (June 2002)
10. Halpin, T.: Objectification. In: Pastor, Ó., Falcão e Cunha, J. (eds.) CAiSE 2005. LNCS, vol. 3520, Springer, Heidelberg (2005)
11. Halpin, T., Curland, M.: Automated verbalization for orm 2. In: Meersman, R., Tari, Z. (eds.). OTM 2006 Workshops, Springer, Heidelberg (2006)
12. Halpin, T., Proper, E.: Subtyping and polymorphism in object-role modelling. Data and Knowledge Engineering 15(3), 251–281 (1995)
13. Horrocks, I., Kutz, O., Sattler, U.: The even more irresistible $\mathcal{SROIQ}$. In: Proceeding of the 10th International Conference on Principles of Knowledge Representation and Reasoning (KR 2006) (2006)
14. Horrocks, I., Sattler, U., Tobies, S.: Practical reasoning for expressive description logics. In: Ganzinger, H., McAllester, D., Voronkov, A. (eds.) LPAR 1999. LNCS, vol. 1705, pp. 161–180. Springer, Heidelberg (1999)
15. Jarrar, M.: Towards Methodological Principles for Ontology Engineering. PhD thesis, Vrije Universiteit Brussel, Brussels, Belgium (May 2005)

16. Jarrar, M.: Towards the notion of gloss, and the adoption of linguistic resources informal ontology engineering. In: Proceedings of the 15th international conference on World Wide Web (WWW2006), May 2006, pp. 497–503. ACM Press, New York (2006)

17. Jarrar, M., Demey, J., Meersman, R.: On using conceptual data modeling for ontology engineering. Journal on Data Semantics (Special issue on Best papers from the ER/ODBASE/COOPIS2002 Conferences) 2800, 185–207 (2003)

18. Jarrar, M., Eldammagh, M.: Reasoning on orm using racer. Technical report, Vrije Universiteit Brussel, Brussels, Belgium (August 2006)

19. Jarrar, M., Heymans, S.: Unsatisfiability reasoning in orm conceptual schemes. In: Illarramendi, A., Srivastava, D. (eds.) Proceeeding of International Conference on Semantics of a Networked World, Munich, Germany, March 2006, vol. LNCS, Springer, Heidelberg (2006)

20. Jarrar, M., Heymans, S.: On pattern-based ontological reasoning. International Journal on Artificial Intelligence Tools (2007)

21. Jarrar, M., Keet, M., Dongilli, P.: Multilingual verbalization of orm conceptual models and axiomatized ontologies. Technical report, Vrije Universiteit Brussel, Brussels, Belgium (February 2006)

22. Jarrar, M., Meersman, R.: Formal ontology engineering in the dogma approach. In: Meersman, R., Tari, Z. (eds.). OTM 2002. LNCS, vol. 2519, pp. 1238–1254. Springer, Heidelberg (2002)

23. Jarrar, M., Verlinden, R., Meersman, R.: Ontology-based customer complaint management. In: Meersman, R., Tari, Z. (eds.). OTM 2003 Workshops. LNCS, vol. 2889, pp. 594–606. Springer, Heidelberg (2003)

24. Cranefield, P.S., Hart, L., Dutra, M., Baclawski, K., Kokar, M., Smith, J.: Uml for ontology development. Knowl. Eng. Rev. 17(1), 61–64 (2002)

25. Simmonds, J., Bastarrica, M.C.: A tool for automatic uml model consistency checking. In: Proceedings of the 20th IEEE/ACM international Conference on Automated softwareengineering, pp. 431–432. ACM Press, New York (2005)

26. van Bommel, P., ter Hofstede, A.H.M., van der Weide, T.P.: Semantics and verification of object-role models. Information Systems 16(5), 471–495 (1991)

27. van der Weide, T.P., ter Hofstede, A.H.M., van Bommel, P.: Uniquest: determining the semantics of complex uniqueness constraints. Comput. J. 35(2), 148–156 (1992)

From Declarative to Imperative UML/OCL Operation Specifications

Jordi Cabot

Estudis d'Informàtica, Multimèdia i Telecomunicació, Universitat Oberta de Catalunya
Rbla. Poblenou 156. E08018 Barcelona, Spain
jcabot@uoc.edu

Abstract. An information system maintains a representation of the state of the domain in its Information Base (IB). The state of the IB changes due to the execution of the operations defined in the behavioral schema. There are two different approaches for specifying the effect of an operation: the imperative and the declarative approaches. In conceptual modeling, the declarative approach is preferable since it allows a more abstract and concise definition of the operation effect and conceals all implementation issues. Nevertheless, in order to execute the conceptual schema, declarative specifications must be transformed into equivalent imperative ones.

Unfortunately, declarative specifications may be non-deterministic. This implies that there may be several equivalent imperative versions for the same declarative specification, which hampers the transformation process. The main goal of this paper is to provide a pattern-based translation method between both specification approaches. To facilitate the translation we propose some heuristics that improve the precision of declarative specifications and help avoid non-determinism in the translation process.

1 Introduction

A Conceptual Schema (CS) must include the definition of all relevant static and dynamic aspects of the domain [12]. Static aspects are collected in structural diagrams. Dynamic aspects are usually specified by means of a behavioral schema consisting of a set of system operations [14] (also known as domain events [19]) that the user may execute to query and/or modify the information modeled in the structural diagram. Without loss of generality, in this paper we assume that structural diagrams are expressed using object-oriented UML class diagrams [21] and that operations are specified in OCL [20].

There are two different approaches for specifying an operation effect: the *imperative* and the *declarative* approaches [28]. In an imperative specification, the conceptual modeler explicitly defines the set of structural events to be applied over the Information Base (IB). The IB is the representation of the state of the domain in the information system. A structural event is an elementary change (insertion of a new object, update of an attribute,...) over the population of the IB.

In a declarative specification, a contract for each operation must be provided. The contract consists of a set of pre and postconditions. A precondition defines a set of

C. Parent et al. (Eds.): ER 2007, LNCS 4801, pp. 198–213, 2007.
© Springer-Verlag Berlin Heidelberg 2007

conditions on the operation input and the IB that must hold when the operation is issued while postconditions state the set of conditions that must be satisfied by the IB at the end of the operation. In conceptual modeling, the declarative approach is preferable since it allows a more abstract and concise definition of the operation effect and conceals all implementation issues [28].

CSs must be executable in the production environment (either by transforming them into a set of software components or by the use of a virtual machine) [18]. To be executable, we must translate declarative behavior specifications into equivalent imperative ones.

The main problem hindering this translation is that declarative specifications are *underspecifications* [28] (also called non-deterministic), that is, in general there are several possible states of the IB that satisfy the postcondition of an operation contract. This implies that a declarative specification may have several equivalent imperative versions. We have a different version for each set of structural events that, given a state of the IB satisfying the precondition, evolve the IB to one of the possible states satisfying the postcondition.

The definition of a postcondition precise enough to characterize a single state of the IB is cumbersome and error-prone [4,26]. For instance, it would require specifying in the postcondition all elements not modified by the operation. There are other ambiguities too. Consider a postcondition as $o.at_1=o.at_2+o.at_3$, where o represents an arbitrary object and at_1, at_2 and at_3 three of its attributes. Given an initial state s of the IB, states s' obtained after assigning to at_1 the value of $at_2 + o.at_3$ satisfy the postcondition. However, states where at_2 is changed to hold the $o.at_1 - o.at_3$ value or where, for instance, a zero value is assigned to all three attributes satisfy the postcondition as well. Strictly speaking, all three interpretations are correct (all satisfy the postcondition), though, most probably, only the first one represents the behavior the conceptual modeler meant when defining the operation.

In this sense, the main contribution of this paper is twofold:

1. We present several heuristics to clarify the interpretation of declarative operation specifications. We believe these heuristics represent usual modelers' assumptions about how the operation contracts should be interpreted when implementing the operations.
2. We define a set of patterns that use these heuristics in order to automatically translate an operation contract into a corresponding imperative operation specification.

As far as we know ours is the first method addressing the translation of UML/OCL operation contracts. Note that the high expressiveness of both languages increases the complexity of the translation process. We believe that the results of our method permit to leverage current model-driven development methods and tools by allowing code-generation from declarative specifications, not currently provided by such methods. Our translation is useful to validate the specification of the operations as well. After defining the operation contract, conceptual modelers could check if the corresponding imperative version reflects their aim and refine the contract otherwise.

The rest of the paper is organized as follows. Section 2 introduces the running example and some basic UML and OCL definitions. Section 3 presents our set of heuristics and Section 4 the list of translation patterns. Section 5 covers some inherently ambiguous declarative specifications. Section 6 sketches some implementation issues. Finally, Section 7 compares our approach with related work and Section 8 presents some conclusions and further research.

2 Running Example

As a running example throughout the rest of the paper we will use the CS of Fig. 1 aimed at (partially) representing a simple e-commerce application. This CS is expressed by means of a UML class diagram [21]. Class diagrams consist of a set of classes (i.e. entity types) related by means of a set of associations (i.e. relationship types). Reified relationship types are called association classes in UML. Class instances are referred to as *objects* while association instances are known as *links*.

The CS contains information on sales (class *Sale*) and the products they contain (class *Product* and association class *SaleLine*). Sales are delivered in a single shipment (class *Shipment* and association *DeliveredIn*) but shipments may include several sales.

The CS includes also the contract of the *replanShipment* operation. This operation checks if shipments to be delivered soon have all their sales ready and replan them otherwise. The operation behavior is specified in OCL [20]. OCL is a formal high-level language used to write expressions on UML models. OCL admits several powerful constructs like iterators (*forAll, exists,…*) and operations over collections of objects (*union, select,…*). In OCL the implicit parameter *self* refers to the object over which the operation is applied. The dot notation is used to access the attributes of an object or to navigate from that object to the associated objects in a related class (the related class is identified by its role name in the association or the own class name when the name is not ambiguous).

For instance, in the precondition the expression *self.shippingDate* returns the value of the *shippingDate* attribute while *self.sale* returns the sales delivered in the shipment represented by the *self* variable. The *exist* iterator applied over this set of sales returns true if at least one sale satisfies the expression *not readyForShipment*.

In the postcondition we specify that there are two different ways of replanning the shipment depending on the value of the *urgent* attribute. We may either simply postpone the shipment until the new date given as an input (when it is not urgent) or to generate a new shipment to hold the sales that are not ready yet (and proceed with the usual shipment for the remaining ones). The expression *sh1.oclIsNew()* indicates that in the final state a new object (represented by the variable *sh1*) must exist and *sh1.oclIsTypeOf(Shipment)* indicates that this object must be instance of *Shipment*. The *includesAll* expression determines that shipment *sh1* must contain all non-ready sales (computed with the expression *self.sale@pre->select(not readyForShipment)*, where @pre indicates that *self.sale* is evaluated in the previous state, that is, in the state of the IB at the beginning of the operation execution), and so forth.

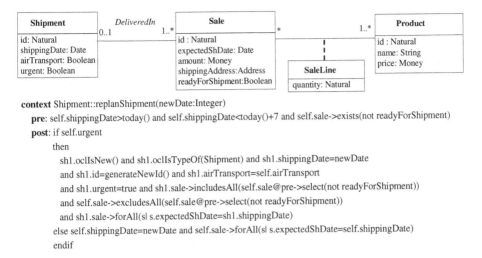

context Shipment::replanShipment(newDate:Integer)
    pre: self.shippingDate>today() and self.shippingDate<today()+7 and self.sale->exists(not readyForShipment)
    post: if self.urgent
        then
            sh1.oclIsNew() and sh1.oclIsTypeOf(Shipment) and sh1.shippingDate=newDate
            and sh1.id=generateNewId() and sh1.airTransport=self.airTransport
            and sh1.urgent=true and sh1.sale->includesAll(self.sale@pre->select(not readyForShipment))
            and self.sale->excludesAll(self.sale@pre->select(not readyForShipment))
            and sh1.sale->forAll(s| s.expectedShDate=sh1.shippingDate)
        else self.shippingDate=newDate and self.sale->forAll(s| s.expectedShDate=self.shippingDate)
        endif

Fig. 1. Our running example

3   Interpreting Declarative Specifications: A Heuristic Approach

Given the contract of an operation *op* and an initial state *s* of an IB (where *s* verifies the precondition of *op*) there exist, in general, a set of final states $set_{s'}$ that satisfy the postcondition of *op*. All implementations of *op* leading from *s* to a state *s'* ∈ $set_{s'}$ must be considered correct. Obviously, *s'* must also be consistent with all integrity constraints in the schema, but, assuming a strict interpretation of operation contracts [24], the verification of those constraints need not to be part of the contract of *op*.

Even though, strictly speaking, all states in $set_{s'}$ are correct, only a small subset $acc_{s'} \subset set_{s'}$ would probably be accepted as such by the conceptual modeler. The other states satisfy the postcondition but do not represent the behavior the modeler had in mind when defining the operation. In most cases $|acc_{s'}| = 1$ (i.e. from the modeler point of view there exists a single state *s'* that really "satisfies" the postcondition).

The first aim of this section is to detect some common OCL operators and expressions that, when appearing in a postcondition, increase the cardinality of $set_{s'}$, that is, the expressions that cause an ambiguity problem in the operation contract. We also consider the classical *frame problem*, which, roughly, appears because postconditions do not include all necessary conditions to state which parts of the IB cannot be modified during the operation execution. Obviously, some of the problems could be avoided by means of reducing the allowed OCL constructs in the contracts but we will assume in the paper that this is not an acceptable solution.

Ideally, once the conceptual modeler is aware of the ambiguities appearing in an operation *op*, he/she should define the postcondition of *op* precise enough to ensure that $acc_{s'} = set_{s'}$. However, this would require specifying the possible state of every single object and link in the new IB state which is not feasible in practice [4,26].

Therefore, the second aim of this section is to provide a set of heuristics that try to represent common assumptions used during the specification of operation contracts. Each heuristic disambiguates a problematic expression *exp* that may appear in a postcondition. The ambiguity is solved by providing a default interpretation for *exp* that identifies, among all states satisfying *exp*, the one that, most probably, represents what the modeler meant when defining *exp*.

With these heuristics, modelers do not need to write long and cumbersome postconditions to clearly specify the expected behavior of the operation. They can rely on our heuristic to be sure that, after the operation execution, the new state will be the one they intended. Our heuristics have been developed after analyzing many examples of operation contracts of different books, papers and, specially, two case studies ([11] and [23]) and comparing them, when available, with the operation textual description. Due to lack of space we cannot provide herein the list of examples we have examined.

In what follows we present our set of heuristics and discuss their application over our running example.

3.1 List of Heuristics

Each heuristic may target different OCL expressions. Note that other OCL expressions can be transformed into the ones tackled here by means of first preprocessing them using the rules presented in [8]. In the expressions, capital letters *X*, *Y* and *Z* represent arbitrary OCL expressions of the appropriate type (boolean, collection,...). The letter *o* represents an arbitrary object. The expression $r_1.r_2...r_{n-1}.r_n$ represents a sequence of navigations through roles $r_1..r_n$.

Heuristic 1: Nothing else changes

-   OCL expressions: –
-   Ambiguity: Possible values for objects and links not referenced in the postcondition are left undefined.
-   Default interpretation: Objects not explicitly referenced in the postcondition should remain unchanged in the IB (they cannot be created, updated or deleted during the transition to the new IB state). Links not traversed during the evaluation of the postcondition cannot be created nor deleted. Besides, for those objects that do appear in the postcondition, only those attributes or roles mentioned in the postcondition may be updated.

Heuristic 2: The order of the operands matters

-   OCL expressions: $X.a=Y$ (and in general any OCL binary operation)
-   Ambiguity: There are three kinds of changes over an initial state resulting in a new state satisfying the above equality expression. We can either assign the value of expression *Y* to *a*, assign *a* to *Y* or assign to *a* and *Y* an alternative value *c*. In $X.a$, *a* represents an attribute or role of the objects returned by *X*.
-   Default interpretation: In the new state *a* must have taken the value of *b*. Otherwise (that is, if the modeler's intention was to define that *b* should take the value of *a*) he/she would have most probably written the expression as $Y.b = X.a$.
    Note that if either operand is a constant value or is defined with the *@pre* operator (referring to the value of the operand in the previous state) just a possible final state exists because the only possible change is to assign its value

to the other operand (as usual, we assume that the previous state cannot be modified). This applies also to other ambiguities described in this section.

Heuristic 3: Do not falsify the *if* clause

- OCL expressions: *if X then Y else Z | X implies Y*
- Ambiguity: Given an *if-then-else* expression included in a postcondition p, there are two groups of final states that satisfy p: 1 – States where the *if* and the *then* condition are satisfied or 2 – States where the *if* condition is false while the *else* condition evaluates to true. Likewise with expressions using *implies*.
- Default interpretation: To evaluate X and enforce Y or Z depending on the true value of X. Implementations of the operation that modify X to ensure that X evaluates to false are not acceptable (even if, for some states of the IB, it could be easier to falsify X in order to always avoid enforcing Y).

Heuristic 4: Change only the last navigation in a navigation chain

- OCL expressions: $X.r_1.r_2...r_{n-1}.r_n=Y$ (or any other operation over objects at r_n)
- Ambiguity: This expression may be satisfied in the final state by adding/removing links to change the set of objects obtained when navigating from r_{n-1} to r_n, by changing any intermediate role navigation r_i or by changing the value of Y.
- Default interpretation: To add/remove the necessary links on the association traversed during the last navigation $(r_{n-1}.r_n)$ in the navigation chain.

Heuristic 5: Minimum insertions over the *includer* collection and no changes on the *included* one

- OCL expressions: X->*includesAll(Y)* | X->*includes(o)*
- Ambiguity: All final states where, at least, the objects in Y (or o) have been included in X satisfy these expressions. However, states that, apart from those objects, add other objects to X also satisfy them as well as states where Y evaluates to an empty set (or o is null) since by definition all collections include the empty collection.
- Default interpretation: The new state s' should be obtained by means of adding to the initial state s the minimum number of links needed to satisfy the expression, that is, a maximum of Y->*size()* links must be created (just one for *includes* expressions). States including additional insertions are not acceptable and neither states where Y is modified to ensure that it returns an empty result.

Heuristic 6: Minimum deletions from the *excluder* collection and no changes on the *excluded* one

- OCL expressions: X->*excludesAll(Y)* | X->*excludes(o)*
- Ambiguity: All final states where, at least, the objects in Y (or o) have been removed from the collection of objects returned by X satisfy these expressions. However, states that, apart from those objects, remove other objects from X also satisfy them as well as states where Y evaluates to an empty set (or o is null) since then, clearly, X excludes all objects in Y.

- Default interpretation: The desired behavior is the one where the new state s' is obtained by means of removing from the initial state s the minimum number of links required to satisfy the expression and where Y has not been modified to ensure that it returns an empty set. Therefore, in s' a maximum of Y->$size()$ links may be deleted (or just one, for *excludes* expressions).

Heuristic 7: Do not empty the source collection of iterator expressions

- OCL expressions: X ->$forAll(Y)$ (and, in general, all other iterator expressions)
- Ambiguity: There are two possible approaches to ensure that a *forAll* expression is satisfied in the new state of the IB. We can either ensure that all elements in X verify the Y condition or to ensure that X results in an empty collection since a *forAll* iterator over an empty set always returns *true*.
- Default interpretation: To ensure that all elements in X verify Y (and not to force X to be empty).

Heuristic 8: Minimum number of object specializations

- OCL expressions: *o.oclIsTypeOf(Cl)* | *o.oclIsKindOf(Cl)*
- Ambiguity: These expressions require o to be instance of class Cl (or instance of a subtype of Cl when using *oclIsKindOf*). Therefore, new states where Cl is added to the list of classes that o is an instance of satisfy the expression. However, states where additional classes have been added or removed from o (assuming multiple classification) satisfy the expression as well.
- Default interpretation: The object o should only be specialized to Cl during the transition to the new state.

Heuristic 9: Minimum number of object generalizations

- OCL expressions: *not o.oclIsTypeOf(Cl)* | *not o.oclIsKindOf(Cl)*
- Ambiguity: These expressions establish that, in the new state, o cannot be an instance of Cl (for *oclIsTypeOf* expressions) or an instance of Cl subtypes (for *oclIsKindOf* expressions). Therefore all states verifying this condition are valid even if they add/remove other classes from the list of classes where o belongs.
- Default interpretation: The object o should only be generalized to a supertype of Cl. If Cl has no supertypes, o must be completely removed from the IB.

3.2 Interpretation of *ReplanShipment* Using Our Heuristics

The expected behavior of *replanShipment* explained in Section 2 is just one of the (many) possible interpretations of *replanShipment* that satisfy its postcondition. Our heuristics prevent these alternative interpretations and ensure the described behavior.

As an example, heuristic 3 discards states where the value of the *urgent* attribute has been set to false (for instance, to avoid creating the new shipment), heuristic 2 ensures that variable *sh1* is initialized with the values of the *self* variable (and not the other way around), heuristic 7 discards states where the expression *self.sale->forAll* is satisfied by means of removing all sales from *self* and so forth.

4 Patterns for a Declarative to Imperative Translation

Given a declarative specification of an operation *op* with a contract including a precondition *pre* and a postcondition *post*, the generated imperative specification for *op* follows the general form:

$$op(param_1...param_n) \{ [if pre then] translate(post) [endif] \}$$

where *translate(post)* is the (recursive) application of our translation patterns over *post*. Testing the precondition is optional. Although usually added in object-oriented programming (*defensive programming* approach), it can be regarded as a redundant check [17] (the client should be responsible for calling *op* only when *pre* is satisfied).

The main purpose of our translation patterns is to draw from the postcondition definition a *minimal* set of structural events that, when applied over an initial state of the IB (that satisfies the precondition), reach a final state that verifies the postcondition. A set of structural events is minimal if no proper subset suffices to satisfy the postcondition [29].

When facing ambiguous OCL expressions, our patterns use the previous heuristics to precisely determine the characteristics of the desired final state and generate the needed structural events accordingly. This ensures that the final state, apart from satisfying the postcondition, is acceptable from the modeler's point of view. Getting rid of ambiguities also guarantees the determinism of the translation process.

As a result, the translation produces an imperative specification of the initial operation that could be used as an input for model-driven development tools in order to (automatically) generate its implementation in a given technology platform.

For the sake of simplicity we focus on the generation of the modifying structural events. We do not provide a translation for queries appearing in the postcondition into a set of primitive *read* events. Since queries do not modify the state of the IB, their translation is straightforward (and, in fact, most imperative languages for UML models allow expressing queries in OCL itself or in some similar language, see [16]).

For each pattern we indicate the OCL expression/s targeted by the pattern and its corresponding translation into a set of structural events. Our patterns do not address the full expressivity of the OCL but suffice to translate most usual OCL expressions appearing in postconditions. Additional OCL expressions can be handled with our method if they are first transformed (i.e. *simplified*) into equivalent OCL expressions (using the transformation rules presented in [8]) covered by our patterns.

4.1 Structural Events in the UML

The set of structural events allowed in UML behavior specifications is defined in the UML metamodel *Actions* packages [21] (structural events are called *actions* in the UML). The list of supported events[1] is the following:

- *CreateObject(Class c)*: It creates a new instance of *c*. This new instance is returned as an output parameter.
- *DestroyObject(Object o)*: It removes *o* from the IB. Optionally, we may indicate in the event that all links where *o* participated must be removed as well.

---

[1] For the sake of clarity, we distinguish between events over attributes and events over association ends (i.e. roles). UML unifies both concepts under the notion of *structural feature*.

- *AddAttributeValue(Attribute at, Object o, Object value)*: It adds *value* to the list of values for the attribute *at* of *o* (attributes may be multivalued in UML)
- *RemoveAttributeValue(Attribute at, Object o)*: It removes all values of attribute *at* in object *o*.
- *CreateLink(Association a, Object o_1, ..., Object o_n)*: It creates a new link for the association *a* relating objects $o_1..o_n$.
- *CreateLinkObject(Association a, Object o_1, ..., Object o_n)*: It creates a new link object (i.e. an association class instance) in *a* relating objects $o_1..o_n$.
- *DestroyLink(Association a, Object o_1, ..., Object o_n)*: It removes from *a* the link (or link object) between objects $o_1..o_n$.
- *RemoveLinkValue(AssociationEnd ae, Object o)*: It removes from *o* the values of the association end (i.e. role) *ae*. This event removes all links of the association *ae.association* (that returns, according to the UML metamodel, the association where *ae* belongs) where *o* participates.
- *ReclassifyObject(Object o, Class[] newClasses, Class[] oldClasses)*: It adds to the list of classes of *o* the classes specified in *newClasses* and removes those in *oldClasses*. Note that this event permits performing several generalizations and specializations at the same time.

Table 1. List of patterns. Column *N* indicates the pattern number. *Expression* describes the OCL expression targeted by each pattern and *Translation* the imperative code excerpt generated for it. In the patterns, B_i stands for a boolean expression, *o* for an object variable and *X* and *Y* for two arbitrary OCL expressions of the appropriate type. *o.r* represents a navigation from *o* to the associated objects in the related class playing the role *r*.

N	Expression	Translation	Description
1	B_1 and ... and B_n	Translate(B_1); ... Translate(B_n);	A set of boolean expressions linked by ANDs are transformed by translating each single expression sequentially.
2	if B_1 then B_2 else B_3	if B_1 then Translate(B_2); else Translate(B_3);	We translate both B_2 and B_3 and execute them depending on the evaluation of B_1 (according to heuristic 3, a translation trying to falsify B_1 is not acceptable).
3	o.at=Y (where at is a univalued attribute)	RemoveAttributeValue(at,o); AddAttributeValue(at,o,Y);	We assign to the attribute *at* of *o* the value *Y*. The previous value is removed. Following heuristic 2, *Y* cannot be modified.
4	o.at=Y (where at is multivalued)	RemoveAttributeValue (at,o); foreach val in Y do AddAttributeValue(at,o,val); endfor;	First, all previous values of *o.at* are removed. Then we assign one of the values of *Y* to each slot of *at*.
5	o.r = Y (where r is a role with a '1' max multiplicity)	RemoveLinkValue(r,o); CreateLink(r.association, o,Y);	A new link relating *o* and *Y* in the association *r.association* is created (*r.association* retrieves the association where *r* belongs to).
6	o.r=Y (when o. r may return many objects)	RemoveLinkValue (r,o); foreach o' in Y do CreateLink(r.association,o,o'); endfor;	We create a new link between *o* and each object in Y.

Table 1. (*continued*)

8	X->forAll(Y)	*foreach o in X do* *if not (o.Y) then Translate(o.Y)* *endif;* *endfor;*	We ensure that each element affected by the *forAll* iterator verifies the Y condition. According to heuristic 7, objects included in X cannot be removed.
9	o.oclIsNew() and o.oclIsTypeOf(Cl)	o:=CreateObject(Cl);	The translation creates a new object of type Cl. This new object is stored in the original postcondition variable. If Cl is an association class *CreateLinkObject* is used instead.
10	o.oclIsNew() and Cl.allInstances()-> includes(c)		
11	not o.oclIsTypeOf(OclAny)	DestroyObject (o);	o is deleted from the IB. This event deletes also all links where o participates. (*OclAny* is the common supertype of all classes in an UML model).
12	not o.oclIsKindOf(Cl) (Cl has no supertypes)		
13	Cl.allInstances() ->excludes(o) (Cl has no supertypes)		
14	o.oclIsTypeOf(Cl)	ReclassifyObject(o,Cl,Cl.generalization.specific);	The class Cl is added to o. Moreover, if Cl has subtypes (retrieved using the navigation *generalization.specific* of the UML metamodel) these subtypes must be removed from o (*oclIsTypeOf* is satisfied iff Cl and the type of o coincide).
15	o.oclIsKindOf(Cl)	ReclassifyObject(o,Cl,[]);	Cl is added to the list of classes of o.
16	not o.oclIsTypeOf(Cl) (Cl<>OclAny)	ReclassifyObject(o, [], Cl);	o is removed from Cl but may remain instance of other classes in the model
17	not o.oclIsKindOf(Cl) (Cl has supertypes)		
18	Cl.allInstances() -> excludes(o) (Cl has supertypes)		
19	o.r->includesAll(Y)	*foreach o' in Y do* *CreateLink(r.association, o, o')* *endfor;*	A new link is created between o and each object in Y. If $o.r$ is a navigation towards an association class, *CreateLinkObject* is used instead.
20	o.r->includes(Y)	CreateLink(r.association,o,Y);	A link is created between o and the single object returned by Y
21	o.r->excludesAll(Y)	*foreach o' in Y* *DestroyLink(r.association,o,o')* *endfor;*	All links between o and the objects in Y are destroyed.
22	o.r->excludes(Y)	DestroyLink(r.association, o,Y)	The link between o and the object in Y is removed.
23	o.r->isEmpty(Y)	*foreach o' in o.r@pre* *DestroyLink(r.association,o,o')endfor;*	All links between o and the objects returned by $o.r$ in the previous state are removed.

4.2 List of Patterns

Table 1 presents our list of translation patterns. The translation is expressed using a simple combination of OCL for the query expressions, the above structural events and, when necessary, conditional and iterator structures.

4.3 Applying the Patterns

Fig. 2 shows the translation of the *replanShipment* operation (Fig. 1). Next to each translation excerpt we show between brackets the number of the applied pattern.

```
context Shipment::replanShipment(newDate:Date)
{
if self.shippingDate>today() and self.shippingDate<today()+7 and self.sale->exists(not readyForShipment)
then
        if self.urgent (2)
        then (1)
          sh1:=CreateObject(Shipment); (9)
          AddAttribueValue(shippingDate, sh1, newDate));  AddAttribueValue(id, sh1, generateNewId()); (3)
          AddAttribueValue(airTransport, sh1, self.airTransport); AddAttribueValue(urgent, sh1, true); (3)
          foreach o in self.sale@pre->select(not readyForShipment) CreateLink(DeliveredIn,sh1,o);  endfor; (19)
          foreach o in self.sale@pre->select(not readyForShipment) DestroyLink (DeliveredIn, self, o); endfor; (21)
          foreach o in sh1.sale (8)
            if not o.expectedShDate=sh1.shippingDate
               then AddAttributeValue(expectedShDate,o,sh1.shippingDate); (3) endif;
          endfor;
        else
          AddAttributeValue(shippingDate,self,newDate); (3)
          foreach o in self.sale (8)
            if not o.expectedShDate=self.shippingDate
               then AddAttributeValue(expectedShDate,o,self.shippingDate); (3) endif;
          endfor;
        endif;
endif;
}
```

Fig. 2. Imperative version of *replanShipment*

5   Translating Inherently Ambiguous Postconditions

In some sense, all postconditions can be considered ambiguous. However, for most postconditions, the heuristics provided in Section 3 suffice to provide a single interpretation for each postcondition.

Nevertheless, some postconditions are inherently ambiguous (also called non-deterministic [2]). We cannot define heuristics for them since, among all possible states satisfying the postcondition, there does not exist a state clearly more appropriate than the others. As an example assume a postcondition including an expression $a>b$. There is a whole family of states verifying the postcondition (all states where a is greater than b), all of them equally correct, even from the modeler point of view or, otherwise, he/she would have expressed the relation between the values of a and b more precisely (for instance saying that $a=b+c$).

We believe it is worth identifying these inherent ambiguous postconditions since most times the conceptual modeler does not define them on purpose but by mistake. Table 2 shows a list of expressions that cause a postcondition to become inherently ambiguous. We also provide a default translation for each expression so that our translation process can automatically translate all kinds of postconditions. Nevertheless, for these expressions user interaction is usually required to obtain a more accurate translation since the default translation may be too restrictive. For instance, for the second group of ambiguous expressions, the user may want to provide a specific constant value instead of letting the translation tool to choose an arbitrary one.

Table 2. List of inherently ambiguous expressions and their possible translation

Expression	Ambiguity description	Default Translation
B_1 or ... or B_n	At least a B_i condition should be true but it is not defined which one(s)	To ensure that B_1 is true
$X<>Y, X>Y, X>=Y,$ $X<Y, X<=Y$	The exact relation between the values of X and Y is not stated	To assign to X the value of Y plus/less a constant value of the appropriate type
$X+Y=W+Z$ (likewise with -, *, /, ...)	The exact relation between the values of the different variables is not stated	To translate the expression $X = W+Z-Y$
$X->exists(Y)$	An element of X must verify Y but it is not defined which one	To force the first element of X to verify Y (a total order relation must exist)
$X->any(Y)=Z$	Any element of X verifying Y could be the one equal to Z	To assign the value of Z to the first element of X verifying Y
$X.at->sum()=Y$	There exist many combinations of single values that once added result in Y	To assign to each object in X a value $Y/X-> size()$ in its attribute at
$X->asSequence()$	There are many possible ways of transforming a collection of elements X into an (ordered) sequence of elements	Order in the sequence follows the total order of the elements in X (a total order relation on X must exist)
$X.r->notEmpty()$	The condition states that the navigation through the role r must return at least an object but it is not stated how many nor which ones.	To assign a single object. The assigned object will be the first object in the destination class (a total order relation on the destination class must exist)
$op_1() = op_2()$	The return value of op_1 and op_2 must coincide. Depending on their definition several alternatives may exist.	Application of previous patterns depending on the specific definition of each operation

6 Tool Implementation

A prototype implementation of the translation presented in this paper has been developed. Given the XMI file representing the CS and the set of OCL operation contracts in a textual form (parsed using the Dresden OCL toolkit [9]), the prototype translates the selected operations.

More specifically, the translation is obtained by means of traversing in preorder the OCL binary tree resulting from representing the OCL postcondition as an instance of the OCL metamodel [20]. For each tree node (where each node represents an atomic subset of the OCL expression: an operation, a constant, an access to an attribute, etc), the prototype chooses and applies the appropriate pattern. The complexity of the translation process is $O(log\ n)$, being n the number of nodes of the tree.

Due to lack of space we cannot show this tree representation nor the details of the preorder traversal algorithm actually performing the translation.

7   Related Work

Two kinds of related work are relevant here: approaches devoted to the problem of improving the precision of declarative specifications (Section 7.1) and model-driven development methods and tools that may include facilities for generating code from operation contracts (Section 7.2).

7.1   Methods to Interpret Declarative Specifications

Methods aimed at disambiguating declarative specifications can be classified in three main groups: (1) methods that extend the contract with additional information, (2) methods that add implicit semantics to the contract expressions and (3) methods that try to characterize all possible new states satisfying the contract postcondition and let the modeler choose the one he/she prefers. This latter group (see [27] and [22] as examples) is not so well-explored and, currently, no method exists that is able to handle contracts defined in a language as expressive as the OCL.

Regarding the first group of methods, several formal languages (such as Z, VDM or JML) force the conceptual modeler to define in the contracts a new clause indicating which objects and links cannot change during the operation execution (*frame axioms*). [13] adapts the notion of frame axioms to OCL contracts. [4] uses a slightly different approach and asks modelers to specify which operations could have effected a change to a particular element. Other approaches, such as [2], combine the OCL with imperative extensions to clarify the semantics of the contract. The main limitations of all these approaches are: (1) they burden the modeler with the task of defining additional information in the contracts, (2) the addition of new elements to the structural diagram may require changing the frame axioms (now there are more elements that "cannot change") and (3) the high expressiveness of the OCL limits their feasibility (for instance, postconditions may state, both, additions and removals over the set of objects returned by a navigation; it is not clear how frame axioms could be used to deal with this situation).

These problems can be avoided when adding implicit semantics to the expressions appearing in a postcondition, as we do in our heuristics proposal. We are aware that our heuristics require some strong assumptions about how the postconditions are specified, yet we believe the assumptions reflect the way conceptual modelers tend to (unconsciously?) specify the postconditions. We are not the first ones in proposing the use of default semantics to simplify ambiguity problems of operation contracts. [4] recognizes that frame axioms could be (semi)automatically generated from the postcondition if assuming some implicit semantics. [26] proposes some basic assumptions regarding object (and collection) creations and removals. [6] proposes a *minimal change* heuristic (the preferred final state is the one with fewer changes wrt the initial one). However, this simple heuristic does not suffice to cover all possible ambiguities (see the different ambiguities commented in Section 3). Some ambiguous OCL expressions and their default interpretation were presented in a preliminary paper [7].

As a trade-off, this kind of methods requires modelers to agree in a given semantics when defining the contracts (either the ones we have assumed in our heuristics or alternative ones). We reckon that alternative approaches could be helpful when dealing with the inherently ambiguous postconditions of Section 5.

7.2 Methods for Code-Generation from Declarative Specifications

As far as we know, ours is the first approach to deal with the declarative-to-imperative translation of OCL operation specifications. Most methods and tools only support imperative specifications (see [16] as a representative example).

There exist several OCL tools allowing the definition of operation contracts (see, among others, [3,5,10,9]). However, during the code-generation phase, contracts are simply added as validation conditions. They are transformed into *if-then* clauses that check at the beginning and at the end of the operation if the pre and postconditions are satisfied (and raise an exception otherwise). The actual implementation of the operation must be manually defined. [1] checks the correctness of an implementation with respect to its contract but does not generate it.

A similar problem is faced in the database field when computing a sequence of updates that make the database to satisfy a given query (see [29] as an example). A typical example is the integrity maintenance problem (see [15] for a survey). Nevertheless, the limited expressivity of these methods (in terms of, both, the constraint definition language and the different types of structural events supported) prevents directly reusing them in the translation of UML/OCL operations.

8 Conclusion and Further Research

We have proposed a new method to transform an operation contract (declarative specification) into a set of structural events (imperative specification). The transformation process uses several heuristics that help draw the events from the OCL expressions included in the contract whenever their interpretation may be ambiguous.

Our translation may be useful to leverage current model-driven development tools, which up to now only support code-generation from imperative specifications. It may also be helpful for validation purposes, since modelers could immediately check which would be the implementation of their declarative specifications.

Our translation process has been validated against two case studies of real-life applications, a Car Rental System [11] and an e-marketplace system [23] as well as with other examples appearing in different books, papers and tutorials. Our patterns have proven to be complete enough to translate most of the examples. Moreover, during the analysis we have detected several inherently ambiguous postconditions. In most cases, and according to the contract information in natural language, the original modelers were unaware of such ambiguities. We believe this is an additional benefit of applying our method.

As a further work, we plan to extend our translation process by combining the basic patterns presented up to now (this has been the main flaw of the method detected during its validation) and by considering the integrity constraints in the generation process to ensure that the generated implementation is consistent with the constraints and, at the same time, that the operation effect is preserved [25]. We are also interested in studying the applicability of our method in the reverse process, that is, in the translation from imperative to declarative specifications. Finally, we plan to work on the integration of our results and our prototype within an existing model-driven development tool.

Acknowledgements

Thanks to the anonymous referees and the people of the GMC group (especially to Anna Queralt) for their useful comments to previous drafts of this paper. This work was partially supported by the Ministerio de Ciencia y Tecnologia and FEDER under project TIN2005-06053.

References

1. Ahrendt, W., Baar, T., Beckert, B., Bubel, R., Giese, M., Hähnle, R., Menzel, W., Mostowski, W., Roth, A., Schlager, S., Schmitt, P.H.: The KeY tool, Integrating object oriented design and formal verification. Software and Systems Modeling 4, 32–54 (2005)
2. Baar, T.: OCL and Graph-Transformations - A Symbiotic Alliance to Alleviate the Frame Problem. In: Bruel, J.-M. (ed.) MoDELS 2005. LNCS, vol. 3844, pp. 20–31. Springer, Heidelberg (2006)
3. Babes-Bolyai. Object Constraint Language Environment 2.0, http://lci.cs.ubbcluj.ro/ocle/
4. Borgida, A., Mylopoulos, J., Reiter, R.: On the frame problem in procedure specifications. IEEE Transactions on Software Engineering 21, 785–798 (1995)
5. Borland. Borland® Together® Architect (2006)
6. Broersen, J., Wieringa, R.: Preferential Semantics for Action Specifications in First-order Modal Action Logic. In: Proc. of the ECAI'98 Workshop on Practical Reasoning and Rationality (1998)
7. Cabot, J.: Ambiguity issues in OCL postconditions. In: Proc. OCL for (Meta-) Models in Multiple Application Domain (workshop co-located with the MODELS'06 Conference), Technical Report, TUD-FI06-04-Sept (2006)
8. Cabot, J., Teniente, E.: Transformation Techniques for OCL Constraints. Science of Computer Programming (to appear), Available online: http://dx.doi.org/10.1016 /j.scico.2007.05.001
9. Dresden. Dresden, OCL Toolkit, http://dresden-ocl.sourceforge.net/index.html
10. Dzidek, W.J., Briand, L.C., Labiche, Y.: Lessons Learned from Developing a Dynamic OCL Constraint Enforcement Tool for Java. In: Bruel, J.-M. (ed.) MoDELS 2005. LNCS, vol. 3844, pp. 10–19. Springer, Heidelberg (2006)

11. Frias, L., Queralt, A., Olivé, A.: EU-Rent Car Rentals Specification. LSI Technical Report, LSI-03-59-R (2003)

12. ISO/TC97/SC5/WG3: Concepts and Terminology for the Conceptual Schema and Information Base (1982)

13. Kosiuczenko, P.: Specification of Invariability in OCL. In: Nierstrasz, O., Whittle, J., Harel, D., Reggio, G. (eds.) MoDELS 2006. LNCS, vol. 4199, pp. 676–691. Springer, Heidelberg (2006)

14. Larman, C.: Applying UML and Patterns: An Introduction to Object-Oriented Analysis and Design and the Unified Process, 2nd edn. Prentice-Hall, Englewood Cliffs (2001)

15. Mayol, E., Teniente, E.: A Survey of Current Methods for Integrity Constraint Maintenance and View Updating. In: Akoka, J., Bouzeghoub, M., Comyn-Wattiau, I., Métais, E. (eds.) ER 1999. LNCS, vol. 1727, pp. 62–73. Springer, Heidelberg (1999)

16. Mellor, S.J., Balcer, M.J.: Executable UML. Object Technology Series. Addison-Wesley, London, UK

17. Meyer, B.: Object-oriented software construction, 2nd edn. Prentice-Hall, Englewood Cliffs (1997)

18. Olivé, A.: Conceptual Schema-Centric Development: A Grand Challenge for Information Systems Research. In: Pastor, Ó., Falcão e Cunha, J. (eds.) CAiSE 2005. LNCS, vol. 3520, pp. 1–15. Springer, Heidelberg (2005)

19. Olivé, A., Raventós, R.: Modeling events as entities in object-oriented conceptual modeling languages. Data Knowl. Eng. 58, 243–262 (2006)

20. OMG: UML 2.0 OCL Specification. OMG Adopted Specification (ptc/03-10-14)

21. OMG: UML 2.0 Superstructure Specification. OMG Adopted Specification (ptc/03-08-02)

22. Penny, D.A., Holt, R.C., Godfrey, M.W.: Formal Specification in Metamorphic Programming. In: Prehn, S., Toetenel, H. (eds.) VDM 1991. LNCS, vol. 551, pp. 11–30. Springer, Heidelberg (1991)

23. Queralt, A., Teniente, E.: A Platform Independent Model for the Electronic Marketplace Domain. LSI Technical Report, LSI-05-9-R (2005)

24. Queralt, A., Teniente, E.: Specifying the Semantics of Operation Contracts in Conceptual Modeling. Journal on Data Semantics VII, 33–56 (2006)

25. Schewe, K.-D., Thalheim, B.: Towards a theory of consistency enforcement. Acta Informatica 36, 97–141 (1999)

26. Sendall, S., Strohmeier, A.: Using OCL and UML to Specify System Behavior. In: Object Modeling with the OCL, The Rationale behind the Object Constraint Language, pp. 250–280. Springer, Heidelberg (2002)

27. Wahls, T., Leavens, G.T., Baker, A.L.: Executing Formal Specifications with Concurrent Constraint Programming. Autom. Softw. Eng. 7, 315–343 (2000)

28. Wieringa, R.: A survey of structured and object-oriented software specification methods and techniques. ACM Computing Surveys 30, 459–527 (1998)

29. Wüthrich, B.: On Updates and Inconsistency Repairing in Knowledge Bases. In: Proc. 9th Int. Conf. on Data Engineering, pp. 608–615 (1993)

An Ontological Metamodel of Classifiers and Its Application to Conceptual Modelling and Database Design

Jeffrey Parsons[1] and Xueming Li[2]

[1] Faculty of Business Administration
Memorial University of Newfoundland
St. John's, NL, Canada A1B 3X5
jeffreyp@mun.ca
[2] Department of Computer Science
Memorial University of Newfoundland
St. John's, NL, Canada A1B 3X5
xueming@cs.mun.ca

Abstract. Classification is a key concept in conceptual modeling. However, the recognition that there might be different kinds of classes has received limited attention in conceptual modeling research. Most work has focused on the concept of role. However, confusion exists on the definition, properties, and representation of role. In this paper, we propose a metamodel of classifiers based on ontological foundations. We focus on the notion of role in the object-oriented and conceptual modeling literature. The metamodel conforms to the fundamental role features identified in the literature and handles several problems associated with role modeling. Furthermore, we contrast conceptual models created using our metamodel to those created using traditional ER or class modeling approaches, and highlight the database design implications of the differences. Using examples, we demonstrate that relational database schemata generated using our approach are more stable with respect to changing requirements.

1 Introduction

Identifying classes can be seen as the central activity in conceptual modeling. According to Sowa, "the selection of categories determines everything that is represented in a computer application or in an entire family of applications." [21, p. 51]. However, most research on the issue treats the construct of "class" uniformly. In reality, to represent the semantics of important real world phenomena it might be useful to distinguish different "kinds" of types. In this paper, we present an ontologically-grounded metamodel of classifiers for conceptual modeling, based on Bunge's ontology [2][3], OntoClean methodology [10][27][11][12], and Guizzardi et al.'s ontological profile [13][14]. We use these ideas to distinguish different kinds of types, and explore implications of the metamodel for conceptual modeling and database design.

C. Parent et al. (Eds.): ER 2007, LNCS 4801, pp. 214–228, 2007.

2 Roles

Role is a fundamental notion for our conceptualization of reality. However, a lot of confusion exists on the definition, properties, and representation of role. Most role models in the literature have been primarily based on implementation considerations. However, Steimann argues that the role concept naturally complements those of object and relationship, standing on the same level of importance [22][23][24].

2.1 What Is a Role?

Sowa introduces the notion of role as capturing *a particular pattern of relationships*: "Subtypes of Entity are of two kinds: *natural types*, which have no required set of linguistic associations; and *role types*, which are subtypes of natural types in some particular pattern of relationships" [20]. For example, Person is a natural type, and Teacher is a subtype of Person in the role of teaching. Sowa further proposes a test for distinguishing role types from natural types: (1) τ is a natural type if something can be identified as type τ in isolation; (2) τ is a role type if something can only be identified as type τ by considering some other entity, action, or state.

Guarino argues that Sowa's test for distinguishing role types from natural types is "too vague to capture intended meaning" [9]. For example, Car is a natural type since it is essentially independent. However, it is also a role type according to Sowa because the existence of a car implies the existence of its engine, which is a part of the car. Guarino therefore proposes a criterion for distinguishing role types from natural types: concept A is called a *role* concept if it is founded (concept A is founded on another concept B if any instance 'a' of A has to be necessarily associated to an instance 'b' of B *which is not related to* 'a' *by a part-of relation*) but not rigid (concept A is rigid if it contributes to the very identity of its instances in such a way that, if 'a' is an instance of A in a particular world, it must be an instance of A in any possible world in order to keep its identity). A concept is called a *natural* concept if it is independent and rigid.

The OntoClean methodology introduces a set of highly general ontological notions (*rigidity*, *identity*, *unity*, and *dependence*) as meta-properties to analyze ontological semantics of various types as well as their relationship [10][27][11][12]. It distinguishes eight different kinds of types based on different combinations of these metaproperties. Moreover, in [13][14], Guizzardi et al. propose a UML profile for ontology representation and conceptual modeling based on a theory of classifiers [14].

Based on OntoClean and Guizzardi et al.'s ontological profile, we propose that a concept A is called a *role* if it is founded and anti-rigid; it is called a *natural* concept if it is independent and rigid; it is called a *phase* if it is independent and anti-rigid.

2.2 Three Different Ways of Representing Roles

There are three different viewpoints on the representation of roles: as named places in relationships; as a form of generalization/specialization; and as separate instances adjoined to the entities playing the roles [22].

2.2.1 Roles as Named Places in Relationships

This view is taken by ER and UML by assigning role names to the entity types participating in relationships. This practice is useful when, in a conceptual model, more than one place in a relationship is played by the same entity type. However, Steimann argues that the main problem with viewing roles as named places in relationships is that, since roles are not modeled as explicit types, "it fails to account for the fact that roles come with their own properties and behavior" [22, p. 88]. Furthermore, since roles are mere labels of types, we argue it is impossible to construct role type generalization/specialization hierarchies leading to better-organized conceptual models.

2.2.2 Roles as a Form of Generalization/Specialization

As discussed in section 2.1, Sowa views role types as subtypes of natural types in some particular pattern of relationships. However, in [1], Al-Jadir and Leonard argue using a number of implementation level examples that inheritance is not flexible enough with respect to object dynamics and schema evolution. A conceptual obstacle with this view is the difficulty of representing roles allowing multiple disjoint types [13][22]. As a consequence, Steimann argues to separate natural types and role types into different type hierarchy and to relate them using a "role-filler" relationship [22].

2.2.3 Roles as Separate Instances Adjoined to the Entities Playing the Roles

In this view, role types are treated as independent types whose instances are existentially dependent on its players (instances of natural types), have role specific state and behavior with separate identity different from their players. A player and its roles are related by a *played-by* relation, thus role instances act as bridges between relationships and its related players [4][8][16][28]. As argued by Steimann in [25] and Masolo et al. in [17], this view is mostly motivated to model some real world situations such as *a person plays exactly three employee roles simultaneously, with different salary and office number* – the so-called counting problem. This approach is problematic because, from an ontological perspective, an object in a conceptual model should correspond to a distinct real world thing [22]. Moreover, requiring each role instance to have a unique identity is artificial.

3 A Metamodel of Classifiers for Conceptual Modeling

In this section, we propose an ontological metamodel of classifiers. Figure 1 summarizes our metamodel. Ontologically, natural type, phase type, and role type model different kinds of *functional schemata* [2] of the same real world things viewed from different perspectives. For clarity, we call instances of a natural type *objects*, instances of a role type *roles*, and instances of a phase type *phases*. Note that, unlike natural types and phase types, there are relationships among role types (because role types are externally dependent, whereas natural/phase types are not). Each role type must associate to at least one other role type (could be the same role type), since roles are based on mutual properties. For example, role type Student must be related to a role type UniversityEnrolled. Instances of natural types and phase types can exist in isolation from any external entities. For an instance of a natural/phase type to interact with other entities in a particular context, it must become an instance of a role type. Since

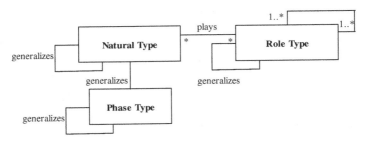

Fig. 1. The classifier metamodel

instances of role types are also instances of natural/phase types, roles can also play roles [18].

4   Implications for Conceptual Modeling

In this section, we explore implications of our metamodel for object-oriented and conceptual modeling as well as information system design and implementation. In particular, we compare it with traditional approaches to conceptual database modeling in order to demonstrate conceptual and practical usefulness of our approach.

4.1   Representing Intrinsic and Mutual Property in UML Diagrams

In Bunge's ontology, a value property of a thing is either an intrinsic property, or a nonbinding mutual property. Intrinsic properties are relatively stable properties of things over their lifetime. In contrast, nonbinding mutual properties are less stable properties in that they can be acquired/dropped by things. Evermann proposes to use attributes of association classes to represent mutual properties [7][6]. Following that idea, since an individual intrinsic property is owned by a thing exclusively, in a UML class diagram Bunge-attribute functions representing general intrinsic properties are modeled as attributes of an *ordinary* class/type placed in the attribute compartment of the class/type. We may call these UML attributes *intrinsic attributes*.

On the other hand, an individual nonbinding mutual property is shared by multiple things, say, for example, A and B. Neither A nor B owns this individual nonbinding mutual property exclusively. As a result, in a UML class diagram, Bunge-attribute functions representing general nonbinding mutual properties shared between things are modeled as attributes placed in the attribute compartment of an association class connecting classes/types whose instances model these things. That is to say, the attribute compartment of an association class between two or more classes/types in a UML class diagram contains a list of attributes each of which models a Bunge-attribute function representing a general nonbinding mutual property shared by things modeled by the functional schemata corresponding to these interconnecting classes/types. We may call these UML attributes *mutual attributes*.

4.2 Representing Natural, Phase, and Role Types in UML Class Diagrams

Furthermore, since natural and phase types are externally independent whereas role types are externally dependent, natural and phase types have only intrinsic properties, and role types have only mutual properties shared with other role types. Thus the attribute compartment of a role type in a UML diagram should be empty. All the (mutual) attributes of the role type are placed in the association class of the association connecting this role type to other role type(s) with which it shares these attributes. Consequently, in a UML conceptual model, we proposed that a role type cannot occur without being related to other role type(s). This rule conforms to the idea that *roles imply patterns of relationships*, since roles depends on external entities [19][20].

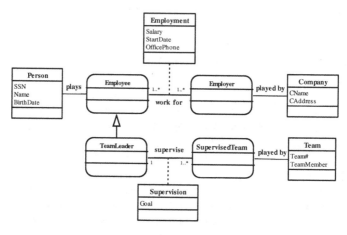

Fig. 2. A UML diagram illustrating natural types and their role types

An example UML diagram illustrating natural types and their role types is shown in Figure 2 (rectangle for natural/phase type and oval for role type). In this figure, Person, Company, and Team are natural types, Employee, Employer, TeamLeader, and SupervisedTeam are role types. A team leader, who is a person, is also an employee working for an employer which is a company. Thus in addition to his/her own mutual attribute (Goal of association class Supervision), he/she also inherits mutual attributes Salary, StartDate and OfficePhone of association class Employment from Employee.

Note that as argued by Wand, Storey, and Weber in [26], in our approach it is not possible for a role type to have optional associations with other role type(s). This is because, for an instance of a natural/phase type to be an instance of a role type, it must have some mutual attributes shared with other entities. For example, a person cannot be an employee without working for an employer.

In addition to natural types and role types, phase types are also useful in object-oriented and conceptual modeling. Examples of phase types include Child, Teenager, and Adult of Person, or Town and Metropolis of City. In a phase type partition of a natural type or phase type, the subtypes should be constructed such that they are mutually disjoint and constitute a *total* partition of this supertype, i.e., an instance of the supertype should have a corresponding instance in exactly one phase subtype. Figure 3 shows a conceptual model including a phase type partition Child, Teenager, and Adult of natural type Person. It indicates that only adult persons can be employees.

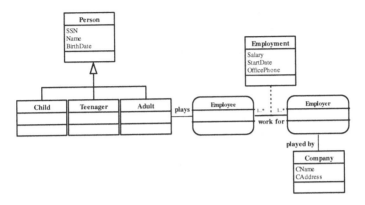

Fig. 3. A conceptual model with a phase type partition

4.3 Object Migration

Since a natural type is rigid, its instances cannot migrate to other natural types in a natural type hierarchy. Phase types however, are anti-rigid, so their instances may migrate to other phase types in the partition of a phase/natural type hierarchy during their lifetime when the distinguishing intrinsic attribute(-s) is changed. An instance of a natural/phase type may become an instance of a role type when it participates in a relationship, thus acquiring some mutual attribute(-s) (It still remains an instance of the natural/phase type). It may further acquire more mutual attributes, thus becoming an instance of a sub role type or a new role type, or it may lose some mutual attributes thus migrate to a super role type or not be an instance of a role type any more.

For example, in Figure 4, Person, Man, and Woman are natural types; Child, Teenager, and Adult are phase types. Note that here and elsewhere our notation here uses the same subtyping mechanism for phases as for natural types, but the notation could be extended to distinguish these concepts. Usually an instance of Man cannot migrate to Woman in his lifetime. But an instance of Child may possibly migrate to Teenager and Adult at some point in time. For role types, in Figure 2, a person may acquire mutual properties Salary, StartDate and OfficePhone shared with an employer thus become an employee. An employee may acquire mutual property Goal shared with a supervised team thus become a team leader.

In a phase type partition of a natural/phase type, object migration between these phase types is subject to some dynamic integrity constraints. For example, in the partition Child, Teenager, and Adult of Person, a person who is a child may migrate from Child to Teenager and further from Teenager to Adult during his/her lifetime, but the reverse direction of migration is forbidden. Similarly, in some role type partitions of

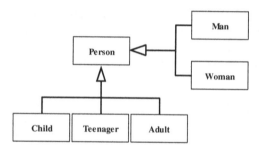

Fig. 4. An example of natural type and phase type partitions

role types (such as UndergraduateStudent and GraduateStudent of Student), instances of a role subtype may migrate to other role subtypes subject to some constraints (e.g., an undergraduate student can migrate to GraduateStudent, but not vice versa).

4.4 The Counting Problem

The counting problem [17][22][28] refers to situations in which instances counted in their roles yield a greater number than the same instances counted by the objects playing the roles. For example, if we count the number of persons served by Air Canada in 2006, we may count 1,000,000 but if we count passengers, we may count 3,000,000.

Existing conceptual modeling languages do not differentiate intrinsic attribute from mutual attribute, nor do they require that all the attributes of a role type should be mutual attributes that are shared by all entities participating in the relationship. Consequently in their approaches, intrinsic attributes which actually are attributes of natural/phase type can occur in a role type, and moreover a role type does not have to be related to other role type(s). This practice may cause *unstable* conceptual models in the situations that a natural/phase type instance can play two or more roles of the same role type simultaneously, i.e. the counting problem. For example, in the Entity-Relationship approach (ER), there is only entity type, no explicit role type. Role types are represented as named places in relationships. As a result, all intrinsic and mutual attributes are placed by modelers in entity types or relationship types arbitrarily. Figure 5 illustrates an ER conceptual model adapted from [5].

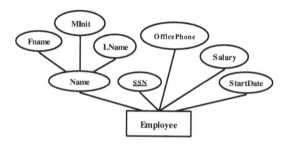

Fig. 5. An ER conceptual model reflecting the 'counting problem' (from [5])

The attributes OfficePhone, Salary and StartDate model Bunge-attribute functions representing general nonbinding mutual properties between, say, employees and employers. In contrast, the attributes Name and SSN model Bunge-attribute functions representing actually general intrinsic properties of persons that play role type Employee. These intrinsic attributes are still valid even after a person ceases to be an employee and thus loses all mutual attributes valid only in the employment relationship. Therefore, instead of belonging to Employee, they should be placed in an additional natural type Person. Figure 6 shows the corresponding model using our metamodel.

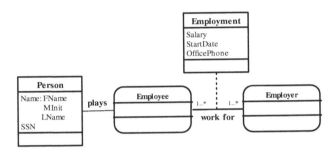

Fig. 6. The corresponding model of Figure 6 using our metamodel

In situations where a person cannot have more than one job at the same time (e.g. a person cannot be a secretary and a technician simultaneously), when mapping conceptual models in Figure 5 and Figure 6 to a relational database schema, we get one relation Employee and two relations Person and Employment respectively. It is usually not necessary to map also Employee and Employer in Figure 6 to two relations in a relational database schema because they have no intrinsic attributes.

However, in situations where, for example, a person can be a secretary and technician simultaneously with different office phones, salaries, and start dates, the corresponding relational database schema of the conceptual model in Figure 5 must be modified. Now attributes OfficePhone, Salary, and StartDate of Employee are multivalued and when mapping this conceptual model to a relational database schema, we need to create a new relation R which includes the three attributes OfficePhone, Salary and StartDate, plus the primary key SSN of Employee as a foreign key in R. The primary key of R is the combination of all four attributes. Thus, unlike in the previous situations, the resulting relational database schema has two relations. It is thus clear that, using ER approach, it is possible that the resulting relational database schema has to evolve after it has already been in existence for some time.

In contrast, for the conceptual model in Figure 6, when a person can be a secretary and a technician at the same time, this fact has no impact on the resulting relational database schema at all. One may simply insert into Employment relation two different records of a person with different employers in order to differentiate different jobs held by the same person. Thus the relational database schema resulting from the conceptual model in Figure 6 is more stable with respect to requirements change and thus more suited to capture evolutionary aspects of real world applications.

Our approach resembles the Object Role Modeling (ORM) approach proposed by Halpin in [15]. Unlike ER modeling (and our approach), ORM does not use attributes. As argued by Halpin, "The first problem with using attributes in the initial models is that they are often unstable. ... So do not agonize over whether to model a particular feature as an attribute or relationship. Just model it as a relationship". However, ORM is not based on formal ontological foundations. As a result, it does not distinguish intrinsic attributes from mutual ones. In our approach, intrinsic attributes are owned by a class/type exclusively and thus should not be modeled as relationships.

4.5 A More Complicated Example

In this section, we present a more complicated example with multiple inheritance. Figure 7 is an ER diagram with a generalization/specialization lattice adapted from [5, p. 84] for a university database. Attributes SSN, Name, Sex, Address, and Birth-Date are intrinsic attributes of natural type Person. Attributes Salary, MajorDept, and PercentTime are mutual attributes of role types Employee, Student, and StudentAssistant respectively. These mutual attributes cannot be owned exclusively by the role types. A corresponding conceptual model of Figure 7 based on our metamodel is illustrated in Figure 8.

In Figure 8, Person and University are natural types (We add to University a key attribute Name). Student, Employee, StudentAssistant, Employer, StudentEmployer, and UniversityEnrolled are all role types. Mutual attribute Salary is shared by Employee (which is played by Person) and Employer (which is played by University). Similarly, mutual attribute MajorDept is shared by Student (which is played by Person) and UniversityEnrolled (which is played by University). Also, mutual attribute PercentTime is shared by StudentAssistant (which is a subtype of role types Employee and Student) and StudentEmployer (which is a subtype of role types Employer and UniversityEnrolled).

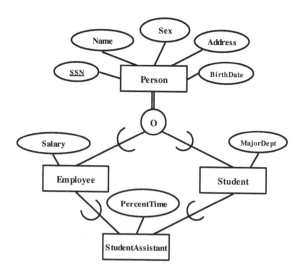

Fig. 7. A generalization/specialization lattice for a university database

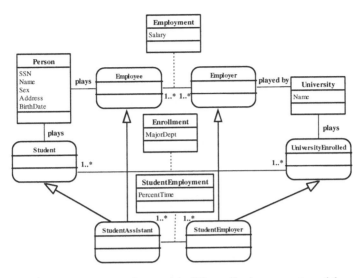

Fig. 8. The corresponding model of Figure 7 using our metamodel

It is clear that the conceptual model in Figure 8 expresses more real world semantics than Figure 7. These real world semantics are implicit in Figure 7, existing only in modelers' mind, while in Figure 8 they are represented explicitly. We deem this a positive aspect of our approach because one of the detrimental effects of the lack of rich, formal languages specific to conceptual modeling is that information system "development projects might begin without explicitly modelling the application domain and instead must rely on implicit assumptions of developers" [7, p 147]. Moreover, in Figure 8, the identifier attribute *Name* of the newly created natural type University is important because it will be used later as part of a combined key attribute to identify each relationship instance of relationship types Employment, Enrollment, and StudentEmployment associated to the role types played by University.

4.6 Union Type (Category) vs. Role Type

In conceptual database modeling, a *union* type or *category* is a subclass (in a single superclass/subclass relationship with more than one superclass, each of which represents a different entity type) which represents a collection of objects that is (a subset of) the union of distinct entity types [5]. For example, Figure 9 (adapted from [5, p. 86]) illustrates two union types Owner and Registered_Vehicle. An owner may own a number of registered vehicles, and a registered vehicle may be owned by a number of owners. An owner of a vehicle can be a person, a bank, or a company. Similarly, a registered vehicle can be a car or a truck.

In a UML model, a subclass may have multiple superclasses. The extension of the subclass is the intersection of the extensions of all superclasses. On the other hand, the extension of a category is (a subset of) the union of the extensions of all superclasses. Each instance of the category must belong to *only one* superclass.

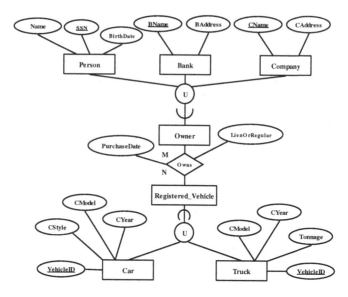

Fig. 9. Two union types: Owner and Registered_Vehicle

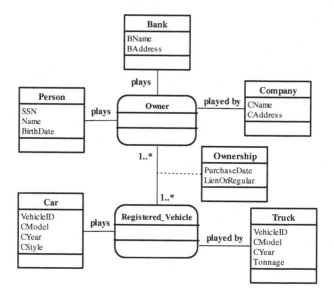

Fig. 10. The corresponding model of Figure 10 using our metamodel

However, we suggest that, instead of being a new modeling concept, a union type or category is actually a role type in our metamodel (which is anti-rigid and dependent). Consequently, we may model Owner and Registered_Vehicle as role types in our metamodel. Figure 10 illustrates the corresponding model based on our metamodel. In Figure 10, Person, Bank, and Company are natural types that can play role type Owner. Similarly, Car and Truck are natural types that can play role type Registered_Vehicle. Since a role type recruits its instances from natural/phase types, an owner can be a person, bank, or company. Similarly, a registered vehicle can be a car or a truck. All attributes of the relationship *Owns* (PurchaseDate and LienOrRegular) are placed in association class Ownership.

Also note that, unlike Figure 9, in Figure 10 the cardinality constraint of Owner and Registered_Vehicle in relationship *Owns* is 1..*. This is because, as we discussed in section 4.2, a role type cannot have optional associations with other role type(s).

4.7 Integrity Constraints

In ER, relationship types usually have certain constraints that limit the possible combinations of entities that may participate in the corresponding relationship set. Among them, the *participation constraint* "specifies whether the existence of an entity depends on its being related to another entity via the relationship type" [5, p. 57]. There are two types of participation constraints – total and partial. An example for total participation constraint is *every employee must work for an employer*. An example for partial participation constraint is *not every employee manages a department*. Total participation is a necessary condition for *existence dependency*. However, as indicated before, in our model, a role type cannot have optional associations (or partial participation) with other role type(s). In fact, in the example for partial participation constraint, instead of role type Employee, it is role type Manager that has a management relationship with role type ManagedDepartment. In this case, the relationship type management is total participation for both Manager and ManagedDepartment.

In a phase type partition of a natural or phase type, the phase subtypes should be constructed such that they are mutually *disjoint* and constitute a *total* partition of this supertype, i.e., any instance of the supertype should have a corresponding instance in exactly one phase subtype. For example, in Figure 11, phase subtypes Child, Teenager, and Adult are mutually disjoint and partition the natural type Person.

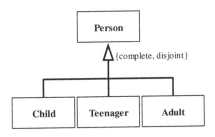

Fig. 11. An example of a phase type partition of natural type Person

Because a phase type partition is a total partition, in a relational database schema, if we insert an entity into a relation that represents the supertype of a phase type partition, this entity must also be inserted into exactly one relation that represents an appropriate phase subtype. For example, in Figure 11, if we insert a person entity that is a child into relation Person, this entity is mandatorily inserted into relation Child. On the other hand, if we delete an entity from *a set of* relations that represent a phase type partition (i.e., this entity does not belong to any phase subtype of the partition any more), this entity must also be deleted from the relation representing the supertype of the phase type partition. In Figure 11, if an adult becomes deceased thus deleted from relation Adult, he or she cannot belong to any phase subtype of partition Person any more, thus is mandatorily deleted from relation Person.

Moreover, Wieringa et al. [28] argue that, to construct taxonomic structures, for each is-a partition of a class the classification principle that governs the division in its subtypes should be *clear*, *unambiguous*, *singular*, and *uniform*. Following the principle, in natural type hierarchies, partitions should be constructed such that its subtypes are mutually disjoint. For example, in Figure 12, natural subtypes Car and Truck are mutually disjoint, as are subtypes Man and Woman.

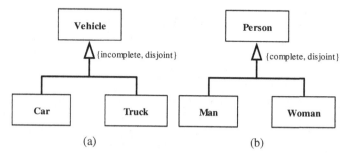

Fig. 12. An example of (a) a *partial* natural type partition, (b) a *total* natural type partition

Note that a natural type partition does not necessarily exhaust its supertype. Figure 12 (a) illustrates a *partial* natural type partition Truck and Car of Vehicle, Figure 12 (b) illustrates a *total* natural type partition Man and Woman of Person. Consequently, in a relational database schema, if we insert an entity into a relation that represents the supertype of a natural type partition, this entity does not necessarily have to be inserted into a relation that represents a natural subtype. For example, in Figure 12 (a), if we insert an entity that is a motorcycle into relation Vehicle, this entity does not have to be inserted into either Car or Truck.

On the other hand, if we delete an entity from *any* relation that represents a subtype of a natural type partition, it must also be deleted from the relation representing the supertype of the partition. For example, in Figure 12(b), if a man/woman entity is deleted from relation Man/Woman, he/she must be deleted from relation Person.

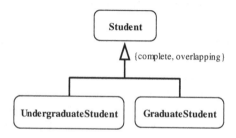

Fig. 13. An example of a total role partition of role type Student

Compared with natural/phase type partition, usually a role type partition can be *overlapping*. This is because an object or phase may play multiple roles simultaneously. For example, in Figure 13, if a person can be an undergraduate student in one university and a graduate student in another, then this partition is overlapping. Furthermore, a role type partition can be *partial* or *total*. Figure 13 illustrates a total partition: every student is either an undergraduate student or a graduate student, or both.

5 Conclusion

This paper proposes a metamodel of classifiers based on distinguishing the notions of natural type, phase type, and role type. We then use the metamodel to suggest extensions to UML class diagrams to capture these distinctions. We further show that the distinctions enable class models to express domain semantics more clearly, and identify some integrity constraints that can be inferred when models adhere to the metamodel.

This approach also has important implications for database design models and can lead to more flexible design that accommodate changing requirements. Further research is needed to examine these implications. In addition, the distinctions we propose among classes lead to diagrams that appear to be more complex than those constructed using traditional approaches. Since conceptual models are important for communication and validation of requirements, work is needed to determine whether the additional complexity impairs or improves the usefulness of models in supporting communication.

References

[1] Al-Jadir, L., Leonard, M.: If we refuse the inheritance. In: Bench-Capon, T.J.M., Soda, G., Tjoa, A.M. (eds.) DEXA 1999. LNCS, vol. 1677, Springer, Heidelberg (1999)

[2] Bunge, M.: Treatise on Basic Philosophy, vol. 3, Ontology I: The Furniture of the World, Boston: Reidel (1977)

[3] Bunge, M.: Treatise on Basic Philosophy vol. 4, Ontology II: A World of Systems, Boston: Reidel (1979)

[4] Dahchour, M., Pirotte, A., Zimanyi, E.: A role model and its metaclass implementation, Information Systems. 29(3), 235–270 (2004)

[5] Elmasri, R., Navathe, S.: Fundamentals of Database Systems, 3rd edn. AddisonWesley, London, UK (2000)

[6] Evermann, J.: The Association Construct in Conceptual Modelling - An Analysis Using the Bunge Ontological Model. In: Pastor, Ó., Falcão e Cunha, J. (eds.) CAiSE 2005. LNCS, vol. 3520, pp. 33–47. Springer, Heidelberg (2005)

[7] Evermann, J., Wand, Y.: Ontology based object-oriented domain modelling: fundamental concepts. Requirements Eng. 10(2), 146–160 (2005)

[8] Gottlob, G., Schrefl, M., Rock, B.: Extending Object-Oriented Systems with Roles. ACM Trans. Inf. Syst. 14(3), 268–296 (1996)

[9] Guarino, N.: Concepts, attributes and arbitrary relations. Data & Knowledge Engineering 8, 249–261 (1992)

[10] Guarino, N., Welty, C.: An overview of OntoClean. In: Staab, S., Studer, R. (eds.) Handbook on Ontologies, pp. 151–159. Springer, Heidelberg (2004)

[11] Guarino, N., Welty, C.: Evaluating ontological decisions with OntoClean, Commun. ACM 45(2), 61–65 (2002)

[12] Guarino, N., Welty, C.: A formal ontology of properties. In: Dieng, R. (ed.) Proceedings of the 12th Int. Conf. On Knowledge Engineering and Knowledge Management. LNCS, Springer, Heidelberg

[13] Guizzardi, G., Wagner, G., Guarino, N., McBrien, P., Rizopoulos, N.: An Ontologically Well-Founded Profile for UML Conceptual Models. In: Persson, A., Stirna, J. (eds.) CAiSE 2004. LNCS, vol. 3084, pp. 112–126. Springer, Heidelberg (2004)

[14] Guizzardi, G., Wagner, G., Sinderen, M.: A Formal Theory of Conceptual Modeling Universals, WSPI (2004)

[15] Halpin, T.A.: Business rules and object-role modeling, DBP&D 9(10) (October 1996)

[16] Loebe, F.: An Analysis of Roles - Toward Ontology-Based Modelling, Master's Thesis, University of Leipzig (2003)

[17] Masolo, C., Guizzardi, G., Vieu, L., Bottazzi, E., Ferrario, R.: Relational Roles and Qua-individuals. In: Roles, an interdisciplinary perspective, AAAI Fall Symposium (2005)

[18] Renouf, D.W., Henderson-Sellers, B.: Towards a Role-Based Framework Approach for User Interfaces. Australian Computer Journal 28(3), 96–106 (1996)

[19] Sowa, J.F.: Conceptual Structures: Information Processing in Mind and Machine. Addison-Wesley, New York (1984)

[20] Sowa, J.F.: Using a lexicon of canonical graphs in a semantic interpreter. In: Evens, M.W. (ed.) Relational Models of the Lexicon, pp. 113–137. Cambridge University Press, Cambridge (1988)

[21] Sowa, J.F.: Knowledge Representation: Logical, Philosophical, and Computational Foundations, Thomson Learning (2000)

[22] Steimann, F.: On the representation of roles in object-oriented and conceptual modeling. Data & Knowledge Engineering 35, 83–106 (2000)

[23] Steimann, F.: A radical revision of UML's role concept. In: Evans, A., Kent, S., Selic, B. (eds.) UML 2000. LNCS, vol. 1939, pp. 194–209. Springer, Heidelberg (2000)

[24] Steimann, F.: Role = Interface: A merger of concepts. Journal of Object-Oriented Programming 14(4), 23–32 (2001)

[25] Steimann, F.: The Role Data Model Revisited. In: Roles, an interdisciplinary perspective, AAAI Fall Symposium (2005)

[26] Wand, Y., Storey, V., Weber, R.: An Ontological Analysis of the relationship Construct in Conceptual Modeling. ACM Transactions on Database Systems 24(4), 494–528 (1999)

[27] Welty, C., Guarino, N.: Supporting ontological analysis of taxonomic relationships. Data & Knowledge Engineering 39(1), 51–74 (2001)

[28] Wieringa, R., Jonge, W., de Spruit, P.: Using Dynamic Classes and Role Classes to Model Object Migration. Theory and Practice of Object Systems 1(1), 61–83 (1995)

Handling Inconsistency of Vague Relations with Functional Dependencies

An Lu and Wilfred Ng

Department of Computer Science and Engineering
The Hong Kong University of Science and Technology
Hong Kong, China
{anlu,wilfred}@cse.ust.hk

Abstract. Vague information is common in many database applications due to internet-scale data dissemination, such as those data arising from sensor networks and mobile communications. We have formalized the notion of a vague relation in order to model vague data in our previous work. In this paper, we utilize Functional Dependencies (FDs), which are the most fundamental integrity constraints that arise in practice in relational databases, to maintain the consistency of a vague relation. The problem we tackle is, given a vague relation r over a schema R and a set of FDs F over R, what is the "best" approximation of r with respect to F when taking into account of the median membership (m) and the imprecision membership (i) thresholds. Using these two thresholds of a vague set, we define the notion of mi-overlap between vague sets and a merge operation on r. Satisfaction of an FD in r is defined in terms of values being mi-overlapping. We show that Lien's and Atzeni's axiom system is sound and complete for FDs being satisfied in vague relations. We study the chase procedure for a vague relation r over R, named VChase(r, F), as a means to maintain consistency of r with respect to F. Our main result is that the output of the procedure is the most object-precise approximation of r with respect to F. The complexity of VChase(r, F) is polynomial time in the sizes of r and F.

1 Introduction

Fuzzy set theory has long been introduced to handle inexact and imprecise data by Zadeh's seminal paper in [1]. In fuzzy set theory, each object $u \in U$ is assigned a single real value, called the *grade of membership*, between zero and one. (Here U is a classical set of objects, called the *universe of discourse*.) In [2], Gau et al. point out that the drawback of using the single membership value in fuzzy set theory is that the evidence for $u \in U$ and the evidence against $u \in U$ are in fact mixed together. In order to tackle this problem, Gau et al. propose the notion of *Vague Sets* (VSs), which allow using interval-based membership instead of using point-based membership as in FSs. We have shown in our previous work [3] that the interval-based membership generalization in VSs is more expressive in capturing vague data semantics.

In a vague relation, each object with a *vague membership* belongs to a VS. A vague membership (also called a vague value) is a subinterval $[\alpha(u), 1 - \beta(u)]$ of the unit interval $[0,1]$, where $0 \le \alpha(u) \le 1 - \beta(u) \le 1$. A true (false) membership function $\alpha(u)$

C. Parent et al. (Eds.): ER 2007, LNCS 4801, pp. 229–244, 2007.
© Springer-Verlag Berlin Heidelberg 2007

$(\beta(u))$ is a lower bound on the grade of membership of u derived from the evidence for (against) u.

In order to compare two vague values, we define the *median membership*, $M_m = (\alpha + 1 - \beta)/2$, which represents the overall evidence contained in a vague value, and the *imprecision membership*, $M_i = (1 - \beta - \alpha)$, which represents the overall imprecision of a vague value. With M_m and M_i, we have the one-to-one correspondence between a vague value, denoted by $[\alpha, 1 - \beta]$, and a *mi-pair* vague value, denoted by $< M_m, M_i >$, for a given object. We further extend the notion of *mi*-overlap to VSs.

Integrity constraints ensure that changes made to the database do not result in a loss of data consistency. The notion of a Functional Dependency (FD) [4], the most fundamental integrity constraints, being satisfied in a vague relation can be formalized in terms values being *mi*-overlapping rather than equal. We show that Lien's and Atzeni's axiom system [5,4] is sound and complete for FDs being satisfied in vague relations. A vague relation is said to be consistent with respect to a set of FDs F if it satisfies F. We define the chase procedure for a vague relation r over R, named $VChase(r, F)$, to tackle the consistency problem with respect to F, defined on vague relations [3]. Our main result is that the output of the procedure is the most *object*-precise (or O-precise in our notation) approximation of r with respect to F.

Here we give a motivating example. Consider a vague relation schema $R = \{S, T\}$, where S stands for the evidence of a sensor ID and T stands for the temperature monitored by a sensor. Here S and T are vague concepts, their values are all represented by VSs. Suppose the attributes S and T share the common universes of discourse, $U = \{0, 1, \ldots, 10\}$. A vague relation r_1 over R is shown in Table 1, where the attributes S and T are vague. The VS $<0.8, 0.1>/0$ means the evidence for "the sensor ID is 0" is 0.8 and the imprecision for it is 0.1. The median membership threshold C and the imprecision membership threshold I are called the *mi-thresholds*. For simplicity, we only show the elements in the values of S and T that satisfy the *mi*-thresholds. Intuitively, this means that the elements in the relation all have strong evidence relative to the thresholds. The saying that two VSs *mi*-overlap means they have at least one common object which satisfies the *mi*-thresholds (i.e., $0.8 \geq C$ and $0.1 \leq I$ in this example). We regard two *mi*-overlapping VSs are similar to each other to some extent and extend the classical FD concept to vague relations. Suppose that the FD $S \rightarrow T$ is specified as a constraint, meaning that same sensor reads same temperature in a vague sense.

We assume a vague relation r_1 over R, where the current temperature may be obtained from different sensors. Thus, at any given time the information may be inconsistent. It can be verified that r_1 satisfies $S \rightarrow T$ and is consistent. Suppose later a vague tuple was inserted into r_1, we have the vague relation r_2 shown in Table 2. It can be verified that r_2 does not satisfy $S \rightarrow T$ and is inconsistent, since the evidence of S shows that the two tuples have the common object 0 *mi*-overlapped, but the values of T do not have a common object and thus do not *mi*-overlap. The vague relation r_2 can be approximated by the less O-precise relation r_3, shown in Table 3. It can be verified that r_3 satisfies $S \rightarrow T$ and is consistent. The vague relation r_3 (one tuple) is in fact the most O-precise approximation of r_2. The transformation from r_2 to r_3 is based on the VChase procedure introduced later.

Table 1. Sensor relation r_1 **Table 2.** Sensor relation r_2 **Table 3.** Sensor relation r_3

S	T
<0.8,0.1>/0	<0.9,0>/0

S	T
<0.8,0.1>/0	<0.9,0>/0
<0.9,0.2>/0	<0.8,0.1>/1

S	T
<0.9,0.1>/0	<0.9,0>/0 +
	<0.8,0.1>/1

We define the merge operation which replaces each attribute value in r by the mi-union of all attribute values with respect to the same reflexive and transitive closure under mi-overlap. This leads to a partial order on merged vague relations and the notion of a vague relation being less O-precise than another vague relation. This partial order induces a lattice on the set of merged vague relations, which we denote by $MERGE(R)$, based on *object*-equivalence (O-equivalence for short) classes. We define the VChase procedure for a vague relation r over R as a means of maintaining consistency of r with respect to F. We investigate the properties of the VChase procedure showing amongst other results that it outputs a consistent vague relation. The output of VChase is unique. VChase can be computed in polynomial time in the sizes of r and F, and the procedure commutes with the merge operation.

The main contributions of this paper are fourfold. First, we develop the notions of median membership and imprecision membership to capture the essential information and in maintain consistency of vague data. Second, we define a partial order on merged vague relations which induces a lattice based on O-equivalence classes. We also define a partial order based on the vague values which induces a complete semi-lattice in each O-equivalence class. Third, we extend the satisfaction of an FD in a vague relation in terms values being mi-overlapping rather than equal and show that Lien's and Atzeni's axiom system is sound and complete for FDs being satisfied in vague relations. Finally, we propose the chase procedure for a vague relation r over R, named VChase, as a means of maintaining consistency of r with respect to a set of FDs F. Our main result is that the output $VChase(r, F)$ of the VChase procedure is the most O-precise approximation of r with respect to F.

The rest of the paper is organized as follows. Section 2 presents some basic concepts related to mi-pair, which are used to enhance vague sets and their operations. In Section 3, we discuss the merge operation, based on the less O-precise order. In Section 4, FDs and the $VChase$ procedure of vague relations are introduced. In Section 5, we give a semantic characterization of the $VChase$ procedure of a vague relation, which is also consistent with respect to a set of FDs. Related work is presented in Section 6. And in Section 7, we offer our concluding remarks.

2   Vague Sets and Mi Memberships

In [6,3,7], some basic concepts related to the vague relational data model are given. Here we explain how and why the median membership and the imprecision membership are useful to represent vague data. We assume throughout V is a vague set and U is the universe of discourse for V.

2.1   Median Memberships, Imprecision Memberships and $\mathcal{M}i$-Pair Vague Sets

In order to compare vague values, we need to introduce two derived memberships for discussion. The first is called the *median membership*, $M_m = (\alpha + 1 - \beta)/2$, which represents the overall evidence contained in a vague value and is illustrated in Fig. 1.

Definition 1 (Median membership). *The* median membership *of an object* $u \in U$ *in a vague set* V, *denoted by* $M_m^V(u)$, *is defined by* $M_m^V(u) = (\alpha(u) + 1 - \beta(u))/2$. *Whenever* V *and* u *are understood from context, we simply write* M_m.

It can be checked that $0 \le M_m \le 1$. In addition, the vague value $[1,1]$ has the highest M_m, which means the corresponding object totally belongs to V (i.e. a crisp value). The vague value $[0,0]$ has the lowest M_m, which informally means that the corresponding object "totally" does not belong to V (i.e. the empty vague value). The higher M_m is, the more crisp the vague value represents.

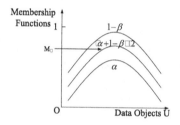

Fig. 1. Median membership of a vague set

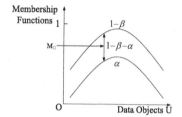

Fig. 2. Imprecision membership of a vague set

The second is called the *imprecision membership*, $M_i = (1 - \beta - \alpha)$, which represents the overall imprecision of a vague value and is illustrated in Fig. 2.

Definition 2 (Imprecision membership). *The* imprecision membership *of an object* $u \in U$ *in a vague set* V, *denoted by* $M_i^V(u)$, *is defined by* $M_i^V(u) = 1 - \beta(u) - \alpha(u)$. *Whenever* V *and* u *are understood from context, we simply write* M_i.

It can be checked that $0 \le M_i \le 1$. In addition, the vague value $[a, a](a \in [0,1])$ has the lowest M_i which means that we know exactly the membership of the corresponding object (that is, reduced to a fuzzy value). The vague value $[0,1]$ has the highest M_i, which informally means that we know "nothing" about the precision of the corresponding object. The higher M_i is, the more imprecise the vague value represents.

Proposition 1. *The median membership and the imprecision membership of an object satisfy the inequality:* $\frac{M_i}{2} \le M_m \le (1 - \frac{M_i}{2})$.

Proposition 1 shows that the median and imprecision memberships actually relate to each other.

Definition 3 (Mi-**pair Vague Set**). *An mi-pair VS vague set, in $U = \{u_1, u_2, \ldots, u_n\}$ is characterized by a median membership function, M_m^V, and an imprecision membership function, M_i^V, where $M_m^V : U \rightarrow [0,1]$, and $M_i^V : U \rightarrow [0,1]$. V is given as follows: $V = \sum_{i=1}^{n} < M_m^V(u_i), M_i^V(u_i) > /u_i$. $<M_m^V(u_i), M_i^V(u_i)>/u_i$ is called an element of V and $<M_m^V(u_i), M_i^V(u_i)>$ is called the (mi-pair) vague value of the object u_i.*

Using M_m and M_i, we have a one-to-one correspondence between a vague value, $[\alpha, 1 - \beta]$, and mi-pair vague value, $<M_m, M_i>$. From now on, a vague set or a vague value refers to an mi-pair vague set or an mi-pair vague value, respectively.

Table 4. A sensor vague relation r

	S	T	L
t_1	$<0.7,0.4>/0 + <0.5,1>/3$	$<0.8,0.3>/0 + <0.6,0.1>/1$	$<0.4,0.3>/0 + <0.6,0.3>/1$
t_2	$<0.8,0.1>/0 + <0.1,0.1>/1$	$<0.9,0.1>/1 + <0.5,0.1>/2$	$<0.6,0.6>/0 + <0.5,0.2>/2$
t_3	$<0.9,0.2>/1 + <0.5,0.1>/2$	$<0.3,0.2>/2$	$<0.2,0.2>/0$
t_4	$<0.5,0.1>/3 + <0.8,0.2>/4$	$<0.4,0.4>/3$	$<0.4,0.2>/3$

Example 1. Let $R = \{S, T, L\}$ be a vague relation schema, where S stands for a sensor ID, T stands for the temperature monitored by a sensor and L stands for a location area ID. A sensor vague relation r having 4 tuples $\{t_1, t_2, t_3, t_4\}$ is shown in Table 4. For those vague elements not listed in the relation, we assume they all have a special vague value $<0, 1>$, which represents the boundary of all vague values, since any median membership is greater than or equal to 0 and any imprecision membership is less than or equal to 1.

2.2   Existence and Overlap of Vague Sets

We next define the concepts of an mi-existing VS and overlapping VSs. The underlying idea is to check if vague values satisfy the predefined mi-thresholds: C as a crisp threshold ($0 \leq C \leq 1$), and I as an imprecision threshold ($0 \leq I \leq 1$).

Definition 4 (Mi-**existing**). *Given V and the mi-thresholds C and I, if $\exists u \in U$, such that $M_m^V(u) \geq C$ and $M_i^V(u) \leq I$, then u is an mi-existing object, $<M_m^V(u), M_i^V(u)>/u$ is an mi-existing element, and V is an mi-existing VS under C and I.*

By Definition 4, it follows that V is not mi-existing if all the objects in V are not mi-existing under C and I.

Definition 5 (Mi-**overlap**). *Given two vague sets V_1 and V_2, if $\exists u \in U$, such that $M_m^{V_1}(u) \geq C$ and $M_m^{V_2}(u) \geq C$, $M_i^{V_1}(u) \leq I$ and $M_i^{V_2}(u) \leq I$, then V_1 and V_2 mi-overlap under mi-thresholds C and I, denoted by $V_1 \sim_{mi} V_2(C, I)$. u is called the common mi-existing object of V_1 and V_2 under C and I. Otherwise, V_1 and V_2 do not mi-overlap under C and I, denoted by $V_1 \nsim_{mi} V_2(C, I)$. We simply write $V_1 \sim_{mi} V_2$ and $V_1 \nsim_{mi} V_2$, if C and I are known from the context.*

By Definition 5, it follows that V_1 and V_2 do not mi-overlap if there is no common mi-existing object of V_1 and V_2 under C and I.

Example 2. Given $C=0.2$ and $I=0.9$, it can be checked that $t_1[L]$ and $t_2[L]$ in Table 4 mi-overlap, i.e. $t_1[L] \sim_{mi} t_2[L](0.2, 0.9)$. However, if $C=0.2$ and $I=0.5$, we find that $t_1[L]$ and $t_2[L]$ do not mi-overlap, that is, $t_1[L] \not\sim_{mi} t_2[L](0.2, 0.5)$.

Using the mi-existing objects of VSs, we define mi-union and mi-intersection of VSs.

Definition 6 (*Mi-union*). *Given two vague sets V_1 and V_2 under the mi-thresholds C and I, the mi-union of V_1 and V_2 is a vague set V_3, written as $V_3 = V_1 \vee V_2$, whose median membership and imprecision membership functions are related to those of V_1 and V_2 given as follows. Let $u \in U$.*

1. *If u is an mi-existing object in both V_1 and V_2,*
   $M_m^{V_3}(u) = max(M_m^{V_1}(u), M_m^{V_2}(u)), M_i^{V_3}(u) = min(M_i^{V_1}(u), M_i^{V_2}(u))$;
2. *If u is an mi-existing object in V_1 but not in V_2,*
   $M_m^{V_3}(u) = M_m^{V_1}(u), M_i^{V_3}(u) = M_i^{V_1}(u)$;
3. *If u is an mi-existing object in V_2 but not in V_1,*
   $M_m^{V_3}(u) = M_m^{V_2}(u), M_i^{V_3}(u) = M_i^{V_2}(u)$;
4. *If u is not an mi-existing object in both V_1 and V_2,*
   $M_m^{V_3}(u) = M_m^{V_1}(u), M_i^{V_3}(u) = M_i^{V_1}(u), \text{if } M_m^{V_1}(u) \geq M_m^{V_2}(u)$;
   $M_m^{V_3}(u) = M_m^{V_2}(u), M_i^{V_3}(u) = M_i^{V_2}(u), \text{otherwise.}$

Since the fourth case of Def. 6 adopts the vague value from either V_1 or V_2, dependent on which has the higher median membership, it guarantees that the mi-union of two non-mi-existing elements cannot "upgrade" to an mi-existing element. That is to say, it always keeps the elements that do not satisfy mi-thresholds to be non-mi-existing.

Definition 7 (*Mi-intersection*). *Using the same set of notations of Definition 6, the mi-intersection of VSs V_1 and V_2 is a VS V_3, written as $V_3 = V_1 \wedge V_2$, is defined as follows:*

1. *If u is an mi-existing object in both V_1 and V_2,*
   $M_m^{V_3}(u) = max(M_m^{V_1}(u), M_m^{V_2}(u)), M_i^{V_3}(u) = min(M_i^{V_1}(u), M_i^{V_2}(u))$;
2. *If u is an mi-existing object in V_1 but not in V_2,*
   $M_m^{V_3}(u) = M_m^{V_2}(u), M_i^{V_3}(u) = M_i^{V_2}(u)$;
3. *If u is an mi-existing object in V_2 but not in V_1,*
   $M_m^{V_3}(u) = M_m^{V_1}(u), M_i^{V_3}(u) = M_i^{V_1}(u)$;
4. *If u is not an mi-existing object in both V_1 and V_2,*
   $M_m^{V_3}(u) = M_m^{V_1}(u), M_i^{V_3}(u) = M_i^{V_1}(u), \text{if } M_m^{V_1}(u) \geq M_m^{V_2}(u)$;
   $M_m^{V_3}(u) = M_m^{V_2}(u), M_i^{V_3}(u) = M_i^{V_2}(u), \text{otherwise.}$

Note that the cases 1 and 4 in Definition 7 are identical to their counterparts in Definition 6.

3   Merge Operation of Vague Relations

In this section, we define the merge of a vague relation r as the operation which replaces each attribute value (represented by a VS) in r by the mi-union of all attribute values with respect to the same reflexive and transitive closure under mi-overlap. This leads to the concept of a less object-precise partial order on merged vague relations.

From now on, we let $R = \{A_1, A_2, \ldots, A_m\}$ be a relation schema and r be a vague relation over R. We also assume common notation used in relational databases [4] such as the projection of a tuple $t[A]$.

The semantics of a vague set, $t[A_i]$, where $t \in r$ and $A_i \in R$, are that an object $u \in U_i$ has the vague value $<M_m(u), M_i(u)>$ in $t[A_i]$. The intuition is that, for those objects which are not mi-existing, we regard their memberships are too weak to consider in the process of chasing the inconsistency with respect to a set of FDs.

We now define the merge operation which replaces each attribute value of a tuple in a vague relation by the mi-union of all attribute values with respect to the same reflexive and transitive closure under mi-overlap.

Definition 8 (Merged relation). *Given $A \in R$ and mi-thresholds C and I, we construct a directed graph $G = (V, E)$, where $V = \pi_A(r)$. An edge $(t_1[A], t_2[A])$ is in E iff $t_1[A] \sim_{mi} t_2[A](C, I)$. Let $G^+ = (V^+, E^+)$ be the reflexive and transitive closure of G. The merge of r, denoted by $merge(r)$, is the vague relation resulting from replacing each $t[A]$ by $\bigvee\{t[A]'|(t[A], t[A]') \in E^+\}$ for all $A \in R$.*

We let $MERGE(R)$ be a collection of all merged relations over R under C and I.

Example 3. Given $C=0.2$ and $I=0.9$, the vague relation $merge(r)$, is shown in Table 5, where r is shown in Table 4. For example, since $t_1[L] \sim_{mi} t_2[L](0.2, 0.9)$ and $t_2[L] \sim_{mi} t_3[L](0.2, 0.9)$, we replace $t_1[L]$, $t_2[L]$ and $t_3[L]$ by $<0.6,0.2>/0 + <0.6,0.3>/1 + <0.5,0.2>/2$. Note that the first two tuples in r (t_1 and t_2) have been merged into a single tuple (t_1') in $merge(r)$. With different mi-thresholds C and I, we may have different merge results. If we set $C=0.2$ and $I=0.5$, then $t_1[L] \not\sim_{mi} t_2[L](0.2, 0.5)$. In this case, we obtain $merge(r)$ shown in Table 6. We see that the first two tuples (t_1' and t_2') are not merged.

Table 5. A relation $merge(r)$ under $C = 0.2$ and $I = 0.9$

	S	T	L
t_1'	<0.8,0.1>/0 + <0.1,0.1>/1 + <0.5,1>/3	<0.8,0.3>/0 + <0.9,0.1>/1 + <0.5,0.1>/2	<0.6,0.2>/0 + <0.6,0.3>/1 + <0.5,0.2>/2
t_2'	<0.9,0.2>/1 + <0.5,0.1>/2	<0.8,0.3>/0 + <0.9,0.1>/1 + <0.5,0.1>/2	<0.6,0.2>/0 + <0.6,0.3>/1 + <0.5,0.2>/2
t_3'	<0.5,0.1>/3 + <0.8,0.2>/4	<0.4,0.4>/3	<0.4,0.2>/3

Table 6. A relation $merge(r)$ under $C = 0.2$ and $I = 0.5$

	S	T	L
t_1'	$<0.8,0.1>/0$ + $<0.1,0.1>/1$ + $<0.5,1>/3$	$<0.8,0.3>/0$ + $<0.9,0.1>/1$ + $<0.5,0.1>/2$	$<0.4,0.2>/0$ + $<0.6,0.3>/1$
t_2'	$<0.8,0.1>/0$ + $<0.1,0.1>/1$ + $<0.5,1>/3$	$<0.8,0.3>/0$ + $<0.9,0.1>/1$ + $<0.5,0.1>/2$	$<0.6,0.6>/0$ + $<0.5,0.2>/2$
t_3'	$<0.9,0.2>/1$ + $<0.5,0.1>/2$	$<0.8,0.3>/0$ + $<0.9,0.1>/1$ + $<0.5,0.1>/2$	$<0.4,0.2>/0$ + $<0.6,0.3>/1$
t_4'	$<0.5,0.1>/3$ + $<0.8,0.2>/4$	$<0.4,0.4>/3$	$<0.4,0.2>/3$

There are two levels of precision we consider in vague sets for handling inconsistency. The first is the *object-precision*, which intuitively means the precision according to the cardinality of a set of mi-existing objects. The second is, given the same object, the vague values have different mi precision, which we term the *value-precision*.

We first define a partial order named *less object-precise* on VSs based on mi-existing objects and extend this partial order to tuples and relations in $MERGE(R)$.

Definition 9 (Less object-precise and object-equivalence). *We define a partial order, less object-precise (or less O-precise for simplicity) between two vague sets V_1 and V_2 as follows:*

$V_1 \sqsubseteq_O V_2$ *if the set of mi-existing objects in V_1 is a superset of the set of those in V_2. We say that V_1 is less O-precise than V_2.*

We extend $\sqsubseteq_O$ in r as follows. Let $t_1, t_2 \in r$. $t_1 \sqsubseteq_O t_2$ if $\forall A_i \in R$, $t_1[A_i] \sqsubseteq_O t_2[A_i]$. We say that t_1 is less O-precise than t_2.

Finally, we extend $\sqsubseteq_O$ in $MERGE(R)$ as follows: Let $r_1, r_2 \in MERGE(R)$. $r_1 \sqsubseteq_O r_2$ if $\forall t_2 \in r_2$, $\exists t_1 \in r_1$ such that $t_1 \sqsubseteq_O t_2$. We say that r_1 is less O-precise than r_2.

We define an object-equivalence between V_1 and V_2, denoted as $V_1 \doteq_O V_2$, iff $V_1 \sqsubseteq_O V_2$ and $V_2 \sqsubseteq_O V_1$. Similar definitions of object-equivalence are extended to tuples and relations.

Thus, an object-equivalence relation on $MERGE(R)$ induces a partition of $MERGE(R)$, which means all vague relations equivalent to each other are put into one O-equivalence class. Given any two vague relations in an O-equivalence class of $MERGE(R)$, each tuple in one vague relation has a one-to-one correspondence in the other vague relation. With in an O-equivalence class of $MERGE(R)$, we still have to consider the second level of precision as follows:

Definition 10 (Less value-precise and value-equivalence). *Let $V_1 \doteq_O V_2$. We define a partial order, less value-precise (or less V-precise for simplicity), between V_1 and V_2 as follows:*

Let $a = <M_m^{V_1}, M_i^{V_1}>$ and $b = <M_m^{V_2}, M_i^{V_2}>$ be the respective vague values of a common mi-existing object u in V_1 and V_2. If $M_m^{V_1} \leq M_m^{V_2}$ and $M_i^{V_1} \geq M_i^{V_2}$ (that is, a is less crisp and more imprecise than b), then we say a is less V-precise than b, denoted as $a \sqsubseteq_V b$.

$V_1 \sqsubseteq_V V_2$ if the vague value of each mi-existing object in V_1 is less V-precise than that of the same object in V_2. We say that V_1 is less V-precise than V_2.

We extend $\sqsubseteq_V$ in r as follows. Let t_1, $t_2 \in r$ and $t_1 \doteq_O t_2$. $t_1 \sqsubseteq_V t_2$ if $\forall A_i \in R$, $t_1[A_i] \sqsubseteq_V t_2[A_i]$. We say that t_1 is less V-precise than t_2.

Finally, we extend $\sqsubseteq_V$ in an O-equivalence class of $MERGE(R)$ as follows. Let $r_1 \doteq_O r_2$. $r_1 \sqsubseteq_V r_2$ if $\forall t_1 \in r_1$, $\exists t_2 \in r_2$ such that $t_1 \sqsubseteq_V t_2$. We say that r_1 is less V-precise than r_2.

We define a value-equivalence, denoted as $V_1 \doteq_V V_2$ iff $V_1 \sqsubseteq_V V_2$ and $V_2 \sqsubseteq_V V_1$. Similar definitions are extended to tuples and relations.

According to Definition 10, we define V-join $\cup$ and V-meet $\cap$ under $\sqsubseteq_V$ of vague values of a given object, that is, $< M_m^x, M_i^x > \cup < M_m^y, M_i^y > = < max\{M_m^x, M_m^y\}$, $min\{M_i^x, M_i^x\} >$ and $< M_m^x, M_i^x > \cap < M_m^y, M_i^y > = < min\{M_m^x, M_m^y\}$, $max\{M_i^x, M_i^x\} >$. It is easy to check that the less V-precise order $\sqsubseteq_V$ induces a complete semi-lattice by using $\cup$ and $\cap$ as shown in Fig. 3.

It can be checked that $<1,0>$ is the top element according to the less V-precise order. Note that for some mi-pair vague values, V-meet may cause the corresponding vague value $[\alpha(u), 1 - \beta(u)]$ beyond the legal range [0,1], which is not valid. From now on, we restrict our discussion to the V-meet that gives rise to valid vague values as a result.

Given any mi-thresholds C and I, if $<C, I>$ is a valid vague value, then we can use $<C, I>$ as a cut-off boundary to construct a complete lattice, rather than the original complete semi-lattice shown in Fig. 3, induced by the less V-precise order $\sqsubseteq_V$. For example, given $<C, I> = <0.5, 0.5>$ (or $<0.6, 0.4>$), which is a valid vague value, in the dotted-line region in Fig. 3, all vague values form a complete lattice, since given any two values in the enclosed region, we have their greatest lower bound and lowest upper bound. However, if $<C, I>$ is not a valid vague value, then we have a complete semi-lattice, since some values in the enclosed region constructed by $<C, I>$ do not have their greatest lower bound. For instance, in the dotted-line region with respect to an invalid vague value $<0.1, 0.3>$, all vague values form a complete semi-lattice, since for $<0.1, 0.2>$ and $<0.2, 0.3>$, we do not have their greatest lower bound.

From Definition 9, we can deduce that $MERGE(R)$ is a lattice based on O-equivalence classes with respect to $\sqsubseteq_O$. In this lattice, each node is an O-equivalence class, in which all vague relations are O-equivalent. The top node is the O-equivalence class of $\emptyset^O$, i.e. the set of vague relations with an empty set of tuples. The bottom node is the O-equivalence class, in which all vague relations have only one tuple and all mi-existing objects in vague relations form the universes of discourse.

Example 4. For simplicity we just assume $U = \{0, 1\}$ and $R = A$, we construct the lattice for $MERGE(R)$ under $C=0.5$ and $I=0.5$ according to O-equivalence classes. As shown in Fig. 4, all O-equivalence classes (the nodes represented by circles) form a lattice based on $\sqsubseteq_O$. Each node in the lattice is actually the set of all vague relations (represented by tables with single attribute) which are O-equivalent to each other. For instance, r_1 and r_2 are two vague relations with two tuples such that $r_1 \doteq_O r_2$. Similarly, we have $r_3 \doteq_O r_4$, where r_3 and r_4 are two vague relations with only one tuple. Inside each node, based on $\sqsubseteq_V$ in Definition 10, all vague relations in the node form a complete lattice (when the cut-off boundary is a valid vague value) or a complete semi-lattice (when the cut-off boundary is not a valid vague value). In the complete (semi-)

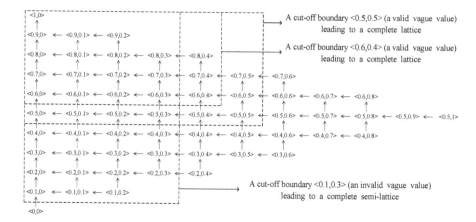

Fig. 3. A complete semi-lattice of vague values of an object u

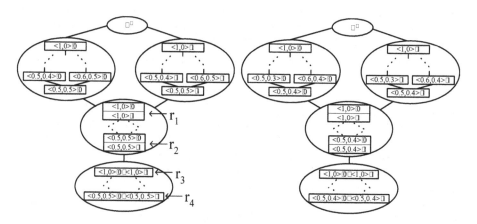

Fig. 4. A lattice of $MERGE(R)$ under C=0.5 and I=0.5

Fig. 5. A lattice of $MERGE(R)$ under C=0.5 and I=0.4

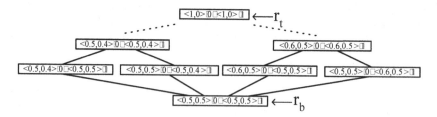

Fig. 6. A lattice within the bottom node of the lattice of MERGE(R) of Fig. 4

lattice, the top element is the vague relation in which all vague values of objects are $<1,0>$, and if the cut-off boundary $<C,I>$ is a valid vague value, then the bottom element is the vague relation in which all vague values of objects are $<C,I>$. For example, in the lattice shown in Fig. 6, which is the bottom node of the lattice in Fig. 4, each table represents a single attribute vague relation. The top is the single attribute vague relation r_t with one tuple $<<1,0>/0+<1,0>/1>$. The bottom is the vague relation r_b with single tuple $<<0.5,0.5>/0+<0.5,0.5>/1>$, and the vague value of each object is $<C,I>$.

Given different mi-thresholds, a lattice induced by $\sqsubseteq_V$ exists inside each node. For instance, we have the lattice of $MERGE(R)$ under $C=0.5$ and $I=0.4$ as shown in Fig. 5. The bottom elements in each node are different from those in Fig. 4, since the mi-thresholds are different.

Now, we extend the mi-existing of VSs given in Definition 4 to tuples as follows: $t[X]$ is mi-existing, if $\forall A \in X$, $t[A]$ is mi-existing, where $X \subseteq R$. We also extend the concept of mi-overlap given in Definition 5 to tuples $t_1, t_2 \in r$ under mi-thresholds C and I as follows: $t_1[X] \sim_{mi} t_2[X](C, I)$, if $\forall A \in X$, $t_1[A] \sim_{mi} t_2[A](C, I)$ where $X \subseteq R$.

Example 5. We can verify that $t_1 \sim_{mi} t_2(0.2, 0.9)$ in the relation shown in Table 4.

4 Functional Dependencies and Vague Chase

Functional Dependencies (FDs) being satisfied in a vague relation r can be formalized in terms values being mi-overlapping rather than equal. The VChase procedure for r is a means of maintaining consistency of r with respect to a given set of FDs.

4.1 Functional Dependencies in Vague Relations

We formalize the notion of an FD being satisfied in a vague relation. Lien's and Atzeni's axiom system is sound and complete for FDs being satisfied in vague relations.

Definition 11 (Functional dependency). *Given mi-thresholds C and I, a* Functional Dependency *over R (or simply an FD) is a statement of the form $X \to_{C,I} Y$, where $X, Y \subseteq R$. We may simply write $X \to Y$ if C and I are known from context. An FD $X \to Y$ is satisfied in a relation r, denoted by $r \vDash X \to Y$, if $\forall t_1, t_2 \in r$, $t_1[X] \sim_{mi} t_2[X](C, I)$, then $t_1[Y] \sim_{mi} t_2[Y](C, I)$, or $t_1[Y]$ or $t_2[Y]$ are not mi-existing.*

A set of FDs F over R is satisfied in r, denoted by $r \vDash F$, if $\forall X \to Y \in F, r \vDash X \to Y$. If $r \vDash F$ we say that r is *consistent* with respect to F (or simply r is consistent if F is understood from context); otherwise if $r \nvDash F$ then we say that r is *inconsistent* with respect to F (or simply r is inconsistent). We let $SAT(F)$ denote the finite set $\{r \in MERGE(R)|r \vDash F\}$.

Example 6. Let $F = \{S \to_{0.2,0.9} TL, L \to_{0.2,0.9} S\}$ be a set of FDs over R, where R is the relation schema whose semantics are given in Example 1. We can verify that $r \vDash S \to_{0.2,0.9} TL$ but that $r \nvDash L \to_{0.2,0.9} S$, where r is the relation shown in Table 4. Thus $r \in SAT(\{S \to_{0.2,0.9} TL\})$ but $r \notin SAT(F)$. Consider also $merge(r)$ shown in Table 5, we have $merge(r) \in SAT(\{S \to_{0.2,0.9} TL\})$ but $merge(r) \notin SAT(F)$. If we change the mi-thresholds from 0.2 and 0.9 to 0.2 and 0.5, the result is different. Let $F = \{S \to_{0.2,0.5} TL, L \to_{0.2,0.5} S\}$ be a set of FDs over R. We can verify that $r \nvDash S \to_{0.2,0.5} TL$ and that $r \nvDash L \to_{0.2,0.5} S$. Thus $r \notin SAT(\{S \to_{0.2,0.5} TL\})$ and $r \notin SAT(F)$. Consider also $merge(r)$ shown in Table 6, we have $merge(r) \notin SAT(\{S \to_{0.2,0.5} TL\})$ and $merge(r) \notin SAT(F)$.

We say that F logically implies an FD $X \to_{C,I} Y$ over R written $F \vDash X \to_{C,I} Y$, whenever for any domain $D, \forall r \in REL_D(R)$, if $r \vDash F$ holds then $r \vDash X \to Y$ also holds.

Here we state the well known Lien's and Atzeni's axiom system [5,4] for incomplete relations as follows:

1. *Reflexivity*: If $Y \subseteq X$, then $F \vdash X \to Y$.
2. *Augmentation*: If $F \vdash X \to Y$ holds, then $F \vdash XZ \to YZ$ also holds.
3. *Union*: If $F \vdash X \to Y$ and $F \vdash X \to Z$ hold, then $F \vdash X \to YZ$ holds.
4. *Decomposition*: If $F \vdash X \to YZ$ holds, then $F \vdash X \to Y$ and $F \vdash X \to Z$ hold.

Definition 12 (Soundness and Completeness of Axiom system). *Whenever an FD $X \to Y$ can be proven from F using a finite number of inference rules from Lien's and Atzeni's axiom system [4], we write $F \vdash X \to Y$.*

Lien's and Atzeni's axiom system is sound if $F \vdash X \to Y$ implies $F \vDash X \to Y$. Correspondingly, Lien's and Atzeni's axiom system is complete if $F \vDash X \to Y$ implies $F \vdash X \to Y$.

The proof of the following theorem is standard [4], which we establish a counter example relation to show that $F \nvdash X \to Y$ but $F \nvDash X \to Y$. Due to lack of space, we omit all proofs in this paper. However, all proofs will be contained in the full version of it.

Theorem 1. *Lien's and Atzeni's axiom system is sound and complete for FDs being satisfied in vague relations.*

4.2 Vague Chase

We define the chase procedure for maintaining consistency in vague relations. Assuming that a vague relation r is updated with information obtained from several different sources, at any given time the vague relation r may be inconsistent with respect to a set of FDs F. Thus we input r and F into the VChase procedure and its output, denoted by $VChase(r, F)$, is a consistent relation over R with respect to F. The pseudo-code for the algorithm $VChase(r, F)$ is presented in Algorithm 1.

We call an execution of line 6 in Algorithm 1 a *VChase step*, and say that the VChase step *applies* the FD $X \to Y$ to the *current state* of $VChase(r, F)$.

Example 7. The vague relation $VChase(r, F)$ is shown in Table 7, where r is shown in Table 4 and $F = \{S \to_{0.2,0.9} TL, L \to_{0.2,0.9} S\}$ is the set of FDs over R. We can verify that $VChase(r, F) \vDash F$, i.e. $VChase(r, F)$ is consistent, and that $VChase(r, F) = VChase(merge(r), F)$, where $merge(r)$ is shown in Table 5. If

Algorithm 1. $VChase(r, F)$

1: Result := r;
2: Tmp := ∅;
3: **while** Tmp ≠ Result **do**
4:     Tmp := Result;
5:     **if** $X \rightarrow_{C,I} Y \in F, \exists t_1, t_2 \in$ Result such that $t_1[X] \sim_{mi} t_2[X](C, I), t_1[Y]$ and $t_2[Y]$ are mi-existing but $t_1[Y] \not\sim_{mi} t_2[Y](C, I)$ **then**
6:         $\forall A \in (Y - X), t_1[A], t_2[A] := t_1[A] \vee t_2[A];$
7:     **end if**
8: **end while**
9: **return** merge(Result);

Table 7. Vague relation $VChase(r, F)$ under C=0.2 and I=0.9

S	T	L
<0.8,0.1>/0 + <0.9,0.2>/1 + <0.5,0.1>/2 + <0.5,1>/3 <0.5,0.1>/3 + <0.8,0.2>/4	<0.8,0.3>/0 + <0.9,0.1>/1 + <0.5,0.1>/2 <0.4,0.4>/3	<0.6,0.2>/0 + <0.6,0.3>/1 + <0.5,0.2>/2 <0.4,0.2>/3

Table 8. Vague relation $VChase(r, F)$ under C=0.2 and I=0.5

S	T	L
<0.8,0.1>/0 + <0.9,0.2>/1 + <0.5,0.1>/2 + <0.5,1>/3 <0.5,0.1>/3 + <0.8,0.2>/4	<0.8,0.3>/0 + <0.9,0.1>/1 + <0.5,0.1>/2 <0.4,0.4>/3	<0.4,0.2>/0 + <0.6,0.3>/1 + <0.5,0.2>/2 <0.4,0.2>/3

$F = \{S \rightarrow_{0.2,0.5} TL, L \rightarrow_{0.2,0.5} S\}$ is the set of FDs over R, we can also verify that $VChase(r, F) \models F$, which is as shown in Table 8, and that $VChase(r, F) = VChase(merge(r), F)$, where $merge(r)$ is shown in Table 6.

From Tables 7 and 8, we see that different mi-thresholds C and I may give rise to different VChase results (the corresponding values of L in the first tuple).

The next lemma shows that $VChase(r, F)$ is less O-precise than $merge(r)$ and unique. Its complexity is polynomial time in the sizes of r and F.

Lemma 1. *The following statements are true:*

1. *VChase(r, F) ⊑$_O$ merge(r).*
2. *VChase(r, F) is unique.*
3. *VChase(r, F) terminates in polynomial time in the sizes of r and F.*

The next theorem shows that the VChase procedure outputs a consistent relation and that it commutes with the merge operation.

Theorem 2. *The following two statements are true:*
1. *VChase(r, F) ⊨ F, i.e. VChase(r, F) is consistent.*
2. *VChase(r, F) = VChase(merge(r), F).*

5   The Most O-Precise Approximation of a Vague Relation

The $VChase(r, F)$ procedure can be regarded as the most O-precise approximation of r, which is also consistent to F. In this section, we first define the *join* of vague relations, which corresponds to the least upper bound of these relations in the lattice $MERGE(R)$ based on O-equivalence classes. (Recall the lattices shown in Figures 4 and 5.) Next, we define the *most O-precise approximation* of r with respect to F to be the *join* of all the consistent and merged relations which are less O-precise than r. Our main result is that $VChase(r, F)$ is the most O-precise approximation of r with respect to F. Thus, the VChase procedure solves the consistency problem in polynomial time in the size of r and F.

We now define the join operation on relations in the lattice of $MERGE(R)$ based on O-equivalence classes.

Definition 13 (Join operation). *The join of two vague relations,* r_1, $r_2 \in MERGE(R)$, *denoted by* $r_1 \sqcup r_2$, *is given by*

$$r_1 \sqcup r_2 = \{t | \exists t_1 \in r_1, \exists t_2 \in r_2 \text{ such that } \forall A \in R, t_1[A] \sim_{mi} t_2[A](C, I),$$
$$t[A] = t_1[A] \wedge t_2[A]\}.$$

It can be verified that the O-equivalence class that consists of $r_1 \sqcup r_2$ is the least upper bound with respect to the O-equivalence classes of r_1 and r_2 in $MERGE(R)$. From now on we will assume that $r_1, r_2 \in MERGE(R)$.

The next theorem shows that if two relations are consistent then their join is also consistent.

Theorem 3. *Let* $r_1, r_2 \in SAT(F)$. *Then* $r_1 \sqcup r_2 \in SAT(F)$.

The most O-precise approximation of a vague relation r over R with respect to F is the join of all consistent relations s such that s is a merged relation that is less O-precise than r.

Definition 14 (Most O-precise approximation). *The most O-precise approximation of a vague relation* r *with respect to* F, *denoted by* $approx(r, F)$, *is given by* $\bigsqcup \{s | s \sqsubseteq_O merge(r) \text{ and } s \in SAT(F)\}$.

The next lemma shows some desirable properties of approximations.

Lemma 2. *The following statements are true:*

1. *approx(r, F) is consistent.*
2. *approx(r, F) $\sqsubseteq_O$ merge(r).*
3. *approx(r, F) $\doteq_O$ merge(r) iff r is consistent.*

The next theorem, which is the main result of this section, shows that output of the VChase procedure is equal to the corresponding most O-precise approximation. Thus, the vague relation $VChase(r, F)$, which is shown in Table 7, is the most O-precise approximation of r with respect to F, where r is the relation over R shown in Table 4 and F is the set of FDs over R specified in Example 6.

Theorem 4. $VChase(r, F) \doteq_O approx(r, F)$.

6   Related Work

The problem of maintaining the consistency with respect to FDs of a relational database is well-known. However, in many real applications, it is too restrictive for us to have FDs hold in relations. For example, the salary of employees is approximately determined by the number of working years. The discovery of meaningful but approximate FDs is an interesting topic in both data mining and database areas [8]. Thus, many research works on approximate FDs have been proposed [9,10,11]. In order to deal with uncertain information including missing, unknown, or imprecisely known data, probability theory [12,13,14,15], fuzzy set and possibility theory-based treatments [16,17] have been applied to extend standard relational databases and FDs [18,19,20,21,22]. Based on vague set theory, we apply some useful parameters such as the median and imprecision memberships to characterize uncertain data objects. The parameters are used to extend various concepts such as satisfaction of FDs in vague relations.

The work in [23] introduces the notion of imprecise relations and FDs being satisfied in imprecise relations in order to cater for the situation when the information may be obtained from different sources and therefore may be imprecise. However, we apply the interval-based vague memberships, which capture positive, neutral and negative information of objects, and extend the "equally likely objects" assumption used in [23]. The imprecise set in [23] can also be considered as the O-equivalent VS in our work.

7   Conclusion

In this paper, we extend FDs to be satisfied in a vague relation. We define the mi-overlap between vague sets and the merge operation of a vague relation r which replaces each attribute value in r by the mi-union of all attribute values with respect to the same reflexive and transitive closure under mi-overlap. We also define a partial order on merged vague relations which induces a lattice on the set of merged vague relations based on O-equivalence classes. Inside each O-equivalence class, we define a partial order based on the vague values of mi-existing objects which induces a complete semi-lattice. Satisfaction of an FD in a vague relation is defined in terms values being mi-overlapping rather than equality. Lien's and Atzeni's axiom system is sound and complete for FDs being satisfied in vague relations. We define the chase procedure VChase as a means of maintaining consistency of r with respect to F. Our main result is that VChase outputs the most O-precise approximation of r with respect to F and can be computed in polynomial time in the sizes of r and F. Our result suggests a mechanical way that maintains the consistency of vague data. It is both interesting and challenging to use the VChase result to provide more effective and efficient evaluation of SQL over vague relations as a future work.

References

1. Zadeh, L.A.: Fuzzy sets. Information and Control 8, 338–353 (1965)
2. Gau, W.-L., Buehrer, D.J.: Vague sets. IEEE Transactions on Systems, Man, and Cybernetics 23, 610–614 (1993)

3. Lu, A., Ng, W.: Vague sets or intuitionistic fuzzy sets for handling vague data: Which one is better? In: Delcambre, L.M.L., Kop, C., Mayr, H.C., Mylopoulos, J., Pastor, Ó. (eds.) ER 2005. LNCS, vol. 3716, pp. 401–416. Springer, Heidelberg (2005)
4. Atzeni, P., Antonellis, V.D.: Relational Database Theory. Benjamin/Cummings (1993)
5. Lien, Y.E.: On the equivalence of database models. J. ACM 29, 333–362 (1982)
6. Lu, A., Ng, W.: Managing merged data by vague functional dependencies. In: Atzeni, P., Chu, W., Lu, H., Zhou, S., Ling, T.-W. (eds.) ER 2004. LNCS, vol. 3288, pp. 259–272. Springer, Heidelberg (2004)
7. Lu, A., Ng, W.: Mining hesitation information by vague association rules. In: Parent, C., Schewe, K.-D., Storey, V.C., Thalheim, B. (eds.) ER 2007. LNCS, vol. 4801, pp. 39–55. Springer, Heidelberg (2007)
8. Bra, P.D., Paredaens, J.: Horizontal decompositions for handling exceptions to functional dependencies. In: Advances in Data Base Theory, pp. 123–141 (1982)
9. Kivinen, J., Mannila, H.: Approximate inference of functional dependencies from relations. Theor. Comput. Sci. 149, 129–149 (1995)
10. Huhtala, Y., Kärkkäinen, J., Porkka, P., Toivonen, H.: Tane: An efficient algorithm for discovering functional and approximate dependencies. Comput. J. 42, 100–111 (1999)
11. King, R.S., Legendre, J.J.: Discovery of functional and approximate functional dependencies in relational databases. JAMDS 7, 49–59 (2003)
12. Barbar, D., Garcia-Molina, H., Porter, D.: The management of probabilistic data. IEEE Trans. Knowl. Data Eng. 4, 487–502 (1992)
13. Dey, D., Sarkar, S.: A probabilistic relational model and algebra. ACM Trans. Database Syst. 21, 339–369 (1996)
14. Ross, R., Subrahmanian, V.S., Grant, J.: Aggregate operators in probabilistic databases. J. ACM 52, 54–101 (2005)
15. Lakshmanan, L.V.S., Leone, N., Ross, R., Subrahmanian, V.S.: Probview: A flexible probabilistic database system. ACM Trans. Database Syst. 22, 419–469 (1997)
16. Bosc, P., Prade, H.: An introduction to the fuzzy set and possibility theory-based treatment of flexible queries and uncertain or imprecise databases. In: Motro, A., Smets, P. (eds.) Uncertainty Management in Information Systems: From Needs to Solutions, pp. 285–324. Kluwer Academic Publishers, Dordrecht (1996)
17. Dubois, D., Prade, H.: Possibility Theory: An Approach to Computerized Processing of Uncertainty. Plenum Press, New York (1988)
18. Dey, D., Sarkar, S.: Generalized normal forms for probabilistic relational data. IEEE Trans. Knowl. Data Eng. 14, 485–497 (2002)
19. Raju, K.V.S.V.N., Majumdar, A.K.: Fuzzy functional dependencies and lossless join decomposition of fuzzy relational database systems. ACM Trans. Database Syst. 13, 129–166 (1988)
20. Bosc, P., Dubois, D., Prade, H.: Fuzzy functional dependencies and redundancy elimination. JASIS 49, 217–235 (1998)
21. Intan, R., Mukaidono, M.: Fuzzy functional dependency and its application to approximate data querying. In: Desai, B.C., Kiyoki, Y., Toyama, M. (eds.) IDEAS, pp. 47–54. IEEE Computer Society, Los Alamitos (2000)
22. Brown, P., Haas, P.J.: Bhunt: Automatic discovery of fuzzy algebraic constraints in relational data. In: Aberer, K., Koubarakis, M., Kalogeraki, V. (eds.) Databases, Information Systems, and Peer-to-Peer Computing. LNCS, vol. 2944, pp. 668–679. Springer, Heidelberg (2004)
23. Levene, M.: Maintaining consistency of imprecise relations. Comput. J. 39, 114–123 (1996)

Querying Incomplete Data with Logic Programs: ER Strikes Back

Andrea Calì[1,2]

[1] Computing Laboratory
University of Oxford
Wolfson Building, Parks Road
Oxford OX1 3QD, United Kingdom
[2] Faculty of Computer Science
Free University of Bozen-Bolzano
piazza Domenicani 3
I-39100 Bolzano, Italy
ac@andreacali.com

Abstract. Since Chen's Entity-Relationship (ER) model, conceptual modelling has been playing a fundamental role in relational data design. In this paper we consider an extended ER model enriched with cardinality constraints, disjunction assertions, and is-a relations among both entities and relationships; we present a framework in which the data underlying an ER schema can be directly queried through the schema by using suitable predicates. In this setting, we consider the case of incomplete data, which is likely to happen, for instance, when data from different sources are integrated. We address the problem of providing correct answers to conjunctive queries by reasoning on the schema. Based on previous results about decidability of the problem, we provide a query answering algorithm based on rewriting the initial query into a recursive Datalog query, in which the information about the schema is encoded. We finally give some complexity results, and we show extensions to more general settings.

1 Introduction

Conceptual data models, and in particular the Entity-Relationship (ER) model [13], have been playing a fundamental role in database design. With the emerging trends in data exchange, information integration, semantic web, and web information systems, the need for dealing with inconsistent and incomplete data has arisen; In this context, it is important to provide *consistent answers* to queries posed over inconsistent and incomplete data [2]. It is worth noticing here that inconsistency and incompleteness of data is considered with respect to a set of constraints (a.k.a. data dependencies); in data integration and exchange such constraints, rather than expressing properties that hold on the data, are used to represent properties of the domain of interest.

We address the problem of answering queries over *incomplete data*, where queries are conjunctive queries expressed over a conceptual schema. As for the conceptual model, we follow [13], and we adopt a well-known (and widely adopted

C. Parent et al. (Eds.): ER 2007, LNCS 4801, pp. 245–260, 2007.

in practice) formalism that we call *Extended Entity-Relationship (EER) Model*, able to represent classes of objects with their attributes, relationships among classes, cardinality constraints in the participation of entities in relationships, and is-a relations among both classes and relationships. We provide a formal semantics to our conceptual model in terms of the relational database model, similarly to what is done in [24]; this allows us for formulating conjunctive queries over EER schemata. In the presence of data that are incomplete w.r.t. to a set of constraints, we need to *reason* about the dependencies in order to provide consistent answers; we do this in a model-theoretic fashion, following the approach of [2,5]. In this paper we present an algorithm, based on encoding the information about the conceptual schema into a *rewriting* of the query, that computes the consistent answers to queries posed on EER schemata, where the data are incomplete w.r.t. the schema. The class of relational constraints we deal with does not fall in cases (in the relational model) for which answering is known to be decidable [7]. Though the decidability of the problem is straightforwardly derived from a work that addresses containment in the context of a Description Logics that is able to capture the EER model [11], our technique can be used in practice, without resorting to costly manipulations of the data: we operate at a purely *intensional level*, reasoning on queries and schemata, and only querying the data at the last step. Moreover, our technique yields an upper bound for the complexity of the problem that is better than the one provided by [11].

The paper is organised as follows. We give necessary preliminaries, including the EER model, in Section 2; in Section 3 we show how to answer queries with the *chase*, a formal tool to deal with dependencies; the query rewriting technique is described in 4, together with extensions to more general cases. Section 5 concludes the paper, discussing related works.

2   Preliminaries and Notation

In this section we give a formal definition of the relational data model, database constraints, conjunctive queries and answers to queries on incomplete data, and the EER formalism, that we use as a conceptual modelling language.

2.1   Data Model, Constraints and Queries

The relational data model. In the relational data model [14], predicate symbols are used to denote the relations in the database, whereas constant symbols denote the objects and the values stored in relations. We assume to have two distinct, fixed and infinite alphabets Γ and Γ_f of constants and *fresh constants* respectively, and we consider only databases over $\Gamma \cup \Gamma_f$. We adopt the so-called *unique name assumption*, i.e. we assume that different constants denote different objects. A *relational schema* $\mathcal{R}$ consists of an alphabet of *predicate* (or *relation*) symbols, each one with an associated arity denoting the number of arguments of the predicate (or attributes of the relation). When a relation symbol R has arity n, it can be denoted by R/n. A *relational database* (or simply database) D over a schema $\mathcal{R}$ is a set of relations with constants as atomic values. We have one relation of arity n for each predicate symbol of arity n in the alphabet $\mathcal{R}$. The relation R^D in D corresponding to the predicate symbol R consists of a set of tuples of constants, that are the tuples satisfying the predicate R in D. When, given a database D for a schema $\mathcal{R}$, a tuple $t = (c_1, \ldots, c_n)$ is in R^D, where $R \in \mathcal{R}$, we say that the fact $R(c_1, \ldots, c_n)$ holds in D. Henceforth, we will use interchangeably the notion of fact and tuple.

Integrity constraints. *Integrity constraints* are assertions on the symbols of the alphabet $\mathcal{R}$ that are intended to be satisfied in every database for the schema. The notion of satisfaction depends on the type of constraints defined over the schema. A database D over a schema $\mathcal{R}$ is said to *satisfy* a set of integrity constraints Σ expressed over $\mathcal{R}$, written $D \models \Sigma$, if every constraint in Σ is satisfied by D. The database constraints of our interest are *inclusion dependencies (IDs)* and *key dependencies (KDs)* (see e.g. [1]). We denote with overlined uppercase letters (e.g. $\bar{X}$) both sequences and sets of attributes of relations. Given a tuple t in relation R^D, i.e. a fact $R(t)$ in a database D for a schema $\mathcal{R}$, and a set of attributes $\bar{X}$ of R, we denote with $t[\bar{X}]$ the *projection* (see e.g. [1]) of t on the attributes in $\bar{X}$.

(i) *Inclusion dependencies (IDs)*. An inclusion dependency between relations R_1 and R_2 is denoted by $R_1[\bar{X}] \subseteq R_2[\bar{Y}]$. Such a constraint is satisfied in a database D iff for each tuple t_1 in R_1^D there exists a tuple t_2 in R_2^D such that $t_1[\bar{X}] = t_2[\bar{Y}]$.

(ii) *Key dependencies (KDs)*. A key dependency over relation R is denoted by $key(R) = \bar{K}$, where $\bar{K}$ is a subset of the attributes of R. Such a constraint is satisfied in a database D iff for each $t_1, t_2 \in R^D$ we have $t_1[\bar{K}] \neq t_2[\bar{K}]$. Observe that KDs are a special case of functional dependencies (FDs) [1].

Queries. A *relational query* is a formula that specifies a set of data to be retrieved from a database. In the following we will refer to the class of *conjunctive queries*. A *conjunctive query* (CQ) Q of arity n over a schema $\mathcal{R}$ is written in the form $Q(\bar{X}) \leftarrow body(\bar{X}, \bar{Y})$ where: Q belongs to a new alphabet $\mathcal{Q}$ (the alphabet of queries, that is disjoint from both Γ, Γ_f and $\mathcal{R}$); $Q(\bar{X})$ is the *head* of the conjunctive query, denoted $head(Q)$; $body(\bar{X}, \bar{Y})$ is the *body* of the conjunctive query, denoted $body(Q)$, and is a conjunction of atoms involving the variables $\bar{X} = X_1, \ldots, X_n$ and $\bar{Y} = Y_1, \ldots, Y_m$, and constants from Γ; the predicate symbols of the atoms are in $\mathcal{R}$, the number of variables of $\bar{X}$ is called the *arity* of Q. Every variable appearing more than once in Q (more than once in the body, or both in the body and in the head) is called *distinguished variable (DV)*; every othervariable is called *non-distinguished variable (NDV)*. We denote with $Var(Q)$ the set of all variables of Q. Given a database D, the answer to Q over D, denoted $ans(Q, D,)$, is the set of n-tuples of constants $(c_1, \ldots, c_n)$, such that, when substituting each x_i with c_i, for $1 \leq i \leq n$, the formula $\exists \bar{Y}.body(\bar{X}, \bar{Y})$ evaluates to *true* in D, where $\exists \bar{Y}$ is a shorthand for $\exists Y_1 \cdots \exists Y_m$.

A Datalog query Π of arity n consists of: (i) A collection of rules of the form $head(\bar{x}) \leftarrow body(\bar{X}, \bar{Y})$, where $body(\bar{X}, \bar{Y})$ is a conjunction of atoms whose predicate symbols are either relation symbols in $\mathcal{R}$ or the head symbol H, and involve $\bar{X} = X_1, \ldots, X_n$ and $\bar{Y} = Y_1, \ldots, Y_m$, where X_i and Y_j are either variables or values of Γ; at least one rule in Π must have the predicate H in the head. *(ii)* A *special rule* ρ (belonging to the above collection) Given a Datalog query Π, the evaluation $\Pi(D)$ of Π over a database D (which is a set of facts), is the evaluation of the special rule ρ, taken as a CQ, over the minimum Herbrand model of $\Pi \cup D$ [1]. We recall that the Herbrand base HB of a Datalog program Π is the set of all ground (without variables) atoms that can be formed with the predicate symbols from Π; a Herbrand interpretation is a subset of HB, and it is a Herbrand model of Π if it a model for Π; it can be proved that positive Datalog programs admit a unique *minimal* Herbrand model.

Homomorphism. Given two sets of atoms (posibly ground, i.e., without variables) A and B, a *homomorphism* μ from A to B is a function from the symbols (variables and constants, but not relation symbols) of A to those of B that sends each constant to itself, and induces a well-defined map from A to B, that is if $R(X_1, \ldots, X_n)$ is in A, then $R(\mu X_1, \ldots, \mu(X_n))$ is in B.

Querying incomplete data. In the presence of incomplete data, a natural way of considering the problem of query answering is to adopt the so-called *sound semantics* or *open-world assumption* [26,21]. In this approach, the data are considered sound but not complete, in the sense that they constitute a piece of correct information, but not all the relevant information. More formally, we consider all databases that satisfy the dependencies, and we consider as answers to a query those that are true in *all* such databases.

Definition 1. *Consider a relational schema $\mathcal{R}$ with a set of IDs Σ, and a database D for $\mathcal{R}$, with $D \models \Sigma_K$; let Q be a conjunctive query of arity n over $\mathcal{R}$. A n-tuple t belongs to the answers to Q w.r.t. D and Σ, which are denoted by $ans(Q, \Sigma, D)$, if and only if, for every database B for $\mathcal{R}$ such that $B \models \Sigma$ and $B \supseteq D$, we have $t \in Q(B)$.*

We will see that, under the database dependencies we consider in this paper, the problem of query answering is mainly complicated by two facts: *(i)* the number of databases that satisfy Σ and that include D can be infinite; *(ii)* there is no bound to the size of such databases.

2.2   The Conceptual Model

In this section we present the conceptual model we shall deal with in the rest of the paper, and we give its semantics in terms of relational database schemata with constraints. Our model incorporates the basic features of the ER model [13] and OO models, including subset (or is-a) constraints on both entities and relationships. Henceforth, we will call our model *Extended Entity-Relationship (EER) model.* An *EER schema* consists of a collection of entity, relationship, and attribute definitions over an alphabet of symbols, partitioned into entity, relationship and attribute symbols. The model is the same as the one in [4], and it can be summarised as follows: *(1)* entities can have attributes; an attribute can

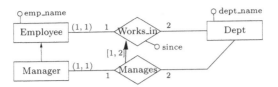

Fig. 1. EER schema for Example 1

be mandatory (instances have at least one value for it), and functional (instances have at most one value for it); *(2)* entities can participate in relationships; a participation of an entity E in a relationship R can be mandatory (instances of E participate at least once), and functional (instances of E participate at most once); *(3)* is-a relations can hold between entities and between relationships; in the latter case, assuming the relationships to have both arity n, a permutation of $(1, \ldots, n)$ specifies the correspondence between the attributes of the two relationships in the is-a relation. We refer the reader to [4] for further details.

Example 1. Consider the EER schema shown in Figure 1, depicted in the usual graphical notation for the ER model (components are indicated by integers for the relationships). The schema describes employees working in departments of a firm, and managers that are also employees, and manage departments. Managers who manage a department also work in the same department, as imposed by the is-a among the two relationships; the permutation $[1, 2]$ labelling the arrow denotes that the is-a holds considering the components in the same order (in general, any permutation of $(1, \ldots, n)$ is possible for an is-a between two n-ary relationships). The constraint $(1, 1)$ on the participation of *Employee* in *Works_In* imposes that every instance of *Employee* participates at least once (mandatory participation) and at most once (functional participation) in *Works_In*; the same constraints hold on the participation of *Manager* in *Manages*. ∎

The semantics of an EER schema is defined by specifying all constraints imposed by EER constructs on databases that satisfy that schema. First of all, we formally define a database schema from an EER diagram. Such a database schema is defined in terms of *predicates*: we define a relational database schema that encodes the properties of an EER schema $\mathcal{C}$.

(a) Each entity E in $\mathcal{C}$ has an associated predicate E of arity 1.
(b) Each attribute A for an entity E in $\mathcal{C}$ has an associated predicate A of arity 2, associating attribute values to entity instances.
(c) Each relationship R among the entities $E_1, \ldots, E_n$ in $\mathcal{C}$ has an associated predicate R of arity n.
(d) Each attribute A for a relationship R among the entities $E_1, \ldots, E_n$ in $\mathcal{C}$ has an associated predicate A of arity $n + 1$, associating attribute values to n-tuples of entity instances.

The conjunctive queries are formulated using the predicates in the relational schema we obtain from the EER schema as described above.

Table 1. Derivation of relation constraints from an EER schema

EER construct	Relational constraint
attribute $A/2$ for an entity E	$A[1] \subseteq E[1]$
attribute $A/(n+1)$ for a relationship R/n	$A[1,\ldots,n] \subseteq R[1,\ldots,n]$
relationship R with entity E as i-th component	$R[i] \subseteq E[1]$
mandatory attribute $A/2$ of entity E	$E[1] \subseteq A[1]$
mandatory attribute $A/(n+1)$ of relationship R/n	$R[1,\ldots,n] \subseteq A[1,\ldots,n]$
functional attribute $A/2$ of entity E	$key(A) = \{1\}$
functional attribute $A/(n+1)$ of a relationship R/n	$key(A) = \{1,\ldots,n\}$
is-a relation between entities E_1 and E_2	$E_1[1] \subseteq E_2[1]$
is-a relation between relationships R_1 and R_2, where components $1,\ldots,n$ of R_1 correspond to components $j_1,\ldots,j_n$ of R_2	$R_1[1,\ldots,n] \subseteq R_2[j_1,\ldots,j_n]$
mandatory participation as i-th component of an entity E in a relationship R	$E[1] \subseteq R[i]$
functional participation as i-th component of an entity E in a relationship R	$key(R) = \{i\}$

Example 2. Consider again the EER schema of Example 1. The elements (predicates) of such a schema are manager/1, employee/1, dept/1, works_in/2, manages/2, emp_name/2, dept_name/2, since/3. Suppose we want to know the names of the managers who manage the toy department (named *toy_dept*). The corresponding conjunctive query is

$$Q(X) \leftarrow \text{manager}(X), \text{emp\_name}(X, Z), \text{manages}(X, Y), \text{dept}(Y),$$
$$\text{dept\_name}(Y, toy\_dept) \qquad \blacksquare$$

Once we have defined the database schema $\mathcal{R}$ for an EER schema $\mathcal{C}$, we give the semantics of each construct of the EER model; this is done by specifying what databases (i.e. extension of the predicates of $\mathcal{R}$) *satisfy* the constraints imposed by the constructs of the EER diagram. We do that by making use of relational database constraints, as shown in Table 1.

The class of constraints we obtain, which is a subclass of key and inclusion dependencies, is a class of relational database dependencies, that we shall call *conceptual dependencies (CDs)* [4] for obvious reasons.

3 Query Answering with the Chase

In this section we introduce the notion of *chase*, which is a fundamental tool for dealing with database constraints [22,23,27,18].; then we show some relevant properties of the chase under conceptual dependencies (CDs) regarding conjunctive query answering, that will pave the way for the query rewriting technique that will be presented in the next section.

The *chase* of a conjunctive query [22,18] is a key concept in particular in the context of functional and inclusion dependencies. Intuitively, given a database, its facts in general do not satisfy the dependencies; the idea of the chase is to convert the initial facts into a new set of facts constituting a database that satisfies the dependencies, possibly by collapsing facts (according to KDs) or adding new facts (according to IDs). When new facts are added, some of the constants need to be *fresh*, as we shall see in the following. The technique to construct a chase is well known (see, e.g., [18]); however we detail this technique here.

3.1 Construction of the Chase

Consider a database instance D for a relational schema $\mathcal{R}$, and a set Σ of dependencies on $\mathcal{R}$; in particular, $\Sigma = \Sigma_I \cup \Sigma_K$, where Σ_I is a set of inclusion dependencies and Σ_K is a set of key dependencies. In general, D does not satisfy Σ, written $D \not\models \Sigma$. In this case, we construct the chase of D w.r.t. Σ, denoted $chase_\Sigma(D)$, by repeatedly applying the rules defined below. We denote with $chase_\Sigma^*(D)$ the part of the chase that is already constructed before the rule is applied.

INCLUSION DEPENDENCY CHASE RULE. Let R, S be relational symbols in $\mathcal{R}$. Suppose there is a tuple t in $R^{chase_\Sigma^*(D)}$, and there is an ID $\sigma \in \Sigma_I$ of the form $R[\bar{Y}_R] \subseteq S[\bar{Y}_S]$. If there is no tuple t' in S^D such that $t'[\bar{X}_S] = t[\bar{X}_R]$ (in this case we say the rule is *applicable*), then we add a new tuple t_{chase} in S^D such that $t_{chase}[\bar{X}_S] = t[\bar{X}_R]$, and for every attribute A_i of S, with $1 \le i \le m$ and $A_i \notin \bar{X}_S$, $t_{chase}[A_i]$ is a fresh value in Γ_f that *follows*, according to lexicographic order, all the values already present in the chase.

KEY DEPENDENCY CHASE RULE. Let R be a relational symbol in $\mathcal{R}$. Suppose there is a KD κ of the form $key(R) = \bar{X}$. If there are two *distinct* tuples $t, t' \in \mathcal{R}^{chase_\Sigma^*(D)}$ such that $t[\bar{X}] = t'[\bar{X}]$ (in this case we say the rule is *applicable*), make the symbols in t and t' equal in the following way. Let $\bar{Y} = Y_1, \ldots, Y_\ell$ be the attributes of R that are not in $\bar{X}$; for all $i \in \{1, \ldots, \ell\}$, make $t[Y_i]$ and $t'[Y_i]$ merge into a combined symbol according to the following criterion: *(i)* if both are constants in Γ and they are not equal, halt the process; *(ii)* if one is in Γ and the other is a fresh constant in Γ_f, let the combined symbol be the non-fresh constant; *(iii)* if both are in Γ_f, let the combined symbol be the one preceding the other in lexicographic order. Finally, replace all occurrences in $chase_\Sigma^*(D)$ of $t[Y_i]$ and $t'[Y_i]$ with their combined symbol.

In the following, we will need the notion of *level* of a tuple in the chase; intuitively, the lower the level of a tuple, the earlier the tuple has been constructed in the chase. Given a database instance D for a relational schema $\mathcal{R}$, and a set Σ of KDs and IDs, the *level* of a tuple t in $chase_\Sigma(D)$, denoted by $level(t)$, is defined as follows: *(1)* if t is in D then $level(t) = 0$; *(2)* if t_2 is generated from t_1 by application of the ID chase rule, and $level(t_1) = k$, then $level(t_2) = k + 1$; *(3)* if a KD is applied on a pair of tuples t_1, t_2, they collapse into a new tuple that gets the minimum of the levels of t_1 and t_2. The algorithm to construct the chase is as follows. We call *chase* of a relational database D for a schema $\mathcal{R}$, according to a set Σ of KDs and IDs, denoted $chase_\Sigma(D)$, the database constructed from the initial database D, by repeatedly executing the following steps, while the KD and ID chase rules are applicable. *(1)* while there are pairs of tuples on which the KD chase rule is applicable, apply the KD chase rule on a pair, arbitrarily chosen; *(2)* if there are tuples on which the ID chase rule is applicable, choose *the one* at the lowest level and apply the ID chase rule on it.

As we pointed out before, the aim of the construction of the chase is to make the initial database satisfy the KDs and the IDs [4], somehow repairing the constraint violations. It is easy to see that $chase_\Sigma(D)$ can be infinite only if the set if IDs in Σ is cyclic [1,18]. In the following we will show how the chase can be used in computing the answers to queries over incomplete databases under dependencies.

3.2   Query Answering and the Chase

In their milestone paper [18], Johnson and Klug proved that, under FDs and IDs, a containment between two conjunctive queries Q_1 and Q_2 can be tested by verifying whether there is a query homomorphism from the body of Q_2 to the chase of the database obtained by "freezing" Q_2, i.e. turning its conjuncts into facts, that sends $head(Q_2)$ to the frozen head of Q_1. To test containment of CQs under IDs alone or *key-based* dependencies (a special class of KDs and IDs), Johnson and Klug proved that it is sufficient to consider a *finite* portion of the chase. The result of [18] was extended in [7] to a broader class of dependencies, strictly more general than keys with foreign keys: the class of KDs and *non-key-conflicting inclusion dependencies (NKCIDs)* [3], that behave like IDs alone because NKCIDs do not interfere with KDs in the construction of the chase. The above results can be straightforwardly extended to answering on incomplete databases, since, as it will be shown later, the chase is a representative of all databases that satisfy the dependencies and are a superset of the initial data.

In a set of CDs, IDs are not non-key-conflicting (or better *key-conflicting*), therefore the decidability of query answering cannot be deduced from [18,7], (though it can derived from [11], as we shall discuss later). In particular, under CDs, the construction of the chase has to face interactions between KDs and IDs; this can be seen in the following example, taken from [4].

Example 3. Consider again the EER schema Example 1. Suppose we have an initial (incomplete) database, with the facts manager(m) and works_in(m, d). If we construct the chase, we obtain the facts employee(m), manages(m, α_1), works_in(m, α_1), dept(α_1), where α_1 is a fresh constant. Observe that m cannot participate more than once to works_in, so we deduce $\alpha_1 = d$. We must therefore replace α_1 with d in the rest of the chase, including the part that has been constructed so far.   ∎

In spite of the potentially harmful interaction between IDs and KDs, analogously to the case of IDs alone [6], it can be proved that the chase is a representative of all databases that are a superset of the initial (incomplete) data, and satisfy the dependencies; therefore, it serves as a tool for query answering.

Note. In the following, we shall make the explicit assumption that the initial, incomplete database satisfies the KDs in the set of constraints. This is not a limitation, since initial violations of KDs can be treated in a separate way, as we explain in Section 4.4.

Lemma 1. *Consider a relational schema $\mathcal{R}$ with a set of CDs Σ, and a database D for $\mathcal{R}$, with $D \models \Sigma_K$. Then, for every database B for $\mathcal{R}$ such that $B \models \Sigma$ and $B \supseteq D$, we have that there exists a homomorphism that sends all tuples of $chase_\Sigma(D)$ to tuples of B.*

Proof (sketch). Similarly to what is done for the analogous result in [6], the result is proved by induction on the application of the ID chase rule, and of the subsequent applications of the KD chase rule.   □

Theorem 1. *Consider a relational schema $\mathcal{R}$ with a set of CDs Σ, and a database D for $\mathcal{R}$, with $D \models \Sigma_K$; let Q be a conjunctive query over $\mathcal{R}$. We have that $Q(chase_\Sigma(D)) = ans(Q, \Sigma, D)$.*

Proof (sketch). The theorem is proved by considering a generic database B such that $B \models \Sigma$ and $B \supseteq D$; by Lemma 1 we derive the existence of a homomorphism μ that sends the facts of $chase_\Sigma(D)$ to those of B; if $t \in Q(chase_\Sigma(D))$, there is a homomorphism λ from the atoms of $body(Q)$ to $chase_\Sigma(D)$; the composition $\lambda \circ \mu$ witnesses $Q(chase_\Sigma(D)) \subseteq ans(Q, \Sigma, D)$; the other inclusion $Q(chase_\Sigma(D)) \supseteq ans(Q, \Sigma, D)$ is proved similarly.   □

Notice that Theorem 1 does not lead to an algorithm for query answering (unless in special cases), since the chase may have infinite size.

4   Answering Queries by Rewriting

In this section we present an efficient technique for computing query answering on incomplete data in the presence of CDs; such technique is based on *query rewriting*; in particular, the answers to a query are obtained by evaluating a query, which is obtained by rewriting the original one according to the dependencies, over the initial incomplete data.

4.1   Query Rewriting

The result of [4] indeed extends to our setting, ensuring decidability of query answering: the consistent answers to a CQ Q over a database D can be computed by evaluating Q over the initial segment of the chase of D, whose size, defined by a maximum level δ_M, depends on the query and on the constraints: in particular, $\delta_M = |\Sigma| \cdot W!$, where W is the maximum number of attributes involved in an ID in Σ, and $|\Sigma|$ is the number of CDs in Σ. However, this strategy would not be efficient in real-world cases, where D has a large size. Our plan of attack is then to rewrite Q according to the CDs on the schema, and then evaluating the rewritten query over the initial data: this turns out to be more efficient in practice, since the size of the data is usually much larger than the size of the schema and dependencies. In particular, the rewritten query is expressed in

Datalog, and it is the union of two set of rules, denoted Π_{Σ_I} and Π_{Σ_K}, that take into account IDs and KDs respectively, plus a set of rules Π_{eq} that simulates equality. Finally, function symbols present in the rules will be eliminated to obtain a Datalog rewriting.

Consider a relational schema $\mathcal{R}$ with a set Σ of CDs, with $\Sigma = \Sigma_I \cup \Sigma_K$, where Σ_I and Σ_K are sets of IDs and KDs respectively. Let Q be a CQ over $\mathcal{R}$; we construct Π_{eq}, Π_{Σ_I} and Π_{Σ_K} in the following way.

Encoding equalities. We introduce a binary predicate $eq/2$ that simulates the equality predicate; to enforce reflexivity, simmetry and transitivity we introduce in Π_{eq} the rules

(a) $eq(X_i, X_i) \leftarrow R(X_1, \ldots, X_n)$ for all R in $\mathcal{R}$ and for all $i \in \{1, \ldots, n\}$
(b) $eq(Y, X) \leftarrow eq(X, Y)$
(c) $eq(X, Z) \leftarrow eq(X, Y), eq(Y, Z)$

Encoding key dependencies. For every KD $key(R) = \{k\}$ (notice from Section 2.2 that in the case of CDs all keys are unary), with R of arity n, we introduce in Π_{Σ_K} the rule

$$eq(X_i, Y_i) \leftarrow R(X_1, \ldots, X_{k-1}, X_k, X_{k+1}, \ldots, X_n),$$
$$R(Y_1, \ldots, Y_{k-1}, Y_k, Y_{k+1}, \ldots, Y_n), eq(X_k, Y_k)$$

for all i s.t. $1 \leq i \leq n$, $i \neq k$.

Encoding inclusion dependencies. The encoding of a set Σ_I of IDs into a set Π_{Σ_I} of rules is done in two steps. Similarly to [5,3], every ID is encoded by a logic programming rule Π_{Σ_I} with function symbols, appearing in Skolem terms that replace existentially quantified variables in the head of the rules; intuitively, they mimick the fresh constants that are added in the construction of the chase. We consider four cases that are possible for an ID σ in a set of CDs:

(1) σ is of the form $R_1[1] \subseteq R_2[1]$, with $R_1/1$, $R_2/1$: we introduce in Π_{Σ_I} the rule $R_2(X) \leftarrow R_1(X)$.
(2) σ is of the form $R_1[k] \subseteq R_2[1]$, with R_1/n, $R_2/1, 1 \leq k \leq n$: we introduce in Π_{Σ_I} the rule $R_2(X_k) \leftarrow R_1(X_1, \ldots, X_n)$.
(3) σ is of the form $R_1[1, \ldots, n] \subseteq R_2[j_1, \ldots, j_n]$, with R_1/n, R_2/n, where $(j_1, \ldots, j_n)$ is a permutation of $(1, \ldots, n)$: we introduce in Π_{Σ_I} the rule $R_2(X_{j_1}, \ldots, X_{j_n}) \leftarrow R_1(X_1, \ldots, X_n)$.
(4) σ is of the form $R_1[1] \subseteq R_2[k]$, with $R_1/1$, $R_2/n, 1 \leq k \leq n$: we introduce in Π_{Σ_I} the rule $R_2(f_{\sigma,1}(X), \ldots, f_{\sigma,j-1}(X), X, \ldots, f_{\sigma,m}(X)) \leftarrow R_1(X)$.

Query maquillage. For technical reasons, and in particular because we need to deal with equalities among values in a uniform way, we need some maquillage (that we call *equality maquillage*) on Q: for every DV X appearing $m \geq 2$ times in $body(Q)$, replace the m occurrences of X with m *distinct* variables $X_1, \ldots, X_m$, not appearing elsewhere in Q, and add (as conjuncts) to $body(Q)$ the atoms $eq(X_1, X_2), eq(X_2, X_3), \ldots, eq(X_{m-1}, X_m)$. Henceforth, we shall denote with Q_{eq} the query after the maquillage.

The following result states that the encoding of IDs by means of the above rules captures the correct inference of facts that is done in the sound semantics.

Theorem 2. *Consider a relational schema $\mathcal{R}$ with a set of IDs Σ_I, a database D for $\mathcal{R}$, with $D \models \Sigma_K$, and a conjunctive query Q over $\mathcal{R}$. Then, the Datalog program $\Pi = Q_{eq} \cup \Pi_{\Sigma_I} \cup \Pi_{\Sigma_K} \cup \Pi_{eq} \cup D$, where Q_{eq} is the special rule, is such that $\Pi(D) = ans(Q, \Sigma, D)$, where we compute $\Pi(D)$ excluding from the result the tuples containing terms with function symbols.*

Proof (sketch). It can be shown that the minimal Herbrand model of $\Pi \cup D$ coincides with $chase_\Sigma(D)$, modulo renaming of the Skolem terms into fresh constants. By applying Theorem 1, the thesis follows.   □

4.2   Elimination of Function Symbols

Now, we want to transform the set of rules Π in another set which has pure (positive) Datalog rules without function symbols. To do that, we adopt a strategy somehow inspired by the elimination of function symbols in the *inverse rules* algorithm [16] for answering queries using views. The problem here is more complicated, due to the fact that function symbols may be arbitrarily nested in the minimal Herbrand model of the program. The idea here is to rely on the fact that there is a finite numbers δ_M of levels in the chase that is sufficient to answer a query [4]. We shall construct a Datalog program that mimicks *only* the first δ_M levels of the chase, so that the function symbols that it needs to take into account are nested up to δ_M times. The strategy is based on the "simulation" of facts with function symbols in the minimal Herbrand model of $\Pi \cup D$ (where D is an initial incomplete database) by means of ad-hoc predicates that are annotated so as to represent facts with function symbols.

More precisely, in order to represent facts of the form $R(t_1, \ldots, t_n)$, where a term $t_i \in \{t_1, \ldots, t_n\}$ is of the form $f_1^{(i)}(f_2^{(i)}(\ldots f_m^{(i)}(d_i) \ldots))$, where d_i is a constant, we introduce a new annotated relation symbol $R^{\bar{\eta}}$ ($\bar{\eta}$ is called *annotation*) of the same arity n as R. Notice that all function symbols have arity 1 by construction. The annotation of the new predicate is $\bar{\eta} = \eta_1, \ldots, \eta_n$: the i-th element, corresponding to the term t_i, is of the form $\eta_i = f_1^{(i)}(f_2^{(i)}(\ldots f_m^{(i)}(\bullet) \ldots))$, where d has been replaced with $\bullet$. The constant d_i appears as the i-th argument of the fact corresponding to $R(t_1, \ldots, t_n)$, that is of the form $R^{\bar{\eta}}(d_1, \ldots, d_n)$. For example, a fact $R(f_{\sigma,1}(d), d, f_{\sigma,3}(d))$ will be represented by a fact $R^{f_{\sigma,1}(\bullet), \bullet, f_{\sigma,3}(\bullet)}(d, d, d)$.

Now, to have a program that yelds the function-free facts as described above, we construct suitable rules that make use of annotated predicates. The idea here is that we want to take control of the nesting of function symbols in the minimal Herbrand model of the program, by explicitly using annotated predicates that represent facts with function symbols; this is possible since we do that only for the (ground) atoms that mimic facts that are in the first δ_M levels of the chase of the incomplete database. Here we make use of the fact, that is not difficult to prove, that the minimal Herbrand model of $\Pi \cup D$ coincides with $chase_\Sigma(D)$, modulo renaming of the Skolem terms into fresh constants (see proof of Theorem 2). Therefore, we are able to transform a (part of a) chase into the corresponding (part of the) minimal Herbrand model.

To do so, we construct a "dummy chase", and transform it, in the following way. Consider a relational schema $\mathcal{R}$ with a set Σ_I of IDs, a database D and a query Q over $\mathcal{R}$:

(1) construct a dummy database for $\mathcal{R}$ by adding a dummy fact $R(c_1, \ldots, c_n)$ for every relation $R/n \in \mathcal{R}$; we denote such a database with B;
(2) we construct $chase_{\Sigma_I}(B)$ up to level δ_M; we denote this initial segment of the chase by $chase_{\Sigma_I}^{\delta_M}(B)$ *(dummy chase)*;
(3) we transform $chase_{\Sigma_I}^{\delta_M}(B)$ by replacing every fact with the corresponding atom in the minimal Herbrand model of $\Pi_{\Sigma_I} \cup B$; we obtain a set of atoms (with function symbols) that we denote with H;
(4) we replace every atom of H with its function-free version that makes use of annotated predicates.

Now, for every pair of atoms f_1, f_2 in H such that f_2 is derived from f_1 by application of the ID chase rule, we introduce the rule $f_2' \leftarrow f_1'$, where f_1', f_2' are obtained from f_1, f_2 (respectively) by replacing every constant with a distinct variable.

Example 4. Consider Example 2; in the dummy chase, we introduce, among the others, the fact employee(c). Since this fact generates, according to the ID σ that is employee$[1] \subseteq$ works_in$[1]$, the fact works_in$(c, f_{\sigma,2}(c))$ (after the transformation of the fresh constants into Skolem terms). Such fact becomes, after introducing the annotated predicate, works_in$^{\bullet, f_{\sigma,2}(\bullet)}(c, c)$. Therefore, we introduce the rule works_in$^{\bullet, f_{\sigma,2}(\bullet)}(X, X) \leftarrow$ employee(X). ∎

Let us initially denote with Π_{DC} the rules obtained from the dummy chase in the way described above; we then iteratively apply the following rewriting rule, adding rules to Π_{DC}. Preliminarly, we need some notation: we denote with $\bar{X}[h]$ the h-th term of a sequence $\bar{X}$, and with $\bar{\eta}[h]$ the h-th element of an annotation $\bar{\eta}$ (which is in turn a sequence).

ALGORITHM FOR THE ELIMINATION OF FUNCTION SYMBOLS. If there is a rule $p(\bar{X}) \leftarrow p_1(\bar{X}_1), \ldots, p(\bar{X}_k)$ in $\Pi \cup \Pi_{DC}$ and:

(1) there are rules in $\Pi_{DC} \cup \Pi$ having predicates of the form $p_1^{\bar{\eta}_1}, \ldots, p_k^{\bar{\eta}_k}$ in their head;
(2) if for some i, j, h, k it holds that $\bar{X}_i[h] = \bar{X}_j[k]$, then $\bar{\eta}_i[h] = \bar{\eta}_j[k]$;

then add to Π_{DC} the rule $p^{\bar{\eta}}(\bar{Y}) \leftarrow p_1^{\bar{\eta}_1}(\bar{Y}_1), \ldots, p_k^{\bar{\eta}_k}(\bar{Y}_k)$, where:

(1) if $\bar{X}[h] = \bar{X}_j[k]$ then $\bar{\eta}[h] = \bar{\eta}_i[k]$ and $\bar{Y}[h] = \bar{Y}_j[k]$;
(2) if $\bar{X}[h]$ is a constant then $\bar{\eta}[h] = \bullet$ (to consider the cases where rules have constants in their head);
(3) if $\bar{\eta}_i[h] = \bar{\eta}_j[k]$ then $\bar{Y}_i[h] = \bar{Y}_j[k]$.

Example 5. Consider Example 2; we have the rule

$$eq(X_1, X_2) \leftarrow \mathsf{manages}(X_1, Y_1), \mathsf{manages}(X_2, Y_2), eq(X_1, X_2)$$

If there are rules having $eq^{f(\bullet),\bullet}$, $\mathsf{manages}^{f(\bullet),\bullet}$ and $\mathsf{manages}^{\bullet,g(\bullet)}$ in the head (we have used f, g as function symbols to have a not too heavy notation here), then we add the rule

$$eq^{f(\bullet),\bullet}(X_1, X_2) \leftarrow \mathsf{manages}^{f(\bullet),\bullet}(X_1, Y_1), \mathsf{manages}^{\bullet,g(\bullet)}(X_2, Y_2), eq^{f(\bullet),\bullet}(X_1, X_2) \ \blacksquare$$

Finally, we denote with $\Pi_{Q,\Sigma}$ the program $Q_{eq} \cup \Pi_{eq} \cup \Pi_{\Sigma_K} \cup \Pi_{DC}$, where Π_{DC} is the result of the addition of rules in the function symbol elimination, and the special rule is the one having $Q_{eq}^{\bullet,\dots,\bullet}$ in the head: the choice on the special rule is important to exclude terms with function symbols from the answer.

Theorem 3. *Consider a relational schema $\mathcal{R}$ with a set of CDs Σ, a database D for $\mathcal{R}$, with $D \models \Sigma_K$, and a conjunctive query Q over $\mathcal{R}$. Then, the Datalog program $\Pi_{Q,\Sigma}$, where the special rule is the one having $Q_{eq}^{\bullet,\dots,\bullet}$ in the head, is such that $\Pi_{Q,\Sigma}(D) = ans(Q, \Sigma, D)$.*

Proof (sketch). The proof is based on the the fact that the minimal Herbrand model of $\Pi_{Q,\Sigma} \cup D$ is a representation of the part of the minimal Herbrand model of $Q_{eq} \cup \Pi_{eq} \cup \Pi_{\Sigma_I} \cup \Pi_{\Sigma_K} \cup D$ that represents the first δ_M levels of $chase_\Sigma(D)$. From Theorem 2, and knowing from [4] that the first δ_M levels of $chase_\Sigma(D)$ suffice for computing the consistent answers to a query, the thesis follows.   □

4.3   (Brief) Considerations on Complexity

We focus on *data complexity*, i.e. the complexity w.r.t. the size of the data, that is the most relevant, being the size of the data usually larger than that of the schema. We recall that the evaluation of a Datalog program is polynomial in data complexity [15]; therefore, being our rewriting in Datalog, we can compute all answers to a CQ in time polynomial w.r.t. the size of the data. This tractability of query answering suggests that our algorithm can be efficient in practical cases.

4.4   Extensions of Results

Dealing with inconsistencies. First of all, as we mentioned in Section 3.2, we have always assumed that the initial, incomplete database satisfies the KDs derived from the EER schema. This assumption does not limit the applicability of our results, since violations of KDs can be treated at least in two ways. *(1) Data cleaning* (see, e.g., [17]): a preliminary cleaning procedure would eliminate the KD violations; then, the results from [4] ensure that no violations will occur in the chase, and we can proceed with the techniques presented in the paper. *(2) Strictly sound semantics*: according to the sound semantics we have adopted, from the logical point of view, strictly speaking, a single KD violation in the initial data makes query answering trivial (any tuple is in the answer, provided it has the same arity of the query); this extreme assumption, not very usable in practice, can be encoded in suitable rules, that make use of inequalities, and that can be added to our rewritings. We refer the reader to [8] for the details. *(3) Loosely-sound semantics*: this assumption is a relaxation of the previous one, and is reasonable in practice. Inconsistencies are treated in a model-theoretic way, and suitable Datalog¬ rules (that we can add to our programs without any trouble, obtaining a correct rewriting under this semantics) encode the reasoning on the constraints. Again, we refer the reader to [8] for further details.

Adding disjointness. Disjointness between two classes, which is a natural addition to our EER model, can be easily encoded by *exclusion dependencies (EDs)* (see, e.g. [20]). The addition of EDs to CDs is not problematic, provided that we preliminarly compute the closure, w.r.t. the implication, of KDs and EDs, according to the (sound and complete) implication rules that are found in [20]. After that, we can proceed as in the absence of EDs.

5   Discussion

Summary of results. In this paper we have presented a conceptual model based on the ER model, and we have given its semantics in terms of the relational database model with integrity constraints. We have considered conjunctive queries expressed over conceptual schemata, and we have tackled the problem of consistently answering queries in such a setting, when the data are incomplete w.r.t. the conceptual schema. We have provided a query rewriting algorithm that transforms a CQ Q into a new (Datalog) query that, once evaluated on the incomplete data, returns the consistent answers to Q. This query rewriting approach keeps the computation at the intensional level, thus avoiding costly manipulations of the data.

Related work. As pointed out earlier, query answering in our setting is tightly related to containment of queries under constraints, which is a fundamental topic in database theory [12,11,18,19]. [5] deals with conceptual schemata in the context of data integration, but the cardinality constraints are more restricted than in our approach, since they do not include functional participation constraints and is-a among relationships. Other works that deal with dependencies similar to those presented here is [9,10], however, the set of constraints considered in these works, represented by the Description Logic language *DL-Lite*, is not comparable to CDs, since it contains some more expressive constructs, but the is-a relation among relationships (which we believe is the major source of complexity) is not considered in it. Also [25] addresses the problem of query containment using a formalism for the schema that is more expressive than the one presented here; however, the problem here is proved to be coNP-hard; our approach, which we believe is more close to real-world cases, achieves better computational complexity by providing a technique that is usable in practice. In [11], the authors address the problem of query containment for queries on schemata expressed in a formalism that is able to capture our EER model; in this work it is shown that checking containment is decidable and its complexity is exponential in the number of variables and constants of Q_1 and Q_2, and double exponential in the number of existentially quantified variables that appear in a cycle of the *tuple-graph* of Q_2 (we refer the reader to the paper for further details). Since the complexity is studied by encoding the problem in a different logic, it is not possible to analyse in detail the complexity w.r.t. $|Q_1|$ and $|Q_2|$, which by the technique of [11] is in general exponential. If we export the results of [11] to our setting, we get an exponential complexity w.r.t. the size of the data for the decision problem[1] of answering queries over incomplete databases. Our work provides a more detailed analysis of the computational cost, showing that the complexity complexity upper bound is polynomial w.r.t. the size of the data; moreover, we provide a technique that does more than solving the decision problem of query answering: it computes all answers to a query in the presence of incomplete data.

Future work. As a future work, we plan to extend the EER model with more constraints which are used in real-world cases, such as covering constraints or more sophisticated cardinality constraints. We also plan to further investigate the complexity of query answering, providing a thorough study of complexity, including lower complexity bounds. Also, we are working on an implementation of the query rewriting algorithm, so as to test the efficiency of our technique on large data sets.

Acknowledgments. This work was partially supported by the EPSRC project "Schema mappings and services for data integration and exchange". I am grateful, for various reasons, and in alphabetical order, to: Leopoldo Bertossi, Benedetto Calì, Jan Chomicki, God, and Michael Kifer.

References

1. Abiteboul, S., Hull, R., Vianu, V.: Foundations of Databases. Addison Wesley Publ. Co, London, UK (1995)
2. Arenas, M., Bertossi, L.E., Chomicki, J.: Consistent query answers in inconsistent databases. In: Proc. of PODS 1999, pp. 68–79 (1999)
3. Calì, A.: Query answering and optimisation in information integration. PhD thesis, Università di Roma "La Sapienza" (February 2003)
4. Calì, A.: Containment of conjunctive queries over conceptual schemata. In: Lee, M.L., Tan, K.-L., Wuwongse, V. (eds.) DASFAA 2006. LNCS, vol. 3882, pp. 270–284. Springer, Heidelberg (2006)
5. Calì, A., Calvanese, D., De Giacomo, G., Lenzerini, M.: Accessing data integration systems through conceptual schemas. In: Kunii, H.S., Jajodia, S., Sølvberg, A. (eds.) ER 2001. LNCS, vol. 2224, Springer, Heidelberg (2001)
6. Calì, A., Calvanese, D., De Giacomo, G., Lenzerini, M.: Data integration under integrity constraints. Information Systems 29, 147–163 (2004)
7. Calì, A., Lembo, D., Rosati, R.: On the decidability and complexity of query answering over inconsistent and incomplete databases. In: Proc. of PODS 2003, pp. 260–271 (2003)

---

[1] The decision problem of query answering amounts to decide whether, given a query Q and a tuple t, t belongs to the answers to Q.

8. Calì, A., Lembo, D., Rosati, R.: Query rewriting and answering under constraints in data integration systems. In: Proc. of IJCAI 2003, pp. 16–21 (2003)

9. Calvanese, D., De Giacomo, G., Lembo, D., Lenzerini, M., Rosati, R.: DL-Lite: Tractable description logics for ontologies. In: Proc. of AAAI 2005, pp. 602–607 (2005)

10. Calvanese, D., De Giacomo, G., Lembo, D., Lenzerini, M., Rosati, R.: Data complexity of query answering in description logics. In: Proc. of the 10th Int. Conf. on the Principles of Knowledge Representation and Reasoning (KR 2006), pp. 260–270 (2006)

11. Calvanese, D., De Giacomo, G., Lenzerini, M.: On the decidability of query containment under constraints. In: Proc. of PODS'98, pp. 149–158 (1998)

12. Edward, P.F.: Containment and minimization of positive conjunctive queries in OODB's. In: Edward, P.F. (ed.) Proc. of PODS'92, pp. 202–211 (1992)

13. Chen, P.: The Entity-Relationship model: Toward a unified view of data. ACM Trans. on Database Systems 1(1), 9–36 (1976)

14. Codd, E.F.: A relational model of data for large shared data banks. Comm. of the ACM 13(6), 377–387 (1970)

15. Dantsin, E., Eiter, T., Gottlob, G., Voronkov, A.: Complexity and expressive power of logic programming. ACM Computing Surveys 33(3), 374–425 (2001)

16. Duschka, O.M., Genesereth, M.R.: Answering recursive queries using views. In: Oliver, M. (ed.) Proc. of PODS'97, pp. 109–116 (1997)

17. Hernández, M.A., Stolfo, S.J.: Real-world data is dirty: Data cleansing and the merge/purge problem. J. of Data Mining and Knowledge Discovery 2(1), 9–37 (1998)

18. David, S., Johnson, D.S., Klug, A.C.: Testing containment of conjunctive queries under functional and inclusion dependencies. J. of Computer and System Sciences 28(1), 167–189 (1984)

19. Kolaitis, P.G., Vardi, M.Y.: Conjunctive-query containment and constraint satisfaction. In: Phokion, G. (ed.) Proc. of PODS'98, pp. 205–213 (1998)

20. Lembo, D.: Dealing with Inconsistency and Incompleteness in Data Integration. PhD thesis, Dip. di Inf. e Sist., Univ. di Roma "La Sapienza" (2004)

21. Lenzerini, M.: Data integration: A theoretical perspective. In: Proc. of PODS 2002, pp. 233–246 (2002)

22. Maier, D., Mendelzon, A.O., Sagiv, Y.: Testing implications of data dependencies. ACM Trans. on Database Systems 4, 455–469 (1979)

23. Maier, D., Sagiv, Y., Yannakakis, M.: On the complexity of testing implications of functional and join dependencies. J. of the ACM 28(4), 680–695 (1981)

24. Markowitz, V.M., Makowsky, J.A.: Identifying extended entity-relationship object structures in relational schemas. IEEE Trans. Software Eng. 16(8), 777–790 (1990)

25. Ortiz, M., Calvanese, D., Eiter, T.: Characterizing data complexity for conjunctive query answering in expressive description logics. In: Proc. of the 21st Nat. Conf. on Artificial Intelligence (AAAI 2006) (2006)

26. Reiter, R.: On closed world data bases. In: Gallaire, H., Minker, J. (eds.) Logic and Databases, pp. 119–140. Plenum Publ.Co. (1978)

27. Vardi, M.: Inferring multivalued dependencies from functional and join dependencies. Acta Informatica 19, 305–324 (1983)

Prioritized Preferences and Choice Constraints

Wilfred Ng

Department of Computer Science and Engineering
The Hong Kong University of Science and Technology
Hong Kong
wilfred@cse.ust.hk

Abstract. It is increasingly recognised that user preferences should be addressed in many advanced database applications, such as adaptive searching in databases. However, the fundamental issue of how preferences impact the semantics and rankings in a relation is not resolved. In this paper, we model a user preference term involving one attribute as a hierarchy of its underlying data values and formalise the notion of Prioritized Preferences (PPs). We then consider multiple user preferences in ranking tuples in a relational table. We examine the impact of a given set of PPs on possible choices in ranking a database relation and develop a new notion of Choice Constraints (CCs) in a relation, r. Given two PPs, X and Y, a CC, $X \leq Y$, is satisfied in r, if the choice of rankings according to Y is no less than that of X. Our main results are related to these two notions of PPs and CCs and their interesting interactions with the well-known Functional Dependencies (FDs). First, we exhibit a sound and complete set of three inference rules for PPs and further prove that for each closed set of PPs, there exists a ranking that precisely satisfies these preferences. Second, we establish a sound and complete set of five inference rules for CCs. Finally, we show the soundness and completeness of two mixed systems of FD-PPs and FD-CCs. All these results are novel and fundamental to incorporating user preferences in database design and modelling, since PPs, CCs and FDs together capture rich semantics of preferences in databases.

1 Introduction

Preference is an important and natural constraint that captures human wishes when seeking information. However, the semantics of preferences were not adequately studied until the recent work in [7,8,2,14]. In these papers, the fundamental nature of different preferences in the form of "I like A better than B" is modelled by a set of orderings defined over data. Still, the impact of preferences as a semantic constraint is not adequately addressed in many ways. For example, in database modelling, traditional constraints like Functional Dependencies (FDs) capture the semantics of the hard fact only, but preferences do not have such semantics as constraints that represent a priority of choices. However, as information becomes abundant over the web, there is a practical need for generating a ranking that satisfies some user preferences in the search result [7,8]. In addition, although FDs are widely recognized as the most important integrity constraint in databases, the interactions of FDs with preferences, to our knowledge, have never been studied in literature.

C. Parent et al. (Eds.): ER 2007, LNCS 4801, pp. 261–276, 2007.

In our modelling, we assume that a user preference is expressed in a sequence of attributes that associate with their respective *preference terms*. We call the attributes involved in preference terms *preference attributes*. The underlying idea is that a user preference is inherent to the ordering relationship between the data projected onto the preference attributes, and thus a *preference hierarchy* can be devised to capture the choices of *preference rankings*. Our approach is to transform a relation to a preference relation, r, which has only natural numbers according to the level of the preference hierarchy. Then a ranking of tuples, $\leq_r$, can be arbitrary defined on r whereas the consistency of $(r, \leq_r)$ is determined by the lexicographical order of the preference attributes. The following example illustrates the use of a preference relation.

Example 1. Suppose a second-hand car relation is defined by the preference attributes *PRICE_RANGE*, *ENGINE_POWER* and *MILEAGE_USED*, which assert the preferences specified by *YOUTH_ CHOICE* (the choice of young customers). The preference increases with first the price range and then the engine power and finally the car's mileage. We adopt the PREFERRING clause proposed in [7] to express the preference terms, which essentially impose an order over their corresponding data domains. The three terms together the respective preference hierarchies are assumed to be prioritized as follows:

First priority: LOWEST(price) $\Rightarrow$ \$5001 $-$ 6000 $<$ \$4001 $-$ 5000 $<$ \$1001 $-$ 2000.
Second priority: HIGHEST(power) $\Rightarrow$ 1000cc $<$ 2000cc $<$ 3000cc.
Third priority: mileage AROUND 30,000km $\Rightarrow$ 10000km $<$ 20000km $<$ 30000km.

A preference relation, r, is generated by mapping the data values in the car relation to natural numbers according to the level of the preference hierarchies of the given preference terms, which is shown in the right-hand side of Figure 1. The overall preference ranking (which is unique in this simplified example but may be more than one in general) in the last column, **Rank**, is determined by the lexicographical order of PRICE, ENGINE and MILEAGE, which is consistent with the tuple ordering, $t_1 <_r \cdots <_r t_5$. Note that some attributes are abbreviated in the table due to width limits.

	PRICE	ENGINE	MILEAGE			PRICE	ENGINE	MILEAGE	Rank
t_1	1001-2000	1500cc	20000km		t_1	1	3	2	1
t_2	4001-5000	3000cc	30000km		t_2	2	1	1	2
t_3	4001-5000	2000cc	20000km	$\Rightarrow$	t_3	2	2	2	3
t_4	4001-5000	1500cc	10000km		t_4	2	3	3	4
t_5	5001-6000	3000cc	10000km		t_5	3	1	3	5

Fig. 1. Transforming the second-hand car relation into a preference relation according to the preference terms of $YOUTH\_CHOICE$

Middle-class adult customers may have different preferences. This gives rise to a different preference relation as shown in Figure 2, where the preference ranking (i.e. **Rank**) is not consistent with the tuple ranking (i.e. $<_r$). The preference terms of MIDDLE CLASS_CHOICE are assumed to be reprioritized as follows:

First priority: price AROUND $4000-$5000.
Second priority: HIGHEST(power).
Third priority: LOWEST(mileage).

Finally, pensioner customers may have another set of preference terms, which give rise to the different preference relation and ranking shown in Figure 3. The preference terms are assumed to be reprioritized as follows:

First priority: LOWEST(price).
Second priority: mileage BETWEEN 20,000km AND 30,000km.
Third priority: power AROUND 2000cc.

	$PRICE$	$ENGINE$	$MILEAGE$	**Rank**		$PRICE$	$ENGINE$	$MILEAGE$	**Rank**
t_1	3	3	2	**5**	t_1	1	2	1	**1**
t_2	1	1	3	**1**	t_2	2	3	1	**3**
t_3	1	2	2	**2**	t_3	2	1	1	**2**
t_4	1	3	1	**3**	t_4	2	2	2	**4**
t_5	2	1	1	**4**	t_5	3	3	2	**5**

Fig. 2. $MIDDLE\ CLASS\_CHOICE$ **Fig. 3.** $PENSIONER\_CHOICE$

Any tuple ranking is *trivially satisfied* in a preference relation r when there are no imposed preference terms. When preference terms are stated by the users, we check if the tuple ranking in r are consistent with a (any) lexicographical order of the sequence of the preference attributes. This gives rise to the notion of *Prioritized Preferences* (PPs) (cf. see Definition 6 in [7] for the motivation for prioritized preferences), and in order to have PP satisfied in r, tuple rankings are restricted to the set of preference rankings. This also gives rise to another notion of Choice Constraints (CCs) being satisfied in a relation. Given two PPs, X and Y, a CC, $X \leq Y$, is satisfied in r, if the choice of preference rankings according to Y is no less than that of X. We focus on three interesting problems related to the semantics of preferences in relations:

1. When there is a tuple ranking that satisfies a set of PPs, what are the rules governing such preference satisfaction?
2. When there is more than one possible tuple ranking that satisfies different PPs, what are the rules of governing the ranking possibilities (CCs)?
3. What are the interactions between FDs, PPs and CCs?

Our main contribution is related to the above problems. We present a spectrum of interesting axiom systems in this paper. With respect to preference satisfaction, we exhibit a sound and complete set of three inference rules for PPs. It is further proved that for each closed set of PPs, there exists a ranking that satisfies these preferences and no others. With respect to the choice of tuple rankings for a given set of PPs, we establish a sound and complete set of five inference rules for CCs. Finally, we study the interactions between PPs and FDs, and between CCs and FDs and formally show the soundness and completeness of two mixed systems of FD-PPs and FD-CCs. All these results are novel and fundamental to incorporating user preferences in database design and modelling, since PPs, CCs and FDs together capture rich semantics of preferences in many database applications in reality.

The rest of the paper is organised as follows. In Section 2, we present some preliminary concepts and notation. In Section 3, we present a sound and complete system with respect to PP satisfaction. In Section 4, we introduce the concept of CCs and present a sound and complete system with respect to CC satisfaction. In Section 5, we discuss the interactions between FDs and PPs and those between FDs and CCs. We present two sound and complete systems of FD-PPs and FD-CCs. In Section 6, we review some related work. In Section 7, we give our concluding remarks.

2   Preliminaries

We assume throughout that X and Y are sequences of attributes and that $X \sim Y$ indicates the fact that X and Y have the same elements. XY denotes the *concatenation* of X and Y (appending Y to X). A *prefix* of X, denoted as $pre(X)$, is a sequence of the form $\langle A_1, \ldots, A_{m_1} \rangle$, where $X = \langle A_1, \ldots, A_m \rangle$ and $1 \leq m_1 \leq m$. A *shuffle* of X and Y, denoted as $shu(X, Y)$, is defined as a sequence of the form $\langle C_1, \ldots, C_{m+n} \rangle$, where there exists two *subsequences* of attributes $\langle C_{i_1}, \ldots, C_{i_m} \rangle = X$ and $\langle C_{j_1}, \ldots, C_{j_n} \rangle = Y$, and the order of the attributes in X and Y is preserved in $shu(X, Y)$.

Lexicographical ordering is a fundamental property of prioritized preferences as illustrated in Example 1, where the preference in $YOUTH\_CHOICE$ can be modelled as a lexicographical ordering of the Cartesian product of the domains $PRICE \times ENGINE \times MILEAGE$ in the preference relation in Figure 1.

We assume the usual terminologies and notation used in the relational data model [1]. In particular, let $R = \{A_1, \ldots, A_n\}$ be the relation schema and $t[A_i]$ $(1 \leq i \leq n)$ denote the *projection* of t onto attribute A_i. A *relation* r defined over R is a finite set of tuples over R. We define $r[A_i] = \{t[A_i] \mid t \in r\}$.

Note that preference terms such as "BETWEEN AND", "HIGHEST", "LOWEST" and "IN" as defined in [7] are equivalent to defining a partial ordering over the tuples induced by the involved preference attributes. Thus, we are able to map the data values into natural numbers according to a preference hierarchy, resulting in a preference relation.

We now assume a relation having one preference attribute, $R = \{A\}$, to illustrate the idea. We first denote by $\mathcal{H}(r, A)$ a *partition* of r, which is a set of pairwise disjoint non-empty subsets of r such that $\bigcup_{T \in \mathcal{H}(r,A)} T = r$, and we call the element $T \in \mathcal{H}(r, A)$ a *preference level* of r induced by A. A *preference hierarchy* of r induced by A is a linearly ordered partition of r, corresponding to the preference term p imposed on A.

Example 2. Consider $r = \{a, b, c, d, e, f\}$ (6 tuples), where $a \leq_A^p c$, $b \leq_A^p c$, $c \leq_A^p e$, $d \leq_A^p e$ and $d \leq_A^p f$. We now show two possible internal hierarchies, $\mathcal{H}(r, A) = \{T_1, T_2, T_3\}$, given in Figure 4, in which each tuple is represented by a node.

Using the bottom-up partition approach, we successively collect the sets of minimal tuples in the subsets of r and construct the preference hierarchy as illustrated in

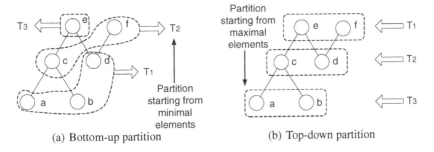

Fig. 4. Two possible preference hierarchies $\mathcal{H}(r, A)$

Figure 4(a). We remark that this method of constructing the preference hierarchy is essentially a matter of convention and another possibility is shown in Figure 4(b) as a comparison. The two conventions can also be used to represent the "like less" and "like more" preferences.

The idea of a preference hierarchies can be straightforwardly generalized to multiple preference attributes. Algorithm 1 shows how to generate a preference relation arising from the preference terms. Essentially, the algorithm collects the minimal tuples of a relation (or its subset) with respect to each preference order using a bottom-up partition.

Algorithm 1. $(PREFERENCE\_RELATION(r, X))$

Input: A relation r, a set of preference attributes X and a set of preference orderings $\leq_A^p$ for all $A \in X$.
Output: A preference relation of r.

1.	**begin**
2.	**for all** $A \in X$, **do**
3.	$i = 0$;
4.	**do until** $r[A] = \emptyset$
5.	Increment i;
6.	Obtain T_i as the set of minimal tuples (wrt $\leq_A^p$) of $r[A]$;
7.	$r[A] := r[A] - T_i$ and $\mathcal{H}(r, A) := \{T_1 <_h \cdots <_h T_i\}$;
8.	**for all** $t \in r$, $A \in X$, **do**
9.	Map $t[A]$ to n in r whenever $t[A] \in T_n$ and $T_n \in \mathcal{H}(r, A)$;
10.	**return** r (with mapped natural numbers on $r[X]$);
11.	**end**

Definition 1 (Preference Relation). Given a relation r over R, a prioritized preference, $X \subseteq R$ and a set of preference terms over X. A preference relation, $(r, \leq_r)$, is the relation (with mapped natural numbers on $r[X]$ returned by Algorithm 1) together with a tuple ranking, $\leq_r$. From now on, we simply call a preference relation a relation whenever no ambiguity arises.

The preference hierarchy generated in Step 7 by Algorithm 1 is unique and therefore Definition 1 is well-defined. The uniqueness of the result of Algorithm 1 is due to the fact that T_n is the unique set of all minimal tuples of $r[A]$ according to $\leq_A^p$. Intuitively, a level $T_n \in \mathcal{H}(r, A)$ captures the "equivalent choices" with respect to a preference term and the hierarchy observes the order arising from the preference term imposed on A. In the special case of linearly ordered preference terms such as HIGHEST(power) or LOWEST(price), T_n is the singleton containing the nth tuple sorted in numerical order.

In our running example, the preference hierarchies of $PRICE$, $MILEAGE$ and $ENGINE\_POWER$ corresponding to the $YOUTH\_CHOICE$ are $\{\{t_1\} <_h \{t_2, t_3, t_4\} <_h \{t_5\}\}$, $\{\{t_2, t_5\} <_h \{t_3\} <_h \{t_1, t_4\}\}$ and $\{\{t_2\} <_h \{t_1, t_3\} <_h \{t_4, t_5\}\}$, respectively.

3   Preferences and Choices

In this section, we present the notion of a *Prioritized Preference* (PP) and its satisfaction over a relation.

The semantics of a preference with multiple attributes, X, is defined according to lexicographical orderings, denoted as $\leq_X^{lex}$, on the Cartesian product of the mapped numerical values via the preference hierarchies of the attributes.

Definition 2 (Prioritized Preference and Choice). A *prioritized preference* (or simply a preference), X, is a sequence of attributes obtained from a relation schema, R. A preference, X, is satisfied in a relation, $(r, \leq_r)$ over R, denoted as $(r, \leq_r) \models X$, if for all $t_1, t_2 \in r$, $t_1[X] <_X^{lex} t_2[X]$ implies that $t_1 <_r t_2$. We call any distinct $\leq_r$ such that $(r, \leq_r) \models X$ a *choice* of rankings wrt X (or simply a choice whenever $(r, \leq_r)$ and X are understood), and denote the number of such distinct ranking choices as $|\, choice(r, X)\,|$. In particular, if the choice is unique, we call the satisfaction arising from the choice the unique satisfaction.

Notably, PPs allow the same attribute appearing several times in a preference X. This is necessary for studying the inference rules later on, since some rules may infer PPs having repeated attributes. However, by removing the repeated occurrence of a particular attribute after its first occurrence in a preference, we can obtain an "equivalent preference" in which each attribute appears at most once. This also implies there exists only a finite number of distinct PPs (up to equivalence) for a given relational schema.

The following proposition follows directly from Definition 2. It means that if a relation satisfies a unique choice, its tuples are simply ordered by $\leq_X^{lex}$. Remarkably, if $X = R$ the satisfaction must be unique, since $\leq_R^{lex}$ is a linear order on r. In addition, if we have all distinct (integer) values for all tuples under any attribute $A \in X$, the satisfaction is also unique. This follows that for any arity-1 relation, i.e. $|\, R\,| = 1$, the satisfaction, if any, must also be unique.

Proposition 1. Given $X = A_1 \cdots A_n$. If $|\, choice(r, X)\,| = 1$, then, for all $t_1, t_2 \in r$, $t_1 <_r t_2$, if and only if $\exists k$, $1 \leq k < n$, such that $t_1[A_1 \cdots A_k] = t_2[A_1 \cdots A_k]$ and $t_1[A_{k+1}] < t_2[A_{k+1}]$. $\square$

	PRICE	MILEAGE	ENGINE	Rank 1	Rank 2
t_1	1	1	1	1	1
t_2	2	2	2	4	4
t_3	2	1	1	2	3
t_4	2	1	1	3	2
t_5	3	1	2	5	5

Fig. 5. Two choices or rankings satisfying the preference terms

For example, it can be checked that the second-hand car relation has a unique satisfaction according to (unique) **Rank** in Figures 1 to 3. However, we may have another set of preference terms, which gives rise to two possible preference rankings, **Rank 1** and **Rank 2**, shown in the two right columns of Figure 5. The preference terms are assumed to be prioritized as follows:

First priority: LOWEST(price).
Second priority: mileage LESS THAN 30,000km.
Third priority: power BETWEEN 1500cc AND 2000cc.

In other words, the relation in the above example should rank as $\{t_1 <_r t_4 <_r t_2 <_r t_3 <_r t_5\}$ or $\{t_1 <_r t_4 <_r t_3 <_r t_2 <_r t_5\}$ in order to satisfy the imposed preference, i.e. we have $|\ choice(r, (price, mileage, power))\ | = 2$.

We now illustrate some non-trivial aspects of preference satisfaction in the following example (assuming usual numerical order $0 < 1$).

Example 3. Let $r = \{t_1 <_r t_2\}$ and $X = ABCD$ as given in Figure 6. It is straightforward to check that $r \models BC$ but not $r \models CB$ and that $r \models ABC$ but not $r \models AC$. However, we will prove later some interesting but non-trivial result such as that $r \models AB$ and $r \models DC$ imply $r \models ADB$ and $r \models ADBC$, as also illustrated in r.

The interesting interactions in the above example motivate our work of establishing a set of inference rules for deriving preferences. In the subsequent discussion, we assume preference satisfaction is restricted to a unique choice of ranking (i.e., $|\ Choice(r, X)\ | = 1$) and say that $(r, \leq_r) \models_u X$ if $(r, \leq_r) \models X$ and there exists no distinct $\leq'_r$ such that $(r, \leq'_r) \models X$. The study of a unique choice of ranking is important, since it affects the way to store and index a preference relation. It may also lead to more efficient evaluation of search queries, for example if the user asks follow-up questions based on existing preference and ranking then we need to evaluate only one relation.

	A	B	C	D
t_1	1	0	1	0
t_2	1	1	0	1

Fig. 6. $r \models BC$ but $r \not\models CB$; $r \models ABC$ but $r \not\models AC$

We now begin to formalise the notion of PP satisfaction as follows.

Definition 3 (PP Satisfaction and Implication). Given a set of preferences, P, and a relation, $(r, \leq_r)$, we say that $(r, \leq_r)$ logically implies P, denoted as $(r, \leq_r) \models_u P$, if and only if $\forall X \in P$, $(r, \leq_r) \models_u X$. In addition, we say that P logically implies X, denoted as $P \models X$, if for any $(r, \leq_r)$, $(r, \leq_r) \models_u P$ implies that $(r, \leq_r) \models_u X$.

From now on, we may lighten the notation of $(r, \leq_r)$ and simply use r to mean a preference relation if $\leq_r$ can be understood.

An *axiom system* [1] for preferences over relations is a set of inference rules that can be used to derive new preferences from P. We denote by $P \vdash X$ the fact that either $X \in P$ or X can be inferred (or derived) from P by using one or more of the inference rules in Definition 4.

Definition 4 (Inference Rules for Prioritized Preferences). Let P be a set of preferences over R, $A \in R$. Let X, Y be non-empty sequences of attributes obtained from R. The inference rules for preferences are defined as follows:

(PP1) *Expansion*: If $P \vdash X$, then $P \vdash XA$.
(PP2) *Shuffle*: If $P \vdash X$ and $P \vdash Y$, then $P \vdash shu(X, pre(Y))$.
(PP3) *Compression*: If $P \vdash XAYAZ$, then $P \vdash XAYZ$.

Unlike most known database constraints, P consists of no reflexivity rule in Definition 4, since there is no trivial preference satisfaction in relations. We also remark that the axiom system comprising these rules is *minimal*, since the three rules given in Definition 4 are independent.

Lemma 1. The axiom system comprising inference rules PP1-PP3 is sound for the satisfaction of PPs in relations.   □

We now show in next theorem that the axiom system comprising the inference rules in Definition 4 is *sound* and *complete* for preference satisfaction in preference relations. The underlying idea in this proof is first to assume that a preference, X, cannot be inferred from the axiom system and then to present a relation as a counter-example in which all the preferences of P' hold except for X (cf. see Theorem 3.21 in [1]). The result is significant since it indicates that the axiom system can be employed as a theorem-proving tool for preferences.

Theorem 1. The axiom system comprising rules PP1 to PP3 is sound and complete for preference satisfaction in relations.

Proof. We now establish the completeness by showing that if $P \nvdash X$, then $P \nmodels X$. Equivalently for the latter, it is sufficient to exhibit a relation as a counter-example, r^c, such that $r^c \models_u P$ but $r^c \nmodels_u X$. Assuming that L is the largest prefix of X such that $P \vdash LQ$ for some $Q \subseteq R$. Let us call this the *L-assumption*.

There are two cases to consider.

In the first case, we assume that $L = X$. We consider the relation $r^c = \{t_1 <_r t_2\}$ shown in Figure 7. Obviously, we have $r^c \nmodels_u X$, since $choice(r^c, X)$ is not unique.

It remains to show that $r^c \models_u P$. Assume to the contrary that $r^c \not\models_u P$. So $\exists X' \in P$ such that $r^c \not\models_u X'$. By the construction of r^c, we have $X' \subseteq X$ (as a set inclusion). By the L-assumption and PP2, it follows that $P \vdash LX'$. So, we have $P \vdash L$ by PP3, which is a contradiction, since we derive X from P.

	X	$R - X$
t_1	$0 \cdots 0$	$0 \cdots 0$
t_2	$0 \cdots 0$	$1 \cdots 1$

	L	B	$R - BL$
t_1	$0 \cdots 0$	1	$0 \cdots 0$
t_2	$0 \cdots 0$	0	$1 \cdots 1$

Fig. 7. A counter-example relation r^c used in the case of $L = X$

Fig. 8. A counter-example relation r^c used in the case of $L \neq X$

In the second case, we assume that $L \neq X$. Let $X = LBQ'$ where $B \notin L$ and $BQ' \subseteq R$. Using a similar technique of the first case, we construct the relation r^c shown in Figure 8, in which $r^c \not\models_u X$.

We now show that $r^c \models_u P$. We assume to the contrary that $\exists p \in P$ such that $r^c \not\models_u p$, where $p = X'$. By the construction of r^c, we have the following two possible cases concerning X'.

(Case of $X' \subseteq L$). By PP1, we expand p by attaching the attribute B. It follows that $P \vdash X'B$. By the L-assumption and PP2, it follows that $P \vdash LX'BQ$. We thus have $P \vdash LBQ$. But LB is the prefix of X and strictly contains L. This leads to a contradiction, since we violate the L-assumption.

(Case of $X' \not\subseteq L$). Let $X' = VBW$ where $V \subseteq L$ and $W \subseteq R$. By the L-assumption and PP2, it follows that $P \vdash LX'$. So by PP3 we have $P \vdash LBW$. But LB is the prefix of X. This leads to the same contradiction, since we also violate the L-assumption. $\square$

4 Choice Constraints

In this section, we consider the case of more than one ranking of r that satisfy X and formalize the notion of a *Choice Constraint* (CC) and their satisfaction in relations. We formulate five inference rules that are proved to be sound and complete for CCs.

Definition 5 (Choice Constraint). Let X and Y be two sequences of non-empty attributes obtained from R. The Choice Constraint (CC), $Y \leq X$, is satisfied in r, written as $r \models Y \leq X$, if and only if, $\mid choice(r, Y) \mid \leq \mid choice(r, X) \mid$. Given a set of CCs, C, we say that r logically implies C, denoted as $r \models C$, if and only if $\forall (Y \leq X) \in C, r \models Y \leq X$. In addition, we say that C logically implies $Y \leq X$, denoted as $C \models Y \leq X$, if for any r, $r \models C$ implies $r \models Y \leq X$.

The study of CCs is related to maintaining the preference rankings in a database, since user preference terms may be removed or added. This is particular important for cache-conscious systems in a client-server architecture, in this case some possible rankings should be evaluated first in order to have quick response in the query evaluation. For example, referring to the $PENSIONER\_CHOICE$ ranking given in Figure 3, if the user is willing to drop the third priority of engine power, then we have two choices. However, dropping the second priority of mileage used does not offer more choices. It can be checked that the relation satisfies the CC, $PRICE, ENGINE \leq PRICE, MILEAGE$.

We are now ready to define a particular axiom system for CC satisfaction in relations.

Definition 6 (Inference Rules for Choice Constraints). Assume that X, Y, Z are non-empty sequences of attributes obtained from R.

(CC1) *Reflexivity*: $C \vdash X \leq X$.
(CC2) *Expansion*: If $C \vdash X \leq Y$ and X is a subsequence of W, then $C \vdash W \leq Y$.
(CC3) *Transitivity*: If $C \vdash X \leq Y$ and $C \vdash Y \leq Z$, then $C \vdash X \leq Z$.
(CC4) *Pseudo Augmentation*: If $C \vdash Y \leq XY$, then $C \vdash YZ \leq XYZ$.
(CC5) *Permutation*: If $X \sim X', Y \sim Y'$ and $C \vdash X \leq Y$, then $C \vdash X' \leq Y'$.

Note that CCs do not have usual augmentation as FDs. The counter example in Figure 9 shows that the statement if $C \vdash B \leq A$, then $C \vdash BC \leq AC$ is false. It can also be checked that $\mid choice(r, A) \mid = \mid choice(r, B) \mid = 2$ but $\mid choice(r, AC) \mid = 1$ and $\mid choice(r, BC) \mid = \mid choice(r, CB) \mid = 2$.

	A	B	C
t_1	0	1	0
t_2	0	0	1
t_3	1	0	1

$choice(r, A) = \{t_1 <_r t_2 <_r t_3; t_2 <_r t_1 <_r t_3\}$
$choice(r, B) = \{t_2 <_r t_3 <_r t_1; t_3 <_r t_2 <_r t_1\}$
$choice(r, AC) = \{t_1 <_r t_2 <_r t_3\}$
$choice(r, BC) = \{t_2 <_r t_3 <_r t_1; t_3 <_r t_2 <_r t_1\}$
$choice(r, CB) = \{t_1 <_r t_2 <_r t_3; t_1 <_r t_3 <_r t_2\}$

Fig. 9. $r \models B \leq A$ but $r \not\models BC \leq AC$

Lemma 2. The following three inference rules can be derived from CC1 - CC5.

(CC6) *Projection I*: If Z is a subsequence of X, then $C \vdash X \leq Z$.
(CC7) *Projection II*: If $C \vdash X \leq Y$ and Z is a subsequence of Y, then $C \vdash X \leq Z$.
(CC8) *Pseudo Union*: If $C \vdash X \leq XY$ and $C \vdash X \leq XZ$, then $C \vdash X \leq XYZ$.

Lemma 3. The axiom system comprising inference rules CC1-CC5 is sound for the satisfaction of CCs in relations.   □

We now establish the completeness of the rules given in Definition 6. First, we introduce two technical concepts of CC *closure* and CC *cover* for establishing the result. Given C, a CC closure, denoted as C^+, is given by $C^+ = \{X \leq Y \mid C \vdash X \leq Y\}$. A CC cover of C, denoted as $cover(C)$, is the set of CCs that have maximal sets of attributes on the right side. Formally, $cover(C) = \{X \leq Y \mid X \leq Y \in C^+ \text{ and } \forall (X \leq Z) \in C^+, Z \subseteq Y \text{ (as sets)}\}$.

Clearly, C and C^+ are equivalent. The following lemma shows that C and $cover(C)$ are equivalent with respect to CC inferencing.

Lemma 4. $C \vdash X \leq Y$ if and only if $cover(C) \vdash X \leq Y$.

Proof. The proof of the "if" part is trivial by the definition of C^+, since $C \vdash C^+$ and $cover(C) \subseteq C^+$. The "only if" part can be established as follow: let $(X \leq Y) \in C$. Then $\exists (X \leq Z) \in cover(C)$ such that $Y \subseteq Z$. If $Y \neq Z$, then we apply CC7 and thus it follows that $cover(C) \vdash X \leq Y$. □

Theorem 2. The axiom system comprising inference rules CC1 to CC5 is sound and complete for the satisfaction of CCs in relations.

Proof. Let $X^+ = \{Y \mid X \leq Y \in cover(C)\}$ and $\mathcal{Y} = \bigcup_{Y \in X^+}(Y - X)$. We now define an *equivalence relation* $\mathcal{E}$ on $\mathcal{Y}$ as follows: for any pair of attributes $A_1, A_2 \in R$, $A_1 \approx_{\mathcal{E}} A_2$ if, for any $Y \in X^+$, $A_1 \in Y$ iff $A_2 \in Y$. Let C is an equivalence class (a set of attributes) induced by $\mathcal{E}$. The collection of all $E = (C - X), \mathcal{P} = \{E_1, \ldots, E_n\}$, forms a partition of $\mathcal{Y}$. We now construct a counter example relation $r^c = \{t_0 <_r t_1 <_t \cdots <_t t_n\}$ as follows. Let $E_0 = X$. We generate an ith tuple for each E_i ($0 \leq i \leq n$) as $t_i[A] = 0$ whenever $A \in E_i$, $t_i[A] = i$ whenever $A \in R - (X \cup \mathcal{Y})$, and 1 otherwise. The schema of r^c is valid, since all $E \in (\mathcal{P} \cup \{X\})$ do not overlap.

By Lemma 3, we know that CC1 to CC5 are sound for CCs. We prove the completeness by showing that if $C \nvdash X \leq Y$, then $C \nvDash X \leq Y$. Equivalently for the latter, it is sufficient to exhibit a relation r^c, such that $r^c \vDash C$ but $r^c \nvDash X \leq Y$. Let r^c be the relation shown in Figure 10.

	X	E_1	E_2	$\cdots$	E_n	$R - (X \cup \mathcal{Y})$
t_0	$0 \cdots 0$	$1 \cdots 1$	$1 \cdots 1$	$\cdots$	$1 \cdots 1$	$0 \cdots 0$
t_1	$1 \cdots 1$	$0 \cdots 0$	$1 \cdots 1$	$\cdots$	$1 \cdots 1$	$1 \cdots 1$
t_2	$1 \cdots 1$	$1 \cdots 1$	$0 \cdots 0$	$\cdots$	$1 \cdots 1$	$2 \cdots 2$
$\vdots$	$\vdots$	$\vdots$	$\vdots$	$\ddots$	$\vdots$	$\vdots$
t_{n+1}	$1 \cdots 1$	$1 \cdots 1$	$1 \cdots 1$	$\cdots$	$0 \cdots 0$	$n+1 \cdots n+1$

Fig. 10. A relation r^c showing that $C \nvDash X \leq Y$

We first show that $r^c \vDash C$. Suppose to the contrary that $r^c \nvDash C$ and thus there exists a CC, $V \leq W \in C$, such that $r^c \nvDash V \leq W$. From the definition of X^+ and $\mathcal{P}$, V and W do not cross more than one E. It follows from the construction of r^c that $\exists A \in W$ such that $A \in R - (X \cup \mathcal{Y})$ and that $V \subseteq X$ or $V \subseteq E_i$ (as sets). In the first case, it follows by CC5 and CC6 that $C \vdash X \leq V$. By CC3, it follows that $C \vdash X \leq W$. Thus, it follows that $C \vdash X \leq A$ by CC6 again. This leads to a contradiction, since $A \in (X \cup \mathcal{Y})$. In the second case, it follows by the definition of E_i and by CC5 and CC6 that $C \vdash X \leq E_i$. By CC6, it follows that $C \vdash X \leq V$. By CC3, it follows that $C \vdash X \leq W$. Thus, $A \in (X \cup \mathcal{Y})$. This leads to the same contradiction again as the first case.

We conclude the proof by showing that $r^c \nvDash X \leq Y$. Suppose to the contrary that $r^c \vDash X \leq Y$; by the construction of r^c, $Y \subseteq E_i$ (as sets). It follows by definition of E_i and by CC6 that $C \vdash X \leq E_i$. By CC3 and CC5, it follows that $C \vdash X \leq Y$. This leads to a contradiction, since we assume $C \nvdash X \leq Y$. □

5 Interaction Rules

In this section we investigate the interactions between FDs and PPs in Section 5.1 and those between FDs and CCs in Section 5.2.

We first state Armstrong's axiom, which is known to be sound and complete for FDs [1]. We also need to adapt the axiom to this context as follows.

Definition 7 (Armstrong's Axiom System). Let X, Y, Z be non-empty sequences of attributes obtained from R, $A \in R$ and F be a set of FDs.

(FD1) *Reflexivity:* If $Y \subseteq X$, then $F \vdash X \to Y$.
(FD2) *Augmentation:* If $F \vdash X \to Y$, then $F \vdash XA \to YA$.
(FD3) *Transitivity:* If $F \vdash X \to Y$ and $F \vdash Y \to Z$, then $F \vdash X \to Z$.
(FD4) *Permutation:* If $X \sim X'$, $Y \sim Y'$, and $F \vdash X \to Y$, then $F \vdash X' \to Y'$.

5.1 Interactions Between FDs and PPs

We show that the axiom system that consists of PP rules in Definition 4, Armstrong's rules in Definition 7 and three new FD-PP interaction rules in Definition 8 is sound and complete for FDs and PPs.

Now, we present the"mixed rules" for the interactions between FDs and PEs.

Definition 8 (Inference Rules for Interactions between FDs and PPs). Let Γ be a mixed set FDs and PPs.

(FD-PP1) *Superkey:* If $\Gamma \vdash X$, then $\Gamma \vdash X \to R$.
(FD-PP2) *Absorption:* If $\Gamma \vdash X \to A$ and $\Gamma \vdash XAY$, then $\Gamma \vdash XY$.
(FD-PP3) *Generation:* If $\Gamma \vdash X \to A$ and $\Gamma \vdash XY$, then $\Gamma \vdash XAY$.

Similar to the concept of implication used in PPs and CCs, we say $r \models \Gamma$, if and only if $r \models \gamma$ for all $\gamma \in \Gamma$. Notably, the statement actually means $r \models f$ for any FD $f \in \Gamma$ and $r \models_u X$ and for any PP $X \in \Gamma$.

Lemma 5. The three interaction rules PF1 to PF3 are sound for the satisfaction of both FDs and PPs in relations.   □

We now show that the collection of the inference rules $\{PP1, PP2, PP3, FD1, FD2, FD3, FD4, FD\text{-}PP1, FD\text{-}PP2, FD\text{-}PP3\}$ is a sound and complete set of rules for proving the implications of FDs and PPs taken together.

Theorem 3. The axiom system comprising inference rules PP1 to PP3, FD1 to FD4, and FD-PP1 to FD-PP3 is sound and complete for the satisfaction of both PPs and FDs in relations.

Proof. We only need to prove the completeness. Let $\Gamma = \Gamma_f \cup \Gamma_p$ where Γ_f is the set of all FDs and Γ_p is the set of all PPs. We now establish the completeness by showing that if $\Gamma \nvdash \gamma$, then $\Gamma \nvDash \gamma$, where γ is either f (an FD) or p (a PP). Equivalently for the latter, it is sufficient to exhibit a relation as a counter-example, r^c, such that $r^c \models \Gamma$ but $r^c \nvDash \gamma$. We let $\Gamma_{p2f} = \{X \to R \mid X \in \Gamma_p\}$.

	X^+	$R - X^+$
t_1	$0 \cdots 0$	$0 \cdots 0$
t_2	$0 \cdots 0$	$1 \cdots 1$

	R
t_1	$1 \cdots 1$
t_2	$0 \cdots 0$

Fig. 11. A counter example relation r^c used in the case $\gamma = X \to A$

Fig. 12. A counter example relation r^c used in the case $\gamma = X$ when $\Gamma_p = \emptyset$

(Case of $\gamma = f$.) Let $\gamma = X \to A$. By FD-PP1, we have $\Gamma \vdash \Gamma_{p2f} \cup \Gamma_f$. Let $X^+ = \{B \mid \Gamma_{p2f} \cup \Gamma_f \vdash X \to B\}$. By the assumption of $\Gamma \nvdash \gamma$, it follows that $A \notin X^+$. We consider the relation $r^c = \{t_1 <_r t_2\}$ shown in Figure 11. Clearly, $r^c \nvDash_u X \to A$. We proceed to show $r^c \vDash \Gamma$. It is straightforward to check that $r^c \vDash \Gamma_f$. It remains for us to show that $r^c \vDash_u \Gamma_p$. Assume to the contrary that there exists $p \in \Gamma_p$ such that $r^c \nvDash_u p$. Let $p = Z$. By construction of r^c, $Z \subseteq X^+$. It follows that $\Gamma_{p2f} \cup \Gamma_f \vdash X \to Z$. But $Z \to R \in \Gamma_{p2f}$. By FD3, it follows that $X \to R$. Thus, $X^+ = R$ and $A \in X^+$. This leads to a contradiction, since by assumption, $A \notin X^+$. This completes the proof of this case, since we have shown $r^c \vDash \Gamma_f \cup \Gamma_p$.

(Case of $\gamma = p$.) Let $\gamma = X$. There are two cases concerning Γ_p to consider.

First, if $\Gamma_p = \emptyset$, then the relation r^c in Figure 12 satisfies $r^c \vDash \Gamma_f$ but $r^c \nvDash_u X$.

Second, if $\Gamma_p \neq \emptyset$, then we assume that X_0 is the largest prefix of X such that $\Gamma \vdash X_0 Q$ for some $Q \subseteq R$. Let us call this the X-assumption. We consider two further cases concerning X_0.

(Case 1:) When $X_0 = X$, we let $X^+ = \{B \mid \Gamma_f \vdash X \to B\}$ and $\Gamma \vdash Z$. We use again the relation shown in Figure 11. (But note that the definition of X^+ in this case is not the same.) It is clear that $r^c \nvDash_u X$ but $r^c \vDash \Gamma_f$. It remains for us to show that $r^c \vDash_u \Gamma_p$. Assume to the contrary that there exists $p \in \Gamma_p$ such that $r^c \nvDash_u p$. Let $p = Z$. By construction of r^c, $Z \subseteq X^+$. But $X_0 = X$ and thus, from the X-assumption, it follows that $\Gamma \vdash XQ$. By $\Gamma_f \vdash X \to X^+$ and FD-PP3, it follows that $\Gamma \vdash X X^+ Q$. By PP2, it follows that $\Gamma \vdash X X^+ Z Q$. By FD-PP1, $\Gamma \vdash Z \to R$. Thus, we have $\Gamma \vdash Z \to Q$. By FD-PP2, it follows that $\Gamma \vdash X X^+ Z$ and by PP3 it follows that $\Gamma \vdash X X^+$. Thus, it follows that $\Gamma \vdash X$, since $\Gamma \vdash X \to X'$. This is a contradiction to the assumption of $\Gamma \nvdash X$.

	X^+	A	$R - X^+ A$
t_1	$0 \cdots 0$	1	$0 \cdots 0$
t_2	$0 \cdots 0$	0	$1 \cdots 1$

Fig. 13. A counter example relation r^c used in the case $\gamma = X$ when $\Gamma_p \neq \emptyset$ (Case 2)

(Case 2:) When $X_0 \neq X$, we let $X = X_0 AQ$ where $A \notin X_0$. We let $X^+ = \{B \mid \Gamma_f \vdash X_0 \to B\}$. Note that $A \notin X^+$. Otherwise, it follows that $\Gamma_f \vdash X_0 \to A$ and by assumption $\Gamma \vdash X_0 Q$, it follows that $\Gamma \vdash X_0 AQ$ by FD-PP3. This leads to a violation of the X-assumption. We now consider the relation, r^c, shown in Figure 13. Clearly,

$r^c \models \Gamma_f$ but $r^c \not\models_u X$. It remains for us to show that $r^c \models_u \Gamma_p$. Assume to the contrary that there exists $p \in \Gamma_p$ such that $r^c \not\models_u p$. Let $p = Z$. By construction of r^c, we have the following two possible cases of Z.

(Case of $Z \subseteq X^+$.) A contradiction can be established similar to the proof of Case 1 when $X = X_0$.

(Case of $Z \not\subseteq X^+$.) Let $Z = VAW$ where $V \subseteq X^+$ and $W \subseteq R$. Since $\Gamma \vdash X_0 Q$ and $\Gamma \vdash VAW$, it follows by PP2 that $\Gamma \vdash X_0 VAWQ$. Since $\Gamma_f \vdash X_0 \rightarrow X^+$, it follows by FD-PP3 that $\Gamma \vdash X_0 X^+ VAWQ$. Thus, by PP3 it follows that $\Gamma \vdash X_0 X^+ AWQ$. Finally, by FD-PP2 and $\Gamma_f \vdash X_0 \rightarrow X^+$, it follows that $\Gamma \vdash X_0 AWQ$. This leads to a contradiction, since we violate the X-assumption. $\square$

5.2   Interactions Between FDs and CCs

We establish two new interaction rules for CCs and FDs. We show that the axiom system that consists of CC rules in Definition 6, Armstrong's rules in Definition 7 and the new FD-CC interaction rules in Definition 9 is sound and complete for FDs and CCs.

Definition 9 (Inference Rules for Interactions between FDs and CCs). Let Σ be a mixed set FDs and CCs.

(FD-CC1) *Reverse*: If $\Sigma \vdash X \rightarrow Y$ and $\Sigma \vdash Y \leq X$, then $\Sigma \vdash Y \rightarrow X$.
(FD-CC2) *Transformation*: If $\Sigma \vdash X \rightarrow Y$, then $\Sigma \vdash X \leq Y$.

Lemma 6. The inference rules FD-CC1 and FD-CC2 are sound for the satisfaction of both FDs and CCs in relations. $\square$

We now prove the axiom system is sound and complete for unary CCs and unary FDs.

Theorem 4. The axiom system comprising inference rules CC1-CC5, FD1-FD4 and CC-FD1-CC-FD2 is sound and complete for the satisfaction of both CCs and FDs in relations.

Proof. We only need to prove the completeness. Let $\Sigma = \Sigma_f \cup \Sigma_c$ where Σ_f is the set of all FDs and Σ_c is the set of all CCs. We now establish the completeness by showing that if $\Sigma \not\vdash \sigma$, then $\Sigma \not\models \sigma$, where σ is either f (an FD) or c (an CC). Equivalently for the latter, it is sufficient to exhibit a relation as a counter-example r^c, such that $r^c \models \Sigma$ but $r^c \not\models \sigma$. We let $\Sigma_{f2c} = \{Y \leq X \mid X \rightarrow Y \in \Sigma_f\}$, which can be derived by the rule FD-CC1.

(*Case of $\sigma = c$.*) We now show that $\Sigma \models \sigma$ if and only if $\Sigma_c \cup \Sigma_{f2c} \models \sigma$. For the "if" part: by CC-FD1, it follows that $\Sigma \models \Sigma_c \cup \Sigma_{f2c}$. Thus, $\Sigma \models \sigma$. For the "only if" part: assume that $\Sigma_c \cup \Sigma_{f2c} \not\models \sigma$. We need to show that $\Sigma \not\models \sigma$.

Let $\sigma = X \leq Y$ and $X_f^+ = \{A \mid \Sigma_f \vdash X \rightarrow A\}$. We then modify the relation based on Figure 10 such that $\forall t \in r^c, t[A] = 1$ whenever $A \in X_f^+$. It follows by FD-CC2 that $X_f^+ \subseteq X \cup \mathcal{Y}$. Then, we can show that the following claim is true.
    (*) Claim: If $r^c \not\models X \rightarrow Y$ and $r^c \models X \leq Y$, then $r^c \not\models Y \rightarrow X$.

By using the claim $(*)$, we are able to check that $r^c \models \Sigma_f$. The proof of $r^c \models \Sigma_c$ but $r^c \not\models X \leq Y$ is similar to Theorem 2.

The result then follows by Theorem 2, since the set of inference rules for CCs in Definition 6 is complete.

(*Case of* $\sigma = f$.) Let FD be $X \to Y$. It can be shown that if $\Sigma \models X \to Y$, then $\Sigma_f \models X \to Y$, or else $\Sigma_f \models Y \to X$. Assume that $\Sigma_f \models X \to Y$. The result immediately follows by Armstrong's axiom. Otherwise, by the completeness of Armstrong's axiom it follows that $\Sigma \vdash Y \to X$. It also follows by FD-CC2 that $\Sigma \models X \leq Y$, since we assume that $\Sigma \models X \to Y$. Thus, it follows by the case of $(\sigma = c)$ in this proof that we have $\Sigma \vdash X \leq Y$. The result follows, since by FD-CC1 we have $\Sigma \vdash X \to Y$. $\square$

6   Related Work

In literature, there is abundant work on data dependencies in relational databases [1] but they have not been used to capture user preferences. It is worth mentioning that in [5,6] the axiom system for partial order dependencies is co-NP, which has limited the applicability of *order comparison dependencies* for decades. Here, with a given set of user preference terms, we override the partial order with a preference hierarchy and generate a preference relation, which simplifies much complex technicalities in establishing the axiom systems.

Preferences are receiving much attention in querying, since DBMSs need to provide better information services in advanced applications [7,8]. In partiuclar, preference SQL [8] is equipped with a "preferring" clause that allows user to specify soft constraints reflecting multiple preference terms.

Our previous work [14] proposes Preference Functional Dependencies (PFDs) as an extension of FDs in relations, which captures the relationship between preferences and preference-dependent data. We emphasize that the constraints considered in this paper are entirely different from PFDs. We study the inference rules for preference constraints (PPs and CCs) in their own right. We neither incorporate preferences into FDs nor classify attributes as the assumptions in [14]. However, we thoroughly study the interactions between PPs, CCs and FDs.

7   Concluding Remarks

We model preference terms as partial orderings on a sequence of attributes and study the implication problem of preference satisfaction in a relation. We first formalize the concept of Prioritized Preferences (PPs), which is a sequence of preference attributes used for ranking a relation. We then establish a novel sound and complete inference system for PPs. The ranking choice is formalized as a set of possible rankings in a relation that satisfies a PP. We propose the concept of Choice Constraints (CCs) which capture the fact that the ranking choice resulting from one preference is less than or equal to another. We then establish a sound and complete inference system for CCs. Finally, we present interesting results on interactions between Functional Dependencies (FDs) and PPs, and between FDs and CCs. The main result of this paper is fundamental, which paves the way to transform the implication problem into a finite procedure for deriving PPs, CCs and FDs from a given set of such constraints. With the established axiom systems, efficient algorithms for checking various kinds of preference satisfaction are to be considered in our future work. It is also interesting to study how to infer and handle vague user preference [10,11], since in real life the user may not be willing to detail and check all the preferences when querying.

Acknowledgements. This work is partially supported by RGC CERG under grant No. HKUST6185/03E and DAG04/05.EG10.

References

1. Atzeni, P., De Antonellis, V.: Relational Database Theory. Benjamin Cummings Publishing Company, Inc (1993)
2. Chomicki, J.: Preference formulas in relational queries. ACM Transaction Database System 28(4), 427–466 (2003)
3. Chomicki, J.: Semantic Optimization Techniques for Preference Queries. Information Systems 32, 670–684 (2006)
4. Garey, M.R., Johnson, D.S.: Computers and Intractability: A Guide to the Theory of NP-Completeness. W.H. Freeman and Co., New York (1979)
5. Ginsburg, S., Hull, R.: Order Dependency in the Relational Model. Theoretical Computer Science 26(1-2), 149–195 (1983)
6. Ginsburg, S., Hull, R.: Sort Sets in the Relational Model. Journal of the Association for Computing Machinery 33(3), 465–488 (1986)
7. Kießling, W., Köstler, G.: Preference SQL - Design, Implementation, Experiences. In: Bressan, S., Chaudhri, A.B., Lee, M.L., Yu, J.X., Lacroix, Z. (eds.) CAiSE 2002 and VLDB 2002. LNCS, vol. 2590, Springer, Heidelberg (2003)
8. Kießling, W., Köstler, G.: Foundations of Preference in Database Systems. In: Bressan, S., Chaudhri, A.B., Lee, M.L., Yu, J.X., Lacroix, Z. (eds.) CAiSE 2002 and VLDB 2002. LNCS, vol. 2590, Springer, Heidelberg (2003)
9. Mannila, H., Raiha, K.-J.: The Design of Relational Databases. Addison-Wesley, London, UK (1992)
10. Lu, A., Ng, W.: Mining hesitation information by vague association rules. In: Parent, C., Schewe, K.-D., Storey, V.C., Thalheim, B. (eds.) ER 2007. LNCS, vol. 4801, pp. 39–55. Springer, Heidelberg (2007)
11. Lu, A., Ng, W.: Handling Inconsistency of Vague Relations with Functional Dependencies. In: Parent, C., Schewe, K.-D., Storey, V.C., Thalheim, B. (eds.) ER 2007. LNCS, vol. 4801, pp. 229–244. Springer, Heidelberg (2007)
12. Ng, W.: Ordered Functional Dependencies in Relational Databases. Information Systems 24(7), 535–554 (1999)
13. Ng, W.: An Extension of the Relational Data Model to Incorporate Ordered Domains. ACM Transactions on Database Systems 26(3) (2001)
14. Ng, W.: Preference Functional Dependencies for Managing Choices. In: Embley, D.W., Olivé, A., Ram, S. (eds.) ER 2006. LNCS, vol. 4215, pp. 140–154. Springer, Heidelberg (2006)

Reasoning over Extended ER Models

A. Artale[1], D. Calvanese[1], R. Kontchakov[2], V. Ryzhikov[1], and M. Zakharyaschev[2]

[1] Faculty of Computer Science
Free University of Bozen-Bolzano
I-39100 Bolzano, Italy
lastname@inf.unibz.it
[2] School of Comp. Science and Inf. Sys.
Birkbeck College
London WC1E 7HX, UK
{roman,michael}@dcs.bbk.ac.uk

Abstract. We investigate the computational complexity of reasoning over various fragments of the Extended Entity-Relationship (EER) language, which includes a number of constructs: ISA between entities and relationships, disjointness and covering of entities and relationships, cardinality constraints for entities in relationships and their refinements as well as multiplicity constraints for attributes. We extend the known EXPTIME-completeness result for UML class diagrams [5] and show that reasoning over EER diagrams with ISA between relationships is EXPTIME-complete even without relationship covering. Surprisingly, reasoning becomes NP-complete when we drop ISA between relationships (while still allowing all types of constraints on entities). If we further omit disjointness and covering over entities, reasoning becomes polynomial. Our lower complexity bound results are proved by direct reductions, while the upper bounds follow from the correspondences with expressive variants of the description logic *DL-Lite*, which we establish in this paper. These correspondences also show the usefulness of *DL-Lite* as a language for reasoning over conceptual models and ontologies.

1 Introduction

Conceptual modelling formalisms, such as the Entity-Relationship model [3], are used in the phase of conceptual database design, where the aim is to capture at best the semantics of the modelled application. This is achieved by expressing the constraints that hold on the entities, attributes and relationships, which represent the domain of interest, through suitable constructors provided by the conceptual modelling language. Thus, on the one hand it would be desirable to make such a language as expressive as possible in order to represent as many aspects of the modelled reality as possible. On the other hand, when using an expressive language, the designer faces the problem of understanding complex interactions that may occur between different parts of the conceptual model under construction and the constraints therein. Such interactions may force, e.g., some class (or even all classes) in the model to become inconsistent in the sense that there cannot exist a database state satisfying all constraints in which the class (respectively, all classes) is populated by at least one object. Or a class may turn

C. Parent et al. (Eds.): ER 2007, LNCS 4801, pp. 277–292, 2007.
© Springer-Verlag Berlin Heidelberg 2007

out to be a subclass of another one, even though this is not explicitly asserted in the model. To understand the consequences, both explicit and implicit, of the constraints in the conceptual model being constructed, it is essential to provide automated reasoning support, especially in those application scenarios where models may become very large and/or have complex interactions between constraints.

In this paper, we address these issues and investigate the computational complexity of reasoning in conceptual modelling languages equipped with various forms of constraints. Our analysis is carried out in the context of the Extended Entity-Relationship (EER) language [14], where the domain of interest is represented through *entities* (representing sets of objects), possibly equipped with *attributes*, and *relationships* (representing relations among objects). Note, however, that all of our results can also be adapted to other conceptual modelling formalisms, such as UML class diagrams[1]. Specifically, the kind of constraints that will be taken into account in this paper are the ones typically used in conceptual modelling, namely:

- *ISA* relations between both entities and relationships;
- *disjointness* and *covering* (referred to as the *Boolean* constructors in what follows) between both entities and relationships;
- *cardinality* constraints for participation of entities in relationships;
- *refinement* of cardinalities for sub-entities participating in relationships; and
- *multiplicity* constraints for attributes.

The hierarchy of EER languages considered in the paper is shown in the table below together with the complexity results for reasoning in these languages (all our languages include cardinality, refinement and multiplicity constraints).

lang.	entities			relationships			complexity
	ISA	disjoint	covering	ISA	disjoint	covering	
	$C_1 \sqsubseteq C_2$	$C_1 \sqcap C_2 \sqsubseteq \bot$	$C = C_1 \sqcup C_2$	$R_1 \sqsubseteq R_2$	$R_1 \sqcap R_2 \sqsubseteq \bot$	$R = R_1 \sqcup R_2$	
ER_{full}	+	+	+	+	+	+	ExpTime [5]
ER_{isaR}	+	+	+	+	−	−	ExpTime
ER_{bool}	+	+	+	−	−	−	NP
ER_{ref}	+	+	−	−	−	−	NLogSpace

In our investigation we exploit the tight correspondences between conceptual modelling formalisms, such as the ER model, and variants of Description Logics (DLs) [11]. DLs [2] are a family of logics studied in knowledge representation that are specifically tailored towards the representation of structured class-based information; quite often these logics enjoy nice computational properties.

It was shown [5] that reasoning with respect to UML class diagrams is an ExpTime-complete problem, and it is easy to see that this result carries over to ER_{full} diagrams as well (cf., e.g., [11]). The upper complexity bound result is established by encoding UML class diagrams in an expressive variant of DL, $\mathcal{DLR}_{ifd}$, reasoning in which is known to be in ExpTime (cf., [7]). The proof of the lower bound is by reduction of

---

[1] See, e.g., http://www.uml.org/

reasoning over knowledge bases in the DL $\mathcal{ALC}$ [2], which is an ExpTime-complete problem. The reduction proposed in [5] makes use of both ISA and the Boolean constructors between relationships. Here we strengthen this result by showing that even if we drop the Booleans between relationships from ER_{full} (obtaining the language denoted by ER_{isaR}) reasoning still stays ExpTime-complete.

We then prove that reasoning in the language ER_{bool}, which essentially corresponds to ER_{isaR} without ISA between relationships, can be done in NP, and is also NP-complete. Thus, quite surprisingly, ISA between relationships turns out to be a major source of complexity for reasoning over schemas, making it jump from NP to Exp-Time. To prove the NP upper complexity bound we again exploit the correspondence with DLs: specifically, we resort to $DL\text{-}Lite_{bool}$, the *Boolean extension* of the tractable DL $DL\text{-}Lite$ [8,9], reasoning in which is an NP-complete problem [1]: we show that ER_{bool} schemas can be captured by knowledge bases in $DL\text{-}Lite_{bool}$ so that the reasoning services carry over. The lower complexity bound is shown by a polynomial reduction of the satisfiability problem in propositional calculus.

Finally, we further restrict the language of ER_{bool} by dropping the covering constructor and obtaining the language called ER_{ref}. We prove that the reasoning problem for ER_{ref} is NLogSpace-complete. The NLogSpace membership is shown by reduction to reasoning in $DL\text{-}Lite_{krom}$, the Krom fragment of $DL\text{-}Lite_{bool}$, which is known to be NLogSpace-complete [1]. Hardness for NLogSpace follows from a reduction of the graph reachability problem to reasoning in ER_{ref}.

The correspondence between conceptual modelling languages like ER_{bool} and ER_{ref} and the $DL\text{-}Lite$ family of DLs, developed and exploited in this paper, shows that both $DL\text{-}Lite_{bool}$ and $DL\text{-}Lite_{krom}$ are useful languages for reasoning over conceptual models and ontologies, even though they are not equipped with all the constructors that are typical of rich ontology languages such as OWL and its variants [4].

Our analysis is similar in spirit to [13], where the consistency checking problem for the EER model equipped with forms of inclusion and disjointness constraints is studied and a polynomial-time algorithm for the problem is given (assuming constant arities of relationships). Such a polynomial-time result is incomparable with the one for ER_{ref}, since ER_{ref} lacks both ISA and disjointness for relationships (both present in [13]); on the other hand, it is equipped with cardinality and multiplicity constraints. We also mention [16], where reasoning over cardinality constraints in the basic ER model is investigated and a polynomial-time algorithm for strong schema consistency is given, and [10], where the study is extended to the case when ISA between entities is also allowed and an exponential algorithm for entity consistency is provided. Note, however, that in [16,10] the reasoning problem is analysed under the assumption that databases are finite, whereas we do not require finiteness in this paper.

The paper is organised as follows. In Section 2, we introduce some members of the $DL\text{-}Lite$ family. Section 3 is devoted to the formal definition of the conceptual modelling language ER_{full} and the relevant reasoning problems. In Sections 4-6, we present the main results of the paper by establishing the computational complexity of reasoning over various fragments of ER_{full}: ER_{isaR}, ER_{bool} and ER_{ref}, respectively. Section 7 concludes the paper.

2   The *DL-Lite* Languages

We consider the extension $DL\text{-}Lite_{bool}$ [1] of the description logic $DL\text{-}Lite$ [8,9]. The language of $DL\text{-}Lite_{bool}$ contains *concept names* $A_0, A_1, \ldots$ and *role names* $P_0, P_1,$ .... Complex *roles* R and *concepts* C of $DL\text{-}Lite_{bool}$ are defined as follows:

$$
\begin{array}{rcl}
R & ::= & P_i \quad | \quad P_i^-, \\
B & ::= & \bot \quad | \quad A_i \quad | \quad \geq q\, R, \\
C & ::= & B \quad | \quad \neg C \quad | \quad C_1 \sqcap C_2,
\end{array}
$$

where $q \geq 1$. Concepts of the form B are called *basic concepts*. A $DL\text{-}Lite_{bool}$ *knowledge base*, $\mathcal{K}$, is a finite set of axioms of the form $C_1 \sqsubseteq C_2$.

A $DL\text{-}Lite_{bool}$ *interpretation* is a structure of the form

$$
\mathcal{I} = (\Delta, A_0^{\mathcal{I}}, A_1^{\mathcal{I}}, \ldots, P_0^{\mathcal{I}}, P_1^{\mathcal{I}}, \ldots), \tag{1}
$$

where Δ is a nonempty set, $A_i^{\mathcal{I}} \subseteq \Delta$ and $P_i^{\mathcal{I}} \subseteq \Delta \times \Delta$, for all i. The role and concept constructors are interpreted in $\mathcal{I}$ as usual:

$$
\begin{array}{rcll}
(P_i^-)^{\mathcal{I}} & = & \{(y, x) \in \Delta \times \Delta \mid (x, y) \in P_i^{\mathcal{I}}\}, & \text{(inverse role)} \\
\bot^{\mathcal{I}} & = & \emptyset, & \text{(the empty set)} \\
(\geq q\, R)^{\mathcal{I}} & = & \{x \in \Delta \mid \sharp\{y \in \Delta \mid (x, y) \in R^{\mathcal{I}}\} \geq q\}, & \text{('at least } q \text{ } R\text{-successors')} \\
(\neg C)^{\mathcal{I}} & = & \Delta \setminus C^{\mathcal{I}}, & \text{('not in } C\text{')} \\
(C_1 \sqcap C_2)^{\mathcal{I}} & = & C_1^{\mathcal{I}} \cap C_2^{\mathcal{I}}, & \text{('both in } C_1 \text{ and } C_2\text{')}
\end{array}
$$

where $\sharp X$ denotes the cardinality of the set X. The standard abbreviations $\top := \neg\bot$, $\exists R := (\geq 1\, R)$ and $\leq q\, R := \neg(\geq q + 1\, R)$ we need are self-explanatory and correspond to the intended semantics. We say that an interpretation $\mathcal{I}$ *satisfies* an axiom $C_1 \sqsubseteq C_2$ if $C_1^{\mathcal{I}} \subseteq C_2^{\mathcal{I}}$. A knowledge base $\mathcal{K}$ is *satisfiable* if there is an interpretation $\mathcal{I}$ that satisfies all the members of $\mathcal{K}$ (such an interpretation $\mathcal{I}$ is called a *model* of $\mathcal{K}$). A concept C is *satisfiable w.r.t. a knowledge base* $\mathcal{K}$ if there is a model $\mathcal{I}$ of $\mathcal{K}$ such that $C^{\mathcal{I}} \neq \emptyset$.

We also consider a sublanguage of $DL\text{-}Lite_{bool}$, the *Krom fragment* $DL\text{-}Lite_{krom}$, where only axioms of the following form are allowed:

$$
B_1 \sqsubseteq B_2 \quad \text{or} \quad B_1 \sqsubseteq \neg B_2 \quad \text{or} \quad \neg B_1 \sqsubseteq B_2,
$$

where B_1, B_2 are basic concepts (i.e., are of the form $\bot$, A_i or $\geq q\, R$).

The following result is proved in [1] and will be used later on:

Theorem 1. *The concept and KB satisfiability problem is* NP*-complete for* $DL\text{-}Lite_{bool}$ *KBs and* NLOGSPACE*-complete for* $DL\text{-}Lite_{krom}$ *KBs.*

3   The Conceptual Modelling Language

In this section, we define the notion of a *conceptual schema* by providing syntax and semantics for the fully-fledged conceptual modelling language ER_{full} (the formalisation adopted here is based on previous presentations in [2,3,11]). First citizens of a conceptual schema are *entities*, *relationships* and *attributes*. Arguments of relationships—specifying the part played by an entity when participating in a particular relationship—are denoted by means of so-called *role names*. Given a conceptual schema, we make the following assumptions about names: relationship and entity names are unique; attribute names are local to entities (i.e., the same attribute can be used by different entities but its type must be the same); role names are local to relationships (this freedom will be limited when considering conceptual models without sub-relationships).

3.1 Syntax

In what follows we make use of the notion of *labelled tuples*. Let X be a finite set $\{x_1, \ldots, x_n\}$ of *labels* and Y a finite set. An *X-labelled tuple over Y* is simply a (total) function $T : X \to Y$. For $x \in X$, we write $T[x]$ to refer to the element $y \in Y$ labelled by x. Given $y_1, \ldots, y_n \in Y$, the expression $\langle x_1 : y_1, \ldots, x_n : y_n \rangle$ stands for the X-labelled tuple T over Y such that $T[x_i] = y_i$, for $1 \leq 1 \leq n$. We also write $(x_i, y_i) \in T$ if $T[x_i] = y_i$. The set of all X-labelled tuples over Y is denoted by $T_Y(X)$.

Definition 1 (ER_{full} Syntax). An ER_{full} *conceptual schema* Σ is a tuple

$$(\mathcal{L}, \text{REL}, \text{ATT}, \text{CARD}_R, \text{CARD}_A, \text{REF}, \text{ISA}, \text{DISJ}, \text{COV}),$$

where

- $\mathcal{L}$ is the disjoint union of alphabets $\mathcal{E}$ for *entity* symbols, $\mathcal{A}$ for *attribute* symbols, $\mathcal{R}$ for *relationship* symbols, $\mathcal{U}$ for *role* symbols, and $\mathcal{D}$ for *domain* symbols. We will call the tuple $(\mathcal{E}, \mathcal{A}, \mathcal{R}, \mathcal{U}, \mathcal{D})$ the *signature* of the schema Σ.
- REL: $\mathcal{R} \to \bigcup_{\nu \subseteq \mathcal{U}, \nu \neq \emptyset} T_{\mathcal{E}}(\nu)$ is a (total) function that assigns to every relation symbol a tuple over the entity symbols labelled with a nonempty set of role symbols: $\text{REL}(R) = \langle U_1 : E_1, \ldots, U_m : E_m \rangle$, where m is the *arity* of R. Note that the roles U_i are pairwise distinct while the entities E_i can be repeated.
- ATT: $\mathcal{E} \to \bigcup_{\alpha \subseteq \mathcal{A}} T_{\mathcal{D}}(\alpha)$ is a (total) function that assigns to every entity symbol a tuple over the domain symbols labelled with some (possibly empty) set of attribute symbols: $\text{ATT}(E) = \langle A_1 : D_1, \ldots, A_h : D_h \rangle$.
- $\text{CARD}_R : \mathcal{R} \times \mathcal{U} \times \mathcal{E} \to \mathbb{N} \times (\mathbb{N} \cup \{\infty\})$ is a *partial* function defining *cardinality constraints*. The value of $\text{CARD}_R(R, U, E)$ may be defined only if $(U, E) \in \text{REL}(R)$.
- $\text{CARD}_A : \mathcal{A} \times \mathcal{E} \to \mathbb{N} \times (\mathbb{N} \cup \{\infty\})$ is a *partial* function defining *multiplicity for attributes*. The value of $\text{CARD}_A(A, E)$ may be defined only if $(A, D) \in \text{ATT}(E)$, for some $D \in \mathcal{D}$.
- REF: $\mathcal{R} \times \mathcal{U} \times \mathcal{E} \to \mathbb{N} \times (\mathbb{N} \cup \{\infty\})$ is a *partial* function defining *refinement* of cardinality constraints for sub-entities (see ISA below). The value of $\text{REF}(R, U, E)$ may be defined only if E ISA E' and $(U, E') \in \text{REL}(R)$. Note that REF subsumes classical cardinality constraints (CARD_R).
- ISA is the union of two binary relations ISA_E and ISA_R, where $\text{ISA}_R \subseteq \mathcal{E} \times \mathcal{E}$ and $\text{ISA}_R \subseteq \mathcal{R} \times \mathcal{R}$. These two binary relations define the ISA hierarchy on entities and relationships, respectively.

- DISJ is the union of two binary relations DISJ_E and DISJ_R, where $\text{DISJ}_E \subseteq 2^{\mathcal{E}} \times \mathcal{E}$ and $\text{DISJ}_R \subseteq 2^{\mathcal{R}} \times \mathcal{R}$. The intended meaning of, say, $(\{E_1, \ldots, E_n\}, E) \in \text{DISJ}_E$ is '$E_1, \ldots, E_n$ are disjoint sub-entities of E.'
- COV is the union of two binary relations COV_E and COV_R, where $\text{COV}_E \subseteq 2^{\mathcal{E}} \times \mathcal{E}$ and $\text{COV}_R \subseteq 2^{\mathcal{R}} \times \mathcal{R}$. The intended meaning of, say, $(\{E_1, \ldots, E_n\}, E) \in \text{COV}_E$ is '$E_1, \ldots, E_n$ are covering sub-entities of E.'

We additionally require that the relations ISA_R, DISJ_R and COV_R may only be defined for relationships of the same arity.

In what follows we use $E_1 \text{ ISA } E_2$ as a shortcut for $(E_1, E_2) \in \text{ISA}$ (similarly for ISA_E and ISA_R) and $\{E_1, \ldots, E_n\} \text{ DISJ } E$ as a shortcut for $(\{E_1, \ldots, E_n\}, E) \in \text{DISJ}$ (similarly for DISJ_E, DISJ_R, COV, COV_E and COV_R).

3.2 Semantics

The following definition specifies the set-theoretic semantics of ER_{full} schemas.

Definition 2 (ER_{full} **Semantics**). Let Σ be an ER_{full} conceptual schema and B_D, for $D \in \mathcal{D}$, a collection of disjoint countable sets called *basic domains*. An *interpretation* for Σ is a pair $\mathcal{B} = (\Delta^{\mathcal{B}} \cup \Lambda^{\mathcal{B}}, \cdot^{\mathcal{B}})$, where

- $\Delta^{\mathcal{B}}$ is a nonempty set, the *interpretation domain*;
- $\Lambda^{\mathcal{B}} = \bigcup_{D \in \mathcal{D}} \Lambda_D^{\mathcal{B}}$, with $\Lambda_D^{\mathcal{B}} \subseteq B_D$ for each $D \in \mathcal{D}$, is the *active domain* such that $\Delta^{\mathcal{B}} \cap \Lambda^{\mathcal{B}} = \emptyset$;
- $\cdot^{\mathcal{B}}$ is a function such that
  (i) $D^{\mathcal{B}} = \Lambda_D^{\mathcal{B}}$, for each $D \in \mathcal{D}$;
  (ii) $E^{\mathcal{B}} \subseteq \Delta^{\mathcal{B}}$, for each $E \in \mathcal{E}$;
  (iii) $R^{\mathcal{B}} \subseteq T_{\Delta^{\mathcal{B}}}(\nu)$, where $\nu = \{U_i \in \mathcal{U} \mid (U_i, E_i) \in \text{REL}(R)\}$, for each $R \in \mathcal{R}$;
  (iv) $A^{\mathcal{B}} \subseteq \Delta^{\mathcal{B}} \times \Lambda^{\mathcal{B}}$, for each $A \in \mathcal{A}$.

An interpretation $\mathcal{B}$ of a schema Σ is called a *legal database state* if it satisfies the following conditions:

1. For each $R \in \mathcal{R}$ with $\text{REL}(R) = \langle U_1: E_1, \ldots, U_m: E_m \rangle$ and each $r \in R^{\mathcal{B}}$, we have $r = \langle U_1: e_1, \ldots, U_m: e_m \rangle$ with $e_i \in E_i^{\mathcal{B}}$, for each $1 \leq i \leq m$. In the following, we adopt the convention to denote such a labelled tuple r as $(e_1, \ldots, e_m)$, and we may use $r[i]$ instead of $r[U_i]$ to denote the U_i/i-component of r—i.e., we simplify the notation by adopting for tuples a *positional* notation instead of the one based on role names.
2. For each $E \in \mathcal{E}$ with $\text{ATT}(E) = \langle A_1: D_1, \ldots, A_h: D_h \rangle$, each $(e, a) \in \Delta^{\mathcal{B}} \times \Lambda^{\mathcal{B}}$ and each $1 \leq i \leq h$, if $(e, a) \in A_i^{\mathcal{B}}$ then $a \in D_i^{\mathcal{B}}$.
3. For each $R \in \mathcal{R}$ with $\text{REL}(R) = \langle U_1: E_1, \ldots, U_m: E_m \rangle$ and each $1 \leq i \leq m$, if $\text{CARD}_R(R, U_i, E_i) = (\alpha, \beta)$ then, for all $e \in E_i^{\mathcal{B}}$,

$$\alpha \quad \leq \quad \#\{(e_1, \ldots, e_i, \ldots, e_m) \in R^{\mathcal{B}} \mid e_i = e\} \quad \leq \quad \beta. \qquad (2)$$

4. For each $E \in \mathcal{E}$ with $\text{ATT}(E) = \langle A_1: D_1, \ldots, A_h: D_h \rangle$ and each $1 \leq i \leq h$, if $\text{CARD}_A(A_i, E) = (\alpha, \beta)$ then $\alpha \leq \#\{(e, a) \in A_i^{\mathcal{B}}\} \leq \beta$, for all $e \in E^{\mathcal{B}}$.

5. For each $R \in \mathcal{R}$ with $\text{REL}(R) = \langle U_1 : E_1, \ldots, U_m : E_m \rangle$, each $1 \le i \le m$ and each $E \in \mathcal{E}$ with $E \text{ ISA } E_i$, if $\text{REF}(R, U_i, E) = (\alpha, \beta)$ then (2) holds for all $e \in E^{\mathcal{B}}$.
6. For all $E_1, E_2 \in \mathcal{E}$, if $E_1 \text{ ISA}_E E_2$ then $E_1^{\mathcal{B}} \subseteq E_2^{\mathcal{B}}$ (similarly for relationships).
7. For all $E, E_1, \ldots, E_n \in \mathcal{E}$, if $\{E_1, \ldots, E_n\} \text{ DISJ}_E E$ then $E_i^{\mathcal{B}} \subseteq E^{\mathcal{B}}$, for every $1 \le i \le n$, and $E_i^{\mathcal{B}} \cap E_j^{\mathcal{B}} = \emptyset$, for all $1 \le i < j \le n$ (similarly for relationships).
8. For all $E, E_1, \ldots, E_n \in \mathcal{E}$, $\{E_1, \ldots, E_n\} \text{ COV}_E E$ implies $E^{\mathcal{B}} = \bigcup_{i=1}^{n} E_i^{\mathcal{B}}$ (similarly for relationships).

3.3   Reasoning Problems

Reasoning tasks over conceptual schemas include verifying whether an entity, a relationship, or a schema is *consistent*, or checking whether an entity (relationship) *subsumes* another entity (relationship, respectively). The model-theoretic semantics associated with a conceptual schema allows us to define formally the following reasoning tasks:

Definition 3 (Reasoning services). Let Σ be an ER_{full} schema.

Schema consistency. Σ is *consistent* if there exists a legal database state $\mathcal{B}$ for Σ such that $E^{\mathcal{B}} \neq \emptyset$, for some entity $E \in \mathcal{E}$.

Strong (schema) consistency. Σ is *strongly consistent* if there exists a legal database state $\mathcal{B}$ for Σ such that $E^{\mathcal{B}} \neq \emptyset$, for *every* entity $E \in \mathcal{E}$.

Entity consistency. An entity $E \in \mathcal{E}$ is *consistent w.r.t. a schema* Σ if there exists a legal database state $\mathcal{B}$ for Σ such that $E^{\mathcal{B}} \neq \emptyset$.

Relationship consistency. A relationship $R \in \mathcal{R}$ is *consistent w.r.t. a schema* Σ if there exists a legal database state $\mathcal{B}$ for Σ such that $R^{\mathcal{B}} \neq \emptyset$.

Entity subsumption. An entity $E_1 \in \mathcal{E}$ *subsumes* an entity $E_2 \in \mathcal{E}$ w.r.t. a schema Σ if $E_2^{\mathcal{B}} \subseteq E_1^{\mathcal{B}}$, for every legal database state $\mathcal{B}$ for Σ.

Relationships subsumption. A relationship $R_1 \in \mathcal{R}$ *subsumes* a relationship $R_2 \in \mathcal{R}$ w.r.t. a schema Σ if $R_2^{\mathcal{B}} \subseteq R_1^{\mathcal{B}}$, for every legal database state $\mathcal{B}$ for Σ.

The reasoning tasks of Schema/Entity/Relationship consistency and Entity subsumption are reducible to each other. Indeed, that Entity subsumption is equivalent to Entity satisfiability is shown in [5]. Schema consistency can be reduced to Entity consistency by extending Σ as follows: let O^* be a fresh entity symbol, $\mathcal{E}^* = \mathcal{E} \cup \{O^*\}$ and $\text{COV}^* = \text{COV} \cup \{(\mathcal{E}, O^*)\}$. Clearly, Σ is consistent iff O^* is consistent w.r.t. Σ^*. For the converse reduction Σ is extended as follows: let O^* be a fresh entity symbol and R_E a fresh relationship symbol, $\mathcal{E}^* = \mathcal{E} \cup \{O^*\}$, $\text{COV}^* = \text{COV} \cup \{(\mathcal{E}, O^*)\}$, $\mathcal{R}^* = \mathcal{R} \cup \{R_E\}$, $\text{REL}(R_E) = \langle U_1 : E, U_2 : O^* \rangle$, $\text{CARD}_R(R_E, U_2, O^*) = (1, \infty)$. Clearly, E is consistent w.r.t. Σ iff Σ^* is consistent.

Relationship consistency can be reduced to Entity consistency by extending Σ as follows: let O^* be a fresh entity symbol, $\mathcal{E}^* = \mathcal{E} \cup \{O^*\}$, $\text{ISA}_E^* = \text{ISA}_E \cup \{(O^*, E)\}$ and REF^* extends REF so that $\text{REF}^*(R, U, O^*) = (1, \beta)$, where E is an entity with $(U, E) \in \text{REL}(R)$ and β is such that $\text{CARD}_R(R, U, E) = (\alpha, \beta)$. Relationship R is consistent w.r.t. Σ iff entity O^* is consistent w.r.t. Σ^*. For the converse reduction, let R_E be a fresh relationship symbol with $\text{REL}(R_E) = \langle U_1 \colon E, U_2 \colon E \rangle$. Then E is consistent iff R_E is consistent.

Finally, we note that, in absence of the covering constructor, Schema consistency cannot be reduced to a single instance of Entity consistency, though it can be reduced to several Entity consistency checks.

4 Reasoning over ER_{isaR} Schemas

The modelling language ER_{isaR} is the subset of ER_{full} without the Booleans between relationships (i.e., $\text{DISJ}_R = \emptyset$ and $\text{COV}_R = \emptyset$) but with the possibility to express ISA between them. In this section we show that reasoning in ER_{isaR} is an EXPTIME-complete problem. The upper bound follows from [5]. The lower bound is established by reducing concept satisfiability w.r.t. $\mathcal{ALC}$ knowledge bases, which is known to be EXPTIME-complete [2], to entity consistency w.r.t. ER_{isaR} conceptual schemas.

We remind the reader that $\mathcal{ALC}$ concepts C are defined as follows:

$$ C \quad ::= \quad A_i \quad | \quad \neg C \quad | \quad C_1 \sqcap C_2 \quad | \quad C_1 \sqcup C_2 \quad | \quad \exists P_i.C \quad | \quad \forall P_i.C, $$

where the last two constructors are interpreted in $\mathcal{I}$ of the form (1) by taking

$$ (\exists P_i.C)^{\mathcal{I}} = \{x \in \Delta \mid \exists y \in \Delta \, ((x,y) \in P_i^{\mathcal{I}} \wedge y \in C^{\mathcal{I}})\}, $$
$$ (\forall P_i.C)^{\mathcal{I}} = \{x \in \Delta \mid \forall y \in \Delta \, ((x,y) \in P_i^{\mathcal{I}} \rightarrow y \in C^{\mathcal{I}})\}. $$

An $\mathcal{ALC}$ knowledge base is a finite set of $\mathcal{ALC}$ concept inclusions $C_1 \sqsubseteq C_2$. It is easy to show (see, e.g., [5, Lemma 5.1]) that one can convert, in a satisfiability preserving way, an $\mathcal{ALC}$ KB $\mathcal{K}$ into a primitive KB $\mathcal{K}'$ that contains only axioms of the form:

$$ A \sqsubseteq B, \quad A \sqsubseteq \neg B, \quad A \sqsubseteq B \sqcup B', \quad A \sqsubseteq \forall R.B, \quad A \sqsubseteq \exists R.B, $$

where A, B, B' are concept names and R is a role name, and the size of $\mathcal{K}'$ is linear in the size of $\mathcal{K}$. Thus, concept satisfiability w.r.t. primitive $\mathcal{ALC}$ KBs is EXPTIME-complete [5].

Let $\mathcal{K}$ be a primitive $\mathcal{ALC}$ KB. We illustrate a satisfiable preserving mapping from $\mathcal{K}$ into an ER_{isaR} schema $\Sigma(\mathcal{K})$: the first three forms of axioms are dealt with in a way similar to [5]. Axioms of the form $A \sqsubseteq \forall R.B$ are encoded in [5] using disjointness and covering (along with ISA) between relationships, which are unavailable in ER_{isaR}. In order to stay within ER_{isaR}, we propose to use reification of $\mathcal{ALC}$ roles (which are binary relationships) to encode the last two forms of axioms. This approach is illustrated in Fig. 1: in (a), $A \sqsubseteq \forall R.B$ is encoded by reifying the binary relationship R with the entity C_R so that the functional relationships R_1 and R_2 give the first and second component of the reified R, respectively; a similar encoding is used to capture $A \sqsubseteq \exists R.B$ in (b). The following lemma shows that ISA between relationships—and so conceptual schemas in ER_{isaR}—are enough to encode $\mathcal{ALC}$ axioms.

Lemma 1. *A concept name E is satisfiable w.r.t. a primitive $\mathcal{ALC}$ KB $\mathcal{K}$ iff the entity E is consistent w.r.t. the ER_{isaR} schema $\Sigma(\mathcal{K})$.*

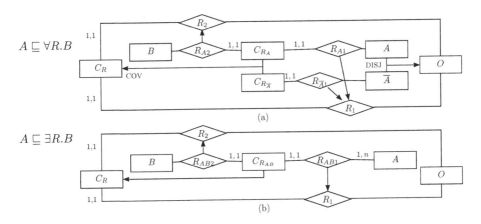

Fig. 1. Encoding axioms: (a) $A \sqsubseteq \forall R.B$; (b) $A \sqsubseteq \exists R.B$

Proof. ($\Leftarrow$) Let $\mathcal{B} = (\Delta^{\mathcal{B}}, \cdot^{\mathcal{B}})$ be a legal database for $\Sigma(\mathcal{K})$ such that $E^{\mathcal{B}} \neq \emptyset$. We construct a model $\mathcal{I} = (\Delta^{\mathcal{I}}, \cdot^{\mathcal{I}})$ of $\mathcal{K}$ with $E^{\mathcal{I}} \neq \emptyset$ by taking $\Delta^{\mathcal{I}} = \Delta^{\mathcal{B}}$, $A^{\mathcal{I}} = A^{\mathcal{B}}$, for all concept names A in $\mathcal{K}$, and $R^{\mathcal{I}} = (R_1^- \circ R_2)^{\mathcal{B}}$, for all role names R in $\mathcal{K}$, where $\circ$ denotes the binary relation composition. Clearly, $E^{\mathcal{I}} \neq \emptyset$. Let us show that $\mathcal{I}$ is indeed a model of $\mathcal{K}$. The cases of axioms of the form $A \sqsubseteq B$, $A \sqsubseteq \neg B$ and $A \sqsubseteq B \sqcup B'$ are treated as in [5]. Let us consider the remaining two cases.

Case $A \sqsubseteq \forall R.B$. Let $o \in A^{\mathcal{I}}$ and $o' \in \Delta^{\mathcal{I}}$ with $(o, o') \in R^{\mathcal{I}}$. We show that $o \in (\forall R.B)^{\mathcal{I}}$. Since $R^{\mathcal{I}} = (R_1^- \circ R_2)^{\mathcal{B}}$, there is $o'' \in \Delta^{\mathcal{B}}$ with $(o, o'') \in (R_1^-)^{\mathcal{B}}$ and $(o'', o') \in R_2^{\mathcal{B}}$. Then $o'' \in C_R^{\mathcal{B}}$ and, by the covering constraint, $o'' \in C_{R_A}^{\mathcal{B}} \cup C_{R_{\overline{A}}}^{\mathcal{B}}$. We claim that $o'' \in C_{R_A}^{\mathcal{B}}$. Indeed, suppose otherwise; then $o'' \in C_{R_{\overline{A}}}^{\mathcal{B}}$, and so there is a unique $a \in \Delta^{\mathcal{B}}$ such that $(o'', a) \in R_{\overline{A}1}^{\mathcal{B}}$ and $a \in \overline{A}^{\mathcal{B}}$; it follows from $R_{\overline{A}1}^{\mathcal{B}} \subseteq R_1^{\mathcal{B}}$ and the cardinality constraint on C_R that $a = o$, contrary to $o \in A^{\mathcal{B}} = A^{\mathcal{I}}$ and the disjointness of A and $\overline{A}$. Since $o'' \in C_{R_A}^{\mathcal{B}}$, there is a unique $b \in \Delta^{\mathcal{B}}$ with $(o'', b) \in R_{A2}^{\mathcal{B}}$ and $b \in B^{\mathcal{B}}$. From $R_{A2}^{\mathcal{B}} \subseteq R_2^{\mathcal{B}}$ and the cardinality constraint on C_R, we conclude that $b = o'$. Thus, $o' \in B^{\mathcal{B}} = B^{\mathcal{I}}$ and $o \in (\forall R.B)^{\mathcal{I}}$.

Case $A \sqsubseteq \exists R.B$. Let $o \in A^{\mathcal{I}}$. Since $o \in A^{\mathcal{I}} = A^{\mathcal{B}}$, there is $o' \in \Delta^{\mathcal{B}}$ with $(o, o') \in (R_{AB1}^-)^{\mathcal{B}}$ and $o' \in C_{R_{AB}}^{\mathcal{B}}$. As $R_{AB1}^{\mathcal{B}} \subseteq R_1^{\mathcal{B}}$, we have $(o, o') \in (R_1^-)^{\mathcal{B}}$, and, as $o' \in C_{R_{AB}}^{\mathcal{B}}$, there is $o'' \in \Delta^{\mathcal{B}}$ such that $(o', o'') \in R_{AB2}^{\mathcal{B}} \subseteq R_2^{\mathcal{B}}$ and $o'' \in B^{\mathcal{B}} = B^{\mathcal{I}}$. Thus, as $R^{\mathcal{I}} = (R_1^- \circ R_2)^{\mathcal{B}}$, we obtain $(o, o'') \in R^{\mathcal{I}}$ and $o'' \in B^{\mathcal{I}}$, i.e. $o \in (\exists R.B)^{\mathcal{I}}$.

($\Rightarrow$) Let $\mathcal{I} = (\Delta^{\mathcal{I}}, \cdot^{\mathcal{I}})$ be an $\mathcal{ALC}$ model of $\mathcal{K}$ such that $E^{\mathcal{I}} \neq \emptyset$. We construct a legal database state $\mathcal{B} = (\Delta^{\mathcal{B}}, \cdot^{\mathcal{B}})$ for $\Sigma(\mathcal{K})$ such that $E^{\mathcal{B}} \neq \emptyset$. Let $\Delta^{\mathcal{B}} = \Delta^{\mathcal{I}} \cup \Gamma$, where Γ is the disjoint union of the $\Delta_R = \{(o, o') \in \Delta^{\mathcal{I}} \mid (o, o') \in R^{\mathcal{I}}\}$, for all $\mathcal{ALC}$ role names R. We set $A^{\mathcal{B}} = A^{\mathcal{I}}$ and $\overline{A}^{\mathcal{B}} = (\neg A)^{\mathcal{I}}$, for all concept names A, $O^{\mathcal{B}} = \Delta^{\mathcal{I}}$, for the entity O, and $C_R^{\mathcal{B}} = \Delta_R$, for all $\mathcal{ALC}$ role names R.

Next, for every $\mathcal{ALC}$ axiom of the form $A \sqsubseteq \forall R.B$, we set

- $C_{R_A}^{\mathcal{B}} = \{(o,o') \in \Delta_R \mid o \in A^{\mathcal{I}}\}, C_{R_{\overline{A}}}^{\mathcal{B}} = \{(o,o') \in \Delta_R \mid o \in (\neg A)^{\mathcal{I}}\},$
- $R_1^{\mathcal{B}} = \{((o,o'),o) \in \Delta_R \times \Delta^{\mathcal{I}} \mid (o,o') \in R^{\mathcal{I}}\},$
- $R_2^{\mathcal{B}} = \{((o,o'),o') \in \Delta_R \times \Delta^{\mathcal{I}} \mid (o,o') \in R^{\mathcal{I}}\},$
- $R_{A1}^{\mathcal{B}} = \{((o,o'),o) \in R_1^{\mathcal{B}} \mid o \in A^{\mathcal{I}}\}, R_{\overline{A}1}^{\mathcal{B}} = \{((o,o'),o) \in R_1^{\mathcal{B}} \mid o \in (\neg A)^{\mathcal{I}}\},$
- $R_{A2}^{\mathcal{B}} = \{((o,o'),o') \in R_2^{\mathcal{B}} \mid o \in A^{\mathcal{I}}\},$

and, for every $\mathcal{ALC}$ axiom of the form $A \sqsubseteq \exists R.B$, we set

- $C_{R_{AB}}^{\mathcal{B}} = \{(o,o') \in \Delta_R \mid o \in A^{\mathcal{I}} \text{ and } o' \in B^{\mathcal{I}}\},$
- $R_1^{\mathcal{B}} = \{((o,o'),o) \in \Delta_R \times \Delta^{\mathcal{I}} \mid (o,o') \in R^{\mathcal{I}}\},$
- $R_2^{\mathcal{B}} = \{((o,o'),o') \in \Delta_R \times \Delta^{\mathcal{I}} \mid (o,o') \in R^{\mathcal{I}}\},$
- $R_{AB1}^{\mathcal{B}} = \{((o,o'),o) \in R_1^{\mathcal{B}} \mid (o,o') \in C_{R_{AB}}^{\mathcal{B}}\}.$
- $R_{AB2}^{\mathcal{B}} = \{((o,o'),o') \in R_2^{\mathcal{B}} \mid (o,o') \in C_{R_{AB}}^{\mathcal{B}}\}.$

It is now easy to show that $\mathcal{B}$ is a legal database state for $\Sigma(\mathcal{K})$ and $E^{\mathcal{B}} \neq \emptyset$.

Since reasoning over $\mathcal{ALC}$ knowledge bases is an EXPTIME-complete problem [2] and ER_{isaR} is a sub-language of ER_{full}, which is also EXPTIME-complete [5], we obtain the following result:

Theorem 2. *Reasoning over ER_{isaR} schemas is* EXPTIME-*complete.*

5   Reasoning over ER_{bool} Schemas

Denote by ER_{bool} the sublanguage of ER_{full} without ISA and the Booleans between relationships (i.e., $\text{ISA}_R = \emptyset$, $\text{DISJ}_R = \emptyset$ and $\text{COV}_R = \emptyset$). We also impose an extra restriction on REL: reusing the same role symbol by different relations is not allowed. More precisely, there is no $U \in \mathcal{U}$ such that $(U, E') \in \text{REL}(R')$ and $(U, E'') \in \text{REL}(R'')$, for some *distinct* $R', R'' \in \mathcal{R}$ and some $E', E'' \in \mathcal{E}$. This restriction does make sense in ER_{bool}, since the language does not allow for sub-relationships.

We first define a polynomial translation τ of ER_{bool} schemas into $DL\text{-}Lite_{bool}$ knowledge bases. Then we show that an entity E is consistent w.r.t. an ER_{bool} schema Σ iff the translation of the entity, $\overline{E}$, is satisfiable w.r.t. the knowledge base $\tau(\Sigma)$. The latter problem is known to be in NP (Theorem 1).

Let Σ be an ER_{bool} schema. Given an entity, domain or relationship symbol N from $\mathcal{E} \cup \mathcal{D} \cup \mathcal{R}$, let $\overline{N}$ be a $DL\text{-}Lite_{bool}$ concept name. Similarly, for an attribute or role symbol $N \in \mathcal{A} \cup \mathcal{U}$, let $\overline{N}$ be a $DL\text{-}Lite_{bool}$ role name. The translation $\tau(\Sigma)$ is defined as the following set of $DL\text{-}Lite_{bool}$ concept inclusions:

$$\tau(\Sigma) = \tau_{dom} \cup \bigcup_{R \in \mathcal{R}} [\tau_{rel}^R \cup \tau_{card_R}^R \cup \tau_{ref}^R] \cup \bigcup_{E \in \mathcal{E}} [\tau_{att}^E \cup \tau_{card_A}^E] \cup$$

$$\bigcup_{\substack{E_1,E_2 \in \mathcal{E} \\ E_1 \text{ISA} E_2}} \tau_{isa}^{E_1,E_2} \cup \bigcup_{\substack{E_1,\dots,E_n,E \in \mathcal{E} \\ \{E_1,\dots,E_n\} \text{DISJ} E}} \tau_{disj}^{\{E_1,\dots,E_n\},E} \cup \bigcup_{\substack{E_1,\dots,E_n,E \in \mathcal{E} \\ \{E_1,\dots,E_n\} \text{COV} E}} \tau_{cov}^{\{E_1,\dots,E_n\},E},$$

where

- $\tau_{dom} = \{\overline{D} \sqsubseteq \neg\overline{X} \mid D \in \mathcal{D},\ X \in \mathcal{E} \cup \mathcal{R} \cup \mathcal{D},\ D \neq X\}$;
- $\tau_{rel}^R = \{\overline{R} \sqsubseteq \exists\overline{U},\ \geq 2\,\overline{U} \sqsubseteq \bot,\ \exists\overline{U} \sqsubseteq \overline{R},\ \exists\overline{U}^- \sqsubseteq \overline{E} \mid (U, E) \in \mathrm{REL}(R)\}$;
- $\tau_{card_R}^R = \{\overline{E} \sqsubseteq\ \geq \alpha\,\overline{U}^- \mid (U, E) \in \mathrm{REL}(R),\ \mathrm{CARD}_R(R, U, E) = (\alpha, \beta),\ \alpha \neq 0\}$
  $\cup\, \{\overline{E} \sqsubseteq\ \leq \beta\,\overline{U}^- \mid (U, E) \in \mathrm{REL}(R),\ \mathrm{CARD}_R(R, U, E) = (\alpha, \beta),\ \beta \neq \infty\}$;
- $\tau_{ref}^R = \{\overline{E} \sqsubseteq\ \geq \alpha\,\overline{U}^- \mid (U, E) \in \mathrm{REL}(R),\ \mathrm{REF}(R, U, E) = (\alpha, \beta),\ \alpha \neq 0\}$
  $\cup\, \{\overline{E} \sqsubseteq\ \leq \beta\,\overline{U}^- \mid (U, E) \in \mathrm{REL}(R),\ \mathrm{REF}(R, U, E) = (\alpha, \beta),\ \beta \neq \infty\}$;
- $\tau_{att}^E = \{\exists\overline{A}^- \sqsubseteq \overline{D} \mid (A, D) \in \mathrm{ATT}(E)\}$;
- $\tau_{card_A}^E = \{\overline{E} \sqsubseteq\ \geq \alpha\,\overline{A} \mid (A, D) \in \mathrm{ATT}(E),\ \mathrm{CARD}_A(A, E) = (\alpha, \beta),\ \alpha \neq 0\}$
  $\cup\, \{\overline{E} \sqsubseteq\ \leq \beta\,\overline{A} \mid (A, D) \in \mathrm{ATT}(E),\ \mathrm{CARD}_A(A, E) = (\alpha, \beta),\ \beta \neq \infty\}$;
- $\tau_{isa}^{E_1, E_2} = \{\overline{E_1} \sqsubseteq \overline{E_2}\}$;
- $\tau_{disj}^{\{E_1, \ldots, E_n\}, E} = \{\overline{E_i} \sqsubseteq \overline{E} \mid 1 \leq i \leq n\} \cup \{\overline{E_i} \sqsubseteq \neg\overline{E_j} \mid 1 \leq i < j \leq n\}$;
- $\tau_{cov}^{\{E_1, \ldots, E_n\}, E} = \{\overline{E_i} \sqsubseteq \overline{E} \mid 1 \leq i \leq n\} \cup \{\overline{E} \sqsubseteq \overline{E_1} \sqcup \cdots \sqcup \overline{E_n}\}$.

Clearly, the size of $\tau(\Sigma)$ is polynomial in the size of Σ (under the same coding of the numerical parameters).

Lemma 2. *An entity E is consistent w.r.t. an ER_{bool} schema Σ iff the concept $\overline{E}$ is satisfiable w.r.t. the DL-Lite$_{bool}$ KB $\tau(\Sigma)$.*

Proof. $(\Rightarrow)$ Let $\mathcal{B} = (\Delta^{\mathcal{B}} \cup \Lambda^{\mathcal{B}}, \cdot^{\mathcal{B}})$ be a legal database state for Σ such that $E^{\mathcal{B}} \neq \emptyset$, where $\{B_D\}_{D \in \mathcal{D}}$ are the domain sets. Define a model $\mathcal{I} = (\Delta^{\mathcal{I}}, \cdot^{\mathcal{I}})$ of $\tau(\Sigma)$ by taking $\Delta^{\mathcal{I}} = \Delta^{\mathcal{B}} \cup \Lambda^{\mathcal{B}} \cup \Gamma$, where Γ is the disjoint union of the $\Delta_R = \{(e_1, \ldots, e_m) \in R^{\mathcal{B}}\}$, for all relationships $R \in \mathcal{R}$, and setting $\overline{D}^{\mathcal{I}} = D^{\mathcal{B}}$, for every $D \in \mathcal{D}$, $\overline{E}^{\mathcal{I}} = E^{\mathcal{B}}$, for every $E \in \mathcal{E}$, $\overline{A}^{\mathcal{I}} = A^{\mathcal{B}}$, for every $A \in \mathcal{A}$, $\overline{R}^{\mathcal{I}} = \Delta_R$, for every $R \in \mathcal{R}$, and, for every $U \in \mathcal{U}$ such that there is $R \in \mathcal{R}$ with $\mathrm{REL}(R) = \langle U_1 : E_1, \ldots, U_m : E_m \rangle$ and $U = U_i$ for some i with $1 \leq i \leq m$,

$$\overline{U}^{\mathcal{I}} = \{((e_1, \ldots, e_m), e_i) \in \Delta_R \times \Delta^{\mathcal{B}} \mid (e_1, \ldots, e_m) \in R^{\mathcal{B}}\}. \tag{3}$$

Clearly, $\overline{E}^{\mathcal{I}} \neq \emptyset$. We now prove that $\mathcal{I}$ is indeed a model of $\tau(\Sigma)$. We guide the proof by considering the translation of the various statements in Σ.

1. We show $\mathcal{I} \models \tau_{dom}$. For any two distinct $D_1, D_2 \in \mathcal{D}$, we have $D_1^{\mathcal{B}} \cap D_2^{\mathcal{B}} = \emptyset$, and so $\mathcal{I} \models \overline{D_1} \sqsubseteq \neg\overline{D_2}$. For all $D \in \mathcal{D}$ and $E \in \mathcal{E}$, since $E^{\mathcal{B}} \subseteq \Delta^{\mathcal{B}}$, $D^{\mathcal{B}} \subseteq \Lambda^{\mathcal{B}}$ and $\Delta^{\mathcal{B}} \cap \Lambda^{\mathcal{B}} = \emptyset$, we have $\mathcal{I} \models \overline{D} \sqsubseteq \neg\overline{E}$. Next, for all $D \in \mathcal{D}$ and $R \in \mathcal{R}$, as $D^{\mathcal{B}} \subseteq \Lambda^{\mathcal{B}}$, $\overline{R}^{\mathcal{I}} = \Delta_R \subseteq \Gamma$ and $\Gamma \cap \Lambda^{\mathcal{B}} = \emptyset$, we have $\mathcal{I} \models \overline{D} \sqsubseteq \neg\overline{R}$.

2. $\mathrm{REL}(R) = \langle U_1 : E_1, \ldots, U_m : E_m \rangle$. Consider all axioms in $\tau_{rel}^R \cup \tau_{card_R}^R \cup \tau_{ref}^R$:

   (a) $\overline{R} \sqsubseteq \exists\overline{U_i}$. Let $r \in \overline{R}^{\mathcal{I}}$. Then r is of the form $(e_1, \ldots, e_m) \in R^{\mathcal{B}}$. By (3), $(r, e_i) \in \overline{U_i}^{\mathcal{I}}$, and so $r \in \exists\overline{U_i}^{\mathcal{I}}$.

   (b) $\geq 2\,\overline{U_i} \sqsubseteq \bot$. Suppose that there are $(r, e), (r, e') \in \overline{U_i}^{\mathcal{I}}$ such that $e \neq e'$. By (3), r is of the form $(e_1, \ldots, e_m)$ and $e = e_i = e'$, contrary to $e \neq e'$.

(c) $\exists \overline{U_i}^- \sqsubseteq \overline{E}_i$. Let $e \in (\exists \overline{U_i}^-)^{\mathcal{I}}$. Then $(r, e) \in \overline{U_i}^{\mathcal{I}}$ for some $r \in \Delta^{\mathcal{I}}$. Since U_i may be involved only in one relation (R in this case) and in view of (3), r is of the form $(e_1, \ldots, e_m) \in R^{\mathcal{B}}$ and $e_i = e$. By the semantics of R, $e \in E_i^{\mathcal{B}}$, from which $e \in \overline{E}_i^{\mathcal{I}}$.

(d) $\exists \overline{U_i} \sqsubseteq \overline{R}$. Let $r \in (\exists \overline{U_i})^{\mathcal{I}}$. Then $(r, e) \in \overline{U_i}^{\mathcal{I}}$ for some $e \in \Delta^{\mathcal{I}}$. Since U_i may be involved only in one relation (R in this case) and by (3), r is of the form $(e_1, \ldots, e_m) \in R^{\mathcal{B}}$ and $e = e_i$. Therefore, $r \in \overline{R}^{\mathcal{I}}$.

(e) $\overline{E} \sqsubseteq \geq \alpha \overline{U_i}^-$ (when $\mathrm{CARD}_R(R, U_i, E_i) = (\alpha, \beta)$ and $\alpha \neq 0$). Let $e \in \overline{E}_i^{\mathcal{I}}$. Then $e \in E_i^{\mathcal{B}}$. We have $\sharp\{(e_1, \ldots, e_m) \in R^{\mathcal{B}} \mid e_i = e\} \geq \alpha$ and, by (3), we obtain $\sharp\{r \mid (r, e) \in \overline{U_i}^{\mathcal{I}}\} \geq \alpha$, from which $e \in (\geq \alpha \overline{U_i}^-)^{\mathcal{I}}$.

(f) $\overline{E} \sqsubseteq \leq \beta \overline{U_i}^-$ (when $\mathrm{CARD}_R(R, U_i, E_i) = (\alpha, \beta)$ and $\beta \neq \infty$). The proof is similar to the previous case.

(g) $\overline{E} \sqsubseteq \geq \alpha \overline{U_i}^-$ (when $\mathrm{REF}(R, U_i, E_i) = (\alpha, \beta)$ and $\alpha \neq 0$). The proof is similar to case 2e.

(h) $\overline{E} \sqsubseteq \leq \beta \overline{U_i}^-$ (when $\mathrm{REF}(R, U_i, E_i) = (\alpha, \beta)$ and $\beta \neq \infty$). The proof is similar to case 2e.

3. $\mathrm{ATT}(E) = \langle A_1 : D_1, \ldots, A_h : D_h \rangle$. Let us consider all axioms in $\tau_{att}^E \cup \tau_{card_A}^E$:

(a) $\exists \overline{A_i}^- \sqsubseteq \overline{D}_i$. Let $a \in (\exists \overline{A_i}^-)^{\mathcal{I}}$. Then there is $e \in \Delta^{\mathcal{I}}$ such that $(e, a) \in \overline{A_i}^{\mathcal{I}}$. As $\overline{A_i}^{\mathcal{I}} = A_i^{\mathcal{B}}$, we have $e \in \Delta^{\mathcal{B}}$ and $a \in \Lambda^{\mathcal{B}}$. It follows that $a \in D_i^{\mathcal{B}}$.

(b) $\overline{E} \sqsubseteq \geq \alpha \overline{A}_i$ (when $\mathrm{CARD}_A(A_i, E) = (\alpha, \beta)$ and $\alpha \neq 0$). Let $e \in \overline{E}^{\mathcal{I}}$. Then $e \in E^{\mathcal{B}}$. Thus, $\sharp\{a \mid (e, a) \in A^{\mathcal{B}}\} \geq \alpha$ and $\sharp\{a \mid (e, a) \in A^{\mathcal{I}}\} \geq \alpha$. Therefore, $e \in (\geq \alpha \overline{A}_i)^{\mathcal{I}}$.

(c) $\overline{E} \sqsubseteq \leq \beta \overline{A}_i$ (when $\mathrm{CARD}_A(A_i, E) = (\alpha, \beta)$ and $\beta \neq \infty$). The proof is similar to the previous case.

4. E_1 ISA E_2. We have $\overline{E}_1^{\mathcal{I}} = E_1^{\mathcal{B}} \subseteq E_2^{\mathcal{B}} = \overline{E}_2^{\mathcal{I}}$, and so $\mathcal{I} \models \tau_{isa}^{E_1, E_2}$.

5. $\{E_1, \ldots, E_n\}$ DISJ E. We have $E_i^{\mathcal{B}} \subseteq E^{\mathcal{B}}$, for $1 \leq i \leq n$, and $E_i^{\mathcal{B}} \cap E_j^{\mathcal{B}} = \emptyset$ for $1 \leq i < j \leq n$. Hence, $\mathcal{I} \models \tau_{disj}^{\{E_1, \ldots, E_n\}, E}$.

6. $\{E_1, \ldots E_n\}$ COV E. Similarly to the previous case.

Thus, $\mathcal{I} \models \tau(\Sigma)$.

($\Leftarrow$) Let $\mathcal{T} = (\Delta^{\mathcal{T}}, \cdot^{\mathcal{T}})$ be a model of $\tau(\Sigma)$ such that $\overline{E}^{\mathcal{T}} \neq \emptyset$. Without loss of generality, we may assume that $\mathcal{T}$ is a *tree model* (see, e.g., [12,6]). We construct domain sets $\{B_D\}_{D \in \mathcal{D}}$ and a legal database state $\mathcal{B} = (\Delta^{\mathcal{B}} \cup \Lambda^{\mathcal{B}}, \cdot^{\mathcal{B}})$ for the ER_{bool} schema Σ by taking $B_D = \Lambda_D^{\mathcal{B}} = D^{\mathcal{B}} = \overline{D}^{\mathcal{T}}$, for $D \in \mathcal{D}$, $\Lambda^{\mathcal{B}} = \bigcup_{D \in \mathcal{D}} \Lambda_D^{\mathcal{B}}$ and $\Delta^{\mathcal{B}} = \Delta^{\mathcal{T}} \setminus \Lambda^{\mathcal{B}}$; further we set $E^{\mathcal{B}} = \overline{E}^{\mathcal{T}}$, for every $E \in \mathcal{E}$, $A^{\mathcal{B}} = \overline{A}^{\mathcal{T}} \cap (\Delta^{\mathcal{B}} \times \Lambda^{\mathcal{B}})$, for every $A \in \mathcal{A}$, and, for every $R \in \mathcal{R}$ with $\mathrm{REL}(R) = \langle U_1 : E_1, \ldots, U_m : E_m \rangle$, we set

$$R^{\mathcal{B}} = \{(e_1, \ldots, e_m) \in T_{\Delta^{\mathcal{T}}}(\{U_1, \ldots, U_m\}) \mid$$
$$\exists r \in \overline{R}^{\mathcal{T}} \text{ such that } (r, e_i) \in \overline{U_i}^{\mathcal{T}} \text{ for } 1 \leq i \leq m\}.$$

Observe that the function $\cdot^{\mathcal{B}}$ is as required by Definition 2 and $E^{\mathcal{B}} \neq \emptyset$. We show now that $\mathcal{B}$ satisfies every assertion of the ER_{bool} schema Σ.

1. $\text{REL}(R) = \langle U_1: E_1, \ldots, U_m: E_m \rangle$. Let $(e_1, \ldots, e_m) \in R^{\mathcal{B}}$. Then there exists $r \in \overline{R}^{\mathcal{T}}$ such that $(r, e_i) \in \overline{U_i}^{\mathcal{T}}$, for $1 \leq i \leq m$. Since $\mathcal{T} \models \exists \overline{U_i}^{-} \sqsubseteq \overline{E_i}$, we obtain $e_i \in \overline{E_i}^{\mathcal{T}}$, and so $e_i \in E_i^{\mathcal{B}}$, for $1 \leq i \leq m$.

2. $\text{ATT}(E) = \langle A_1: D_1, \ldots, A_h: D_h \rangle$. Let $(e, a_i) \in \Delta^{\mathcal{B}} \times \Lambda^{\mathcal{B}}$ with $(e, a_i) \in A_i^{\mathcal{B}}$, for $1 \leq i \leq h$. Then $(e, a_i) \in \overline{A_i}^{\mathcal{T}}$. As $\mathcal{T} \models \exists \overline{A_i}^{-} \sqsubseteq \overline{D_i}$, we have $a_i \in \overline{D_i}^{\mathcal{T}}$, from which $a_i \in D_i^{\mathcal{B}} \subseteq \Lambda^{\mathcal{B}}$.

3. $\text{CARD}_R(R, U, E) = (\alpha, \beta)$. Then we have $\text{REL}(R) = \langle U_1: E_1, \ldots, U_m: E_m \rangle$ such that $U_i = U$ and $E_i = E$, for some U_i and E_i, $1 \leq i \leq m$. We have to show that, for every $e \in E^{\mathcal{B}}$,

$$\alpha \leq \sharp\{(e_1, \ldots, e_m) \in R^{\mathcal{B}} \mid e_i = e\} \leq \beta.$$

Consider the lower and upper bounds.

(a) We may assume that $\alpha \neq 0$. Since $\mathcal{T} \models \overline{E} \sqsubseteq \geq \alpha \overline{U}^{-}$ and $E^{\mathcal{B}} = \overline{E}^{\mathcal{T}}$, there exist at least α distinct $r_1, \ldots, r_\alpha \in \Delta^{\mathcal{T}}$ such that $(r_j, e) \in \overline{U}^{\mathcal{T}}$, for $1 \leq j \leq \alpha$. Since $\mathcal{T} \models \exists \overline{U} \sqsubseteq \overline{R}$, we have $r_1, \ldots, r_\alpha \in \overline{R}^{\mathcal{T}}$. And since $\mathcal{T} \models \overline{R} \sqsubseteq \exists \overline{U_i}$ and $\mathcal{T} \models \geq 2 \overline{U_i} \sqsubseteq \bot$, for all $1 \leq i \leq m$, there are uniquely determined $e_k^j \in \Delta^{\mathcal{T}}$ such that $(r_j, e_k^j) \in \overline{U_k}^{\mathcal{T}}$ and $e_i^j = e$, for all $1 \leq j \leq \alpha$ and $1 \leq k \leq m$. Since $\mathcal{T}$ is a tree-like model, we have $e_k^j \neq e_{k'}^{j'}$ whenever $k \neq i$, $k' \neq i$ and either $k \neq k'$ or $j \neq j'$. Therefore, we have shown that exactly one tuple corresponds to each object in $\overline{R}^{\mathcal{T}}$ and vice versa. Then, by construction, $(e_1^j, \ldots, e_m^j) \in R^{\mathcal{B}}$ and $e_i^j = e$, for all $1 \leq j \leq \alpha$. It follows that $\sharp\{(e_1, \ldots, e_m) \in R^{\mathcal{B}} \mid e_i = e\} \geq \alpha$.

(b) We may assume that $\beta \neq \infty$. The proof is similar to the previous item.

4. $\text{CARD}_A(A, E) = (\alpha, \beta)$. Let $e \in E^{\mathcal{B}} = \overline{E}^{\mathcal{T}}$. Consider the lower and upper bounds:

(a) We may assume $\alpha \neq 0$. Since $\mathcal{T} \models \overline{E} \sqsubseteq \geq \alpha \overline{A}$ and $\mathcal{T} \models \exists \overline{A}^{-} \sqsubseteq \overline{D}$, for some D with $(A, D) \in \text{ATT}(E)$, we have $\sharp\{a \in D^{\mathcal{B}} \mid (e, a) \in \overline{A}^{\mathcal{T}}\} \geq \alpha$. Finally, as $A^{\mathcal{B}} = \overline{A}^{\mathcal{T}} \cap (\Delta^{\mathcal{B}} \times \Lambda^{\mathcal{B}})$, we obtain $\sharp\{a \mid (e, a) \in A^{\mathcal{B}}\} \geq \alpha$.

(b) We may assume $\beta \neq \infty$. The proof is similar to the previous case.

5. $\text{REF}(R, U, E) = (\alpha, \beta)$. The proof is the same as in case 3.

6. E_1 ISA E_2. This holds in $\mathcal{B}$ since $\mathcal{T} \models \overline{E_1} \sqsubseteq \overline{E_2}$ and $E_i^{\mathcal{B}} = \overline{E_i}^{\mathcal{T}}$, for $i \in \{1, 2\}$.

7. $\{E_1, \ldots, E_n\}$ DISJ E. This holds in $\mathcal{B}$ since $\mathcal{T} \models \overline{E_i} \sqsubseteq \overline{E}$, for all $1 \leq i \leq n$, and $\mathcal{T} \models \overline{E_i} \sqsubseteq \neg \overline{E_j}$, for all $1 \leq i < j \leq n$, and $E_i^{\mathcal{B}} = \overline{E_i}^{\mathcal{T}}$, for $1 \leq i \leq n$.

8. $\{E_1, \ldots E_n\}$ COV E. Similar to the previous case.

It follows from this lemma and the mutual reducibility between the various reasoning problems in ER_{bool} that we have the following complexity result:

Theorem 3. *Reasoning over ER_{bool} conceptual schemas is NP-complete.*

Proof. The upper bound follows from Lemma 2 and Theorem 1. To prove NP-hardness we provide a polynomial reduction of the 3SAT problem, which is known to be NP-complete, to the entity consistency problem. Let an instance of 3SAT be given by a set ϕ of 3-clauses $c_i = a_i^1 \vee a_i^2 \vee a_i^3$ over some finite set Λ of literals. We define an ER_{bool} schema Σ_ϕ as follows:

- the signature $\mathcal{L}$ of Σ_ϕ is given by $\mathcal{E} = \{\overline{a} \mid a \in \Lambda\} \cup \{\overline{c} \mid c \in \phi\} \cup \{\overline{\phi}, \top\}$, $\mathcal{A} = \emptyset$, $\mathcal{R} = \emptyset$, $\mathcal{U} = \emptyset$, $\mathcal{D} = \emptyset$;
- $\overline{\phi}$ ISA $\overline{c}$, for all $c \in \phi$;
- $(\mathcal{E} \setminus \{\top\})$ COV $\top$, $\{\overline{a}, \overline{\neg a}\}$ COV $\top$, for all $a \in \Lambda$,

  $\{\overline{a_i^1}, \overline{a_i^2}, \overline{a_i^3}\}$ COV $\overline{c}_i$, for all $c_i \in \phi$, $c_i = a_i^1 \vee a_i^2 \vee a_i^3$;
- $\{\overline{a}, \overline{\neg a}\}$ DISJ $\top$, for all $a \in \Lambda$;
- ATT, REL, CARD$_R$, CARD$_A$, REF are empty functions.

Now we show the following claim:

Claim. ϕ is satisfiable iff the entity $\overline{\phi}$ is consistent w.r.t. the schema Σ_ϕ.

$(\Rightarrow)$ Let $\mathcal{J} \models \phi$. Define a legal database state $\mathcal{B} = (\Delta^\mathcal{B}, \cdot^\mathcal{B})$ by taking $\Delta^\mathcal{B} = \{o\}$, $\top^\mathcal{B} = \{o\}$ and, for every $\overline{E} \in \mathcal{E} \setminus \{\top\}$, $\overline{E}^\mathcal{B} = \{o\}$ if $\mathcal{J} \models E$ and $\overline{E}^\mathcal{B} = \emptyset$ if $\mathcal{J} \not\models E$. We show that $\mathcal{B}$ is indeed a legal database state for Σ_ϕ. Since $\mathcal{J} \models \phi$, we have $\mathcal{J} \models c_i$ for all $c_i \in \phi$, and, by construction, $\overline{c}_i^\mathcal{B} = \{o\}$. This means that every ISA assertion in Σ_ϕ is satisfied by $\mathcal{B}$. Consider now some $c_i \in \phi$. Then $\mathcal{J} \models a_i^k$ for at least one of a_i^1, a_i^2 or a_i^3, which means that $\overline{a_i^k}^\mathcal{B} = \{o\}$. It follows that the assertion $\{\overline{a_i^1}, \overline{a_i^2}, \overline{a_i^3}\}$ COV $\overline{c}_i$ holds in $\mathcal{B}$. The assertion $(\mathcal{E} \setminus \{\top\})$ COV $\top$ holds, since $\overline{E}^\mathcal{B} \subseteq \{o\}$, $\overline{\phi}^\mathcal{B} = \{o\}$ and $\top^\mathcal{B} = \{o\}$, for every $\overline{E} \in \mathcal{E} \setminus \{\top\}$. It should also be clear that every assertion $\{\overline{a}, \overline{\neg a}\}$ COV $\top$, for $a \in \Lambda$, holds in $\mathcal{B}$. Since only one of $a, \neg a$ is satisfied by $\mathcal{J}$, the other one will be interpreted in $\mathcal{B}$ as the empty set, so every assertion in DISJ holds, too. Thus, $\mathcal{B}$ is a legal database state for Σ_ϕ, with $\overline{\phi}^\mathcal{B} \neq \emptyset$.

$(\Leftarrow)$ Let $\mathcal{B} = (\Delta^\mathcal{B}, \cdot^\mathcal{B})$ be a legal database state for Σ_ϕ such that $o \in \overline{\phi}^\mathcal{B}$, for some $o \in \Delta^\mathcal{B}$. Construct a model $\mathcal{J}$ for ϕ by taking, for every propositional variable p in ϕ, $\mathcal{J} \models p$ iff $o \in \overline{p}^\mathcal{B}$. We show that $\mathcal{J} \models \phi$. Indeed, as $o \in \overline{\phi}^\mathcal{B}$ and $\overline{\phi}$ ISA $\overline{c}_i$, we have $o \in \overline{c}_i^\mathcal{B}$, for $1 \leq i \leq n$. Since, for every c_i, we have $\{\overline{a_i^1}, \overline{a_i^2}, \overline{a_i^3}\}$ COV $\overline{c}_i$, there is a_i^k in c_i such that $o \in (\overline{a_i^k})^\mathcal{B}$. Now, if a_i^k is a variable then, by the construction of $\mathcal{J}$, we have $\mathcal{J} \models a_i^k$, and so $\mathcal{J} \models c_i$. Otherwise, $a_i^k = \neg p$ and, since $\{\overline{a_i^k}, \overline{p}\}$ DISJ $\top$, $o \notin \overline{p}^\mathcal{B}$. Therefore, by the construction of $\mathcal{J}$, $\mathcal{J} \not\models p$, i.e., $\mathcal{J} \models a_i^k$, and so $\mathcal{J} \models c_i$.

6 Reasoning over ER_{ref} Schemas

Denote by ER_{ref} the modelling language without the Booleans and ISA between relationships, but with the possibility to express ISA and disjointness between entities (i.e., ISA$_R = \emptyset$, COV$_R = \emptyset$, DISJ$_R = \emptyset$ and COV$_E = \emptyset$). Thus, ER_{ref} is essentially ER_{bool} without the covering constructor.

In this section we show that checking entity consistency in ER_{ref} is an NLOGSPACE-complete problem. Consider the reduction τ from Section 5. It is not difficult to check that τ is *logspace bounded*. At the same time, for every ER_{ref} schema Σ, the knowledge base $\tau(\Sigma)$ is a *DL-Lite$_{krom}$* knowledge base, because we do not have τ_{cov} in this case. Thus, as a consequence of Lemma 2, the problem of entity consistency for ER_{ref} can be logspace reduced to the NLOGSPACE-complete problem of concept satisfiability w.r.t. *DL-Lite*$_{krom}$ knowledge bases [1]. So the entity consistency problem w.r.t. ER_{ref} schemas is in NLOGSPACE as well.

To establish the lower bound, we consider the reachability problem in oriented graphs, or the MAZE problem, which is known to be NLOGSPACE-hard; see, e.g., [15]. Let $G = (V, E, s, t)$ be an instance of MAZE, where s, t are the initial and terminal vertices of (V, E), respectively. We can encode this instance in ER_{ref} using the following schema Σ_G:

$$\overline{u} \text{ ISA } \overline{v}, \quad \text{for all } (u, v) \in E, \quad \text{and} \quad \{\overline{s}, \overline{t}\} \text{ DISJ } \overline{O},$$

where $\overline{O}$ is a fresh entity. Clearly, we have the following:

Claim. The terminal node t is reachable from s in $G = (V, E, s, t)$ iff the entity $\overline{s}$ is *not* consistent w.r.t. Σ_G.

As NLOGSPACE=CONLOGSPACE (by the Immerman-Szelepcsényi theorem; see, e.g., [15]) and the above reduction is logspace bounded, it follows that the problem of entity consistency in ER_{ref} is NLOGSPACE-hard. This result coupled with the membership in NLOGSPACE showed above gives us the following complexity result:

Theorem 4. *The entity consistency problem for ER_{ref} is NLOGSPACE-complete.*

7   Conclusion

This paper provides new complexity results for reasoning over Extended Entity-Relationship (EER) models with different modelling constructors. Starting from the EXP-TIME result [5] for reasoning over the fully-fledged EER language, we prove that the same complexity holds even if we drop the Boolean constructors (disjointness and covering) on relationships. This result shows that ISA between relationships (with the Booleans on entities) is powerful enough to capture EXPTIME-hard problems. To illustrate that the presence of relationship hierarchies is a major source of complexity in reasoning, we show that avoiding them makes reasoning in ER_{bool} an NP-complete problem. Another source of complexity is covering constraints: indeed, we show that without relationship hierarchies and covering constraints reasoning problem is NLOGSPACE-complete.

The paper also establishes a tight correspondence between conceptual modelling languages and the *DL-Lite* family of description logics. Such a correspondence shows the usefulness of *DL-Lite* for representing and reasoning over conceptual models and ontologies.

Acknowledgements. The authors were partially supported by the EU funded projects Tones, KnowledgeWeb and InterOp and the U.K. EPSRC grant GR/S63175. We are grateful to the referees for their helpful remarks and suggestions.

References

1. Artale, A., Calvanese, D., Kontchakov, R., Zakharyaschev, M.: DL-Lite in the light of first-order logic. In: Proc. of the 22nd Nat.Conf. on Artificial Intelligence (AAAI 2007) (2007)

2. Baader, F., Calvanese, D., McGuinness, D., Nardi, D., Patel-Schneider, P.F.: The Description Logic Handbook: Theory, Implementation and Applications. Cambridge University Press, Cambridge (2003)

3. Batini, C., Ceri, S., Navathe, S.B.: Conceptual Database Design, an Entity-Relationship Approach. Benjamin and Cummings Publ. Co. (1992)

4. Bechhofer, S., van Harmelen, F., Hendler, J., Horrocks, I., McGuinness, D.L., Patel-Schneider, P.F., Stein, L.A.: OWL Web Ontology Language reference. W3C Recommendation, Available at (February 2004), http://www.w3.org/TR/owl-ref/

5. Berardi, G.D., Calvanese, D., Giacomo, D.: Reasoning on UML class diagrams. Artificial Intelligence 168(1–2), 70–118 (2005)

6. Blackburn, P., de Rijke, M., Venema, Y.: Modal Logic. Cambridge Tracts in Theoretical Computer Science, vol. 53. Cambridge University Press, Cambridge (2001)

7. Calvanese, G.D., Giacomo, D.: Expressive description logics. In: Baader. F., et al. (eds.) [2], ch.5, pp. 178–218 (2003)

8. Calvanese, D., De Giacomo, G., Lembo, D., Lenzerini, M., Rosati, R.: DL-Lite: Tractable description logics for ontologies. In: Proc. of the 20th Nat. Conf. on Artificial Intelligence (AAAI 2005), pp. 602–607 (2005)

9. Calvanese, D., De Giacomo, G., Lembo, D., Lenzerini, M., Rosati, R.: Data complexity of query answering in description logics. In: Proc. of the 10th Int. Conf. on the Principles of Knowledge Representation and Reasoning (KR 2006), pp. 260–270 (2006)

10. Calvanese, D., Lenzerini, M.: On the interaction between ISA and cardinality constraints. In: Proc. of the 10th IEEE Int. Conf. on Data Engineering (ICDE'94), pp. 204–213. IEEE Computer Society Press, Los Alamitos (1994)

11. Calvanese, D., Lenzerini, M., Nardi, D.: Unifying class-based representation formalisms. J. of Artificial Intelligence Research 11, 199–240 (1999)

12. Chagrov, A., Zakharyaschev, M.: Modal Logic. Oxford Logic Guides 35 (1997)

13. Di Battista, G., Lenzerini, M.: Deductive entity-relationship modeling. IEEE Trans. on Knowledge and Data Engineering 5(3), 439–450 (1993)

14. ElMasri, R.A., Navathe, S.B.: Fundamentals of Database Systems, 5th edn. Addison Wesley Publ.Co. (2007)

15. Kozen, D.: Theory of Computation. Springer, Heidelberg (2006)

16. Lenzerini, M., Nobili, P.: On the satisfiability of dependency constraints in entity-relationship schemata. Information Systems 15(4), 453–461 (1990)

On Order Dependencies for the Semantic Web

David Toman[1,2] and Grant Weddell[1]

[1] David R. Cheriton School of Computer Science
University of Waterloo, Canada
{david,gweddell}@uwaterloo.ca
[2] Faculty of Computer Science
Free University of Bozen-Bolzano, Italy
david@inf.unibz.it

Abstract. We consider the problem of adding both equality and order generating dependencies to Web ontology languages such as OWL DL that are based on description logics. Such dependencies underlie a number of problems that relate, for example, to web service composition, to document ordering, and to lower level algorithmic issues in service plan generation and evaluation.

1 Introduction

RDF underlies a vision of the Semantic Web in which both data and metadata are viewed as a set of *subject/property/object* triples that can be associated with web resources denoted by *Universal Resource Identifiers* (URIs) [13]. To support reasoning, there has been a progression of further standards for inferring the existence of additional triples. This is accomplished by adding interpretations for particular RDF properties. For example, in the case of property *subClassOf*, the RDF Schema standard mandates inferring the triple

$$x/subClassOf/\text{ITEM}$$

from the pair of triples

$$x/subClassOf/\text{SALEITEM}$$

and

$$\text{SALEITEM}/subClassOf/\text{ITEM}, \tag{1}$$

where ITEM and SALEITEM are now viewed as *concepts*.

The current best practices for these standards, measured in terms of established reasoning technology, are the *description logic* (DL) based fragments of the OWL web ontology language, called OWL Lite and OWL DL [22]. Building

C. Parent et al. (Eds.): ER 2007, LNCS 4801, pp. 293–306, 2007.

on RDF Schema, they enable a collection of triples to encode more general concepts such as *anything not on sale* or *an item with a reliable supplier*. In this paper, we use a more abstract and compact syntax developed for description logics in which collections of triples encoding such concepts can be specified more succinctly as

$$\neg SALEITEM$$

and as

$$ITEM \sqcap \forall Supplier.RELIABLE,$$

respectively. We do this also for *subClassOf* RDF triples, such as (1) above, which we now refer to as *inclusion dependencies*, and write instead as

$$CONCEPT_1 \sqsubseteq CONCEPT_2. \tag{2}$$

For example, (1) above is now written $SALEITEM \sqsubseteq ITEM$.

A collection of inclusion dependencies of the form (2) defines an OWL DL *ontology* that can be used by other protocols for the semantic web, such as the RDF query language SPARQL [15]. In this setting, XML can be used as a transport language for RDF in the sense that an XML document is an ordered forest of RDF triples that in turn encode OWL DL concepts and inclusion dependencies. However, the significance of *ordering* in XML is currently beyond any real capacity of OWL DL, or even full OWL, to account for any consequent logical significance, e.g., to inform a SPARQL query engine by way of an ontology that the order in which various ITEM concepts occur in a document correlates in some way with their *Price*.

An obvious approach to remedy this is to reconsider the underlying description logic for OWL DL, to consider in particular how concept descriptions can be enriched to capture metadata relating to order. Knowledge of the relevance of document order in XML would not only be useful to a SPARQL query engine in helping to address lower level algorithmic and performance issues, e.g., avoiding sort costs when reporting on the supplier for a given item in order of increasing cost, but also by other web services that reason in turn about web service composition in which attributes are used to abstract temporal artifacts such as events.

In this paper, we consider a new concept constructor for description logics with the potential of endowing OWL DL with an ability to capture knowledge about ordering. Instances of this constructor are called *path order dependencies* (PODs). They are a generalization of *path functional dependencies* (PFDs) that have been considered in the context of a DL dialect called $\mathcal{DLF}$ [19,20,21], which we also use. This dialect is *feature based* and therefore more functional in style as opposed to the more common *role based* derivatives of $\mathcal{ALC}$ such as OWL DL. As a consequence, it is much easier to incorporate PODs.

Example 1. To illustrate using PODs, consider an ontology of ITEM concepts of relevance, say, to an online supplier of photography equipment. The supplier maintains an XML document of the ITEM concepts in such a way that sub-trees defining the concepts satisfy a major sort on their *ProductCode* feature and a minor sort on their *Price* feature. This knowledge can now be captured by an inclusion dependency using two instances of the proposed POD concept constructor as follows:

$$\text{ITEM} \quad \sqsubseteq \quad (\text{ITEM} : \{DocOrder^<\} \to \{ProductCode^{\leq}\})$$
$$\sqcap \ (\text{ITEM} : \{DocOrder^<, ProductCode^=\} \to \{Price^{\leq}\}).$$

As a second example, the supplier in question can capture an inherent ordering for SALEITEM concepts in which their relative ordering by virtue of their *Price* is preserved by their *DiscountPrice* by adding the following:

$$\text{SALEITEM} \quad \sqsubseteq \quad \text{ITEM}$$
$$\sqcap \ (\text{SALEITEM} : \{Price^<\} \to \{DiscountPrice^<\}.$$

Note that, in comparison to OWL DL, $\mathcal{DLF}$ is a worthwhile basis for study since it is already sufficient to simulate the DL dialect $\mathcal{ALCQI}$ in an intuitive fashion using *role reification* [19]. In essentially the same way, $\mathcal{ALCQI}$ can in turn simulate $\mathcal{SHIQ}$ without transitive roles, a large subset of OWL DL that includes OWL Lite. With regard to the above hypothetical metadata about item ordering in a document, the examples are expressed in terms of the DL dialect $\mathcal{DLFD}_{reg}$, the extension of $\mathcal{DLF}$ considered in this paper.

Our contributions relate to $\mathcal{DLFD}_{reg}$ and are as follows.

1. We define a guarded condition for PODs for which the associated implication problem remains decidable and indeed unchanged from $\mathcal{DLF}$; and
2. We show how a slight relaxation of this condition leads to undecidability.

1.1   Related Work

In addition to OWL DL, description logics have been used extensively as a formal way of understanding a large variety of languages for specifying meta-data, including ER diagrams, UML class and object diagrams, relational database schemata, and so on [14].

The form of order dependencies introduced in this paper is a generalization of a relational variant [17], and is also a generalization of regular PFDs introduced in [19]. Less expressive first order PFDs were introduced and studied in the context of object-oriented data models [8,23]. An FD concept constructor was proposed and incorporated already in Classic [4], an early DL with a PTIME reasoning procedure, without changing the complexity of its implication problem. The generalization of this constructor to PFDs alone leads to EXPTIME completeness of the implication problem [10]; this complexity remains unchanged in the presence of additional concept constructors common in rich DLs such as roles, qualified number restrictions, and so on [17,18].

In [5], the authors consider a DL with functional dependencies and a general form of keys added as additional varieties of dependencies, called a *key box*. They show that their dialect is undecidable for DLs with inverse roles, but becomes decidable when unary functional dependencies are disallowed. This line of investigation is continued in the context of PFDs and inverse features, with analogous results [20]. We therefore disallow inverse features in this paper to exclude an already known cause for undecidability.

PFDs have also been used in a number of applications in object-oriented schema diagnosis and synthesis [2,3], in query optimization [6,9] and in the selection of indexing for a database [16].

Order dependencies have been considered in the context of the relational model [7], and as a special case of constraint-generating dependencies for the relational model [1]. A form of key dependency with left hand side feature paths has been considered for a DL coupled with various concrete domains [12,11]. In this case, the authors explore how the complexity of satisfaction is influenced by the selection of a particular concrete domain together with various syntactic restrictions on the key dependencies themselves. Note that this earlier work strictly separates objects that serve as "domain values," and can therefore be ordered, from abstract objects such as tuples. This makes such approaches less applicable in the RDF setting in which no such distinction exists, where both objects and values can in turn be object-attribute-value triples.

The remainder of the paper is organized as follows. Section 2 that follows defines the syntax and semantics for $\mathcal{DLFD}_{\mathrm{reg}}$. Our main results are then presented in Section 3. We conclude with a summary and a discussion of remaining issues and open problems in Section 4.

2   Definitions

The syntax and semantics of the $\mathcal{DLFD}_{\mathrm{reg}}$ dialect of description (or feature) logics are given by the following.

Definition 2 (Syntax and Semantics of $\mathcal{DLFD}_{\mathrm{reg}}$). Let F be an arbitrary finite set of attribute names. We define a *path language* L to be a regular language over the alphabet F. We use *regular expressions* as the surface syntax for such languages with Id standing for the empty word in L. We use $L^{\approx}$ to denote a regular language in which every word $\mathsf{Pf}^{\sim} \in L^{\approx}$ is a concatenation of a word from $\mathsf{Pf} \in L$ with a symbol $\sim \in \{<, \leq, =, \geq, >\}$. We denote by $L^{\sim}$ the regular sublanguage $\{\mathsf{Pf}^{\sim} \mid \mathsf{Pf}^{\sim} \in L^{\approx}\}$ in which all words end with the same symbol $\sim$.

Let C be primitive concept description(s). We define *derived concept descriptions* using the grammar in Figure 1. A concept formed by an application of the final production in the grammar is called a *regular path order dependency* (POD).

An *inclusion dependency* $\mathcal{C}$ is an expression of the form $D \sqsubseteq E$.

The *semantics* of expressions is given with respect to a structure $(\Delta, \leq, \cdot^{\mathcal{I}})$, where Δ is a domain of "objects"; $\leq$ is a linear order on Δ; and $(.)^{\mathcal{I}}$ an in-

SYNTAX:		SEMANTICS: DEFN OF "$(\cdot)^{\mathcal{I}}$"
D	$::=\quad C$	$(C)^{\mathcal{I}} \subset \Delta$
	$\mid\quad D_1 \sqcap D_2$	$(D_1)^{\mathcal{I}} \cap (D_2)^{\mathcal{I}}$
	$\mid\quad \forall L.D$	$\bigcap_{\mathsf{Pf} \in L} \{x : (\mathsf{Pf})^{\mathcal{I}}(x) \in (D)^{\mathcal{I}}\}$
	$\mid\quad \neg D$	$\Delta \setminus (D)^{\mathcal{I}}$

E	$::=\quad D$	
	$\mid\quad E_1 \sqcap E_2$	$(E_1)^{\mathcal{I}} \cap (E_2)^{\mathcal{I}}$
	$\mid\quad E_1 \sqcup E_2$	$(E_1)^{\mathcal{I}} \cup (E_2)^{\mathcal{I}}$
	$\mid\quad \forall L.E$	$\bigcap_{\mathsf{Pf} \in L} \{x : (\mathsf{Pf})^{\mathcal{I}}(x) \in (E)^{\mathcal{I}}\}$
	$\mid\quad D : L_1^{\approx} \to L_2^{\approx}$	$\{x : \forall y \in (D)^{\mathcal{I}}. \bigwedge_{\mathsf{Pf}^{\sim} \in L_1^{\approx}} (\mathsf{Pf})^{\mathcal{I}}(x) {\sim} (\mathsf{Pf})^{\mathcal{I}}(y)$
		$\Rightarrow \bigwedge_{\mathsf{Pf}^{\sim} \in L_2^{\approx}} (\mathsf{Pf})^{\mathcal{I}}(x) {\sim} (\mathsf{Pf})^{\mathcal{I}}(y)\}$

Fig. 1. Syntax and Semantics of $\mathcal{DLFD}$reg

terpretation function that fixes the interpretations of primitive concepts to be subsets of Δ and of primitive attributes in F to be total functions over Δ. The interpretation is extended to words over F as follows: $(Id)^{\mathcal{I}} = \lambda x.x$ and $(f.\mathsf{Pf})^{\mathcal{I}} = (\mathsf{Pf})^{\mathcal{I}} \circ (f)^{\mathcal{I}}$, and to derived concept descriptions, cf. Figure 1.

An interpretation *satisfies an inclusion dependency* $\mathcal{C}$ of the form $D \sqsubseteq E$ if $(D)^{\mathcal{I}} \subseteq (E)^{\mathcal{I}}$.

A *terminology* $\mathcal{T}$ consists of a finite set of inclusion dependencies. The *logical implication problem* asks if $\mathcal{T} \models \mathcal{C}$ holds; that is, if all interpretations that satisfy each constraint in $\mathcal{T}$ must also satisfy $\mathcal{C}$ (the posed question).

Note that the notation $\mathsf{Pf}^{\sim} \in L^{\approx}$ stands for the fact that *the path (string)* $\mathsf{Pf}^{\sim}$ *belongs to the language* $L^{\approx}$. The paths are in turn interpreted as (compositions of) total functions over the domain Δ. Hence the conjunctions in the semantic definition of a POD range over all words in an appropriate regular language and define order among objects in the range of their interpretations.

The two-level syntax is needed to prevent any occurrence of a POD on the left-hand side of an inclusion dependency or within the scope of negation. Removing this restriction leads to undecidability [21].

Example 3. Recall our introductory example relating to ITEM concepts maintained by a hypothetical online supplier. Now suppose the supplier has a second XML document containing a sequence of subtrees encoding SUPPLIES concepts, and that this document satisfies the following property:

> *a traversal of the root nodes for the* SUPPLIES *elements correlates with a major sort of the* ITEM *component of each element, and a minor sort of the wholesale price.*

When added to a terminology, the following inclusion dependency formally captures this property:

SUPPLIES $\sqsubseteq$ $\forall Iref$.ITEM
$\qquad\qquad\sqcap$ (SUPPLIES : $\{DocOrder^<\} \rightarrow \{Iref^\leq\}$)
$\qquad\qquad\sqcap$ (SUPPLIES : $\{DocOrder^<, Iref^=\} \rightarrow WholesalePrice^\leq$).

To paraphrase the final line: *if the first of a pair of arbitrary SUPPLIES concepts precedes the second in a given document and if both refer to the same items, then the wholesale price of the first will not exceed the wholesale price of the second.*

3   Reasoning in $\mathcal{DLFD}_{\text{reg}}$

The question of *logical implication* is central to the use of logic-based approaches to conceptual modeling of the artifacts in the semantic Web. This section shows the main results relating to the logical implication problem with respect to PODs.

3.1   Undecidability for General Order Dependencies

The general implication problem for $\mathcal{DLFD}_{\text{reg}}$ is, unfortunately, undecidable:

Proposition 4 ([21]). *The implication problem for $\mathcal{DLFD}_{\text{reg}}$ becomes undecidable when dependencies of the form $D : \{\} \rightarrow \{f^=\}$ are allowed. This is the case even when all dependencies are restricted to finite languages and are equality-generating.*

Path-functional dependencies with empty left-hand sides allow one to simulate *nominals*—concept descriptions whose interpretation must correspond to a singleton set; this can be enforced, e.g., for a concept C, by the inclusion dependency $C \sqsubseteq C : \{\} \rightarrow \{Id^=\}$.

Decidability can be reobtained by requiring any regular languages occurring in PFDs to be non-empty [19]. However, this restriction does not suffice for the more general case of PODs.

Theorem 5. *The implication problem for $\mathcal{DLFD}_{\text{reg}}$ is undecidable. This remain true when all regular languages occurring in PODs are non-empty.*

Proof: (sketch) The above dependency with an empty left-hand side can be simulated by the order dependency $C : Id^\leq \rightarrow \{Id^=\}$. The remainder follows from a reduction of a tiling problem to the implication problem, expanding on the reduction proposed in [21]. $\qquad\qquad\qquad\qquad\qquad\qquad\qquad\qquad\qquad\qquad\square$

3.2   Decidability for Guarded Order Dependencies

To regain decidability, we define a subset of PODs called *guarded PODs*. Intuitively, we require all the PODs appearing in the terminology to be satisfied by trees whose nodes are ordered by the $\leq$ relation top-down and left-to-right (breadth-first).

Definition 6 (Guarded Order Dependency)

An order dependency $D_1 \sqsubseteq D_2 : L_1^\approx \rightarrow L_2^\approx$ is guarded if it satisfies the following conditions:

1. if $= \subseteq \sim$ for all $\mathsf{Pf}^\sim \in L_1^\approx$ then also $= \subseteq \sim$ for all $\mathsf{Pf}^\sim \in L_2^\approx$,
2. if $< \subseteq \sim$ for all $\mathsf{Pf}^\sim \in L_1^\approx$ then also $< \subseteq \sim$ for all $\mathsf{Pf}^\sim \in L_2^\approx$, and
3. if $> \subseteq \sim$ for all $\mathsf{Pf}^\sim \in L_1^\approx$ then also $> \subseteq \sim$ for all $\mathsf{Pf}^\sim \in L_2^\approx$,

where $\subseteq$ denotes set inclusion among the interpretations of the binary relations denoted by $\{<, \leq, =, \geq, >\}$.

For the remainder of the paper, we assume all PODs are guarded. The ramification of definition is that guarded order dependencies in a terminology cannot, on their own, lead to inconsistency. This is in contrast to the general case where, e.g., $\top \sqsubseteq \top : \{f^<\} \rightarrow \{f^>\}$ is not satisfiable.

To aid the decision procedure for the guarded case, we simplify terminologies of $\mathcal{DLFD}_{\text{reg}}$ implication problems as follows:

Definition 7. A $\mathcal{DLFD}_{\text{reg}}$ implication problem $\mathcal{T} \models \mathcal{C}$ is simple if each inclusion dependency in $\mathcal{T}$ is of the form $D_1 \sqsubseteq D_2$ or the form $D_1 \sqsubseteq D_2 : L_1^\approx \rightarrow L_2^\approx$. In the former case, the dependency is described as pure; in the latter case, the dependency is called an order dependency.

It is easy to see that unrestricted implication problems can be always reduced to reasoning w.r.t. simple terminologies only—called simple implication problems:

Lemma 8. Let $\mathcal{T}$ be an arbitrary $\mathcal{DLFD}_{\text{reg}}$ terminology and $\mathcal{C}$ an arbitrary subsumption constraint. Then there is a simple terminology $\mathcal{T}'$ such that $\mathcal{T} \models \mathcal{C}$ if and only if $\mathcal{T}' \models \mathcal{C}$.

Proof: (sketch) $\mathcal{T}'$ introduces additional primitive concept descriptions to name subconcepts on the right-hand sides of concept descriptions in $\mathcal{T}$.   □

For each simple $\mathcal{DLFD}_{\text{reg}}$ implication problem $\mathcal{T} \models \mathcal{C}$, we define a corresponding $\mathcal{DLF}_{\text{reg}}$ satisfiability problem. There are two cases to consider depending on $\mathcal{C}$.

Pure Posed Questions. For simple terminologies that use guarded ordered dependencies only and for a pure constraint $\mathcal{C}$, the logical implication problem can be reduced to the implication problem that does not involve ordered dependencies:

Lemma 9. *Let T be a simple $\mathcal{DLFD}_{\text{reg}}$ terminology and C a pure inclusion dependency. Also let T' be the set of all pure inclusion dependencies in T. Then $T \models C$ if and only if $T' \models C$.*

Proof: Consider a tree model of $T' \cup \{\neg C\}$ with nodes ordered by their breadth-first traversal number. This model satisfies all (possible) guarded order dependencies, hence it is a model of $T \cup \{\neg C\}$. The other direction is immediate as $T' \subseteq T$. □

The decidability of this problem is then an immediate consequence of the following proposition, since T' is a $\mathcal{DLF}_{\text{reg}}$ terminology.

Proposition 10 ([19]). *The implication problem for $\mathcal{DLF}_{\text{reg}}$ is decidable and complete for EXPTIME.*

In addition, whenever $T \not\models D \sqsubseteq D'$, there is a F-tree with nodes labeled by sets of concept descriptions that serves as a model of T and whose root label contains the concepts D and $\neg D'$.

General Posed Questions. Due to the undecidability issues connected with allowing order dependencies in the scope of negation, it is not possible to express a negation of a posed question as a concept description. We develop an alternative solution, based on construction in [8,24]. We introduce the solution by an example.

Example 11. Consider a terminology T and a posed question of the form $D \sqsubseteq D' : L_1^{\approx} \to L_2^{\approx}$. To falsify such an order dependency, *two* objects are needed, one in the interpretation of D and another in the interpretation of D'. Hence, by Lemma 9, both D and D' must be satisfiable with respect to T', the *pure part* of T. Note that the two models witnessing the satisfiability of D and D', if they exist, are F-trees that differ only in the labeling of nodes by concept descriptions.

To simulate the two models and the effects of the posed question using only a single F-tree, we define a $\mathcal{DLF}_{\text{reg}}$ terminology consisting of the following components that simulate the effects of the original assertions in this new interpretation:

- T_1' and T_2', that are two copies of T' in which all primitive concept descriptions C have been renamed to C_1 and C_2, respectively;
- $T_{1,2}$, that captures the effects of order dependencies in T on the two interpretations. These effects are captured by auxiliary primitive concept descriptions $\text{Aux}_{1,2}^{\sim}$ and $\mathcal{DLF}_{\text{reg}}$ constraints of the form

$$((D_1 \sqcap D_2') \sqcup (D_1' \sqcap D_2)) \sqcap (\forall L_1^{<}.\text{Aux}_{1,2}^{<}) \sqcap \ldots \sqcap (\forall L_1^{>}.\text{Aux}_{1,2}^{>}) \sqsubseteq$$
$$(\forall L_2^{<}.\text{Aux}_{1,2}^{<}) \sqcap \ldots \sqcap (\forall L_2^{>}.\text{Aux}_{1,2}^{>})$$

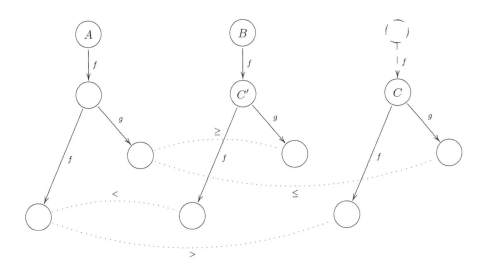

Fig. 2. Counterexample for Example 12

created for each $D \sqsubseteq D' : L_1^{\approx} \to L_2^{\approx} \in \mathcal{T}$ where $L_i^{\approx} = L_i^{<} \cup \ldots \cup L_i^{>}$ is a partition of $L_i^{\approx}$ according to the order predicate associated with the individual words (and for $i = 1, 2$). Intuitively, membership in $\mathsf{Aux}_{1,2}^{\sim}$ concepts stands for the $\sim$ relationship between *corresponding* objects in the two tree interpretations that are encoded by this model.

- A terminology $\mathcal{A}$ of auxiliary assertions that govern the interactions of the $\mathsf{Aux}_{1,2}^{\sim}$ concepts in accordance with the axioms of linear order. In addition, assertions governing the *existence* of nodes in the *copies* of the tree are also included here (e.g., the fact that in an actual counterexample, such as the one in Figure 2, the rightmost root node is not necessarily present).

Counterexamples to the posed question $D \sqsubseteq D' : L_1^{\approx} \to L_2^{\approx}$ are then captured as objects satisfying the concept

$$D_1 \sqcap D_2' \sqcap (\forall L_1^{<}.\mathsf{Aux}_{1,2}^{<}) \sqcap \ldots \sqcap (\forall L_1^{>}.\mathsf{Aux}_{1,2}^{>}) \sqcap \neg((\forall L_2^{<}.\mathsf{Aux}_{1,2}^{<}) \sqcap \ldots \sqcap (\forall L_2^{>}.\mathsf{Aux}_{1,2}^{>})).$$

Hence the logical implication is reduced to concept satisfiability w.r.t. a modified terminology.

However, allowing arbitrary $\mathcal{DLFD}_{\text{reg}}$ inclusion dependencies as posed questions, e.g., in which order dependencies occur within other positive concept constructors, involves an additional construction which extends an earlier form used in the simpler case of path-functional dependencies [21]:

Example 12. A counterexample to the constraint

$$A \sqsubseteq (B : \{ff^{<}\} \to \{fg^{<}\}) \sqcup \forall \{f\}.(C : \{f^{>}\} \to \{g^{>}\})$$

is shown in Figure 2. Observe with this case that the distinct C object must occur at *different* levels when compared to an A-rooted forest. Such a counterexample, however, cannot be constructed in the presence of a terminology $\{B \sqsubseteq \forall\{f\}.C, C \sqsubseteq C : \{f^>\} \rightarrow \{g^>\}\}$. Hence the example posed question is a logical consequence of this terminology.

The examples suggest a need for multiple *root objects* in counterexample interpretations, with the roots themselves occurring at different levels. Our overall strategy is to therefore reduce a logical implication problem to a negation of a consistency problem in an alternative formulation in which objects in a satisfying counterexample *denote up to ℓ possible copies in a counterexample interpretation for the original problem*, where ℓ is the number of occurrences of PODs in the posed question.

To encode this one-to-many mapping of objects, we require a general way to have ℓ copies of concepts occurring in a given membership problem. We therefore write D_i to denote the concept description D in which all primitive concepts C are replaced by C_i. For a simple terminology $\mathcal{T}$ we then define

$$\mathcal{T}^i = \{\mathsf{Nd}_i \sqcap D_i \sqsubseteq E_i \mid D \sqsubseteq E \in \mathcal{T} \text{ pure}\}, \text{ and}$$

$$\mathcal{T}^{i,j} = \{\mathsf{Nd}_i \sqcap \mathsf{Nd}_j \sqcap D_i \sqcap D'_j \sqcap (\bigsqcap_{L_1^\sim \subseteq L_1^\approx} \forall L_1^\sim.\mathsf{Aux}_{0,i}^\sim) \sqsubseteq (\bigsqcap_{L_2^\sim \subseteq L_2^\approx} \forall L_2^\sim.\mathsf{Aux}_{0,i}^\sim),$$

$$\mathsf{Nd}_i \sqcap \mathsf{Nd}_j \sqcap D_j \sqcap D'_i \sqcap (\bigsqcap_{L_1^\sim \subseteq L_1^\approx} \forall L_1^\sim.\mathsf{Aux}_{0,i}^\sim) \sqsubseteq (\bigsqcap_{L_2^\sim \subseteq L_2^\approx} \forall L_2^\sim.\mathsf{Aux}_{0,i}^\sim)$$

$$\mid D \sqsubseteq D' : L_1^\approx \rightarrow L_2^\approx \in \mathcal{T} \}.$$

For a concept description E we define

$$\mathsf{ToCon}(E) = \begin{cases} D_0 & \text{if } E\ (= D) \text{ is POD free,} \\ \mathsf{ToCon}(E_1) \sqcap \mathsf{ToCon}(E_2) & \text{if } E = E_1 \sqcap E_2, \\ \mathsf{ToCon}(E_1) \sqcup \mathsf{ToCon}(E_2) & \text{if } E = E_1 \sqcup E_2, \\ \forall L.\mathsf{ToCon}(E_1) & \text{if } E = \forall L.E_1, \text{ and} \\ \neg(\mathsf{Nd}_i \sqcap D_i \sqcap (\bigsqcap_{L_1^\sim \subseteq L_1^\approx} \forall L_1^\sim.\mathsf{Aux}_{0,i}^\sim)) \sqcup (\bigsqcap_{L_2^\sim \subseteq L_2^\approx} \forall L_2^\sim.\mathsf{Aux}_{0,i}^\sim) \\ \qquad \text{otherwise, when } E = D : L_1^\approx \rightarrow L_2^\approx \end{cases}$$

where i in the last equation is the index of the POD in the original posed question.

In the above, we have introduced primitive concepts $\mathsf{Aux}_{i,j}^\sim, 0 \le i \ne j \le \ell$, to express that the ith and jth object copies are related by $\sim$, and $\mathsf{Nd}_i, 0 \le i \le \ell$, to assert that the ith copy exists. The following auxiliary sets of constraints are therefore defined to account for the axioms of equality and of linear orders, and for the fact that features in $\mathcal{DLFD}_{\mathrm{reg}}$ denote total functions.

$$\mathcal{A}(\ell) = \{\mathsf{Aux}_{i,j}^{\sim} \sqcap \mathsf{Aux}_{j,k}^{\sim} \sqsubseteq \mathsf{Aux}_{i,k}^{\sim} \mid 0 \le i < j < k \le \ell \,\}$$

$$\cup \ \{\mathsf{Aux}_{i,j}^{<} \sqcap \mathsf{Aux}_{i,j}^{=} \sqsubseteq \bot, \mathsf{Aux}_{i,j}^{<} \sqcap \mathsf{Aux}_{i,j}^{>} \sqsubseteq \bot,$$
$$\mathsf{Aux}_{i,j}^{=} \sqcap \mathsf{Aux}_{i,j}^{>} \sqsubseteq \bot \mid 0 \le i \ne j \le \ell \,\}$$

$$\cup \ \{\top \sqsubseteq \mathsf{Aux}_{i,j}^{<} \sqcup \mathsf{Aux}_{i,j}^{=} \sqcup \mathsf{Aux}_{i,j}^{>} \mid 0 \le i \ne j \le \ell \,\}$$

$$\cup \ \{\mathsf{Aux}_{i,j}^{=} \sqsubseteq \mathsf{Aux}_{j,i}^{=}, \mathsf{Aux}_{i,j}^{<} \sqsubseteq \mathsf{Aux}_{j,i}^{>} \mid 0 \le i \ne j \le \ell \,\}$$

$$\cup \ \{\mathsf{Aux}_{i,j}^{\le} \sqsubseteq \mathsf{Aux}_{j,i}^{<} \sqcup \mathsf{Aux}_{i,j}^{=},$$
$$\mathsf{Aux}_{i,j}^{\le} \sqsubseteq \mathsf{Aux}_{i,j}^{<}, \mathsf{Aux}_{i,j}^{<} \sqsubseteq \mathsf{Aux}_{i,j}^{\le} \mid 0 \le i \ne j \le \ell \,\}$$

$$\cup \ \{\mathsf{Aux}_{i,j}^{\gtrsim} \sqsubseteq \mathsf{Aux}_{j,i}^{>} \sqcup \mathsf{Aux}_{i,j}^{=},$$
$$\mathsf{Aux}_{i,j}^{\gtrsim} \sqsubseteq \mathsf{Aux}_{i,j}^{>}, \mathsf{Aux}_{i,j}^{>} \sqsubseteq \mathsf{Aux}_{i,j}^{\gtrsim} \mid 0 \le i \ne j \le \ell \,\}$$

$$\cup \ \{(\mathsf{Aux}_{i,j}^{=} \sqcap C_i) \sqsubseteq C_j \mid 0 \le i \ne j \le \ell \text{ and } C \text{ a primitive concept}\}$$

$$\cup \ \{\mathsf{Aux}_{i,j}^{=} \sqsubseteq \forall f.\mathsf{Aux}_{i,j}^{=} \mid 0 \le i \ne j \le \ell \text{ and } f \in F \text{ a primitive feature}\}$$

$$\cup \ \{\mathsf{Nd}_i \sqsubseteq \forall f.\mathsf{Nd}_i \mid 0 \le i \le \ell \text{ and } f \in F \text{ a primitive feature}\}$$

Theorem 13. *Let $\mathcal{T}$ be a simple terminology and $D \sqsubseteq E$ an inclusion dependency containing ℓ occurrences of the POD concept constructor. Then $\mathcal{T} \models D \sqsubseteq E$ if and only if*

$$\left(\bigcup_{0 \le i \le \ell} \mathcal{T}_i\right) \cup \left(\bigcup_{0 \le i < j \le \ell} \mathcal{T}_{i,j}\right) \cup \mathcal{A}(\ell) \models (\mathsf{Nd}_0 \sqcap D_0 \sqcap \neg\mathsf{ToCon}(E)) \sqsubseteq \bot.$$

Proof: (sketch) Given an interpretation $\mathcal{I}$ such that $\mathcal{I} \models \mathcal{T}$ and $\mathcal{I} \not\models D \sqsubseteq E$ we construct an interpretation $\mathcal{J}$ as follows. First, in the construction, we use a many-to-one map $\delta : \Delta^{\mathcal{I}} \to \Delta^{\mathcal{J}}$ to associate objects in $\mathcal{I}$ with those in $\mathcal{J}$. The range of δ serves as the domain of the interpretation $\mathcal{J}$. For the counterexample object $o \in (D \sqcap \neg E)^{\mathcal{I}}$ we set $\delta o \in (\mathsf{Nd}_0)^{\mathcal{J}}$. Then, for all $o \in \Delta$ and $0 \le i \ne j \le \ell$ we define the map δ and the interpretation $\mathcal{I}$ as follows:

- $\delta o \in (\mathsf{Nd}_i)^{\mathcal{J}} \wedge (f)^{\mathcal{I}}(o) = o' \Rightarrow \delta o' \in (\mathsf{Nd}_i)^{\mathcal{J}} \wedge (f)^{\mathcal{J}}(\delta o) = \delta o'$,
- $\delta o \in (\mathsf{Nd}_i)^{\mathcal{J}} \wedge o \in (D)^{\mathcal{I}} \Rightarrow \delta o \in (D)^{\mathcal{J}}$ for D a POD free concept,
- $\delta o = \delta o' \wedge \delta o \in (\mathsf{Nd}_i)^{\mathcal{J}} \wedge \delta o' \in (\mathsf{Nd}^j)^{\mathcal{J}} \wedge (\mathsf{Pf})^{\mathcal{I}}(o) \sim (\mathsf{Pf})^{\mathcal{I}}(o') \Rightarrow \delta o \in (\mathsf{Aux}_{i,j}^{\sim})^{\mathcal{J}}$, and
- $\delta o \in (\mathsf{Nd}_i)^{\mathcal{J}} \wedge o \notin (D : L_1^{\approx} \to L_2^{\approx})^{\mathcal{I}}$ where $D : L_1^{\approx} \to L_2^{\approx}$ is the i-th POD constructor in E. Thus there must be $o' \in \Delta$ such that $o' \in (D)^{\mathcal{I}}$ and the pair o, o' falsifies the POD; we set $\delta o = \delta o'$ and $\delta o' \in (\neg(\mathsf{Nd}_i \sqcap D_i \sqcap (\sqcap_{L \sim \sqsubseteq L_1^{\approx}} \forall L^{\sim}.\mathsf{Aux}_{0,i}^{\sim})) \sqcup (\sqcap_{L \sim \sqsubseteq L_2^{\approx}} \forall L^{\sim}.\mathsf{Aux}_{0,i}^{\sim}))^{\mathcal{J}}$.

Note that, due to the syntactic restrictions imposed on the uses of POD constructors, a complement of an POD can be enforced only in the counterexample of the description E. Spurious occurrences of negated PODs in the interpretation $\mathcal{I}$ are therefore ignored as the interpretation itself satisfies all PODs in $\mathcal{T}$.

It is easy to verify that $\delta o \in (\mathsf{Nd}_0 \sqcap D_0 \sqcap \neg\mathsf{ToCon}(E))^{\mathcal{J}}$ for $o \in (D \sqcap \neg E)^{\mathcal{I}}$. By inspecting all inclusion dependencies in $\mathcal{T}$ we have $\mathcal{J} \models \mathcal{T}_i$ as $\mathcal{I} \models \mathcal{T}$. Furthermore, the construction of $\mathcal{J}$ enforces $\mathcal{J} \models \mathcal{A}(\ell)$.

On the other hand, given a tree-shaped interpretation $\mathcal{J}$ of $(\mathsf{Nd}_0 \sqcap D_0 \sqcap \mathsf{ToCon}(E))$ that satisfies all assertions in

$$(\bigcup_{0 \leq i \leq \ell} \mathcal{T}_i) \cup (\bigcup_{0 \leq i < j \leq \ell} \mathcal{T}_{i,j}) \cup \mathcal{A}(\ell),$$

we construct an interpretation $\mathcal{I}$ of $\mathcal{T}$ that falsifies $D \sqsubseteq E$ as follows:

- $\Delta^{\mathcal{I}} = \{(o, i) : o \in (\mathsf{Nd}_i)^{\mathcal{J}}, 0 \leq i \leq \ell \text{ and } o \notin (\mathsf{Aux}_{j,i}^=)^{\mathcal{J}} \text{ for any } 0 \leq j < i\}$,
- $(f)^{\mathcal{I}}((o, i)) = (o', j)$ whenever $(f)^{\mathcal{J}}(o) = o'$ where j is the smallest integer such that $o \in (\mathsf{Aux}_{j,i}^=)^{\mathcal{J}}$ if such value exists and i otherwise; and
- $(o, i) \in (D)^{\mathcal{I}}$ whenever $(o, i) \in \Delta^{\mathcal{J}}$ and $o \in (D_i)^{\mathcal{J}}$.

The values $(o, i) \in \Delta^{\mathcal{J}}$ are ordered by the breadth-first number of o in $\mathcal{I}$ and then consistently with the interpretation of the $\mathsf{Aux}_{i,j}^{\sim}$ descriptions in $\mathcal{I}$.

It is easy to verify that $(o, 0)$ falsifies $D \sqsubseteq E$ whenever o belongs to $(\mathsf{Nd}_0 \sqcap D_0 \sqcap \neg\mathsf{ToCon}(E))$, and such an object must exist by our assumptions. Also, $\mathcal{I} \models \mathcal{T}$, as otherwise by cases analysis we get a contradiction with $\mathcal{J} \models (\bigcup_{0 \leq i \leq \ell} \mathcal{T}_i) \cup (\bigcup_{0 \leq i < j \leq \ell} \mathcal{T}_{i,j}) \cup \mathcal{A}(\ell)$. $\qquad\square$

Corollary 14. *The implication problem for guarded $\mathcal{DLFD}_{\mathrm{reg}}$ is decidable and EXPTIME-complete.*

Proof: Follows immediately from Proposition 10 and Theorem 13 above. $\square$

4   Summary

In this paper, we have explored the possibility of adding a very general form of equality and order generating dependencies based on regular languages to Web ontology languages deriving from description logics. In particular, we have introduced a description logic dialect called $\mathcal{DLFD}_{\mathrm{reg}}$ that incorporates such dependencies as a new concept constructor, and have explored the computational properties of the associated implication problems.

4.1   Remaining Issues and Open Problems

The negative results that relate to the possibility of admitting nominals to $\mathcal{DLFD}_{\mathrm{reg}}$ is unfortunate indeed [21], since OWL DL requires this ability. An important open problem is to devise other restrictions on the PODs concept constructor or on occurrences of this constructor in an implication problem that allows effective reasoning in the presence of nominals.

Another direction of research leads towards tractable dialects. Again, preliminary investigations suggest that there might be a polynomial time procedure for the implication problem for a fragment of $\mathcal{DLFD}_{reg}$ that excludes negation, disallows defined concepts, and requires ordering concepts that occur in terminologies to satisfy a syntactic condition similar to the *regularity* condition in [10].

References

1. Baudinet, M., Chomicki, J., Wolper, P.: Constraint-generating dependencies. J. Comput. Syst. Sci. 59(1), 94–115 (1999)
2. Biskup, J., Polle, T.: Decomposition of Database Classes under Path Functional Dependencies and Onto Constraints. In: Foundations of Information and Knowledge Systems, pp. 31–49 (2000)
3. Biskup, J., Polle, T.: Adding inclusion dependencies to an object-oriented data model with uniqueness constraints. Acta Informatica 39, 391–449 (2003)
4. Borgida, A., Weddell, G.: Adding Uniqueness Constraints to Description Logics (Preliminary Report). In: International Conference on Deductive and Object-Oriented Databases, pp. 85–102 (1997)
5. Calvanese, D., De Giacomo, G., Lenzerini, M.: Identification Constraints and Functional Dependencies in Description Logics. In: Proc. of the 17th Int. Joint Conf. on Artificial Intelligence (IJCAI), pp. 155–160 (2001)
6. De Haan, D., Toman, D., Weddell, G.: Rewriting Aggregate Queries using Description Logics. In: Description Logics 2003, pp. 103–112. CEUR-WS vol.81 (2003)
7. Ginsburg, S., Hull, R.: Order Dependency in the Relational Model. TCS 26, 149–195 (1983)
8. Ito, M., Weddell, G.: Implication Problems for Functional Constraints on Databases Supporting Complex Objects. Journal of Computer and System Sciences 49(3), 726–768 (1994)
9. Khizder, V.L., Toman, D., Weddell, G.: Reasoning about Duplicate Elimination with Description Logic. In: Rules and Objects in Databases (DOOD, part of CL'00), pp. 1017–1032 (2000)
10. Khizder, V.L., Toman, D., Weddell, G.: On Decidability and Complexity of Description Logics with Uniqueness Constraints. In: International Conference on Database Theory ICDT'01, pp. 54–67 (2001)
11. Lutz, C., Areces, C., Horrocks, I., Sattler, U.: Keys, Nominals, and Concrete Domains. In: Proc. of the 18th Int. Joint Conf. on Artificial Intelligence (IJCAI), pp. 349–354 (2003)
12. Lutz, C., Milicic, M.: Description Logics with Concrete Domains and Functional Dependencies. In: European Conference on Artificial Intelligence (ECAI), pp. 378–382 (2004)
13. Resource Description Framework (RDF), http://www.w3.org/RDF/
14. Sattler, U., Calvanese, D., Molitor, R.: Relationships with other formalisms. In: The Description Logic Handbook: Theory, Implementation, and Applications, vol. 4, pp. 137–177. Cambridge University Press, Cambridge (2003)

15. SPARQL Query Language for RDF, http://www.w3.org/TR/rdf-sparql-query/
16. Stanchev, L., Weddell, G.: Index Selection for Embedded Control Applications using Description Logics. In: Description Logics 2003, vol. 81, pp. 9–18. CEUR-WS (2003)
17. Toman, D., Weddell, G.: On Attributes, Roles, and Dependencies in Description Logics and the Ackermann Case of the Decision Problem. In: Description Logics 2001, vol. 49, pp. 76–85. CEUR-WS (2001)
18. Toman, D., Weddell, G.: Attribute Inversion in Description Logics with Path Functional Dependencies. In: Description Logics 2004, vol. 104, pp. 178–187. CEUR-WS (2004)
19. Toman, D., Weddell, G.: On Reasoning about Structural Equality in XML: A Description Logic Approach. Theoretical Computer Science 336(1), 181–203 (2005)
20. Toman, D., Weddell, G.: On the Interaction between Inverse Features and Path-functional Dependencies in Description Logics. In: Proc. of the 19th Int. Joint Conf. on Artificial Intelligence (IJCAI), pp. 603–608 (2005)
21. Toman, D., Weddell, G.: On Keys and Functional Dependencies as First-Class Citizens in Description Logics. In: Proc. of the Third Int. Joint Conf. on Automated Reasoning (IJCAR), pp. 647–661 (2006)
22. Web Ontology Language (OWL) (2004), http://www.w3.org//OWL/
23. Weddell, G.: A Theory of Functional Dependencies for Object Oriented Data Models. In: International Conference on Deductive and Object-Oriented Databases, pp. 165–184 (1989)
24. Weddell, G.: Reasoning about Functional Dependencies Generalized for Semantic Data Models. TODS 17(1), 32–64 (1992)

Collection Type Constructors in Entity-Relationship Modeling

Sven Hartmann and Sebastian Link*

Information Science Research Centre, Massey University, New Zealand
{s.hartmann,s.link}@massey.ac.nz

Abstract. Collections play an important part in everyday life. Therefore, conceptual data models should support collection types to make data modeling as natural as possible for its users. Based on the fundamental properties of endorsing order and multiplicity of its elements we introduce the collection types of rankings, lists, sets and bags into the framework of Entity-Relationship modeling. This provides users with easy-to-use constructors that naturally model different kinds of collections. Moreover, we propose a transformation of extended ER schemata into relational database schemata. The transformation is intuitive and invertable introducing surrogate attributes that preserve the semantics of the collection. Furthermore, it is a proper extension to previous transformations, and results in a relational database schema that is in Inclusion Dependency Normal Form. In addition, we introduce a uniqueness constraint that identifies collections uniquely and guarantees referential integrity at the same time.

1 Introduction

The Entity-Relationship (ER) model has evolved into one of the most popular conceptual data models since its introduction in the late 1970s [5]. It is established as an excellent communication tool between systems analysts, database designers, managers and potential database users during the crucial process of identifying user information requirements. The ER model provides a well-defined semantics that is vital for a successful implementation of the information system under consideration, and offers modeling features that very much resemble the structure of natural languages [8].

Complex application domains, such as CAD/CAM, meta-modeling, hypermedia, office automation and life sciences, have resulted in the introduction of extended ER features [16,18]. These aim at providing natural modeling capabilities that adequately reflect complex object types that are inherent in everyday life activities. The most popular of these modeling constructors are the *tuple* and *cluster* constructor that represent aggregation and disjoint union [6,18]. Other kinds of very common complex objects are collections such as lists, sets, and

* This research is supported by the Marsden Fund Council from Government funding, administered by the Royal Society of New Zealand.

C. Parent et al. (Eds.): ER 2007, LNCS 4801, pp. 307–322, 2007.

bags. Such constructors are present in many other data models including semantic data models [9], the nested relational data model [13], object-oriented
data models [2], semi-structured data models [1] and XML [4], as well as sequence
data models [11] and spatio-temporal data models [15]. In order to serve as a
conceptual data model for these various approaches it is essential that the ER
model supports these constructors in such a way that users are able to naturally
take advantage of these extended capabilities. A further motivation to incorporate collection types into the framework of ER modeling is that they represent
very often the modeling counterpart of *plurals* in natural languages [8].

Contributions. Since different types of collections do occur in everyday life
conceptual data models should directly support the modeling of collections.
Therefore, we introduce *collection type constructors* into the *formal* framework
of Entity-Relationship modeling. Our constructors have a well-defined semantics and are very simple to utilise. Indeed, a collection type U has just a single
object type component C that can model either finite lists, sets or bags of objects over C. The popularity of the ER model in the conceptual design phase is
mainly due to its well-defined, intuitive and simple-to-use features. We strongly
believe that our collection type constructors extend and enhance these characteristics further. In order to implement the conceptual design the conceptual
database schema is usually mapped to a logical schema. The question is then
how to map collection types and collections to object types and objects, respectively, of the logical data model. Our second objective is to address this question
for the relational model of data which is still the de-facto standard model for
most commercial database systems. While there are many different ways of implementing such a transformation our choice has several distinctive features: *i)*
it extends the standard transformation of ER schemata [3,6,18] to relational
database schemata to encompass collection types; *ii)* it is invertable preserving the semantics inherent in the collections at hand by introducing surrogate
attributes that describe the membership relation of objects and collections, the
position of an object within a list, and the multiplicity of an object within a bag;
iii) the resulting relational database schema is in Inclusion Dependency Normal
Form with respect to its functional and inclusion dependencies [10]. Finally, we
propose an additional constraint that uniquely identifies collections within the
relational database, and guarantees referential integrity at the same time.

Related Work. Complex-value databases have been studied extensively in the
database literature [13], and we do not attempt to cite every work. It is therefore surprising that relatively little work has been done on extending the ER
approach in this direction. Although nested attributes (multivalued attributes)
have been introduced on the *attribute level* [14,16,18] the term collection type
usually refers only to set-valued attributes. While tuple and cluster constructors are well-known features of ER modeling [18] collection constructors have
not been properly investigated yet. This restricts the modeling capabilities unnecessarily, as we will demonstrate in this paper. Modeling collections has been
discussed in other data models such as UML and ORM [7] but there is no provi-

sion of direct constructors for different collections. Instead, an annotation of the conceptual schema is proposed that guides the mapping process from conceptual to lower levels. In sharp contrast, our approach provides constructors for directly modeling collections, and our invertable transformation *automatically* encodes the structural properties of these collections into the relational database schema. It is therefore *different* from a simple flattening of complex structures. An alternative approach to modeling collections [17] encodes the structural properties of collections within an extensional uniqueness constraint. Our proposed transformation automatically derives a single constraint that identifies collections uniquely and guarantees referential integrity at the same time. Thus, the structural properties of collections are directly modeled on the conceptual model, and our transformation automatically encodes their distinctive properties on the logical level. It is therefore our strong belief that collection type constructors are very natural and useful features that increase the modeling capabilities of the ER approach without complicating the underlying theory.

2   Entity-Relationship Modeling

Since we intend to introduce new constructors into the ER framework, and since many different ER models do exist we will use this section to provide a common framework and to fix the semantics of the basic ER data model [5] and many of its extensions [3,6,18].

Entity Types. An *entity type* $E = (attr(E), id(E))$ consists of a name E, a finite and non-empty set of attributes $attr(E)$ such that each attribute $A \in attr(E)$ has a domain $dom(A)$, and a key $id(E) \subseteq attr(E)$ whose elements are called key attributes. An *entity* over E is a mapping $e : attr(E) \rightarrow \bigcup_{A \in attr(E)} dom(A)$ such that $e(A) \in dom(A)$ holds for all $A \in attr(E)$. An *entity set* E^t over E is a finite set of entities over E that satisfy the unique key value property, i.e., for all $e_1, e_2 \in E^t$ with $e_1(A) = e_2(A)$ for all $A \in id(E)$ we must have $e_1 = e_2$. We use $ent(E)$ to denote the set of all entities of an entity type E. We do not consider *weak* entity types due to their lack of a formal foundation and the problems caused by the identification of weak entities [18, pp.34-38].

Example 2.1. We can specify an entity type CLIENT as follows: its attribute set is $attr(\text{CLIENT}) = \{\text{Name, Birthday, Address, Phone}\}$ with domain assignment $dom(\text{Name})=\text{STRING}$, $dom(\text{Birthday})=\text{DATE}$, $dom(\text{Address})=\text{STRING}$, and $dom(\text{PHONE})=\text{NUMBER}$. The key attributes of CLIENT are $id(\text{Client}) = \{\text{Name, Birthday}\}$. An entity set may consist of the following three clients:

(John Fox, 08/08/1980, 88 Main Street, 3508888),
(John Fox, 02/12/1967, 23 Te Awe Awe, 3539465), and
(Lisa Hunter, 02/12/1967, 7 Park Ave, 356 1154).

Note that none of these clients has the same values on all key attributes.   □

Relationship Types. A *relationship type* $R = (comp(R), attr(R), id(R))$ consists of a name R, a finite, non-empty set of components $comp(R)$, a finite set of attributes $attr(R)$ such that each attribute $A \in attr(R)$ has a domain $dom(A)$, and a key $id(R) \subseteq comp(R) \cup attr(R)$ whose elements are called key components and key attributes, respectively. A *relationship* over R is a mapping $r : comp(R) \cup attr(R) \rightarrow \bigcup_{E \in comp(R)} ent(E) \cup \bigcup_{A \in attr(E)} dom(A)$ such that $r(E) \in ent(E)$ for all $E \in comp(R)$ and $r(A) \in dom(A)$ for all $A \in attr(E)$. A *relationship set* R^t over R is a finite set of relationships over R that satisfy the unique key value property, i.e., for all $r_1, r_2 \in R^t$ with $r_1(X) = r_2(X)$ for all $X \in id(R)$ we must have $r_1 = r_2$. We refer to entity and relationship types jointly as *object types*. Note that we use *set semantics* to describe relationships [18]. At the moment, $comp(R)$ consists of entity types only. However, we will discuss other options for components shortly.

Example 2.2. Let COPY=({CopyNo,Title,Year,Director},{CopyNo}) be an entity type and let RENTAL=({CLIENT,COPY}, {RentalDay, DueDay},{COPY, RentalDay}) be a relationship type. The two relationships

> ((John Fox,08/08/1980,88 Main Street,3508888),(001.001,The
> Godfather,F.F.Coppola, 1972),04/01/2007,06/01/2007),
> ((John Fox,02/12/1967,23 Te Awe Awe,3539465),(001.002,The
> Godfather,F.F.Coppola, 1972),05/01/2007,06/01/2007).

form a relationship set over RENTAL.   □

Relationship Types with Role Names. It may well occur that a relationship type must be used to model relationships between objects of the same component. In order to avoid confusion we associate distinct *role names* with the components. Role names can also be utilised to improve the readability of the ER diagram. As an example, we may specify the relationship type DESCENDANT with components $comp(\text{DESCENDANT}) = \{Child : \text{CLIENT}, Parent : \text{CLIENT}\}$, an empty attribute set and key $id(\text{DESCENDANT}) = comp(\text{DESCENDANT})$.

Specialisation and Generalisation. Sometimes, objects in the target of the database can be represented by more than just a single abstract concept. The idea to derive a *subtype* from a more general *supertype* is known as *specialisation*. A subtype inherits all features of its supertype, but often adds some new properties. A subtype U may be modelled as a unary relationship type whose single component is just its supertype C. Clearly, U may have some additional attributes, and we may use C as the key for U, i.e. $U = (\{C\}, attr(U), \{C\})$. Note that every object of type C gives rise to at most one object of type U.

Occasionally, it is desirable to model alternatives, e.g., having a relationship to various kinds of objects. The idea to derive a new abstract concept that is more general than several other abstract concepts is known as *generalisation*. A *cluster type* U consists of a finite, non-empty set $comp(U)$ of components $C_1, \ldots, C_n$, normally $n \geq 2$. We denote this cluster type by $C_1 \oplus \cdots \oplus C_n$. Clusters model disjoint unions, i.e., an object set $\mathcal{I}(U)$ associated with a cluster type U is the disjoint union of its component's object sets $\mathcal{I}(U) = \bigcup_{i=1}^{n} \{(i, o) \mid o \in \mathcal{I}(C_i)\}$.

Higher-Order Relationship Types. So far, we have only allowed entity types to occur as components of relationship types. However, best practice suggests to allow also relationship types and cluster types to occur as components of another relationship type. For convenience, we call these kinds of types jointly *object types*. Entity types are object types without components while all other object types have at least one component. We need to ensure that the components of an object type are well-defined. For that we assign an order to each object type. Let U be an object type with component set $comp(U)$. The *order* of U is 0 if U is an entity type, and k if all components of U have order less than k and at least one of its components has order $k - 1$. It is simple to extend the definitions of relationship and relationship set, correspondingly [18].

An *Entity-Relationship schema* (ER schema) is a finite set $\mathcal{S}$ of object types such that for each object type U in $\mathcal{S}$ and each of its components C or $p : C$ in $comp(U)$ we have that the object type C belongs to $\mathcal{S}$ as well. An *instance* $\mathcal{I}$ of an ER schema $\mathcal{S}$ assigns each object type U in $\mathcal{S}$ an object set $\mathcal{I}(\mathcal{U})$ such that for each relationship type or cluster type U in $\mathcal{S}$, for each of its components C or $p : C$, and for each object $o \in \mathcal{I}(U)$ we have that $o(C)$ or $o(p : C)$ belongs to $\mathcal{I}(C)$. An *Entity-Relationship diagram* (ER diagram) of an ER schema $\mathcal{S}$ is a directed graph with the elements of $\mathcal{S}$ as nodes, and with edges from a node U to a node C for all components $C \in comp(U)$, and edges from node U to node C labelled with p for all components $p : C \in comp(U)$. An example of an ER-diagram is given in Figure 1.

Nested Attributes. Due to lack of space we will not go into details concerning the treatment of nested attributes [14,16,18].

3   Syntax, Semantics and Examples of Collection Types

In database practice it becomes often desirable to model collections of objects. For example, a course might be taught by more than a single lecturer and the readings of this course may consist of a ranking of books. In such cases it is advantageous to have an abstract concept modeling a finite collection of objects of the same type. That is, we would like to derive a new object type from a given one by applying some kind of collection constructor. On the basis of endorsing an order between elements of a collection and/or multiplicity of elements within a collection we can naturally distinguish between four kinds of collections:

1. lists in which duplicates are allowed and order matters,
2. sets in which duplicates are not allowed and order does not matter,
3. bags in which duplicates are allowed and order does not matter, and
4. rankings (also known as ordered sets) in which duplicates are not allowed and order does matter.

A *list-,set-,bag-* or *ranking*-type U has a single component C, i.e. $comp(U) = \{C\}$. We use the following notation for collection types: double brackets allow duplicates while single brackets disallow duplicates. We write $\{\cdot\}$ to represent the absence of order, and $[\cdot]$ to represent its presence. Consequently, we denote a list type by $U[\![C]\!]$, a set type by $U\{C\}$, a bag type by $U\{\{C\}\}$ and a ranking type by $U[C]$, respectively. We write $U(C)$ to refer to a collection type without emphasising its particular type, i.e., $(\cdot)$ denotes one of the four collection brackets. The object set $\mathcal{I}(U)$ associated with a collection type $U(C)$ is just a set of finite lists (sets, bags, or rankings, respectively) of objects in $\mathcal{I}(C)$. The *key* of a collection type $U(C)$ is the collection type $U(C)$ itself: to identify any collection within a set $\mathcal{I}(U)$ of collections we need to know the collection. Collection types are visualised using a circle around the corresponding bracket and drawing a (labelled) edge to its component. Figure 1 shows an example. An *object type* may now refer to an entity, relationship, cluster or collection type, and an *object* to an entity, relationship or a collection. The definitions of higher-order relationship type, ER schema and ER diagram carry over. For an *instance* $\mathcal{I}$ of an ER schema $\mathcal{S}$ we add the requirement that for each collection type U in $\mathcal{S}$, and for its single component C or $p : C$, for each collection $O \in \mathcal{I}(U)$ we have that every $o \in O$ belongs to $\mathcal{I}(C)$. Note that this does not add any additional requirement for the empty collection in $\mathcal{I}(U)$.

Examples of Rankings. An object of a ranking type $U[C]$ is a finite ranking of C-objects, i.e., the C-objects in the ranking are totally ordered and the same C-object cannot occur more than once in the same ranking. Examples in which ranking types are useful modeling constructs can be found in everyday life. As a simple example consider an entity type WEBSITE with attributes *Name, Contents, URL* and *Size*. The key of WEBSITE is simply *URL*. The result of a web-search can then be modelled by a ranking of websites, i.e., we define the ranking type WEBSEARCH[WEBSITE].

Examples of Lists. An object of a list type $U[\![C]\!]$ is a finite list of C-objects, i.e., the C-objects in the list are totally ordered and the same C-object may occur repeatedly in the same list. A very simple example is a bit sequence in which we have an entity type BIT with a single (key) attribute *value* with domain $\{0, 1\}$. The list type SEQUENCE$[\![$BIT$]\!]$ models all finite lists of bits, i.e., $0, 1$-values.

Examples of Sets. An object of a set type $U\{C\}$ is a finite set of C-objects, i.e., the C-objects in the set occur precisely once and there is no order between them. The set type is significant whenever there is no preference between the elements and only the occurrences of distinct elements matter. For instance, one may be interested in the collection of all *distinct* articles a customer bought, or the collection of all students a professor has supervised. As a simple example we look at profiles of customers that purchase MP3s. In this particular case customers will not buy the same MP3 more than once (since they can copy it afterwards). Moreover, the order in which the customer selects the MP3s of a single purchase is not of interest. We may obtain the entity type MP3=$(\{song, artist, album, genre\}, \{song, artist\})$, and the relationship type PLAYER with component set {CUSTOMER,ORDER{MP3}}, attribute set {*day,price*} and key {CUSTOMER,ORDER{MP3},day}.

Examples of Bags. An object of a bag type $U\{\{C\}\}$ is a finite bag of C-objects, i.e., a C-object in the bag may occur repeatedly but there is no order between them. A simple example for using bag types are shopping profiles in which customers buy articles. The emphasis in this example is on the total price of the purchase. It therefore matters how many times the same article is purchased. We may use an entity type PRODUCT with attributes *p-ID, name, description* and *price* where *p-ID* forms the key, and a relationship type SHOPPING with components CUSTOMER and bag type BAG{{PRODUCT}}, attributes *time* and *type-of-payment*, and key {CUSTOMER,*time*}.

An Example. Consider the following ER schema of a university example:

- ACADEMIC=({Name, Phone, Office}, {Name}),
- BOOK=({ISBN, Price, Title}, {ISBN}),
- COURSE=({No, Title}, {No}),
- STAFF{ACADEMIC}, READINGS[BOOK]
- TEACHING=({COURSE,Lecturers:STAFF,Tutors:STAFF,READINGS},{Year},
             {COURSE,Lecturers:STAFF,Year})

Note that the key on TEACHING says that in every year the same course cannot be taught by the same set of lecturers. The corresponding ER diagram is illustrated in Figure 1.

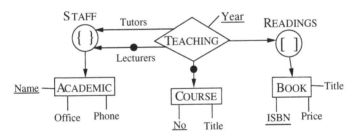

Fig. 1. ER diagram

4   Transformation to the Relational Model

An ER schema is the result of the conceptual design phase and serves as input for the following design steps, in particular the logical design phase. The framework of the latter is the relational model of data (RDM). Therefore, one needs to transform an ER schema with its abstract concepts into an RDM schema that uses flat relation schemata only. While the collection type constructors provide simple-to-use modeling features the transformation will actually reveal how these features can be implemented in relational tables. Our transformation does not simply flatten any nested structures but preserves the structural properties of collections, and makes therefore the mapping invertable.

4.1   Notions from the Relational Model of Data

In order to describe our transformation for collection types we will repeat fundamental notions from the RDM and summarise the transformation of object types different from collection types. This will also illustrate how neatly our extension fits into the current framework, and how the modeling capabilities extend without changing much of the underlying theory.

Let $\mathcal{D}$ denote a set of domains, i.e., a set of countably infinite sets. A *relation schema* R consists of a finite set $attr(R)$ of *attributes* and a *domain assignment* $dom : attr(R) \rightarrow \mathcal{D}$. A *tuple* over a relation schema R (for short: an R-*tuple*) is a mapping $t : attr(R) \rightarrow \bigcup_{D \in \mathcal{D}} D$ with $t(A) \in dom(A)$ for all $A \in attr(R)$. A *relation* over a relation schema R is a finite set r of R-tuples. For $X \subseteq R$ let $t[X]$ denote the projection of t on X. A *relational database schema* is a finite, non-empty set $\mathcal{S}$ of relation schemata. An *instance* $\mathcal{I}$ of a relational database schema $\mathcal{S}$ assigns to each $R \in \mathcal{S}$ a relation $\mathcal{I}(R)$ over R. A *key* on a relation schema R is a subset $K \subseteq attr(R)$ restricting relations r over R to satisfy $t_1[K] \neq t_2[K]$ for all $t_1, t_2 \in r$. A *key* K is called *minimal* if and only if no proper subset of K is a key. A *foreign key* on a relation schema R in a schema $\mathcal{S}$ is a sequence of attributes $A_1, \ldots, A_n \in attr(R)$ together with a minimal key $K = \{B_1, \ldots, B_n\}$ of some relation schema $S \in \mathcal{S}$ with $dom(A_i) = dom(B_i)$ $(i = 1, \ldots, n)$ restricting instances $\mathcal{I}$ of $\mathcal{S}$ to satisfy the inclusion dependency $R[A_1, \ldots, A_n] \subseteq S[B_1, \ldots, B_n]$, i.e., for each tuple $t \in \mathcal{I}(R)$ there must exist a tuple $t' \in \mathcal{I}(S)$ with $t[A_i] = t'[B_i]$ for all $i = 1, \ldots, n$. We use the notation $[A_1, \ldots, A_n] \subseteq S[B_1, \ldots, B_n]$ for a foreign key on R.

4.2   Transformation of Entity and Relationship Types

The transformation starts with entity types, and then continues with relationship types of order 1, then 2 and so on.

An entity type is simply just a different notation of a relation schema. The transformation is therefore very simple. The entity type $E = (attr(E), id(E))$ leads to a relation schema E' with $attr(E') = attr(E)$. The domain assignment for the attributes of E and E' is the same. Furthermore, E leads to a minimal key $id(E)$ on E'. Consider entity types as relationship types of order 0. For the entity types of the university example from Figure 1 we obtain

- ACADEMIC$'$ = {Name, Phone, Office} with minimal key {Name},
- BOOK$'$ = {ISBN, Price, Title} with minimal key {ISBN},
- COURSE$'$ = {No, Title} with minimal key {No}.

Suppose that we have transformed all relationship types of order n, and let $R = (comp(R), attr(R), id(R))$ be a relationship type of order $n + 1$. For each component $S \in comp(R)$ we choose pairwise disjoint sets

$$k\_attr(S) = \{S.A \mid A \text{ key attribute of } S'\}$$

of new attribute names not occurring in $attr(R)$. Similarly, for a component $r : S \in comp(R)$ we choose $k\_attr(r : S) = \{r.A \mid A \text{ key attribute of } S'\}$. The relationship type R results in the new relation schema R' with

$$attr(R') = \bigcup_{X \in comp(R)} k\_attr(X) \cup attr(R).$$

For the domain assignment we have $dom(S.A) = dom(A)$, $dom(r.A) = dom(A)$, and $dom(A)$ remains unchanged for $A \in attr(R)$. Furthermore, R leads to the minimal key

$$\bigcup_{X \in id(R) \cap comp(R)} k\_attr(X) \cup (id(R) \cap attr(R)) \text{ on } R'$$

and each component $S \in comp(R)$ defines a foreign key

$$[S.A_1, \ldots, S.A_n] \subseteq S'[A_1, \ldots, A_n]$$

on R'. In case of role names each component $r : S \in comp(R)$ defines a foreign key $[r.A_1, \ldots, r.A_n] \subseteq S'[A_1, \ldots, A_n]$ on R'. The transformation of an ER instance into its corresponding relational database instance is straightforward.

4.3 Transformation of Cluster Types

Clusters are used in conceptual design to model alternatives. The RDM does not provide a similar concept and one therefore transforms ER schemata with clusters into equivalent ER schemata without clusters [18]. This is only necessary as a pre-processing step before the actual transformation takes place. In general, clusters provide a convenient way to model objects in the target of the database. We do not recommend to avoid clusters as the size of an ER schema increases dramatically, and will therefore become much harder to comprehend.

4.4 Transformation of Collection Types

In the following we use U' to denote the name of the relation schema that corresponds to $U(C)$. For each collection type $U(C)$ the set $attr(U')$ of attributes of U' contains the set

$$k\_attr(C) = \begin{cases} \{C.A \mid A \text{ is key attribute of } C'\}, & \text{if } C \text{ is not a collection type} \\ \{C'_{ID}\}, & \text{otherwise.} \end{cases}$$

and an additional surrogate attribute U'_{ID}. The attribute U'_{ID} identifies collections and, therefore, enables us to associate objects with collections in flat relations. The domain $dom(U'_{ID})$ is a set of surrogates.

Elements of bags may occur multiple times. Thus, a bag type $U\{\{C\}\}$ defines an additional attribute U'_{Mul} in $attr(U')$. It accommodates the information on the multiplicity of a bag's elements, and its domain is the set of positive integers.

Elements of rankings and lists have a position. Thus, a ranking or list type $U(C)$ defines an additional attribute U'_{Pos} in $attr(U')$. It accommodates the information on the position of an ordered collection's elements, and its domain is the set of non-negative integers.

In summary, for each collection type $U(C)$ in the ER schema, a relation schema U' with attributes $k\_attr(C) \cup \{U'_{ID}\}$ is generated. For ordered collection types this relation schema will also contain an attribute U'_{Pos}, and for a bag type also U'_{Mul}. For the collection types of the example from Figure 1 we obtain

- STAFF$'$ = {ACADEMIC.Name, Staff$'_{ID}$}, and
- READINGS$'$ = {BOOK.ISBN, Readings$'_{ID}$, Readings$'_{Pos}$}.

Keys. An ordered collection type $U(C)$ defines the minimal key {U'_{ID}, U'_{Pos}} on U'. That is, a tuple over U' is uniquely identified by the collection (the value in the U'_{ID}-column) and the position in this collection (the value in the U'_{Pos}-column). The difference between rankings and lists is that elements in a ranking uniquely determine the position within the ranking. In a list, however, the same element may occur in different positions. Thus, ranking types $U[C]$ result in the specification of a further minimal key, namely $k\_attr(C) \cup \{U'_{ID}\}$ on U'.

A bag type $U\{\{C\}\}$ defines the minimal key $k\_attr(C) \cup \{U'_{ID}\}$. That is, a tuple over U' is uniquely identified by the bag (the value in the U'_{ID}-column) and the values that identify the element of the bag (the values in the $k\_attr(C)$-columns). In other words, every element of every bag has a fixed multiplicity.

A set type $U\{C\}$ defines the minimal key $attr(U')$. That is, a tuple over U' can only be uniquely identified by the set (the value in the U'_{ID}-column) and the values that identify the element of the set (the values in the $k\_attr(C)$-columns). This is a consequence of the fact that the same element may occur in different sets, and different sets may have different elements.

In the university example, the minimal key on STAFF$'$ is STAFF$'$ itself, and the minimal keys on READINGS$'$ are

$$\{\text{Readings}'_{ID}, \text{Readings}'_{Pos}\} \text{ and } \{\text{BOOK.ISBN}, \text{Readings}'_{ID}\}.$$

Foreign Keys. Let $U(C)$ denote an arbitrary collection type. If the object type C is not a collection type, then C defines a foreign key $[C.A_1, \ldots, C.A_n] \subseteq C'[A_1, \ldots, A_n]$ on U'. In the university example, the foreign key on STAFF$'$ is [ACADEMIC.Name] $\subseteq$ ACADEMIC$'$[Name], and the foreign key on READINGS$'$ is [BOOK.ISBN] $\subseteq$ BOOK$'$[ISBN].

If C is the collection type $V(D)$, then $k\_attr(C) = \{V'_{ID}\}$ and V'_{ID} uniquely identifies the collection but not the V'-tuple since the same V'_{ID}-value may be associated with different D-objects in the V'-relation (namely with all the elements of the collection V'_{ID} denotes). Consequently, we do not obtain a foreign key in this case. It is important to note at this point that we also do not specify the inclusion dependency $U'[V'_{ID}] \subseteq V'[V'_{ID}]$. The reason for this is the empty collection. Without the use of null values an empty collection of type $U(C)$ cannot be modelled in the U'-relation since empty collections do not have any elements. However, in the V'_{ID}-column of a U'-relation we may use a surrogate value to represent the empty collection. This surrogate value cannot occur in the V'_{ID}-column of the V'-relation. On the other hand, the use of the null value *not exists* for $k\_attr(C)$-values permits the introduction of a U'_{ID}-value for the empty collection in the U'-relation. However, no attributes in $k\_attr(C)$ can then be used as key attributes, and we would have to deal with incomplete information. Therefore, we prefer not to represent the empty collection in the U'-relation.

A Uniqueness Constraint. We will now introduce an additional constraint for those relation schemata that result from the transformation of collection types.

The purpose of the U'_{ID} attribute is to define the membership of elements in collections and to uniquely identify collections in the relational database instance. That is, any two U'_{ID}-entries in the database instance are the same precisely when they denote the same collection. In fact, if two different surrogate values from $dom(U'_{ID})$ occur in any relation, then these surrogate values denote different collections of type $U(C)$. That is, there must be a C-object t which separates the two collections **in the U'-relation**. Let $\mathcal{S}'$ denote the relational database schema obtained from transforming all object types of the ER schema $\mathcal{S}$. The active domain $adom_{\mathcal{S}'}(U'_{ID})$ is the union of all those values from $dom(U'_{ID})$ that occur in any U'_{ID}-column of an R-relation for any $R \in \mathcal{S}'$.

$$\forall id_1, id_2 \in adom_{\mathcal{S}'}(U'_{ID}).(id_1 \neq id_2 \Rightarrow \exists t \in \prod_{A \in k\_attr(C)} dom(A).$$

$$((id_1, t) \in U'[U_{ID}, k\_attr(C)] \wedge (id_2, t) \notin U'[U_{ID}, k\_attr(C)]) \vee$$
$$((id_1, t) \notin U'[U_{ID}, k\_attr(C)] \wedge (id_2, t) \in U'[U_{ID}, k\_attr(C)])).$$

By abuse of notation $U'[X]$ denotes the projection of the U'-relation to the attributes in $X \subseteq U'$. Our uniqueness constraint really serves two purposes. Firstly, it guarantees that each collection can be identified uniquely by its surrogate from $dom(U'_{ID})$. Note that this is similar to the *extensional uniqueness constraint*, introduced by ter Hofstede et al. [17], which says that two sets are equal if and only if they have the same extension (i.e. the same elements). Secondly, our uniqueness constraint guarantees referential integrity over the RDM schema, i.e., it is a weak inclusion dependency saying that every element from $adom_{\mathcal{S}'}(U'_{ID})$ must also occur in the U'_{ID}-column of the U'-relation or denotes the empty collection. Notice that the constraint also eliminates the possibility that the empty collection is denoted by different surrogates. The uniqueness constraint is specified on the active domain of the U'_{ID} attribute in those U' that result from a collection type $U(C)$. In the university example we obtain the following uniqueness constraint on the active domain of $Staff'_{ID}$:

$$\forall id_1, id_2 \in adom(Staff'_{ID}).(id_1 \neq id_2 \Rightarrow \exists t \in dom(\text{ACADEMIC.Name}).$$
$$((id_1, t) \in \text{STAFF}' \wedge (id_2, t) \notin \text{STAFF}') \vee ((id_1, t) \notin \text{STAFF}' \wedge (id_2, t) \in \text{STAFF}')).$$

Accordingly, we can define the uniqueness constraint for the active domain of $Readings'_{ID}$.

4.5   Object Types with Collection Type Components

The transformation described in Section 4.2 remains the same in the presence of collection types in the ER schema $\mathcal{S}$ taking into consideration the definition of $k\_attr(X)$ from Section 4.4. The only difference is now that a collection type component U of the relationship type R does not define an inclusion dependency $R'[U'_{ID}] \subseteq U'[U'_{ID}]$ on R'. In fact, the unique surrogate value from $adom_{\mathcal{S}'}(U'_{ID})$ that may violate such an inclusion dependency is treated as if it denotes the corresponding empty collection. The relationship type TEACHING from the university example in Figure 1 results in the relation schema TEACHING$'$ with

– attributes COURSE.No, Lecturers:Staff$'_{ID}$, Tutors:Staff$'_{ID}$, Readings$'_{ID}$, Year,
– minimal key {COURSE.No, Lecturers:Staff$'_{ID}$, Year}, and
– foreign key [COURSE.No] ⊆ COURSE$'$[No].

Notice that we cannot specify any of the following inclusion dependencies:

– TEACHING$'$[Lecturers:Staff$'_{ID}$] ⊆ STAFF$'$[Staff$'_{ID}$],
– TEACHING$'$[Tutors:Staff$'_{ID}$] ⊆ STAFF$'$[Staff$'_{ID}$],
– TEACHING$'$[Readings$'_{ID}$] ⊆ READINGS$'$[Readings$'_{ID}$].

Rather than formalising the transformation of collections from the ER instance into flat relations we will use this section to illustrate this mapping by some examples. Therefore, consider the following, artificially small, ER database over our university schema.

COURSE	
No	Title
157266	Data Modeling
157357	IS Security

BOOK		
Title	ISBN	Price
ER Modeling	3540654704	138.-
DB Design	0201565234	90.-
Cryptography	0130914290	87.-
Viruses	0471007684	123.-

ACADEMIC		
Name	Office	Phone
Sven	2.09	7308
Sebastian	2.10	2717
Ernie	2.33	0077
Bert	2.33	0077

READINGS
[3540654704, 0201565234]
[0130914290, 0471007684]

STAFF
{Sven, Sebastian}
{Sebastian}
{Ernie, Bert}
∅

TEACHING				
COURSE	Year	READINGS	Lecturers:STAFF	Tutors:STAFF
157266	2007	[3540654704, 0201565234]	{Sven, Sebastian}	{Ernie, Bert}
157357	2007	[0130914290, 0471007684]	{Sebastian}	∅

This database will be transformed into the following relational database. We omit the representations of COURSE$'$, BOOK$'$ and ACADEMIC$'$ since these are just the same relations as the ones over COURSE, BOOK and ACADEMIC, respectively.

READINGS$'$		
ISBN	Readings$'_{ID}$	Readings$'_{Pos}$
3540654704	1	1
0201565234	1	2
0130914290	2	1
0471007684	2	2

STAFF$'$	
Name	Staff$'_{ID}$
Sven	2
Sebastian	2
Sebastian	1
Ernie	3
Bert	3

TEACHING$'$				
CourseNo	Year	Readings$'_{ID}$	Lecturers:Staff$'_{ID}$	Tutors:Staff$'_{ID}$
157266	2007	1	2	3
157357	2007	2	1	0

Notice how the nested STAFF-relation is represented as STAFF$'$-relation: every non-empty set S in the STAFF-relation is represented by a unique surrogate $n_S \in dom(\text{Staff}'_{ID})$, and for every element $e \in S$ the tuple $(e, n_S) \in dom(\text{Name}) \times dom(\text{Staff}'_{ID})$ represents this membership in the STAFF$'$-relation.

Notice that the active domain of Staff$'_{ID}$ consists of $0, 1, 2, 3$ where 0 denotes the empty set. In fact, the value 0 is the unique surrogate that violates the inclusion dependency TEACHING$'$[Tutors:Staff$'_{ID}$] $\subseteq$ STAFF$'$[Staff$'_{ID}$].

4.6   Another Example for Mapping Collection Types and Collections

In order to illustrate the transformation for ER schemata in which collection types are nested we consider the following simple example of an ER schema:

WEBSITE=({URL,Name,Size},{URL}), and the two collection types
SEARCH[WEBSITE] and MONITOR{{SEARCH}}.

Our transformation yields the following relational database schema

- WEBSITE$'$={URL,Name,Size} with minimal key {URL},
- SEARCH$'$ = {WEBSITE.URL, SEARCH$'_{ID}$, SEARCH$'_{Pos}$} with
  minimal keys {SEARCH$'_{ID}$, SEARCH$'_{Pos}$} and {WEBSITE.URL, SEARCH$'_{ID}$},
  and foreign key [WEBSITE.URL] $\subseteq$ WEBSITE$'$[URL]
- MONITOR$'$ = {SEARCH$'_{ID}$, MONITOR$'_{ID}$, MONITOR$'_{Mul}$} with
  minimal key {SEARCH$'_{ID}$, MONITOR$'_{ID}$}.

For the database instance level we consider the following ER instance.

WEBSITE		
URL	Name	Size
http://www.sigmod.org/	SIGMOD Website	27.9 KB
http://www.acm.org/	ACM Website	26.75 KB
http://www.westwardlook.com/	Westward Website	Unknown

SEARCH
[http://www.sigmod.org/,http://www.acm.org/,http://www.westwardlook.com/]
[http://www.sigmod.org/,http://www.westwardlook.com/]
[ ]

MONITOR
{{ [http://www.sigmod.org/,http://www.acm.org/,http://www.westwardlook.com/], [ ], [ ], [ ], [http://www.sigmod.org/, http://www.westwardlook.com/], [http://www.sigmod.org/,http://www.westwardlook.com/] }}
{{ [http://www.sigmod.org/,http://www.westwardlook.com/], [http://www.sigmod.org/,http://www.westwardlook.com/], [http://www.sigmod.org/,http://www.westwardlook.com/] }}

This ER database can be represented as the following relational database. We omit the representation of WEBSITE$'$ since this is just the same relation as the one over WEBSITE.

SEARCH′		
WEBSITE.URL	SEARCH′$_{ID}$	SEARCH′$_{Pos}$
http://www.sigmod.org/	1	1
http://www.acm.org/	1	2
http://www.westwardlook.com/	1	3
http://www.sigmod.org/	2	1
http://www.westwardlook.com/	2	2

MONITOR′		
MONITOR′$_{ID}$	SEARCH′$_{ID}$	MONITOR′$_{Mul}$
1	0	3
1	1	1
1	2	2
2	2	3

Note that the value 0 in the SEARCH′$_{ID}$-column of the MONITOR′-relation denotes the empty ranking [ ] since it is not present in the SEARCH′$_{ID}$-column of the SEARCH′-relation. The active domain of SEARCH′$_{ID}$ is $\{0, 1, 2\}$.

5   Properties of the Transformation

Our transformation enjoys several nice properties. Firstly, it is a proper extension of the standard transformation for ER schemata that only include relationship types and cluster types of any order [18].

Secondly, it preserves the semantics of its collection types, i.e., the values stored on the surrogate attributes that occur in a relation schema permit the reconstruction of the original collection in a straightforward manner. Basically, two objects belong to the same collection over $\mathcal{I}(U)$ precisely when they have been assigned the same U'_{ID}-value in the U'-relation. Moreover, the U'_{Pos}-value determines the position of an object in a ranking or a list. Finally, the U'_{Mul}-value denotes the multiplicity of an object within a bag. These properties make the transformation invertible. However, for a collection type $U(C)$ it cannot be decided whether the empty collection was an element of $\mathcal{I}(U)$ given the corresponding U'-relation. If $U(C)$ is the component of another object type O and a surrogate violates the inclusion dependency $O'[U'_{ID}] \subseteq U'[U'_{ID}]$, then the uniqueness constraint tells us that this surrogate represents the empty collection in the corresponding O'-relation. According to the definition of an ER instance the empty collection must have been an element of $\mathcal{I}(U)$. Mappings from relational databases to ER databases without collections have been studied previously [12].

Thirdly, some of the semantics of collections is reflected by keys on relation schemata that result from the transformation. For instance, since every C-object in a ranking over $U[C]$ determines its position within the ranking we obtain the functional dependency $\{U'_{ID}\} \cup k\_attr(C) \rightarrow U'_{Pos}$, i.e., U'_{ID} and $k\_attr(C)$ form a minimal key on U'. In lists, however, a C-object may occur in several positions of the list, but the list and the position within this list uniquely determine the C-object in this position (this is also true for rankings), i.e., $\{U'_{ID}, U'_{Pos}\}$

forms a minimal key on U'. Moreover, a bag and its C-object element together uniquely determine the multiplicity of the C-object, i.e., $\{U'_{ID}\} \cup k\_attr(C)$ forms a minimal key for U'. In the special case of a set the multiplicity of an element is fixed to 1, and therefore there is no need for the surrogate attribute U'_{Mul} (this is a good example for a non-standard functional dependency, namely $\emptyset \to U'_{\mathrm{Mul}}$).

Fourthly, the transformation results in a relational database schema that is in Inclusion-Dependency Normal Form with respect to the set of functional and inclusion dependencies obtained. Thus, it enjoys several desirable semantic properties [10] such as the absence of value and attribute redundancies and update anomalies. In fact, the transformation shows that the only functional dependencies defined on any of the resulting relation schemata are keys, and the inclusion dependencies are non-circular (due to the strict hierarchy of ER schemata) and key-based. It should be noted, however, that our uniqueness constraint implies some kind of weak inclusion dependency that is not key-based. It is future work to investigate the precise impact of the uniqueness constraints on design desiderata.

Finally, the transformation involving collection types does not result in a unique database instance since there are several choices for the values on the surrogate attributes. However, if the uniqueness constraint is satisfied, then it does not matter what these values are. Collections can be uniquely identified, and the relationship between different tables is guaranteed to be meaningful. In fact, every value occurring within the active domain of U'_{ID} either denotes the empty collection or it occurs in the relation over U' and references a unique collection. This results in a generalisation of the extensional uniqueness constraint introduced by ter Hofstede et al. [17].

6   Conclusion and Future Work

Entity-Relationship models use tuple- (aggregation) and cluster constructors to generate more complex object types from simpler ones. Collection types, however, have not been introduced into the formal framework of Entity-Relationship modeling. Previous work on this subject has either suggested to encode properties of collections into constraints [17] or annotate conceptual schemata and leave the burden of their implementation to lower design phases [7]. These solutions make it unnecessarily difficult for the designer to model collections naturally, and therefore to discuss the approximation of the target database with its users. This, in turn, defeats the purpose of a conceptual data model. In order to overcome these shortcomings we have introduced four collection type constructors into the ER framework. These have a well-defined semantics, and are intuitive and easy to use. The implementation of the collection types in relational tables can be done automatically by a transformation algorithm that enjoys many desirable properties.

In the future we would like to investigate the applicability of collection types to mappings into other data models such as XML [4] and sequence data models [11]. Several relational database management systems are now object-relational. It might be interesting to provide mapping algorithms that directly take into account the collection types supported by such systems. It seems also desirable to provide query languages for the extended ER model, and to investigate integrity constraints in the presence of collection types.

References

1. Abiteboul, S., Buneman, P., Suciu, D.: Data on the Web: From Relations to Semistructured Data and XML. Morgan Kaufmann Publishers, San Francisco (2000)
2. Atkinson, M., Bancilhon, F., DeWitt, D., Dittrich, K., Maier, D., Zdonik, S.: The object-oriented database system manifesto. In: Proceedings of the International Conference on Deductive and Object-Oriented Databases, pp. 40–57 (1989)
3. Batini, C., Ceri, S., Navathe, S.B.: Conceptual Database Design: An Entity-Relationship Approach. Benjamin Cummings (1992)
4. Bray, T., Paoli, J., Sperberg-McQueen, C.M., Maler, E., Yergeau, F.: Extensible markup language (XML) 1.0 (third edition) W3C recommendation 04 (february 2004), http://www.w3.org/TR/2004/REC-xml-20040204/
5. Chen, P.P.: The entity-relationship model: Towards a unified view of data. Transactions on Database Systems 1, 9–36 (1976)
6. Elmasri, R., Navathe, S.: Fundamentals of Database Systems, 4th edn. Addison-Wesley, London, UK (2003)
7. Halpin, T.: Modeling collections in UML and ORM. In: EMMSAD (2000), http://www.orm.net/pdf/EMMSAD2000.pdf
8. Hartmann, S., Link, S.: English sentence structures and EER modeling. In: The Fourth Asia-Pacific Conference on Conceptual Modelling. Conferences in Research and Practice in Information Technology, vol. 67, pp. 27–35 (2007)
9. Hull, R., King, R.: Semantic database modeling: Survey, applications and research issues. ACM Computing Surveys 19(3) (1987)
10. Levene, M., Vincent, M.: Justification for inclusion dependency normal form. IEEE Trans. Knowl. Data Eng. 12(2), 281–291 (2000)
11. Li, J., Ng, S., Wong, L.: Bioinformatics adventures in database research. In: Calvanese, D., Lenzerini, M., Motwari, R. (eds.) ICDT 2003. LNCS, vol. 2572, pp. 31–46. Springer, Heidelberg (2003)
12. Markowitz, V., Makowsky, J.: Identifying extended entity-relationship object structures in relational schemas. IEEE Trans. Softw. Eng. 16(8), 777–790 (1990)
13. Paredaens, J., De Bra, P., Gyssens, M., Van Gucht, D.: The Structure of the Relational Database Model. Springer, Heidelberg (1989)
14. Parent, C., Spaccapietra, S.: Complex objects modeling: An entity-relationship-approach. In: Nested Relations and Complex Objects. LNCS, vol. 361, pp. 272–296. Springer, Heidelberg (1987)
15. Parent, C., Spaccapietra, S., Zimányi, E.: Spatio-temporal conceptual models: Data structures + space + time. In: ACM-GIS, pp. 26–33 (1999)
16. Schek, H., Scholl, M.: The relational model with relation-valued attributes. Inf. Syst. 11(2), 137–147 (1986)
17. ter Hofstede, A., van der Weide, T.: Deriving identity from extensionality. International Journal of Software Engineering and Knowledge Engineering 8(2), 189–221 (1998)
18. Thalheim, B.: Entity-Relationship Modeling: Foundations of Database Technology. Springer, Heidelberg (2000)

Schema Exchange: A Template-Based Approach to Data and Metadata Translation

Paolo Papotti and Riccardo Torlone

Università Roma Tre
{papotti,torlone}@dia.uniroma3.it

Abstract. In this paper we study the problem of schema exchange, a natural extension of the data exchange problem to an intensional level. To this end, we first introduce the notion of schema template, a tool for the representation of a class of schemas sharing the same structure. We then define the schema exchange notion as the problem of (i) taking a schema that matches a source template, and (ii) generating a new schema for a target template, on the basis of a set of dependencies defined over the two templates. This framework allows the definition, once for all, of generic transformations that work for several schemas. A method for the generation of a "correct" solution of the schema exchange problem is proposed and a number of general results are given. We also show how it is possible to generate automatically a data exchange setting from a schema exchange solution. This allows the definition of queries to migrate data from a source database into the one obtained as a result of a schema exchange.

1 Introduction

In the last years, we have witnessed an increasing complexity of database applications, especially when several data sources need to be accessed, transformed and merged. There is a consequent growing need for advanced tools and flexible techniques supporting the management, the exchange, and the integration of different and heterogeneous sources of information.

In this trend, the data exchange problem has received recently great attention, both from a theoretical [12,13] and a practical point of view [19]. In a data exchange scenario, given a set of correspondences between a source and a target schema, the goal is the automatic generation of queries able to transform data over the source into a format conforming to the target.

In this paper, we address the novel problem of *schema exchange*, which naturally extends the data exchange scenario to *sets* of similar schemas. To this aim, we first introduce the notion of *schema template*, which is used to represent a class of different database schemas sharing the same structure. Then, given a set of correspondences between the components of a source and a target template, the goal is the translation of any data source whose schema conforms to the source template into a format conforming to the target template. This framework allows the definition, once for all, of "generic" transformations that

C. Parent et al. (Eds.): ER 2007, LNCS 4801, pp. 323–337, 2007.

works for different but similar schemas, such as the denormalization of a pair of relation tables based on a foreign key between them.

To tackle this problem, we introduce a formal notion of *solution* for a schema exchange setting and propose a technique for the automatic generation of solutions. This is done by representing constraints over templates and correspondences between them with a special class of first order formulas, and then using them to generate the solution by chasing [2] the source schema. Moreover, we show how it is possible to generate automatically a data exchange setting from a schema exchange solution. This allows the definition of a set of queries to migrate data from a source database into the database obtained as a result of the schema exchange.

From a practical point of view, in our scenario the user can: (i) describe a collection of databases presenting structural similarities, by means of a source template T_1, (ii) define the structure of a possible transformation of the source through a target template T_2, (iii) define how to exchange information from the source to the target by means of simple correspondences, graphically represented by lines between T_1 to T_2, and (iv) translate any data source over a schema matching with T_1 into a format described by a schema matching with T_2.

We advocate that the relational model is adequate for implementing such approach. In particular we show how existing repositories for relational database management systems can be profitably used for such purpose. In fact, templates can be stored in tables and can be then queried using a standard relational query language, independently of whether or not they are associated with some data.

To our knowledge, the notion of schema exchange studied in this paper is new. In general, we can say that our contribution can be set in the framework of *metadata management*. Metadata can generally be thought as information that describes, or supplements, actual data. Several studies have addressed metadata related problems, such as, interoperability [15,20], annotations and comments on data [7,10,14], data provenance [9], and a large list of more specific problems, like data quality [17]. While the list is not exhaustive, it witnesses the large interest in this important area and the different facets of the problem.

Most of the proposed approach focus on a specific kind of metadata and are not directly applicable to other cases without major modifications. Bernstein set the various problems within a very general framework called *model management* [3,4,5]. In [6] the authors show the value of this framework to approach several metadata related problems, with a significant reduction of programming effort. Our contribution goes in this direction: as in model management, schemas and mappings are treated as first class citizens. In particular, the schema exchange problem has some points in common with the *ModelGen* operator. The ModelGen operator realizes a *schema translation* from a source data model M_s to a target data model M_t. For instance, the ModelGen operator could be used to translate an Entity-Relationship schema into a schema for an XML document (e.g., a DTD). Several approaches to this problem have been proposed in the last years [1,8,16,18]. In this paper, we provide a novel contribution to this problem by studying a framework for schema translation with a clear and precise semantics, that can be at the basis of an innovative tool supporting an important activity of model management.

The structure of the paper is as follows. In Section 2 we briefly set the basic definitions and recall some results of the data exchange problem. In Section 3, we introduce the notions of template and schema exchange and we show how they can be implemented with the relational database technology. In Section 4 we describes how templates and schemas are related and, in Section 5 we show how a data exchange problem can be obtained from a schema exchange setting. Finally, in Section 6, we draw some conclusions and sketch future directions of research.

2   Preliminaries

2.1   Basics

A *(relational) schema* **S** is composed by a set of *relations* $R(A_1, \ldots, A_n)$, where R is the *name* of the relation and $A_1, \ldots, A_k$ are its *attributes*. Each attribute is associated with a set of values called the *domain* of the attribute. An instance of a relation $R(A_1, \ldots, A_n)$ is a set of tuples, each of which associates with each A_i a value taken from its domain. An instance I of a schema **S** contains an instance of each relation in **S**.

A *dependency* over a schema **S** is a first order formula of the form: $\forall \mathbf{x}(\phi(\mathbf{x}) \rightarrow \chi(\mathbf{x}))$ where $\phi(\mathbf{x})$ and $\chi(\mathbf{x})$ are formulas over **S**, and **x** are the free variables of the formula, ranging over the domains of the attributes occurring in **S**.

As usual, we will focus on two special kind of dependencies: the tuple generating dependencies (tgd) and the equality generating dependencies (egd), as it is widely accepted that they include all of the naturally-occurring constraints on relational databases. A tgd has the form: $\forall \mathbf{x}(\phi(\mathbf{x}) \rightarrow \exists \mathbf{y}(\psi(\mathbf{x}, \mathbf{y})))$ where $\phi(\mathbf{x})$ and $\psi(\mathbf{x}, \mathbf{y})$ are conjunction of atomic formulas, whereas an egd has the form: $\forall \mathbf{x}(\phi(\mathbf{x}) \rightarrow (x_1 = x_2))$ where $\phi(\mathbf{x})$ is a conjunction of atomic formulas and x_1, x_2 are variables in **x**.

2.2   Data Exchange

In the relational-to-relational data exchange framework [12], a data exchange setting is described by $M = (\mathbf{S}, \mathbf{T}, \Sigma_{st}, \Sigma_t)$, where: (i) **S** is a source schema, (ii) **T** is a target schema, (iii) Σ_{st} is a finite set of *s-t* (source-to-target) tgds $\forall \mathbf{x}(\phi(\mathbf{x}) \rightarrow \exists \mathbf{y}(\chi(\mathbf{x}, \mathbf{y})))$ where $\phi(\mathbf{x})$ is a conjunction of atomic formulas over **S** and $\chi(\mathbf{x}, \mathbf{y})$ is a conjunction of atomic formulas over **T**, and (iv) Σ_t is a finite set of tgs or egds over **T**. Given an instance I of **S**, a solution for I under M is an instance J of **T** such that (I, J) satisfies $\Sigma_{st} \cup \Sigma_t$. A solution may have distinct labeled nulls denoting unknown values.

In general, there are many possible solutions for I under M. A solution J is *universal* if there is a homomorphism from J to every other solution for I under M. A homomorphism from an instance I to an instance J is a function h from constant values and nulls occurring in I to constant values and nulls occurring in J such that: (i) it is the identity on constants, and (ii) (with some abuse of notation) $h(I) \subseteq J$.

In [13] it was shown that a universal solution of I under M can be obtained by applying the chase procedure to I using $\Sigma_{st} \cup \Sigma_t$. This procedure takes as input an instance I and generates another instance by applying *chase steps* based on dependencies in $\Sigma_{st} \cup \Sigma_t$. There are two kinds of chase steps: (1) a tgd $\forall \mathbf{x}(\phi(\mathbf{x}) \to \exists \mathbf{y}(\psi(\mathbf{x}, \mathbf{y})))$ can be applied to I if there is a homomorphism h from $\phi(\mathbf{x})$ to I; in this case, the result of its application is $I \cup h'(\psi(\mathbf{x}, \mathbf{y}))$, where h' is the extension of h to $\mathbf{y}$ obtained by assigning fresh labeled nulls to the variables in $\mathbf{y}$; (2) an egd $\phi(x) \to (x_1 = x_2)$ can be applied to I if there is a homomorphism h from $\phi(\mathbf{x})$ to I such that $h(x_1) \neq h(x_2)$; in this case, the result of its application is the following: if one of $h(x_1)$ and $h(x_2)$ is a constant and the other is a variable then the variable is changed to the constant, otherwise the values are equated unless they are both constants, since in this case the process *fails*. The chase of I is obtained by applying all applicable chase steps exhaustively to I.

3 Schema Exchange Semantics

In this section we define the schema exchange problem as the application of the data exchange problem to *templates* of schemas.

3.1 Schema Templates

We fix a finite set $\mathcal{C}$ of *construct names*. A *construct* $C(p_0, p_1, \ldots p_k)$ has a name C in $\mathcal{C}$ and a finite set $p_1, \ldots, p_k$ of distinct *properties*, each of which is associated with a set of values called the *domain* of the property. In principle, the set $\mathcal{C}$ can contain construct names from different data models so that we can define transformations between schemas of different models. In this paper however, for sake of simplicity, we focus on schema exchange between schema templates of relational schemas; the approach can be extended to other types of templates, but challenging issues already arise in the relational case.

Therefore, we fix the following relational construct names and properties:

Construct Names	Properties (domain)
Relation (or R)	name (strings)
Attribute (or A)	name (strings), nullable (booleans), in (strings)
AttributeKey (or AK)	name (strings), in (strings)
AttributeFKey (or AFK)	name (strings), in (strings), refer (strings)

Note that the Relation construct is associated only to the name property, whose domain is a set of strings. The same domain is also associated with the property in of the constructs Attribute, AttributeKey and AttributeFKey, and the property refer of the construct AttributeFKey: these properties are used to specify references between constructs. Clearly, other properties can be considered for every construct. For instance, we could associate the properties type and has_default with the construct Attribute.

Basically, a template is a set of constructs with a set of dependencies associated with them, which are used to specify constraints over single constructs and semantic associations between different constructs.

Definition 1 (Template). *A (schema) template is a pair* $(\mathbf{C}, \Sigma_{\mathbf{C}})$, *where* $\mathbf{C}$ *is a finite collection of constructs and* $\Sigma_{\mathbf{C}}$ *is a set of dependencies over* $\mathbf{C}$.

Example 1. An example of a template $\mathcal{T} = (\mathbf{C}, \Sigma_{\mathbf{C}})$ contains the following set of constructs:

$$\mathbf{C} = \{\ \mathsf{Relation(name)}, \mathsf{AttributeKey(name, in)}, \mathsf{Attribute(name, nullable, in)},$$
$$\mathsf{AttributeFKey(name, in, refer)}\}$$

and the dependencies:

$$\Sigma_{\mathbf{C}} = \{\ d_1 = \mathsf{AttributeKey}(n_K, n_R) \rightarrow \mathsf{Relation}(n_R),$$
$$d_2 = \mathsf{Attribute}(n_A, u, n_R) \rightarrow \mathsf{Relation}(n_R),$$
$$d_3 = \mathsf{AttributeFKey}(n_F, n_R, n'_R) \rightarrow \mathsf{Relation}(n_R), \mathsf{Relation}(n'_R),$$
$$d_4 = \mathsf{Attribute}(n_A, u, n_R) \rightarrow (u = \mathtt{true})\}$$

The tgds d_1 and d_2 state the membership of keys and attributes to relations, respectively. The dependency d_3 states the membership of a foreign key to a relation and its reference to another relation. Finally, the egd d_4 states that we are considering only relations with attributes that allow null values.

For simplicity, in the following we will omit the membership dependencies between constructs (like d_1, d_2 and d_3 in Example 1), assuming that they belong to $\Sigma_{\mathbf{C}}$.

Let us now introduce the notion of e-schemas. Basically, an e-schema corresponds to the *encoding* of a (relational) schema and is obtained by instantiating a template.

Definition 2 (E-schemas). *An e-schema component S over a construct C is a function that associates with each property $p_1, \ldots, p_k$ of C a value a_i taken from its domain. A e-schema S over a template $(\mathbf{C}, \Sigma_{\mathbf{C}})$ is a finite set of e-schema components over constructs in $\mathbf{C}$ that satisfy $\Sigma_{\mathbf{C}}$.*

Example 2. A valid e-schema for the template of Example 1 is the following:

Relation

name
EMP
DEPT

AttributeKey

name	in
EmpName	EMP
DeptNo	DEPT

Attribute

name	nullable	in
Salary	true	EMP
Building	true	DEPT

AttributeFKey

name	in	refer
Dept	EMP	DEPT

It is easy to see that this e-schema represents a relational table EMP with EmpName as key, Salary as attribute and Dept as foreign key, and a relational table DEPT with DeptNo as key and Building as attribute.

Note that e-schemas in Example 2 remind the common way commercial databases use to store metadata in catalogs. We can therefore easily verify whether a relational schema stored in a DBMS matches a given template definition: this can be done by querying the catalog of the system and checking the satisfaction of the dependencies.

In the following, an e-schema component over a construct $C(p_1, \ldots, p_k)$ will be called a *relation* component if $C = $ Relation, an *attribute* component if $C = $ Attribute, a *key* component if $C = $ AttributeKey, a *foreign key* component if $C = $ AttributeFKey. Moreover, we will denote an e-schema component over a construct $C(p_1, \ldots, p_k)$ by $C(p_1 : a_i, \ldots, p_k : a_k)$. Alternatively, we will use, for each construct, a tabular notation with a column for each property.

3.2   Schema Exchange

Given a source template $T_1 = (\mathbf{C}_1, \Sigma_{\mathbf{C}_1})$, a target template $T_2 = (\mathbf{C}_2, \Sigma_{\mathbf{C}_2})$, and a set $\Sigma_{\mathbf{C}_1 \mathbf{C}_2}$ of *source-to-target dependencies*, that is, a set of tgds on $\mathbf{C}_1 \cup \mathbf{C}_2$, we denote a *schema exchange setting* by the triple $(T_1, T_2, \Sigma_{\mathbf{C}_1 \mathbf{C}_2})$.

Definition 3 (Schema exchange). *Let $(T_1, T_2, \Sigma_{\mathbf{C}_1 \mathbf{C}_2})$ be a schema exchange setting and S_1 a source e-schema over $(\mathbf{C}_1, \Sigma_{\mathbf{C}_1})$. The schema exchange problem consists in finding a finite target e-schema S_2 over $(\mathbf{C}_2, \Sigma_{\mathbf{C}_2})$ such that $S_1 \cup S_2$ satisfies $\Sigma_{\mathbf{C}_1 \mathbf{C}_2}$. In this case S_2 is called a solution for S_1 or, simply a solution.*

Example 3. Consider a schema exchange problem in which the source template $T_1 = (\mathbf{C}_1, \Sigma_{\mathbf{C}_1})$ and the target template $T_2 = (\mathbf{C}_2, \Sigma_{\mathbf{C}_2})$ are the following:

$$\mathbf{C}_1 = \{ \text{ Relation(name), AttributeKey(name, in), Attribute(name, in)} \}$$

$$\mathbf{C}_2 = \{ \text{ Relation(name), AttributeKey(name, in), Attribute(name, in),}$$
$$\text{AttributeFKey(name, in, refer)} \}$$

with the corresponding membership constraints in $\Sigma_{\mathbf{C}_1}$ and in $\Sigma_{\mathbf{C}_2}$.

Assume now that we would like to split relations over T_1 into a pair of relations over T_2 related by a foreign key. This scenario is graphically shown (informally) in Figure 1 and is precisely captured by the following set of tgds $\Sigma_{\mathbf{C}_1, \mathbf{C}_2}$:

$$\Sigma_{\mathbf{C}_1, \mathbf{C}_2} = \{ \text{ Relation}(n_R), \text{AttributeKey}(n_K, n_R), \text{Attribute}(n_A, n_R) \rightarrow$$
$$\text{Relation}(n_R), \text{AttributeKey}(n_K, n_R), \text{AttributeFKey}(n_F, n_R, n'_R),$$
$$\text{Relation}(n'_R), \text{AttributeKey}(n_F, n'_R), \text{Attribute}(n_A, n'_R) \}$$

Consider now the following e-schema valid for T_1:

Relation
name
EMP

AttributeKey	
name	in
EmpName	EMP

Attribute	
name	in
DeptName	EMP
Floor	EMP

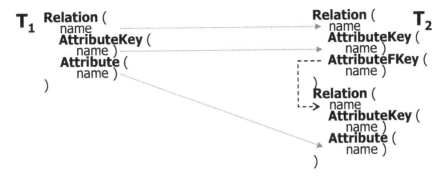

Fig. 1. Schema exchange scenario for Example 3

This e-schema has one relation called EMP with EmpName as key and two attributes: DeptName and Floor. A possible solution S'_1 for this setting is:

Relation	AttributeKey		Attribute		AttributeFKey		
name	name	in	name	in	name	in	refer
EMP	EmpName EMP		DeptName N_0		N_1	EMP	N_0
N_0	N_1	N_0	Floor N_2		N_3	EMP	N_2
N_2	N_3	N_2					

where $N_0, \ldots, N_3$ are labelled nulls. This solution contains three relations: EMP, N_0 and N_2. Relation EMP has EmpName as key and N_1, N_3 as foreign keys for N_0 and N_2, respectively. Relation N_0 has N_1 as key and DeptName as attribute. Finally, relation N_2 has N_3 as key and Floor as attribute. There are several null values because the dependencies in Σ_{C_1,C_2} do not allow the complete definition of the target e-schema.

Consider now another solution S'_2:

Relation	AttributeKey		Attribute		AttributeFKey		
name	name	in	name	in	name	in	refer
EMP	EmpName EMP		DeptName N_0		N_1	EMP	N_0
N_0	N_1	N_0	Floor N_0				

with N_0 and N_1 as labelled nulls. This solution contains two relations named EMP and N_0. Relation EMP has EmpName as key and N_1 as foreign key, relation N_0 has N_1 as key and DeptName and Floor as attributes.

Two issues arise from Example 3: which solution to choose and how to generate it. Solution S'_2 in the example seems to be less general than S'_1. This is captured precisely by the notion of homomorphisms. In fact, it is easy to see that, while there is a homomorphisms from S'_1 to S'_2, there is no homomorphism from S'_2 to S'_1. It follows that S'_2 contains "extra" information whereas S'_1 is a more general solution. As in data exchange [12,13], we argue that the "correct" solution is the most general one, in the sense above. This solution is called universal.

Definition 4 (Universal solution). *A solution S of the schema exchange problem is* universal *if there exists a homomorphism from S to all other solutions.*

The following result follows from analogous results of the data exchange problem.

Theorem 1. *Let* $(T_1, T_2, \Sigma_{C_1C_2})$ *be a data exchange setting and* S_1 *be an e-schema over* T_1. *The chase procedure over* S_1 *using* $\Sigma_{C_1C_2} \cup \Sigma_{C_2}$ *terminates and generates a universal solution.*

4   Decoding and Encoding of Relational Schemas

In this section we describe how the notion of e-schema introduced in Section 3 can be converted into a "standard" relational schema, and vice versa.

4.1   Relational Decoding

Basically, the transformation of an e-schema in a relational schema requires the definition of formulas that describe the semantics of the various components of an e-schema, according to the intended meaning of corresponding constructs.

Let S be an e-schema over a template $T = (\mathbf{C}, \Sigma_\mathbf{C})$. The *relational decoding* of S, denoted by R-DEC(S), is a pair $(\mathbf{S}, \Sigma_\mathbf{S})$ where:

- **S** contains a set of objects $R(A_1, \ldots, A_n)$ for each relation component $S \in \mathsf{S}$ such that:
  - $S(\mathsf{name}) = R$ and
  - $R = S_i(\mathsf{in})$ for the attribute components $S_1, \ldots, S_k$ in S such that $S_i(\mathsf{name}) = A_i$.
- $\Sigma_\mathbf{S}$ contains an egd over $R(A_1, \ldots, A_n) \in \mathbf{S}$ of the form:

$$R(x_1, x_2, \ldots, x_n), R(x_1, x'_2, \ldots, x'_n) \rightarrow (x_2 = x'_2, \ldots, x_n = x'_n)$$

  for each key component $S \in \mathsf{S}$ such that:
  - $S(\mathsf{name}) = A_1$ and
  - $S(\mathsf{refer}) = R$.
- $\Sigma_\mathbf{R}$ contains a tgd over a pair of relation schemas $R(A_1, \ldots, A_k, \ldots, A_n)$ and $R'(A'_k, A'_1, \ldots, A'_n)$ in $\mathbf{S}$ of the form:

$$R(x_1, \ldots, x_k, \ldots, x_m) \rightarrow R'(x_k, x'_1, \ldots, x'_n)$$

  for each foreign key component $S \in \mathsf{S}$ such that:
  - $S(\mathsf{name}) = A_k$,
  - $S(\mathsf{in}) = R$,
  - $S(\mathsf{refer}) = R'$, and
  - $R' = S'(\mathsf{in})$ for the key component S' in S such that $S'(\mathsf{name}) = A'_k$.

Example 4. Let us consider the e-schema S of Example 2 reported below:

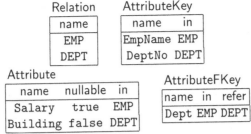

The relational representation of S is: R-DEC(S) = $(\mathbf{S}, \Sigma_\mathbf{S})$ where:

$$\mathbf{S} = \{\text{EMP}(\text{EmpName}, \text{Salary}, \text{Dept}), \text{DEPT}(\text{DeptNo}, \text{Building})\}$$

$$\begin{aligned}
\Sigma_\mathbf{S} = \{\ &\text{EMP}(x_1, x_2, x_3), \text{EMP}(x_1, x_2', x_3') \to (x_2 = x_2', x_3 = x_3'), \\
&\text{DEPT}(x_1, x_2), \text{DEPT}(x_1, x_2') \to (x_2 = x_2'), \\
&\text{EMP}(x_1, x_2, x_3) \to \text{DEPT}(x_3, x_2')\}
\end{aligned}$$

In the same line, a procedure for the *encoding* of a relational schema, that is for the transformation of a relational schema $(\mathbf{S}, \Sigma_\mathbf{S})$ into an e-schema S, can also be defined. This procedure will be illustrated in the following section.

4.2 Relational Encoding

Let $\mathbf{S}$ be a relational schema with a set of dependencies $\Sigma_\mathbf{S}$. The *encoding* of $\mathbf{S}$, denoted by R-ENC$(\mathbf{S}, \Sigma_\mathbf{S})$, is an e-schema S such that:

- for each relation $R(A_1, \ldots, A_n)$ in $\mathbf{S}$, S has a relation component m such that $m(\text{name}) = R$ and, for each attribute $A_i \in R$, S has an attribute component m_i such that:
  - $m_i(\text{name}) = A_i$,
  - $m_i(\text{nullable}) =$ true if A_i is nullable,
  - $m_i(\text{in}) = R$;
- for each egd in $\Sigma_\mathbf{S}$ of the form:

$$R(x_1, x_2, \ldots, x_n), R(x_1, x_2', \ldots, x_n') \to (x_2 = x_2', \ldots, x_n = x_n')$$

  over a relation schema $R(A_1, \ldots, A_n) \in \mathbf{S}$, S has a key component m such that:
  - $m(\text{name}) = A_i$, and
  - $m(\text{in}) = R$;
- for each tgd in $\Sigma_\mathbf{S}$ of the form:

$$R(x_1, \ldots, x_k, \ldots, x_m) \to R'(x_k, x_1', \ldots, x_n')$$

  over a pair of relation schemas $R(A_1, \ldots, A_k, \ldots, A_m)$ and $R'(A_1', \ldots, A_n')$ in $\mathbf{S}$, S has a foreign key component m such that:
  - $m(\text{name}) = A_k$,
  - $m(\text{in}) = R$, and
  - $m(\text{refer}) = R'$.

5   From Schema to Data Exchange

In this section we propose a transformation process that generates a data exchange from a given schema exchange setting.

5.1   Metaroutes and Value Correspondences

Before discussing the transformation process, two preliminary notions are needed. First of all, in order to convert the schema exchange setting into a *data* exchange setting, we need to keep track of the correspondences between the source schema and the solution of the schema exchange problem. This can be seen as an application of the data provenance problem to schema exchange. To this end, by extending to our context a notion introduced in [11], we make use of *metaroutes* to describe the relationships between source and target metadata.

Definition 5. *Let S be an e-schema and Σ be a set of dependencies. A metaroute for S is an expression of the form:*

$$I_0 \rightarrow_{\sigma_1, h_1} I_1 \ldots I_{n-1} \rightarrow_{\sigma_n, h_n} I_n$$

where $I_0 \subseteq S$ and, for each $I_{i-1} \rightarrow_{\sigma_i, h_i} I_i$ ($1 \leq i \leq n$), it is the case that I_i is the result of the application of a chase step on I_{i-1} based on the dependency $\sigma_i \in \Sigma$ and the homomorphism h_i.

Note that, since a reduced number of elements are involved in schema exchange, we can store all the metaroutes and we do not need to compute them partially and incrementally as in [11].

Metaroutes and homomorphisms are then used to derive *value correspondences* between source and target schemas.

Definition 6. *A* value correspondence *over two schemas S and S' is a triple $v = (t \in R, t' \in R', t.A_i = t'.A_j)$ where $R \in S$, $R' \in S'$, and $A_i = A_j$ is a set of equalities over the attributes of R and R', respectively.*

5.2   The S-D Transformation Process

Given a relational database over a schema S_1 and schema exchange setting $(\mathcal{T}_1, \mathcal{T}_2, \Sigma_{C_1 C_2})$ such that the encoding S_1 of S_1 is an instance of $\mathcal{T}_1$, we aim at generating a target database over a schema S_2 such that the encoding S_2 of S_2 is a universal solution for S_1. We call such generation process S-D *transformation* and it can be summarized as follows.

1. S_1 is encoded into an e-schema S_1;
2. the chase procedure is applied to S_1 using $\Sigma_{C_1 C_2}$ and metaroutes are generated during the execution of the procedure: each chase step based on the dependency $\sigma_i \in \Sigma$ and the homomorphism h_i adds an element $I_{i-1} \rightarrow_{\sigma_i, h_i} I_i$ to the metaroute;
3. the result S_2 of the chase procedure is decoded into a schema S_2;

4. for each attribute A occurring in $\mathbf{S}_2$: (i) we select the metaroute $I_0 \to_{\sigma_1,h_1} I_1 \ldots I_{n-1} \to_{\sigma_n,h_n} I_n$ such that A occur in I_n, and (ii) A is annotated in $\mathbf{S}_1$ and $\mathbf{S}_2$ with $h^{-1}(A)$, where $h = h_1 \circ \ldots \circ h_n$;
5. the annotations of the attributes in $\mathbf{S}_1$ and $\mathbf{S}_2$ are used to derive value correspondences between them;
6. a data exchange setting is generated from $\mathbf{S}_1$ and $\mathbf{S}_2$ using the generated value correspondences, on the basis of the method presented in [19].

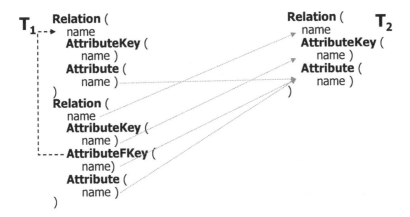

Fig. 2. Schema exchange scenario for Example 5

Example 5. Let us consider the schema exchange setting described graphically in Figure 2 and represented by the following set of tgds $\Sigma_{\mathbf{C}_1,\mathbf{C}_2}$:

$$\{ v_1 = \mathsf{Relation}(n_r), \mathsf{AttributeKey}(n_k, n_r), \mathsf{Attribute}(n_a, n_r), \mathsf{Relation}(n'_r),$$
$$\mathsf{AttributeKey}(n'_k, n'_r), \mathsf{Attribute}(n'_a, n'_r), \mathsf{AttributeFKey}(n_f, n'_r, n_r) \to$$
$$\mathsf{Relation}(n'_r), \mathsf{AttributeKey}(n'_k, n'_r), \mathsf{Attribute}(n'_a, n'_r), \mathsf{Attribute}(n_f, n'_r),$$
$$\mathsf{Attribute}(n_a, n'_r) \}$$

Intuitively, the only constraint occurring in $\Sigma_{\mathbf{C}_1,\mathbf{C}_2}$ specifies that the target is obtained by joining two source relations according to a foreign key defined between them. Now consider the following source schema:

$$\mathbf{S} = \{\mathsf{DEPT}(\mathsf{id}, \mathsf{dname}), \mathsf{EMP}(\mathsf{id}, \mathsf{ename}, \mathsf{dep})\}$$

$$\Sigma_{\mathbf{S}} = \{ \mathsf{DEPT}(x_1, x_2), \mathsf{DEPT}(x_1, x'_2) \to (x_2 = x'_2),$$
$$\mathsf{EMP}(x_1, x_2, x_3), \mathsf{EMP}(x_1, x'_2, x'_3) \to (x_2 = x'_2, x_3 = x'_3),$$
$$\mathsf{EMP}(x_1, x_2, x_3) \to \mathsf{DEPT}(x_3, x'_1)\}$$

The encoding of $\mathbf{S}$ is the e-schema S that follows:

Relation		AttributeKey			Attribute			AttributeFKey		
	name		name	in		name	in		name	in	refer
s_1	DEPT	s_3	id	DEPT	s_5	dname	DEPT	s_7	dep	EMP	DEPT
s_2	EMP	s_4	id	EMP	s_6	ename	EMP				

Let $\{s_1, \ldots, s_7\}$ be the e-components of S. The application of the chase based on the given tgd produces the set of e-schema components $\{t_1, \ldots, t_5\}$:

Relation		AttributeKey			Attribute	
	name		name	in		name	in

t_1 EMP t_2 id   EMP

t_3 ename EMP
t_4 dep   EMP
t_5 dname EMP

The metaroute generated by this chase step is: $\{s_1, \ldots, s_7\} \to_{v_1, h_1} \{t_1, \ldots, t_5\}$, where h_1 is the homomorphism:

$$\{\, n_r \mapsto \text{DEPT}, n_k \mapsto \text{id}, n_a \mapsto \text{dname}, n'_r \mapsto \text{EMP}, n'_k \mapsto \text{id}, n'_a \mapsto \text{ename}, n_f \mapsto \text{dep}\}$$

The chase ends successfully and produces an e-schema S' whose decoding is the schema $(\mathbf{S}', \Sigma_{\mathbf{S}'})$ where:

$$\mathbf{S}' = \{\text{EMP}(\text{id}, \text{ename}, \text{dep}, \text{dname})\}$$

$$\Sigma_{\mathbf{S}'} = \{\, \text{EMP}(x_1, x_2, x_3, x_4), \text{EMP}(x_1, x'_2, x'_3, x'_4) \to (x_2 = x'_2, x_3 = x'_3, x_4 = x'_4)\}$$

Now, on the basis of the above metaroute, source and target schema can be annotated as follows:

$$\mathbf{S} = \{\text{DEPT}(\text{id}[n_k], \text{dname}[n_a]), \text{EMP}(\text{id}[n'_k], \text{ename}[n'_a], \text{dep}[n_f])\}$$
$$\mathbf{S}' = \{\text{EMP}(\text{id}[n'_k], \text{ename}[n'_a], \text{dep}[n_f], \text{dname}[n_a])\}$$

The value correspondences between $\mathbf{S}$ and $\mathbf{S}'$ easily follow:

$vc_1 = (d \in \mathbf{S}.\text{DEPT}, e \in \mathbf{S}'.\text{EMP}, d.\text{dname} = e.\text{dname})$
$vc_2 = (e \in \mathbf{S}.\text{EMP}, e' \in \mathbf{S}'.\text{EMP}, e.\text{id} = e'.\text{id}, e.\text{ename} = e'.\text{ename}, e.\text{dep} = e'.\text{dep})$

We then obtain the data mapping scenario reported graphically in Figure 3. In the spirit of [19] we are now able to automatically generate a data exchange setting. Given the source schema $\mathbf{S}$, the target schema $\mathbf{S}'$ with its constraints, and the value correspondences we obtain the following tgd:

$$t_1 = \mathbf{S}.\text{EMP}(ss, en, d), \mathbf{S}.\text{DEPT}(d, dn) \to \mathbf{S}'.\text{EMP}(ss, en, d, dn)$$

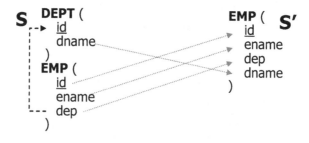

Fig. 3. Data exchange scenario for Example 5

A number of general results can be shown. First, the fact that the output of the S-D process is a "correct" result, that is, the solution of the data exchange problem reflects the semantics of the schema exchange problem given as input. In order to introduce the concept of correctness in this context, a preliminary notion is needed.

Given a tgd t, an *encoding* of t is the tgd obtained by applying the encoding procedure defined in Section 4 considering the atoms of the formula as they were relational schemas and using the dependencies in $\Sigma_{\mathbf{S}}$ for the left side of t and the dependencies $\Sigma_{\mathbf{S}'}$ for the right side of t. Note that the tgd we obtain is defined on templates.

For instance, given the tgd t_1 of the example above, the encoding of t_1 is the following tgd on templates:

$v_2 = $ Relation(EMP), AttributeKey(ss, EMP), Attribute(en, EMP),
    AttributeFKey(d, EMP, DEPT), Relation(DEPT), AttributeKey(d, DEPT),
    Attribute(dn, DEPT) $\rightarrow$ Relation(EMP), AttributeKey(ss, EMP),
    Attribute(en, EMP), Attribute(d, EMP), Attribute(dn, EMP)

This tgd v_2 is different from the original tgd v_1 for the schema exchange scenario described in Example 5. However, it can be verified that they generate the same output S' on the given input S. This exactly captures the fact that the data exchange problem obtained as output fulfills the semantics of the schema exchange problem given as input.

This intuition is captured by the following correctness result.

Theorem 2. *Let* $(\mathbf{S}, \mathbf{S}', \Sigma_{\mathbf{SS}'})$ *be the output of the* S-D *transformation process when* $(\mathcal{T}_1, \mathcal{T}_2, \Sigma_{\mathbf{C}_1\mathbf{C}_2})$ *and* $\mathbf{S}$ *are given as input and let* $\overline{\Sigma}$ *be the set of s-t tgds obtained by encoding the s-t tgds in* $\Sigma_{\mathbf{SS}'}$. *The e-schema* $\mathbf{S}'$ *is a universal solution of the schema exchange setting* $(\mathcal{T}_1, \mathcal{T}_2, \overline{\Sigma})$.

The following completeness result can also be shown. We say that a data exchange setting is *constant-free* if no constants are used in formulas.

Theorem 3. *Any constant-free data exchange setting can be obtained from the* S-D *transformation process over some schema exchange setting.*

6   Conclusion and Future Work

We have introduced the schema exchange problem, a generalization of data exchange. This problem consists of taking a schema that matches a source template, and generating a new schema for a target template, on the basis of a set of dependencies defined over the two templates. To tackle this problem, we have presented a method for the generation of a "correct" solution of the problem and a process aimed at automatically generating a data exchange setting from a schema exchange solution.

We believe that several interesting directions of research can be pursued within this framework. We just sketch some of them.

- *Expressive power of the framework.* A challenging issue to be investigated is the precise identification of the class of schema and data transformations that can be defined with the framework we have defined. This is clearly related with the formulas used to express the mappings between templates. For instance, it is an open problem to identify the formalism needed to express a schema exchange that operates over a specific number of columns.
- *Metaquerying.* A template is actually a schema and it can therefore be queried. A query over a template is indeed a *meta* query since it operates over meta-data. There are a number of meta-queries that are meaningful. For instance, we can retrieve with a query over a template the pairs of relations that can be joined, being related by a foreign key. Also, we can verify whether there is a join path between two relations.
- *Special class of solutions.* Given a schema exchange problem, can we verify whether all the solutions of the problem satisfy some relevant property? For instance, we would like to obtain only relations that are acyclic or satisfy some normal form. We are also investigating under which conditions a schema exchange problem generates a data exchange setting with certain properties, e.g., the fact that the dependencies belong to some relevant class.
- *Combining data and metadata.* The framework we have presented can be extended to support mappings and constraints involving data and metadata at the same time. This scenario also allows the user to specify the transformation of metadata into data and vice versa. For instance, we could move the name of a relational attribute into a tuple of a relation.

References

1. Atzeni, P., Cappellari, P., Bernstein, P.A.: Model-independent schema and data translation. In: Ioannidis, Y., Scholl, M.H., Schmidt, J.W., Matthes, F., Hatzopoulos, M., Boehm, K., Kemper, A., Grust, T., Boehm, C. (eds.) EDBT 2006. LNCS, vol. 3896, pp. 368–385. Springer, Heidelberg (2006)
2. Beeri, C., Vardi, M.Y.: A Proof Procedure for Data Dependencies. J. ACM 31(4), 718–741 (1984)
3. Bernstein, P.A.: Applying Model Management to Classical Meta Data Problems. In: CIDR, pp. 209–220 (2003)
4. Bernstein, P.A., Melnik, S.: Model Management 2.0: Manipulating Richer Mappings. In: Bernstein, P.A., Melnik, S. (eds.) SIGMOD, pp. 1–12 (2007)
5. Bernstein, P.A., Levy, A.Y., Pottinger, R.A.: A Vision for Management of Complex Models. SIGMOD Record 29(4), 55–63 (2000)
6. Bernstein, P.A., Rahm, E.: Data Warehouse Scenarios for Model Management. In: Laender, A.H.F., Liddle, S.W., Storey, V.C. (eds.) ER 2000. LNCS, vol. 1920, pp. 1–15. Springer, Heidelberg (2000)
7. Bhagwat, D., Chiticariu, L., Tan, W.C., Vijayvargiya, G.: An Annotation Management System for Relational Databases. In: VLDB, pp. 900–911 (2004)
8. Bowers, S., Delcambre, L.M.L.: The uni-level description: A uniform framework for representing information in multiple data models. In: Song, I.-Y., Liddle, S.W., Ling, T.-W., Scheuermann, P. (eds.) ER 2003. LNCS, vol. 2813, pp. 45–58. Springer, Heidelberg (2003)

9. Buneman, P., Khanna, S., Tan, W.C.: Why and Where: A Characterization of Data Provenance. In: Van den Bussche, J., Vianu, V. (eds.) ICDT 2001. LNCS, vol. 1973, pp. 316–330. Springer, Heidelberg (2000)
10. Buneman, P., Khanna, S., Tan, W.C.: On Propagation of Deletion and Annotations Through Views. In: PODS, pp. 150–158 (2002)
11. Chiticariu, L., Tan, W.C.: Debugging Schema Mappings with Routes. In: VLDB, pp. 79–90 (2006)
12. Fagin, R., Kolaitis, P.G., Popa, L.: Data exchange: getting to the core. ACM Trans. Database Syst. 30(1), 174–210 (2005)
13. Fagin, R., Kolaitis, P.G., Miller, R.J., Popa, L.: Data exchange: Semantics and Query Answering. Theor. Comput. Sci. 336(1), 89–124 (2005)
14. Geerts, F., Kementsietsidis, A., Milano, D.: MONDRIAN: Annotating and querying databases through colors and blocks. In: ICDE, pp. 82–93 (2006)
15. Lakshmanan, L.V.S., Sadri, F., Subramanian, S.N.: SchemaSQL: An extension to SQL for multidatabase interoperability. ACM Trans. Database Syst. 26(4), 476–519 (2001)
16. McBrien, P., Poulovassilis, A.: Data Integration by Bi-Directional Schema Transformation Rules. In: ICDE, pp. 227–238 (2003)
17. Mihaila, G., Raschid, L., Vidal, M.-E.: Querying "quality of data" metadata. In: IEEE META-DATA, IEEE Computer Society Press, Los Alamitos (1999)
18. Papotti, P., Torlone, R.: Heterogeneous Data Translation through XML Conversion. J. Web Eng. 4(3), 189–204 (2005)
19. Popa, L., Velegrakis, Y., Miller, R.J., Hernández, M.A., Fagin, R.: Translating Web Data. In: Bressan, S., Chaudhri, A.B., Lee, M.L., Yu, J.X., Lacroix, Z. (eds.) CAiSE 2002 and VLDB 2002. LNCS, vol. 2590, pp. 598–609. Springer, Heidelberg (2003)
20. Wyss, C.M., Robertson, E.: Relational Interoperability. TODS 30(2) (2005)

A Conceptual Modeling Methodology Based on Niches and Granularity

Sonia Berman and Thembinkosi Daniel Semwayo

Computer Science Department, University of Cape Town, South Africa
{sonia,dsemwayo}@cs.uct.ac.za

Abstract. This paper presents a methodology for conceptual modeling which is based on a new modeling primitive, the niche, and associated constructs granularity and reconciliation. A niche is an environment where entities interact for a specific purpose, playing specific roles, and according to the norms and constraints of that environment. Granularity refers to the relative level of power or influence of an entity within a niche. Reconciliation is a relationship from N entities onto one reconciled entity, and represents explicitly a situation where two or more different perspectives of the same entity have been reconciled, by negotiation, into a single consensus view. The methodology we propose provides a systematic method of designing conceptual models along with a process for normalising inappropriate relationships. Normalising is a prescriptive process for identifying and remedying inconsistencies within a model based on granularities. Drawing on a number of case studies, we show how niches and granularity make complexity easier to manage, highlight inaccuracies in a model, identify opportunities for achieving project goals, and reduce semantic heterogeneity.

1 Introduction

Conceptual modeling is a difficult task. It requires a group of people, typically from different fields of expertise, to understand a complex situation and to agree on an appropriate set of abstractions that captures correctly and completely the characteristics and interactions of the entities involved. While data models such as the ER model or UML provide many useful constructs to simplify this problem, there is little prescriptive guidance on how to develop a model, or how to evaluate one that has been designed. Errors and omissions in a conceptual model can have far-reaching consequences, as physical systems that are built from these models can be faulty; incorrect or incompatible data can be collected; and data can be integrated and analysed inappropriately leading to invalid conclusions about the real world.

We aim to improve on conceptual modeling by proposing a methodology that can address these problems, specifically:

- providing mechanisms to handle complexity so as to reduce inaccuracies and omissions in the model
- prescribing a sequence of steps to carry out, and constraints to check, so that the task is tackled in a systematic way

C. Parent et al. (Eds.): ER 2007, LNCS 4801, pp. 338–358, 2007.

- reducing semantic heterogeneity – the phenomenon whereby different people use different terms for the same concept, or use the same term with subtly different meanings - as occurs particularly with multi-disciplinary teams
- where applicable, depicting the situation in a way that highlights where interventions can achieve project goals – i.e. where there is an opportunity for improving the real-world situation being modeled

In studying a number of projects where we acted as consultants, we realized that many of the modeling problems arose because entities and relationships were described in isolation, rather than in the context of the particular sphere in which they operated. As a result, much was omitted from the models altogether because certain interaction contexts weren't considered at all, and because the different roles that entities play in different contexts were not recognised. We accordingly introduce early in the methodology the notion of a ***niche*** (system context or sphere of operation) to ensure that such errors and omissions are minimized. We further observed that missing entities and roles were more likely to be noticed when the team was asked to consider the relative levels of influence (power, impact or status) of entities in each context. This often showed e.g. how an individual can have greater influence in one niche in which s/he operates than in another niche, because of different roles s/he plays in these different contexts. We have named this meta-property of an entity within a niche its ***granularity*** or granular level, and the methodology requires that designers assign granularities to entities after niches have been determined. Constraints on relationships involving entities of differing granularity (unequal relationships) are then checked: either they are modeling errors or else they are anomalies in the real world. Such anomalies highlight a vital aspect of the domain being modeled, namely interactions which are suboptimal. In many domains, such as the socio-economic projects we have tackled, a key objective is to improve the status quo; interaction anomalies indicate precisely where improvements are possible. In addition to niches and granularity, we propose a ***reconciles*** relationship which serves to explicitly document where semantic heterogeneity has been identified and resolved. This indicates where and how differing views of the same entity have been replaced by a consensus view after negotiation among the design team.

In sections 2 and 3, the paper describes the new modeling constructs and the proposed methodology. Thereafter we discuss experiments in which the methodology has been applied, highlighting advantages and disadvantages noted during those workshops and case studies. Section 5 presents related work, and we conclude with a summary of the main ideas and some suggestions for future research.

2 New Modeling Primitive and Associated Constructs

In this section we introduce the niche modeling primitive and its associated constructs: granularity and reconciliation. We show why they are needed, how to recognise them and introduce them into a model, and when to do so. We also discuss what effects, if any, poor use of the new constructs would have.

2.1 Niches

When describing the entities in a domain and the relationships between them, it is important to bear in mind the different contexts in which interactions occur. In any project, it is important that no interaction context is forgotten, and that the entities and their relationships are accurately depicted by taking into account the conditions and norms that apply in that specific context. Drawing on the biological notion, we define a niche as a specific context in which entities interact for a specific functional purpose, favouring particular individuals or groups, and behaving according to the conventions and constraints of that particular environment. In a niche there is a stable pattern of behaviour and structuring of the community, and interactions take place accordingly. A niche frequently exhibits emergent properties, which are attributes that do not necessarily apply to the individual members but do apply to the niche as a whole.

A niche can be defined as a 7-tuple (S, T, M, N, H, A, P) where

S is a spatial location occupied by this niche

T is a time interval

M is a non-empty set of member entities present at location S for part of time interval T

N is a non-empty set of interactions between entities, the normal behaviour in that niche

H is a hierarchical structuring of the entities M based on relative impact/influence/power

i.e. H is a function mapping every m in M onto a granular level g i.e. $H(m)=g$

A is a set of attributes of the niche which aren't attributes of its members M

P is a possibly empty set of environmental parameters that hold at location S during time T

An example of a niche attribute is its functional purpose or its quality/performance. The environmental parameters describe domain conditions that make the niche viable – e.g. in an ecological domain these would be climate factors, whereas in a business domain these would be political and economic factors. We note further the following niche constraints:

If $m \in M$ then $H(m)$ is unique i.e. every entity has exactly one granular level in a niche.

If $m1 \in M$ and $m2 \in M$ and $m1$ is-part-of $m2$ then $H(m1) \leq H(m2.)$

If $m1 \in M$, $m2 \in M$, $R \in N$ and $R(m1,m2)$ then $\exists t \in T$ s.t. $In(S,t,m1)$ and $In(S,t,m2)$ i.e. for two entities to interact in a niche they must exist in that niche at the same time.

For all $m \in M$, $\exists t \in T$ s.t. $In(S,t,m) = $ false i.e. entities do not have to remain in a niche throughout its existence.

Considering the familiar example of an academic environment, it should be clear that individuals behave differently in a staff meeting (administration) than they would in a research meeting, because these are two different niches. An academic might play the role of subordinate in a staff meeting if she were a junior lecturer, the role of critic at a research paper presentation, and the role of student in a meeting with her thesis supervisor. In each of these niches we can identify relationships between academics, but the nature of these relationships varies according to the niche in which the interaction takes place. The functional purpose of the staff meeting, the paper presentation and the supervision meeting differs, with interactions favouring the head of department, the speaker and the supervisor, respectively. Even in this simple example it is evident that, without considering these niches, modelers may well have used only one "meeting" relationship between academic staff entities, and failed to recognise the different roles that they play and the extra data that should be collected accordingly.

To determine the niches in a domain, it is generally best to examine the life-cycle of the key entities and the value chain of that domain. The value chain concept was first used for business system modeling [1] but has since been applied in other contexts. It comprises the sequence of core, value-adding activities of a system. For example, in the business world, the niches would be purchasing, infrastructure, production, sub-contracting, management, marketing, etc. In education the niches would be application, registration, tuition, examination, qualification, administration, infrastructure, etc. Some niches will be sufficiently well understood by designers to be modeled directly, but most will be too complex and require decomposition into sub-niches, resulting in one or more hierarchies comprising niches nested within each other. Most conceptual modelers are able to identify the value chain for their project, to identify those nodes which require further decomposition, and to find appropriate sub-niches for these – simply because they are familiar with the domain and hence with its processes and sub-sections. What is the danger of choosing the wrong niches? If designers can articulate for each niche its functional purpose, favoured members and behavioural norms, then there is little chance that the niche is not a valid context or environment within the project domain. But even if a "wrong niche" should be included, it still gives the same modeling benefits: it forces designers to think about where their entities and relationships will be found, how this affects their behaviour, what exists around them, how these influence each other, which entities are more favoured, and for what purpose they interact; producing a better model as a result. It focuses the mind not only on what entities exist in a relationship, but also on where, why and how they interact. Including entity life-cycles and domain value chain diagrams ensures that all contexts - the full scope of the project - is modeled, reducing the risk of significant omissions.

Because of its usefulness in identifying niches, we include a value chain diagram (figure 1) as part of our model, where any node can be shown at the head of a hierarchy of sub-niches into which it has been divided.

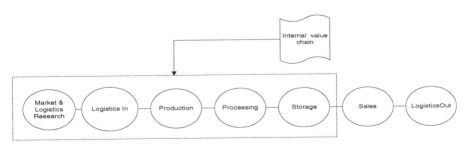

Fig. 1. Value chain diagram

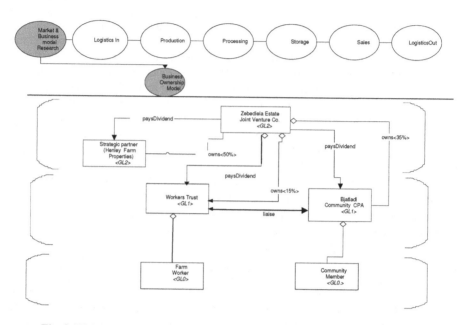

Fig. 2. Niche model showing business ownership of an agricultural estate property

The model for each niche or sub-niche is drawn below the niche, as shown in figure 2.

2.2 Granularity

An important property of a relationship is the relative level of influence, power or impact of the entities involved. We call this the granular level or granularity of the entity, which is always given relative to a base entity – the main object in the project – which has granularity zero. Entities with similar impact, influence or power would thus also have granularity 0, those with less would have granularity of -1, those with even less have granularity of -2, and so on; while those with greater influence have granularity of +1, those with still more influence have +2, etc. Granularity is relative, it is not meaningful as an absolute measure but only in comparison with other entities, as it reflects the level at which an entity operates in a particular context relative to others in that niche.

For example, where humans interact, their relative power, status or influence indicates their granularity. In most institutions, status or ranking within the hierarchy is well-known, and interactions between individuals with very different granularity (status) rarely if ever occur. If we are to model a niche correctly, we must take cognisance of the granularity of entities in a relationship in order to determine whether the correct entities are being modeled in that context. To take the familiar example of a university model, a relationship between the Vice-Chancellor and a student is contrary to the norms and constraints of the environment, unless that student is a particular student such as a StudentLeader who has higher status/granularity than his peers. In an agricultural example, rainfall has higher granularity (impact or influence) than a farmer, so if these two entities appear in a relationship there is again an anomaly that should be addressed – here the rainfall entity should be replaced by another that operates at the correct level of influence and scale for the farm context, such as a local water source like a dam or irrigation channel. Modeling with entities at the correct granular level for the niche/context reduces the chances of collecting incorrect data, such as rainfall figures for an area rather than information about farm dams and irrigation systems. Similarly, collecting data about students who meet with the Vice-Chancellor would be useless without information about the student body they represent. Thus we see that granularity aids the designer in finding the right abstractions to represent real-world phenomena, by making it far more likely that entities at the right level for the niche/context will be used.

By annotating entities with their granularity (denoted GL for Granular Level and written after the entity name, as shown in figure 2) the relationships in a model can be studied to detect inequalities or anomalies, which imply that there is either a problem in the model or in the real world situation. Often modelers will realise in such cases that they have failed to recognise that an entity is playing a particular role in some context/niche, different from its other interactions in other niches. This in turn will highlight the need for either a generalisation hierarchy (e.g. MonopolySupplier *is-a* Supplier, or StudentLeader *is-a* Student) or an aggregation (e.g. Supplier *is-part-of* SupplierGroup, or Student *is-part-of* StudentCommitee) to be added to the model, and the entity in the relationship replaced with a new entity such as MonopolySupplier or SupplierGroup. If granularity is not taken into account in modeling, data is typically collected for the entities at differing resolutions, and so some of the data goes unused.

As granularity is a measure of gravitas or influence, it is only applicable to entities, not relationships; only to the actors or agents that are involved in interactions according to their power/impact/status. The granularity of an aggregate or composite entity cannot be less than the granularity of any of its component parts. For example, a Union entity representing an organised group of people cannot have lower granularity than its constituent union member entities. There is no corresponding constraint for *is-a* (subtype/generalization) hierarchies; if S *is-a* T then an S may have greater influence/power than a T entity, or it may have less, depending on the nature of the specialization. For example, StudentLeader *is-a* Student with higher granularity than Student in many niches, but StudentTeacher *is-a* Teacher with lower granularity than Teacher in many niches.

Like many aspects of modeling, granularity assignment is subjective. It will require the design team interrogating the clients or domain experts about relative levels of influence, just as they would ask them about other aspects of relationships such as cardinality or participation constraints. Modeling a niche however reduces subjectivity significantly, as the context and scale of activity is defined. We note further that incorrect use of granularity in a model will not introduce new modeling errors. It would mean that entities in a relationship are depicted as having equal influence when in fact the one has less power/impact than the other. Essentially the model is then no worse than it would have been if granularity were not used at all – a modeling error or omission remains undetected because there has also been an error in granularity assignment. The chances of this occurring when a domain is well understood are slight however, because granularity is considered for every relationship, and again when checking the level associated entities across aggregation / composition hierarchies. Lastly we note that granularity will not add value to conceptual modeling if the application is so simple that multiple levels do not exist; while checking relative impact/status of entities in such systems may not provide new insights, however, it will cause developers to carefully consider design decisions they have made. Most systems are more complex than they appear to be however, so such simple systems will be rare. Granularity is useful in separating concerns when complexity is revealed even in a simple study – for example in a retail scenario, small-businesses and big-businesses differ in granularity and exhibit different roles, attributes and relationships in different contexts.

2.3 Reconciliation

Semantic heterogeneity is a well-known problem in modeling and design. It refers to two kinds of situation: one where different individuals use different terms without

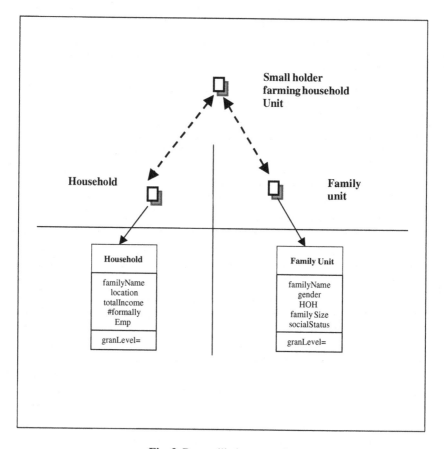

Fig. 3. Reconciliation example

realising that they have the same real-world object in mind; the other where people all use the same term for a concept without realising that they have differing ideas of what exactly is meant by that term. Thus e.g. a botanist may speak of miombo scrubland and a geographer of tree-bush savanna without realising that they are referring to the same thing, since a botanist describes vegetation according to function and the dominant species in the area whereas a geographer provides a structural description according to the relative proportions of tree, bush and grass. Or two individuals may discuss "household" without realising that the economist means a unit with an income and location, while the sociologist has in mind a group of people living together with a range of ages, incomes, genders, etc.

When niches and granularity are used in modeling, we find that semantic heterogeneity is detected and resolved as a bonus side-effect. For example, when granularity is considered, the difference between a geologist's and an engineer's concept of a rock profile becomes evident because the geologist works at a much bigger scale or granularity than does the engineer. When designing in the context of a financial niche, the economists' notion of a household as an income-generating object is the view shared by the whole team; and when modeling the sociological niche all designers see the household as a group of separate individuals with different ages, genders, etc. We represent explicitly in our models the reconciling of entities wherever this occurs: if e.g. Household is an entity with different attributes in different niche models, the reconcile diagram shows how a consolidated Household entity is derived from these, as shown in figure 3.

In this example, differences in granularity would have led the design team to realise that the household of the sociological niche was in fact a composition of people, one of whom is the head-of-household who was viewed as "the household" itself in the financial niche. By representing this in a reconcile diagram as well, the possibility of different interpretations is highlighted and the chances of incorrect future development or data collection are reduced. The utility of this construct lies therefore in explicitly including as part of a model the fact that people had different perceptions of an entity, to indicate the similarities and differences between these views, and to show how the differing views were unified. Without this, future model users will be unaware that there are different ways of looking at the entity, let alone how to relate each others' perspectives to their own.

3 The Design Methodology

In our experience, conceptual modeling is typically done by groups of individuals who first discuss and agree on their goal and objectives as a project team, and then brainstorm the entities involved and the relationships between them. A complex picture emerges, which the team must then improve upon in order to remove errors, redundancy and inconsistency; to discover and remedy omissions; and to decide which abstractions to use in depicting the situation. As this is a complex process, a consultant or facilitator is typically engaged to manage and assist.

3.1 A Systematic Approach to Conceptual Modeling

We propose a methodology which requires a facilitator, skilled in conceptual modeling, to guide the team, and which commences in the normal way as described above. The steps of the methodology are as follows:

1. Define the goal of the project, and list the *objectives* to be met in order to achieve this goal.
2. Draw a *value chain diagram* depicting the main contexts or niches (spheres of operation) in which interactions take place.
3. Consider each node of the value chain, and draw an ER model for the entities and interactions that take place in this context. If a node is too large or complex, decompose it into sub-niches first and develop a model for each sub-niche. We call the resulting set of models the *niche models*.
4. Choose a key entity, that is central to the project goal and that occurs in most (if not all) niche models, and assign this a granularity of zero. For each niche model in which this key entity appears, assign *granularities* to all other entities, based on their relative level of influence/power – those with less influence being assigned negative granularities, etc. For any remaining niche model, assign granularities to entities in a similar way. Flag relationships involving entities of different granularity. An example is shown in figure 4.
5. *Normalize* flagged relationships: identify missing generalizations (role identification) or aggregations (composite entities), remedying the model and removing the relationship flag wherever these are found. For each relationship that is still flagged, consider whether this is an opportunity for achieving a project objective. If so, introduce the corresponding intervention in the model by adding dashed entities and relationships to represent these proposed changes to the status quo. Any relationships that are still flagged represent unsolved problems in the real world. The result of normalising the model of figure 4 is shown in figure 5. Here, specific operational staff for providing direct help to farmers have been identified through normalization.
6. Finally, create *reconcile* diagrams to record every situation where divergent views of the same entity were merged, or were resolved through generalisation, aggregation or composition.

We distinguish sortals from other entities – these are ontological entities like "person" that inarguably exist independent of context, and have a stable set of attributes. Other entities in the model are aggregations, compositions or specialisation of sortals. Sortals are useful for obtaining cross-niche perspectives, since the same sortal will appear in several niches corresponding to different roles played in different contexts. An over-arching view of the niche models is easily formulated by taking some key entity and looking at all the relationships in which it participates. If all occurrences of the subtypes of a sortal are considered across all niches, one gets a global picture of the interactions that such entities can be involved in. In one case study, for example, this highlighted the fact that an individual could be a community member, a leader, a shareholder and a director, and be financially rewarded repeatedly in each separate role.

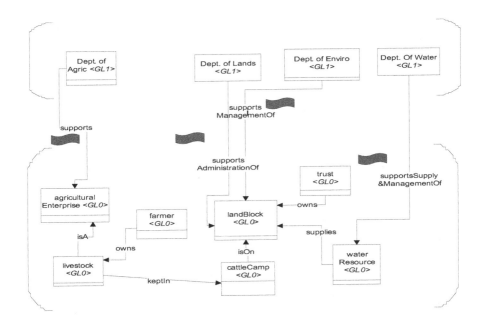

Fig. 4. Flags highlight cross-granular relationships in a niche model

3.2 Relationship Normalisation

Normalisation in step five of the methodology involves examining the entities in each flagged relationship to detect any missing specialisations or aggregations. Where these do not apply, this means the relationship is problematic in the real world, rather than being a modeling error. In this case, normalisation requires that the project team apply their mind to this opportunity or challenge that has just been highlighted. If they come up with a practical solution, they include it in the model as a possible intervention/strategy (denoted using dashed lines); otherwise the flags remain, as annotations that highlight anomalous relationships in the system. The designers thus leave a flag in place whenever they have checked that the correct entities are indeed being used and the relationship does in reality involve entities of unequal power/influence. In projects where a goal is to improve the system being modeled, the team would first look for ways of remedying the situation, and only leave the flag in place where these do not exist. When our methodology is not followed, intervention strategies suggested in such projects are often doomed to fail precisely because the niche is not taken into account; suggestions don't address problems in the context of the sphere of operation, and the crucial factor of relative impact levels is not considered.

As an example, a relationship between a farmer and a bank would be flagged because the granularity (power/influence) of the bank is greater than that of the farmer. This can be remedied by an intervention such as the introduction of a farmer's union or grouping of some sort, which would have more influence than a single individual. In other situations specialisation, rather than composition, is needed. A flagged relationship between Field and HighValueCrop is an example, where the

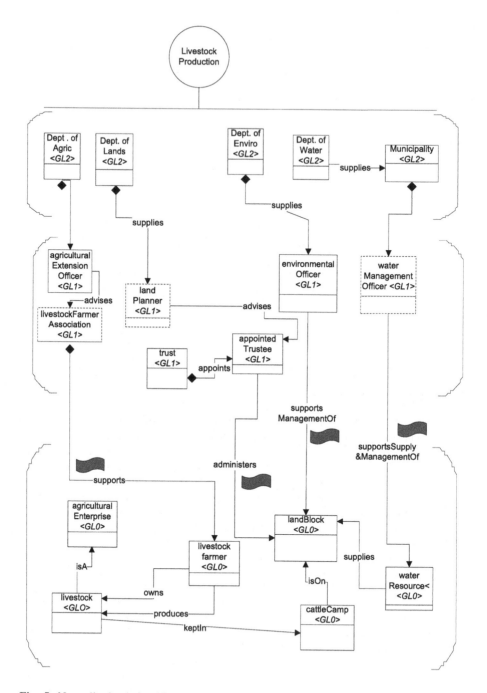

Fig. 5. Normalised relationships, with intervention opportunities/plans shown using dotted rectangles

latter has a higher granularity because it represents a crop which is sold on global rather than local markets. To handle this flagged relationship requires that the Field be a special type of field that can support a HighValueCrop, e.g. one which is irrigated and treated appropriately. Thus a specialisation of Field, called say HighValueField, is required here. Additional entities and relationships providing the extra inputs that such a field requires (irrigation etc.) have to be added to the model at the same time. This might be an intervention opportunity, or it might simply be rectifying a modeling error – if in fact the fields being modeled are already being irrigated and treated, this aspect may simply have been omitted in the model, despite being crucial to the production of a HighValueCrop. The flagging of cross-granularity relationships brings the problem to the modeler's attention, thus increasing the chance of such an omission being remedied. Similarly, in the previous example, it is possible that a farmer's union does already exist but was erroneously omitted from the model; the flagged relationship highlights the need to model that the bank is approached by a group representative rather than an individual. For the example in figure 5, relationships between high-level government departments and the lower-granularity entities that they support have a considerable gap in power/influence level. The intervention that emerges, viz. to consult the appropriate official in that department, is explicitly added to the model, but using dashed notation to indicate a future plan rather than an existing situation.

Note that these normalisation examples also illustrate how semantic heterogeneity is reduced as a natural side-effect of using our methodology. Often designers use the same term but have different subtypes in mind, e.g. all will speak of a "field", but some will have in mind a HighValueField (irrigated, fertilised, etc.) and others not; or they will all use the word "farmer" but some will mean subsistence-farmer and others commercial-farmer. Our methodology brings such discrepancies to light and ensures that the generalisation hierarchy for "field" or "farmer" is added to the model. In step 6, reconcile diagrams are also produced, so that there is a record of the fact that conflicting definitions of "field" and "farmer" have been resolved, and how.

4   Experiments

While the model and methodology were still being developed, we applied it in a number of projects involving multi-disciplinary teams. In these initial experiments, which we call the workshops, we explained the new concepts, facilitated application of the methodology, and then pointed out the benefits of our approach. We evaluated the usability of the methodology through questionnaires and interviews. As a result of these three initial workshops the model, methodology and tools were improved considerably based on observations and feedback.

Then, after the model and methodology had been developed, we used them in a number of case studies for clients in the field. As it isn't possible to "prove" that a methodology is beneficial, these case studies were done in an attempt to demonstrate by example the validity, applicability, and advantages of our methodology over conventional modeling practices. In each case study therefore, the initial design produced by the team was compared to the final model obtained after applying our methodology, in order to discover any differences and identify which benefits and shortcomings, if any, were introduced using our approach.

4.1 Initial Workshops

Our initial experiments were conducted while the model and methodology were being refined. By observing novices discussing, questioning and applying our approach we were able to evaluate its usability and identify ways in which it could be improved or extended. For each of the workshops we drew up a pro forma plan of our expectations beforehand, started the workshop by introducing the new concepts, facilitated application of the methodology by the team while a co-worker observed, and obtained feedback from participants through questionnaires and interviews.

The aims of the workshops were to:

1. determine whether participants appreciated the danger of inaccurate and incomplete models
2. discover whether participants felt that they knew how to solve such problems
3. establish the validity of niches, granularity and reconciles
4. assess the applicability of the methodology
5. evaluate the usability of our approach
6. elicit user perceptions of the model and methodology
7. gauge whether the methodology reduced semantic heterogeneity

At the first workshop a multi-disciplinary team from such diverse fields as computer science, engineering, ecology, geography, zoology, geology, biology and financial management, tackled the problem of integrated coastal zone management. In this workshop, as a first step, only granularity was introduced; the project was small enough to manage complexity by modeling within a single broad context, without niches. With the aid of the facilitator (ontological engineer), the team assigned granularities to entities and normalised cross-granular relationships; they were even able to identify interventions to improve the status quo. For example, a relationship between the DistrictTourismAuthority and the CommunityOrganisation, entities with different granularity, led to the team identifying a potential strategic partnership to remove this anomaly.

At the start of the workshop, nine of the fifteen participants were aware of the dangers of modeling errors. Of these nine however, only two realised that such errors would not be "automatically" corrected in software. After the workshop, all but one of the participants were convinced of the dangers of poor modeling. All but one were convinced that granularity was valid and useful, while 13 of the 15 felt it was applicable in their domain (2 unsure). On a rating scale from 1 to 5, two subjects chose 5 (our approach much better than other methodologies), 12 chose 4 (better), and one chose 3 (same as others). Comments noted i.a. the following benefits: "improved data classification", "the modeling process (is) more specific", "assist in focusing (the) project", and "able to minimise risk". From observations during the workshop, it was clear that normalisation involving specialisation hierarchies for different roles contributed significantly to a reduction in semantic heterogeneity. Clearly a key factor in avoiding semantic heterogeneity lies in distinguishing between entities and entity roles.

In the second workshop a team of engineers and geologists, amongst others, modeled a gold mining project using the full methodology, including niches and granularity, under the guidance of a facilitator. Granularity was particularly useful here because of the natural tendency for engineers to describe rocks and related objects at a far smaller scale than do geologists. Participants were able to model with niches, and found them particularly useful for defining emergent properties, i.e. properties of the group or niche that cannot be traced back to properties of the individuals in that niche. It was also noted that niches and granularity helped the team to define attributes at the correct scale or level of detail, because the context and impact level was taken into account. Usability results were similar to the first workshop: all but one were convinced that granularity was valid and useful. Five subjects felt the methodology was applicable in their field, three were unsure and one thought is was not applicable in his domain. On the rating scale of 1 to 5, one participant rated the methodology 3 (same as others), three people rated it 4 (better than others) and five participants rated it 5 out of 5 (much better than other methodologies).

The third workshop was a follow-up study in which the same group who had attended workshop one, set about refining and extending the model they had produced there. It was encouraging to see that they had assimilated the ideas to the extent that they required only a brief introduction to remind them how the methodology worked. They also found using niches helpful in handling the increased complexity of the extended task. Overall the workshops indicated that the model and methodology were usable and broadly applicable, and led to improvements not only in the methodology itself but also in the toolkit we used to support the process.

4.2 Modeling Toolkit

In the first workshop, we customised the Poseidon UML modeling tool [2] to suit our model, and the facilitator used this during the modeling exercise. It was discovered that participants who were not computer scientists struggled to understand these diagrams, which hampered rather than helped the process, because of its sophisticated interface and the richness of the diagrams and repositories it displayed. For the next workshop, we used a far simpler tool which was geared specifically to support our methodology. Surprisingly, the use of this simpler tool during the design was still problematic, with discussion often relating to the tool rather than the task at hand. For the final workshop we used a tablet on which designs were hand-drawn, and found that this worked far better. The facilitator would input these hand-drawn diagrams to our simple tool each night, and discuss this with the group the next morning. At that stage the team was not attempting to be creative but rather to understand the implications of what they had previously designed, and were able to assimilate lessons learned from inputting diagrams into the tool. Thus we conclude that a tool should not be used during creative design phases, but rather when a design is being reviewed, evaluated and refined.

4.3 Case Studies

Using our methodology we have developed models for the following projects: a system for monitoring sustainability in land reform projects; a citrus farm development study; an eco-tourism investigation; a knowledge base for the Department of Water and Forestry; a feasibility study for the establishment of a land and water management regional database; a small business linkages system for the City of Cape Town and for the provincial government; and a strategy development tool for the South African Land Reform Programme. In this section we briefly describe aspects of one case study to illustrate some of the benefits of using our approach.

The Eastern Cape Development Corporation (ECDC) exists to improve the standard of living of a South African rural community, the Dwesa Cwebe. The community, represented by a Dwesa Cwebe Land Trust (DCLT), has a joint venture company with the ECDC - called the Operational Structure (OPS) - each owning 50% of the shares.

OPS owns the local Haven Bashe hotel which is operated by a private entrepreneur. It is hoped that in the long run the ECDC will relinquish ownership in OPS.

4.3.1 Initial Conceptual Model

The multi-disciplinary project team first used the conventional approach of stating project objectives, brainstorming to identify pertinent entities, and then drawing up a conceptual model indicating these entities and the relationships between them. We first outline this initial modeling that took place. Two objectives were identified to meet the project goal:

1. Create employment opportunities linked to the Haven Bashe hotel
2. Create employment opportunities linked to the Dwesa Cwebe nature reserve lodges and chalets.

Brainstorming was then done as a team, to share ideas and explore the problem collectively, mind-mapping the thoughts that emerged. From this mind-map a conceptual model was drawn as shown in figure 6.

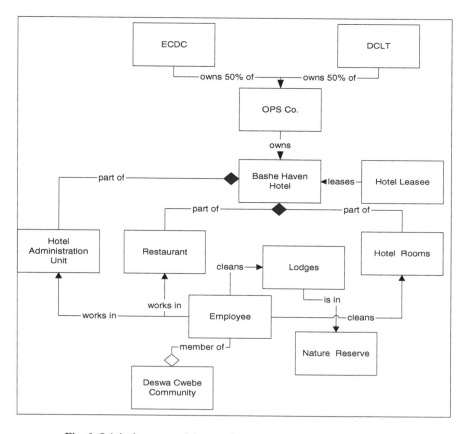

Fig. 6. Original conceptual data model, before applying our methodology

It was observed that

- No more then 50 persons are employed by the hotel and surrounding Nature Reserve. The community has a population of 2382 households. Unemployment is therefore rife.
- Although the DCLT owns 50% of the hotel, it has not been able to leverage the full potential offered by the tourism industry.

The model provided a static, given, hopeless situation from the community's point of view.

4.3.2 Applying the Methodology

At this stage our methodology was applied by the team, with the author as facilitator. First, the value chain, niches and sub-niches were identified for the project, as shown in figure 7.

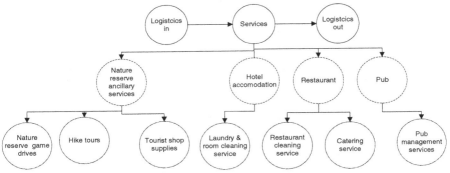

Fig. 7. Haven Bashe Project value chain and niches

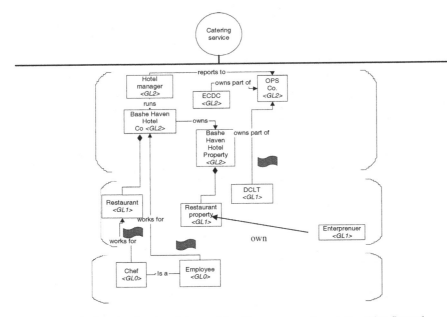

Fig. 8. Catering Service niche model, with cross-granular relationships flagged

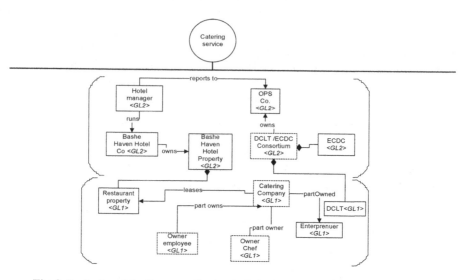

Fig. 9. Revised model, after normalisation had yielded some innovative interventions

It was clear that the use of the value chain and its decomposition into sub-niches was considerably broadening the team's view of the problem, and bringing new aspects to bear that had not emerged in the earlier brainstorming or modelling sessions. Models were then drawn up for each sub-niche, granularities assigned to entities, and cross-granular relation-ships flagged. The resulting model for the Catering Service niche is shown in figure 8.

After normalising the flagged relationships, the model was refined to obtain that of figure 9. In so doing, intervention opportunities were identified. An idea emerged of forming a catering company part-owned by the chef and other restaurant employees. This effectively gave greater influence/power to those community members working in the restaurant. As a direct result of distinguishing the service niche from the broader project context, a strategy of forming separate enterprises serving the tourism industry was born, thus better leveraging opportunities offered by the hotel and nature reserve; and at the same time giving the workers from the community part ownership of these service enterprises.

There were several other situations where benefits arose from identifying and exploring specific niches and examining the granularity of the entities interacting there. For example, it was established that there was a relationship between the hotel lessee and the ECDC (nepotism) and this was a source of friction with the DCLT, resulting in an environment so fraught with suspicion and non-cooperation that it almost paralysed the project. As another example, the granularities of the "equal partners" in the joint venture company differed, since the ECDC, being a quasi-government organization, were in a privileged position (with access to information such as future plans, etc.) and were more highly skilled than the members of the Trust. Relations between the ECDC and the DCLT were particularly acrimonious with all parties seeing the DCLT as a "poor relation". Another strategy emerged in trying to resolve this difference in granularity: it was decided that the ECDC and the

DCLT form a consortium that owned the OPS, so that they could be a single entity working together, rather than being seen as two rivals.

As a result of studying granularities and identifying intervention opportunities such as those illustrated above, the objectives of the Haven Bashe project were re-stated as follows:

1. Participate in the opportunities provided for the Haven Bashe hotel as employees and owners
2. Participate in the tourism industry by providing tourist related services inside and outside the Dwesa Cwebe nature reserve.

This represented a significant shift in the expected strategic outcomes compared to the original approach. From this and many other case studies, our methodology was seen to be highly useful in developing better models and in identifying ways of achieving project goals.

5 Related Work

In a previous paper [3] we proposed using niches in GIS system design. This paper follows on that work, describing a model and methodology for using niches, granularity and reconciliations that we have used extensively in many real-world projects. We are not aware of any other model that incorporates such modeling constructs, nor of any comparable methodology. In ecological modeling the focus is on spatial granularity, the cartographic scale of representation, at the expense of other important variables such as time, context and functional granularity. For example, [4] emphasise the importance of describing ecological entities at the relevant spatio-temporal scale, and state that "There is no reason to assume that concepts, theories or components, defined on some scale of resolution, will necessarily be applicable to ecosystem phenomena at some other scale level" [5]. In geographical information system modeling, recent thinking [6] is that the traditional approach of identifying separate layers or themes (e.g. vegetation, rainfall, slope) is inadequate because ecosystems are not disjoint but are connected wholes. [5] proposes that the rate of change within an ecosystem be used to group ecological processes into functional hierarchies. For example, bio-chemical processes such as photosynthesis occur within short time spans, while tree growth takes years, soil erosion decades, and denudation hundreds of years.

In [7] an ecosystem is defined as a system describing the relationships of organisms to their physical environment and to one another. A niche (also called a habitat, ecotope, biotope or micro-landscape) is an ecological whole with its own meta-properties, containing members that interact under specific environmental conditions, and favouring particular members or groups of members [7]. They refer to a niche as "a location in space that is defined additionally by a specific constellation of ecological parameters such as degree of slope, exposure to sunlight, soil fertility, foliage density, and so on".

The suggestion that the functional niche be used as a fundamental unit of investigating ecological systems appears in [8,9]. Smith [7] defines an ecological niche as a containment space bounded by spatial and/or temporal parameters favouring specific groups of members. That entities interact with each other according to the ecosystem or environment in which they exist is also recognised by [9] who refers to niches as socio-economic units, and physical behavioural units. While these researchers advocate that niches are used in studying ecological phenomena, they offer no suggestions for incorporating this into conceptual models, nor do they propose any method for using them in the design process. They also give no indication as to whether they have put their idea into practice when tackling real problems. This paper therefore takes their work further by presenting a way of including niches in a model and methodology, and by reporting on its successful usage in a number of workshops and case studies.

Our methodology differs from other conceptual modeling methods not only in its use of niches, granularity and reconciliation, but also in the starting point of design. Booch[10] begins with a description of the system's function and structure, as do others such as OPM[11] and Insyde[12]. Many UML-based methodologies [13,14,15,16,17] commence with a problem description and a set of use cases, and thus also focus on processes rather than on the value chain and the environments in which interactions occur. Most modeling methodologies offer little guidance to designers, with steps indicating what to do when (e.g. identify entities, then subtypes, then relationships [18], or specify process-events, then objects, then constraints[12]) but not how to do so, with little if any help in detecting errors or omissions. A few like [12,18] mention the problem of semantic heterogeneity, but fail to include this explicitly in the model. A methodology that offers more guidance than most is TCM[19] which uses noun-phrase analysis to detect possible entities, verb-phrase analysis to detect potential associations, Chen's English Sentence Structure to determine attributes [20] and class category lists[21,22,23,24,25] to validate entities. TCM gives elimination rules to for entities and for associations. It also recommends that class categories (a given list of entity kinds such as person-role, event, etc.) be used as a checklist to detect omissions. However it does not take context or sphere of operation into account, and does not provide guidelines for discovering when inappropriate entities or entity roles have been used.

6 Conclusion

Conceptual modeling requires dealing with complexity, handling semantic heterogeneity (where different individuals use different vocabularies or attach subtly different meanings to terms), and choosing appropriate abstractions to represent the real world. A systematic, prescriptive method of undertaking such a difficult task is clearly needed. This paper presented such a methodology for conceptual modeling. It comprises the following six steps: setting objectives; identifying niches; designing niche models; assigning and checking granularities; normalising relationships; and recording reconciliations.

We introduced the notion of a niche as a basis for the methodology because of the importance of taking immediate context into account during design. A niche is an environment with a particular functional purpose that favours specific entities, in which interactions take place according to set norms and constraints. Within each niche we model not only entities, attributes and relationships, but also the granularity of entities. This we define as the relative level of influence, power or impact of the entity compared with others in the environment. This is an important tool for detecting errors and omissions in a model, because during the normalization process all relationships involving entities of differing granularity are systematically checked and remedied where necessary. We show how these remedial actions lead to the identification of missing aggregates or composition entities, or indicate the need for new specializations/roles for an entity. Without the use of granularity and normalization, such modeling inaccuracies typically go undetected. We further show that normalization can identify intervention opportunities were the status quo in the real world can be improved, because it highlights anomalies that exist and requires designers to think creatively about such problems.

Our methodology has been applied in a number of case studies and shown to be valid, applicable and useable. It improved the quality of models produced and also greatly reduced semantic heterogeneity. By virtue of modeling in the context of a specific niche, the chances of seeing a situation with discipline-specific biases are vastly reduced. Furthermore, normalizing cross-granularity relationships causes two different views of an entity to be recognized as different roles that the entity plays in different niches, and this is then resolved in the corresponding generalisation hierarchy. As a final step, the methodology requires that all instances in which semantic heterogeneity was resolved be explicitly recorded using a simple reconciles relationship that we developed for this purpose.

In future, we plan to investigate the potential of our model and methodology across a more diverse set of case studies. While we have applied them in many different situations, these have thus far all been socio-ecological projects. We need to explore the methodology in other domains, particularly in the business world. Another aspect that needs further work is that of defining more precisely the role of the facilitator (ontological engineer). Until now, the author has acted as facilitator, and questions remain as to how a facilitator should best be trained for such work and, once trained, how best s/he should proceed before, during and after each modeling session. A further important part of the research is the creation of domain ontologies from the models produced with our methodology. We have already done this for socio-economic upliftment projects, where we are now re-using our ontology in new projects quite successfully. However the general problem of converting models that incorporate niches, granularity and reconciliations into a suitable ontology needs further exploration.

References

1. Porter, M.E.: Competitive Advantage: Creating and Sustaining Superior Performance. Free Press, New York (1985)
2. Poseidon for UML, Community Edition, http://www.gentleware.com
3. Semwayo, D.T., Berman, S.: Representing ecological niches in a conceptual model. In: Wang, S., Tanaka, K., Zhou, S., Ling, T.-W., Guan, J., Yang, D.-q., Grandi, F., Mangina, E.E., Song, I.-Y., Mayr, H.C. (eds.). ER 2004 LNCS, vol. 3289, pp. 31–42. Springer, Heidelberg (2004)

4. Cheng, T., Molenaar, M.: A process-oriented spatio-temporal data model to support physical environmental modeling. In: Cheng, T., Molenaar, M. (eds.) Proceedings of the 8th International symposium on spatial data handling, pp. 418–430 (1997)

5. O'neill, R.V., DeAngelis, D.L., et al.: A hierarchical concept of ecosystems. Princeton University Press, Princeton (1986)

6. Smith, B., Varci, A.C.: The Formal Structure of Ecological Contexts, in Modeling and using Context. In: Bouquet, P., Brezillon, P., Serafini, L. (eds.) Proceedings of the Second International and Interdisciplinary Conference, pp. 339–350. Springer, Heiderberg (1999)

7. Smith, B.: Objects and their Environments: From Aristotle to Ecological Ontology. Communications of the ACM 45(2), 79–79 (2002)

8. Raper, J.: Defining Spatial Socio-Economic Units: Retrospective and Prospective, in Life & Motion of Socio-economic units, Taylor Francis, 2001 Multidimensional Geographic Information Science. Taylor Francis (2000)

9. Frank, A., Raper, J., Cheylan (eds.): Life and motion of socio-economic units. Taylor Francis (2001)

10. Booch, G.: Object-Oriented Analysis and Design with Applications, 2nd edn. Benjamin Cummings (1994)

11. Liu, H., Gluch, D.P.: Conceptual Modeling with the Object-Process Methodology in Software Architecture. Journal for Computing Sciences in Colleges, 10–21 (2004)

12. King, R., McLeod, D.: A Database Design Methodology and Tool for Information Systems, ACM Trans. ACM Trans. on Office Information Systems 3(1), 2–21 (1985)

13. Maciaszek, L.A.: Requirement Analysis and System Design: Developing Information Systems with UML. Addison-Wesley, London, UK (2001)

14. Rosenberg, D.: Use Case Driven Object Modeling with UML: A Practical Approach. Addison-Wesley, London, UK (1999)

15. Rumbaugh, J., Blaha, M., et al.: Object-Oriented Modeling and Design. Prentice-Hall, Prentice (1991)

16. Siau, L.: Unified Modeling Language: Systems Analysis, Design and Development Issues. Idea Publishing, USA (2001)

17. Stevens, P., Pooley, R.: Using UML: Software Engineering with Objects and Components. Addison-Wesley, London, UK (1999)

18. Teorey, J.J., Yang, D., Fry, J.P.: A Logical Design Methodology for Relational Databases Using the Extended Entity-Relationship Model. Computing Surveys 18(2), 197–222 (1986)

19. Song, I.-Y., Yano, K., Trujillo, J., Mora, S.L.: A Taxonomic Class Modelling Methodology for Object-Oriented Analysis. In: Proc. EMMSAD (2003)

20. Chen, P.P.: English Sentence Structure and Entity-Relationship Diagrams. Information Sciences, 127–149 (1983)

21. Bahrami, A.: Object-Oriented Systems Development. McGraw-Hill, New York (1999)

22. Larman, C.: Applying UML and Patterns, 2nd edn. Prentice-Hall, Prentice (2001)

23. Richter, C.: Designing Flexible Object-Oriented Systems with UML. Macmillan Technical Publishing (1999)

24. Ross, R.G.: Entity Modeling: Techniques and Applications, Database Research Group Inc (1988)

25. Starr, L., Executable, U.M.L.: Executable UML: How to Build Class Models. Prentice Hall, Prentice (2001)

As We May Link: A General Metamodel for Hypermedia Systems

Beat Signer and Moira C. Norrie

Institute for Information Systems, ETH Zurich
CH-8092 Zurich, Switzerland
{signer,norrie}@inf.ethz.ch

Abstract. Many hypermedia models have been proposed, including those specifically developed to model navigational aspects of web sites. But few hypermedia systems have been implemented based on metamodelling principles familiar to the database community. Often there is no clear separation between conceptual and technical issues in the models and their implementations are not based on an explicit representation of a metamodel. This results in a loss of generality and uniformity across systems. Based on principles of metamodel-driven system development, we have implemented a platform that can support various categories of hypermedia systems through the generality and extensibility of the metamodel. We present our metamodel and show how it generalises concepts present in a range of hypermedia and link server systems.

1 Introduction

The vision presented by Vannevar Bush in his paper *As We May Think* [1] is often accredited as being the origin of hypermedia systems. Since then, many hypermedia models and systems have been developed, but they are all based on the same underlying model of information spaces as interlinked collections of resources. Variations abound according to the precise nature of the links and resources, how they can be authored and accessed and also the application domains considered. This has led to numerous categories of systems including open hypermedia, adaptive hypermedia, physical hypermedia and spatial hypermedia. Of course, the most famous of all hypermedia systems is the World Wide Web and the hypermedia community has actively investigated ways of extending the underlying technologies and tools to enable more advanced and flexible features to be supported. At the same time, hypermedia models have been adopted by the web engineering community as a basis for modelling navigation and adaptation in model-based approaches to web site development.

However, a study of the hypermedia literature reveals a lack of clear, conceptual models that are general and flexible enough to support the development of a wide range of hypermedia systems and applications. In some cases, conceptual and technical issues are combined into the same model, while other approaches integrate application-specific concepts into the core of the model. Further, in contrast to database systems, implementations are rarely metamodel-driven. This

C. Parent et al. (Eds.): ER 2007, LNCS 4801, pp. 359–374, 2007.

means that a metamodel is not represented explicitly in the system resulting in, not only a loss of flexibility, but also the introduction of major restrictions in the model during the implementation process.

Our goal was to produce a general platform for the development of hypermedia systems based on principles of metamodel-driven engineering and extensibility. This meant defining a core link metamodel that is general enough to support features of many different systems and free from implementation issues. In addition, the core metamodel was designed with extensibility in mind so any type of resource and link could be supported. For example, in the implemented system, we currently support text and XHTML documents, images, videos, Flash movies, databases, RFIDs, interactive paper documents and program components as resources that can be linked together. In addition, each type of resource can have one or more selectors defined to enable links to and from elements within resources. We support both navigational and structural links as well as links with multiple targets, multiple sources and also links over links.

In this paper, we present our metamodel and show how it generalises existing hypermedia models in terms of supporting concepts of these models either directly in the core model or through extensibility. At the same time, we use this as an example to show the benefits that can be attained by using a conceptual metamodel as the basis for system engineering.

We start in Sect. 2 by describing the range of existing hypermedia models and systems in order to identify the requirements of a general metamodel and also highlight some of the problems of existing model definitions. Section 3 then presents the core of our metamodel in terms of link concepts. In Sect. 4, we show how a user model is integrated into the core metamodel. The concept of layers is introduced in Sect. 5 and we describe how this can be used to support nested links. Section 6 shows how the core model was extended to support structural links as well as navigational links. In Sect. 7, we discuss some key features of the implementation. Concluding remarks are given in Sect. 8.

2   Background

Over the last two decades a variety of hypermedia models for different domains and purposes have been proposed. We first review some of the best known in order to show the variety of features supported and part of the history of how these models evolved. We then discuss some general limitations of the proposed models and implementations in order to motivate our approach for a general metamodel supporting different hypermedia domains.

In an attempt to generalise concepts from different hypertext systems, the *Dexter* hypertext reference model [2] introduced three abstraction layers. The storage layer describes a network of interlinked nodes (components) whereas the within-component layer deals with the content and structure within those nodes. User interaction with hypermedia content is handled by the runtime layer. A limitation of the Dexter model is the fact that all data has to be encapsulated within the components and data not forming part of the hypermedia structure itself cannot be addressed. Furthermore, the Dexter model does not specify in detail how anchors can be used to address parts of composite components. The *DeVise Hypermedia* (DHM) system [3] for cooperative hypermedia addressed some of these limitations by extending the Dexter model. Around the same time, the *Amsterdam Hypermedia Model* (AHM) [4] added concepts of time and context to the Dexter model to investigate ways of combining multimedia and hypertext concepts to support the linking of dynamic multimedia information. In addition to the original navigational hypermedia models, spatial [5] and taxonomic hypermedia [6] models were also investigated in the mid-90s.

Adaptive hypermedia systems enable the content and link structure to be adapted dynamically based on the user context by integrating a user concept into the model [5]. *AHAM* [7] is a reference model for adaptive hypermedia systems that extends the storage layer of the Dexter model with a user model.

Open Hypermedia architectures address interoperability between hypermedia systems and the *Open Hypermedia Protocol* (OHP) was developed for the exchange of navigational link information. OHP was specified using DTDs resulting in a lack of detail due to the limited expressiveness of the chosen "specification language". The *Fundamental Open Hypertext Model* (FOHM) [8], an extension of OHP, attempts to provide a common data model for navigational, spatial and taxonomic hypermedia by providing operations for these three domains. However, a drawback of FOHM is its limitation to exactly those three domains, ignoring other existing hypermedia domains. The issue of limited extensibility in terms of structural abstractions necessary to support different hypermedia domains was addressed by *Component-based Open Hypermedia Systems* (CB-OHS) [9]. In many open hypermedia systems, the controlled sharing of information seems to be difficult since the majority of approaches do not consider user management and the issues of *data* and *link ownership* in their core model.

A distinguishing feature of open hypermedia systems is the fact that they use external link servers to deal with links between resources. Managing links separately from resources allows for greater flexibility in supporting features such as bidirectional links, multi-source and multi-target links and link groups. Importantly, it also enables the removal of the sharp distinction between the authors and users of links since users can create links between resources without having access rights to modify those resources. Well known link servers include *Chimera* [10], *Microcosm* [11] and *Hyper-G* along with its successor *Hyperwave* [12]. Similar issues of embedding links in resources as opposed to managing them separately arose in the context of the World Wide Web and the hypermedia community have contributed to the development of the *XML Linking Language* (XLink) [13] which allows links to be managed separately as well as providing more flexibility in terms of defining and accessing links. The XLink standard is based on the *Hypermedia/Time-based Structuring Language* (HyTime) [14]. As part of the Semantic Web initiative, the Annotea project [15] uses these ideas to allow users to create and share annotations of web resources.

More recently, physical hypermedia models for bridging the physical and digital worlds have been proposed. For example, *HyperReal* [16] is a mixed reality model that introduces the concept of map components for managing geographical data. In addition, existing hypermedia solutions have also been challenged by new ideas such as the structural computing approach that treats structure as a first-class citizen and no longer puts the focus on the data [17].

As outlined, there is a wide variety of hypermedia models and systems. While there have been some attempts to provide reference models such as Dexter and FOHM, most hypermedia models and systems are isolated solutions for specific domains (e.g. navigational or spatial hypertext) or even specific applications. Although the Dexter model was instrumental in providing a common vocabulary, its specification is not detailed enough to enable information exchange between different systems based on the Dexter model or one of its extensions. Many models for hypermedia systems have claimed to be general and extensible and yet these have often disappeared only to be replaced by another hypermedia model. There is little or no support for evolution between these models with the result that applications and data are lost between implementations.

In our opinion, one of the causes for this situation is the lack of well-defined conceptual models on which implementations are based. Often models are presented as a mix of architectural, technical and conceptual features. As a result, the concepts become obfuscated and restrictions are introduced unnecessarily due to technicalities of the envisaged implementation.

Designing a system around a well-defined conceptual metamodel leads to increased generality and flexibility of both the model and the system. The use of metamodels as a basis for specifying and implementing hypermedia models is not widespread. In the field of web engineering where hypermedia models have been adapted to model navigation and adaptivity in web sites, metamodels are more commonly used and there have been efforts to define common metamodels (e.g. [18]). However, in this case, the metamodels tend to be focussed on the specific needs of web engineering.

Summarising, we feel that there is a need for a general framework to support the development of different categories of hypermedia systems and that this framework should be based on a general, extensible metamodel for hypermedia. The core of this metamodel has to be powerful enough to support the specification and modelling of different hypermedia domains in terms of a small set of fundamental link concepts. The development of the framework should be based on an implementation of the metamodel with the explicit representation of concepts of the metamodel in terms of metadata. While such a metamodel-driven approach to implementation is well-known to the conceptual modelling and database communities, along with its advantages in terms of flexibility and support for evolution, it is relatively rare to find it outside these communities and, in particular, in hypermedia systems. The result is that often model concepts are mapped to implementation-specific approximations that introduce restrictions and the model itself is hard-coded and static.

In the remainder of the paper, we present such a metamodel, the *resource-selector-link* (RSL) model, and describe how it was used to implement a general cross-media information platform called iServer [19]. We highlight how the RSL model generalises concepts found in the range of hypermedia models mentioned above. Further we show how extensibility for domain-specific requirements is supported through a combination of concept specialisation in the metamodel and plug-in components in the architecture.

3   Link Metamodel

Our general metamodel for hypermedia systems was defined using the semantic, object-oriented data model OM [20]. OM is a data model that integrates concepts from both entity relationship and object-oriented data models. The OM model is intended as a basis for efficient data management as well as semantic expressiveness, and a family of object-oriented database platforms have been realised based on this model including the OMS Java data management system [21]. Using OM together with OMS allowed us to directly implement the metamodel and we were able to exploit powerful features of the OM model such as multiple classification and ordered collections in the metamodelling process. For that reason, we choose to use the OM modelling notation here rather than a more commonly used alternative. However, it is important to note that, even if another implementation platform were used, it would prove beneficial to base the system design on our OM metamodel which provides rich classification structures over objects and associations together with a full operational model.

The OM model supports information modelling through a two-level structure of classification and typing, dealing with these on separate layers. *Typing* deals with representation and entities are represented by objects with attributes, methods and triggers defined for the corresponding object types. *Classification* deals with semantic roles and a particular classification is represented by a named *collection* of objects with a specified member type. In addition, OM provides a high-level *association* construct which enables associations between entities to be classified and manipulated directly.

The OM model differs from many conceptual models in that it is intended as an operational model for data management as well as for system design. Thus the OM model defines a full operational model over objects, collections and associations as well as constructs for their definition. The expressive features of the OM model enable us to capture the semantics of application domains in terms of a simple, but powerful set of constructs. Its support for the direct representation and manipulation of associations is particularly useful in supporting link management in systems that offer hypermedia functionality. For more details about the OM model and its additional features please refer to [20].

In this section, we focus on the core link functionality of our general model whereas other parts of the RSL metamodel are presented in Sect. 4 to Sect. 6. The schema of the core link model is shown in Fig. 1. The shaded rectangular shapes denote collections of objects (classification) where the name of the collection is given in the unshaded part and the name of the associated type in the shaded part. The type serves both as a constraint on membership in the collection and also as the default view of objects accessed through that collection. Thus, links

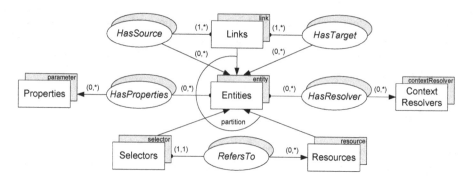

Fig. 1. Core link metamodel

are represented by objects of type `link` grouped into the `Links` collection. The shaded ovals represent *associations between entities* of two collections.

The most general concept within our hypermedia metamodel is the generic notion of an `entity` (similar to components in the Dexter model). Note that all instances of entities are further classified and grouped by the collection `Entities`. While an entity represents only an abstract concept, there are three specific forms of entities described by three different subtypes: the `resource`, the `selector` and the `link` types.

The simplest type of entity is the `resource` type representing an entire information unit. While a `resource` is still an abstract concept, all types of media to be handled by the hypermedia system have to provide a specific extension of the `resource` type based on a plug-in mechanism. Our implementation of the hypermedia model, known as iServer, currently supports a variety of different resource types for web pages, movie and sound clips, images, Flash movies, physical objects marked with RFID tags as well as interactive paper. Note that we have a subtyping relationship between the `resource` and `entity` type but the specialisation of resources is also reflected in the model by designing `Resources` as a subcollection of the `Entities` collection.

Often we want to define links between not only entire resources but also specific parts of resources. For example, the anchor of a link within a web page addresses a specific part of an HTML document using the `href` anchor tag. Therefore, as a second subtype of the `entity` type, we introduce the concept of a `selector` which is a construct enabling parts of the related resource to be addressed (similar to reference objects in FOHM [8]). Again the specialisation of `Entities` is reflected by the `Selectors` subcollection. An association `RefersTo` represents the fact that a selector is always associated with exactly one resource, whereas each resource can have more than one referencing selector. The cardinality constraints specified at the source and target points of the associations indicate the possible level of participation of individual objects. Thus (`1,1`) at the source point of the `RefersTo` association indicates that each selector is always associated with exactly one resource, whereas the (`0,*`) cardinality constraint at the target means that each resource can have zero or more referencing selectors. A `selector` is an abstract concept that has to be extended to support concrete types of media. For example, the selector to address parts of an XHTML document resource could be an XPointer expression, whereas the selector to specify parts of a movie clip could be a temporal selector with a start and an end time.

After providing a mechanism to allow entities to be referenced by a link, we now provide a specification for the links themselves. A link within our hypermedia metamodel is always directed and leads from one or more *sources* to one or more *targets*. A source may either be an entire `resource` or parts of a resource addressed by a `selector`. This is reflected in the model by making the collection `Entities` the target collection of both the `HasSource` and `HasTarget` associations. Furthermore, the `(1,*)` cardinality constraint at the source point of both associations indicates that each link must have at least one and possibly many sources and targets. In this way, we support multi-target links as well as links with multiple sources. The `(0,*)` at the target point of the `HasSource` and `HasTarget` associations specifies that there is no limit on the number of links for which an entity may be the source or target. Note that by ensuring that each link has at least one source and target entity, we prevent any occurrence of dangling links as proposed in the Dexter model and guarantee that the system is always in a consistent state where links can be resolved. For cases where the source or target entity is not available at link creation time, special placeholder elements could be used and replaced at a later time.

While there are many existing hypermedia models dealing with multi-target links, we found that links with multiple source anchors are not supported by most systems. However, from our experience of integrating information across different digital and physical information spaces, we can say that the concept of multi-source links is very powerful. For example, if the same information is published on different output channels (e.g. a web page and an interactive paper document) the semantics of a single link is maintained by associating it with two different sources for the two different types of media triggering the link resolution. Also note that since the underlying OM model provides bidirectional associations as a higher-level construct, all the associations used within the cross-media link model are also bidirectional. This enables us to, not only get all the link targets for a specific link source, but also to find the corresponding link sources given a specific target object.

By also modelling `Links` as a subcollection of `Entities`, we gain the flexibility to create links whose sources or targets are defined by other links. This means that we can annotate any link with supplementary information. While other systems also support the annotation of links with additional information, our approach of using the metamodel's link functionality for annotating links entails the advantage that links can not only be annotated with textual information but with any arbitrary entity. This means that we can use resources, parts of resources or even other links to annotate a link. For example, we could have a web page with links to additional information and these links could then be annotated by other users with textual comments or links to different web resources etc. A final remark about the three core concepts (resource, selector and link) is that a `partition` is specified over the `Resources`, `Selectors` and `Links` subcollections to denote that each entity belongs to exactly one of these three categories.

To provide some additional flexibility for future extensions, each entity can be associated with a set of properties which are stored as a set of string tuples in an entity's property attribute. These properties, represented by key/value pairs, are not predefined by a system implementing the model. They can be defined individually to customise an entity's behaviour for specific application domains. For example, one could define a link property `onActivate` which would represent the action to be taken when a link is activated. Possible values could be `openInline` to open the link target within the current resource or `openNew` to display the link target in a separate view. This is similar to concepts in XLink [13] where the `actuate` attribute is used to define the traversal behaviour and the `show` attribute defines where a link should be shown (e.g. in the same or in a new window). However, we try to be as flexible as possible by not predefining a set of properties but rather introducing an abstract property set which can be extended for specific domains. Another example is to provide a flexible "typing" of links by introducing a property with the name `type` and assigning the appropriate values to it as proposed in the Dexter model. For instance, we could introduce a special type for links which represent annotations and treat them in a specific way. As an alternative, we could also introduce domain- or application-specific subcollections of `Links` as a means of classifying links. This combination of being able to associate properties to links and also classifying them provides a very flexible and powerful way of representing link taxonomies.

Finally, our core model provides functionality for the context-dependent handling of entities. Each entity can be associated with a set of context resolvers which are then used to compute an entity's visibility. A `contextResolver` basically returns a boolean value representing an entity's accessibility based on data managed by the hypermedia model as well as any other available contextual information. If multiple context resolvers are associated with a single entity, the entity will only be visible if all context resolvers return positive feedback. While the context resolver is an abstract concept, various domain- and application-specific context resolver extensions can be registered with the system.

By introducing the concept of context-dependent information at the very core of our model (i.e. at the entity level), we gain the flexibility of having context-dependent resources, selectors and links operating independently of each other. For example, a link with multiple targets may be accessible in a given context while, for the same context, some of its target entities may be inaccessible. The implementation of adaptive hypermedia functionality mentioned in the previous section is just one of the domains that can be supported by the context resolver concept. Entities can be easily tagged with different properties which will then be used in the decision process of specific context resolvers. A built-in context resolver for handling access rights has to be provided by all systems implementing our hypermedia metamodel and is presented in the next section as part of the user management component.

4   User Model

In order to support both personalisation and the sharing of links and resources, we need a notion of *data ownership* combined with different levels of access rights. While most early hypermedia systems did not deal with an explicit representation of users as part of the model, some adaptive hypermedia models (e.g. AHAM [7]) introduced the concept of user models in the core of the system. However, while those user models typically deal with the aggregation and storage of user access patterns, our user model only provides functionality for managing data ownership and access rights at the entity level. The richer user models investigated by the adaptive hypermedia community could be integrated as a domain-specific extension of our metamodel. Note that even more recent link models such as the XLink standard do not provide the concept of data ownership nor do they deal with the definition of link access rights. By defining the access rights at the entity level, we can define individual permissions for links, resources and selectors. The representation of the fundamental user management component in our model is illustrated in Fig. 2.

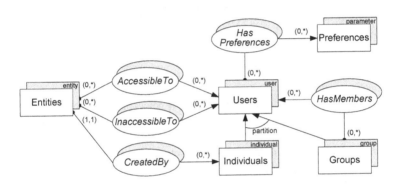

Fig. 2. User management

A `user` can either be an `individual` or a `group`. Users can be classified in different groups represented by the collection `Groups`, where a `group` itself can be part of other groups. Each `entity` is created by exactly one individual user having full control over its content. Note that the collaborative authoring of links and resources is possible due to the fact that the creator can define read and write access rights for other groups of users or individuals. The two associations `AccessibleTo` and `InaccessibleTo` are introduced to define access rights in a flexible way. The set of individuals having access to a specific entity is defined by the groups and individuals associated by `AccessibleTo` minus the groups and individuals defined through the `InaccessibleTo` association. In addition, there exists a constraint that access rights defined for an individual always have priority over access rights that have been defined for a group. More formally, a group $\mathcal{G}$ is defined by some subgroups $\mathcal{G}_i$ and some individuals I_k that it contains, i.e. $\mathscr{G} = \{\mathscr{G}_1, \ldots, \mathscr{G}_m, I_1, \ldots, I_n\}$. The expanded set of individuals who are members of a group is given by

$$\mathscr{E}(\mathscr{G}) = \bigcup_{g \in \mathscr{G}} \mathscr{E}(g) \quad \text{with} \quad \mathscr{E}(I) \equiv \{I\}.$$

For a specific entity e, let $\mathscr{G}_a(e)$ denote the set of groups explicitly specified as having access to e and $\mathscr{G}_x(e)$ those explicitly denied access. Correspondingly, let $\mathscr{I}_a(e)$ denote the set of individuals explicitly specified as having access to e and $\mathscr{I}_x(e)$ those explicitly denied access. Then $\mathscr{A}(e)$, the set of individuals having access to entity e is defined as

$$\mathscr{A}(e) = \mathscr{I}_a(e) \cup (\mathscr{E}(\mathscr{G}_a(e)) \setminus \mathscr{E}(\mathscr{G}_x(e)) \setminus \mathscr{I}_x(e)).$$

This allows us to define complex access rights for an individual entity of the form "the entity should be visible to everybody except one specific group of users and two particular individuals". The activation of a link may depend on the user and even the user role. An author of a cross-media application based on our hypermedia metamodel may not only define different selectors for different users but also link the same selector to different information resources based on the user profile. Note that a specific context resolver can be used for ensuring entity access control based on the presented user model.

5   Layers

We have already introduced the concept of a selector to address parts of a resource as a link source or target entity. However, so far we have not explained how we deal with the case that the parts of a resource defined by different selectors overlap. For example, we could have one selector which specifies a paragraph within an XHTML document, while another selector specifies a word within that paragraph. The overlapping selectors can create a link resolution problem in terms of not knowing which link to activate when the word is selected. This is the problem of supporting so-called nested links. In the case of HTML, this problem does not arise as overlapping anchors are not allowed, but this is also quite restrictive and therefore a number of hypermedia models support some form of overlapping anchors (strictly nested and/or partly overlapping). But, even if nested link anchors are supported, it is often the case that the link resolution behaviour in the case of overlapping anchors cannot be specified. For example, the XLink specification allows for nested and overlapping link anchors but does not provide any functionality to control their behaviour. To become more flexible in defining the semantics of nested link source and target anchors, we introduce the concept of layers shown in Fig. 3.

Each selector is associated with exactly one layer and we do not allow overlapping selectors on the same layer, thereby forcing overlapping link source selectors to be defined on separate layers. In the case that a concrete selection would return several links by activating multiple overlapping selectors, by definition, the link bound to the selector on the uppermost layer will be selected.

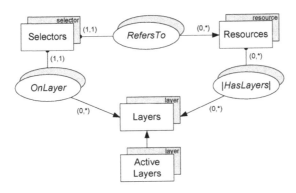

Fig. 3. Layers

The OM model supports collections of four different behaviours—sets, bags, rankings and sequences—to cater for collections with and without multiple occurrences of elements and with or without an explicit ordering. This also applies to associations. A selector's associated resource defines the set of available layers over the association |HasLayers| and the vertical bars indicate that this is a totally ordered association (ranking) that provides an explicit ordering of the layers. Furthermore, it is possible to activate and deactivate specific layers by adding them to or removing them from the ActiveLayers collection. The order defined by this association is used to choose the appropriate layer in the case that a selection addresses multiple overlapping selectors. Note that a selector can only be associated with a layer defined by its related resource over the |HasLayers| association.

Specific layers may be activated, deactivated and dynamically reordered enabling us to generate context-dependent links by resolving a particular selection to different selectors depending on the current set of active layers and the order of layering defined by the associated resource. An application may also control the navigational behaviour by switching the active layer set as a result of a user repeatedly providing the same selection.

6   Structural Links

As explained earlier, links are already first class objects in our model. By using links to describe structural components as well as navigational relationships between different resources, we place structure on the same level as resources and navigational links. Note that we do not give priority to structure over data as sometimes proposed by structural computing [17] but rather consider them to be on the same level.

In Fig. 4, we present an extension of our metamodel that distinguishes between structural and navigational links between resources. The collection Links introduced in Sect. 3 is partitioned into Navigational Links and Structural Links. By modelling structural links as a subcollection of regular links, they can be used to define a structure over arbitrary entities (e.g. resources, selectors and even links).

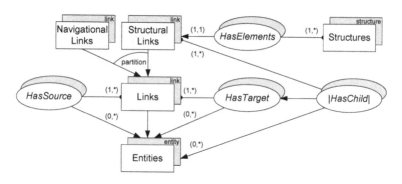

Fig. 4. Navigational and structural links

All structures are handled by the `Structures` collection and a single structure is related to its structural links by the `HasElement` association. It is necessary to have such an explicit grouping of structure elements since parts of structures might be reused by other structures as shown later in this section. Furthermore, structural links are a specialisation of general links since we have to introduce an order for the substructure relationship. For example, if we want to model the structure of a document with different chapters and sections within a chapter, we have to know the order of the chapter within the entire document as well as the order of the sections within the chapters. The order over such substructure relationships is introduced by the ordered |`HasChild`| subassociation of the `HasTarget` association. Therefore, the `Structures` and |`HasChild`| components provide us with information about all of the components belonging to a specific structure as well as their structural relationships.

A first type of structure that can be defined based on the new concepts is a structural relationship of different resources. An example of such a *structure over data* is a regular document containing chapters, sections, paragraphs etc. It is up to an application to define different domain-specific structures. Note that since we have a clear separation of data and structure, it is possible to reuse the same resource in different structures by transclusion as suggested by Nelson [22]. The context-dependent link resolution, discussed earlier as an example to support adaptive hypermedia, is also available for structural links. Therefore, the structure of a specific resource may change based on the user accessing it or any other context resolver-based adaptation.

Structural links can not only be defined directly over resources but we can also define a *structure over structures*. It is important to know that each structural link within a structure defines a substructure containing the structural link's source elements and all of its children (recursively). This implies that we can superimpose any structure on top of existing structural components and, of course, the structural composition of data and substructures can also be combined. Note that to address a substructure we do not define a structural link to the `structure` element but rather to the corresponding structural link defining the substructure. An example of such a reuse of a substructure component could be a chapter of a document (e.g. a technical specification in an appendix) that is structurally referenced by different documents.

Last but not least, we can also specify a *structure over links*. This enables us to put different navigational links in relation to each other. A simple example would be the structure of an ordered list of navigational links defined by a single structural link. Such an ordered list of navigational links could be used to represent trails and tours, which are two well-known concepts available in many hypermedia models and systems. While we have indicated some examples for *structure over data*, *structure over structures* and *structure over links*, it is beyond the scope of this paper to discuss the potential applications of structural links in detail. We also point out that we are still investigating the implications of this powerful concept for different domains.

7   Implementation

The RSL metamodel presented in this paper is implemented using the OMS Java data management system [21]. The resulting iServer platform [19] for cross-media information management has been used over the last five years in a variety of projects for linking digital and physical information resources and, specifically, for the implementation of the iPaper framework [23] for interactive paper.

Since the metamodel was implemented on the OMS Java data management system, the iServer platform provides a Java API for accessing data as well as metadata. We have also implemented a Web Service interface providing the same functionality as the Java API to offer a more general language independent programming interface for the iServer platform. Other extensions include a distributed version of the platform where different distributed iServer instances can exchange link information based on peer-to-peer technology.

Different media-specific plug-ins for the resource and selector concepts have been developed including plug-ins for XHTML documents, movie and sound clips, still images, Flash movies, physical hypermedia based on RFID tagged physical objects and interactive paper. For a given resource type, there may be varying types of selectors based on the requirements of specific applications. In Table 1, we suggest time spans to be used as a candidate for movie selectors. However, a specific application might need to link movies based on spatial information within the movie whereas others might need to define links based on a combination of temporal and spatial information. The iServer architecture therefore supports the definition of different selectors for a single resource type.

To illustrate the flexibility of the iServer model and framework, we would like to provide some more details about the iWeb resource plug-in for linking XHTML documents. Similar to other link server approaches proposed by the hypertext community, our iWeb plug-in uses iServer as an external link repository for web pages. In contrast to most existing link servers, the iServer-based approach results in a flexible cross-media solution capable of integrating arbitrary digital or physical resources.

Table 1. iServer plug-ins

Medium	Resource	Selector
paper	document page	shape
web page	XHTML document	XPointer
movie	mpeg file, avi file etc.	time span
movie	mpeg file, avi file etc.	shape
sound	mp3 file, wav file etc.	time span
image	gif file, jpeg file etc.	shape
database	database workspace	query
physical object	RFID space	RFID tag

The definition of a selector for XHTML documents was straightforward since we could build on work already done in the context of XLink [13]. XLink uses the XML Pointer Language (XPointer) to address a specific part of an XML document. By using XPointer expressions as XHTML selectors within the iServer framework, we can define any part of an XHTML document as a link source or link target. However, as explained earlier, we obtain some additional features not available in the XLink language such as the well-defined semantics for multi-layered link resolution or the link ownership and access right control.

To integrate the link metadata stored in iServer with existing XHTML pages, we implemented an extension for the Firefox web browser. When a new web page is requested by the user, it is first downloaded from the server and immediately visualised in the browser. In a second step, the iWeb browser extension starts to parse the web page and augment it with supplemental link information that is acquired by contacting the iServer Web Service based on specific JavaScript functionality. As soon as the integrated web page has been rendered by the browser extension, the page gets redisplayed in the browser's main window.

The general resource and selector concepts together with the multi-layer functionality have proven to be powerful enough to support the integration of digital and physical objects. Different authoring tools haven been developed for creating and browsing link information managed by the iServer platform. For example, the iWeb Firefox extension can be used to augment arbitrary XHTML web documents in a similar way to the Annotea [15] project. Another authoring tool developed based on QuickTime technology enables parts of movie clips to be linked based on temporal selectors. An active component mechanism implemented on top of the iServer platform supports links to pieces of program code that can used as link targets and are executed when a link is activated [23].

A wide variety of applications have been developed using the iServer platform. These include several applications which use the iPaper plug-in to support interaction between paper and digital resources including an interactive guide for the Edinburgh festivals [24], PaperPoint [25], a paper-based interface for PowerPoint presentations and Print-n-Link [26], a system to support the reading of scientific publications. In addition, iServer has been used to support a number of interactive media installations designed by artists.

Although the system has been extended significantly over the last few years, this always happened as an evolutionary rather than a revolutionary process. This means that, even if the core of the model was extended, all applications evolved with the changes of the model due to our database-driven approach and even our first applications are still operational. For example, the recent extension of the framework to support structural links did not affect the operation of existing applications or the data managed by these applications. However, any new or existing application can now make use of the new structural links functionality. For instance, an application for the publishing of interactive paper documents now uses the structural link functionality to define a domain-specific document model.

8   Conclusion

We have presented RSL, a general metamodel for hypermedia systems dealing with data, structure and navigation information based on a core set of link concepts. Our conceptual modelling approach led naturally to a very general and flexible link model that integrates various concepts of existing hypermedia models. In addition, the RSL model caters for cross-media linking and provides extensibility for the introduction of new resource types. To show the flexibility of the model, we also described the iServer framework for cross-media information spaces which is based on RSL and supports a rich variety of applications.

References

1. Bush, V.: As We May Think. Atlantic Monthly 176(1), 101–108 (1945)
2. Halasz, F.G., Schwartz, M.: The Dexter Hypertext Reference Model. Communications of the ACM 37(2) (1994)
3. Grønbæk, K., Trigg, R.H.: Design Issues for a Dexter-based Hypermedia System. Communications of the ACM 37(2), 40–49 (1994)
4. Hardman, L., Bulterman, D.C.A., van Rossum, G.: The Amsterdam Hypermedia Model: Adding Time and Context to the Dexter Model. Communications of the ACM 37(2), 50–62 (1994)
5. Brusilovsky, P.: Methods and Techniques of Adaptive Hypermedia. User Modeling and User-Adapted Interaction 6(2–3), 87–129 (1996)
6. Parunak, H.: Don't Link Me In: Set Based Hypermedia for Taxonomic Reasoning. In: Proc. of Hypertext '91, San Antonio, USA, pp. 233–242 (December 1991)
7. Bra, P.D., Houben, G.J., Wu, H.: AHAM: A Dexter-Based Reference Model for Adaptive Hypermedia. In: Proc. of Hypertext 1999, Darmstadt, Germany (February 1999)
8. Millard, D., Moreau, L., Davis, H., Reich, S.: FOHM: A Fundamental Open Hypertext Model for Investigating Interoperability between Hypertext Domains. In: Proc. of Hypertext 2000 (May 2000)
9. Nürnberg, P.J., Leggett, J.J., Wiil, U.K.: An Agenda for Open Hypermedia Research. In: Proc. of Hypertext 1998, Pittsburgh, USA, pp. 198–206 (June 1998)

10. Anderson, K.M., Taylor, R.N., E. J., Whitehead, J.: Chimera: Hypermedia for Heterogeneous Software Development Environments. ACM Transactions on Information Systems 18(3), 211–245 (2000)
11. Hall, W., Davis, H.C., Hutchings, G.: Rethinking Hypermedia: The Microcosm Approach. Kluwer Academic Publishers, Dordrecht (1996)
12. Maurer, H.: Hyperwave: The Next Generation Web Solution. Addison-Wesley, London, UK (1996)
13. De Rose, S.J: XML Linking. ACM Computing Surveys 31(4) (1999)
14. Newcomb, S.R., Kipp, N.A., Newcomb, V.T.: The "HyTime": Hypermedia/Time-based Document Structuring Language. Communications of the ACM 34(11), 67–83 (1991)
15. Kahan, J., Koivunen, M.R., Prud'Hommeaux, E., Swick, R.R.: Annotea: An Open RDF Infrastructure for Shared Web Annotations. In: Proc. of WWW10, 10th International World Wide Web Conference, Hong Kong (May 2001)
16. Romero, L., Correia, N.: HyperReal: A Hypermedia Model for Mixed Reality. In: Proc. of Hypertext 2003, Nottingham, UK, pp. 2–9 (August 2003)
17. Nürnberg, P.J., schraefel, m.c: Relationships Among Structural Computing and Other Fields. Journal of Network and Computer Applications 26(1), 11–26 (2003)
18. Koch, N., Kraus, A.: Towards a Common Metamodel for the Development of Web Applications. In: Lovelle, J.M.C., Rodríguez, B.M.G., Gayo, J.E.L., Ruiz, M.d.P.P., Aguilar, L.J. (eds.) ICWE 2003. LNCS, vol. 2722, pp. 497–506. Springer, Heidelberg (2003)
19. Signer, B.: Fundamental Concepts for Interactive Paper and Cross-Media Information Management. PhD thesis, ETH Zurich, Switzerland (2006)
20. Norrie, M.C.: An Extended Entity-Relationship Approach to Data Management in Object-Oriented Systems. In: Proc. of ER '93, 12th International Conference on the Entity-Relationship Approach, Arlington, USA, pp. 390–401 (1993)
21. Kobler, A., Norrie, M.C.: OMS Java: A Persistent Object Management Framework. In: Java and Databases. Hermes Penton Science, pp. 46–62 (May 2002)
22. Nelson, T.: Literary Machines. Mindful Press (1982)
23. Norrie, M.C., Signer, B., Weibel, N.: General Framework for the Rapid Development of Interactive Paper Applications. In: Proc. of CoPADD 2006, 1st International Workshop on Collaborating over Paper and Digital Documents, Banff, Canada, pp. 9–12 (2006)
24. Belotti, R., Decurtins, C., Norrie, M.C., Signer, B., Vukelja, L.: Experimental Platform for Mobile Information Systems. In: Proc. of MobiCom 2005, 11th Annual International Conference on Mobile Computing and Networking, Cologne, Germany, pp. 258–269 (August 2005)
25. Signer, B., Norrie, M.C.: PaperPoint: A Paper-Based Presentation and Interactive Paper Prototyping Tool. In: Proc. of TEI 2007, First International Conference on Tangible and Embedded Interaction, Baton Rouge, USA, pp. 57–64 (February 2007)
26. Norrie, M.C., Signer, B., Weibel, N.: Print-n-Link: Weaving the Paper Web. In: Proc. of DocEng 2006, ACM Symposium on Document Engineering, pp. 34–43. Amsterdam, The Netherlands (2006)

A Goal Oriented Approach for Modeling and Analyzing Security Trade-Offs

Golnaz Elahi[1] and Eric Yu[2]

[1] Department of Computer Science, University of Toronto, Canada, M5S 1A4
gelahi@cs.toronto.edu
[2] Faculty of Information Studies, University of Toronto, Canada, M5S 3G6
yu@fis.utoronto.edu

Abstract. In designing software systems, security is typically only one design objective among many. It may compete with other objectives such as functionality, usability, and performance. Too often, security mechanisms such as firewalls, access control, or encryption are adopted without explicit recognition of competing design objectives and their origins in stakeholder interests. Recently, there is increasing acknowledgement that security is ultimately about trade-offs. One can only aim for "good enough" security, given the competing demands from many parties. In this paper, we examine how conceptual modeling can provide explicit and systematic support for analyzing security trade-offs. After considering the desirable criteria for conceptual modeling methods, we examine several existing approaches for dealing with security trade-offs. From analyzing the limitations of existing methods, we propose an extension to the i* framework for security trade-off analysis, taking advantage of its multi-agent and goal orientation. The method was applied to several case studies used to exemplify existing approaches.

Keywords: Security Trade-offs, Trade-off Analysis, Goal Modeling, Goal Model Evaluation.

1 Introduction

"Security is about trade-offs, not absolutes."
Ravi Sandhu

In designing software systems, security is typically only one design objective among many. Security safeguards may conflict with usability, performance, and even functionality. For example, if usability concerns are not addressed in the design of a secure system, users respond by circumventing security mechanisms [29, 30]. Achieving a balance between the intrusiveness of security mechanisms [25] and usability goals is an important consideration in designing successful secure software systems. Security goals can have their own contradictions because confidentiality, integrity, privacy, accountability, availability, and recovery from security attacks often conflict fundamentally. For example, accountability requires a strong audit trail and end-user authentication, which conflicts with privacy needs for user anonymity [25].

C. Parent et al. (Eds.): ER 2007, LNCS 4801, pp. 375–390, 2007.

Ultimately, security is about balancing the trade-offs among the competing goals of multiple actors. In current practice, security designers often adopt security mechanisms such as firewalls, access control, or encryption without explicit recognition of, and systematic treatment of competing design objectives originating from various stakeholders. This motivates the question: what conceptual modeling techniques can be used to help designers analyze security trade-offs to achieve "good enough" security?

The remaining parts of the paper are structured as follows. In section 2, we consider the criteria for a suitable conceptual modeling technique for dealing with security trade-offs. In section 3, a number of existing approaches to security trade-off analysis are reviewed and compared to the introduced criteria. From analyzing the limitations of existing methods, we propose a conceptual modeling technique for modeling and analyzing security trade-offs in a multi-actor setting. In section 4, the meta-model of security concepts is introduced, and proposed extensions and refinements to the i* notation are presented. In section 5, we describe the goal model evaluation and trade-off analysis technique. Section 6 summarizes the results of some case studies. Finally, section 7 discusses results and limitations of the approach.

2   Conceptual Modeling Criteria for Security Trade-Offs Analysis

Trade-off analysis in software design refers to achieving the right balance among many competing goals. When some goals are not sufficiently satisfied, designers need to explore further alternatives that can better achieve those goals without detrimentally hurting others. Each potential solution can have positive effects on some goals while being negative on others. A careful and systematic process for security trade-off analysis can be very challenging, because a wide range of security mechanisms, solutions and frameworks need to be considered.

To support security trade-off analysis a conceptual modeling technique should model three kinds of concepts: i) Goals, ii) Actors and iii) Security specific concepts.

i) Goals: Security trade-offs are conflicts among design objectives that originate from stakeholder goals. While selecting a solution among security alternatives is difficult, the more fundamental problem is that designers need to decide about alternatives security mechanisms subject to multiple factors such as cost, time-to-market, non-functional requirements (NFRs), security policies, standards, and individual goals of various stakeholders. Therefore, the "goal" concept is a basic modeling construct required in the conceptual modeling technique for dealing with trade-offs. The technique should provide means for structuring the contributions to goals and modeling the extents and measures of goals satisfaction, contribution and competition. The measures could be quantitative or qualitative. Quantitative approaches can greatly simplify decision making, but can be difficult to apply due to lack of agreed metrics or unavailability of accurate measures. The modeling technique should be able to support analysis despite inaccurate or incomplete knowledge about goals.

ii) Actors: Design objectives typically come from multiple sources and stakeholders such as system's users, administrators, top managers, project managers, and customers. The conceptual modeling technique should be able to model multiple actors that impose competing goals on the designer, and should provide means to trace back goals to the actors. The modeling technique should be able to model trade-offs that occur within a single actor or across multiple actors.

iii) Security Specific Concepts: The conceptual modeling technique that enables security trade-off analysis should model security specific concepts such as threats, vulnerabilities, and safeguards. Threats can be viewed as malicious actors' goals. Conflicts among stakeholders' goals are usually unavoidable, and the designer needs to balance the trade-offs among conflicting goals. In contrast, threats and attacks must be mitigated. In addition, decision makers need a measurable expression of the security level of solutions [21]; therefore, the modeling technique should provide means to model to what extent attacks are successful, how attacks influence on goals, whether countermeasures control the threats, and whether the goals are at risk.

The modeling concepts need to be accompanied with a procedure for evaluating security alternatives. The proper trade-off analysis method should evaluate the impact of each alternative on goals and potential threats. It should answer to what extent the goals are satisfied or denied, threats are contained, and vulnerabilities are patched. The procedure should be able to analyze the trade-offs in the face of incomplete or inaccurate knowledge about goals' contributions and security measures.

3 Existing Approaches to Security Trade-Off Analysis

Many approaches have been proposed to model security aspects of the software systems. The notion of "abuse case" [14] and UMLsec modeling language [15] are examples of security specific conceptual modeling approaches for modeling security requirements and aspects of the system.

In recent years, agent and goal oriented frameworks in Requirements Engineering have emerged as new approaches to the analysis and design of complex software systems. Examples of such frameworks are KAOS [1], the NFR framework [10], the i* framework [7], and Tropos [2]. Several approaches such as [3, 5, 6, 16, 17, 18] propose frameworks for modeling and analyzing security concepts by taking advantage of agent and goal oriented techniques. The majority of these approaches employ qualitative trade-off analysis, while [16] suggests a quantitative approach for analyzing security requirements. In [22], probabilistic inference on security influence diagrams is used to support trade-off analysis using Bayesian Belief Nets (BBN). The approach in [23] proposes a framework of core security requirements artefacts to describe the security requirements. The meta-model of the core artefacts includes concepts such as assets, threats, security goals, functional requirements, and security requirements. In [20], using the core security artefacts, the authors propose a framework for security requirements elicitation and analysis.

In this section, we review three selected methods for modeling and analyzing security trade-offs as representative of existing approaches. We study Architecture Tradeoff Analysis Method (ATAM) [11] as a general purpose and widely used architectural trade-off analysis method which considers security. We study agent and goals oriented approaches for dealing with security trade-offs. Security Verification and security solution Design Trade-off analysis (SVDT) [21] and Aspect-Oriented Risk-Driven Development (AORDD) [27] are studied as representatives of quantitative analysis methods. We study how well these approaches are matched with the criteria discussed in the previous section.

3.1 ATAM

Bass et al. [11] introduces a framework to model quality attributes and architectural options using the notion of scenarios and tactics respectively. A quality attribute scenario is a quality-attribute-specific requirement, and consists of six parts: Source of stimulus, Stimulus, Environment, Artifact, Response, and Response measure. Achievement of quality scenarios relies on tactics. ATAM is an evaluation method to analyze whether an architecture decision satisfies particular quality goals. ATAM helps designers to prioritize scenarios and evaluate alternative tactics using a "Quality Attribute Utility Tree". Scenarios that have at least one high priority of importance or difficulty are chosen for a detail analysis to examine if the selected tactics satisfy the scenario.

The result of the analysis is an "Architectural Approach Analysis" table for each quality scenario. In this table, evaluators identify and record sensitivity, tradeoff, risks and non-risks points for alternative tactics. Sensitivity and tradeoff points are architectural decisions that have effect on one or more quality attributes, the former positively and the latter negatively. In ATAM, a risk is defined as an architectural decision that may lead to undesirable consequences, and non risk points are defined in the opposite way. The conceptual elements related to trade-offs in ATAM may be captured in a meta-model as in Fig. 1.

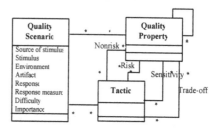

Fig. 1. Meta-model of trade-off elements in ATAM

3.2 SVDT/AORDD Approach

Houmb et al. [21] propose the SVDT approach using UMLsec for modeling security solutions. UMLsec is used to specify security requirements, and UMLsec tools verify if the design solutions satisfy the security requirements. Design solutions that pass the verification are then evaluated using security solution design trade-off analysis. A complementary framework on AORDD provides a risk assessment process and cost-benefic trade-off analysis. AORDD and SVDT use BBN to compute Return on Security Investment (RoSI).

Fig. 2 illustrates the relationship between the main concepts involved in AORDD risk assessment, which specifies the structure of the inputs to the AORDD cost-benefit trade-off analysis. The result of risk assessment is a list of misuses which need security treatments. This list, alternative security treatments, and fixed trade-off parameters such as budget, time-to-market, and policies are fed into the BBN to compute the RoSI.

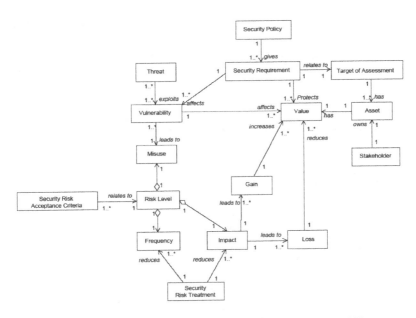

Fig. 2. ARODD risk assessment main concepts and relation [27]

3.3 Secure Tropos/i*

The proposed approaches in [3, 5, 6, 17, 18] take advantage of the i* and Tropos frameworks. In these approaches, systems are modeled as intentional agents collaborating or competing with each other to achieve their goals. Security issues arise when some actors, while striving to achieve their own goals, intentionally or unintentionally threaten other actors' goals; therefore, agent and goal oriented approaches provide a suitable basis for dealing with competing goals of multiple actors.

The approach in [3] suggests using relationships among strategic actors for analyzing security requirements. In [3], potential attackers of the systems are distinguished from

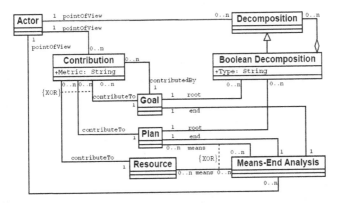

Fig. 3. Part of Tropos meta-model for goals and related concepts [31]

other actors of the system. [5] proposes a methodological framework for dealing with security requirements based on the i* notation. In [6], a framework known as Secure Tropos for modeling and analyzing security requirements based on the notions of trust, ownership, and permission delegation is developed. In [17, 18], the "threat" and "security constraint" modeling elements are added to the i* meta-model. "Threat" elements are employed in the "security diagram" to express potential violation against the security goals, and "security constraints" are used to impose security requirements on actors' dependencies. The meta-model of related concepts to the Tropos goal model, which is the core of all these approaches, is depicted in Fig. 3.

3.4 Limitations of Existing Approaches

In ATAM, trade-offs among quality scenarios and tactics in the "Architectural Approach Analysis" table are indirect and implicit, since trade-off and risk points, instead of referring to quality scenarios, refer to affected quality properties. ATAM lacks considering the impact of each tactic on stimuli of security scenarios (attacks). The impact of tactics on quality attributes are not captured qualitatively or a quantitatively. Finally, the framework of scenarios, tactics and ATAM method does not provide means to model and analyze security concepts specifically.

SVDT and AORDD rely on quantitative computation and probabilistic inference for trade-off analysis. This requires the software designers obtain the quantitative measures of the impact of misuses and solutions. The major limitation is the inaccuracy or unavailability of qualitative data on the impact of misuses and solutions especially in the early stages of the development lifecycle.

Generally, the suggested BBN topologies in SVDT and AORDD do not consider a more general source of trade-off inputs such as NFRs and functionalities, and the trade-off inputs to the designed BBN are limited to factors such as budget, laws and regulation. Besides, the AORDD meta-model of risk assessment concepts (Fig. 2) does not consider the relation between "security risk treatment" and other entities such as "security requirement", "threat", and "vulnerability". The AORDD meta-model could be strengthen by considering more general concepts such as goals, other quality requirements, and actors.

In SVDT and AORDD, the trade-off inputs and information are given to a BBN, and the final RoSI is computed automatically, which makes the analysis efficient. Since, the relationships between various states of the variables are specified in terms of the node probability matrix in BBN, this automatic trade-off analysis process can be traced by the designer. However, it may be difficult for the designer to follow what aspects of the design caused the difference in the final results.

Although agent and goal oriented approaches provide a proper conceptual basis for modeling and analyzing security trade-offs, a mechanism for such analysis has not been elaborated in these frameworks. The method in [5] lacks a direct and explicit way to model the competition among malicious and non-malicious actors' goals, and trade-off modeling among goals is limited to the non-malicious actors. The proposed framework in [6] does not support modeling security concepts such as malicious behavior. In [17, 18], threats are modeled explicitly as a distinct construct in the "security diagram", but they are not traced to the threats' source actors, and the relation between countermeasures and threats are not elaborated.

Table 1 summarizes a comparison of the studied approaches based on the evaluation criteria from section 2.

Table 1. A comparison of existing approaches based on the criteria of the conceptual modeling technique for security trade-off analysis

Method Requirement	ATAM	SVDT/AORDD	i*/Tropos
Goals	Expressed in terms of scenarios	Limited to security requirements and fixed BBN parameters	Explicit goals
Relations of goals	Not model explicitly	Limited to UMLsec models	Modeled using contribution links
Extents of goal satisfaction	Not expressed	Quantitatively	Qualitatively
Goals contribution structure	Utility tree doesn't capture the contributions of scenarios	Not modeled	Modeled in terms of sub goals and contribution links
Multiple actors	Expressed implicitly by multiple stimuli sources	Not modeled	Modeled in terms of agents/actors/ roles/ positions
Trade-off within a single actor or across actors	Single actor	Single actor	Single and multiple actors
Security Specific Trade-off Concepts	Not modeled	Some concepts are modeled	Some concepts are modeled
Trade-off analysis method	Qualitative analysis	Quantitative analysis	Qualitative and quantitative analysis

4   The Security Trade-Offs Modeling Notation

We propose a meta-model of security concepts for systematically addressing security trade-offs (Fig. 4), considering the limitations of existing approaches and reviewing well known security knowledge sources such as NIST's guidelines and standards like [19], CERT [26], and widely used textbooks such as [4, 13]. The core of the meta-model is the concepts of goals and actors guided by the criteria of the conceptual modeling technique that enables security trade-offs analysis.

The proposed notation builds upon the i* framework which provides a notation to model *actors*, their *goals* and intentional *dependencies* and competitions among the actors. Actors achieve goals on their own or depend on each other for goals to be achieved, tasks to be performed, and resources to be furnished. Quality goals, which do not have clear-cut criteria for satisfaction degree, are modeled as softgoals. *Means-ends* relation between goals and tasks is used to model alternative ways to achieve a goal [8]. However, the i* notation lacks explicit modeling constructs for concepts such as threats and vulnerabilities. In this section, we propose some extensions to the i* notation, which provide conceptual structures for modeling and analyzing security trade-offs.

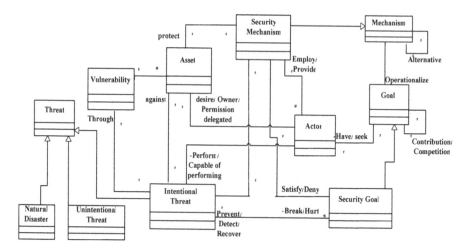

Fig. 4. Meta-model of security concepts used in proposed modeling notation

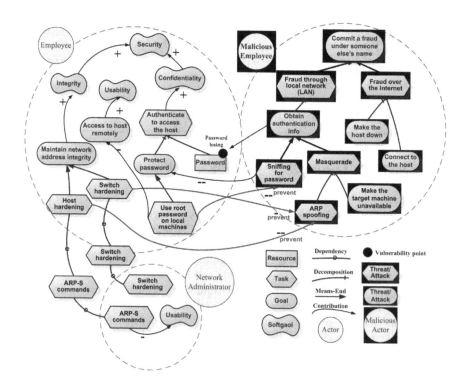

Fig. 5. Example of a multi-actor system modeled using the proposed notation

4.1 Malicious Actor, Goals and Tasks

Actors depend on, or compete with each other to achieve their goals. Meanwhile, malicious actors try to achieve their own goals. Representing a malicious actor with a different modeling construct in i* was first employed in [3] by highlighting them with a black shadow rectangle. This notation was used to model malicious goals in [5]. We make use of this notation in which malicious goals, softgoals, tasks, and actors are highlighted by a black shadow rectangle. By distinguishing malicious modeling elements from non-malicious ones, we emphasize studying the attackers' goals and tasks. Although attacker's behavior might be partially unknown and generic, an important aspect of trade-off analysis depends on studying attackers' options and the risks they pose to other actors' goals.

A security threat is any malicious behavior that interferes with the achievement of other actors' goals. For example, in Fig. 5, Malicious Employee is the malicious actor whose goal is to Commit a fraud under someone else's name, either through the local network or over the Internet. Threats might be unintentional or caused by natural disasters. In this paper, we mainly focus on the security threats caused by actors with malicious intent.

4.2 Assets, Services and Vulnerabilities Points

An asset is any thing that has a value for the organization [13]. Physical resources, information, and people can be counted as assets. In this way, the asset concept is well matched with the "resource" modeling element in i*. Assets can be the services an organization offer or receive, and in this case, can be represented by tasks or goals that actors offer to the "depender" actors.

In security analysis, a vulnerability point is any weakness in, or back door to the system [13]. For example, it is said that *buffer overflow* and *password cracking* are the most common vulnerability points of many computer systems [4]. Generally, a vulnerability point corresponds to an asset or service, and attackers usually try to achieve malicious goals through a vulnerability to reach an asset. In the i* notation, tasks are usually decomposed to goals, softgoals, other tasks, and resources. In this way, harm of an attack can be indicated by the cost of the failed task that relies on the compromised assets. In a similar approach in [20, 23], threats are described in terms of assets, the action that exploits the assets, and the subsequent harm.

Although vulnerability that arises from dependencies among actors is a fundamental concept in i* in [5], there is no explicit modeling construct in i* to represent vulnerability points. We add the vulnerability point modeling element to i*, accompanied with a graphical notation to connect a vulnerability point to the corresponding attacks, and to attach it to a resource. For example, in Fig. 5, to protect confidentially employees are authenticated by the host. Hence, Password is one of the employees' assets they need to protect. On the other hand, Password losing is one of the most important vulnerability points in computer systems. Sniffing for password is an attack against the goal of Protect password. Through this attack and Password losing vulnerability point, the goal of Fraud under someone else's name can be satisfied, and the attacker gains a valuable asset: the Password.

4.3 Relation Between Attacks and Security Mechanisms

In the i* notation, relation between softgoals and other elements is modeled by contribution links [7]. If an element hurts a softgoal, yet not enough to prevent it, the contribution link type is "-". If the element is sufficient to prevent a softgoal, the contribution link type is "--". This qualitative approach is used to model the impact of attacks on softgoals and the impact of security mechanisms on malicious tasks and goals. In security engineering, various mechanisms have different effects on attacks. Contribution of mechanisms to attacks are categorized as 1) Prevent 2) Detect 3) Recover [13]. These categories are added as attributes on the contribution links. "Detect" and "Recover" contribution links may partially mitigate the effect of attacks. Mechanisms which are related to the attacks with "Detect" contribution links can not control any attack. Similarly, "Recover" contribution links indicate that the mechanisms can not control the attack either, but the mechanism would be used to recover the system after the attack. This link would be useful to express availability and integrity goals that rely on recovering the system after the failure. To sufficiently counteract an attack, security mechanisms must be related to the attack with a "Prevent" contribution link.

4.4 Expressing Trade-Offs by the Proposed Conceptual Structure

The proposed approach provides the means to model goals, and trace them back to the source actors. In this approach, trade-offs among goals are modeled by contribution links. Through contribution link types of -, --, + and ++ [10], the qualitative effect of alternative solutions are propagated to the other goals. The i* notation offers the conceptual structure to model trade-offs between refined sub-goals of high level goals as well. For example, in Fig. 5, the employee can Use root password on local machines to completely prevent the attack of Sniffing for password [4]. However, this security solution contributes negatively to the Access to host remotely goal, and it has negative influence on the Usability softgoal consequently. In this way, the trade-off among usability and security is modeled through relationships among their refined sub-goals.

5 Trade-Off Analysis and Decision Making

In the previous section, we proposed a conceptual modeling technique for modeling security trade-offs. In this part, we propose a trade-off analysis method for use with the trade-off model. Designers need to balance the trade-offs to mitigate the security risks and yet satisfy the goals of multiple actors. A goal is at risk when it may be denied (partially or fully) by the successful behavior of malicious actors. Partially or fully denial of goals are expressed through contribution links of type "-" and "--". Hence, for trade-off analysis designers need to examine available alternative security solutions, and verify the impacts of each one on attacks and goals to finally select the one which fits with goals of multiple actors. Goal model evaluation is the procedure to ensure that actors' top level goals are satisfied by the choices they have made [12]. The security goal model evaluation, consisting of interactive qualitative reasoning, is based on the method proposed in [10] and refined in [12]. Fig. 6 depicts the proposed security trade-off analysis procedure.

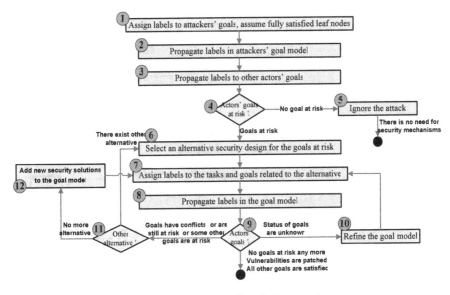

Fig. 6. Security trade-off analysis procedure

In the first step, evaluator assumes that attackers are successful in performing tasks and satisfying their goals, since attackers are usually external actors that designer has no sure knowledge of their abilities and skills. Therefore, the leaf nodes in attackers' goal model are labeled fully satisfied. This assumption does not imply that the risk of attacks is definite, as it is possible that evaluation of attackers' goal model yields to denial of higher goals of attacker. The leaf labels are propagated to upper goals. Once the impact of malicious actors' behavior is propagated to the entire goal model, the evaluator assigns labels to the tasks and goals that operationalize security mechanism (step 7). This label indicates the evaluator's judgment about the success of the actor in performing a security task or achieving a security goal. This judgment could be based on knowledge of previous experiences, empirical studies, or subjective knowledge [21].

In step 9, the goal model indicates which goals are fully or partially satisfied or denied for the examined security solution. The procedure iterates until a security design solution is found that, based of the evaluator's perception, satisfies an acceptable configuration of goals. However, the evaluator may prefer to examine further alternatives to select the security design solution that satisfies more goals. After evaluating an alternative, the status of some goals may be unknown, prompting the designer to elaborate on the models (step 10). In case of conflict of goals, other alternatives should be examined to resolve the conflicts (step 11). An example of security goal model evaluation is shown in Fig. 7.

Propagation of the labels is based on the contribution types and rules summarized in Table 2. [12] provides details about aggregation rules for multiple contributions. The rules provided in Table 2 are merely valid for the "Prevent" contribution type, as we discussed earlier that recovering from, or detecting an attack do not lead to controlling the attack.

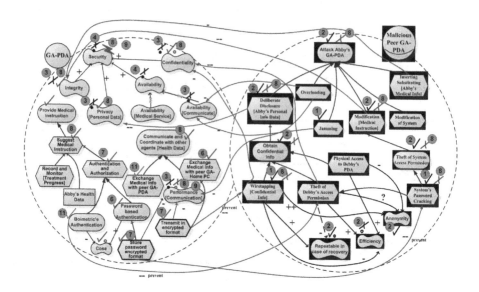

Fig. 7. Part of the attacker and countermeasures model for the Guardian Angel case study annotated with the evaluation steps introduced in Fig. 6

Table 2. Evaluation labels and propagation rules from [10, 12]

Child Node		Contribution Type (Prevent)				
Label Name	Symbol	++	+	-	- -	?
Satisfied	✓	✓	✓.	✗	✗	?.
Weakly Satisfied	✓.	✓.	✓.	✗	✗	?.
Conflict	⇌	⇌	⇌	⇌	⇌	?.
Unknown	?.	?.	?.	?.	?.	?.
Weakly Denied	✗.	✗.	✗.	✓.	✓.	?.
Denied	✗	✗	✗.	✓.	✓.	?.

6   Case Studies

In developing the proposed notation, we modeled a number of NIST guidelines [19] and security engineering knowledge in [4], using the extended i* notation. In addition to example cases, we applied the notation to three example cases originally used to illustrate other approaches to security trade-offs [28]. In the first example case, we modeled and analyzed the eSAP system, an agent-based health and social care system, which was used as the case study system in [16, 17, 18]. In the second example case system, we modeled and analyzed a simple Course Registration system, using the proposed extensions to the i* and the framework proposed in [11]. Due to space limitations, we present only a third case study in the following. Details of the case studies can be found in [28].

The Guardian Angel (GA) [9] is a patient and physician supporting system using software agents, which is studied in [5]. In vulnerability analysis in [5], each dependency is examined as a potential threat against the system. In this approach, each actor is studied in two roles: its regular role, and its potential malicious role. One of the actors in the dependency relation is substituted by its corresponding attacker. For each malicious actor, a number of attacks and threats are identified, the impact of threats and corresponding security safeguards are added to the goal model. However, resulting models do not capture goals and intentions of the attacker. The goal model evaluation is limited to evaluating impact of security safeguards on threats, while the safeguards may affect other goals such as performance and usability. Generally, the approach in [5] does not consider modeling security mechanisms in terms of the trade-offs they impose to the other goals.

Fig. 7 gives a part of the trade-off models and analysis of GA system using the proposed approach in this paper. The model captures the potential intentions behind an attack, since deciding among different countermeasures depends on the attacker's goals. For example, the designer needs to differentiate between goals of a professional hacker and intentions of a curious kid to select proper security mechanisms. The resulting goal model captures the effects of each alternative attack on malicious and non-malicious actors' goals and softgoals. As a result, the designer can evaluate the risk of threats, and select a more appropriate countermeasure for attackers' behavior based on the consequence of malicious actors' behavior. In the goal model of Fig. 7, the designer decides to employ Authentication and Authorization with Password based Authentication (Steps 6 and 7). The goal model evaluation yields a fully satisfied Privacy goal with Confidentiality partially satisfied, while Performance is partially denied.

7   Conclusion and Future Work

In this paper, we began by considering the criteria for a conceptual modeling technique that enables designers to model and analyze security trade-offs among competing goals of multiple actors to achieve a good-enough security level. We studied existing approaches to trade-off analysis, and identified limitations of these approaches. Based on the evaluation criteria and limitation of previous works, we proposed extensions to the i* notation for modeling and analyzing security trade-offs of a multi-actor system. The proposed modeling notation is accompanied with a qualitative trade-off analysis procedure based on goal model evaluation methods. The procedure provides the designers with assessment of security mechanisms' impact on actors' goals and threats. Table 3 gives the comparison of the proposed approach with the evaluation criteria.

Although the i* notation provides the proper basis for modeling and analyzing trade-offs, the models become complex and inefficient when the goal models scale. Another limitation of the proposed approach is that a comprehensive source of knowledge of security mechanisms and corresponding contributions does not exist.

Table 3. Comparison of proposed approach with the conceptual modeling technique's criteria

Method Requirements	Suggested approach
Goals	Modeled using goals and softgoals elements of i*
Relations of goals	Modeled using i* goal dependency modeling. Competition and trade-offs are modeled by contribution links and relation between attacks and goals.
Extents and measures of goals	Modeled qualitatively by contribution links of type -, - -, +, ++
Inaccurate or incomplete knowledge	Modeled by unknown contribution links, and goal model evaluation propagates them to related elements
Goals contribution structure	Structured by sub-goals, task decomposition, contribution links
Multiple actors	Multiple malicious and non malicious actors can be modeled
Trade-off within a single actor or across actors	Trade-off within a single actor or across actors can be modeled
Security specific trade-off concepts	Modeled by security extensions to i* notation derived from the meta-model
Trade-off analysis method	Security goal model evaluation technique supports qualitative trade-off analysis

In future work, we aim to conduct empirical studies of how security designers make trade-offs in practice, and to adapt the proposed systematic trade-off analysis framework for integration into everyday design practice. We will also build a security requirements and design knowledge base to gather and catalogue reusable knowledge about security trade-offs. Tool support for managing and applying security knowledge will also be studied.

Acknowledgments. Financial support from Natural Science and Engineering Research Council of Canada and Bell University Labs is gratefully acknowledged.

References

1. Dardenne, A., van Lamsweerde, A., Fickas, S.: Goal-Directed Requirements Acquisition. The Science of Computer Programming 20, 3–50 (1993)
2. Castro, J., Kolp, M., Mylopoulos, J.: A requirements-driven development methodology, In Proc. of the 13th Int. Conf. on Advanced Information Systems Engineering, CAiSE'01. In: Dittrich, K.R., Geppert, A., Norrie, M.C. (eds.) CAiSE 2001. LNCS, vol. 2068, pp. 108–123. Springer, Heidelberg (2001)
3. Liu, L., Yu, E., Mylopoulos, J.: Analyzing Security Requirements as Relationships among Strategic Actors. In: 2nd Symp. on Requirements Engineering for Information Security (SREIS) (2002)
4. Anderson, R.: Security Engineering: a guide to Building dependable Distributed systems. John Wiley and Sons, Chichester (2001)

5. Liu, L., Yu, E., Mylopoulos, J.: Security and Privacy Requirements Analysis within a Social Setting. In: IEEE Joint Int. Conf. on Requirements Engineering, pp. 151–161. IEEE Computer Society Press, Los Alamitos (2003)

6. Giorgini, P., Massacci, F., Mylopoulos, J., Zannone, N.: Modeling Security Requirements through Ownership, Permission and Delegation. In: 13th IEEE Int. Requirements Engineering Conf, pp. 167–176. IEEE Computer Society Press, Los Alamitos (2005)

7. Yu, E.: Modeling Strategic Relationships for Process Reengineering, PhD thesis, Department of Computer Science, University of Toronto, Canada (1995)

8. Yu, E.: Towards Modelling and Reasoning Support for Early-Phase Requirements Engineering. In: Proc. of the 3rd IEEE Int. Symp. on Requirements Engineering, pp. 226–235 (1997)

9. Szolovits, P., Doyle, J., Long, W.J.: Guardian Angel: Patient-Centered Health Information Systems: MIT/LCS/TR-604, Available at: http://www.ga.org/ga

10. Chung, L., Nixon, B.A., Yu, E., Mylopoulos, J.: Non-Functional Requirements in Software Engineering. Kluwer Academic Publishing, Dordrecht (2000)

11. Bass, L., Clements, P., Kazman, R.: Software Architecture in Practice, 2nd edn. Addison Wesley, London, UK (2003)

12. Horkoff, J.: Using i* Models for Evaluation, Masters Thesis, University of Toronto, Department of Computer Science (2006)

13. Pfleeger, C.P., Pfleeger, S.L.: Security in Computing, 3rd edn. Prentice-Hall, Englewood Cliffs (2002)

14. McDermott, J., Fox, C.: Using Abuse Case Models for Security Requirements Analysis. In: McDermott, J., Fox, C. (eds.) Proc.15th. IEEE Annual Computer Security Applications Conf., pp. 55–64. IEEE Computer Society Press, Los Alamitos (1999)

15. Jürjens, J.: Secure Systems Development with UML. Springer Academic Publishers, Germany (2004)

16. Bresciani, P., Giorgini, P., Mouratidis, H.: On Security Requirements Analysis for Multi-Agent Systems. In: Lucena, C., Garcia, A., Romanovsky, A., Castro, J., Alencar, P.S.C. (eds.) Software Engineering for Multi-Agent Systems II. LNCS, vol. 2940, pp. 35–48. Springer, Heidelberg (2004)

17. Mouratidis, H., Giorgini, P., Manso, G., Philp, I.: A Natural Extension of Tropos Methodology for Modelling Security. In: Proc. of the Workshop on Agent-oriented methodologies, at OOPSLA, pp. 91–103 (2002)

18. Mouratidis, H., Giorgini, P.: Manso, Modelling Secure Multiagent Systems. In: the 2nd Int. Conf. on Autonomous Agents and Multiagent Systems, pp. 859–866 (2003)

19. Grance, T., Stevens, M., Myers, M.: Guide to Selecting Information Technology Security Products, Recommendations of the National Institute of Standards and Technology, NIST Special Publication 800–836 (2003)

20. Haley, C.B., Moffett, J.D., Laney, R., Nuseibeh, B.: A framework for security requirements engineering. In: Software Engineering for Secure Systems Workshop (SESS'06), pp. 35–42 (2006)

21. Houmb, S.H., Georg, G., Jürjens, J., France, R.: An Integrated Security Verification and Security Solution Design Trade-off Analysis. In: Integrating Security and Software Engineering: Advances and Future Visions, pp. 190–219. IDEA Group Publishing, USA (2007)

22. Johnson, P., Lagerstrom, R., Norman, P., Simonsson, M.: Extended Influence Diagrams for Enterprise Architecture Analysis. In: Enterprise Distributed Object Computing Conference, EDOC '06. 10th IEEE Int., pp. 3–12. IEEE Computer Society Press, Los Alamitos (2006)

23. Moffett, J.D., Haley, C.B., Nuseibeh, B.: Core Security Requirements Artefacts, Department of Computing, The Open University, Milton Keynes UK, Technical Report 2004/23 (2004)
24. Mayer, N., Rifaut, A., Dubois, E.: Towards a Risk-Based Security Requirements Engineering Framework, 11th Int. Workshop on Requirements Engineering: Foundation for Software Quality (REFSQ'05) (2005)
25. Sandhu, R.: Good-Enough Security: Toward a Pragmatic Business-Driven Discipline," IEEE Internet Computing, Vol. IEEE Internet Computing 07(1), 66–68 (2003)
26. US-CERT Vulnerability Notes Database, United States Computer Emergency Readiness Team, http://www.kb.cert.org/vuls
27. Houmb, S.H., Georg, G.: The Aspect-Oriented Risk-Driven Development (AORDD) Framework. In: Proc. of the Int. Conf. on Software Development (SWDC.REX), pp. 81–91 (2005)
28. Elahi, G., Yu, E.: A Goal Oriented Approach for Modeling and Analyzing Security Trade-Offs, Technical Report, University of Toronto, Department of Computer Science, Available (2007), at http://istar.rwth-aachen.de/tiki-index.php?page=Security+Requirements+Engineering
29. Sasse, M.A.: Computer Security: Anatomy of a Usability Disaster, and a Plan for Recovery, Workshop on Human-Computer Interaction and Security Systems, CHI 2003, Fort Lauderdale (2003)
30. De Witt, A.J., Kuljis, J.: Aligning Usability And Security-A Usability Study Of Polaris. In: Proc. of the Symp. On Usable Privacy and Security (2006)
31. Susi, A., Perini, A., Mylopoulos, J.: The Tropos Metamodel and its Use. Informatica 29, 401–408 (2005)

Rapid Business Process Discovery (*R*-BPD)

Aditya Ghose, George Koliadis, and Arthur Chueng

Decision Systems Lab (DSL)
School of Computer Science and Software Engineering
University of Wollongong, NSW 2522 Australia
{aditya,gk56,ac83}@uow.edu.au

Abstract. Modeling is an important and time consuming part of the Business Process Management life-cycle. An analyst reviews existing documentation and queries relevant domain experts to construct both mental and concrete models of the domain. To aid this exercise, we propose the Rapid Business Process Discovery (R-BPD) framework and prototype tool that can query heterogeneous information resources (e.g. corporate documentation, web-content, code e.t.c.) and rapidly construct proto-models to be incrementally adjusted to correctness by an analyst. This constitutes a departure from building and constructing models toward just editing them. We believe this rapid mixed-initiative modeling will increase analyst productivity by significant orders of magnitude over traditional approaches. Furthermore, the possibility of using the approach in distributed and real-time settings seems appealing and may help in significantly improving the quality of the models being developed w.r.t. being consistent, complete, and concise.

1 Introduction

Modeling is an important, expensive, time-consuming and labour-intensive part of the business process lifecycle. The first major step in managing a business process is *discovery* (or *understanding*) [1] [2]), with subsequent improvement initiatives driven by a need to "understand existing processes and evolve these processes in ways that maintain their strengths" [3]. In this paper we report on a project to build a tool-kit *that would shift the focus in modeling from model-building to model-editing*. Our aim is to address the *model acquisition bottleneck*, a version of the well-known *knowledge acquisition bottleneck* [4]. Our guiding premise is that most organizations maintain enterprise repositories of (sometimes legacy) documents and models which can provide rich sources of information that could be mined to extract "first-cut" process models. Our premise is also that by extracting such "first-cut" models (henceforth referred to as *proto-models*) and presenting them to an analyst for editing, such a toolkit can significantly enhance analyst productivity. Given that organizations are often loathe to invest the resources required for significant modeling exercises, the availability of such a toolkit can make modeling-in-the-large a viable option in many instances.

C. Parent et al. (Eds.): ER 2007, LNCS 4801, pp. 391–406, 2007.

We classify the artefacts (henceforth called *source artefacts*) typically available in an enterprise repository into two categories: *text* and *model*. Text artefacts are documents such as memos, manuals, requirements documents, design documents, mission/vision statements, meeting minutes etc. Model artefacts could be models in a variety of notations, including UML design models, or enterprise models or rule models. We define two categories of model extraction techniques: text-to-model extraction (for extracting process models from text artefacts) and model-to-model extraction (for extracting process models from models in other notations). We describe the R-BPD (*Rapid* Business Process Discovery) toolkit in which instances of these extraction techniques have been implemented. Additional R-BPD examples and code fragments that could not be included in this paper due to space constraints are available at [5].

The R-BPD can potentially extract a large number of (sometimes small) process proto-models from an enterprise repository. Some of these proto-models might in fact be alternative descriptions of the same process. We describe heuristic techniques for establishing model identity to deal with such situations. When multiple models that seem to describe the same process are identified, we need to cross-validate these against each other. We use *model consistency* as a basis for cross-validation, i.e., alternative consistent descriptions of the same process are viewed as supporting each other. We define a lightweight structural check for consistency and provide examples. Finally, we describe how the R-BPD toolkit can also support traceability and change management.

Our research relies, for its conceptual foundations, on several other areas of inquiry. Knowledge acquisition and modeling "can be the most time consuming portion of the knowledge engineering process" [6], and has been termed as the "bottleneck" in expert systems design [7]. This issue covers the inherent difficulties (inc. time and resources required) in eliciting complete and concise knowledge from experts.

Some of the major considerations include:

- the *choice* of approach (or combination) to use for acquiring specific types of knowledge, as captured by the differential access hypothesis [7] [8];
- the tradeoff between the *acquirability* (i.e. usability by a particular audience) and *expressive power* (or applicability) of languages used to represent knowledge [6], which may be reduced via the combined use of multiple languages and views on a domain of interest;
- and, *bias* that "is the result of cognitive heuristics" and is mostly introduced when: individual or group experience is overestimated; there is inappropriate emphasis on specific phenomena; small sample sizes are used; there is over-confidence in levels of certainty; or, there is over-estimation of data completeness [9].

Automated knowledge acquisition shells provide an interesting approach toward a solution. Such shells iteratively construct and propose queries to experts to discover computable representations of the domain [10]. In particular, the Requirements Apprentice [11] project contributes a system (as a mediator) for applying knowledge acquisition techniques to support the "transition between informal and formal specifications..." [11]. The apprentice "avoids involvement with the surface syntax of natural language [specifications]" [11] to ensure the "deeper" problems in natural language understanding are not encountered.

A growing body of literature has been established on Workflow Mining [12]. These approaches focus on extracting meaningful process models by analyzing event logs that are generated by transactional information systems. They have also been extended to mine social networks [13] and decision junctions [14]. In [15], an extended scope for workflow mining is proposed, which allows for the discovery of activities and social phenomena in combination with traditional approaches that capture precedence relationships between activities. Activities are induced from similar sets of ordered database transactions. Once activities are discovered, traditional mining techniques are applied to business process traces to discovery precedence relationships. In addition, the approach used to induce activities is applied to the discovery of roles by analyzing the similarity between the behaviors of actors.

The area of multi-viewpoint software engineering [16] [17] [18] provide methodological and automated approaches for checking and resolving consistency among distributed modeling perspectives. In particular, [3] describes a means for managing inconsistencies among distributed process descriptions. Our work contributes an automated means and tool for managing inconsistencies during the rapid discovery of processes and process architectures.

Model Driven Architecture (MDA) is primarily concerned with the automated transformation of models from abstract domain descriptions directly into implementable solutions (see [19] for a taxonomy of approaches). Our approach for model-to-model translation (see Section 3) extends and partially automates the constrained development method we presented in [20] for managing business process model (BPMN, see Figure 4) lifecycles with organizational models (i*, see Figure 3). In essence, [20] described an methodology to managing process lifecycles with explicit high-level organizational models by guiding the derivation or maintenance of one type of model given the availability of the other. This was achieved by: 1/ Establishing a correspondence between elements within the models that describe aspects of the process; 2/ Annotating sets of elements common to both models with semantics in natural language (with the intent of automated translation into structured, formal notation); 3/ Applying specific rules and procedures for determining consistency between such models; and, 4/ Using the results of the consistency check to help guide refinement and co-evolution of the models toward correctness.

To date, we have also developed the Enterprise Process Lifecycle Management (EPLM) toolkit (see Figure 1) above a commercial CASE platform [21] for experimentation. The EPLM partially automates the procedures described in [20]. This paper extends [20] by contributing a means to rapidly extract and identify partial proto-process models from a variety of sources and incrementally combine them toward completeness and correctness.

In [22], an approach for discovery is described, which proposes a three-layered language for representing business processes and the use of model checking techniques for verifying constructed models against business requirements that are specified a-priori. They presume the correctness of the requirements provided and cannot resolve inconsistencies, manage change and evaluate correctness within and across the inter-relationships between models constructed in a such a variety of languages.

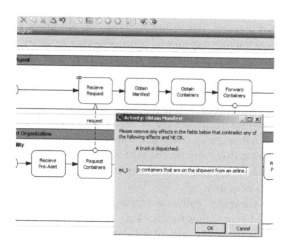

Fig. 1. Enterprise Process Life-cycle Manager (EPLM) Prototype

2 Text-to-Model Extraction

To support process discovery, we employ both *text-to-model* and *model-to-model* translation as follows. The examples presented follow from an *R*-BPDTk test case based on a tutorial provided by BEA Systems [23].

The intent of our approach for text-to-model extraction is to look for cues within text documents that suggest "snippets" of process models. In the *R*-BPDTk, we use two sets of techniques for text-to-model extraction:

- *Template-Based Extraction:* Here we construct templates of commonly occurring textual cues for processes, and extract proto-models by scanning documents for instances of these patterns. For example, one such cue that we currently use in the *R*-BPDTk simply extracts sentences that conform to the pattern:

  "**If** < *condition/event* >, [*then*] < *action* >."

  For example. "**If** *the credit check fails, the customer service representative is assigned the task of notifying the customer to obtain correct credit information, and the process becomes manual from this point on.*

- *Information extraction-based:* Here we use NLP toolkits such as NLTk [24] to extract verb phrases, verbs, temporal connectives etc. as the building blocks for process models.

  For example we can extract noun phrases (*np*) such as "the customer", verb phrases (*vp*) such as "notifying", and extract possible activities (*a*) by looking for < *vp, np* > pairs or possible role/assignments from < *np, a* > pairs where *np* refers to an actor.

Both these approaches provide a rapid means to extract, interpret and summarize the knowledge contained within text documents. This is not to say that the machine interpretation will always be valid, however analyst support and automated identification and cross-validation functions will help to unearth inconsistencies (e.g. where the *np* in an assignment pair is found to be an inanimate *object* rather than an *actor* - also see Section 4). In addition, other advanced and efficient methods are available that may help in reducing errors, for example when interpreting temporal relationships [25].

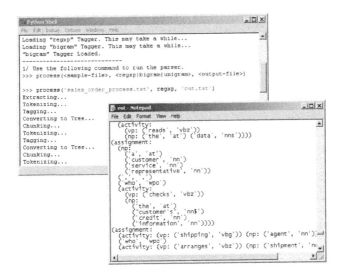

Fig. 2. *R*-BPDTk Prototype

The following fragment shows output from the *R*-BPD tool that assigns an activity to a role. The activity in question is "check customer credit information" and the role in question is that of "customer service representative". A combination of template-based extraction and analysis using the NLTk toolkit is used to identify both the role and its relationship to the activity.

```
(assignment:
  (np:
    ('a', 'at')
    ('customer', 'nn')
    ('service', 'nn')
    ('representative', 'nn'))
  (',', ',')
  ('who', 'wpo')
  (activity:
    (vp: ('checks', 'vbz'))
    (np:
      ('the', 'at')
      ("customer's", 'nn$')
      ('credit', 'nn')
      ('information', 'nn'))))
```

This second fragment indicates a precedence relationship between two activities - specifically that "order cancellation" may only occur prior to "shipping".

```
(rule:
  ('before', 'cs')
  (activity: (vp: ('shipping', 'vbg')))
  (',', ',')
  (np_act:
    (np: ('the', 'at') ('order', 'nn'))
    ('can', 'md')
    ('be', 'be')
    (activity:
      (vp: ('cancelled', 'vbd'))
      (pp: ('by', 'in')
        (np: ('notification', 'nn')))
      (pp: ('from', 'in') (np: ('the', 'at')
      ('customer', 'nn')))))
  ('.', '.'))
```

3 Model-to-Model Extraction

The intent of model-to-model extraction is to obtain elements of process models that might be described in other existing models. For instance, a sequence diagram can be viewed as a fine-grained proto-process model. We can conceive of the following two alternative approaches for model-to-model extraction:

– *Syntactic mappings between notations:* In this approach, hand-crafted mapping functions are used to map models in a variety of different notations (e.g., use case diagrams, sequence diagrams, state diagrams etc.) to a process modeling notation. Our current work is primarily based on this approach. Let N_i and N_j be two distinct modeling notations. Let $f_{N_i,N_j}^{syn} : M_{N_i} \rightarrow M_{N_j}$ where M_{N_i} and M_{N_j} are the sets of all possible models expressible in N_i and N_j respectively, be a function that maps a model in N_i to a model in N_j. That is, the function generates an N_j model that expresses as much of the input model (in N_i) as can be expressed in N_j. We shall refer to such functions as *syntactitc transformation functions* and note that such functions can be realized using QVT languages in the model-driven architectures framework (although our current implementation does not use a QVT language). We provide a complete example of a syntactic transformation function below, and outline another instance.

Consider an $i*$ [26] in Figure 3, mapped to the BPMN process model [27] in Figure 4. In this case, the function $f_{i*,BP}^{syn}$ mapped: activities in $i*$ to process models in BPMN; the child nodes of activities in an $i*$ model to activities within the BPMN process model; actors in an $i*$ model to pools/lanes in the BPMN model; and, resource dependencies between activities in the $i*$ model to message flow links in the BPMN model. The BPMN model could then be easily edited to refine sequencing information and additional activities, that may also trigger some change in the $i*$ model if a reverse mapping were applied.

– *Mappings based on semantic correspondences:* Here we would rely on semantic correspondences that exist between languages to establish what statements can be said in another language, and how they should be represented syntactically. In this case, analyst involvement will mainly be required where either N_i or N_j is an informal notation. Where the semantics for both N_i and N_j are well-understood, we would require a function $f_{N_i,N_j}^{sem} : Sem_{N_i} \rightarrow Sem_{N_j}$, where Sem_{N_i} and Sem_{N_j} represent the semantic domains of N_i and N_j respectively. Our current implementation does not adopt this approach but [20] provides some preliminary indications of how an analyst-driven "mized" approach might look like.

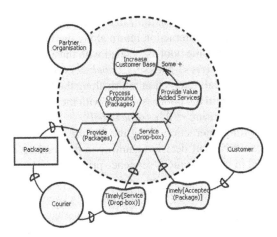

Fig. 3. A Partial Organizational Model

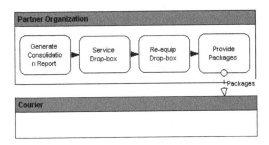

Fig. 4. An Outbound Package Process

The following describes a syntactic transformation function that maps UML Interaction Diagrams to BPMN models:

1. Represent each object in the UML interaction diagram as a pool within the BPMN model.

2. Traverse the lifeline of each object in the UML interaction diagram from beginning to end, creating activities within the corresponding BPMN pool using the following rules. The sequence of these activities in the BPMN model reflect the sequence of the corresponding interactions on the lifeline.

   (a) For each internal message along the lifeline, include an activity within the objects associated pool labeled with the $< MessageLabel >$ as the activity label.

   (b) For each outgoing call interaction along the lifeline, include an activity within the pool associated with the corresponding object of the following form: $Request < MessageLabel >$.

   (c) For each incoming call interaction along the lifeline, include an activity within the pool within the pool associated with the corresponding object of the following form: $Receive < MessageLabel > Request$.

   (d) For each outgoing call interaction return along the lifeline, include an activity within the pool within the pool associated with the corresponding object of the following form: $Return < MessageLabel >$.

   (e) For each incoming call interaction return along the lifeline, include an activity within the pool within the pool associated with the corresponding object of the following form: $Receive < MessageLabel >$.

   (f) For each outgoing interaction along the lifeline guarded by a state invariant, include an exclusive-OR decision gateway in the sending objects' pool in the BPMN model in the contiguous sequence prior to the $Request$ / $Return$ message of that outgoing interaction, and after the prior activity in the object's lifeline. Label the flow on the BPMN model between the exclusive gateway and the aforementioned $Request$ / $Return$ message with the conditional expression. The decision gateway thus obtained may violate BPMN syntax - for instance, in Figure 6, the decision gateway labelled with the guard condition $order.CreditCheck='Approved'$ does not actually achieve an X-OR split. Such models are nonetheless of interest because they are proto-models and it is assumed that they would be edited/refined by analysts.

3. For each interaction between two objects in the interaction diagram, introduce a message flow link between the corresponding activities in the BPMN model and label the message flow with the argument[s] of the interaction.

Figure 6 is an example of a BPMN model thus extracted from a UML interaction digram (depicted in Figure 5).

As another instance of a syntactic transformation function, consider an $i*$ [26] in Figure 3, mapped to the BPMN process model [27] in Figure 4. In this case, the function $f_{i*,BP}^{syn}$ mapped: activities in $i*$ to process models in BPMN; the child nodes of activities in an $i*$ model to activities within the BPMN process model; actors in an $i*$ model to pools/lanes in the BPMN model; and, resource dependencies between activities in the $i*$ model to message flow links in the BPMN model. The BPMN model could then be easily edited to refine sequencing information and additional activities, that may also trigger some change in the $i*$ model if a reverse mapping were applied.

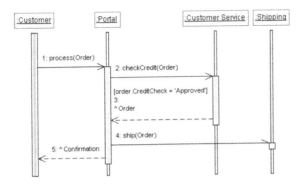

Fig. 5. Process Sales Order Interaction Diagram

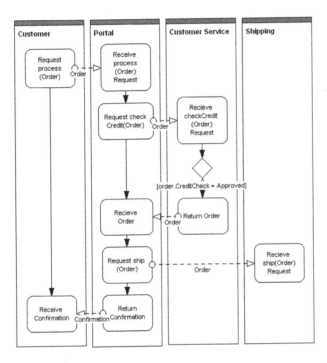

Fig. 6. BPMN Proto-Process Model Extracted from Sales Order Interaction Diagram

4   Model Identity and Cross-Validation

Distinct process models obtained via model-to-model extraction and text-to-model extraction might actually describe the same process. This presents both an opportunity and a challenge. The opportunity lies in the ability to *cross-validate* distinct models of the same process against each other. The challenge relates to the problem of establishing *model identity*, i.e., determining whether two distinct process models refer to the same process.

Determing model identity is a difficult problem. The *R*-BPD tool generates proto-models from multiple sources. Consider a process model m_1 generated from one or more text documents and process model m_2 extracted from one or more legacy UML Interaction Diagrams. m_1 and m_2 might indeed be alternative descriptions of the same process, but determining whether this is the case is the problem of model identity. One approach would be to relegate that decision to the analyst. It would, however, be useful if the tool were able to establish tentative identity relationships between distinct process models and use these to perform cross-validation across models (discussed below). The process of establishing model identity can be decomposed into three steps. First, we need to resolve *naming conflicts* (i.e., the use of distinct names for the same concept - "shipment" and "consignment" for instance). We use an *enterprise ontology* for this purpure. Second, we need to resolve *abstraction conflicts*, which relates to the problem of describing the same process at varying levels of abstraction. Here too we require an enterprise ontology. Within such an ontology, background rules such as $Performs_1(ProcessingSystem, Read, Order) \land Performs_2(ProcessingSystem, AppendID, Order) \Rightarrow Performs_3(ProcessingSystem, Recieve, Order)$ permit us to relate finer-grained descriptions of a process (containing, say, $Step_1$ and $Step_2$) with more abstract descriptions of the same process (containing $Step_3$) (this rule corresponds to the natural language statement *"The order is recieved by a processing system, which reads the data and appends an ID number to the order."*).

Having resolved naming conflicts and having established relationships between descriptions at different levels of abstraction, the third step involves actually establishing whether two process models indeed describe the same process. In general terms, this involves devising a *similarity function* that takes as input a pair of process models and produces as output a similarity measure. If the similarity measure meets a pre-specified threshold, the two models are deemed to describe the same process. In the current implementation of the *R*-BPD tool, we use a simple structural similarity function the exploits a graph encoding of BPMN models (our approach resembles that of [28] in some respects). In the resulting digraph (V, E), each node is of the form $< ID, nodetype, owner >$ and each edge is of the form $<< u, v >, edgetype >$. Each event, activity or gateway in a BPMN model maps to a node, with the *nodetype* indicating whether the node was obtained from an event, activity or gateway respectively in the BPMN model. The ID of nodes of type *event* or *activity* refers to the ID of the corresponding event or activity in the BPMN model. The ID of a *gateway* type node refers to the condition associated with the corresponding gateway in the BPMN model. The *owner* attribute of a node refers to the role associated with the pool from which the node was obtained. The *edgetype* of an edge can be either *control* or *message* depending on whether the edge represents a control flow or message flow in the BPMN model. To obtain a similarity measure between two process models, we first encode the process models into digraphs d_i and d_j as described above. We then compute the total number of nodes plus edges on which the two digraphs thus obtained agree, denoted by $| intersect(d_i, d_j) |$. Note that we assume that both *naming conflicts* and *abstraction conflicts* have been resolved via reference to the enterprise ontology. We relax the identity requirement for nodes in relation to the *owner* attribute - two nodes are also deemed to be identical if they agree on the *ID* and *nodetype* and the *owner* attribute of at least one of the nodes is null. This permits us to deal with proto-models where some owner roles are yet to be assigned. The similarity measure is given by $min(|$ $intersect(d_i, d_j)$ $|/|$ d_i $|, |$ $intersect(d_i, d_j)$ $|/|$ d_j $|)$, where for a digraph d, $| d |$ represents the total number nodes and edges in d. The threshold is a tunable parameter - setting it low would generate a large number of potentially incorrect identity relationships, while setting it too high might lead to potential identities being ignored by the tool. The similarity measure described above is one of several that could be used in this context, reflecting alternative intuitions and it is not our intention to suggest that this might be the best similarity measure to use. Much remains to be done in exploring the effectiveness of alternative means of assessing similarity and suggesting model identity.

When an identity relation is indicated between a pair of process models extracted from distinct source artefacts, it is useful to *cross-validate* these models, i.e., to determine if the models support each other. In our current implementation, we use *model consistency* as the basis for cross-validation. If a pair of process models deemed to represent the same process is mutually consistent, then they are viewed supporting each other. On the other hand, an inconsistent pair of models of the same process generates a trigger for analysts to manually check the corresponding source artefacts and also to manually resolve the inconsistency. We outline below a lightweight, structural approach to determining process model consistency that has been implemented in our tool. We note that a semantic approach to consistency would be more desirable, but is somewhat difficult due to the absence of consensus on the most effective means of describing BPMN semantics.

In the context of formal languages, two distinct theories in the language are deemed to be consistent if and only if a model (in the sense of model-theoretic semantics) exists that satisfies both theories. In our context, process models may be viewed as (syntactic) theories, or descriptions of processes, while individual process instances may be viewed as playing the role of semantic models (snapshots of the world being syntactically described). A pair of process models may therefore be deemed to be consistent if a process instance exists that satisfies both models. The consistency check that we have implemented performs lightweight, structural analysis of the digraphs obtained from BPMN models in the manner described above.

Let m_1 and m_2 be two graphical process models that we have initially determined to be identical. As with the similarity measure, we assume that naming and abstraction conflicts have been resolved with reference to an enterprise ontology. As before, we will permit pair of nodes to be deemed to be identical even if the owner role for one of them is undefined. We say that m_1 is *consistent* with m_2 (with d_1 and d_2 representing the corresponding digraphs, respectively) *iff* the following properties hold:

1. The sub-graphs within d_1 and d_2 defined by the nodes common to d_1 and d_2 are *isomorphic*.
2. For each incoming edge connecting a common node to a node that does not belong to the intersection in one digraph, there does not exist a corresponding incoming edge connecting the same common node in the other. Similarly, for each outgoing

edge connecting a common node to a node that does not belong to the intersection in one digraph, there does not exist a corresponding outgoing edge connecting the same common node in the other.

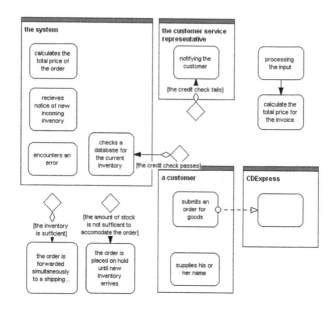

Fig. 7. BPMN Proto-Process Model Fragments Extracted from Text

Example: Figure 8 (m_T) summarizes some fragments of a Sales Order proto-process model that has been extracted from a sample text using the R-BPD prototype. The (ontological) correspondences established in Table 1 between m_U (Figure 6) and m_T (Figure 8) provide an initial basis with which to determine consistency.

Application of the consistency check reveals the following:

- In m_T, the node and edge pair "credit check passes $\rightarrow$", and the m_U "CreditCheck = Approved $\rightarrow$ node and edge pair violate consistency rule (2).
- In m_T the node and edge pair "[submits an order for goods] $\rightarrow$", and the m_U "[Request process(Order)] $\rightarrow$ (Portal)" also violate consistency rules (2).

Such inconsistencies that arise during discovery may be either resolved in an automated or mediated manner. Given much of the available information has been extracted and summarized, such inconsistencies require only minimal analyst involvement and may even help unearth previously unknown and valuable process change information [3]. During the resolution of the first inconsistency (Figure 8 (a)), the analyst has chosen to differentiate the previously identified node and place it under control of 'the system' with the subsequent activity. Such information would in most cases be only available to an expert within the domain and may place the change out of scope of the R-BPDTk. Finally, the second inconsistency results in an update of the domain ontology signifying an association between "CDExpress", "portal", and "the system". The acquisition

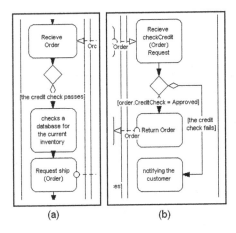

Fig. 8. Analyst Meditation and Inconsistency Resolution

Table 1. Figures 6 and 8 Correspondence

	Figure 6 (UML)	Figure 8 (Text)
Roles	Portal	the system
	Customer Service	the customer service representative
	Customer	a customer
Nodes	Request process(Order)	submit an order for goods
	order.CreditCheck=Approval	credit check passes

of such information would be valuable during subsequent or revised iterations of discovery.

The *R*-BPD procedure continues until the correspondences and combinations of proto-process models have been established up-to some fixed-point. We can then apply additional metrics to determine where further analyst mediation may be required.

5   Managing Traceability and Change During *R*-BPD

The extraction of process models from artefacts in an enterprise repository helps establish critical traceability links, which can be leveraged in a variety of ways. If a proto-model is deemed to be incorrect by an analyst and is found to have been extracted from a *live* artefact, an immediate alert (to the owners of the artefact, e.g., the authors of a document) is triggered. such an alert does not oblige revision of the source artefact - it merely signals that disagreements (between the analyst in question and the artefact owners) on the process being described might exist and might require resolution. The actual resolution of such a disagreement is outside the scope of our tool. Similar alerts can also be issued to the owners of the source artefacts of process models that are changed for other extraneous reasons. Such alerts may be viewed as suggestions to revisit these source artefacts in light of the changes made to the process models extracted from them.

6 Experimental Evaluation Using *R*-BPDTk

In preliminary experimental evaluation, we explored the effectiveness of: (1) an implemented interaction diagram to BPMN extraction module; and (2) an implemented text to BPMN extraction module. We ran each with ten sets of inputs (*ten* interactions diagrams in the former instance and *ten* pieces of text in the latter). For simplicity, the implementations were configured to generate one process proto-model for each input. The ten proto-models generated in each instance were evaluated by an independent analyst, who partitioned the set into usable and non-usable subsets.

The preliminary results look promising:

- The analyst found all of the ten sequence diagram translations into proto-process models extremely useful in developing subsequent business process models.
- The analyst found three proto-models to be useless from our set of ten proto-models extracted from text. Of these three however, one description actually contained close to no process relevant knowledge, suggesting that the problem did not reside in our tool.
- Seven of the ten proto-models extracted from text were deemed to be useful by the analyst.
- Finally, two of the ten proto-models extracted from text were deemed to be extremely useful in extracting the aspects of the process described in the text.

These results indicate that the combination of both models will yield significantly improved results during subsequent experiments. We are currently pursuing the integration of such modules with a capability to incorporate and propagate analyst edits across the system during iterations of business process model discovery.

7 Conclusion

We have discussed the *R*-BPD method for rapidly discovering business process knowledge from a wide variety of sources. The approach can work in conjunction with any means for eliciting or extracting information, including the choice of notation used (which may help improve differential access and acquirability). *R*-BPD allows for the rapid extraction and summarization of process knowledge from large samples of artifacts, as well as the possibility of distributed elicitation and negotiation of consistency among domain experts. In future work we propose to extend the toolkit to enable finer grained traceability between process models and source artefacts, relating elements of an extracted process model to components of source artefacts (such as paragraphs of text, or elements of a UML interaction diagram). This would permit a more sophisticated set of functionalities driven by analyst edits to generated proto-models. We also propose to explore alternative, and possibly semantic, notions of model identity and consistency. Finally, industry-scale empirical evaluation needs to be conducted.

References

1. Smith, H., Fingar, P.: Business Process Management: The Third Wave. Meghan-Kiffer Press, Tampa, FL (2003)
2. van der Aalst, W.M., ter Hofstede, A.H., Weske, M.: Business process management: A survey. In: van der Aalst, W.M.P., ter Hofstede, A.H.M., Weske, M. (eds.) BPM 2003. LNCS, vol. 2678, pp. 1–12. Springer, Heidelberg (2003)
3. Sommerville, I., Sawyer, P., Viller, S.: Manging process inconsistency using viewpoints. IEEE Transactions on Software Engineering 25, 784–799 (1999)
4. Gruber, T.R.: Automated knowledge acquisition for strategic knowledge. Machine Learning 4, 293–336 (1989)
5. RBPD: Rapid model discovery project, http://www.dsl.uow.edu.au/projects/rmd/
6. Boose, J.H.: Knowledge aquisition, methods, and mediating representations. In: First Japanese Knowledge Aquisition for Knowledge-Based Systems Workshop (JKAW'90) (1990)
7. Hoffman, R.R., Shadbolt, N.R., Burton, M., Klein, G.: Eliciting knowledge from experts: A methodological analysis. Organizational Behaviour and Human Decision Processes 62, 129–158 (1995)
8. Young, R.M., Gammack, J.: The role of psychological techniques and intermediate representations in knowledge elicitation. In: Proceedings of the First European Workshop on Knowledge Acquisition and Knowledge-based Systems (1987)
9. Shore, B.: Bias in the development and use of an expert system: Implications for lifecycle costs. Industrial Management and Data Systems 4, 18–26 (1996)
10. Hoffman, R.R.: Bibliography: Automated knowledge elicitation, representation, and instantiation. In: Bibliography: Automated knowledge elicitation, representation, and instantiation, pp. 346–358. Erlbaum, Hillsdale, NJ (1992)
11. Reubenstein, H.B., Waters, R.C.: The requirements apprentice: Automated assistance for requirements acquisition. IEEE Trans. Softw. Eng. 17(3), 226–240 (1991)
12. de Medeiros, A., van der Aalst, W., Weijters, A.: Workflow mining: Current status and future directions. In: Meersman, R., Tari, Z., Schmidt, D.C. (eds.). OTM 2003. LNCS, vol. 2888, Springer, Heidelberg (2003)
13. van der Aalst, W.M.P., Song, M.: Mining social networks: Uncovering interaction patterns in business processes. In: Desel, J., Pernici, B., Weske, M. (eds.) BPM 2004. LNCS, vol. 3080, pp. 244–260. Springer, Heidelberg (2004)
14. Rozinat, A.W.M.P.v.d.A.: Decision mining in prom. In: Business Process Management. (2006) 420–425
15. Ellis, C.A., Rembert, A.J., Kim, K.-H., Wainer, J.: Beyond worflow mining. In: Dustdar, S., Fiadeiro, J.L., Sheth, A. (eds.) BPM 2006. LNCS, vol. 4102, Springer, Heidelberg (2006)
16. Sommerville, I., Sawyer, P.: Viewpoints: Principles, problems and a practical approach to requirements engineering. Annals of Software Engineering 3, 101–130 (1997)
17. Easterbrook, S., Nuseibeh, B.: Using viewpoints for inconsistency management. BCS/IEE Software Engineering Journal, 31–43 (January 1996)
18. Easterbrook, S., Finkelstein, A., Kramer, J., Nuseibeh, B.: Co-ordinating distributed viewpoints: the anatomy of a consistency check. Technical Report 94/7, Department of Computing, Imperial College, London (1994)
19. Czarnecki, K., Helsen, S.: Classification of model transformation approaches. In: Proc. OOPSLA'03 Workshop on Generative Techniques in the Context of Model-Driven Architecture (2003)

20. Koliadis, G., Vranesevic, A., Bhuiyan, M., Krishna, A., Ghose, A.: A combined approach for supporting the business process model lifecycle. In: Proc. of the 10th Pacific Asia Conference on Information Systems (PACIS'06) (2006)
21. Holocentric (2007), http://www.holocentric.com
22. Xu, K., Lianchen, L., Wu, C.: A three-layered method for business process discovery and its application in manufacturing industry. Computers in Industry 58, 265–278 (2007)
23. BEA: Introduction to business process management and the sample workflows. Accessed: 27.02.07 (2007), http://edocs.bea.com/wli/docs70/bpmtutor/ch1.htm
24. Klein, E.: Computational semantics in the natural language toolkit. In: Proceedings of the 2006 Australasian Language Technology Workshop (ALTW2006), pp. 26–33 (2006)
25. Pham, S., Hoffmann, A.: Efficient knowledge acquisition for extracting temporal relations. In: Proceedings of the Australasian language technology workshop, pp. 87–95 (2005)
26. Yu, E.: Models for supporting the redesign of organizational work. In: Proceedings of Conf. on Organizational Computing Systems (COOCS'95), Milpitas, CA: USA, August 13-16 1995, pp. 225–236 (1995)
27. White, S.: Business process modeling notation (bpmn), Technical report, OMG Final Adopted Specification 1.0 (2006), http://www.bpmn.org
28. Lu, R., Sadiq, S.: Managing process variants as an information resource. In: Dustdar, S., Fiadeiro, J.L., Sheth, A. (eds.) BPM 2006. LNCS, vol. 4102, Springer, Heidelberg (2006)

Ontology-Driven Business Modelling: Improving the Conceptual Representation of the REA Ontology

Frederik Gailly and Geert Poels

Faculty of Economics and Business Administration, Ghent University, Belgium
{Frederik.Gailly,Geert.Poels}@UGent.be

Abstract. Business modelling research is increasingly interested in exploring how domain ontologies can be used as reference models for business models. The Resource Event Agent (REA) ontology is a primary candidate for ontology-driven modelling of business processes because the REA point of view on business reality is close to the conceptual modelling perspective on business models. In this paper Ontology Engineering principles are employed to reengineer REA in order to make it more suitable for ontology-driven business modelling. The new conceptual representation of REA that we propose uses a single representation formalism, includes a more complete domain axiomatization (containing definitions of concepts, concept relations and ontological axioms), and is proposed as a generic model that can be instantiated to create valid business models. The effects of these proposed improvements on REA-driven business modelling are demonstrated using a business modelling example.

1 Introduction

Business modelling is a research domain that is gradually moving to more in depth analyses that aim at providing toolkits for representing, analysing, assessing and changing business models [1]. The goal of business modelling is to create semantically faithful and pragmatically usable representations of business domain artefacts (e.g. transactions, processes, value chains). As Ontology also aims at creating real-world representations, *business domain ontologies* (e.g. [2-8]) may offer support for business modelling in the sense that their representation can be seen as a reference model for concrete business models. This reference model describes concepts, concept relations and axioms that are potentially relevant for business models. Ontology-driven business modelling thus means that a business domain ontology is used to constrain the contents and structure of the business model, thereby helping to identify and organize relevant objects, relationships and other knowledge [9]. When emphasizing their use for ontology-driven business modelling, we will refer to business domain ontologies as *business modelling ontologies*.

The Resource Event Agent (REA) ontology [5] is one such ontology that has been proposed as a business modelling ontology. The origin of REA is an accounting data model [10] that has been extended first into an enterprise information architecture and later into a full-scale business domain ontology. This gradual development and extension in scope has resulted in the coexistence of multiple conceptualizations that

C. Parent et al. (Eds.): ER 2007, LNCS 4801, pp. 407–422, 2007.
© Springer-Verlag Berlin Heidelberg 2007

all provide partial (and not necessarily consistent) views of REA and that are represented in different (and not always compatible) formats. This lack of a definite reference for business modellers, preferably in a representation format useful for business modelling, may hinder REA's application as a business modelling ontology. This paper therefore proposes a new conceptual representation of REA with the goal of increasing the applicability of REA as a business modelling ontology. The development of this new conceptual representation was guided by proven Ontology Engineering principles as recommended in a new business domain ontology reengineering methodology [11].

The paper also elaborates a business modelling example to illustrate that the newly developed representation offers a better reference for business modellers than the current REA representations. The example illuminates the interpretation problems that may arise when instantiating the generic business model that can be inferred from the currently available REA representations and shows that these problems are avoided when using our proposal. The paper emphasizes especially that the inclusion of basic domain axioms in the generic business model makes the business model instantiations more correct.

In the next section we motivate the choice of REA as our object of study. REA is also compared to alternative business modelling ontologies. Section three briefly discusses the Ontology Engineering principles on which the development of a new conceptual representation for REA is based. The currently available representations of REA are summarized in section four. The business modelling example is also introduced in that section. The new conceptual representation of REA is presented in the fifth section and is subsequently used as a reference for the same business modelling example as in section four, thereby illustrating the value of our proposal (i.e. less interpretation problems and a more complete model). Section six ends with conclusions.

2 REA as a Business Modelling Ontology

The three main business modelling ontologies are REA [5], the e^3-value ontology [4], and the e-Business Model Ontology (e-BMO) [6]. Although these ontologies all focus on the creation and transfer of economic value (which is why they are sometimes called *business model ontologies* [7] to distinguish them from so-called *enterprise model ontologies* (or *generic enterprise models*) like TOVE [2] and EO [3] that are more focused on organizational structure, activities and management [7]), they have a different purpose.

Considering the envisioned applications of business modelling we can roughly distinguish two groups of business modelling ontologies: on the one hand e^3-value and e-BMO that mainly approach a business model as a conceptual representation of a business 'case' (i.e. the management perspective [1]) and on the other hand REA that regards the business model as the core of the conceptual schema of a business software or database application. The REA point of view is closer to the conceptual modelling perspective on 'business' models and together with its level of detail makes REA the primary candidate for ontology-driven modelling of single or interrelated business processes. It must be noted that given its origin in data modelling, the resulting models can be characterized as structural models (i.e. *domain* models) rather than behavioural models (i.e. *process* models). It must also be noted that, given REA's accountability and control perspective on business reality (which clearly influences REA's conceptualization of business reality), REA business models are particulary useful in the development of intra/inter-enterprise systems that focus on accounting information processing.

REA's potential as a business modelling ontology has been recognized by a number of international standardization efforts for e-collaboration systems (e.g. ISO Open-EDI initiative, UN/CEFACT, OAG, eBTWG). REA was the basis for the business process ontology in the UMM business process and information model construction methodology [12], the ECIMF system interoperability enabling methodology [13] and the Open-EDI business transaction ontology which is part of the ISO/IEC 15944-4 standard.

Apart from the aforementioned initiatives (in which the REA developers were actively involved), there are few documented accounts of REA-driven business modelling in practice (although REA is taught in accounting information systems or database courses in more than 100 business schools or faculties [14]). In [15] we identified plausible reasons for this lack of wide-scale application of REA in ontology-driven business modelling and system engineering: the ontological concepts and the relations between the concepts are not strictly defined, the ontological axioms are confusing (mixing up types and instances of concepts), and there is neither a generally accepted conceptualization nor a uniform representation of the ontology. Furthermore, the view on REA expressed in textbooks such as [16] differs in some aspects from the 'official' view of the REA developers as in [17, 18] which is still different from REA's adoption in international standards like ISO/IEC 15944-4.

The success of ontology-driven business modelling depends in large extent on the quality of the conceptual backbone: the business domain ontology. Ontology research has proposed sound methodological guidelines for developing ontologies. However REA was developed in an ad-hoc manner and the developers focused more on the theoretical background of the ontology (events accounting and Micro-Economic theories) than on the representation, formalization and computational correctness of the ontology (although they did perform in [5] an ontological analysis using Sowa's classification of ontological categories). It is our position that applying sound Ontology Engineering principles to existing business domain ontologies to redesign them, will improve these ontologies and will increase their capability as a driver for business modelling.

3 Redesigning Business Domain Ontologies

Based on the METHONTOLOGY framework [19] we have published in [11] a three-phased reengineering methodology for business domain ontologies. The first phase is *Reverse Engineering* during which the conceptualization of the business domain ontology is recovered starting from the currently available representations, in whatever format they are available. In the following *Restructuring* phase the recovered conceptualization is redesigned by applying ontology evaluation and redesign techniques. The resulting redesigned conceptualization is subsequently transformed into a reengineered, formal ontology representation during the *Forward Engineering* phase.

The reengineering activities of these phases have been executed for the REA-ontology and have resulted in a formal REA-ontology representation. The *Reverse Engineering* and *Restructuring* of REA are described in sections four and five respectively. In the current section (section three) we explain the Ontology Engineering principles that were used during the *Restructuring* phase and that resulted in an improved conceptual representation of the REA-ontology. These principles were chosen in function of our goal, i.e. improving REA as a business modelling ontology. We wish to stress that our aim was not to evaluate or change the content of the REA-ontology, but to improve the representation of REA's conceptualization of business reality to make it more suitable as a generic business model.

The mapping rules that were subsequently used to *Forward Engineer* this improved conceptual representation into a formal representation in OWL can be found in [11] and are not repeated here.

3.1 Ontology Modelling Using Conceptual Modelling Languages

A first principle is to model domain ontologies using conceptual modelling languages (e.g. ER, UML, ORM ...) [20-22]. Conceptual modelling languages help conceptualizing the ontology (i.e. creating a conceptual representation) because they offer representations that are close to how humans perceive the world [23]. We see at least three advantages of using a well-defined graphical modelling language such as UML for conceptually representing a business modelling ontology:

- A graphical representation balances understandability and precision. For the average business modeller an UML diagram is easier to understand than a formal representation in a knowledge representation language, but still causes less interpretation problems and ambiguity than an informal, textual description. Using a graphical conceptual modelling language, ontology developers can make domain semantics explicit whilst still being able to effectively communicate these semantics to the business modeller.
- UML can be used both for representing the ontology and for representing business models, allowing for a smoother transition between description (ontology) and specification (model). In fact, by using a common representation language the ontology may act as a generic model that can be instantiated to obtain a concrete business model.
- There exist mapping rules in both directions between UML and the knowledge representation (or web ontology) languages RDF and OWL [24]. The formalization of an ontology's conceptual representation will therefore be facilitated if UML is used as the ontology modelling language.

3.2 Ontology Restructuring Based on the DOGMA Double Articulation Principle

The ontology double articulation principle proposed by Jarrar [25] stipulates that a domain ontology should be divided into a domain axiomatization and a number of application axiomatizations. The domain axiomatization represents the ontology's intended meaning which is shared and public. An application axiomatization specifies which parts of the domain axiomatization are relevant for an intended application and adds application-specific rules that constrain the relevant concepts. The DOGMA approach to ontology engineering [22] captures the domain axiomatization in an ontology base and the different application axiomatizations in a commitment layer.

The distinction between an ontology base and a commitment layer within the conceptual representation of a business domain ontology is highly relevant for ontology-driven business modelling. For instance, the Model-Driven Architecture (MDA) prescribes the use of a Computation-Independent Model (CIM) as an abstraction of the system from the end user's viewpoint. The CIM is a representation of the problem domain focusing on the system requirements rather than a representation of the software artefacts in the solution space for that problem domain. If a business application is developed, then the CIM is what we have called a business model and business modelling ontologies can be used to develop the CIM.

The CIM typically contains a domain model which describes the concepts of the domain, their relations and the domain rules that apply, and a requirements model which adds application-specific issues. According to [26] domain ontologies can be employed for representing the domain model of the CIM, but the parts of the CIM that deal with requirements are application-specific and cannot be grasped by ontologies. We agree with this in so far that only the domain axiomatization, represented as a generic business model, should be used for developing the CIM's domain model (through instantiation). Therefore the ontology base should be application-independent. However, the application-specific parts of the CIM together with the domain model form a business model whose development can also be driven by the business modelling ontology's commitment layer on condition that it contains appropriate mechanisms for mediating between the domain axiomatization and the intended application.

Business domain ontologies would benefit from the double articulation principle as it would increase the reusability of their ontology base (because of application-independence) as well as their applicability for ontology-driven business modelling.

4   Current Conceptualization of REA

The *Reverse Engineering* of REA was mainly an ontology 'unification' effort, focusing on the commonalities in the existing representations and underlying interpretations. In case of doubt we referred to the 'official' version of the ontology as described by the REA developers in their most recent papers (i.e. [17, 18]).

4.1 Reverse Engineering: Ontology Unification

The conceptualization of a business process according to REA originates in the REA accounting data model developed by McCarthy [10]. This model was originally conceived as a semantic data model for creating accounting databases. According to this model there are three kinds of objects that can be identified in any economic exchange or conversion process: Economic Resources, Economic Agents and Economic Events. The REA ontology further extended this classification with the

Commitment concept which refers to a promise or obligation of economic agents to perform an economic event in the future (e.g. accepting a sales order is a promise to deliver the ordered goods or services) and the Contract concept which refers to a collection of mutual commitments and applicable terms (e.g. an accepted sales order obliges the enterprise to deliver and the customer to pay). Table 1 gives an overview of the definitions of the basic operational REA concepts related to the business process level.

Table 1. Definitions of basic operational REA concepts – business process level

Concept	Definition
Economic Resource	A thing that is scarce and has utility for economic agents and is something users of business applications want to plan, monitor and control.
Economic Agent	Is an individual or organization capable of having control over economic resources, and transferring or receiving the control to or from other individuals or organizations.
Economic Event	Represents either an increment or a decrement in the value of economic resources that are under control of the enterprise.
Commitment	Is a promise or obligation of economic agents to perform an economic event in the future
Contract	Is a collection of increment and decrement commitments and terms.

In [5, 18] a knowledge layer has been proposed on top of the operational business process level. The typification abstraction is used to provide concept descriptions that apply to a kind of objects (e.g. describing the characteristics of different types of sales like cash sales, credit sales, etc.). The type images of the operational concepts are named Economic Resource Type, Economic Agent Type, Economic Event type, Commitment Type and Contract Type [17, 18]. A second abstraction used is grouping which refers to the group-membership special form of aggregation and groups objects together in collections based on something they have in common. For each operational concept group images can be defined, instead of or jointly with type images. These group images are not explicitly named in the ontology.

Figure 1 (UML class diagram) is another representation of REA that shows named concept relations. Economic resources are associated with the economic events that cause their inflow or outflow (*stockflow relationships*). Economic events that result in resource inflows (e.g. purchases) are paired by economic events that result in resource outflows (e.g. cash disbursements) (*duality relationships*). The *participation relationships provide* and *receive* identify the economic agents involved in economic events.

A commitment specifies a promise to perform some type of economic event and will eventually be related to an economic event of the specified type by a *fulfilment relationship. Reciprocity relationships* are analogous to duality relationships, but relate commitments instead of economic events. These reciprocity relationships can be reified as contracts (the Contract concept is not shown in figure 1). Both commitments and contracts can also be typified (i.e. the Commitment Type and Contract Type concepts, again not shown in figure 1). *Specify relationships* exist between commitments and the economic agent types that are scheduled to participate in some type of economic event. They also exist between commitments and the economic resource types that are needed or are expected by future economic events. It is also possible that a commitment specifies the actual economic resource or economic agents involved in some type of economic event, but this special case (called *reservation relationship* for the relation between commitments and economic resources in [5, 18]) has not been included in figure 1. Finally, the relations between type images (or group images if relevant) are referred to as *policy relationships*, as they express business policies (e.g. which type of agent can or should be involved in which type of event).

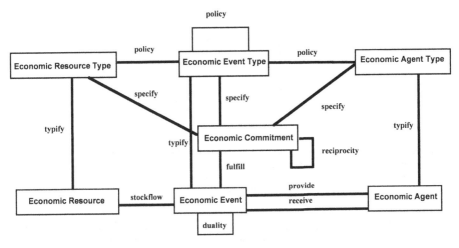

Fig. 1. REA concept relations at the business process level (partly)

Next to the REA concepts and relationships between the concepts, the ontology also includes three axioms which are only defined in a textual format in the REA literature:

- *Axiom 1 (the stockflow axiom)*: At least one inflow event and one outflow event exist for each economic resource; conversely inflow and outflow events must affect identifiable resources.
- *Axiom 2 (the duality axiom)*: All events effecting an outflow must be eventually paired in duality relationships with events effecting an inflow and vice-versa.
- *Axiom 3 (the participation axiom)*: Each economic event needs to have at least one provide and one receive relationship with an economic agent.

4.2 Business Modelling Example

The business modelling example represented in this section by means of an REA-model is the order and sale process of an online bookstore like Amazon.com or BarnesandNoble.com. This process does not include purchase and delivery activities. This means that we assume for simplicity's sake that all books offered for sale are available and that the bookshop has a contract with different types of couriers that take care of delivery. The business model is described from the viewpoint of the bookstore and could be used for the development of a system that registers the order and sale of books as well as payment collection. The customer orders one or more book titles which are added to his purchase cart. At the end of the order the customer must go to his purchase cart and select the sale type which determines how the order will be delivered and will be paid for. The actual sale is only registered when the products are delivered to the customer and a delivery notification from the courier is received. Important to notice is that the order commitment has a specify relationship with the customer and not with a customer type because the order identifies the customer to which must be delivered.

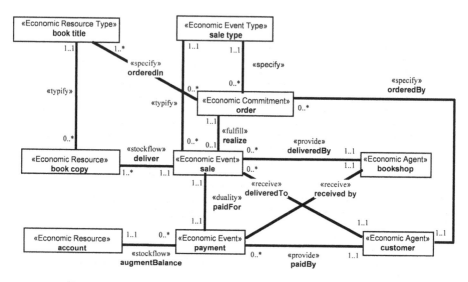

Fig. 2. REA-model for an order and sale process of an online bookshop

The REA business model example of figure 2 has been developed by a naive business modeller and reflects a subjective (and wrong) interpretation of some of the REA axioms. The modeller has for instance enforced the duality axiom by making the paidFor relationship one-to-one and mandatory for both roles, thereby ensuring that each sale must be paid for and that each payment relates to a sale. However, in practice, it could be that a payment has not yet resulted in a delivery of the books when the customer uses a credit card for the payment of the books. Vice versa, ordered books may have been delivered, but the payment not collected in the sense that the account balance has not been augmented yet. The example also shows a strict (but wrong) interpretation of the stockflow axiom in the sense that every economic resource must have an inflow relationship with an economic event <u>and</u> an outflow relationship with an economic event. However, a book copy may have been delivered to the bookshop by a publisher (outside the scope of the model) but may not have been sent to a customer yet, so a mandatory relationship with a sale event is a too strong constraint.

The REA-model is also not complete because an order also creates a commitment for the customer to pay for the ordered books. The generic model that can be derived from figure 1 does not explicitly show that dual economic events fulfill reciprocal commitments, so this omission is understandable.

One could argue that the incompleteness and incorrectness of the model could easily be avoided and that a non-naive modeller would not make these mistakes. This is true, but the point we wish to make here is that the currently available REA representations do not seem helpful to avoid such problems. Hence they provide insufficient guidance for ontology-driven business modelling.

5 Improved Conceptual Representation of REA

Based on the Ontology Engineering principles described in section three the REA conceptualization described in the previous section can be restructured in order to make the REA-ontology better suited for ontology-driven business modeling.

5.1 Restructuring Phase: Ontology Redesign

We have used the UML class diagram of figure 1 as the basis for an improved conceptual REA representation (see figure 3). Adding some new classes, relationships and multiplicities to figure 1 makes it possible to include the basic REA axioms. At the same time, the definition of the concept relations can be made more explicit, complete and consistent. The additional classes are specializations of existing classes: Increment Economic Event, Decrement Economic Event, Increment Commitment, Decrement Commitment, Increment Economic Event Type, and Decrement Economic Event Type. Less commonly used, but supported by UML 2.0, is the specialization of

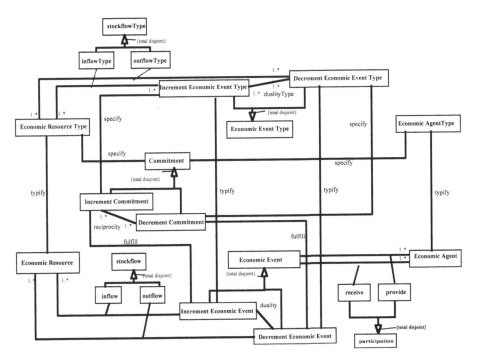

Fig. 3. The redesigned REA conceptualization (ontology base)

associations: inflow(Type) and outflow(Type) as specializations of the stockflow(Type) association and provide and receive as specializations of the participation association. The specializations of the stockflow(Type) and participation associations redefine their parent associations by specializing the types of the association ends and/or adding additional multiplicity constraints.

These new classifications add formerly implicit semantics to the conceptual representation. The diagram shows, for instance, that inflows relate increment events to resources, outflows relate decrement events to resources, increment events fulfil increment commitments, decrement events fulfil decrement commitments, increment commitments specify increment economic event types and decrement commitments specify decrement economic event types. While common-sense, none of these semantics has been explicitly represented in the current REA representations. Incorporating these relations in a generic business model allows constraining the structure of concrete business models.

The extensions make it also possible to represent the basic REA axioms using multiplicities, further constraining the business models that can be considered as 'valid' w.r.t. REA. The main problem with the axioms as originally formulated is that it not always clear whether they are defined at the operational level or at the knowledge level, i.e. whether they apply to instance concepts or type concepts. The REA axioms are explicitly specified in the class diagram as follows:

- The *stockflow axiom* consists of two parts. The first part states that at least one inflow event and one outflow event exist for every economic resource. However, a company can own a resource it has acquired but not used, consumed or sold yet. Clearly, the first part of the axiom must be interpreted at the knowledge level and actually means that each type of economic resource must be related by at least one type of inflow relationship to an increment economic event type and by at least one type of outflow relationship to a decrement economic event type. As a result the first part of the axiom can be represented by a relationship between Economic Resource Type and Increment Event Type and a relationship between Economic Resource Type and Decrement Event Type. The participation of Economic Resource Type objects in both types of relationships is mandatory.

- The second part of the axiom states that inflow and outflow events must affect identifiable resources. This can be modelled at the operational level and is represented by a mandatory participation of Increment Economic Event objects in inflow relationships and a mandatory participation of Decrement Economic Event objects in outflow relationships.

- The *duality axiom* prescribes that all events effecting an outflow must be eventually paired in duality relationships with events effecting an inflow and vice-versa. This axiom can only be modelled at a knowledge level because it could for example be possible that in reality the purchase of a product has not yet been paid by the company. At the knowledge level however we can say that every sale must result in a payment (given certain boundary conditions that exclude for instance philanthropic behaviour). In our class diagram this constraint is added by making the participation in the dualityType relationships mandatory for both roles.

- The *participation axiom* implies that each economic event must have a provider and a receiver. This axiom can be modelled on the operational level by making the participation of Economic Event objects in provide and receive relationships mandatory.

The redesigned conceptual representation makes it also possible to add additional domain axioms that can be inferred from existing descriptions. For instance, analogously to the duality axiom, there could be a reciprocity axiom which defines that every increment commitment must be paired with at least one decrement commitment, and vice versa. Important to notice is that this new axiom can be defined at the operational level because of the economic reciprocity principle of capitalist market economies (i.e. this principle underlies every contract).

Following the double articulation principle, policy relationships should be removed from the ontology base and stored in a commitment layer because they are used to model application-specific rules. According to Geerts and McCarthy [18] "the policy definitions are essentially non-normative in nature; i.e. there are no domain-specific rules to structure the descriptions that are part of the policy infrastructure". Based on this observation we conclude that policy relationships are not part of the business domain axiomatization but that they can be used to add application-specific constraints to the business domain axiomatization. Also cardinality heuristics for the different concept relations (see e.g. [27]) logically belong to a commitment layer and not to the ontology base.

Figure 3 must therefore be considered as the ontology base of the improved conceptual REA representation and the business models that are deployed based on this reference model can be considered as specific application axiomatizations. It is important to notice that the multiplicities shown in figure 3 are only used to define ontological axioms. The

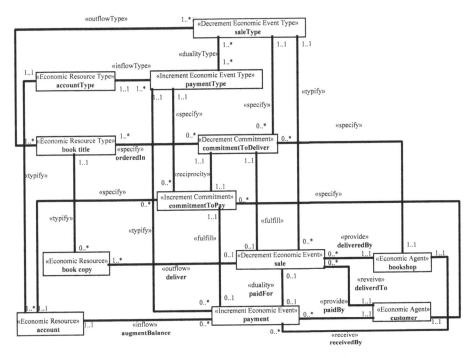

Fig. 4. REA-model for an order and sale order process using the redesigned REA conceptualization

relationship ends where no multiplicities are shown, have no participation or cardinality constraints that directly result from REA domain axioms. Likewise, the stockflowType and dualityType relationships are only added to allow for the definition of axioms. Their semantics as policy specifications would be considered an application axiomatization. Important to notice is also that the inclusion of these relationship types makes it necessary to add typify relationships between the association(s) (classes) at the operational and knowledge levels. These typify relationships are hidden in figure 3 in order to reduce the complexity of the class diagram.

5.2 Business Modelling Example Based on the Redesigned REA Conceptualization

Figure 4 presents the REA-model of the order and sale process of an online bookshop, but now based on an instantiation of the improved REA conceptual representation. During the instantiation process, multiplicity constraints can be strengthened but not weakened. Therefore, the generic business model shown in figure 3 forces the business modeller to take basic business laws (captured in the REA axioms) into account in a manner that relies less on the modeller's subjective interpretation of business reality.

The main improvements in the REA-model of the online bookshop's order and sale process can be summarized as follows:

- One of the most distinguishing characteristics of the REA-ontology is the enforcement of the principle of economic reciprocity. The instantiation of the generic business model forces the business modeler to explicitly distinguish between an increment economic commitment (commitmentToPay) and a decrement economic commitment (commitmentToDeliver). These commitments and the reciprocity relationship between them could be collapsed into a contract (order), but anyway the inclusion of specify (or reservation) and fulfill relationships for both reciprocal parts of the contract would lead to a more complete business model, allowing for more business applications than the model in figure 2 (e.g. the reservation relationship between commitmentToPay and account allows the budgeting of incoming cash flows).

- At the knowledge level the modeling of the decrement economic event type saleType forces the developer to also include an increment economic event type (paymentType) which adds to the model the different types of payment the customer can choose from. For every saleType there is at least one valid paymentType and vice-versa.

- The generic business model in figure 3 also avoids the interpretation problems that may arise with the formerly only informally described REA axioms. For instance, business modellers will feel no need to specify the duality axiom at the operational level, as it is automatically present when instantiating the knowledge level concepts and relations of figure 3. Hence, according to figure 4, there can be a sale without a corresponding payment and vice-versa. The complete execution of an order can at all times be controlled by referring to the reciprocal commitments that are fulfilled by these events.

- Likewise, figure 4 reflects a correct interpretation of the stockflow axiom and allows book copies to exist even if they are not related to sales. The knowledge level shows that the bookshop only offers book titles that it can sell (though not shown in the figure, the economic resource type book title may be further typified such that in application axiomatizations book types can be distinguished and related to sales types, e.g. modes of delivery).

6 Conclusion: Contribution, Related Work and Future Research

This paper proposed a new conceptual representation of the REA ontology that increases the applicability of this business *domain* ontology as a business *modelling* ontology. This new representation, developed using Ontology Engineering principles, is an improvement over the existing, heterogeneous and partial REA representations. The new REA representation is *uniform* (using a single representation formalism), *unified* (including definitions of concepts, concept relations and axioms) and more *useful* for ontology-driven business modelling. The proposed UML class diagram makes the semantics of REA's business conceptualization explicit and thus presents an understandable reference model for business modellers.

A major change that we introduced was the incorporation of basic business domain axioms in the class diagram, instead of describing them separately (and informally) as in the 'old' REA. The class diagram thus acts as a generic business model for generating and validating concrete business models. Instantiating this generic model constrains the business modeller's subjective interpretation of business reality and assures that basic business laws are respected in the generated models.

The restructured REA conceptualization also provides a better basis for further analysis, comparison and consensus amongst researchers on REA's domain axiomatization (hence making the ontology more *shared*). It may, for instance, improve the reference ontology of business model ontologies (REA, e^3-value and e-BMO) proposed in [7]. The purpose of this reference ontology is not to present an all encompassing ontology of the business domain, but to compare the three component ontologies, relate them, and identify opportunities for extension and revision. To integrate REA in the reference ontology a choice had to be made between different views on REA as found in the literature (in particular [28], [16], and [12] were used, though these references do not present the 'official' and latest REA version as found in [17, 18]). Many mappings of REA into the reference ontology are based on the explicit distinction between increments and decrements or between inflows and outflows. By using our improved REA representation, this distinction would be incorporated by means of specialization structures and not by attributes as currently done. Using our representation as the REA reference model would make the reference ontology more up-to-date and semantically richer and would facilitate the inclusion of the basic REA axioms into the reference ontology.

In related work [11] we proposed a representation of our restructured REA conceptualization in OWL-DL. The use of this web ontology language (grounded in Description Logics) operationalizes REA such that it can be used at run-time by so-called *ontology-driven information systems* [9] to support information integration and system interoperability. The *formal* specification of REA (based on UML-OWL mapping rules) would not have been possible without a uniform and unified conceptual representation.

This work was further extended in [29] where we used OMG's UML-OWL profile [30] for graphically representing the REA-ontology. Using this profile makes the back-and-forward transformations between graphical and machine-readable ontology representations straightforward and automatic. Ontology-driven business models can now be very easily represented in a formal ontology language such as OWL offering opportunities to be validated by reasoners and to be queried by ontology query languages (e.g. for auditing and internal control purposes). Specifically for REA business models, a lot of useful information about the business domain which would normally be hard-coded in business applications can now be added to a machine-readable representation of the business model. For instance, a semantic rule language like SWRL could now be used to specify business policies that are executed by rule engines to update the company's ontology. In [29] we also experimented with the knowledge representation framework Protégé and the owlViz and ontoViz ontology visualization plug-ins to obtain a more structured presentation of the REA-ontology that can be used for further analysis and application in business modelling.

Future work can extend this research in at least three directions. Firstly, our redesign of REA was aimed at increasing REA's applicability as a business modelling ontology by improving its representation as a generic business model. However, we did not evaluate or change the content of the ontology (i.e. the question of external validity). For this evaluation, an ontological analysis can be conducted (this is another well-known Ontology Engineering principle (see e.g. [31])). REA's ontological analysis using Sowa's classification in [5] is a starting point, but should be repeated using other upper-level ontologies (e.g. SUMO, BWW, Dolce, OntoClean, GFO, ...).

Secondly, a clear limitation of the current study is that the improved usefulness of our new conceptual representation for REA-driven business modelling is not empirically tested (it is merely illustrated using a toy example). We believe that the proposed changes should also be evaluated by business modellers in order to measure and demonstrate the benefits of using our proposed representation instead of the 'old' version(s). In future work we plan to use the user evaluations based quality model for conceptual models developed by Maes and Poels [32] for this purpose.

Thirdly, the generalizability of our reengineering methodology must be investigated. It is clear that the different ontology engineering principles and techniques employed in each of the reengineering phases depend on the specific reengineering goal, but we must also evaluate whether the methodology itself is independent of the business domain ontology to which it is applied. We will therefore also reengineer other business domain ontologies than REA and eventually the reengineered formal and conceptual representations of these ontologies will be used for the development of small scale applications in the context of ontology-driven systems and ontology-driven system development in order to demonstrate the value of the reengineered business domain ontologies for business.

References

1. Pateli, A.G., Giaglis, G.M.: A research framework for analysing eBusiness models. European Journal of Information Systems 13, 302–314 (2004)
2. Fox, M.S.: The TOVE Project: A Common-sense Model of The Enterprise. In: Belli, F., Radermacher, F. (eds.) Industrial and Engineering Applications of Artificial Intelligence and Expert Systems, pp. 25–24. Springer, Berlin (1992)

3. Ushold, M., King, M., Moralee, S., Zorgios, Y.: The Enterprise Ontology. The Knowledge Engineering Review: Special Issue on Putting Ontologies to Use 13, 31–89 (1998)
4. Gordijn, J.: Value based requirements engineering: Exploring innovative e-commerce ideas. Vrije Universiteit, Amsterdam (2002)
5. Geerts, G.L., McCarthy, W.E.: An Ontological Analysis of the Economic Primitives of the Extended-REA Enterprise Information Architecture. International Joural of Accounting Information Systems 3, 1–16 (2002)
6. Osterwalder, A.: The Business Model Ontology - a proposition in a design science approach. Ecole des Hautes Etudes Commerciales. University of Lausanne, Lausanne (2004)
7. Andersson, B., Bergholtz, M., Edirisuriya, A., Ilayperuma, T., Johannesson, P., Grégoire, B., Schmitt, M., Dubois, E., Abels, S., Hahn, A., Gordijn, J., Weigand, H., Wangler, B.: Towards a Reference Ontology for Business Models. In: Embley, D.W., Olivé, A., Ram, S. (eds.) ER 2006. LNCS, vol. 4215, Springer, Heidelberg (2006)
8. Dietz, J.L.G.: Enterprise Ontology: Theory and Methodology. Springer, New York (2006)
9. Guarino, N.: Understanding, building and using ontologies. International Journal of Human-Computer Studies 46, 293–310 (1997)
10. McCarthy, W.E.: The REA Accounting Model: A Generalized Framework for Accounting Systems in A Shared Data Environment. The Accounting Review, 554–578 (july 1982)
11. Gailly, F., Poels, G.: Towards Ontology-driven Information Systems: Redesign and Formalization of the REA Ontology. In: Gailly, F., Poels, G. (eds.). BIS 2007. LNCS, vol. 4439, Springer, Heidelberg (2007)
12. UN/CEFACT: UN/CEFACT Modeling Methodology (UMM) User Guide. (2003)
13. ECIMF: E-Commerce Integration Meta-Framework. Final draft. ECIMF Project Group (2003)
14. McCarthy, W.E.: The REA Modelling Approach to Teaching Accounting Information Systems. Issues in Accounting Education 18, 427–441 (2003)
15. Gailly, F., Poels, G.: Towards a Formal Representation of the Resource Event Agent Pattern International Conference on Enterprise Systems and Accounting (ICESAcc), Greece (2006)
16. Hruby, P.: Model-driven design using business patterns. Springer, New York (2006)
17. Geerts, G., McCarthy, W.E.: The Ontological Foundation of REA Enterprise Information Systems (2005)
18. Geerts, G., McCarthy, W.E.: Policy-Level Specification in REA Enterprise Information Systems. Journal of Information Systems Fall (2006)
19. Gómez-Pérez, A., Rojas, M.D.: Ontological Reengineering and Reuse. In: Fensel, D., Studer, R. (eds.) 11th European Workshop on Knowledge Acquisition, Modeling and Management, pp. 139–156. Springer, Heidelberg (1999)
20. Kogut, P., Cranefield, S., Hart, L., Dutra, M., Baclawski, K., Kokar, M.K., Smith, J.: UML for ontology development. Knowledge Engineering Review 17, 61–64 (2002)
21. Spaccapietra, S., Parent, C., Vangenot, C., Cullot, N.: On Using Conceptual Modeling for Ontologies. In: Bussler, C.J., Hong, S.-k., Jun, W., Kaschek, R., Kinshuk, Krishnaswamy, S., Loke, S.W., Oberle, D., Richards, D., Sharma, A., Sure, Y., Thalheim, B. (eds.) Web Information Systems – WISE 2004 Workshops. LNCS, vol. 3307, pp. 22–23. Springer, Heidelberg (2004)
22. Spyns, P.: Object Role Modelling for ontology engineering in the DOGMA framework. In: Meersman, R., Tari, Z., Herrero, P. (eds.) On the Move to Meaningful Internet Systems 2005: OTM 2005 Workshops. LNCS, vol. 3762, pp. 710–719. Springer, Heidelberg (2005)

23. Mylopoulos, J.: Information modeling in the time of the revolution. Information Systems 23, 127–155 (1998)
24. OMG: Ontology Definition Metamodel (ODM) - Sixth Revised Submission to OMG/ RFP ad/2003-03-40. Object management Group (2006)
25. Jarrar, M.: Towards Methodological Principles for Ontology Engineering. STARLAB. Vrije Universiteit Brussel, Brussel (2005)
26. Assmann, U., Zchaler, S., Wagner, G.: Ontologies, Meta-Models, and the Model-Driven Paradigm. In: Calero, C., Ruiz, F., Piattini, M. (eds.) Ontologies for Software Engineering and Software Technology (2006)
27. Dunn, C.L., Cherrington, J.O., Hollander, A.S.: Enterprise Information Systems: A Pattern Based Approach. McGraw-Hill, New York (2005)
28. Geerts, G., McCarthy, W.E.: An Accounting Object Infrastructure for Knowledge Based Enterprise Models. IEEE Intelligent Systems and Their Applications 14, 89–94 (1999)
29. Gailly, F., Laurier, W., Poels, G.: Positioning REA as a Business Domain Ontology. Resource Event Agent -25 (REA-25) Conference, Newark, Delaware, USA (2007)
30. Ontology, O.M.G.: Definition Metamodel: OMG Adopted Specification (ptc/06-10-11). Object Management Group (2006)
31. Gómez-Pérez, A., Fernández-López, M., Corcho, O.: Ontological Engineering. Springer, Heidelberg (2004)
32. Maes, A., Poels, G.: Evaluating Quality of Conceptual Models Based on User Perceptions. In: Embley, D.W., Olivé, A., Ram, S. (eds.) ER 2006. LNCS, vol. 4215, Springer, Heidelberg (2006)

A Comparison of Two Approaches to Safety Analysis Based on Use Cases

Tor Stålhane and Guttorm Sindre

Dept. of Computer and Info. Science, Norwegian Univ. of Sci. and Tech (NTNU)
{stalhane,gutters}@idi.ntnu.no

Abstract. Engineering has a long tradition in analyzing the safety of mechanical, electrical and electronic systems. Important methods like HazOp and FMEA have also been adopted by the software engineering community. The misuse case method, on the other hand, has been developed by the software community as an alternative to FMEA and preliminary HazOp for software development. To compare the two methods misuse case and FMEA we have run a small experiment involving 42 third year software engineering students. In the experiment, the students should identify and analyze failure modes from one of the use cases for a commercial electronic patient journals system. The results of the experiment show that on the average, the group that used misuse cases identified and analyzed more user related failure modes than the persons using FMEA. In addition, the persons who used the misuse cases scored better on perceived ease of use and intention to use.

Keywords: Safety engineering, FMEA, misuse cases, experiment.

1 Introduction

Due to the growing dependency of IT, an increasing number of safety-critical software systems are being developed and fielded, and potentially disastrous problems with these systems tend to stem more from requirements defects than from coding errors [1]. Similar concerns can be raised for security. Safety and security analysis are complex disciplines in their own right, demanding their own expertise and sometimes applying heavyweight methods. It is a challenge that many pieces of software for which there are safety or security concerns will be developed by mainstream software developers not having such expertise and perhaps not being able to apply these heavyweight methods [2]. As noted by Lutz [3], better integration of formal and informal methods is one important direction for the engineering of safe software systems, and so is better integration between safety engineering and mainstream software engineering. While formal methods have advantages in supporting rigorous analysis, informal methods may enable increased creativity and the involvement of diverse groups of stakeholders in the safety engineering process.

This paper concerns itself with modelling approaches in the informal end of the spectrum, and especially with a focus on integrating the safety analysis with mainstream software engineering approaches. Over the last decade, use cases [4] have grown in popularity to become a major technique in early stage of software requirements analysis.

C. Parent et al. (Eds.): ER 2007, LNCS 4801, pp. 423–437, 2007.

To achieve an informal approach to the development of safety related software systems, integrated with mainstream software engineering practices, it seems natural to investigate if safety techniques could be based on use cases. There are two ways to achieve this:

- Combining use cases with one or more safety techniques, e.g., let use case diagrams and textual use cases be the input to existing safety analysis techniques.
- Adapting use cases to deal with safety directly, for instance by extensions of diagrams and / or textual descriptions

An interesting topic for research would be the relative merits of these two alternative approaches – when would it be most feasible to combine use cases with existing safety techniques, and when would it be most feasible to use adaptations of use cases to analyze safety with one integrated modelling technique? This paper tries to explore this question, by means of an experimental comparison of these two alternatives. Notably, the need for more experimental evaluations of modelling approaches was explicitly called for in a panel at ER'06 [5].

The rest of the paper is structured as follows: Section 2 reviews related work. Section 3 presents the two techniques compared in the experiment. Section 4 presents the experimental design, and section 5 presents the results from the experiment. Section 6 discusses threats to validity, whereupon section 7 concludes the paper and indicates some directions for future work.

2 Related Work

The idea of combining use cases or scenarios with safety analysis is not entirely new. [6] proposed to apply use cases as input for performing safety analysis by means of the safety engineering techniques Functional Hazard Assessment (FHA) [7] and HazOp [8]. A similar combination of use cases and FHA is also discussed in [9]. More generally, the application of use cases to analyze safety and express safety cases is recommended in [10], and [11] discusses informally some industrial experiences with using UML for developing mission-critical systems. [12] proposes a formalization of use cases to deal with the specification of fault-tolerant systems.

Abuse cases [2] and misuse cases [13] are slight extensions to use cases, used to capture negative functionality - events that should not happen in the system. These techniques were originally proposed for eliciting security requirements, but misuse cases have also been considered in connection with safety, [14], [15]. In the CORAS project, misuse cases was combined with other UML notations such as sequence diagrams, also specifically adapted for safety analysis [16].

Other adaptations of UML have also been proposed to address safety concerns, but then on the design level. [17] discusses some extensions to UML specifically for modelling safety constraints, primarily achieved by profiles of packages, class and component diagrams. [18] briefly discusses an application of Safe-UML for modelling in the railway domain, and a more detailed UML profile for modelling safety critical systems in this domain is proposed in [19]. In [20], UML design models consisting of activity diagrams and state machines are used as a starting point for a so-called "exploration game" to improve the models to better address safety hazards. Use cases and FMEA have been used together to analyse system robustness [21]. FMEA has also been used to analyse process reliability and has turned out to be a methods that is easy to learn and use [22].

For security aspects, there are also several additional adaptations of UML. For instance, [23] and [24] look at adaptations of UML class diagrams and activity diagrams to design secure data warehouses and business processes, respectively, and [25] and [26] look at secure systems design by means of UML more in general. In [27], inverted icons à la misuse case diagrams are also employed to extend UML activity diagrams, to capture negative actions of attackers in business processes. Similarly, [28] indicates that inverted icons can also be used to capture dependability threats in other types of conceptual models, such as information models and Petri net based workflow models.

Of the above works, many are mainly related to design, i.e., analyzing safety or security of a system where the design is already known or at least outlined, whereas our work is focused on an early identification of hazards based on available use case diagrams. Most closely related to our work are therefore [6] – combining use cases with traditional safety analysis techniques – and [14], [15], [16] – combining use cases with misuse cases for safety analysis. This paper is different from the above in that it *compares* two such approaches, while previous papers primarily present their own modelling approach. A somewhat related paper comparing approaches is [29], but this used a case study rather than a controlled experiment, analyzed security, not safety, and partly looked at different modelling approaches, comparing misuse cases with Common Criteria and Attack Trees. Some comparison between misuse cases and various safety approaches is also provided in [30], but in that paper the comparison is primarily from the perspective of misuse cases and it is also purely conceptual, not backed by any empirical results on the effectiveness of the various representations.

3 The Techniques to be Compared

3.1 Misuse Cases

Misuse cases [13] were originally proposed for eliciting security requirements, but they have also been used for safety analysis, misuse cases then being accidents causing harm in the system [14]. The diagram of Fig. 1 shows the human operator functions related to an automated system used to keep the water level in a tank constant while delivering steam to an industrial process. This is done by filling the tank through one valve and emptying it through another valve when needed. If the pressure in the tank becomes too high, a relief valve should open automatically as the pressure exceeds the critical pressure pre-set by the operator. The operator may also manually empty the tank (for instance if the relief valve fails to work when the pressure becomes too high) or manually fill the tank (if the automatic adjustment of water level does not work). A misuse case such as "Set too high pressure" may have a "threatens" relationship to one or more use cases (in this case "Set critical pressure"). It is also possible that one misuse case may "aggravate" the effect of another, or that a use case may have a "mitigates" relationship to that misuse case. Such relationships are not exemplified in Figure 1.

Fig. 1. Example safety-oriented misuse case diagram for a boiler tank system

An example of a textual representation is shown in Table 1. Here, threats (corresponding to misuse cases) can be added in a third column called "Threats", and mitigations can be added in a fourth column. An essential idea of misuse case analysis is that the representation format causes only a limited overhead if use cases are already applied in a project, which is often the case in mainstream software projects. Moreover, the informality and simplicity of the technique makes it suitable for supporting brainstorming about threats at an early stage of development. For a more complete coverage of misuse case analysis, the reader is referred to [13] and [15].

3.2 Failure Mode and Effect Analysis

FMEA [31] is short for Failure Mode Effect Analysis, a method that tries to identify how a component or system can fail (the failure modes) and then analyze the effect of these identified failure modes. The FMEA process consists of the following steps:

- Decide the level where we want to identify components. For the experiment reported here, the granularity of component was a use case function. If using FMEA in a later development stage where, e.g., the proposed architecture or detailed design is known, the design modules could have been components in the analysis.
- Identify the failure modes. A failure mode is a way the component can fail – deliver a wrong result. Again we can choose several levels. If an operator is entering a numerical value we can choose between several alternatives, e.g., just one failure mode for "wrong value", or two failure modes: "too high value" and "too low value". Usually, we should only split a failure mode such as "wrong number" up into several failure modes if they will have different effects.

Table 1. Column format use case with safety issues for the boiler

Use case name	"Empty tank manually"		
User actions	System response	Threats	Mitigations
	System alarms operator of high pressure	System fails to raise alarm; Operator fails to notice alarm	2 independent alarms; Use both sound and blinking lights
Operator issues command to empty tank		Operator fails to react (e.g., incapacitated?) Operator gives wrong command, e.g., filling tank	Alarm backup operator; Auto sanity check, disallow filling at high pressure
	System opens valve to sewer	System fails to relay command to valve; Valve is stuck	
Operator reads pressure		Operator misreads and stops tank emptying too soon	Maintain alarm blinking until situation normal
	Pressure returns to normal	This is not achieved, see exceptions	
Operator stops tank emptying and logs the event. This ends the use case.			
Exceptional paths			
	Opening valve is insufficient to normalize pressure		
Operator issues command to reduce temperature		Operator gives wrong command, e.g., increase temperature	Automatic sanity check, disallow temp increase at high pressure
	Pressure returns to normal		
Operator logs the event. This ends the use case.			

All identified failure modes are registered in an FMEA table, see Table 2 for an example. For each failure mode, the following information is included:

- Consequences of each failure mode. FMEA identifies three types of consequences (1) local consequences - related to the component that we are analyzing, (2) system consequences - related to the system we are analyzing and which the component is a part of, and (3) global consequences – not decided by the failing component or system alone but a relationship between the system and the environment it is operating in. In the experiment, the participants were asked to consider only local and system consequences.
- Corrective action – identification of possible barriers and mitigations of each failure mode. There are several ways to handle an identified failure mode. We can use (1) removal – remove the possibility of this particular failure mode, (2) barriers – prevent this particular failure mode from having a dangerous effect

and (3) mitigations – reduce the effect of this particular failure mode. In the experiment, participants could use all three strategies but only on a high level of description – i.e., they were not expected to design or describe the solution in any detail.

- P – probability index. This index indicates how probable it is that this failure mode occurs.
- C – failure consequence. This index indicates how severe the effect of the failure mode will be if it becomes a failure event.
- R – failure risk. This index is the product of a failures consequence and its probability, i.e. we have R = P * C.

The P, C, and R columns were not used in the experiment, on the grounds that assigning numerical values for the likelihood of failures would be little more than speculation from the participants' perspective. Table 2 shows two example FMEA tables, in the format used in the experiment. The failure modes are from the same example as the misuse case diagram of Figure 1 and the textual misuse case of Table 1, concentrating on the use case functions "Empty tank manually" and "Set critical pressure", respectively.

Table 2. FMEA tables for two of the use case functions of Fig. 1

Unit	Empty tank manually		
Failure mode	Local effect	System effect	Corrective action
Valve will not open	Cannot empty tank	*Accident* – too high pressure	• Valve status indicator
Valve will not close	Cannot fill tank	No steam delivered	• Duplicate valve • Must be possible to turn valve without motor

Unit	Set critical pressure		
Failure mode	Local effect	System effect	Corrective action
Pressure set too high	Too high pressure in the tank	*Accident* – too high pressure	Reasonability check on pressure. Cannot exceed defined, hard coded limit
Pressure set too low	Too low pressure in the tank	No steam delivered	Reasonability check on pressure. Cannot go below defined, hard coded limit

One of the important ideas behind use cases is that it should serve as a vehicle of communication between users and software developers. The FMEA method is easy to use and easy to learn and should thus be a good method to combine with use cases.

4 The Experiment

4.1 Research Approach

Our experiment was a combination of a quantitative and a qualitative study. The goal of the experiment was to study two methods for failure mode analyses – FMEA and Misuse Case (MUC). We will arrive at our conclusions based on the answer to the research questions:

- RQ1 – do we identify more failure modes when using one of the methods? If the answer is yes – is one of the methods uniformly better, i.e., outperforming the other method for all types of failure modes?
- RQ2 – is one of the methods better than the other when it comes to important characteristics such as easy to learn, and easy to use?

The data analysis for RQ1 consists of two steps (1) categorizing the failure modes into a common set for both methods and (2) a t-test used to compare the two data sets. We will answer RQ1 by use of t-tests – one for the total number of failure modes identified from each method and one for the number of failure modes identified in each of the three categories primary user, system, and secondary user.

The data analysis for RQ2 is done by using the t-test on the coded scores in the usual way – using a Likert scale where strongly disagree to strongly agree is coded as 1 to 5. The questions used to answer RQ2 were based on the TAM model [32].

We have observed that there are purists who do not like to use the t-test on Likert scale data, but we are not going to repeat this discussion. Instead the reader is referred to [33] where this discussion is summed up and, hopefully, brought to an end.

4.2 Experiment Design

The students participating in the experiment were randomly divided into two groups, one using FMEA for the analysis task and the other using MUC. Both groups solved their tasks under equal conditions - same room, same time-frame. The experiment consisted of four steps, namely (1) studying the four page tutorial describing the respective methods, (2) filling in the pre-experiment questionnaire, (3) performing an FMEA or a Misuse Case (MUC) analysis, with the help of the tutorial, and (4) filling in the post-experiment questionnaire. We allocated 20 minutes for studying the tutorial and completing the pre-experiment questionnaire, 50 minutes for doing the analysis and 10 minutes for completing the post-experiment questionnaire. Based on our own observations, no group seemed to have problems with finishing their tasks within the allocated time frame.

The students were instructed to identify as many failure modes as possible. A failure mode was defined as any system event that could threaten the well being of one or more patients.

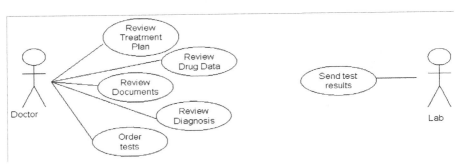

Fig. 2. The use case diagram that was input for the experiment

The use case to be analyzed stems from a system for electronic patient journals and is shown in the use case diagram of Figure 2. The doctor has five functions – he can review (i.e., read and update) the patient's treatment plan, the patient's drug data, the diagnosis and other documents, and order tests from the lab. The lab sends test results back to the doctor.

5   Experiment Results and Analysis

5.1   Identified Failure Modes

A simple t-test (Table 3) shows that the MUC is better than FMEA when it comes to number of failure modes identified, with a p-value less than 0.01 which is satisfactory. The standard deviation for the whole data set is 2.87, giving an effect size of $(8.48 - 5.86) / 2.87 = 0.91$, which is a moderate (0.6) to large (1.2) effect [34].

Table 3. Comparison of failure mode identification by the two techniques

	FMEA	MUC
Mean	5,86	8,48
Variance	5,33	7,96
Observations	21,00	21,00
Hypothesized Mean Difference	0,00	
df	38	
t Stat	-3,29	
P(T<=t) one-tail	0,00	
t Critical one-tail	1,69	
P(T<=t) two-tail	0,00	
t Critical two-tail	2,02	

Table 4. Comparison of system-internal failure modes identified by the two techniques

	FMEA System	MUC System
Mean	2,76	3,29
Variance	2,99	5,21
Observations	21,00	21,00
Hypothesized Mean Difference	0,00	
df	37	
t Stat	-0,84	
P(T<=t) one-tail	0,20	
t Critical one-tail	1,69	
P(T<=t) two-tail	0,41	
t Critical two-tail	2,03	

The failure modes identified stem from three distinct areas – the doctor, which is the main user, the computer system, and the lab – the secondary user. Splitting the data according to these three categories, only the first category (doctor-related failure modes) shows a significant difference. The t-test summary of Table 4 shows the result from comparing the failure modes related to the system itself.

In order to check the influence of factors like the participants' experience with writing use cases or using other UML related methods, we performed a best subset regression analysis with the answers to the pre-experiment questionnaire as independent variables and the number of failure modes identified as the dependent variable. The regression analysis showed us that there exists no set of pre-experiment factors which gave an adjusted R^2 greater than 0.13. A sequence of ANOVAs confirms this conclusion. The only factor that gave a p-value less than 0.10 was the experiment type – FMEA vs. MUC. Even pre-experiment question 5 which asked for the participants' experience with making use cases gave us a p-value of 0.53.

The next question is then – is MUC uniformly better than or as good as FMEA? The easy way to answer this question is to start with a bar plot. The bar plots for the three areas of analysis – primary user failures, system failures, and secondary user failures – are shown below. From left to right we see the number of failure modes identified for primary user, system and secondary user. The grey bars show the FMEA results while the black bars show the MUC results.

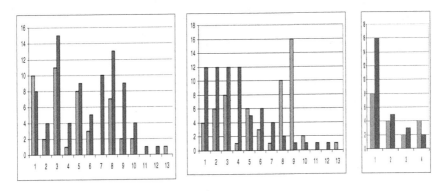

Fig. 3. Number of identified failure modes for primary user, system and secondary user

If we interpret "much more" as more than 25% more, and only consider the failure modes that are identified by at least half of the participants in at least one of the groups, the most important differences are:

- For primary user, the persons that used MUC found much more of the failure modes 3, 6, 7, 8 and 9 – select wrong test (3), set incorrect drug dosage (6), incorrect review of drug data (7), diagnosis (8) or document (9). All in all MUC is better than FMEA for 11 out of 13 failure modes – approximately 85%.

- For the system, the persons that used MUC found much more of the failure modes 1, 2, 3, 4 and 6 – show incorrect info on treatment plan (1), drug data (2), diagnosis (3) or document (4) and test results not arriving. The persons that used FMEA found much more of the failure modes 8 and 9 – data not available (8) and data lost (9). All in all MUC is better than FMEA for 8 out of 13 failure modes – approximately 61%.

- For the secondary user, the persons that used MUC found much more of the failure mode 1 – lab enters wrong results. All in all MUC is better than FMEA for 3 out of 4 failure modes – 75%.

From these observations, we see a pattern. MUC is significantly better for identification of failure modes related to the primary user. The analysis of system failure modes also shows that MUC usually is much better than FMEA when it comes to identifying failure modes related to the user's interaction with the system. The only cases where FMEA performs better are related to the network communication. The network was not included in the use case but became a natural part of the results from the FMEA.

5.2   Learning and Using the Methods

In order to answer RQ2 – is one of the two methods FMEA and MUC easier to use – we used the TAM model [32] with the three factors Perceived ease of use (PEOU), Perceived usefulness (PU) and Intention to use (IU) – see Fig. 4. We used a post-experiment questionnaire with four questions for each factor to measure them.

The answers to the questionnaire were scored on a five point Likert scale. We have used t-test to compare the scores given by the MUC group and the FMEA group – see Table 5. Using a p-value of 0.10 we got the following results:

- PEOU – questions Q1, Q3, Q7 and Q8. For all but one question, the MUC group scored higher than the FMEA group. For the last question (Q8), the scores were the same.
- ITU – questions Q4, Q6, Q9 and Q12. For all but one question, the MUC group scored higher than the FMEA group. For the last question (Q12), the scores were the same.
- PU – questions Q2, Q5, Q10 and Q11. For the first question, the MUC group did better, while the scores were the same for the three last questions.

Based on the summary above it is reasonable to claim that MUC is better than FMEA for perceived ease of use and intention to use, while they are equally good when it comes to perceived usefulness.

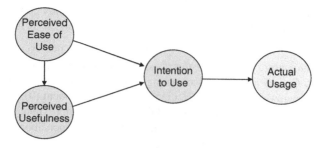

Fig. 4. The factors in the TAM model

All the response mean values were larger for the MUC group than for the FMEA group. From Table 5, we see that eight of the effects are in the range 0.2 to 0.6 which falls in the category small to medium. Two effects are even smaller – Q10 and Q11. The only questions which generate a medium to large effect – 0.6 to 1.2 – are Q6 and Q7. A simple correlation analysis of all answers to the post-experiment questionnaire also shows that the correlation between Q6 and Q7 are small – 0.15 for the FMEA group and 0.00 for the MUC group.

Table 5. Effect sizes for MUC vs. FMEA for the TAM questions

Question id	Question area	Effect size
Q1	The method was easy to learn	0.4
Q2	The method helped me to identify threats	0.5
Q3	The method was easy to understand	0.6
Q4	I will use the method in the future for similar problems during my studies	0.5
Q5	The method worked better than just using common sense	0.4
Q6	I will use the method in the future for similar problems at work	0.7
Q7	I was never confused when using the method	0.9
Q8	The method made the search for threats more systematic	0.3
Q9	I would support a suggestion for using the method at work	0.5
Q10	The diagrams and tables were easy to draw	0.1
Q11	The method helped me to focus on the important threats	0.1
Q12	If I worked as a freelance I would use this method in a discussion with my customer	0.3

The small effect sizes may lead us to assume that the participants answered the questions at random. However, if this was the case we have an equal probability of getting a higher score for FMEA users and for MUC users for each question. If the participants answered the questions randomly, the probability of getting a higher score for MUC than for FMEA for all 12 questions is 2^{-12} or less than 0.002. We will thus reject the idea of random answers.

6   Threats to Validity

We will use the categories defined in [35] as a starting point for our discussion on threats to validity. We will look at each threat in a short section before giving a sum-up of our validity claims.

6.1 Conclusion Validity

Conclusion validity is concerned with our ability to draw the right conclusions about the relationship between the treatment and the outcome. An important question here is sample size. We have claimed a medium to large effect – ES = 0.9. We will denote the type I error probability by α and the type II error probability by β. The following relationship holds:

$$N = \frac{4(u_{\alpha/2} + u_\beta)^2}{ES^2} \qquad (1)$$

If we use $\alpha = 0.05$ and $\beta = 0.20$, we get $N = 26/0.9^2$ which gives use an N-value of 32. Since we have 42 participants, we have a sufficient number of observations for our conclusion.

For the post-experiment questions, the situation is different. In only one case is the effect size large enough to be observed with a sample size of 42. In one other case, the effect size is almost large enough.

6.2 Internal Validity

Internal validity is concerned with the relationship between treatment and outcome – was it the treatment that caused the outcome? The analysis reported in section 5.1 shows that using the method MUC or FMEA explain the difference, while factors like UML experience and use case experience did not explain the observed differences in the number of failure modes identified. Thus, we are confident that it was the difference in analysis method that caused the observed differences in the number of failure modes identified.

For the post-experiment questionnaire, the situation is more difficult. There are no combinations of pre-experiment factors that can explain more than 25% of the variation in observed values for any of the post-experiment questions. The variation in experiment type can only explain the observed variations for two of these questions.

6.3 Construct Validity

Construct validity is concerned with the relationship between theory and observations – was the experiment realistic? The realism of the experiment is lacking in two ways: (1) little training with a new method and (2) the quality of the result has no influence, neither on a real product nor on the participant's working situation. However, the above-mentioned threats will influence both groups in the same way. Since we are only looking for differences between two methods and not for any absolute measure of efficiency this should not influence our conclusions of the two methods' relative merits.

6.4 External Validity

External validity is concerned with generalization – where and when are the conclusions applicable and can we generalize from our experiments to industrial practice? The important problem here is whether we can generalize our results to the software industry. Experiments on defect detection performed by Runeson [36] found no significant difference between graduate students and professionals. As shown by [37] generalization is not a question of students vs. professional developers – it is mainly a question of level of competence. UML competence did not seem to influence the results. The only competence that could influence the results in a significant way is the domain competence – in our case competence related to hospital work and working with patient journals.

6.5 Our Claims to Validity

Based on the discussions above, we claim that there are no serious threats to validity for our conclusions on the number of identified failure modes – RQ1. For factors related to ease of use, we see problems related to conclusion validity due to the small effect sizes.

7 Conclusion and Future Work

Our research questions were whether one of the two methods MUC or FMEA was better than the other one for identifying failure modes and if one of the methods was easier to learn and to use. Based on the data analysis and the identified threats to validity, we offer the following conclusions: When the system's requirements are described as use cases

- MUC is better than FMEA for analysing failure modes related to user interactions.
- FMEA is better than MUC for analysing failure modes related to the inner working of the system.
- MUC will create less confusion and in general be easier to use than FMEA.

In order to reap maximum benefits, both methods should be used together – MUC for the user interfaces and FMEA for the rest of the system.

Those who used MUC in the experiment found the method easier to understand. They were seldom confused and were more willing to use their method again than were the participants who used the FMEA.

There are still a lot of data from our experiment that are not analysed – especially data pertaining to identified consequences and suggested mitigations. These data will be analysed later. In addition, we want to study how easy it is to use the results from MUC and FMEA to implement the small example system including possible mitigations.

References

1. Firesmith, D.G.: Engineering Safety Requirements, Safety Constraints, and Safety-Critical Requirements. Journal of Object Technology 3, 27–42 (2004)
2. McDermott, J., Fox, C.: Using Abuse Case Models for Security Requirements Analysis. In: Dignum, F.P.M., Greaves, M. (eds.) Issues in Agent Communication. LNCS, vol. 1916, Springer, Heidelberg (2000)
3. Lutz, R.R.: Software Engineering for Safety: A Roadmap. In: Finkelstein, A. (ed.) The Future of Software Engineering, pp. 213–226. ACM Press, New York (2000)
4. Jacobson, I., Christerson, M., Jonsson, P., Overgaard, G.: Object-Oriented Software Engineering: A Use Case Driven Approach. Addison-Wesley, Boston (1992)
5. Poels, G., Burton-Jones, A., Gemino, A., Parsons, J., Ramesh, V.: Experimental Research on Conceptual Modeling: What Should We Be Doing and Why? In: Embley, D.W., Olivé, A., Ram, S. (eds.) ER 2006. LNCS, vol. 4215, pp. 544–547. Springer, Heidelberg (2006)
6. Allenby, K., Kelly, T.: Deriving Safety Requirements Using Scenarios. In: Nuseibeh, B., Easterbrook, S. (eds.) Fifth IEEE International Symposium on Requirements Engineering (RE'01), Toronto, Canada, pp. 228–235. IEEE Computer Society Press, Los Alamitos (2001)

7. Guidelines, S.A.E.: Methods for Conducting the Safety Assessment Process on Civil Airborne Systems and Equipment. Society of Automotive Engineers (1996)

8. Redmill, F., Chudleigh, M., Catmur, J.: System Safety: HAZOP and Software HAZOP. Wiley, Chichester, UK (1999)

9. Kim, H.-K., Chung, Y.-K.: Automatic Translation from Requirements Model into Use Cases Modeling on UML. In: Gervasi, O., Gavrilova, M., Kumar, V., Laganà, A., Lee, H.P., Mun, Y., Taniar, D., Tan, C.J.K. (eds.) ICCSA 2005. LNCS, vol. 3482, pp. 769–777. Springer, Heidelberg (2005)

10. Hause, M.: Use-cases to aid safe design. Electronics Systems and Software 2, 38–41 (2004)

11. Pettit IV, R.G., Street, J.A.: Lessons Learned Applying UML in the Design of Mission-Critical Software. In: Nunes, N.J., Selic, B., Rodrigues da Silva, A., Toval Alvarez, A. (eds.) UML Modeling Languages and Applications. LNCS, vol. 3297, pp. 129–137. Springer, Heidelberg (2005)

12. Ebnenasir, A., Cheng, B.H.C., Konrad, S.: Use Case-Based Modeling and Analysis of Failsafe Fault-Tolerance. In: Glinz, M. (ed.) 14th IEEE International Requirements Engineering Conference (RE'06), St.Louis, USA, pp. 343–344. IEEE Computer Society Press, Los Alamitos (2006)

13. Sindre, G., Opdahl, A.L.: Eliciting Security Requirements with Misuse Cases. Requirements Engineering 10, 34–44 (2005)

14. Alexander, I.F.: Initial Industrial Experience of Misuse Cases in Trade-Off Analysis. In: Pohl, K. (ed.) 10th Anniversary IEEE Joint International Requirements Engineering Conference (RE'02), Essen, Germany, pp. 9–13. IEEE Computer Society Press, Los Alamitos (2002)

15. Alexander, I.F.: Misuse Cases, Use Cases with Hostile Intent. IEEE Software 20, 58–66 (2003)

16. Gran, B.A., Fredriksen, R., Thunem, A.P.-J.: An Approach for Model-Based Risk Assessment. In: Heisel, M., Liggesmeyer, P., Wittmann, S. (eds.) SAFECOMP 2004. LNCS, vol. 3219, pp. 311–324. Springer, Heidelberg (2004)

17. Jürjens, J.: Developing Safety-Critical Systems with UML. In: Stevens, P., Whittle, J., Booch, G. (eds.) (UML 2003). LNCS, vol. 2863, pp. 144–159. Springer, Heidelberg (2003)

18. Hungar, H.: UML-basierte Entwicklung sikkerheitskritische Systemen im Bahnbereich. Dagstuhl Workshop on Model-Based Development of Embedded Systems, Dagstuhl, Germany (January, 9-13), pp. 63-64. Tech Univ Braunschweig (2006)

19. Berkenkötter, K., Hannemann, U., Peleska, J., HYBRIS,: HYBRIS - Efficient Specification and Analysis of Hybrid Systems - Part III: RCSD - A UML 2.0 Profile for the Railway Control System Domain (Draft Version). Univ. Bremen, Germany (2006)

20. Tenzer, J.: Exploration games for safety-critical system design with UML 2.0. In: Fernandez, E.B., et al. (eds.): 3rd International Workshop on Critical Systems Development with UML, CSDUML'04, Lisbon, Portugal, 12 Oct, Technical Report I0415. pp. 41-55. Technische Universität München, (2004)

21. Stålhane, T., Pham, H.T.: Assessment and Analysis of Robustness for a Web-Based System. In: Isaias, P., et al. (eds.) IADIS International Conference on WWW/Internet, Murcia, Spain, 5-8 October, IADIS Press (2006)

22. Lauritzen, T., Stålhane, T.: Safety Methods in Software Process Improvement. In: Richardson, I., Abrahamsson, P., Messnarz, R. (eds.) Software Process Improvement. LNCS, vol. 3792, pp. 95–105. Springer, Heidelberg (2005)

23. Fernandez-Medina, E., Trujillo, J., Villaroel, R., Piattini, M.: Extending UML for Designing Secure Data Warehouses. In: Atzeni, P., Chu, W., Lu, H., Zhou, S., Ling, T.-W. (eds.) ER 2004. LNCS, vol. 3288, Springer, Heidelberg (2004)

24. Rodriguez, A., Fernandez-Medina, E., Piattini, M.: Capturing Security Requirements in Business Processes through a UML 2. In: Roddick, J.F., Benjamins, V.R., Si-Saïd Cherfi, S., Chiang, R., Claramunt, C., Elmasri, R., Grandi, F., Han, H., Hepp, M., Lytras, M., Mišić, V.B., Poels, G., Song, I.-Y., Trujillo, J., Vangenot, C. (eds.). ER 2006. LNCS, vol. 4231, Springer, Heidelberg (2006)

25. Lodderstedt, T., Basin, D., Doser, J.: SecureUML: A UML-Based Modeling Language for Model-Driven Security. In: Jézéquel, J.-M., Hussmann, H., Cook, S. (eds.). UML 2002. LNCS, vol. 2460, pp. 426–441. Springer, Heidelberg (2002)

26. Jürjens, J.: Sound methods and effective tools for model-based security engineering with UML. In: Inverardi, P., Jazayeri, M. (eds.) ICSE 2005. LNCS, vol. 4309, pp. 322–331. Springer, Heidelberg (2006)

27. Sindre, G.: Mal-activity diagrams to capture attacks on business processes. In: Sawyer, P., Paech, B., Heymans, P. (eds.). REFSQ 2007. LNCS, vol. 4542, pp. 355–366. Springer, Heidelberg (2007)

28. Sindre, G., Opdahl, A.L.: Capturing Dependability Threats in Conceptual Modelling. In: Krogstie, J., et al. (eds.) Conceptual Modelling in Information Systems Engineering, pp. 247–260. Springer, Heidelberg (2007)

29. Diallo, M.H., Romero-Mariona, J., Sim, S.E., Richardson, D.J.: A Comparative Evaluation of Three Approaches to Specifying Security Requirements. REFSQ'06, Luxembourg (2006)

30. Sindre, G.: A look at misuse cases for safety concerns. In: Henderson-Sellers, B., et al. (eds.) IFIP WG8.1 Working Conference on Situational Method Engineering: Fundamentals and Experiences (ME'07), Geneva, Switzerland. IFIP Series, Springer, Heidelberg (2007)

31. Stamatis, D.H.: Failure Mode and Effect Analysis: FMEA from theory to execution. American Society for Quality (ASQ), Milwaukee, Wisconsin (1995)

32. Davis, F.D., Bagozzi, R.P., Warshaw, P.R.: User Acceptance of Computer Technology: A Comparison of Two Theoretical Models. Management Science 35, 982–1003 (1989)

33. Tukey, J.W.: Data analysis and behavioral science or learning to bear the quantitative's man burden by shunning badmandments. In: Jones, L.W. (ed.) The Collected Works of John W. Tukey, Wadsworth, Monterey, CA. Tukey, vol. III, pp. 187–389 (1986)

34. Hopkins, W.G.: A New View of Statistics. University of Queensland, Australia, Brisbane (2001)

35. Wohlin, C., Runeson, P., Höst, M., Ohlsson, M.C., Regnell, B., Wesslén, A.: Experimentation in Software Engineering: An Introduction. Kluwer Academic, Norwell, MA, USA (2000)

36. Runeson, P.: Using Students as Experiment Subjects – An Analysis on Graduate and Freshmen Student Data. In: Linkman, S. (ed.) 7th International Conference on Empirical Assessment & Evaluation in Software Engineering (EASE'03), pp. 95–102. Keele University, Staffordshire, UK (2003)

37. Arisholm, E., Sjøberg, D.I.K.: Evaluating the Effect of a Delegated versus Centralized Control Style on the Maintainability of Object-oriented Software. IEEE Transactions on Software Engineering 30, 521–534 (2004)

Using Unified Modeling Language for Conceptual Modelling of Knowledge-Based Systems

Mohd Syazwan Abdullah[1], Ian Benest[2], Richard Paige[2], and Chris Kimble[2]

[1] Faculty of Information Technology, Universiti Utara Malaysia (UUM),
06010 UUM-Sintok, Kedah, Malaysia
syazwan@uum.edu.my
[2] Department of Computer Science, University of York,
Heslington, York, YO10 5DD, United Kingdom
{idb,paige,kimble}@cs.york.ac.uk

Abstract. This paper discusses extending the Unified Modelling Language by means of a profile for modelling knowledge-based system in the context of Model Driven Architecture (MDA) framework. The profile is implemented using the eXecutable Modelling Framework (XMF) Mosaic tool. A case study from the health care domain demonstrates the practical use of this profile; with the prototype implemented in Java Expert System Shell (Jess). The paper also discusses the possible mapping of the profile elements to the platform specific model (PSM) of Jess and provides some discussion on the Production Rule Representation (PRR) standardisation work.

1 Introduction

Knowledge-based systems (KBS) were developed for managing codified knowledge (explicit knowledge) in Artificial Intelligence (AI) systems [1]. These were known as expert systems and were originally created to emulate human expert reasoning [2]. KBS are developed using knowledge engineering (KE) techniques [2], which are similar to those used in software engineering (SE), but they emphasise knowledge rather than data or information processing. Both KE and SE development processes have the same objective: to develop the system given the user requirements, in order to solve a particular problem related to the domain [2]. Systems development in SE involves the following iterative stages regardless of the methodology adopted: gathering and analysing user requirements, designing the system by translating user requirements into a software specification using conceptual models, coding the software specification into computer programs, testing the program to ensure the agreed results are produced, implementing the system and maintaining the system throughout its intended life span.

The KE processes for constructing a KBS in general are: requirements analysis involving identifying the scope for the KBS, designing the system by identifying the sources of expert knowledge for the KBS and how to represent them, acquiring the knowledge from the expert through knowledge acquisition techniques and constructing the knowledge base with instances of the domain knowledge, coding the system on target application languages or shells, testing the system to ensure the inference

C. Parent et al. (Eds.): ER 2007, LNCS 4801, pp. 438–453, 2007.
© Springer-Verlag Berlin Heidelberg 2007

mechanism is working properly and producing the correct results, implementing the system incrementally and performing maintenance on the system [5, 26, 29]. In comparison with SE, the KE has one additional stage: that of knowledge acquisition (KA). This stage is vital in KBS development as the KBS is designed around the domain expert's knowledge of solving problems for a particular task, such as diagnosis, assessment and so on. The acquired knowledge is then used to populate the knowledge base in the form of rules, with which the system will perform reasoning. However, in SE there is no KA stage as the system is intended to capture information rather than reason with it and the actual dataset of the database will be populated by the system user when the system is deployed [26, 29]. Therefore, it may be concluded that the KA stage differentiates the SE and KE domains when developing software systems.

Central to this is the conceptual modelling of the system during the analysis and design stages of KBS development (known as knowledge modelling). A number of KE methodologies have emphasised the use of models, for example: CommonKADS, Model-based and Incremental Knowledge Engineering (MIKE), Knowledge Acquisition and Representation Language (KARL) and others [3]. KBS continue to evolve as the need to have a stable technology for managing knowledge grows; its current role as an enabler in knowledge management initiatives has led to its wider acceptance [4]. It has matured from a non-scalable technology [1, 5]. Once restricted to the research laboratory, it is now used for demanding commercial applications and is a tool widely accepted by industry [6, 7]. As a result, the Object Management Group (OMG), which governs object-oriented software modelling standards, has started the standardisation process for production rule representation (PRR) [8] and knowledge-based engineering (KBE) services [9]. The standardisation of PRR is vital as it allows interoperability of rules between different inference engines – much needed by industry [10, 11].

The major problem with conceptual modelling of KBS (*known as knowledge modelling*) is that there is no standard language available to model the knowledge for developing a KBS. Most of the languages used are adapted from SE. The languages used in knowledge modelling are project based using a mix of notations such as Unified Modeling Language (UML), Integrated Definition Method (IDEF), Structured Analysis and Design Technique (SADT) etc. The SE community has adopted UML as the *de facto* standard for modelling object-oriented systems and the KE community should do the same. This would be beneficial in the long-term as KBS can be easily integrated into other enterprise systems [4] particularly if their designs were based on a standard language; it would help facilitate communication and sharing of blueprints among developers [12].

Research has shown that neither technical nor economic factors determine whether KBS technology will be successfully adopted, but rather it is the organisational and managerial environment that is the main determinant [13, 14]. Gill [13] highlights one of the problems: the management of the development team. KBS projects are specialised in nature requiring team members to have knowledge of both the problem domain and the development tools. As a result, the team members are skilful individuals and the success of the project is threatened if one or more leave the team mid-way through the development or during the maintenance period. But a KBS that is designed using an appropriate, well-understood, standard language for conceptual modelling along with a methodologically sound representation technique should be readily understood by new team members. Conceptual models (CM) are a description of the software system at different level of abstractions [15] and are popular in SE domain for providing an overview of concepts and relationships of the real-world, eliminate costly errors during analysis and design stages prior to construction and facilitates better communications between different people in the project team [16]. The importance of CM in software systems development are reflected through Model Driven Architecture (MDA) technique as models rather than codes have become the important artifacts of software development [17].

This paper is organised thus. Section 2 discusses the UML extensibility mechanicsm. Section 3 describes the knowledge modelling profile, and section 4 illustrates how the profile can be used to develop a KBS. Section 5 provides some discussion and finding on the use of the profile in PRR standardisation, while section 6 concludes with directions for future work.

2 UML, Model Driven Architecture and UML Profile Mechanism

UML is a general-purpose modelling language [18] that may be used in a wide range of application domains. Although UML is very popular and widely used as the modelling language for business applications, its use for knowledge modelling is limited. This is due to the fact that the usage of UML in modelling KBS has not been standardised [8], as there is no commonly agreed consensus on what KBS and KE concepts should be represented in a KBS design, and how rules should be defined and modelled. Nevertheless, there have been several attempts to use UML for knowledge modelling but such comprehensive efforts are only reflected in CommonKADS [26]. UML can be extended to model domains that it does not currently support, by extending the modelling features of the language in a controlled and systematic fashion.

The OMG's Model Driven Architecture (MDA) – a model-driven engineering framework – provides integration with, and interoperability between, different models developed using its standards [18] (such as UML, Meta-Object Facility (MOF), and others). The growth of MDA will fuel the demand for more meta-models to cater for domain specific modelling requirements [18, 19]. Profiles have defined semantics and syntax, which enables them to be formally integrated into UML, though of course they must adhere to the profile requirements proposed by OMG. Previous profile development for knowledge modelling has concentrated only on certain task types such as product design and product configuration [20]. In contrast, the work described here emphasises the development of a generic profile for modeling the design knowledge of a KBS. Developing a meta-model for knowledge modelling will enable it to be integrated into the MDA space allowing the relation between the knowledge models and other language models to be understood. It provides for seamless integration of different models in different applications within an enterprise. The OMG [21, 22] defines two mechanisms for extending UML: profiles and meta-model extensions. Both extensions have (unfortunately) been called profiles [18].

The "lightweight" extension mechanism of UML [22] is profiles. It contains a predefined set of Stereotypes, TaggedValues, Constraints, and notation icons that collectively specialize and tailor the existing UML meta-model. The main construct in the profile is the stereotype that is purely an extension mechanism. In the model, it is marked as «stereotype» and has the same structure (attributes, associations, operations) as that defined by the meta-model. However, the usage of stereotypes is restricted; changes in the semantics, structure, and the introduction of new concepts to the meta-model are not permitted [23]. The "heavyweight" extension mechanism for UML (known as the meta-model extension) is defined through the MOF specification [24] which involves the process of defining a new meta-model [23]. This approach should be favoured if the semantic gap between the core modelling elements of UML and the newly defined modelling elements is significant [18].

The work presented in this paper exploits the profile extension using the XMF (eXecutable Meta-modelling Framework) approach [25] as we believe that the knowledge modelling concepts can be modelled by tailoring existing UML meta-models without having to introduce new meta-concepts to UML. Furthermore, this will enable the profile to have readily available tool support, which will be a significant advantage for knowledge modellers in adopting UML over other languages. The OMG only specifies what profiles should constitute and not how to design them. By adopting the XMF approach, the profile development is structured into well-defined stages that are easy to follow and methodologically sound. The XMF is a newly developed object-oriented meta-modelling language, and is an extension to existing standards for meta-models such as MOF and UML. XMF offers an alternative approach in profile design, which allows modification, or addition, of new modelling constructs; and these are easily integrated into the core meta-model of UML. This work uses the XMF approach in designing the profile and implementing it in the Mosaic tool. Although XMF core meta-model differs slightly from UML meta-model, and the same is true for Eclipse ECore meta-model, nevertheless the fundamentals are still the same. Furthermore, the knowledge modelling profile only extends the UML meta-class Class and Associations. However, only the profile concepts' extension to Class can be defined using Mosaic, as associations are implemented as built-in modelling features which are directly available to use at the model level.

3   UML Profile for Knowledge Modelling

The concepts for the knowledge modelling profile are re-used from the existing BNF definition of the CommonKADS Conceptual Modelling Language (CML) [26]; this provides a well-defined and well-established main set of concepts for the domain. Most of these elements are generally adopted in the KBS literature [1, 27-29] and are widely used for representing concepts in KBS in the KE domain. The Knowledge Modelling profile was implemented using the XMF Mosaic by defining a meta-profile that allows for the definition of the knowledge modelling profile stereotypes, which in turn enables the construction of a knowledge model as an instance of the profile meta-model. To achieve this, the profile is defined as an extension to the XCore meta-model (the XMF-Mosaic's MOF based meta-model, similar to the definition of the UML meta-model) in the form of a meta-package for the profile. An important feature of the stereotypes is the inheritance of the modelling capabilities of UML meta-class elements. Meta-package is a mechanism in XMF-Mosaic that enables the content of the profile package to be viewed as an instance of the XCore meta-model class. The profile meta-model used here is the derived meta-model of CommonKADS and defined as the complete knowledge modelling abstract syntax meta-model in [32] as shown in Figure 1.

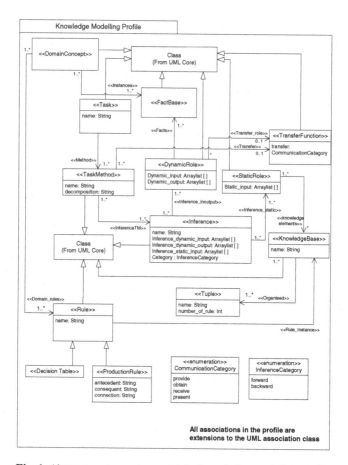

Fig. 1. Abstract syntax meta-model for knowledge modeling profile

The discussion of XCore meta-model here is related to implementing the profile in the XMF-Mosaic tool. Although the knowledge modelling profile meta-model is in UML, it is compatible with XMF-Mosaic because the elements that the profile extends are the standard MOF features in both tools. Furthermore, using various UML tools in implementing a UML profile is different as these tools have distinct implementation procedures or concepts in defining the profile in the tool, but this does not change the profile definition. Figure 2 shows the knowledge modelling profile stereotypes defined in XMF-Mosaic.

A Concept class is used to represent structural things and these have attributes contained in them; it is similar to class in the UML meta-model. When the attributes are used in rules they are known as knowledge elements. A Concept is linked to the Rule class in the model. Concepts are diagrammatically associated with FactBase; as the values of the attributes are stored here and are extracted during the reasoning process of the inference. The instances of each attribute, contained in the FactBase class, are accessed by the dynamic role, which passes them to the inference process that matches the premise with the consequent part of an implication rule.

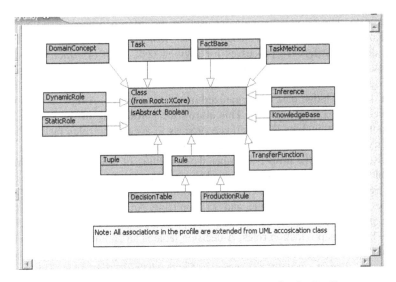

Fig. 2. Extension of the UML with stereotypes for the Profile

Task class defines the reasoning function and specifies the overall input and output of the task. Each task will have an associated task method that executes the task. The structure of the task, its task method, and the set of associated inference processes can be defined with the knowledge model from the problem-solving method library. The task-type, knowledge model, will help in identifying the inference structure needed to perform the desired task. Task method can be decomposed into sub-tasks for certain task-types. Task method class will specify the type of inference that is to be performed. The control structure of the method captures the inference reasoning strategy, which is described using an activity diagram. If the inference process requires additional input, either from the user or from an external entity, the task method will invoke a transfer function. Such functions are used to transfer additional information between the reasoning processes.

The Dynamic Role class specifies the 'information' flow of attribute instances from the concepts. It also specifies the outputs that arise from executing the inference sets. The output of this inference process is the 'result' of matching the antecedent of the rule with the consequent part. Depending on what the KBS is reasoning about, if it is not the final output of the system, then the output can be used in another inference. The Static Role class is the function responsible for fetching the collection of domain knowledge (rules) from the knowledge base prior to an active inference. Inferences do not access the knowledge base directly, but request the necessary rules related to the particular inference from the static roles. In some KBS shells this is similar to posting the rules to the inference process or similar to setting which rule should be fired. This allows the inference process to handle a specific reasoning task and invoke those rules that are appropriate.

An Inference class executes a set of algorithms for determining the order in which a series of non-procedural, declarative statements are to be executed. The inference process infers new knowledge from information/facts that are already known. The Task Method invokes this. The input (information/fact) used by this process is provided by the dynamic role. The result of the inference process is then passed to the dynamic role. The knowledge element used in the inference is accessed through the Static Role, which fetches the group of rules from the knowledge base. There are several different inference processes for a given task, most of which are run in the background by the inference engine. The knowledge base class contains domain knowledge, represented as rules, which are used by the inference process. The contents of the knowledge base are organized in tuples (records). A tuple is used to group rules according to their features. This allows the partitioning of the knowledge base into modules that enables the inference process to access the rules faster. The maintainability of the rules is enhanced when it is organised in this manner.

The Rule class of the profile describes the modelling of rules within the domain concept. Rule class is used to represent knowledge elements in KBS and is viewed as 'information about information'. Rule class allows for rules to be in different formats. There are two types of rule: implication rule, and decision table. An implication rule is of the form: 'if-then' premise followed by an action. This type of representation is widely used in KBS; they are known as production rules. A decision table is an addition to the rule class. It is introduced here because certain rules are best expressed in the form of a decision table, even though they are usually converted to flattened production rules. This paper only concentrates on rule-based KBS as it is the one widely adopted by industry [10, 11] and is the focus of OMG's PRR [8] and KBE [9] standardisation work.

4   Case Study – The Clinical Practice Guidelines KBS

The purpose of this case study was to show the usefulness of the knowledge modelling profile in capturing the KBS requirements and to see the implementation value of the profile when building a KBS from scratch. To demonstrate that the profile is capable in bridging the gap between domain analysis and system implementation, a prototype KBS was built using the Java Expert System Shell (Jess) [29]. The possible mapping between the profile elements and Jess meta-model is also presented. The case study is based on the Clinical Practice Guideline (CPG) recommendations for managing patients with venous leg ulcers described in [30]. The CPG contains recommendations for assessment of ulcers patients, the management of treatment using compression therapy, cleaning and dressing of the ulcers, education and training of care through sharing of knowledge and quality assurance issues related to provision of leg ulcer care. Each of these categories is further divided into several related factors grouped together functionally. The guideline is evidence-based and these recommendations are gathered from systematic review reports complied by researchers in patient health care. The guideline contains recommendation statements, which were graded based on the following three strength of evidence: I- Generally consistent findings in a majority of multiple acceptable studies; II- Either based on a single acceptable study, or a weak or inconsistent finding in multiple acceptable studies; and III- Limited scientific evidence which does not meet all the criteria of acceptable studies of good quality.

4.1 Modelling and Development of Clinical Practice Guidelines KBS

The CPG recommendation was implemented as a KBS application for educational purposes to list the recommendations based on evidence strength using the following classification (a) evidence strength only; (b) evidence strength and category; (c) category only; and (d) factors, evidence and category. The rules for the KBS was defined based on these classifications (in the actual recommendation, each recommendation has a brief explanation rather than ID as I1, II2, III4, etc which are much more convenient for discussions.).

The first stage in modelling KBS applications is to determine the nature of the problem [29] that the system should tackle and what the applicable task types available in the task catalogue are [2, 26]. The CPG can be regarded as a classification task, since the system classifies the recommendation based on four pre-defined criteria. To avoid any confusion, this task is referred to as a recommendation task, which is implemented using the task method 'match method', which consists of a single 'match' inference. This is shown in the task decomposition diagram in figure 3.

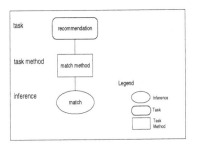
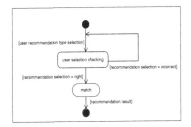

Fig. 3. Task decomposition diagram for CPG based on CommonKADS [26] notation   **Fig. 4.** CPG UML activity diagram

The control structure of this match method is shown using the activity diagram and is shown in figure 4. This is a straight-forward reasoning system as there are no loops in the recommendation matching process. The system user makes a recommendation type selection, and the resulting selection combinations are checked to ensure that they are valid. The selection is then matched with the recommendation value and the result is obtained. If incorrect selections are made, the selection process is repeated. Once the KBS task requirements and functionality have been determined, the knowledge model of the system is constructed using the knowledge modelling profile stereotypes. Most of the stereotypes of the profile were used, except for transfer function, as the CPG system does not need any input from external sources during the reasoning process and does not need any decision tables, as the rules for the system are represented by production rules. Figure 5 shows the knowledge model of the CPG application.

The KBS domain concept 'CPG' is composed of the five category of recommendations which are represented as domain concept 'CPGManagement', 'CPGCleansing', 'CPGQualityAssurance', 'CPGAssessment' and 'CPGEducation' shown at the top section of figure 5. Each of the domain concepts has three attributes (name, factors and evidence strength) upon which four types of rules for the system were defined based on their values. The instances of these attribute are stored in the fact base of the system which are accessed by dynamic role to get the facts for the inference reasoning process. The inference executes the reasoning task based on the task method specification which only specifies a single inference execution for the CPG system. The production rules of the system are stored in the knowledge base which are organised into tuples.

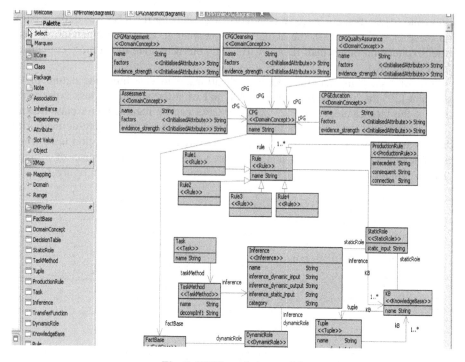

Fig. 5. CPG knowledge model

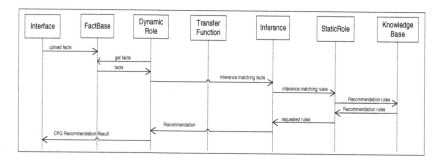

Fig. 6. Sequence Diagram of CPG system

KBS design is very much different to that of a conventional system, as the overall aim of the KBS is to gather the needed facts to fire the rules. In doing so, completing the whole reasoning cycle involves activation of different processes and message passing between objects. As a result, it is difficult to capture these vital information using object diagram due to the fact that several snapshots are needed to gather the whole picture. However, this limitation was solved with the aid of another type of UML diagram, namely the sequence diagram. Using sequence diagrams, the processing elements of the KBS gathered from the profile are listed as objects with an additional Interface object to model the flow of logic that captures the dynamic behaviour of the KBS as shown on figure 6. The input from the user is entered through the interface which becomes the fact for the system when the recommendation type selection question has been answered. These facts are gathered by dynamic role and the inference engine gets these facts and matches them with the rule gathered from the knowledge base to provide the recommendation.

Table 2. Jess Program Summary for CPG System

```
;; Module MAIN
(deftemplate CPG) deftemplate S-C-F)
(deftemplate question)(deftemplate answer)
(deftemplate recommendation)
;;Module Question
(deffacts question-data)(defglobal ?*crlf* = "")
;; Module ask
(defmodule ask)(deffunction ask-user (?question
?type))(defmodule startup)
;; Module interview
(defmodule interview)
(defrule request-strength => assert ask strength)))
(defrule assert-user-fact
   (answer (ident strength)text ?i))(answer (ident
cate_gory)    (text ?d))(answer (ident factors_type)
(text ?j))=>  (assert (user (strength ?i) (cate_gory
?d)(factors_type ?j))))
;; Module recommend
(defmodule recommend)( defrule S-C-F-1-0-0
 user (strength ?i&:(= ?i 1))(cate_gory ?d&:
( = ?d 0))factors_type ?j&:(= ?j 0))) => assert
recommendation (S-C-F STR1) (explanation "Strength
equals 1 Recommendation ( I1 , I2 , I3 , I4 )") )))

;; Module report
```

The CPG prototype recommendation system was implemented using Java Expert System Shell (Jess) rule engine, which is a popular variation of the CLIPS rule engine developed in Java. Jess was chosen as the implementation platform as it is the reference implementation of the JSR 94 Java Rule Engine API that defines standard API for Java developer to interact with a Java rule engine widely used in commercial products and open source software projects.

The system receives the user input value for the strength, category and factor which are the facts for the system to fire the rules through the interview module based on the questions from the question module and the ask module performing error checking on the answers. In the recommendation module, the CPG rules are defined (evidence strength only; category only; evidence strength and category; and factors, evidence and category) and these rules are matched against the facts to fire the activated recommendation rule. The report module produces the recommendation report of the system which contains the explanation and the recommendation value. Table 2 presents portion of the Jess program summary for CPG system and the sample screenshot is shown in figure 7.

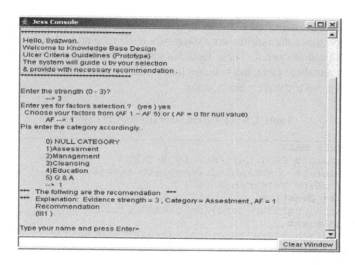

Fig. 7. Sample screenshot of the CPG system

4.2 Possible Mapping of the Profile to Jess

One of the key motivations for the MDA is in providing transformations between models (i.e. from a Platform Independent Model (PIM) such as a UML model or a profile model to Platform Specific Model (PSM) of a specific implementation platform such as Jess). The meta-model of Jess which defines the PSM is shown in figure 8. The purpose of this mapping is to translate a model of the profile into Jess implementation to prove that the profile is capable in bridging the gap between domain analysis and system implementation.

However, the profile meta-model elements cannot be directly mapped to all elements of the Jess meta-model and only partial mapping are technically possible. This limitation is due to the declarative nature of expert system shells programming and the need to have different level of abstraction between general KBS conceptual model and detail model of the implementation platform to enable model transformation in generating the specific program code. However, it is acknowledged that the knowledge modelling profile was very useful in understanding the KBS requirements for the CPG recommendations. This limitation is further discussed in detail on section 5.

Table 3 lists the possible mapping of the profile elements to the Jess. The domain concept elements of the profile can be mapped to `deftemplate`, `defclass` or `definstance` of Jess. However, for the CPG system, only `deftemplate` was used to represent the CPG domain concept which has three different slots for strength, factor type and category. The factbase element of the profile can be mapped to `deffacts` and for the CPG system; the question-data were used to gather the needed facts for the application. There are no direct mapping for task and task method to Jess but `defmodule` can be used to divide the application into structured modules. To perform the reasoning process, inference is activated through the function 'run', which is a Jess function that starts the pattern matching process. The dynamic role can be mapped to the Jess function 'assert' which asserts all facts into the working memory of the inference engine. In the CPG system, this can be seen in the interview module in getting the facts to the working memory and asserting the recommendations.

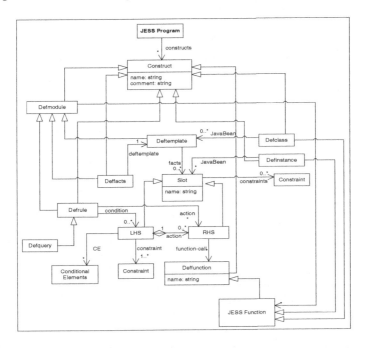

Fig. 8. Jess Meta-model

Table 3. Possible mapping of the Knowledge Modelling

Profile Concepts	mapping	JESS Concepts
DomainConcept	=	Deftemplate (Frame) Slot, Defclass Definstance
FactBase	=	Deffacts
Task	≈	Defmodule
Task Method	≈	Defmodule
Inference	≈	Deffunction – run ( )
Dynamic role	≈	Deffunction – assert ( )
Static Role	≈	Defmodule - focus
Transfer function	≈	Defunction
Knowledge base	≈	Defmodule - focus
Tuple	≈	Defmodule – focus (rules partition)
Rule	=	Defrule
• Implication Rule	=	Defrule - LHS, RHS
o Antecedent	=	Deffunction, Conditional Elements
o Consequent	=	Defquery

There is no direct mapping for knowledge base and tuple, but the `defmodule` constructs of Jess allows large number of rules to be physically organised into logical groups. Modules also provide a control mechanism that only allows the module that has the *focus* to fire the rule in it, and only one module can be in focus at a time. In the CPG system, the recommend module is used to organise the rules into knowledge base and static role can be mapped to the focus function of Jess since all the CPG rules for the inference engine are contained here. The role of transfer function in obtaining additional information can be mapped to the `defmodule` construct that implements the appropriate functions to get this information.

Table 4. CPG `'S-C-F-1-0-0'` rule

```
1 defrule S-C-F-1-0-0
2 user (strength ?i&:(= ?i 1))
3 cate_gory  ?d&:(= ?d 0))
4 factors_type ?j&:(= ?j 0)))
5 => assert recommendation S-C-F STR1) (explanation
6 "Strength equals 1 Recommendation I1,I2,I3,I4)"))))
```

The rule element of the profile can be mapped directly to the `defrule` construct of Jess in which the antecedent part corresponds to the left-hand side (LHS) of the rule and the consequent part corresponds to the right-hand side (RHS) of the rule. The following example of manual mapping the CPG system rule 'S-C-F-1-0-0' shown in table 4 would help demonstrate this better.

In line 1, we define the rule using defrule which states the name of the rule – in this case strength = 1, category = null and factor = null S-C-F-1-0-0 which will list all recommendation of strength values of 1. Line 2, 3 and 4 is the LHS of the rule which consists of facts matching patterns and line 5 and 6 contains the function call (RHS) which asserts the recommendations values.

5 Discussions Related to OMG PPR Standardisation Work

The following discussions are intended to provide useful information regarding KBS modelling in the context of the OMG Production Rule Representation standardisation work. The PPR work mainly requires the use of activity diagrams to model the relationship between rulesets to action states. However, in this work we have identified that the use of activity diagram is limited to model a particular process of the system. Furthermore, class diagram can only provide partial snaphots of the system at a particular point in time which is less meaningful in complex inference cycles. To overcome this limitation, we have used the sequence diagram which clearly helps to understand the flow of logic in the system as shown in section 4.2.

The profile described in this paper would help in understanding how rules are related to the domain concept elements in the KBS and the processes that are involved in activating the rule to fire with the help of activity and sequence diagram.

Furthermore, the profile only shows the categories of rule which can be modelled in a single diagram with the other model elements. Thus the profile would help overcome the current problem of omitting rules from the model.

Mapping the profile to PSM is only limited to domain concept, factbase and implication rule. The rest of the profile elements are useful to describe the KBS and usually implemented differently as runtime concepts in various rule engines. Nevertheless, this proves that the most important work in designing and developing KBS is writing the rules based on the domain concepts which attribute values stored in the fact base will activate the rules. As such, the standardisation work in PRR should first emphasise on agreeing standard representation of rule elements in writing rules which are portable across different inference engines.

6 Conclusion and Future Work

This paper presented an extension to UML using the (lightweight) profile mechanism for knowledge modelling that allows the relevant structural properties of KBS to be represented at conceptual level. This allows knowledge models to be built using an object-oriented approach based on the standard modelling language that is widely adopted. The profile was implemented in an object-oriented meta-modelling language tool, XMF Mosaic that allows easier visual implementation of profile which diagrams are similar to the common UML editors.

The profile has been successfully tested on several case studies. This includes designs from scratch and re-engineering of existing KBS and the results are encouraging. Currently work has concentrated on building an Eclipse plug-in to support the profile as it is a popular implementation tool for UML profiles. The plug-in allows profile-compliant diagrams to be drawn and validated, and XML or XMI representations produced. The infrastructure in the Eclipse makes this mapping straightforward to implement. The future work in this area involves studying how to automate the generation of Jess code from the profile elements that can be mapped to Jess meta-model. The work in automating the generation of Jess code from models is still in a work in progress [31].

References

1. Giarratano, J.C., Riley, G.D.: Expert Systems: Principles And Programming. Course Technology, Boston, Massachusetts (2004)
2. Studer, R., Benjamins, R.V., Fensel, D.: Knowledge Engineering: Principles and methods. Data & Knowledge Engineering, 25(1), 161–197 (1998)
3. Gomez-Perez, A., Benjamins, V.R.: Overview of Knowledge Sharing and Reuse Components: Ontologies and Problem-Solving Methods. In: IJCAI-99 Workshop on Ontologies and Problem-Solving Methods (KRR5), Stockholm, Sweden (1999)
4. Ergazakis, K., Karnezis, K., Metaxiotis, K., Psarras, I.: Knowledge Management in Enterprises: A Research Agenda. Intelligent Systems in Accounting, Finance and Management 13(1), 17–26 (2005)
5. Awad, E.M.: Building Expert Systems: Principles, Procedures, and Applications. West Publishing, Minneapolis (1996)

6. Liebowtiz, J.: If you are a dog lover, build expert system; if you are a cat lover, build neural networks. Expert System with Applications 21, 63 (2001)
7. Preece, A.: Evaluating Verification and Validation Methods in Knowledge Engineering, in Micro-Level Knowledge Management. In: Roy, R. (ed.) Evaluating Verification and Validation Methods in Knowledge Engineering, in Micro-Level Knowledge Management, R, pp. 123–145. San Francisco, Morgan-Kaufman (2001)
8. Production, O.M.G.: Rule Representation - Request for Proposal, Object Management Group: Needham, USA. p. 57 (2003)
9. Services, O.K.: for Engineering Design - Request for Proposal, Object Management Group: Needham, MA, US. p. 32 (2004)
10. McClintock, C.: ILOG's position on Rule Languages for Interoperability. In: W3C Workshop on Rule Languages for Interoperability, Washington, D.C, USA (2005)
11. Krovvidy, S., Bhogaraju, P., Mae, F.: Interoperability and Rule Languages. In: W3C Workshop on Rule Languages for Interoperability, Washington, DC, USA (2005)
12. Abdullah, M.S., Benest, I., Evans, A., Kimble, C.: Knowledge Modelling Techniques for Developing Knowledge Management Systems. In: Abdullah, M.S., Benest, I., Evans, A. (eds.) 3rd European Conference on Knowledge Management, Dublin, Ireland (2002)
13. Gill, G.T.: Early Expert Systems: Where Are They Now? MIS Quarterly 19(1), 51–81 (1995)
14. Tsui, E.: The role of IT in KM: where are we now and where are we heading. Knowledge Management 9(1), 3–6 (2005)
15. Juristo, N., Moreno, A.M.: Introductory paper: Reflections on Conceptual Modelling. Data & Knowledge Engineering 33(2), 103–117 (2000)
16. Dieste, O., Juristo, N., Moreno, A.M., Pazos, J., Sierra, A.: Conceptual Modelling in Software Engineering and Knowledge Engineering: Concepts, Techniques and Trends. In: Chang, S.K. (ed.) Handbook of Software Engineering & Knowledge Engineering, pp. 733–766. World Scientific Publishing, Hackensack, NJ (2002)
17. Jézéquel, J.-M., Hussmann, H., Cook, S.: A Metamodel for the Unified Modeling Language. In: Jézéquel, J.-M., Hussmann, H., Cook, S. (eds.). UML 2002. LNCS, vol. 2460, Springer, Heidelberg (2002)
18. Muller, P.-A., Studer, P., Bezivin, J.: Platform Independent Web Application Modeling. In: Stevens, P., Whittle, J., Booch, G. (eds.). UML 2003. LNCS, vol. 2863, Springer, Heidelberg (2003)
19. Brown, A.W.: Expert's voice - Model driven architecture: Principles and practice. Software and Systems Modelling 3(4), 314–327 (2004)
20. Abdullah, M.S., Kimble, C., Paige, R., Benest, I.: Developing UML Profile for Modelling Knowledge-Based Systems. In: Aßmann, U., Aksit, M., Rensink, A. (eds.) MDAFA 2003. LNCS, vol. 3599, Springer, Heidelberg (2005)
21. OMG. UML 2.0 InfrastructureFinal Adopted Specification, [cited 2004 5 April], Available from (2003), http://www.omg.org
22. OMG, Requirements for UML Profile. 1999, Object Management Group: Framingham, MA. p. 8.
23. Perez-Martinez, J.E.: Heavyweight extensions to the UML metamodel to describe the C3 architectural style. ACM SIGSOFT Software Engineering Notes, 28–3 (2003)
24. OMG. MOF Specification version 1.4. 2002 [cited 2004 5 April], Available from, http://www.omg.org
25. Clark, T., Evans, A., Sammut, P., Willians, J.: Metamodelling for Model-Driven Development (draft) (To be published 2004), http://albini.xactium.com

26. Schreiber, G., Akkermans, H., Anjewierden, A., De Hoog, R., Shadbolt, N., De Velde, W.: Knowledge Engineering and Management: The CommonKADS Methodology. MIT Press, Massachusetts (1999)
27. Cuena, J., Molina, M.: The role of knowledge modelling techniques in software development: a general approach based on a knowledge management tool. International Journal of Human-Computer Studies 52, 385–421 (2000)
28. Håkansson, A.: UML as an approach to Modelling Knowledge in Rule-based Systems. In: The Twenty-first SGES International Conference on Knowledge Based Systems and Applied Artificial Intelligence (ES2001), Peterhouse College, Cambridge, UK (2001)
29. Friedman-Hill, E.: Jess in Action: Rule-Based System in Java. Manning Publications, Greenwich, US (2003)
30. Clinical, R.C.N.: Practice Guidelines: The management of patients with venous leg ulcers. Royal College of Nursing Institute, London (1998)
31. Wu, C.G. (2004) Modelling Rule-Based Systems with EMF. Accessed at http://www.eclipse.org/articles
32. Abdullah, M.S., Profile, A U.: for Conceptual Modelling of Knowledge-Based Systems, Unpublished PhD Thesis, University of York (2006)

Tracing the Rationale Behind UML Model Change Through Argumentation

Ivan J. Jureta and Stéphane Faulkner

Information Management Research Unit (IMRU), University of Namur, Belgium
iju@info.fundp.ac.be, stephane.faulkner@fundp.ac.be

Abstract. Neglecting traceability—i.e., the ability to describe and follow the life of a requirement—is known to entail misunderstanding and miscommunication, leading to the engineering of poor quality systems. Following the simple principles that (a) changes to UML model instances ought be justified to the stakeholders, (b) justification should proceed in a structured manner to ensure rigor in discussions, critique, and revisions of model instances, and (c) the concept of argument instantiated in a justification process ought to be well defined and understood, the present paper introduces the UML Traceability through Argumentation Method (UML-TAM) to enable the traceability of design rationale in UML while allowing the appropriateness of model changes to be checked by analysis of the structure of the arguments provided to justify such changes.

1   Introduction

In a noted discussion of the traceability problem [10], Gotel and Finkelstein define traceability as follows:

> "Requirements traceability refers to the ability to describe and follow the life of a requirement, in both a forwards and backwards direction (i.e., from its origins, through its development and specification, to its subsequent deployment and use, and through all periods of on-going refinement and iteration in any of these phases)."

Ensuring proper traceability through specialized concepts, techniques, and methods is argued to reduce the number of iterations in the construction and change of requirements engineering (RE) artifacts, thus helping keep the software development project under time, budget, and other constraints. However, if traceability is neglected, misunderstanding and miscommunication are bound to appear, compounding the loss of implicit information guiding requirements change and increasing the risk of poor project results [6,20,25].

This paper focuses on the problem of tracing the rationale behind changes local to one or spanning across several different kinds of models in the Unified Modeling Language (UML) [18]. To address the problem, the UML Traceability through Argumentation Method (UML-TAM) is suggested to enable the traceability of design rationale in UML while allowing the appropriateness of model

C. Parent et al. (Eds.): ER 2007, LNCS 4801, pp. 454–469, 2007.

changes to be checked by analysis of the structure of the arguments provided to justify such changes.

As the related research efforts are numerous, the following section (§2) first positions the present work within the relevant literature. The problem of interest is then identified and contributions outlined (§3), and is followed by a description of the case study (§4). The conceptual basis of UML-TAM is then presented (§5). It is followed by an illustration of its use in the case study (§6). The paper closes with conclusions and indications on directions for future effort (§7).

2   Background and Related Work

Complexity of the traceability problem, its span over the various activities in software development, along with the trade-off between extensive traceability and budget and time constraints make elusive the construction of an encompassing traceability approach still applicable to realistic settings—methods specialized for particular traceability sub-problems, combined with domain-specific expertise on when and how to apply them in a given project seem to be the choice in research and industry. In light of the various methods suggested in related research efforts, situating the results of the present paper is facilitated by classification over five taxonomic dimensions: traceability data types, scope, degree of automation, conceptual foundations, and framework specificity. Each is considered in turn below.

2.1   Traceability Data Types

Traceability data types, as suggested by Dömges and Pohl [6], distinguish methods according to the content of traceability information being recorded:

- *Bi-directional links* between the stakeholder expectations, derived requirements, and software components enable validation of system functionality by stakeholders and impact analysis of requirements change on the system. Ramesh and colleagues [25] indicate that such benefits can be achieved, although at high initial cost of implementing and applying traceability policies. A framework allowing the capture of bi-directional links has been proposed by Pohl [21] and later extended to allow configuration to project-specific traceability needs [22], in both cases focusing on the recording of what changes are made, by whom, when, and how.
- *Contribution structures* aim at clearly relating the requirements to stakeholders to facilitate negotiation, search for additional information, and revision. Gotel [11] introduced contribution structures in RE to allow the recording of detailed information on stakeholders and the requirements they provide, hence ensuring traceability of the requirements to the people and systems from which these emanate.
- *Design rationale* records the reasoning that led to particular modeling and other software development decisions, in the aim of arriving at a shared understanding of models and other artifacts, and their purpose in the given

project. Usually, a design rationale approach is employed to record such traceability information (Louridas and Loucopoulos give an overview [16]).

– *Process data* which relates to the planning and control of activities in the software development project.

2.2 Scope

Gotel and Finkelstein [10] introduce a separation of pre-Requirements Specification (pre-RS) from post-RS traceability. *Pre-RS*, which concerns the life of stakeholder expectations until they are converted to requirements, has been treated in the various RE frameworks proposed over the last decade—for instance, the introduction of goals in requirements models facilitates traceability, for goals make explicit (at least in part) the rationale for the inclusion of more specific requirements [30]. *Post-RS* focuses on the evolution of requirements in the steps following RE, i.e., the various activities involved in deploying the requirements. Automated traceability methods (below) focus on post-RS.

2.3 Degree of Automation

The degree of automation concerns the support allowed by or provided with a traceability method to reduce manual effort and facilitate analyses of trace information. Haumer and colleagues [12] and Jackson [13] both suggest manual traceability techniques focused on simplicity, while allowing rich trace recording (e.g., video, audio, etc.). Such an approach becomes difficult to manage efficiently for realistic systems, leading to, among other, Egyed's proposal [7] where models and software are aligned using traces generated by observation of software operation through the running of various test scenarios. Antoniol and colleagues [1] and Pinheiro and Goguen [19] both rely on formal methods for traceability, with the difficulty of avoiding obsolescence of formal trace specifications.

2.4 Conceptual Foundations

Conceptual foundations discriminate according to the main concepts employed in recording traceability information (e.g., goals, scenarios, aspects). Egyed [7] generates design traceability information by iteratively running test *scenarios* on already operational software, so as to verify whether the models implementing the tested functionality correspond to the behavior of the observed system. A preliminary proposal from Naslavsky and colleagues [17] focuses on traceability between scenarios and the use thereof to relate requirements to code. Ubayashi and colleagues [28] propose a method for dealing with model evolution using model transformations based on *aspect* orientation, the main benefit thereof being the separation of concerns over traceability information. Torenzo and Castro [27] also seem to separate concerns, albeit through specialized *views* and not aspects. In an overview of goal-oriented RE [30], Van Lamsweerde observes that the refinement links in goal refinement trees, in which an abstract goal is made more precise through refinement, can be read as traceability links making *goal*-orientation a favorable approach to aligning abstract and precise, operational information about a system. The concept of *argument* appears in design rationale approaches (for an overview, see [16]) which enable the recording of reasoning behind decisions. For instance, Ramesh and Dhar [24] suggest an approach involving concepts specialized for the RE: in addition to classical concepts—position, argument, issue—introduced in IBIS [5], REMAP [24] integrates the notion of requirement, design object, decision, and constraint.

2.5   Framework Specificity

Framework specificity classifies approaches according to whether they are specialized or not for a particular software development framework. Briand and colleagues [3] suggest bi-directional links be extracted automatically from changes in UML models, whereby each identified type of UML model refinement (each refinement being a kind of model change) has associated traceability information, thus facilitating impact analysis in model evolution. Letelier [15] suggests a roughly defined metamodel of traceability information to collect when working with UML and requirements expressed in textual form; the aim is to ensure that bi-directional links are known during UML modeling, while very limited support is provided for design rationale recording.

3   Problem Outline and Contributions

The work presented in the remainder enables the recording of design rationale behind changes local to one or spanning across several different kinds of UML models. It is thus framework-specific and both pre- and post-RS (this depending on how UML is employed), while relying on the concept of argument. Because informally or formally expressed information is allowed into arguments to allow adaptability of the method to project specificities, automation is limited, this entailing selective application of the method. The present work is a response to the following observations, each highlighting a difficulty in current research:

- UML traceability rarely aims to record the rationale behind modeling decisions, and when this is attempted, as in Letelier's work [15], very limited attention is given to what kind of rationale information is to be recorded and how, and if/how it can be analyzed.
- Automated traceability by taxonomies of UML change/refinement types lacks the recording of design rationale—in the efforts cited in §2, traceability information answers *what* changes are made, but not *why* they are made. It is therefore possible to determine who, when, and how made a particular appropriate or inappropriate decision, but it is difficult/impossible to determine why the decision is made, hence limiting the potential to learn from mistakes or reinforce appropriate modeling behavior.
- Framework-independent traceability methods that use arguments in recording design rationale, such as REMAP [24] only provide techniques for trace capture—how to analyze such information remains unknown.

Following the simple principles that (a) changes to UML model instances ought be justified to the stakeholders, (b) justification should proceed in a structured manner to ensure rigor in discussions, critique, and revisions of model instances, and (c) the concept of argument instantiated in a justification process ought to be well defined and understood, the present paper introduces the UML Traceability through Argumentation Method (UML-TAM) for capturing and analyzing design rationale in UML modeling. The salient properties of the method are:

- *Adaptability.* Both informal and formal, and qualitative and quantitative information is allowed into arguments, to ensure that few constraints are placed on the stakeholders employing it to record design rationale.
- *Active rationale analysis.* Where available methods focus on ensuring design rationale is recorded (passive rationale traceability), UML-TAM provides specialized analyses for confronting arguments and avoiding ill-structured rationale which unavoidably leads to inappropriate modeling choices.
- *Sound conceptual foundations.* By relying on formal definitions of the concept of argument established in AI, and using it as a central concept, UML-TAM avoids ambiguity and aims to facilitate the learning of the method to the stakeholders (it merely requires the understanding of the notion of argument and the argumentation and justification processes).
- *Justification of modeling choices.* While recording arguments is certainly relevant, confronting them through a justification process to discriminate among alternative changes of model instances is critical. Justification thus provides a means for selecting among alternative sets of arguments to arrive at justifiably appropriate modeling choices.

4   Case Study

Following the classical meeting scheduler case study [29], a variant serves herein to illustrate the salient features of the method.[1] The aim is to design a system for scheduling meetings and meeting rooms. A user can request a meeting room of a chosen size and for a chosen period of time, and can schedule a meeting. A user can cancel any of the mentioned two until the beginning of the meeting time. An email is sent to participants any time the meeting is scheduled or canceled. When defining a meeting, the user provides a list of attendees, meeting time and room, and gives a brief description of the topic. It is further assumed that there is a Post Office package which delivers messages to designated users, and an Employee Management package which provides employee reference and email address. Fig.1(a) shows the initial use case which represents most of the described

---

[1] As noted above, UML-TAM is not intended for recording rationale behind all modeling decisions for it is not automated and thus impractical—contributions are primarily conceptual and not related to efficiency per se in the present paper. An accessible case study, appropriate for the constraints of the present format, thus introduces the method, while scalability and cost to industrial projects are under study.

functionality but is incomplete and serves as a starting point in moving toward a more extensive use case diagram to illustrate the use of UML-TAM in tracing rationale for change. Fig.1(b) gives an initial class diagram, and is used in the remainder to illustrate traceability within class diagram with UML-TAM.

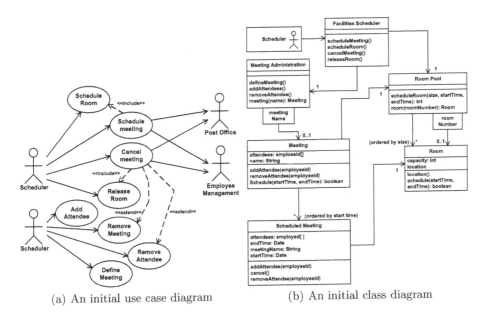

(a) An initial use case diagram   (b) An initial class diagram

Fig. 1. Some initial UML diagrams for the case study

5   Traceability Through Argumentation in UML-TAM

Returning to the initial use case digram in Fig.1(a), it is not difficult to notice it is incomplete at least with regards to the following plausible situations:

- If the room of requested size is not available at the requested period, various alternative responses by the system can be identified: e.g., it may record a failed request for a room for statistics on room availability; another option is to communicate the unavailability to the user and ask for a different period.
- If an attendee is added as a participant to a recurrent meeting, should the system assume that this person is to attend all occurrences of the meeting in the future, or should the user specify this? Same applies when an attendee of a recurrent meeting is removed from the list of participants—does the removal apply for all occurrences of the meeting or only the next one?
- A participant informed of a meeting may have another engagement for the same period. Fig.1(a) gives no explicit mechanisms for ensuring the scheduler knows what participants to expect. The system could, e.g., connect to employees' electronic agendas and return availability information when the scheduler adds a participant and the meeting period.

It should be apparent from the above that providing a revised use case diagram alone—i.e., without additional information on why that particular revision is more adequate than another one—may be appropriate only in case the stakeholders are of similar background, share a precise idea of what the system is expected to do, and so on. In most realistic settings, however, this is not satisfactory, for various stakeholders would participate, each bringing a different perspective on the system grounded in different backgrounds and interests. The very presence of alternatives in both system functionality and of options in the representation of functionality (e.g., at the level of use cases: what to wrap in an existing use case, what requires an additional use case, and so on) makes it appropriate to make explicit the reasons (i.e., arguments) that aim to justify the functionality and representation decisions. One thus observes that three components are needed for ensuring traceability of rationale in UML: (1) a design rationale approach (below: TAM-Design Rationale, TAM-DR), which indicates when and how the engineer proceeds to making explicit the alternatives in functionality and/or modeling; (2) an argumentation framework, which, as soon as the alternatives are known, enables the argumentation of each alternative, the confrontation and comparison of arguments, ending in a justified choice of one alternative; (3) specialized means for connecting the content of UML diagrams with the content of rationale traces (referred to in the remainder as TAM-Connectors) produced through the use of the design rationale approach and associated argumentation and justification techniques.

5.1   UML-TAM Design Rationale

Having identified an engineering problem, design rationale literature (and as usual in problem solving) suggests the engineer should identify alternative solutions, compare them according to some relevant criteria, subsequently choose one alternative, and act upon the prescription given in the alternative. In the classical IBIS approach [5], the aforementioned problem is termed *issue* whereas *positions* (i.e., alternative solutions) resolve issues, and *arguments* support or object to positions. A problem in the present setting appears whenever alternative system structures can be chosen to translate stakeholder expectations into a UML representation, or when several modeling options exist for a chosen alternative system structure (i.e., one knows what to model, but syntax and semantics of the model permit various ways of modeling this). Based on work from Louridas and Loucopoulos [16], which integrates common characteristics of established design rationale approaches, a design rationale approach specialized for rationale traceability in UML-TAM involves the following steps (see, Fig.2):

1. *Problem setting* consists of identifying a discrepancy between the content of the given UML model instance and the content it should represent—e.g., some newly acquired information is not represented therein, or the given representation uses questionable modeling choices.
2. Based on the problem statement produced in 1 above, *problem analysis* leads to the identification of *alternative solutions*.

3. *Evaluation* then consists of providing arguments for or against each alternative solution. Such *argumentation* is followed by a *justification* of a choice of (i.e., *Decision* on) a particular alternative.
4. Having selected the alternative, the affected UML model instances need to be changed according to the adopted solution. The process is reinitiated as new problems are identified.

As shown in Fig.2, content of alternatives and arguments can give itself rise to new problem statements. Activities of the given process rely mainly on the domain- and problem-specific knowledge of the stakeholders. Argumentation and justification activities require specialized concepts and techniques outlined in §5.2 and §5.3. The use of the given concepts and techniques is exemplified in §6.

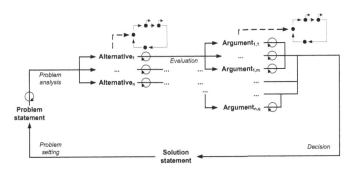

Fig. 2. Overview of the UML-TAM design rationale process

5.2   UML-TAM Argumentation Framework

Argumentation modeling literature [4] in the artificial intelligence field focuses on formalizing commonsense reasoning in the aim of automation. An *argumentation model* is a static representation of an *argumentation process*, which can be seen as a search for arguments, where an argument consists of a set of rules chained to reach a conclusion. Each rule can be rebutted by another rule based on new information. To formalize such defeasible reasoning, elaborate syntax and semantics have been developed (e.g., [4,26,2]) commonly involving a logic to formally represent the argumentation process and reason about argument interaction. A structured argumentation framework (i.e., a model and processes employing the model) is needed herein for a rigorous justification process in the *Evaluation* step of TAM-DR. To arrive at a structured argumentation system, the concept of argument is first defined below, followed by a set of argument relationships, and the justification process.

Argument. Assuming a first-order language $\mathcal{L}$ defined as usual, let $\mathcal{K}$ be a consistent set of formulae (i.e., $\mathcal{K} \nvdash \bot$), each a piece of information, and let $\mathcal{K} \equiv \mathcal{K}_N \cup \mathcal{K}_C$. Members of the set $\mathcal{K}_N$, called *necessary knowledge*, represent facts about the universe of discourse and are taken to be formulae which contain variables. Necessary knowledge is assumed unquestionable. The set $\mathcal{K}_C$, called *contingent knowledge*, are information that can be put in question or argued for. It is then said that the knowledge a stakeholder a can use in argumentation is given by the pair (K_a, Δ_a), where K_a is a consistent subset of $\mathcal{K}$ (i.e., $K_a \subset \mathcal{K}$ and $K_a \not\vdash \perp$), and Δ_a is a finite set of *defeasible rules* of the form $\alpha \hookrightarrow \beta$. The relation $\hookrightarrow$ between formulae α and β is understood to express that "reasons to believe in the antecedent α provide reasons to believe in the consequent β". In short, $\alpha \hookrightarrow \beta$ reads "α is reason for β".

Let A a set of stakeholders, $K \equiv \bigcup_{a \in A} K_a$, and $\Delta \equiv \bigcup_{a \in A} \Delta_a$. Given (K_a, Δ_a) and $P \subset \Delta_a^{\downarrow}$, where $\Delta_a^{\downarrow}$ is a set of formulae from Δ_a instantiated over constants of the formal language, P is an *argument* for $c \in \mathcal{K}_C$, denoted $\langle P, c \rangle_K$, if and only if: 1) $K \cup P \vdash c$ (K and P derive c); 2) $K \cup P \not\vdash \perp$ (K and P are consistent); and 3) $\not\exists P' \subset P, K \cup P' \vdash c$ (P is minimal for K). Where "$\vdash$" is called the *defeasible consequence* [26] and is defined as follows. Define $\Phi = \{\phi_1, \ldots, \phi_n\}$ such that for any $\phi_i \in \Phi$, $\phi_i \in K \cup \Delta^{\downarrow}$. A formula ϕ is a defeasible consequence of Φ (i.e., $\Phi \vdash \phi$) if and only if there exists a sequence $B_1, \ldots, B_m$ such that $\phi = B_m$, and, for each $B_i \in \{B_1, \ldots, B_m\}$, either B_i is an axiom of $\mathcal{L}$, or B_i is in Φ, or B_i is a direct consequence of the preceding members of the sequence using modus ponens or instantiation of a universally quantified sentence. This argument definition is well-understood in the AI literature [4,23].

Argumentation. While an argument can be constructed by combining explicitly expressed knowledge (e.g., from a knowledge base), the aim here is to start from a conclusion and build arguments that support it from the knowledge that stakeholders provide and that can be related to the conclusion. Argumentation of a conclusion R consists of recursively defining an argument tree AT_R as follows:

1. Define R as the root of the tree AT_R and set $c = R$;
2. Let $\langle P, c \rangle$. Identify $p_1, \ldots, p_n$ s.t. $\{p_1, \ldots, p_n\} = P$, $P \subseteq K \cup \Delta^{\downarrow}$;
3. Define a node for each premise $p_i \in P$ and define an edge from that node to c. Draw the edge "$\longrightarrow$" if $p \in K$, or "$\longmapsto$" in case $p \in \Delta^{\downarrow}$;
4. Set $c = p_i$ and repeat steps 2 and 3 for each $i = 1, \ldots, n$, until the argument tree has been constructed to a satisfactory extent.

Argument Relationships. Of particular interest in argumentation is to confront arguments and reject some conclusion in favor of other. It is therefore necessary to define several simple relationships between arguments.

Two arguments $\langle P_1, c_1 \rangle$ and $\langle P_2, c_2 \rangle$ *disagree*, denoted by $\langle P_1, c_1 \rangle \bowtie_K \langle P_2, c_2 \rangle$, if and only if $\mathcal{K} \cup \{c_1, c_2\} \vdash \perp$.

Instead of seeking contradiction of conclusions, a *counterargument* relation looks for incompatibility of a conclusion with the conclusion of a subargument of another argument. $\langle P_1, c_1 \rangle$ *counterargues* at c the argument $\langle P_2, c_2 \rangle$, denoted by $\langle P_1, c_1 \rangle \not\hookrightarrow^c \langle P_2, c_2 \rangle$, if and only if there is a subargument $\langle P, c \rangle$ of $\langle P_2, c_2 \rangle$ such that $\langle P_2, c_2 \rangle \bowtie_K \langle P, c \rangle$ (i.e., $\langle P, c \rangle \subset \langle P_2, c_2 \rangle$ and $\mathcal{K} \cup \{c_1, c\} \vdash \perp$).

In case two arguments are such that one counterargues the other, it is necessary to determine which of the two is to be maintained. An argument $\langle P_1, c_1 \rangle$ *defeats at* c an argument $\langle P_2, c_2 \rangle$, denoted by $\langle P_1, c_1 \rangle \gg^c \langle P_2, c_2 \rangle$, if and only if there is a subargument $\langle P, c \rangle$ of $\langle P_1, c_1 \rangle$ such that (1) $\langle P_1, c_1 \rangle \not\leftrightarrow^c \langle P_2, c_2 \rangle$ (that is, $\langle P_1, c_1 \rangle$ counterargues $\langle P_2, c_2 \rangle$ at c); and (2) $\langle P_1, c_1 \rangle \succ^c \langle P, c \rangle$ ($\langle P_1, c_1 \rangle$ is more *specific* than $\langle P, c \rangle$). In a dialectical tree (see below), defeat is represented by "$\not\leftrightarrow$" directed from the conclusion of the argument that defeats to the node which is defeated. The specificity relation "$\succ^c$" is an order relation over arguments, defined so that arguments containing more information, i.e., which are more specific, are preferred over other. An argument $\langle P_1, c_1 \rangle$ is *strictly more specific than* $\langle P_2, c_2 \rangle$, denoted by $\langle P_1, c_1 \rangle \succ^c \langle P_2, c_2 \rangle$ if and only if (1) $\forall e \in \mathcal{K}_C$ such that $\mathcal{K}_N \cup \{e\} \cup P_1 \mathrel{\vdash\!\!\!\sim} c_1$ and $\mathcal{K}_N \cup \{e\} \mathrel{\not\vdash\!\!\!\sim} c_1$, also $\mathcal{K}_N \cup \{e\} \cup P_2 \mathrel{\vdash\!\!\!\sim} c_2$; and (2) $\exists e \in \mathcal{K}_C$ such that: (2.1) $\mathcal{K}_N \cup \{e\} \cup P_2 \mathrel{\vdash\!\!\!\sim} c_2$; (2.2) $\mathcal{K}_N \cup \{e\} \cup P_1 \mathrel{\not\vdash\!\!\!\sim} c_1$; (2.3) $\mathcal{K}_N \cup \{e\} \mathrel{\not\vdash} c_2$.

Justification. Argument defeat is employed when attempting to justify a particular conclusion. The *justification* process consists of recursively defining and labeling a *dialectical tree* $\mathcal{T} \langle P, c \rangle$ as follows:

1. A single node containing the argument $\langle P, c \rangle$ with no defeaters is by itself a dialectical tree for $\langle P, c \rangle$. This node is also the root of the tree.
2. Suppose that $\langle P_1, c_1 \rangle, \ldots, \langle P_n, c_n \rangle$ each defeats $\langle P, c \rangle$. Then the dialectical tree $\mathcal{T} \langle P, c \rangle$ for $\langle P, c \rangle$ is built by placing $\langle P, c \rangle$ at the root of the tree and by making this node the parent node of roots of dialectical trees rooted respectively in $\langle P_1, c_1 \rangle, \ldots, \langle P_n, c_n \rangle$.
3. When the tree has been constructed to a satisfactory extent by recursive application of steps 1 and 2 above, label the leaves of the tree *undefeated* (U). For any inner node, label it undefeated if and only if every child of that node is a *defeated* (D) node. An inner node will be a defeated node if and only if it has at least one U node as a child. Do step 4 below after the entire dialectical tree is labeled.
4. $\langle P, c \rangle$ is a *justification* (or, P justifies c) if and only if the node $\langle P, c \rangle$ is labeled U.

Dialectical trees are shown in the UML-TAM traceability templates in Figures 4 and 5, in §6; arguments are drawn enclosed in boxes, a dialectical tree relates such boxes with the defeat relationship. The content of arguments is informally expressed, and can be replaced (pending some adjustments) with first-order formulae. However, the informal character thereof does not affect the ability to manually determine relationships between arguments, as they have been presented above, and consequently to proceed to justification. Having formal foundations, as suggested in the present subsection contributes to the precision of the conceptual bases for the argumentation and justification activities.

5.3   UML-TAM Connectors

Connectors in UML-TAM relate information used and produced with the design rationale, and argumentation and justification techniques to the content of the UML diagrams whose rationale traceability is to be ensured. Fig.3 shows the metamodel, written in UML class diagram notation, integrating the relevant concepts of UML-TAM and relating them to the UML 2.0 metamodel [18]

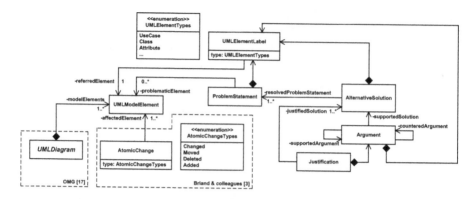

Fig. 3. Metamodel relating UML-TAM to the UML 2.0 metamodel

through the *UMLDiagram* class. Although the illustration §6 discusses the traceability in use case and class diagrams, the metamodel does not limit the potential for bridging UML-TAM and other UML diagrams.

The part of the metamodel proper to UML-TAM integrates the concept of ProblemStatement, AlternativeSolution, Argument, and Justification, each following the definitions given in previous subsections. Note the ProblemStatement can be associated to no UMLModelElement, which occurs when the ProblemStatement results in the addition of new UMLModelElement instances into a UMLDiagram instance. The metamodel is linked to a part of the metamodel underlying the bi-directional link traceability approach from Briand and colleagues [3]: AtomicChange is a modification applicable to the UML diagram, whose execution gives rise to a number of traceability links to ensure that information about what changed and how is captured. The types of atomic changes given in the figure are the basic ones, whereby more extensive taxonomies are suggested by refining each of the four activities, and this depending on the syntax of the underlying UML diagram [3]. An important practical consequence of the above metamodel is that UML-TAM can be thus be combined to automated traceability methods and applied selectively, when stakeholders explicitly identify problems which in turn entail the use of UML-TAM for resolution.

As the content of arguments can be informal or formal, labels are used to highlight the relevant elements of the UML model being mentioned in arguments, alternative solutions, and/or problem statement. The UMLElementLabel concept is thus introduced in the metamodel in Fig.3. In Fig.4, labels are placed within arguments and the alternative solution, whereas the problem statement (the title of the UML-TAM traceability template) does not contain explicit references to elements of the use case diagram, and therefore contains no labels.

The approach to relate the UML artifacts and those produced in UML-TAM is straightforward: as soon as a justified alternative solution is found, and the stakeholders no longer provide arguments to defeat it (i.e., the justification process ends), change is performed in the corresponding UML diagram. A template is filled out—it contains a snapshot showing the original structure of the

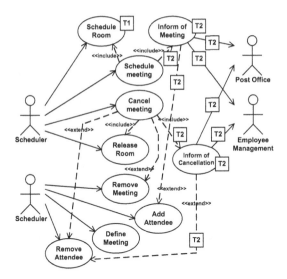

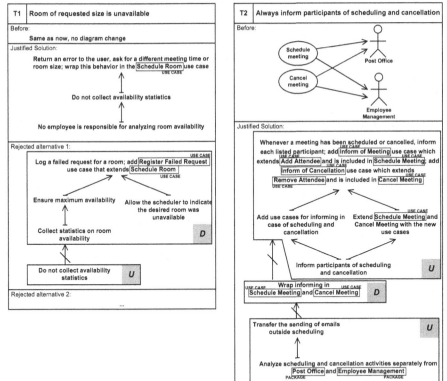

Fig. 4. The modified use case diagram with accompanying rationale traceability information produced with UML-TAM

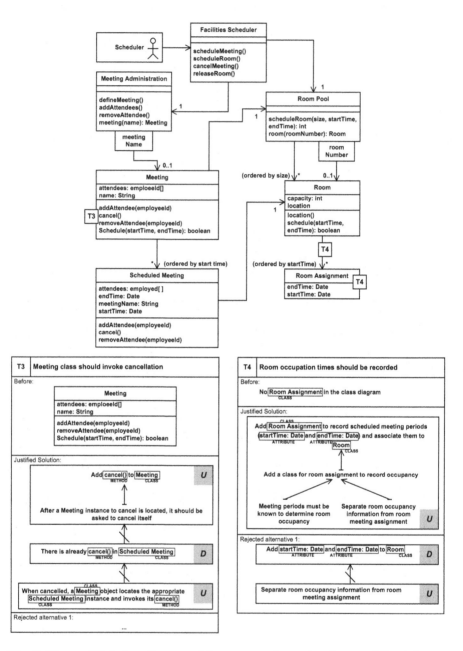

Fig. 5. The modified class diagram with accompanying rationale traceability information produced with UML-TAM

part of the diagram that is being changed, the problem statement, the alternative solutions, the justification, and all arguments provided for each alternative solution.

6   Applying UML-TAM

It has been observed earlier that the initial use case diagram shown in Fig.1(a) is incomplete in several respects. Using UML-TAM, two changes were performed leading to the use case diagram in Fig.4. There, labels are placed on the elements of the diagram to relate them to *traceability templates* used in UML-TAM to summarize information used and produced in moving from the initial version of the diagram to that presented in Fig.4. Each template contains four parts: (i) a label (e.g., T1, T2) for relating the elements of the diagram to the template; (ii) a title, which is the problem statement requiring diagram change; (iii) the dialectical tree for the justified alternative solution; and (iv) the dialectical trees for the rejected alternative solutions. Following the metamodel in Fig.3, information referring to UML diagram elements and appearing in the template is labeled following the kind of UML element the information refers to.

Figures 4 and 5 are self-explanatory and show modified initial use case and class diagrams obtained by applying UML-TAM. Each has been constructed by applying the UML-TAM. Practical experience with UML-TAM that goes beyond the simple, yet illustrative case presented here leads to several observations about the practical use of the proposed method. For instance, it has been empirically observed that nonmonotonic reasoning is hard for humans [8]. Effort involved in finding arguments in UML-TAM is considerable and appears to confirm the cited empirical result. Some techniques derived from theory are particularly hard to apply in practice: for instance, comparing arguments for specificity appeared counterintuitive and was thus seldom used. Prior experience and resources about the debated domain are relevant sources of arguments, so that referring to these is suggested. Although the difficulties are considerable when applying argumentation and justification, a significant benefit is that these techniques lead to the externalization of information usually left implicit in UML modeling. The information made explicit is available to a number of stakeholders who can, through argumentation and justification, question and revise the modeling decisions. Moreover, lessons can be learned from past modeling problems as sources of the problems (such as, e.g., fallacious argumentation) can be identified by going back to the recorded arguments. UML-TAM is therefore of interest for projects in which particularly high degree of rigor is required, as in the case of, e.g., safety-critical systems.

7   Conclusion and Future Work

The UML Traceability through Argumentation Method presented herein introduces rigorous argumentation and justification when tracing the rationale behind UML modeling decisions. The main contributions are: (1) The information about the design rationale used in modeling is usually lost or, when available, stated in an unstructured manner. UML-TAM provides a simple, yet precise means for representing this information, analyzing it for problematic rationale (by justification), and using it to arrive at justifiably appropriate modeling decisions. (2) Both qualitative and quantitative, informal and formal information can be put into arguments allowing the application of the method to a wide range of settings. (3) When combined with traceability approaches focused on answering how, what, when, and who modified a UML diagram, UML-TAM allows answering and discussing *why* a change was needed. (4) By applying argumentation and justification activities, the modeler can claim that a modeling choice is appropriate or not, while relying on solid and well understood conceptual foundations and rigorous processes for their use. Modeling choices can thus be claimed as justified, or questioned through a step-by-step process. Following the outline of related research efforts §2, the proposed method advances the rationale traceability literature, while ensuring compatibility with approaches focusing on traceability of other types of information—this is accomplished by focusing the method on a precise traceability issue, proposing connection points for relating the method to compatible approaches, and avoiding overlap with related techniques.

Current effort includes the exploration of benefits of formalizing arguments in combination with various UML formalizations, to attempt automated analysis of argument and associated UML diagram structures. Experimentation is currently performed to improve usability in industrial settings.

Acknowledgments. The authors thank Alex Borgida for insightful remarks on the paper [14] presented at the 14th International Conference on Requirements Engineering, which helped shape the ideas herein. The first author acknowledges funding from the Belgian ICM/CIM Doctoral Fellowship Program.

References

1. Antoniol, G., Canfora, G., De Lucia, A.: Maintaining traceability during object-oriented software evolution: a case study. In: Proc. Int. Conf. Softw. Maintenance (1999)
2. Besnard, P., Hunter, A.: A logic-based theory of deductive arguments. Intell. 128(1–2), 203–235 (2001)
3. Briand, L.C., Labiche, Y., Yue, T.: Automated Traceability Analysis for UML Model Refinements. Carleton Univ. Technical Report, TR SCE-06-06, ver.2 (August 2006)
4. Chesñevar, C.I., Maguitman, A.G., Loui, R.P.: Logical Models of Argument. ACM Comput. Surv. 32(4), 337–383 (2000)
5. Conklin, J., Begeman, M.L.: gIBIS: A hypertext tool for exploratory policy discussion. ACM Trans. Inf. Syst., 6(4) (1988)
6. Dömges, R., Pohl, K.: Adapting Traceability Environments to Project-Specific Needs. Comm. ACM 41(12), 54–62 (1998)
7. Egyed, A.: A Scenario-Driven Approach to Traceability. Proc. Int. Conf. Softw. Eng., 123–132 (2001)
8. Ford, M., Billington, D.: Strategies in Human Nonmonotonic Reasoning. Computat. Intel. 16(3), 446–468 (2000)
9. Gotel, O.C.Z., Finkelstein, A.C.W.: An Analysis the Requirements Traceability Problem. Tech. Rep. TR-93-41, Dept. of Computing, Imperial College (1993)
10. Gotel, O.C.Z., Finkelstein, A.C.W.: An analysis of the requirements traceability problem. In: Proc. Int. Conf. Req. Eng., pp. 94–101 (1994)

11. Gotel, O.C.Z.: Contribution Structures for Requirements Engineering. Ph.D. Thesis, Imperial College of Science, Technology, and Medicine, London, England (1996)
12. Haumer, P., Pohl, K., Weidenhaupt, K., Jarke, M.: Improving Reviews by Extending Traceability. In: Proc. Annual Hawaii Int. Conf. on System Sciences (1999)
13. Jackson, J.: A Keyphrase Based Traceability Scheme. IEE Colloq. on Tools and Techn. for Maintaining Traceability During Design (1991)
14. Jureta, I.J., Faulkner, S., Schobbens, P.-Y.: Justifying Goal Models. Proc. Int. Conf. Req. Eng., 119–128 (2006)
15. Letelier, P.: A Framework for Requirements Traceability in UML-Based Projects. In: Proc. Int. Worksh. on Traceability in Emerging Forms of Softw. Eng. (2002)
16. Louridas, P., Loucopoulos, P.: A Generic Model for Reflective Design. ACM Trans. Softw. Eng. Meth. 9(2) (2000)
17. Naslavsky, L., Alspaugh, T.A., Richardson, D.J., Ziv, H.: Using Scenarios to Support Traceability. Proc. Int. Worksh. on Traceability in emerging forms of software engineering, 25–30 (2005)
18. OMG. UML 2.0 Superstructure Specification. Object Management Group, Final Adopted Specification ptc/03-08-02 (2003)
19. Pinheiro, F.A.C., Goguen, J.A.: An Object-Oriented Tool for Tracing Requirements. IEEE Software 13(2), 52–64 (1996)
20. Pohl, K.: Process-Centered Requirements Engineering. Advanced Software Development Series. J.Wiley & Sons Ltd, Taunton, England (1996)
21. Pohl, K.: PRO-ART: Enabling Requirements Pre-Traceability. Proc. Int. Conf. Req. Eng., 76–85 (1996)
22. Pohl, K., Dömges, R., Jarke, M.: Towards Method-Driven Trace Capture. Proc. Conf. Adv. Info. Syst. Eng., 103–116 (1997)
23. Prakken, H., Vreeswijk, G.: Logical systems for defeasible argumentation. In: Gabbay, D., Guenther, F. (eds.) Handbook of Philosophical Logic, Kluwer, Dordrecht (2002)
24. Ramesh, B., Dhar, V.: Supporting systems development by capturing deliberations during requirements engineering. IEEE Trans. Softw. Eng. 18(6), 498–510 (1992)
25. Ramesh, B., Stubbs, C., Powers, T., Edwards, M.: Implementing requirements traceability: A case study. Annals of Softw. Eng. 3, 397–415 (1997)
26. Simari, G.R., Loui, R.P.: A mathematical treatment of defeasible reasoning and its implementation. Artificial Intelligence 53, 125–157 (1992)
27. Toranzo, M., Castro, J.: A Comprehensive Traceability Model to Support the Design of Interactive Systems. In: Guerraoui, R. (ed.) ECOOP 1999. LNCS, vol. 1628, pp. 283–284. Springer, Heidelberg (1999)
28. Ubayashi, N., Tamai, T., Sano, S., Maeno, Y., Murakami, S.: Model evolution with aspect-oriented mechanisms. In: Proc. Int. Worksh. Principles of Softw. Evol. (2005)
29. van Lamsweerde, A., Darimont, R.: Massonet Ph.: The Meeting Scheduler Problem: Preliminary Definition. Université catholique de Louvain (1992)
30. van Lamsweerde, A.: Goal-Oriented Requirements Engineering: A Guided Tour. In: Proc. Int. Conf. Req, pp. 249–263 (2001)

Exploring Alternatives for Representing and Accessing Design Knowledge About Enterprise Integration

Karthikeyan Umapathy and Sandeep Purao

College of IST, Penn State University, University Park, PA
{kumapathy,spurao}@ist.psu.edu

Abstract. Enterprise integration refers to solutions that facilitate meaningful interactions among heterogeneous legacy applications. The scale, complexity and specificity of most enterprise integration efforts mean that design knowledge for enterprise integration has resisted codification. Important exceptions to this include: use of Business Process Models (BPM) to understand integration requirements; and Enterprise Integration Patterns (EIP), which present designers with abstract descriptions of recurring design tactics for integrating applications. The two, however, can be at odds. BPM encourages the control flow perspective; whereas EIP codifies an operational perspective. Mapping between the two to develop coherent solutions, therefore, tends to be problematic. To bridge the gap, we suggest an approach that builds on the theory of speech acts. We develop essential components of such an approach, including a re-representation of EIP as structures of speech acts, a characterization of tasks in BPM with action types, and a mapping between speech acts and action types. These components are accompanied by inference rules that produce a mapping between sets of tasks in a business process and structures of speech acts to allow reasoning on identification of appropriate EIPs for given set of tasks. We demonstrate usefulness of the proposed approach by application to industry cases.

Keywords: Enterprise integration, design knowledge, patterns, business process modeling, BPMN, speech acts, action types, ontology reasoner.

1 Introduction

Designing enterprise integration solutions is difficult for several reasons including heterogeneity of platforms and programming languages, the autonomous nature of legacy applications [1], diversity and complexity of systems [2], and difficulties related to understanding requirements for integration [2].

To overcome these difficulties, designers can utilize many integration tactics [3]. These include the use of business process models (BPM) [4] and use of design knowledge in the form of enterprise integration patterns (EIP) [5] to devise solutions in response to the integration requirements. The two, BPM and EIP, however follow different perspectives. BPM embody a control-flow perspective [4], whereas EIP describe operational solutions abstracted to reflect codified wisdom from past experiences [5, 6]. Mapping the two, therefore, remains a challenge for enterprise integration solution developers, who must exploit (a) knowledge of integration requirements as expressed in

C. Parent et al. (Eds.): ER 2007, LNCS 4801, pp. 470–484, 2007.

the BPM, (b) design knowledge as expressed in the EIP, and (c) rules or heuristics that dictate application of the latter to the former.

In addition to the cognitive roadblocks that developers may face, the primitives used by the two perspectives also tend to be different. The BPM techniques are used for modeling business activities and dependencies among activities through constructs such as sequencing, splits, joins, and iterations, i.e., they follow a control-flow perspective [4]. The EIP [5], on the other hand, use constructs such as message, channel, one-way, request-response and others that build abstract solutions to connect systems that perform business activities, i.e. they follow an operational perspective [6]. Translation across the two, therefore, remains a significant concern.

The *objective* of this paper is to explore a specific alternative, speech act theory [7] and language-action perspective [8], for bridging this gap. We argue for and develop several components towards this objective. Together, the contribution of these components is to help enterprise integration solution developers to overcome this gap between integration requirements and design knowledge about enterprise integration. The paper reviews prior work; develops parsimonious sets of speech acts and action types and mechanisms such as for rules and heuristics for inferring the mapping between BPM fragments and EIPs. Three cases, of which one is described in significant detail, demonstrate usefulness of the technique.

2 Background

The two elements, BPM and EIP address two sides of a solution approach for enterprise integration. The first is useful for eliciting requirements; the second provides abstract representations of design knowledge.

2.1 Eliciting Enterprise Integration Requirements

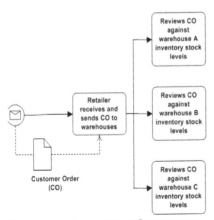

Fig. 1. A business process fragment represented using BPMN

To understand how the existing systems must interact, the tasks performed by these systems must be identified and logically interlinked to form end-to-end processes [9]. These tasks typically represent the flow of business tasks, decision points, events, and the logic for executing a process. Logical interlinking of these tasks, therefore, follows control-flow constructs defined by the Workflow Management Coalition [10]. Representations for visually depicting these tasks include BPM techniques which are, in part, based on ideas contained in Petri Nets [4], i.e. following control constructs. Business Process Modeling Notation (BPMN) [11] has been proposed as a standard for modeling business processes. It provides graphical notations for developing BPM that are easily understandable by all stakeholders [11].

Fig 1 shows a fragment of BPM developed using BPMN. Business process models developed using BPMN allow identification of tasks performed by disparate systems, tasks that can be automated, kinds of exchanges that take place between systems and areas where business rules need to be enforced [12]. BPM, therefore, help determine how to integrate systems, and thus represent integration requirements.

2.2 Design Knowledge for Enterprise Integration

The design of a solution, however, requires drawing on insight, prior experience or codified knowledge. The design activity, therefore, often involves identification of issues and exploration of various design strategies that may address those issues [13]. Design strategies that can be employed to address specific design problems are known as design knowledge [14]. Design knowledge typically consists of abstractions of design strategies and their associated relationships [15]. Depending on the design domain, these abstractions may consist of recurring patterns of geometrical, topological, temporal, causal, and functional descriptions and relations [16]. Explicitly capturing design strategies in the form of patterns has been shown to aid in transferring design knowledge to other designers [17].

The idea of patterns as a design solution was introduced by Christopher Alexander in the building construction architectures domain [18], and first popularized in the software design domain by Gamma et al. [19]. A pattern is domain-independent abstraction of common design structure for recurring design problem. Each pattern describes when it can be applied, its design constraints, consequences and trade-offs of applying it in a particular contexts [19]. When related patterns are woven together they form a "pattern language" which captures the relationship between solutions and problems [5]. Patterns have been proposed for conceptual design [20], in different domains for detailed design [19], and have been demonstrated to be viable for conceptual design of new systems [21].

2.2.1 Enterprise Integration Patterns (EIP)

In the enterprise integration domain, such a pattern language, consisting of sixty-five patterns has been proposed [5]. These patterns are abstract, i.e., they do not provide implementation code or wrappers; instead, they provide recurring solutions that designers can use to solve integration problems. For instance, publish-subscribe channel (shown in the fig 2) describes how channels may be designed to deliver a copy of a particular event to each receiver, who may have subscribed to a channel. Hohpe and Woolfe [5] organize the patterns into seven categories: integration styles, endpoint patterns, system management patterns, channel patterns, message construction patterns, routing patterns, and transformation patterns. The first three categories suggest different ways of exchanging documents, producing or consuming messages and managing performance of messaging systems respectively;

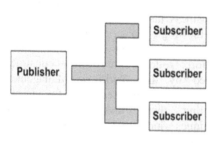

Fig. 2. Publish-subscribe channel pattern

while the last four categories outline different ways of integrating systems based on how they transport, construct, route and transform messages respectively. Patterns contained in these four categories, which focus on operational flow between applications to suggest abstract solutions to integrate them [6], are the focus of this research.

2.3 Problem: A Mismatch Between Control-Flow and Operational-Flow

As outlined earlier, this mismatch between the two perspectives between BPM and EIP represents the key problem we address in this paper. One possibility to address this problem includes analogical reasoning [22]. A prerequisite to this, however, is a clear mapping between a problem domain and the solution domain [21]. With this mapping, inferences may be drawn to apply the latter to the former. We explore the feasibility of Language-Action to facilitate this mapping.

3 An Alternative Based on Language-Action Perspective

We start our arguments with the observation that a naive approach to accessing design solutions (EIP) based on integration requirements (BPM) is to utilize structural similarities between them [16]. For instance, a requirement with one-to-many relationship (i.e., first task performed by single performer while following set of tasks performed by two or more performers) would lead to choice of following patterns: message router, publish-subscribe channel, content-based router, dynamic router, recipient list, competing consumers, and message dispatcher. As the example demonstrates, structural similarity alone cannot lead to appropriate selection of EIP. Further, each pattern has a specific purpose and associated constrains of its usage [23], which may make some of them more appropriate for a situation versus others, Both functional and structural similarities must, therefore, be employed to access and identify EIP for a set of requirements [16]. For instance with above example, if the first performer is sending an event message to a set of performers who have subscribed for that particular topic, then the appropriate pattern would be publish-subscribe pattern.

We argue that the language-action perspective [8] and specifically, speech act theory [7] is appropriate for representing such functional attributes of both BPM and EIP. The speech acts represents a viable candidate for this mapping because they focus on the use of language as performance of actions necessary to accomplish tasks, and message exchanges that take place in aid of those actions [24]. Lim et al. [25] suggest that, enterprise integration are represented by *interactions* among participants in a business process. The EIP contain integration tactics to support such *interactions* among participants [5]. These *interactions* can be operationalized with the use of structures of speech acts [26], because speech acts codify different actions that participants must perform to engage in these *interactions* [27] (e.g. promises, orders, requests, declarations among others).

Following these arguments, we develop the mapping between BPM and EIP with *interactions* as the starting point. An interaction is defined as a sequence of interrelated speech acts performed by least two performers [26]; including an 'initiator' and a 'responder' [28]. Speech act theory [7] argues that language can be used not only to describe a situation or fact, but also to perform action [29]. In our case, speech acts represent performance of actions by each participant in an interaction. Sequences of speech acts, thus, codify the interaction. An important prerequisite for ensuring that appropriate speech acts are selected are *action types* that reflect the performers' intent [30]. Action types represent high-level business actions performed by participants through means of communication directed towards other participant(s) [31].

The mapping between BPM developed using BPMN notations and EIP, then, must contain an element that identifies *interactions* in the business processes. Interactions in the BPM can be identified by detecting a sequence of tasks in a business process, where there are changes in the performer. Task(s) carried out by one performer (initiator) are labeled as the first part of the interaction, and those carried out by the other performer (responder) are identified as the second part of interaction. Each task in the interaction with associated action type can be mapped against a small set of possible speech acts. These interactions among speech acts (compiled from the set of tasks) can be mapped against representation of EIPs as sequences of speech acts. Fig 3 below provides overview of this mapping.

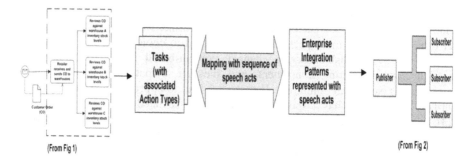

Fig. 3. Mapping sets of tasks against integration patterns

3.1 Components Facilitating Mapping

The components necessary for mapping described above include: (i) a parsimonious set of speech acts appropriate for representing EIPs, (ii) representing EIPs as sequences of speech acts, (iii) a set of action types that depict high-level business actions to categorize tasks in BPMs, and (iv) associations between action types and speech acts.

3.1.1 A Parsimonious Set of Speech Acts
To obtain this set of speech acts, we gathered an initial set of speech acts that are relevant to the enterprise integration domain (see, for example, [30] and [24]). Moore [30] suggests that speech act theory provides appropriate foundation for automated electronic messaging systems and identifies 23 speech acts that can aid in this automation. Johannesson and Perjons [24] develop design principles for modeling

business processes in the context of enterprise integration domain and suggest 12 speech acts that can be used to represent different message types that are typically found in the business processes. A combination of these two resources provided the initial set of speech acts for our research. This initial set was examined, and speech acts that were overlapping were discarded. The combined set was further refined by aggregating speech acts that represented specializations of other speech acts. For instance, the 'Query' speech act can encompass the 'Request' speech act as both represent intent of the initiator asking for certain information or action from the responder. The refinement resulted in 9 speech acts, which are: Acknowledge, Cancel, Commit, Direct, Disagree, Fulfill, Inform, Propose, and Query. Table 1 provides brief description of the parsimonious set of speech acts.

Table 1. A parsimonious set of speech acts

Speech Acts	Description	Source	Comment
Acknowledge	Acknowledge successful completion of an exchange or transaction	Moore 2001	
Cancel	Cancel an established commitment or contract	Johannesson and Perjons 2001 and Moore 2001	
Commit	Committing to a course of action or an obligation	Moore 2001	These two speech acts were dropped because they were unemployable in the context of EIP
Disagree	Participant may disagree on an issue with other participants		
Direct	An attempt to get the recipient to perform a desired action		
Fulfill	Participants completing certain material or economic actions	Johannesson and Perjons 2001 and Moore 2001	
Inform	Providing information that will be useful for other participants actions		
Propose	Proposing to create, change or cancel a contract, commitment, or any other economic event		
Query	Requesting for more information		

3.1.2 Representing EIP with Speech Acts

The parsimonious set of speech acts was used to identify sequences of speech acts that can represent each EIP of interest. Fig 4 shows a few examples, where an EIP is represented as a sequence of speech acts along with the rationale.

We acknowledge this set of speech acts may not be comprehensive. It is not our intent to arrive at a comprehensive list of speech acts. Any such claim is clearly subject to empirical assessment. Instead, we focus on ensuring that the EIP of interest can be described by this parsimonious set. We were able to devise structures of speech to represent each EIP.

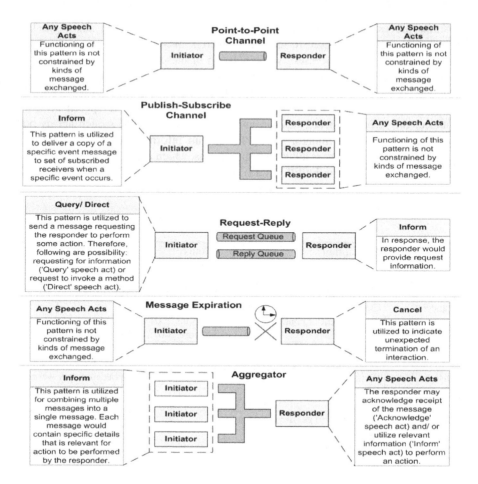

Fig. 4. Enterprise integration patterns as sequence of speech acts

3.1.3 Characterizing Task Types in BPM with Action Types

To categorize task types in BPM, high-level business actions were obtained from different business activity behaviors described in the Unified Modeling Language (UML) specification [32]. UML is widely used for modeling BPM and software application design solutions [33]. The UML specification describes about 54 different possible activities; each activity description was interpreted with respect to their applicability to seven speech acts. From this review, we identified 16 different activities relevant to this mapping. These 16 action types were transformed into their simple forms, for easier comprehension. For instance, the 'AcceptCallAction' action type was found relevant for the 'Acknowledge' speech act, and was transformed into 'Accept call with no receipt send'. After this transformation, the 16 action types were further reduced to 11 action types by aggregating action types that can encompass other action types into single action type. For instance, 'Accept call with no receipt send' and 'Accept event with no receipt send' action types that are relevant to 'Acknowledge' speech act were aggregated into 'Accept with no receipt send' action type. Table 2 provides shows the action types with mapping against speech acts.

Table 2. Mapping between speech acts and action types

Action Types	Speech Acts
Accept with no receipt send	Acknowledge
Reject with no receipt send	Cancel
Invocation	Direct
Declare completion of task	Fulfill
Accept and send receipt	Inform
Provide information	
Raise Exception	
Reject and send receipt	
Propose to perform task	Propose
Request for Information	Query
Request to cancel task	

3.1.4 Inferring Mapping Between BPM and EIP with Speech Acts

Armed with the choices and representations described above, it is possible to construct mechanisms for inferring a mapping between requirements (BPM fragments) and solutions (EIP). An infrastructure to implement this mapping would require a knowledge base that captures relationship and constraints among concepts such as task, action types, speech acts and EIP [34]. The ontology we develop allows such a description of concepts and expresses relationships and constraints between concepts [36] – it follows the view of an ontological representation as "an explicit specification of a conceptualization" [35] The declarative formalism we use for this purpose is the Web Ontology Language (OWL) [37].

An advantage of OWL is the ability to make inferences using the OWL knowledge base with the use of OWL reasoners. We utilize Bossam OWL Reasoner [38] to make inference on appropriate EIPs for a given set of tasks. Bossam is a RETE-based forward chaining rule engine with native support for reasoning over OWL ontologies [39]. The Bossam inference engine translates OWL classes and restrictions as facts, i.e., relationships among action types, speech acts and EIPs are declared as a set of facts. Rules can then be developed to make inferences about appropriate EIPs over this declared set of facts.

A final input to the execution of rules in the Bossam OWL Reasoner is interactions in the business process as an additional set of facts. The Bossam OWL Reasoner, then, suggests a mapping between interactions identified and sequence of speech acts that are appropriate for the identified interactions. The inference for each identified interaction is constructed as a sequence of speech acts, which is then declared as an additional set of facts to the Bossam OWL Reasoner. Bossam OWL Reasoner then infers a mapping between the interactions and EIPs using this sequence of speech acts. So far, more than 25 rules have been developed for this inference. Table 3 shows an example.

Table 3. Heuristic for inferring mapping between EIP and BPMN with speech acts

Pattern	Inference Rule
Aggregator	If Interaction *ind* has Many to One association between initiator *y* and responder *b* AND Relevant speech act for action performed by Initiator(s) *y* is *Inform* AND Relevant speech act for action performed by Responder *b* is *Inform*
	Then Appropriate pattern for identified Interaction *ind* is *Aggregator*
Command Message	If Interaction *ind* has One to One association between initiator *y* and responder *b* AND Relevant speech act for action performed by Initiator(s) *y* is *Direct*
	Then Appropriate pattern for identified Interaction *ind* is *Command Message*
Point-to-Point Channel	If Interaction *ind* has One to One association between initiator *y* and responder *b*
	Then Appropriate pattern for identified Interaction *ind* is *Point-to-Point Channel*

4 Application

The mapping developed was applied to three examples. The first was drawn from ITSO Speedy Rentals scenario developed by IBM [40]; the second came from the supply chain management (SCM) scenario [41] developed by the Web Services Interoperability Organization (WS-I); and the third was the Widget-Gadget Corp scenario developed by Hohpe and Woolfe [5]. The inference engine was used to identify mappings for these examples. Table 4 shows a summary of results. Due to space constraints, the first, drawn from IBM [40] is described in more detail.

Table 4. Summary of application of the mapping to the three examples

Case	Source	Interactions Identified	BOSSAM Rules invoked	Number of distinct EIPs identified
1	IBM	11	8	3
2	WS-I	4	7	4
3	Hohpe and Woolfe	6	9	5

4.1 The Speedy Rentals Scenario from IBM

To demonstrate application the mapping developed in this paper, we use ITSO Speedy Rentals scenario developed by IBM [40]. The particular business process identified for this demonstration is the "Vehicle fulfillment process." In this process, the customer reserves a vehicle and reaches a rental agreement with ITSO Speedy Rentals. The rental agency then reserves a vehicle based on customer's request. If the vehicle is not available for the selected group, a vehicle from the next group level is selected. When the vehicle is collected by the customer, a rental agreement is initiated and its status is set to 'active.' The customer takes possession of the vehicle for the agreed duration. If a vehicle is not returned at the planned date and time, the customer must be contacted and a new return date, time, and location is confirmed. The existing rental agreement should be updated with the new details. At the time of the final payment calculation, a discount will be applied to ITSO Speedy Rentals loyalty club members. A final invoice is generated and given to the customer upon completion and return. After receiving payment from customer, rental agreement is terminated. Fig 5 shows the model for the vehicle fulfillment process drawn with the BPMN notation.

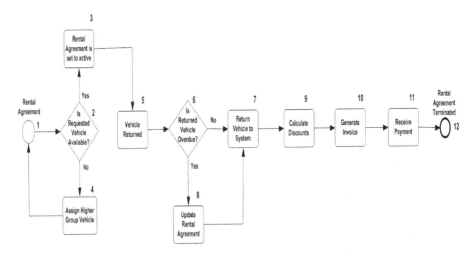

Fig. 5. Business process model for vehicle fulfillment process

In this process, 11 interactions can be identified. The tasks are marked in the figure and the interactions listed in table 5, columns 1 through 4. For each task in the identified interactions, based on its action type appropriate speech act is identified by declaring these tasks and action types as facts to the Bossam OWL reasoner. Running Bossam OWL reasoner with this fact set allows generation of a mapping between tasks and relevant speech acts. Table 5 shows these results. For instance, the action type for task 1 is 'Accept and send receipt' as the customer accepts and enters into a rental agreement. The associated speech act for 'Accept and send receipt' action type is 'Inform;' therefore, the Bossam OWL Reasoner would map task 1 to the 'Inform' speech act.

The speech acts of initiator and responder forms a sequence of speech acts for each interaction. These speech act sequences are declared as facts to the Bossam OWL Reasoner. Running Bossam OWL reasoner with this set of facts provides a mapping between interactions identified and EIPs appropriate for these interactions. For instance, interaction 2 is a many-to-one interaction (2, 3 and 4), with the 'Inform' speech act for initiator and the 'Acknowledge' and 'Inform' speech acts for responders. The Bossam OWL Reasoner suggests Content-Based Router as an appropriate EIP for this interaction. Table 6 shows these results.

The EIPs identified for each interaction, thus, point to plausible implementation strategies for connecting the performers for tasks involved in the interaction. For example, interaction 2 requires performance of tasks from the vehicle reservation system and the rental agent. The EIP identified, content-based router, suggests that the capability of the vehicle reservation system be augmented to include such routing, and the interface of the rental agent system be augmented to respond to such routing messages. A further use of the results is to examine the capabilities required for a performer system by examining all interactions in which it participates. For example,

Table 5. Speech act sequence for identified interactions for the speedy rental scenario

Interactions	Tasks	Performer	Role	Action Type	Speech Act
1	1	Customer	Initiator	Accept and send receipt	Inform
	2	Vehicle Reserve System	Responder	Provide information	Inform
2	2	Vehicle Reserve System	Initiator	Provide information	Inform
	3	Rental Agent	Responder	Accept with no receipt send	Acknowledge
	4	Rental Agent	Responder	Provide information	Inform
3	4	Rental Agent	Initiator	Provide information	Inform
	1	Customer	Responder	Accept and send receipt	Inform
4	3	Rental Agent	Initiator	Accept with no receipt send	Acknowledge
	5	Customer	Responder	Declare completion of task	Fulfill
5	5	Customer	Initiator	Declare completion of task	Fulfill
	6	Rental Agent	Responder	Provide information	Inform
6	6	Rental Agent	Initiator	Raise Exception	Inform
	7	Vehicle Reserve System	Responder	Accept and send receipt	Inform
	8	Customer	Responder	Provide information	Inform
7	8	Customer	Initiator	Provide information	Inform
	7	Vehicle Reserve System	Responder	Accept and send receipt	Inform
8	7	Vehicle Reserve System	Initiator	Accept and send receipt	Inform
	9	Member Discounts	Responder	Provide information	Inform
9	9	Member Discounts	Initiator	Provide information	Inform
	10	Invoice	Responder	Provide information	Inform
10	10	Invoice	Initiator	Provide information	Inform
	11	Customer	Responder	Provide information	Inform
11	11	Customer	Initiator	Provide information	Inform
	12	Rental Agent	Responder	Declare completion of task	Fulfill

the vehicle reservation system participates in interaction 1 (as responder), in interaction 2 (as initiator), interaction 6 (as responder), interaction 7 (as responder), and interaction 8 (as initiator). The different EIPs identified for these interactions include: point-to-point channel, content-based router, and content enricher. Hohpe and Woolfe [5] describe the capabilities and interfaces that different parties to these patterns must possess. Such prescriptions can then guide the development of integration solutions for each performer participating in the process.

Table 6. Enterprise Integration Patterns suggested for the identified interactions

Interactions	Speech Act Sequence	Patterns Identified
1	Inform, Inform	Point-to-Point Channel
2	Inform, Acknowledge, Inform	Content-Based Router
3	Inform, Inform	Point-to-Point Channel Content Enricher
4	Acknowledge, Fulfill	Point-to-Point Channel
5	Fulfill, Inform	Point-to-Point Channel
6	Inform, Inform, Inform	Content-Based Router
7	Inform, Inform	Point-to-Point Channel Content Enricher
8	Inform, Inform	Point-to-Point Channel
9	Inform, Inform	Point-to-Point Channel Content Enricher
10	Inform, Inform	Point-to-Point Channel
11	Inform, Fulfill	Point-to-Point Channel

5   Discussion

In this paper, we argue for, and develop essential components of, an approach to facilitate the representation, translation and access to design knowledge about enterprise integration. The components we develop include a parsimonious set of speech acts and action types, both building on prior work that provides a basis for the translation. The translation includes a re-representation of EIPs as structures of speech acts, a characterization of tasks in BPM with action types, and a mapping between speech acts and action types. These are accompanied by a set of rules that can be used to infer the mapping between BPM and EIP. As a consequence of these representations and rules, we demonstrate an approach to map integration requirements (captured as BPMN specifications following a control-flow perspective) against design knowledge (available as EIPs following the operational perspective).

Accessing and identifying appropriate design knowledge like EIP is merely a starting point in the process of designing enterprise integration solutions. As described towards the end of the previous section, after identifying appropriate EIP for each interaction in the business process, the identified patterns must be considered for each performer in the interaction, and then composed according to the interaction sequences described in the business process. Such a composition of integration patterns would describe conversations among systems that are being integrated. Thus, possible design solutions suggested by integration patterns can be implemented using web service conversation specifications. A possible mechanism to translate this composition into a web service conversation specification is described in [42].

In this paper, we have also demonstrated applicability of this mapping and the overall solution approach to multiple examples, including one in-depth, for the Speedy Rental scenario developed by IBM. We are currently refining a research prototype that will allow designers to develop business process models using BPMN, access and select appropriate integration patterns, and convert them into web service conversation specifications with the help of mechanisms described in this paper. We believe that the approach we have outlined and its components, as described in this paper would improve the quality and internal consistency of the design solution, and reduce the effort required to access and select appropriate EIPs. As part of future work, an empirical evaluation is planned to assess whether these outcomes can be obtained.

References

1. Hasselbring, W.: Information System Integration. Communications of the ACM 43, 32–38 (2000)
2. Dalal, N.P., Kamath, M., Kolarik, W.J., Sivaraman, E.: Toward an Integrated Framework for Modeling Enterprise Processes. Communications of the ACM 47, 83–87 (2004)
3. Themistocleous, M., Irani, Z., Kulj, J., Love, P.E.D.: Extending the information system lifecycle through enterprise application integration: a case study experience. In: Annual Hawaii International Conference on System Sciences, vol. 37, pp. 228–235. IEEE, Los Alamitos (2004)
4. Aalst, W.M.P.: Business Process Management: A Survey. Business Process Management (BPM): International Conference. In: van der Aalst, W.M.P., ter Hofstede, A.H.M., Weske, M. (eds.) BPM 2003. LNCS, vol. 2678, pp. 1–12. Springer, Heidelberg (2003)
5. Hohpe, G., Woolf, B.: Enterprise Integration Patterns. Addison-Wesley, London, UK (2004)
6. Aalst, W.M.P., Hofstede, A.H.M.t., Kiepuszewski, B., Barros, A.P.: Workflow Patterns. Distributed and Parallel Databases 14, 5–51 (2003)
7. Searle, J.R.: Speech acts: An essay in the philosophy of language. Cambridge, Cambridge, England (1969)
8. Weigand, H.: Two Decades of the Language-Action Perspective: Introduction. Communications of the ACM 49, 44–46 (2006)
9. Zhu, J., Tian, Z., Li, T., Sun, W., Ye, S., Ding, W., Wang, C.C., Wu, G., Weng, L., Huang, S., Liu, B., Chou, D.: Model-driven business process integration and management: A case study with the Bank SinoPac regional service platform. IBM Journal of Research and Development 48, 649–670 (2004)
10. Terminology, W.: Workflow Management Coalition Terminology & Glossary. The Workflow Management Coalition Specification (1999). http://www.wfmc.org/standards/docs/TC-1011_term_glossary_v3.pdf
11. BPMN: Business Process Modeling Notation Specification. Object Management Group, Inc. (OMG) (2006), http://www.bpmn.org/Documents/OMG
12. Popkin, J.: Improving Regulatory Compliance With Business Process Modeling. Business Integration Journal (2005), http://bijonline.com/index.cfm?section=article&aid=212

13. Gero, J.S.: Design prototypes: a knowledge representation schema for design. AI Magazine 11, 26–36 (1990)
14. Purcell, T., Sodersten, K.: Design Education, Reflective Practice, and Design Research. Design Thinking Research Symposium Delft University of Technology, The Netherlands (2001)
15. Kalay, Y., Swerdloff, L., Majkowski, B.: Process and Knowledge in Design Computation. Journal of Architectural Education 43, 47–53 (1990)
16. Goel, A.K.: Design, analogy, and creativity. IEEE Expert 12, 62–70 (1997)
17. Schmidt, D.C.: Using design patterns to develop reusable object-oriented communication software. Communications of the ACM 38, 65–74 (1995)
18. Alexander, C., Ishikawa, S., Silverstein, M.: A Pattern Language: Towns, Buildings, Construction. Oxford University Press, USA (1977)
19. Gamma, E., Helm, R., Johnson, R., Vlissides, J.: Design Patterns: Elements of Reusable Object-Oriented Software. Addison-Wesley, London, UK (1994)
20. Coad, P., North, D., Mayfield, M.: Object Models: Strategies, Patterns, and Applications. Prentice-Hall, Englewood Cliffs (1995)
21. Purao, S., Storey, V.C., Han, T.: Improving Analysis Pattern Reuse in Conceptual Design: Augmenting Automated Processes with Supervised Learning. Information Systems Research 14, 269–290 (2003)
22. Gentner, D.: Structure-mapping: A theoretical framework for analogy. Cognitive Science: A Multidisciplinary Journal 7, 155–170 (1983)
23. Vokáč, M., Tichy, W., SjØberg, D.I.K., Arisholm, E., Aldrin, M.: A Controlled Experiment Comparing the Maintainability of Programs Designed with and without Design Patterns-A Replication in a Real Programming Environment. Empirical Software Engineering 9, 149–195 (2004)
24. Johannesson, P., Perjons, E.: Design Principles for Process Modelling in Enterprise Application Integration. Information Systems 26, 165–184 (2001)
25. Lim, S.H., Juster, N., Pennington, A.: The Seven Major Aspects of Enterprise Modelling and Integration: A Position Paper. ACM SIGGROUP Bulletin 18, 71–75 (1997)
26. Aakhus, M.: Felicity conditions and genre: Linking act and conversation in LAP style conversation analysis. International Working Conference on the Language-Action Perspective on Communication Modelling (2004)
27. Bach, K., Harnish, R.M.: Linguistic Communication and Speech Acts. MIT Press, Cambridge, MA (1979)
28. Christiansson, M.-T.: Interaction Analysis - An important part of Inter-organizational Business and IS development. International Working Conference on the Language-Action Perspective on Communication Modelling (LAP) (1998)
29. Goldkuhl, G., Ågerfalk, P.J.: Actability: A Way to Understand Information Systems Pragmatics. International Workshop on Organisational Semiotics, Staffordshire University, Stafford, UK (2000)
30. Moore, S.A.: A Foundation for Flexible Automated Electronic Communication. Information Systems Research 12, 34–62 (2001)
31. Lind, M., Goldkuhl, G.: Generic Layered Patterns for Business Modelling. International Working Conference on the Language-Action Perspective on Communication Modelling (LAP) (2001)
32. UML: Unified Modeling Language. Object Management Group (OMG) (2005), http://www.uml.org/

33. Gardner, T.: UML Modeling of Automated Business Processes with a mapping to BPEL4WS. European Workshop on Object Orientation and Web Services (EOOWS) (2003)

34. Sowa, J.F.: Knowledge Representation: Logical, Philosophical, and Computational Foundations, Brooks/Cole, Pacific Grove. CA (2000)

35. Gruber, T.R.: A Translation Approach to Portable Ontology Specifications. Knowledge Acquisition 5, 199–220 (1993)

36. Wang, X., Chan, C.W., Hamilton, H.J.: Design of Knowledge-Based Systems with the Ontology-Domain-System Approach. International conference on Software Engineering and Knowledge Engineering. ACM Press, New York (2002)

37. OWL: OWL Web Ontology Language Overview. W3C (2004), http://www.w3.org/TR/owl-features/

38. Bossam: Bossam Rule/OWL Reasoner. Minsu Jang (2006), http://mknows.etri.re.kr/bossam/FrontPage

39. Jang, M., Sohn, J.-C.: An Extended Rule Engine for OWL Inferencing. International Workshop on Rules and Rule Markup Languages for the Semantic Web, Hiroshima, Japan, pp. 128–138 (2004)

40. ITSO Speedy Rentals: Patterns: SOA Foundation - Business Process Management Scenario. IBM (2006), http://www.redbooks.ibm.com/redbooks/pdfs/sg247234.pdf

41. Scenario, S.C.M.: Supply Chain Management Use Case Model. Web Services-Interoperability Organization (2003), http://www.ws-i.org/SampleApplications/SupplyChainManagement/2003-12/SCMUseCases1.0.pdf

42. Umapathy, K., Purao, S.: Designing Enterprise Solutions with Web Services and Integration Patterns. IEEE International Conference on Services Computing (SCC), pp. 111–118. IEEE Computer Society Press, Los Alamitos (2006)

Mining and Re-engineering Transactional Workflows for Reliable Executions*

Walid Gaaloul, Sami Bhiri, and Armin Haller

DERI – National University of Ireland
IDA Business Park, Galway, Ireland
{walid.gaaloul,sami.bhiri,armin.haller}@deri.org

Abstract. A continuous evolution of business process parameters, constraints and needs, hardly foreseeable initially, requires from the business process management systems a continuous design and a reliable process model. In this paper, we are interested in developing a reactive design through a process log analysis ensuring process re-engineering and execution reliability.

We propose to analyse workflow logs to discover workflow transactional behavior and to improve and correct related recovery mechanisms subsequently. Our approach starts by collecting workflow logs. Then, we build, by statistical analysis techniques, an intermediate representation specifying elementary dependencies between activities. These dependencies are refined to mine the transactional workflow model. The analysis of the discrepancies between the discovered model and the initially designed model enables us to detect design gaps, concerning particularly the recovery mechanisms. Thus, based on this mining step, we apply a set of rules on the initially designed workflow to improve workflow reliability.

1 Introduction

The increasing use of Workflow Management Systems (WfMS) in companies expresses their undeniable importance to improve the efficiencies of their processes and reduce costs. In spite of an established potential, WfMS show some limits to ensure a correct and reliable execution. Due to the complex design process and the initially unforeseeable character of other parameters which appear after the execution phase (users' evolution needs, unexpected execution exception, etc), it is impossible to easily foresee and initially realize all necessary parameters for a "perfect" design. The main problem is how to ensure that the specified workflow model guaranties reliable executions and efficient recovery mechanisms. Most previous approaches develop a set of techniques to analyze and check model correctness in their respective workflow model [1,2,3]. Although powerful, these approaches may fail to ensure reliable workflow execution in some cases.

It is neither possible nor intended by workflow designers to model all failures: the process description will become complex very soon [4]. Furthermore, workflow errors

---

* This material is based upon works supported by the EU funding under the SUPER project (FP6-026850).

C. Parent et al. (Eds.): ER 2007, LNCS 4801, pp. 485–501, 2007.

and exceptions are commonly not detected until the workflow model is executed. In addition, a great diversification of company services and products lead to a continuous process evolution. New requirements emerge and existing processes change ("the only constant is change"). Consequently, the alignment of the processes to the observed evolutions requires a permanent attention and reaction during process life cycle. To maintain this alignment it is important to detect changes, i.e. the deviations of the described or prescribed behavior.

It is obvious that the discovery, and the analysis of workflow interactions at runtime, would enable the designer to be alerted of design gaps and then better understand and correct failure handling and recovery techniques. Indeed, this kind of analysis is very useful in showing cause effect relationships and to analyse the discrepancies between the discovered model and the initially designed model. These discrepancies can be used to detect initial design gaps which may be used in a re-engineering process. In this paper, we describe new workflow mining [5] techniques which are able to discover a workflow model by log analysis, and allow to improve its transactional behavior. These workflow mining techniques are suitable tools to detect process changes during the execution which can reflect process evolution.

In this article, we will illustrate our ideas using a running example (see Figure 1) showing the need for discovering transactional behavior to improve workflow reliability. We consider a car rental scenario. This workflow acts as a broker offering to its customers a set of choices made from their choices expressed in the Customer Requirements Specification (CRS) activity. The Customer Identity Check (CIC) activity checks the customer ID while the Car checking availability (CCA) activity and the parking localisation (PL) provide available cars information and the respective car rental companies supplier. Afterwards, the customer makes his choice and agrees on rental terms in the CA activity. Then, the customer is requested to pay either by credit card (CC), by check (CH), or by cash (SH). Finally, the bill is sent to the customer by the send Bill (SB) activity.

To deal with workflow failures and ensure a reliable execution, designers specify additional transactional interactions (dotted arrow). In our example, it was specified that if CA fails then DBC compensates already executed activities and the car rental discovery process (CIC, CCA and PL) should be restarted. To ensure the payment if CC fails, we specify that CH or SH as alternatives. Besides, SH has the capability to be (re)executed until success in case of failure. As for the failures of CCA (the workflow instance does

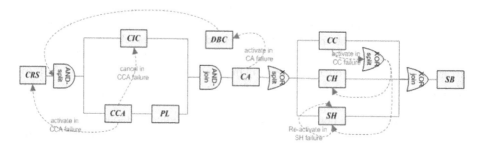

Fig. 1. Example of workflow

not find any car propositions), the workflow instance cancels the CIC execution and restarts CCA execution to (re)specify the client requirements. Workflow designers did not provide failure handling mechanisms for the other activities and suppose that these activities never fail.

Let us suppose now that in reality (by observation of sufficient execution cases) CCA never fails but CIC can fail. This means there is no need to specify a recovery mechanism for CCA, but if CIC fails we should cancel concurrent activities of the car rental discovery process and resume workflow execution. Starting from workflow logs (sufficient workflow execution cases), we propose workflow mining techniques that detect these transactional design gaps and provide help to correct them.

The remainder of this paper is structured as follows. First, we describe in section 2 the structure of workflow event logs. After that, we detail our approach for mining workflow recovery techniques (section 3). We mainly proceed in two steps. First, we discover workflow patterns using statistical analysis of logs. After that, we extract workflow transactional dependencies. Based on these mined results, we use a set of rules to improve workflow failure handling and recovery, and consequently process reliability (section 4). Finally, we discuss in section 5 related works, implementation and perspectives issues, before concluding.

2   Workflow Event Log Analysis

2.1   Workflow Event Logs Structure

The workflow specification might not be concerned with the details of the internal execution of activities. However, it has to deal, at least, with the externally visible completion events (such as cancelled, failed, and terminated). Currently, most WfMS log all events occurring during process execution. We suppose that it is possible to record events such as (i) each event is referred to one activity (i.e. a well defined step in the workflow), (ii) each event refers to one case (i.e. a workflow instance), and (iii) events are completely ordered. Thus, we expect that events are detectable and collectable, which means that WfMS are required to capture and keep a workflow log. Any information system such as ERP, CRM, or WfMS using transactional systems offers this information in a certain form [5]. Data warehouses storing these workflow logs were proposed in the literature [6,7]. These data warehouses simplify and accelerate workflow mining techniques' requests over these databases.

Definition 1 (WorkflowLog)
An EventStream *represents the history of a worflow instance events as a tuple* stream *(*sequenceLog, SOccurrence*) where:*
    SOccurrence : int *is the instance number.*
    sequenceLog : Event* *is an ordered events set belonging to a workflow instance, where an event is defined as tuple e* Event= *(*activityId, state*)*
A WorkflowLog *is a set of* EventStreams. WorkflowLog=(*workflowID*, {EventStream$_i$, $0 \leq i \leq$ *number of workflow instances*}) *where* EventStream$_i$ *is the event stream of the* i^{th} *workflow instance.*

Based on actual workflow log collecting propositions, we present, in Definition 1, our workflow log model. A WorkflowLog is composed of a set of EventStreams . Each EventStream traces the execution of one case (instance). It consists of a set of events (Event) that captures the activities life cycle performed in a particular workflow instance. An Event is described by the activity identifier and the activity execution result state (canceled, failed and terminated). In the following we present an EventStream extracted from the workflow example of Figure 1 representing 5th workflow instance:

L = EventStream(5, [**Event**("CRS", terminated), **Event**("CCA", terminated), **Event**("CIC", terminated), **Event**("PL", terminated), **Event**("CA", terminated), **Event**("CC", terminated), **Event**("SB", terminated)]))

2.2 Logs Statistical Analysis

As workflow execution flows are described through event dependencies, we propose to build, by analysing statistically the WorkflowLog, Statistical Dependency Tables (SDT) reporting log elementary events dependencies. An elementary events dependency is a relation linking an Event e_i to an other Event e_j and expresses that there is an EventStream where the event e_i precedes directly the occurrence of the event e_j. These tables, which are based on the frequency table [8], report for each event a, the following information: (i) The overall frequency of this event (denoted $\#a$) and (ii) the causal dependencies to previous events b_i (denoted $SDT(a, b_i)$). The size of SDT is N*N, where N is the number of workflow events. The (m,n) table entry is the frequency of the nth event immediately preceding the mth event. Table 1 represents a fraction of the initial SDT of our motivating workflow example. For instance, in this table $SDT((SB, terminated), (SH, terminated))$=0.35 expresses that if SB occurs then we have 35% of chance that SH occurs directly before SB in the workflow logs.

We demonstrated in [9] a correlation between the workflow dependencies and the log statistics expressed in SDT (Theorem 1). Thus, each dependency between two workflow events is expressed by a positive value in the corresponding SDT entry. This expresses a relation of equivalence between the positive entries in SDT and the dependencies between the concerned events. Thus, the first event of this statistical dependency is considered as a pre-condition of the second and reciprocally the second event is considered as a post-condition of the first.

THEOREM 1 (CORRELATION BETWEEN SDT AND ACTIVITIES DEPENDENCIES)
Let wft a workflow which does not contain short loop spanning only two activities. $\forall a, b \in wft$ where a immediately precedes $b \Leftrightarrow SDT((b, terminated), (a, terminated)) > 0 \wedge SDT((a, terminated), (b, terminated)) = 0$.

---

3   Transactional Workflow Mining

WfMS are expected to recognize and handle errors to support reliable and consistent execution of workflows. However as [10] pointed out, the introduction of some kind of transactions in WfMSs is unavoidable to guarantee reliable and consistent workflow executions. Transactional workflows have been introduced in [11] to clearly recognize the relevance of transactions in the context of workflows. The integration of transactions into workflows was motivated by research efforts concerning database transaction models for advanced applications [12]. In contrast to database transaction models, transactional workflows focus on consistency issues from a business point of view rather than from a database point of view. The motivation behind modelling workflow transactional behavior is to add the capability in the workflow to handle exceptional circumstances that would otherwise leave the workflow in an unacceptable state. Basically, the transactional behavior is used in case of failures and define recovery mechanisms supporting the automation of failure handling during runtime.

Within transactional workflow models, we distinguish between the control flow and the transactional behavior which is described through the activity's transactional properties and transactional flow depicting respectively the intra and the inter activity transactional dependencies.

Control Flow: Within a workflow instance where all activities are executed without failure or cancellation, the control flow defines activity dependencies. In order to enhance reusability and common comprehension, we use the workflow patterns [13] as an abstract description of a reoccurring class of dependencies to describe the control flow as a patterns composition.

Activities Transactional Properties: Every activity can be associated to a life cycle statechart that models the possible states through which the executions of this activity can go, and the possible transitions between these states. The transactional properties of an activity depend on the intra-activity state dependencies. The main transactional properties that we are considering are *retriable* and *pivot* [14] (Figure 2). An activity a is said to be retriable (a^r) *iff* it is sure to complete even if it fails. a is said to be pivot (a^p) *iff* once the activity successfully completes, its effects remain and cannot be semantically undone or reactivated.

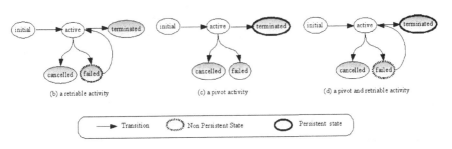

(b) a retriable activity   (c) a pivot activity   (d) a pivot and retriable activity

Transition   Non Persistent State   Persistent state

Fig. 2. Activity transactional properties

Transactional Flow: During the execution of a transactional workflow, it has to be decided, after an activity execution failure (i.e observation of failed state), whether an inconsistent state was reached. According to this decision either a recovery procedure has to be started or the process execution can continue according to the control flow (if the activity failure does not affect the execution of the workflow instance). Recovery mechanisms which are specified by transactional dependencies allow the failed activity to react to reach a coherent state. The goal is to recover the failed workflow to a semantically acceptable state. Thus, the incoherent state of failure can be corrected and the execution can resume thanks to the recovery mechanism which put the failed instance to a coherent point. A coherent point is an execution step of the workflow (equivalent to a save point in database transactions) which represents an acceptable intermediate execution state. It is also a decision point where certain actions can be taken to either solve the problem that caused the failure or choose an alternative execution path to avoid this problem [15]. Designers define for each failed activity, according to their business needs the localisation of the coherent point. For instance, in our example, in case of CCA failures, it was specified that the workflow resumes its execution from the coherent point located on CRS.

In the following, we describe a set of techniques and algorithms for transactional workflow mining. We proceed in three steps by discovering: (i) the workflow patterns composing its control flow (section 3.1), the transactional flow (section 3.2) and the activities transactional properties (section 3.3) including its recovery mechanisms.

3.1   Mining Workflow Patterns

In this section we focus on discovering "elementary" routing workflow patterns: *Sequence, AND-split, OR-split, XOR-split, AND-join, OR-join*, and *M-out-of-N* patterns composing the control flow. As we have mentioned, these patterns describe the control flow interactions for activities executed without "exceptions" (*i.e.* they reached successfully their terminated state). Thus, there is no need to use the events dependencies relating to (failed or cancelled) states which concern only workflow transactional behavior (see next sections). For these reasons, we need to filter workflow logs and take only EventStreams executed without failures or cancellations. Thus, the minimal condition to discover workflow patterns is to have workflow logs containing at least the terminated event state. This feature allows us to mine control flow from "poor" logs which contain only terminated event state. Thus, we build a control flow SDT (noted SCfT) that captures only events dependencies with terminated state in successful executions. Therefore we do not differentiate between activities dependencies and events dependencies (i.e. we do not need to mention the event states as we are interested only in terminated states).

However, SDT presents some problems to express correctly activity dependencies especially relating to concurrent or parallel behavior. In the following, we detail these issues and propose solutions to overcome them (more details can be found in [16]). If we assume that each EventStream from a WorkflowLog stems from a sequential (i.e no concurrent behaviour) workflow, a zero entry in SDT represents a causal independence and a non-zero entry a causal dependency (*i.e.* sequential or conditional dependency). However, in case of concurrent behavior EventStreams may contain interleaved events sequences from concurrent threads. As a consequence, some entries, in SDT, can indicate non-zero entries that do not correspond to dependencies. For example, the EventStream given in section 2 "suggests" causal dependencies between CCA and CIC erroneously in one direction, and CIC and PL in another direction. Indeed, CIC comes just before CCA and CIC comes immediately before PL in this EventStream. These relations will be reported by erroneous entries which are different to zero in SDT. These entries are erroneous because there is no causal dependencies between these activities. Formally, two activities A and B are concurrent *iff* $SDT((A, terminated), (B, terminated))$ and $SDT((B, terminated), (A, terminated))$ entries in SDT are different from zero. Based on this definition we proposed in [16] an algorithm to discover activity parallelism and mark related entries by a negative value (solution 1).

Besides, an activity might not depend on its immediate predecessor in the EventStream, but it might depend on another "indirectly" preceding activity. As an example of this behavior, CIC is logged between CCA and PL in the EventStream given in section 2. As consequence, CCA does not occur always immediately before PL in the workflow logs. Thus we will have $SDT((PL, terminated), (CCA, terminated))) < 1$ which is an under-evaluated. In fact, the right value is 1 because the execution of PL depends exclusively on CCA. To discover these indirect dependencies, we introduced in [16] the notion of activity concurrent window [16]. An activity concurrent window (ACW) is related to the activity of its last event and covers its directly and indirectly preceding activities (solution 2). Now using these two solutions, we can compute the SCfT (Table 1) which will be used to discover workflow patterns.

Table 1. SCfT and activities Frequencies (#)

SCfT((x,y)	CRS	CIC	CCA	PL	CA	CC	CH	SH	SB
CRS	0	0	0	0	0	0	0	0	0
CIC	1	0	-1	-1	0	0	0	0	0
CCA	1	-1		0	0	0	0	0	0
PL	0	-1	1	0	0	0	0	0	0
CA	0	1	0	1	0	0	0	0	0
CC	0	0	0	0	1	0	0	0	0
CH	0	0	0	0	1	0	0	0	0
SH	0	0	0	0	1	0	0	0	0
SB	0	0	0	0	1	0	0.43	0.35	0.22

$$\#CRS = \#CIC = \#CCA = \#PL = \#CA = \#SB = 100$$
$$\#CC = 43\#CH = 35\#SH = 22$$

The last step is the identification of workflow patterns through a set of rules. Each pattern has its own features which abstract statistically its causal dependencies, and represent its unique identifier. These rules allow, if a workflow log is complete, to discover the set of workflow patterns included in the mined workflow. Our control flow mining rules are characterized by a "local" workflow mining approach. Indeed, these rules proceed through a local log analysis that allows us to recover partial results of mining workflow patterns. To discover a particular workflow pattern we need only Events related to the activities of this pattern. Thus, even using only fractions of workflow logs, we can discover correctly corresponding workflow patterns.

Due to the lack of space we present here only rules related to the *XOR-split* $(A, B_1, B_2, \ldots, B_n)$ pattern which chooses after the A activity execution one of the $\{B_1, B_2, \ldots, B_n\}$ activities (Table 2). We refer to our previous works [16,17] for the other patterns mining rules. The *XOR-split* pattern rule specifies that (i) there is no concurrent behavior between $\{B_1, B_2, \ldots, B_n\}$ through ($\forall 0 \leq i, j \leq n$; $SCfT((A_i, A_j) \neq -1$) formula and (ii) the execution of A depends on the termination of one of the $\{B_1, B_2, \ldots, B_n\}$ through ($\Sigma_{i=0}^{n} (\#A_i) = \#B \wedge \Sigma_{i=0}^{n} SCfT((B, A_i) = 1)$ formula. For instance, using Table 1 we mine that this pattern links CC, CH, SH and SB. In fact, the SCfT's entries of these activities indicate non concurrent behaviour between CC, CH and SH ($SCfT(CC, CH) = SCfT(CH, SH) = SCfT(SH, CC) \neq -1$) and SB execution depends on the termination of CC, CH and SH ($SCfT(SB, CC) + SCfT(SB, CH) + SCfT(SB, SH) = 1$).

Table 2. Mining rules of *XOR-split* workflow pattern

Pattern	rules
XOR-split	$(\Sigma_{i=0}^{n} (\#A_i)=\#B) \wedge (\Sigma_{i=0}^{n} \text{SCfT}(B, A_i)=1) \wedge (0 \leq i, j \leq n; SCfT(A_i, A_j) \neq -1)$

3.2 Mining Activities Transactional Dependencies

Similar to the discovery of workflow patterns, we build statistical transactional dependencies tables STrD that report only event dependencies captured after activity failures. These dependencies provide a convenient way to specify and reason about workflow transactional behavior expressed in terms of transactional properties and transactional flow. To calculate these dependencies we use the same definition, except that we capture only event dependencies after activity failures. In practical terms, each STrD is related to an activity "*act*" and captures statistically workflow behavior after *act* fails. ITR_{act} is a STrD, built to capture transactional inter-activities dependencies after *act* failure. We note that *act*'s dependencies before the failure are not reported in ITR_{act}.

Definition 2 (Inter-activities transactional dependencies table)
We denote by ITR_{act} inter-activity transactional dependencies table that reports event dependencies after act failures. Each entry in $ITR_{act}(e_1, e_2)$ is an event dependency where for i=1 or i=2:

$\checkmark (e_i.state = \text{failed} \wedge e_i.activity = act;\,) \vee$

$\checkmark \exists str : EventStream; Evt_i, Evt_j : Event \in str |\ (Evt_j.activity = act \wedge Evt_j.state = \text{failed} \wedge Evt_i.activity = e_i.activity \wedge Evt_i.state = e_i.state \wedge Evt_i < Evt_j).$

To build ITR_{act}, we use only logs where *act* fails keeping only the events dependencies after its failure. The dependencies located before *act* fails report the control flow. We distinguish two types of inter-activities transactional dependencies in ITR_{act} (*c.f.* definition 2). The first category reports the event dependencies where we can find the failed event of *act* (e.state = failed $\wedge$ e.activity = act). The second category reports any dependencies where there is an activity executed after the failure of *act*. In this set of activities, we can find activities which are not in the discovered control flow. Indeed, the recovery mechanisms can require, to compensate the *act* failure, "new" compensation activities which semantically undo *act*'s execution effects. Table 3.a represents a fraction of ITR_{act} of our motivating workflow example after CA fails.

Table 3. Fractions of Statistical Transactional Dependencies tables of CA Activity

(a) ITR_{CA} table

ITR_{CA}	CA,f	DBC,t	CIC,t	CCA,t	PL,t
CA,f	0	0	0	1	1
DBC,t	1	0	0	0	0
CIC,t	0	1			
CCA,t	0	1			
PL,t	0	0			

(b) ATR_{CA} tables

ATR_{CA}^{CIC}	t	f	a
t	1	0	0
f	0	0	0
c	0	0	0

ATR_{CA}^{CCA}	t	f	a
t	1	0	0
f	0	0	0
c	0	0	0

ATR_{CA}^{PL}	t	f	a
t	1	0	0
f	0	0	0
c	0	0	0

t=terminated, f=failed, c=cancelled

After the failure of an activity, the recovery process can be initialized by an alternative dependency that activates another activity, which is located through a related coherent point, to resume instance execution. Table 4 describes the statistical log rules that enable us to discover the alternative dependencies related to an activity A_i using ITR_{A_i}. These dependencies are deduced if we observe a positive entry between the event reporting A_i failure and the event reporting A_j execution in ITR_{A_i}. According to the localization of A_j, we identify two types of alternative dependencies: a forward (respectively backward) alternative if A_j is after (respectively before) A_i in the discovered control flow. If A_j is is not in the discovered control flow then we mine an alternative forward (respectively backward) if there is an activity A_k in the control flow such as A_j is executed before A_k in ITR_{A_i} and A_k is after (respectively before) A_i in the control flow.

For instance in our motivating example, we can deduce from table 3.a that we have a backward alternative dependency from CA to DBC (ITR_{CA} ((DBC, terminated), (CA, failed)) = 1 $\wedge$ ITR_{CA} ((CIC, terminated), (DBC, activate)) = 1 $\wedge$ $SCfT(CA, CIC) > 0$). Besides, we can observe the execution of a "new" activity (*i.e, DBC*) which does not exist in the discovered control flow. Indeed, the backward or forward recovery can also entail compensating the already terminated activities through "new" activities which semantically undo the failed activity [18].

An activity failure can cause a cancellation (non-regular or abnormal end) of one or more active activities. Table 4 describes the statistical log rules that specifies rules to discover the cancellation dependencies of an activity A_i based on ITR_{A_i}. These dependencies are deduced if we observe a positive entry between the event reporting A_i failure and the event reporting the cancellation of A_j in ITR_{A_i}.

Table 4. Statistical log properties of inter-activity transactional dependencies

Dependencies	Rules
$depAlt(A_i, A_j)$	ITR_{A_i} ((A_j, terminated), (A_i, failed)) $\neq 0$ ✓**Backward alternative:** $SCfT(A_i, A_j) > 0 \vee \exists A_k \mid SCfT(A_i, A_k) > 0 \wedge$ ITR_{Ai} ((A_k, terminated), (A_j, failed))> 0 ✓**Forward alternative:** $SCfT(A_j, A_i) > 0 \vee \exists A_k \mid SCfT(A_k, A_i) > 0 \wedge$ ITR_{Ai} ((A_k, terminated), (A_j, failed))> 0
$depCnl(A_i, A_j)$	ITR_{A_i} ((A_j, cancelled), (A_i, failed))> 0

3.3 Mining Activities Transactional Properties

The activity transactional properties are discovered through the STrD intra-activity transactional dependencies table ATR (c.f. definition 3). Indeed, if activity act fails, a table ATR_{act}^{A} is built for each A activity executed after the failure of act to capture the internal state dependencies between the events of A. Thus, ATR_{act} extracts from instances logs where act fails the dependencies between the internal events of its following activities. The table 3.b captures the intra-activities transactional dependencies of CIC, CCA and PL after the failure of CA (ATR_{CA}^{CIC}, ATR_{CA}^{CCA}, ATR_{CA}^{PL}). In particular, we observe that CIC could be re-executed after the failure of CA so far it reaches terminated state (ATR_{CA}^{CIC}(c,c)= 1).

Definition 3 (Intra-activities transactional dependencies table)
We denote by ATR_{act}^{A} the Intra-activities transactional dependencies table that reports the A's intra-event dependencies after act failures. These dependencies are extracted from a workflow log projection taking only A events from instances related to act failures. Each entry in ATR_{act}^{A} is an event dependency where for i=1 or i=2 :
$\checkmark$ *(e_i.activity = A;) $\wedge$*
$\checkmark \exists str$: $EventStream; Evti, Evtj$: $Event \in str|$ *(Evtj.activity = act $\wedge$ Evtj.state= failed $\wedge$ Evti.activity = A $\wedge$ Evti.state= e_i.state $\wedge$ Evtj.occurTime < Evti.occurTime).*

An activity a is retriable a^r if it always finishes successfully after a finished number of activations. This property defines a recovery mechanism which is generally used if the failure of the retriable activity is without consequences. In other words, the general effect of its failure does not influence the execution of the other activities. Thus, this type of activity, that we can also call neutral activity or idempotent, can be executed multiple times without consequences. Table 5 describes the statistical log rules that enable us to discover the retriable transactional property of a based on ITR_a. This property is mined if we observe in ATR_a^a an entry equal to 1 between the event reporting the state failed of a and the event reporting the state terminated of a and we also observe in ITR_a an entry equal to 1 between the events failed and terminated of a.

An activity a is pivot a^p if once it terminates without failure, it can not be re-executed, thus its execution effects are persistent. Table 5 describes the statistical log rules that enable to mine the transactional property pivot of a based on ITR_a. This property is mined if we do not observe any ATR^a tables reporting a positive entry between a's terminated state and and a's terminated, failed or cancelled state.

Now using these statistical specifications we can discover activity transactional properties from StrD tables. For instance, we can deduce from table 3.b that the CIC, CCA

Table 5. Statistical log properties of intra-activities transactional dependencies

properties	rules
a^r	$ATR_{a^r}^{a^r}(terminated, failed)=1 \wedge ITR_{a^r}((a^r, terminated, (a^r, failed)) = 1$
a^p	$\nexists act|(act \neq a^p \wedge ATR_{act}^{a^p}("x", terminated) \neq 0 \wedge ("x"= \text{terminated} \vee "x"= \text{failed} \vee "x"= \text{canceled}))$

and PL activities are not pivot. Indeed, these activities are re-executed after reaching a terminated state when CA fails: $(ATR_{CA}^{CIC}(t,t)= ATR_{CA}^{CCA}(t,t)= ATR_{CA}^{PL}(t,t)= 1)$.

4   Transactional Behavior Re-engineering

In this section, we focus on the correction and the improvement of the transactional behavior of the mined workflow. Basically, we use process mining for Delta Analysis (section 4.2), i.e. to compare the real process, represented by the discovered workflow, to the initially designed process. By comparing the initially designed process to the discovered process, the discrepancies between these two models can be detected and used to improve, in particular, the transactional behavior. We propose, thereafter, a set of rules that allow to correct or to remove, if necessary, any erroneous or omittable transactional behavior and thus to reduce the number of tries to resume workflow execution after an activity fails. By erroneous or useless transactional behaviors, we mean initially designed transactional flow which is not necessary or does not coincide with the execution. These transactional behaviors can simply be expensive and a cause for additional errors. The correction and improvement rules (section 4.3) depend on transactional consistency semantics (section 4.1). The transactional behavior specifications must respect these semantic rules linking the control with the transactional flow.

4.1   Semantic Relations Within Recovery Mechanisms

The specification of the recovery mechanisms defined through the transactional behavior should respect rules which are partially dependent on the control flow to ensure reliable execution. Concretely, these semantic relations are described in Rule 1 and are inspired from [19] which specifies and proves the potential transactional dependencies of workflow patterns. The first rule expresses the fact that a cancellation dependence can occur only between concurrent activities. Whereas the second rule specifies the localisation of the coherent point for some patterns. The third rule specifies which activities should be recoverable. The last rule is a consequence of the persistent feature of the pivot activity. These relations are independently common to all transactional workflows applications. These relations can be enriched to include other rules dependent on business semantics. Moreover, our transactional model can be extended. Indeed, further transactional properties or transactional dependencies can be added which consequently will restructure these semantic relations to integrate these modifications.

RULE 1 (SEMANTIC RELATIONS)
- ✓ **R1:** For the *XOR-split*, *XOR-join* and *sequence* patterns:
  No cancellation dependency in these patterns;
- ✓ **R2:** For the *AND-join* and the *M-out-of-N* patterns:
  No coherent point located in parallel activities;
- ✓ **R3:** Except parallel flow outside *AND* or *XOR* patterns compositions:
  All activities should be recoverable in case of failure;
- ✓ **R4:** For the *sequence, AND-split, XOR-split, OR-split, XOR-join*:
  No backward recovery for pivot activities.

4.2   Delta Analysis

At run time users can deviate from the initially designed workflow. Delta Analysis (Figure 3) between the initially designed and the discovered process allow us to monitor these deviations. The analysis of these deviations is fundamental for a new re-engineering phase. Indeed, a deviation can become a current practice rather than to be a rare exception. In this case, the correction and the reliability of the initially designed process are uncertain and a re-engineering phase based on the discrepancies between the two models is required.

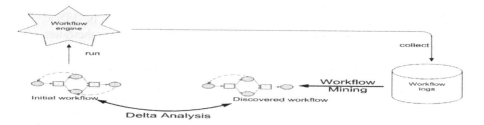

Fig. 3. Delta analyse for workflow re-engineering

Independently of the chosen comparison technique [20,21], a delta analysis process aims to detect the discrepancies between the discovered and the initial models. These discrepancies can be exploited: (option 1) to motivate the process users to be closer to the initially designed process if the discrepancies do not express a real evolution or (option 2) to correct and improve the process model to be as close as possible to the "execution" reality. We propose a set of rules to correct and improve the transactional behavior according to option 2. These rules respect the semantic relations between the transactional flow and the control flow as described in Rule 1. We note a_{nt} the transactional behavior of the activity a at the initial design phase. a_{dcvr} indicates the discovered transactional behavior of a. And, a_{cr} indicates the corrected transactional behavior or improved a.

4.3   Correcting and Improving the Transactional Behavior

The correction rules (Rule 2) allow to remove the initially designed recovery mechanisms which are not in the discovered workflow. These erroneous mechanisms can be expensive for the WfMS which should provide the necessary means to support them. The first three rules, witch are inspired from the semantic relation **R3**, express that if we discover that an activity never fails then any recovery mechanisms initially designed (for instance, retriable property, alternative or cancellation dependencies) are not necessary and should be removed. The last rule **S4** is inspired from the semantic relation **R1** indicating that suspension or cancellation dependencies can exist only between parallel activities. Thus, if we discover that two non-concurrent activities (e.g. activities belonging to the parallel flows of the *M-out-of-N* or *OR-split* patterns, due to their partial concurrent behavior) then we should suppress this transactional behavior.

For instance, if you discover in our motivating example that CCA never fails it indicates a discrepancy between the discovered model and the initially designed model. Then we can conclude: (i) by applying **S1**, there is no need to specify CCA as recoverable and thus, we suppress the alternative transactional dependency between CCA and CRS, (ii) by applying **S2**, there is no need to cancel CIC when CCA fails. Thus, we suppress the cancellation dependency between CIC and VSC. Figure 4 shows these corrections on our motivating example crossed out.

RULE 2 (SUPPRESSING OMITTABLE TRANSACTIONAL BEHAVIORS)
✓**S1:** $\nexists ITR_{a_{dc}} \wedge a_{nt}^r \Rightarrow a_{cr}^{\not{q}}$;
✓**S2:** $\nexists ITR_{a_{dc}} \wedge depAlt(a_{nt}, b_{nt}) \Rightarrow depAlt(a_{cr}, b_{cr}) =$ false
✓**S3:** $\nexists ITR_{a_{dc}} \wedge depCnl(a, b) \Rightarrow depCnl(a_{cr}, b_{cr}) =$ false
✓**S4:** $SCfT(b_{dc}, a_{dc}) \geq 0 \wedge depSus(a_{nt}, b_{nt}) =$true$\Rightarrow depSus(a_{cr}, b_{cr}) =$ false

---

We also define rules proposing suggestions of recovery mechanisms for discovered activities that failed without an initially designed recovery mechanisms (Rule 3). However, not every failed activity does necessarily require a recovery mechanism. The choice of specifying a recovery mechanism depends on a designers business choice. However, respecting **R3** in Rule 1 we have to guarantee that if we discover that an initially designed activity can fail and induce the instance failure, a recovery mechanism for this activity has to be defined.

RULE 3 (SUGGESTING ADDITIONAL RECOVERY MECHANISMS)
For each transactional activity $a \in Wf$ a transactional workflow, which is not initially recoverable but we discover that it fails, we propose the following suggestions as recovery mechanism:
✓**A1.1:** a is neutral $\Rightarrow a_{cr}^r$
✓**A1.2:** (b is a's coherent point) $\wedge SCfT(b_{dc}, a_{dc}) > 0 \Rightarrow depAlt(a_{cr}, b_{cr}) =$ true
✓**A1.3:** (b is a's coherent point)$\wedge SCfT(a_{dc}, b_{dc}) \geq 0 \wedge b_{dc}^{\not{q}} \Rightarrow depAlt(a_{cr}, b_{cr}) =$true
✓**A2:** $SCfT(a_{dc}, b_{dc}) = -1 \Rightarrow depAnl(a_{cr}, b_{cr}) =$ true

---

The rules **A1.1**, **A1.2** and **A1.3** suggest three different propositions specifying recovery mechanisms for discovered failed activity. The rule **A1.1** proposes to specify the retriable property as recovery mechanism if the activity is neutral. The rule **A1.2** suggests a forward alternative dependency in case we have an activity representing a coherent point located after the failed activity. Rule **A1.2** respects the semantic rule **R2** that indicates that the coherent point should not be in concurrence with the failed activity. The rule **A1.3** suggests an alternative backward dependency in case we have an activity representing a coherent point located before the failed activity. This rule **A1.3** respects the semantic rule **R2** that indicates that there are no pivot activities between the coherent point and the failed activity. We note that the specification of the coherent points and their localizations depend on the designer's choices. Finally, **A2** rule suggests a transactional cancellation dependencies from the discovered failed activities to its concurrent activities respecting the semantic rule **R1**.

For instance, if you discover in our workflow example the fact that VD can fail. This induces a discrepancy between the discovered model and the initially designed model which indicates that VD never fails. If you suppose that CIC is not neutral, we can suggest: (i) by applying **A1.2**, a forward alternative recovery where the coherent point is located on CA. (ii) otherwise by applying **A1.3**, we can suggest to specify a backward recovery to CRS, if the concurrent activities CCA and PL are not pivot. Finally, by applying **A2**, we can suggest to specify cancellation dependencies between CIC and (CCA and PL). Figure 4 shows these suggestions on our motivating example in green. These suggestions could be entirely or partially applied w.r.t to a designer's business choices.

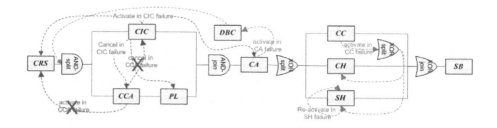

Fig. 4. Correcting and improving transactional flow

5   Discussion

In this paper we have presented an original approach to ensure reliable workflow transactional behavior. Different from previous works, our approach starts from effective executions, while previous works use only specification properties which only reflect the designer's assumptions. Our approach allows to address process evolution requirements and to correct potential design errors after runtime. Indeed, our approach starts from workflow logs and uses a set of mining techniques to discover the workflow control flow and the workflow transactional behavior. Then, based on Delta Analysis between the initially designed model and the discovered workflow, we use a set of rules to improve its recovery mechanisms.

So far previous works in workflow mining seem to focus on control flow mining perspectives. Van der Aalst et al. proposes in [5] an exhaustive survey. Compared to existing works, our control flow mining approach dynamically deals with concurrent behavior through concurrent windows that only requires additional calculus where it is needed. Furthermore, we give an original control flow mining approach through the discovery of workflow patterns which are well-known structures giving an abstract description of a recurrent class of control flow interactions. Besides, we propose a set of control flow mining rules that are characterized by a workflow pattern discovery. These rules proceed through a local log analysis that allow us to correctly recover partial results even if we have only fractions of a workflow log.

A first discussion related to the workflow recovery issue was presented in [22]. The necessity of workflow recovery concepts was partly addressed in [10]. Especially, the concept of business transactions, introduced in [23], describes some basic workflow recovery ideas in detail. However, to the best of our knowledge, there are practically no approaches in workflow mining that address the issue of failure handling and recovery, except our works [24,17] which proposes techniques for discovering workflow transactional behaviour. This paper may be seen as a first step in this area. Particulary there are only few research activities in process re-engineering based on process logs analysis. We can mention for example, recent work of van der Aalst et al. [25] for retrospective checks of security violations which shows how a specific mining algorithm can be used to support intrusion detection. In the same context, Rozinat et al. [26] are interested in the potential use of log analysis to measure process alignments, i.e. to compare the execution behavior with the intended behavior. However, this work does not describe how to use the results of this process alignment to improve or correct the process. In addition, there is other work related to process performance analysis for dynamic execution checking [27].

We have implemented our workflow patterns mining approach as a plug-in within the ProM framework which is a process mining plugable environment [17]. We are also implementing our transactional flow mining and re-engineering in our WorkflowMiner prototype. We have already implemented the control flow mining in this prototype. Due to the lack of space we can refer to [28] for a thorough description on the WorkflowMiner architecture. In our future work we are trying to enhance workflow recovery mining techniques by enriching workflow logs and extracting data flow dependencies. We are also interested in applying process mining techniques in composite Web services [29].

References

1. ter Hofstede, A.H.M., Orlowska, M.E., Rajapakse, J.: Verification problems in conceptual workflow specifications. Data Knowl. Eng. 24(3), 239–256 (1998)
2. van der Aalst, W.M.P.: The Application of Petri Nets to Workflow Management. The Journal of Circuits, Systems and Computers 8(1), 21–66 (1998)
3. Adam, N.R., Atluri, V., Huang, W.-K.: Modeling and analysis of workflows using petri nets. J. Intell. Inf. Syst. 10(2), 131–158 (1998)
4. Eder, J., Liebhart, W.: Workflow recovery. In: Conference on Cooperative Information Systems, pp. 124–134 (1996)
5. van der Aalst, W.M.P., van Dongen, B.F.: Workflow mining: A survey of issues and approaches. In: Data and Knowledge Engineering (2003)
6. Eder, J., Olivotto, G.E., Gruber, W.: A data warehouse for workflow logs. In: Proceedings of the First International Conference on Engineering and Deployment of Cooperative Information Systems, pp. 1–15. Springer, Heidelberg (2002)
7. zur Muehlen, M.: Process-driven management information systems - combining data warehouses and workflow technology. In: Gavish, B. (ed.) Proceedings of the 4th International Conference on Electronic Commerce Research (ICECR-4), Dallas (TX), pp. 550–566. Southern Methodist University (2001)
8. Cook, J.E., Wolf, A.L.: Event-based detection of concurrency. In: Proceedings of the 6th ACM SIGSOFT international symposium on Foundations of software engineering, pp. 35–45. ACM Press, New York (1998)

9. Gaaloul, W.: La Découverte de Workflow Transactionnel pour la Fiabilisation des Exécutions. Phd thesis, Université Henri Poincaré - Nancy 1, LORIA(November 3, 2006)
10. Georgakopoulos, D., Hornick, M., Sheth, A.: An overview of workflow management: from process modeling to workflow automation infrastructure. Distrib. Parallel Databases 3(2), 119–153 (1995)
11. Sheth, A., Rusinkiewicz, M.: On transactional workflows. Special Issue on Workflow and Extended Transaction Systems IEEE Computer Society (1993)
12. Elmagarmid, A.K.: Database transaction models for advanced applications. Morgan Kaufmann Publishers Inc, San Francisco (1992)
13. van der Aalst, W.M.P., Barros, A.P., ter Hofstede, A.H.M., Kiepuszewski, B.: Advanced Workflow Patterns. In: Scheuermann, P., Etzion, O. (eds.) CoopIS 2000. LNCS, vol. 1901, pp. 18–29. Springer, Heidelberg (2000)
14. Elmagarmid, A., Leu, Y., Litwin, W.: A multidatabase transaction model for interbase. In: Proceedings of the sixteenth international conference on Very large databases, pp. 507–518. Morgan Kaufmann Publishers Inc, San Francisco (1990)
15. Du, W., Davis, J., Shan, M.-C.: Flexible specification of workflow compensation scopes. In: Proceedings of the international ACM SIGGROUP conference on Supporting group work: the integration challenge, pp. 309–316. ACM Press, New York (1997)
16. Gaaloul, W., Baïna, K., Godart, C.: Towards mining structural workflow patterns. In: Andersen, K.V., Debenham, J.K., Wagner, R. (eds.) DEXA. LNCS, vol. 3588, pp. 24–33. Springer, Heidelberg (2005)
17. Gaaloul, W., Godart, C.: A workflow mining tool based on logs statistical analysis. In: Maurer, F., Ruhe, G. (eds.) SEKE, pp. 37–44 (2006)
18. Kiepuszewski, B., Muhlberger, R., Orlowska, M.E.: Flowback: providing backward recovery for workflow management systems. In: Proceedings of the 1998 ACM SIGMOD international conference on Management of data, pp. 555–557. ACM Press, New York (1998)
19. Bhiri, S., Perrin, O., Godart, C.: Extending workflow patterns with transactional dependencies to define reliable composite web services. In: AICT/ICIW, p. 145. IEEE Computer Society (2006)
20. van der Aalst, W.M.P.: Exterminating the dynamic change bug: A concrete approach to support workflow change. Information Systems Frontiers 3(3), 297–317 (2001)
21. Basten, T., van der Aalst, W.M.P.: Inheritance of behavior. J. Log. Algebr. Program. 47(2), 47–145 (2001)
22. Jin, W.W., Rusinkiewicz, M., Ness, L., Sheth, A.: Concurrency control and recovery of multidatabase work flows in telecommunication applications. In: Proceedings of the 1993 ACM SIGMOD international conference on Management of data, pp. 456–459. ACM Press, New York (1993)
23. Leymann, F.: Supporting business transactions via partial backward recovery in workflow management systems. In: Proceedings of BTW 1995, pp. 51–70. Springer, Heidelberg (1995)
24. Gaaloul, W., Bhiri, S., Godart, C.: Discovering workflow transactional behaviour event-based log. In: Meersman, R., Tari, Z. (eds.) OTM 2004. LNCS, vol. 3290, Springer, Heidelberg (2004)
25. van der Aalst, W.M.P., de Medeiros, A.K.A.: Process mining and security: Detecting anomalous process executions and checking process conformance. Electr. Notes Theor. Comput. Sci. 121, 3–21 (2005)
26. Rozinat, A., van der Aalst, W.M.P.: Conformance testing: Measuring the fit and appropriateness of event logs and process models. In: Business Process Management Workshops, pp. 163–176 (2005)
27. Grigori, D., Casati, F., Castellanos, M., Dayal, U., Sayal, M., Shan, M.-C.: Business process intelligence. Comput. Ind. 53(3), 321–343 (2004)

28. Baïna, K., Gaaloul, W., ElKhattabi, R., Mouhou, A.: A new workflow patterns and performance analysis tool. In: Dubois, E., Pohl, K. (eds.) CAiSE 2006. LNCS, vol. 4001, Springer, Heidelberg (2006)
29. Rouached, M., Gaaloul, W., van der Aalst, W.M.P., Bhiri, S., Godart, C.: Web service mining and verification of properties: An approach based on event calculus. In: Meersman, R., Tari, Z. (eds.) OTM 2006. LNCS, vol. 4275, pp. 408–425. Springer, Heidelberg (2006)

Cross: An OWL Wrapper for Reasoning on Relational Databases

Pierre-Antoine Champin[1], Geert-Jan Houben[2], and Philippe Thiran[3]

[1] LIRIS, Université Claude Bernard Lyon 1
`pchampin@liris.cnrs.fr`
[2] Vrije Universiteit Brussel
`Geert-Jan.Houben@vub.ac.be`
[3] Facultés Universitaires Notre-Dame de la Paix, Namur
`pthiran@fundp.ac.be`

Abstract. One of the challenges of the Semantic Web is to integrate the huge amount of information already available on the standard Web, usually stored in relational databases. In this paper, we propose a formalization of a logic model of relational databases, and a transformation of that model into OWL, a Semantic Web language. This transformation is implemented in Cross, as an open-source prototype. We prove a relation between the notion of legal database state and the consistency of the corresponding OWL knowledge base. We then show how that transformation can prove useful to enhance databases, and integrate them in the Semantic Web.

1 Introduction

One of the challenges of the Semantic Web (SW) vision is to integrate, in a machine-consumable form, the huge amount of information already available on the standard Web. The long-term goal is to allow software agents to aggregate information from heterogenous sources in order to handle complex user queries. However, a great amount of the information available on the web is stored in relational databases (RDBs). From that perspective, the Semantic Web can benefit from the abundant literature on reverse engineering [1] and data integration [2] in the field of RDBs. On the other hand, SW technologies shed a new light on those classical problems, and provide new tools and methodologies, but also new challenges to the field.

Enhancing RDBs with semantically rich languages is indeed not a new idea: description logics (DLs), that happen to be one of the foundations of SW technologies, have already been considered as a unifying formalism for conceptual data models [3,4]. However, the proposed approaches were not deployed on large-scale legacy databases, notably because conceptual models of RDBs are not always available in practice. On the other hand, there have been some efforts to bridge the gap between RDBs and SW languages, but paradoxically, they have

C. Parent et al. (Eds.): ER 2007, LNCS 4801, pp. 502–517, 2007.
© Springer-Verlag Berlin Heidelberg 2007

been neglecting the reasoning issue, either focusing on the syntactical level [5] or undecidable formalisms [6].

Our goal is to draw experience from all those works to provide a sound and practical approach to integrating RDBs in the SW. That approach will make it possible 1/ to use SW technologies and tools for the benefit of database engineering and re-engineering, and 2/ to smoothly integrate legacy RDBs in the Semantic Web, possibly to perform data integration with other RDBs, native RDF data sources, or even Web Services.

In this paper, we formally define an abstraction of RDBs, focusing on their logical model, and show how this fits into OWL, an SW language based on description logics. More precisely, we prove a relation between the notion of *legal database state* and the consistency of the corresponding OWL knowledge base. We then present Cross, an open-source implementation of our approach, which introduces the notion of *semantic values*.

1.1   Running Example

Along the paper, we will use as a running example the database schema described in Figure 1, which is a subset of the information system of an imaginary university. That schema describes students, the courses they attend, and their scholarship if any. It also represents the prerequisites between courses, and which courses involve practical work (practical courses).

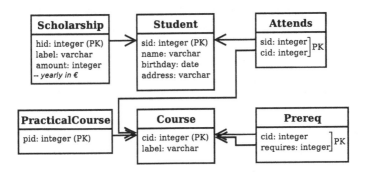

Fig. 1. An example RDB schema. PK represent primary keys. Arrows represent foreign keys.

1.2   Structure of the Paper

In Section 2 we motivate our work by a number of use cases. We then give a formal description of OWL in Section 3. Section 4 describes our formalization of RDBs logical model, that we call the ODBC model. In Section 5, we define a correspondence between both models and prove the equivalence between ODBC weak legality and OWL consistency. We present in Section 6 Cross, a working implementation of our approach. Finally we conclude and discuss some further work.

2   Motivations

OWL [7] is a knowledge representation language based on description logics and is a recomendation of the W3C. It has a well-defined formal semantics, that we will recap in Section 3. Its high expressive power allows complex inferences to be performed on OWL knowledge bases, hence the relevance of mapping relational databases to OWL. More precisely, we consider three interesting directions for such reasoning: schema reasoning and enriching, querying the data, and ensuring interoperability.

Schema reasoning and enriching. As suggested by [3], converting models into description logics brings the power of DL inference to those models, as well as additional expressiveness. The first interest of our approach w.r.t. RDBs is indeed to allow to reason about relational schemas[1], and discover implicit relations between their tables or columns.

But beyond reasoning about the schemas, mapping relational schemas to OWL allows to express *additional* constraints about them. Such constraints sometimes fit in the relational model but were omitted at design time; one can add for example in our running example axioms stating that all students must have a name. Sometimes, on the other hand, the constraints do not fit in the relational model (e.g. like cardinality constraints): we can state for example that no more than 30 students can attend a given course. We are aware that most RDB management systems (RDBMSs) allow to express that kind of constraint (e.g. using the CHECK or TRIGGER keywords from SQL), but this type of constraint is expressed in an imperative form, which makes it suited for consistency checking but unfortunately not for reasoning.

Querying the data. What we just said about the schema is, in theory, also true for the data: OWL inference engines do provide so-called $\mathcal{A}$-box reasoning services, and even elaborate query languages like SPARQL [8]. In practice, however, this is only possible with knowledge bases of a modest size, far below the size of the average corporate database. The main reason is that current inference engines must load the whole knowledge base in memory in order to reason with it. Research is being pursued on the field of distributed reasoning [9] in order to overcome this limitation, but is still at a preliminary stage.

However, we believe that an OWL mapping of the sole schema of an RDB can be used to reason about queries in order to optimize them. We will develop this point in Section 6.3.

---

[1] [3] actually advocate *finite model* reasonning for that purpose. Although OWL reasonners currently do not provide that kind of reasonning, we believe that "classical" OWL reasonning can nevertheless prove useful.

Interoperability. Ontologies are widely recognized as a means to achieve inter-operability between heterogeneous sources of data [10]. A wealth of approaches has hence been proposed to map several relational schemas to a global ontology. However, by first translating *each* relational schema into an ontology, we also make a number of recent work on ontology aligning [11] applicable to legacy relational databases, with the opportunity to take advantage of additional knowledge enriching the schema.

3   OWL Semantics and Inferences

We recap in this section the formal semantics of OWL [7], a recommendation of the W3C to express ontologies on the SW, and present the inference services that it enables[2]. Although OWL is usually represented in XML, we favor in this paper a more compact notation which common in the DL literature [12].

Table 1. OWL constructors syntax and semantics. C and D denote concept expressions; P denotes a property symbol; n denotes a natural integer; $\#s$ denotes the cardinality of set s.

Class constructors	Syntax	Semantics
Predefined classes	$\top$	$\Delta^{\mathcal{I}}$
	$\bot$	$\emptyset$
Set operators	$C \sqcup D$	$C^{\mathcal{I}} \cup D^{\mathcal{I}}$
	$C \sqcap D$	$C^{\mathcal{I}} \cap D^{\mathcal{I}}$
	$\neg C$	$\Delta^{\mathcal{I}} \setminus C^{\mathcal{I}}$
Quantifiers	$\exists P.C$	$\{x \mid \exists (x,y) \in P^{\mathcal{I}}, y \in C^{\mathcal{I}}\}$
	$\forall P.C$	$\{x \mid \forall (x,y) \in P^{\mathcal{I}}, y \in C^{\mathcal{I}}\}$
Cardinality restriction	$(\leq n\, P)$	$\{x \mid \#\{y \mid (x,y) \in P^{\mathcal{I}}\} \leq n\}$
	$(\geq n\, P)$	$\{x \mid \#\{y \mid (x,y) \in P^{\mathcal{I}}\} \geq n\}$
	$(= n\, P)$	$\{x \mid \#\{y \mid (x,y) \in P^{\mathcal{I}}\} = n\}$
Property constructors	Syntax	Semantics
Property inverse	P^{-}	$\{(x,y) \mid (y,x) \in P^{\mathcal{I}}\}$

In OWL, a domain of interest is modeled as a set of individuals, classes denoting sets of individuals, and properties denoting binary relationships between individuals. OWL provides a number of constructors allowing to define complex classes and properties from a set of atomic classes and properties (see table 1). Features of the domain of interest are represented in an OWL knowledge base, defined hereafter.

---

[2] Actually, OWL has three dialects (called species): Lite, DL and Full. Only the first two of them are description logics. OWL-Full, on the other hand has an expressiveness beyond the one of DLs, but no decidable inference algorithm. In the following, mentions to OWL will only refer to its first two species. Note also that we omit on purpose some features of OWL which are not relevant to this work.

Definition 1. *An OWL knowledge base $\mathcal{O}$ is defined by $\langle \mathcal{L}_\mathcal{O}, \mathcal{T}_\mathcal{O}, \mathcal{A}_\mathcal{O} \rangle$, where:*

- *$\mathcal{L}_\mathcal{O}$ is a finite alphabet partitioned into a set $\mathcal{C}_\mathcal{O}$ of class symbols, a set $\mathcal{P}_\mathcal{O}$ of property symbols and a set $\mathcal{O}_\mathcal{O}$ of individual symbols.*
- *$\mathcal{T}_\mathcal{O}$ is a set of axioms as described in table 2, equivalent to the $\mathcal{T}$-box in the DL literature.*
- *$\mathcal{A}_\mathcal{O}$ is a set of facts as described in table 2, equivalent to the $\mathcal{A}$-box in the DL literature.*

Table 2. Syntax and semantics for OWL axioms and facts. C and D denote concept expressions; P and Q denote property expressions; i and j denote individual symbols; S denote a set of individual symbols.

	Syntax	Semantics
Class axioms	$C \sqsubseteq D$	$C^\mathcal{I} \subseteq D^\mathcal{I}$
Property axioms	$P \sqsubseteq Q$	$P^\mathcal{I} \subseteq Q^\mathcal{I}$
	transitive(P)	$\forall x, y, z \in \Delta^\mathcal{I}, (x,y) \in P^\mathcal{I} \wedge (y,z) \in P^\mathcal{I}$ $\implies (x,z) \in P^\mathcal{I}$
Facts	$i : C$	$i^\mathcal{I} \in C^\mathcal{I}$
	$\langle i, j \rangle : P$	$(i^\mathcal{I}, j^\mathcal{I}) \in P^\mathcal{I}$
	$i = j$	$i^\mathcal{I} = j^\mathcal{I}$
	$i \neq j$	$i^\mathcal{I} \neq j^\mathcal{I}$
	all-different(S)	$\forall i \neq j \in S, i^\mathcal{I} \neq j^\mathcal{I}$

The semantics of an OWL knowledge base is defined by means of an interpretation $\mathcal{I} = (\Delta^\mathcal{I}, \cdot^\mathcal{I})$, consisting of an interpretation domain $\Delta^\mathcal{I}$ and an interpretation function $\cdot^\mathcal{I}$. The latter maps every individual symbol i to an element $i^\mathcal{I} \in \Delta^\mathcal{I}$, every class C to a subset $C^\mathcal{I} \subseteq \Delta^\mathcal{I}$, every property P to a relation $P^\mathcal{I} \subseteq \Delta^\mathcal{I} \times \Delta^\mathcal{I}$, while respecting the semantics of constructors as defined in table 1. An interpretation is said to satisfy a statement (axiom or fact) if it verifies the semantics of that statement as defined in table 2. An interpretation satisfying all the statements of a knowledge base $\mathcal{O}$ is said to be a *model* of that knowledge base.

A knowledge base is said to be *consistent* if it has at least one model. An axiom is said to be *entailed* by a knowledge base if every model of that knowledge base satisfies that axiom. A class C is said to be *satisfiable* under a knowledge base if that knowledge base does not entail $C \sqsubseteq \bot$, i.e. if there is at least one model $\mathcal{I}$ such that $C^\mathcal{I}$ is not empty. A class C is said to *subsume* another class D under a knowledge base if that knowledge base entails $D \sqsubseteq C$.

The problems of checking consistency, entailment, satisfiability and subsumption, are provably decidable. Several inference engines are available for OWL; we are using Pellet [13].

4   Formalizing the ODBC Model

In this section, we formalize the schema and data instance of relational databases. Although this kind of formalization is classical for conceptual data models such as the Entity-Relationship model [3,14], it has never been proposed, to the best of our knowledge, for logical data models. This makes former propositions difficult to apply for legacy databases where the conceptual model is not directly available, while logical models are. Of course, such models vary amongst the various RDBMS implementations. Nevertheless, they share a number of common notions, on which we chose to focus, and which makes it possible to port an application from one system to another. Indeed, those notions are captured by standard APIs for accessing arbitrary relational databases; this is why we named our model after one of the most popular such API: ODBC. It is not however limited to that API; other standards such as JDBC provide basically the same abstraction for relational databases, which demonstrates that the common notions they both capture are widely accepted and robust.

In the following, $tuple(S)$ denotes the set of all tuples on S (i.e. finite sequences of elements of S) of any length (including 1); if t is a tuple, $|t|$ is its length, and we note $e \in t$ if e is one of the elements of t.

Definition 2. *An ODBC schema $\mathcal{S}$ is defined by $\langle \mathcal{L}_\mathcal{S}, f_\mathcal{S}^T, f_\mathcal{S}^D, \mathcal{C}_\mathcal{S}^N, f_\mathcal{S}^C, f_\mathcal{S}^{ref} \rangle$, where:*

- *$\mathcal{L}_\mathcal{S}$ is a finite alphabet partitioned into a set $\mathcal{T}_\mathcal{S}$ of table symbols, a set $\mathcal{C}_\mathcal{S}$ of column symbols, a set $\mathcal{U}_\mathcal{S}$ of uniqueness constraint symbols, a set $\mathcal{F}_\mathcal{S}$ of foreign key constraint symbols and a set $\mathcal{D}_\mathcal{S}$ of domain symbols; each domain symbol D has an associated pre-defined basic domain $D^{\mathcal{B}_\mathcal{D}}$. We do not assume the various basic domains to be pairwise disjoint, and we suppose that, given two basic domains d_1 and d_2, the set-relation between them is known (inclusion, disjointness, etc.).*
- *$f_\mathcal{S}^T : \mathcal{C}_\mathcal{S} \cup \mathcal{U}_\mathcal{S} \cup \mathcal{F}_\mathcal{S} \to \mathcal{T}_\mathcal{S}$. Intuitively, each column, uniqueness constraint or foreign key constraint belongs to a unique table.*
- *$f_\mathcal{S}^D : \mathcal{C}_\mathcal{S} \to \mathcal{D}_\mathcal{S}$. Intuitively, each column has an associated datatype.*
- *$\mathcal{C}_\mathcal{S}^N \subseteq \mathcal{C}_\mathcal{S}$ is a subset of the column symbols. Intuitively, it denotes the columns that are required to have a value (marked NOT NULL in SQL schemas).*
- *$f_\mathcal{S}^C : \mathcal{U}_\mathcal{S} \cup \mathcal{F}_\mathcal{S} \to tuple(\mathcal{C}_\mathcal{S})$. Intuitively, each uniqueness constraint and foreign key constraint K applies to an ordered tuple of columns. Those columns must obviously all belong to the same table as K. Formally, it must hold that $\forall c \in f_\mathcal{S}^C(K), f_\mathcal{S}^T(c) = f_\mathcal{S}^T(K)$.*
- *$f_\mathcal{S}^{ref} : \mathcal{F}_\mathcal{S} \to \mathcal{U}_\mathcal{S}$. Intuitively, each foreign key references columns with a uniqueness constraint. It must hold, for every F in $\mathcal{F}_\mathcal{S}$, that it references a uniqueness constraint with the same number of columns, i.e. $|f_\mathcal{S}^C(f_\mathcal{S}^{ref}(F))| = |f_\mathcal{S}^C(F)|$. Note that we assume without loss of generality that the order of the columns in the foreign key matches the order of the columns in the referenced uniqueness constraint.*
- *For each table $T \in \mathcal{T}_\mathcal{S}$, there is at least one uniqueness constraint symbol $U \in \mathcal{U}_\mathcal{S}$ such that $f_\mathcal{S}^T(U) = T$ and $\forall C_i \in f_\mathcal{S}^C(U), C_i \in \mathcal{C}_\mathcal{S}^N$. U is known as the primary key of T.*

About the last point of that definition , we are aware that not all RDBMSs impose the existence of a primary key for every table. However, the use of primary keys is usually considered as good practice and rarely omitted.

Definition 3. *An* ODBC *database state $\mathcal{B}$ corresponding to a schema $\mathcal{S}$ is defined by $\langle \Delta^{\mathcal{B}}, \cdot^{\mathcal{B}} \rangle$ where $\Delta^{\mathcal{B}}$ is a non-empty finite set assumed to be disjoint from all basic domains (and sets of tuples over the basic domains), and $\cdot^{\mathcal{B}}$ is a function mapping:*

- *every domain $D \in \mathcal{D}_{\mathcal{S}}$ to the corresponding basic domain $D^{\mathcal{B}_D}$,*
- *every table symbol $T \in \mathcal{T}_{\mathcal{S}}$ to a subset $T^{\mathcal{B}}$ of $\Delta^{\mathcal{B}}$,*
- *every column symbol $C \in \mathcal{C}_{\mathcal{S}}$ to a relation $C^{\mathcal{B}} \subseteq T_C^{\mathcal{B}} \times \mathcal{V}$ where*
  - *$T_C = f_{\mathcal{S}}^T(C)$ is the table to which C belongs,*
  - *$\mathcal{V} = \bigcup_{D \in \mathcal{D}_{\mathcal{S}}} D^{\mathcal{B}_D}$ is the union of all the basic domains.*

It is furthermore assumed, for every table T, that no two rows have the same values for the columns composing the primary key of T.

Intuitively, $\Delta^{\mathcal{B}}$ can be regarded as the set of objects represented by the database; those objects are typically represented by *table rows* in the database, but a single object may be represented in several tables (i.e. an element $r \in \Delta^{\mathcal{B}}$ may belong to several $T^{\mathcal{B}}$). This allows in particular to take into account *inheritance*, which can be simulated by some patterns in relational schemas, or is even explicitly managed by some RDBMSs. Columns model attributes of those objects, hence they are represented as relations between the set of objects and the basic data domains.

The last sentence of the definition, stating that primary key constraints must be satisfied by *any* database state (rather than legal ones only) may seem misplaced. However, we need rows to be identified in some way, so we assume that this particular constraint os necessarily enforced (which, we already mentioned, is most often the case).

Note that function $\cdot^{\mathcal{B}}$ is not defined over constraint symbols (uniqueness or foreign key); indeed, those symbols do not represent elements of a database state, but merely constraints that must hold between its elements. However, for convenience, we extend the definition of $\cdot^{\mathcal{B}}$ on constraint symbols: for each $K \in \mathcal{U}_{\mathcal{S}} \cup \mathcal{F}_{\mathcal{S}}$, if $T = f_{\mathcal{S}}^T(K)$ and $f_{\mathcal{S}}^C(K) = \langle C_1, \ldots, C_k \rangle$:

$$K^{\mathcal{B}} \doteq \{(r, \langle v_1, \ldots, v_k \rangle) \mid r \in T^{\mathcal{B}}, (r, v_i) \in C_i^{\mathcal{B}}, i \in \{1, \ldots, k\}\}$$

Definition 4. *A database state $\mathcal{B}$ is said to be* legal *for a schema $\mathcal{S}$ if it satisfies the following conditions:*

- *For each $C \in \mathcal{C}_{\mathcal{S}}$*
  - *$C^{\mathcal{B}} \subseteq f_{\mathcal{S}}^T(C)^{\mathcal{B}} \times f_{\mathcal{S}}^D(C)^{\mathcal{B}}$ (range)*
  - *$\forall (r_1, v_1), (r_2, v_2) \in C^{\mathcal{B}}, r_1 = r_2 \implies v_1 = v_2$ (functionality)*
  - *$\forall C \in \mathcal{C}_{\mathcal{S}}^N, \exists r \in f_{\mathcal{S}}^T(C)^{\mathcal{B}} \implies \exists (r, v) \in C^{\mathcal{B}}$ (not null)*
- *For each $U \in \mathcal{U}_{\mathcal{S}}, \forall (r_1, t_1), (r_2, t_2) \in U^{\mathcal{B}}, t_1 = t_2 \implies r_1 = r_2$ (uniqueness)*
- *For each $F \in \mathcal{F}_{\mathcal{S}}, \forall (r, t) \in F^{\mathcal{B}}, \exists (r', t) \in f_{\mathcal{S}}^{ref}(F)^{\mathcal{B}}$ (reference)*

That definition of legality straightforwardly captures the constraints usually enforced by RDBMSs according to the definition of relational schemas. However, it does not have an exact correspondence in OWL (we will explain that in the next section). In the following, we will therefore need a weaker notion of legality, defined thereafter.

Definition 5. *An database state $\mathcal{B}$ is said to be* weakly legal *for a schema $\mathcal{S}$ if it satisfies all the conditions from definition 4, except for the* reference *condition.*

5   From the ODBC Model to OWL

In this section, we propose a correspondence between the ODBC model and the OWL model, and prove the equivalence between weak legality of an ODBC database state and consistency of the corresponding OWL knowledge base.

Definition 6. *Let $\mathcal{S}$ be an ODBC schema. The OWL knowledge base $\psi(\mathcal{S}) = \langle \mathcal{L_O}, \mathcal{T_O}, \mathcal{A_O} \rangle$ is defined as follows.*
  The set $\mathcal{C_O}$ of class symbols contains the following elements:

- *the predefined symbols* Row, *and* Data,
- *for each table symbol $T \in \mathcal{T_S}$, a new class symbol $\psi(T)$,*
- *for each domain symbol $D \in \mathcal{D_S}$, a new class symbol $\psi(D)$.*

The set $\mathcal{P_O}$ of property symbols contains for each symbol $S \in \mathcal{C_S} \cup \mathcal{U_S} \cup \mathcal{F_S}$, a new property symbol $\psi(S)$.
  The set $\mathcal{T_O}$ contains the following axioms:

- *the predefined axioms:*

$$\text{Row} \sqsubseteq \neg\text{Data} \tag{6.1}$$
$$\top \sqsubseteq \text{Row} \sqcup \text{Data} \tag{6.2}$$

- *for each table symbol $T \in \mathcal{T_S}$, the axiom:*

$$\psi(T) \sqsubseteq \text{Row} \tag{6.3}$$

- *for each domain symbol $D \in \mathcal{D_S}$, the axiom:*

$$\psi(D) \sqsubseteq \text{Data} \tag{6.4}$$

- *for each domain symbol $D_1, D_2 \in \mathcal{D_S}$ with $D_1^{\mathcal{B}_D} \subseteq D_2^{\mathcal{B}_D}$, the axiom:*

$$\psi(D_1) \sqsubseteq \psi(D_2) \tag{6.5}$$

- *for each domain symbol $D_1, D_2 \in \mathcal{D_S}$ with $D_1^{\mathcal{B}_D} \cap D_2^{\mathcal{B}_D} = \emptyset$, the axiom:*

$$\psi(D_1) \sqsubseteq \neg\psi(D_2) \tag{6.6}$$

- *for each symbol $S \in \mathcal{C_S} \cup \mathcal{U_S} \cup \mathcal{F_S}$ with $T = f_{\mathcal{S}}^T(S)$, the axioms:*

$$(\geq 1\,\psi(S)) \sqsubseteq \psi(T) \tag{6.7}$$
$$\top \sqsubseteq (\leq 1\,\psi(S)) \tag{6.8}$$

– for each column symbol $C \in \mathcal{C}_S$ with $D = f_S^D(C)$, the axiom:

$$\top \sqsubseteq \forall \psi(C).\psi(D) \tag{6.9}$$

– for each column symbol $C \in \mathcal{C}_S^N$ with $T = f_S^T(C)$, the axiom:

$$\psi(T) \sqsubseteq \exists \psi(C).\top \tag{6.10}$$

– for each symbol $K \in \mathcal{U}_S \cup \mathcal{F}_S$, the axiom:

$$\top \sqsubseteq \forall \psi(K).\mathsf{Data} \tag{6.11}$$

– for each symbol $K \in \mathcal{U}_S \cup \mathcal{F}_S$ with $T = f_S^T(K)$ such that all columns C_i of K are in $\mathcal{C}_S^N$:

$$\psi(T) \sqsubseteq \exists \psi(K).\top \tag{6.12}$$

– for each uniqueness constraint symbol $U \in \mathcal{U}_S$, the axiom:

$$\top \sqsubseteq\; \leq 1\, \psi(U) \tag{6.13}$$

The sets $\mathcal{O}_\mathcal{O}$ of individual symbols and $\mathcal{A}_\mathcal{O}$ of facts are empty.

Intuitively, the transformation ψ maps every table row to an individual of class Row and every data value to an instance of class Data[3]. Tables are mapped to subclasses of Row, while domains are mapped to subclasses of Data. Columns are mapped to functional properties between rows and values. The constraints expressed in the schema are translated into corresponding OWL axioms.

Itis worth noting that, since axioms can not involve a *set* of properties, while relational constraints (uniqueness and foreign key) may involve several columns, ψ also creates a property for every constraint, whose values will be the tuple of values associated to that constraint. In our running example, a row of table *Attends* with values $(sid : 1, cid : 2)$ will e.g. be mapped to an individual with three properties: $\psi(sid)$ with value 1, $\psi(cid)$ with value 2, and $\psi(attends\_fk)$ with value $(1, 2)$.

Definition 7. *Let $\mathcal{B}$ be an ODBC database state corresponding to a schema $\mathcal{S}$. The OWL knowledge base $\psi(\mathcal{B}) = \langle \mathcal{L}_\mathcal{O}, \mathcal{T}_\mathcal{O}, \mathcal{A}_\mathcal{O} \rangle$ is defined as follows.*

The sets $\mathcal{C}_\mathcal{O}$ of class symbols, $\mathcal{P}_\mathcal{O}$ of property symbols and $\mathcal{T}_\mathcal{O}$ of axioms are defined according to $\psi(\mathcal{S})$ (see definition 6).

The set $\mathcal{O}_\mathcal{O}$ of individual symbols contains the following elements:

– *for each $r \in \Delta^\mathcal{B}$, a new individual symbol $\psi(r)$,*
– *for each $v \in \bigcup_{S \in \mathcal{C}_S \cup \mathcal{U}_S \cup \mathcal{F}_S} S^{\mathcal{B}_D}$, a new individual symbol $\psi(v)$,*

---

[3] We represent data values with OWL instances rather than concrete values (literals) because only the former allow to capture the semantics of a key (inverse-functional properties). See [15] for a discussion on that issue.

The set $\mathcal{A}_\mathcal{O}$ contains the following facts:

— *for* $V = \{\psi(v) \mid (r, v) \in \bigcup_{S \in \mathcal{C}_\mathcal{S} \cup \mathcal{U}_\mathcal{S} \cup \mathcal{F}_\mathcal{S}} S^{\mathcal{B}_\mathcal{D}}\}$,

$$\text{all-different}(V) \tag{7.1}$$

— *for each* $T \in \mathcal{T}_\mathcal{S}$, *for each* $r \in T^\mathcal{B}$,

$$\psi(r) : \psi(T) \tag{7.2}$$

— *for each* $S \in \mathcal{C}_\mathcal{S} \cup \mathcal{U}_\mathcal{S} \cup \mathcal{F}_\mathcal{S}$, *for each* $(r, v) \in S^\mathcal{B}$,

$$\langle \psi(r), \psi(v) \rangle : \psi(S) \tag{7.3}$$

— *for each* $S \in \mathcal{C}_\mathcal{S} \cup \mathcal{U}_\mathcal{S} \cup \mathcal{F}_\mathcal{S}$, *for each* $r \in f_\mathcal{S}^T(S)^\mathcal{B}$ *such that* $\nexists (r, v) \in S^\mathcal{B}$:

$$\psi(r) : (\leq 0\, \psi(S)) \tag{7.4}$$

— *for each* $v \in \bigcup_{C \in \mathcal{C}_\mathcal{S}} C^{\mathcal{B}_\mathcal{D}}$, *for each* $D \in \mathcal{D}_\mathcal{S}$, *if* $v \in D^{\mathcal{B}_\mathcal{D}}$,

$$\psi(v) : \psi(D) \tag{7.5}$$

else:

$$\psi(v) : \neg\psi(D) \tag{7.6}$$

Theorem 1. *Let $\mathcal{B}$ be an ODBC database state corresponding to a schema $\mathcal{S}$. The corresponding OWL knowledge base $\psi(\mathcal{B})$ has a model if and only if $\mathcal{B}$ is weakly legal for $\mathcal{S}$.*

The proof of this theorem is not included because of space limitation. It can be found in [16].

Limitation of the theorem. We now discuss and explain the reason of theorem 1 applying only to *weakly* legal database states, rather than strongly legal ones. We recall that a weakly legal state is not required to satisfy the "reference" constraint, i.e. that it may contain foreign keys pointing to non-existent rows. One may notice that the translation ψ of an ODBC schema into an OWL knowledge base contains no axiom about the foreign keys; it is tempting to believe that that limitation of the theorem would be alleviated by the addition of the following axiom, for all $F \in \mathcal{F}_\mathcal{S}$:

$$\top \sqsubseteq \forall \psi(F).(\geq 1\, \psi(f_\mathcal{S}^{ref}(F))^-)) \tag{7.7}$$

which states that every foreign key property must point to the value of *some* row for the corresponding uniqueness constraint. However, that axiom can be validated by $\psi(\mathcal{B})$ even if $\mathcal{B}$ does not satisfy the "reference" condition.

This is due to the fact that foreign key constraints in RDBMSs strongly rely on the so called *closed world assumption*: any information absent from the database is considered false. For example, in the schema given in Figure 1, assume a row in *Scholarship* with value 123 for *hid*, while no row in *Student* has value 123 for *sid*. This is a violation of the foreign key constraint. On the other hand, OWL reasoning is based on the *open world assumption*: any information absent from the knowledge base is considered unknown, neither true nor false. So in our example, the fact that $\mathcal{A}_\mathcal{O}$ does not contain an individual with value 123 for $\psi(sid)$ does *not* mean that such an individual does not exist, and since nothing prevents its existence, there is a model $\mathcal{I}$ of $\psi(\mathcal{B})$ containing that individual, even if it has no corresponding row in $\mathcal{B}$. The closed *versus* open world issue is a well-known difference between database systems and knowledge representation systems, and we will address it in more detail in the next section.

An inverse transformation. Another tempting idea is that, given an ODBC schema $\mathcal{S}$, any OWL knowledge base consistent with $\psi(\mathcal{S})$ would correspond to a weakly legal database state $\mathcal{B}$. This happens to be wrong as well, for two reasons. The first one is again related to the closed *versus* open world issue: a consistent knowledge base may be *underspecified* with regard to the schema. For example, a row may have no explicit value for a column $C \in \mathcal{C}_\mathcal{S}^N$; this is not inconsistent as long as it is not stated either that the row *does not* have any value for C[4].

Another problem comes from the redundancy introduced by ψ in the knowledge base: a uniqueness constraint U spanning two columns C_1 and C_2 is represented by a property of its own $\psi(U)$, independent, in the OWL knowledge base, of $\psi(C_1)$ and $\psi(C_2)$. It is therefore possible for an instance to have a tuple value for $\psi(U)$ different from its values for $\psi(C_1)$ and $\psi(C_2)$, which can of course not be represented by a database state. Furthermore, this makes it possible for two individuals to have different values for $\psi(U)$ even if their values for $\psi(C_1)$ and $\psi(C_2)$ are identical, making them artificially respect the uniqueness constraint. For those two reasons, an inverse transformation ψ^- can not exist in the general case.

6   Cross: An Implementation

In this section, we present Cross, an implementation of our approach presented before. This implementation is an open-source software, available at http://liris.cnrs.fr/~pchampin/dev/cross. We first stress a number of differences between the theoretical model and the actual implementation, and develop the most saillant of them: semantic values. Additionally we show the benefits of using Cross in the motivating use cases described in Section 2.

6.1   Differences to the Theoretical Model

There are three differences between the theoretical model described above and the actual implementation. In the following we describe those differences and explain why they do not affect the validity of theorem 1.

---

[4] A statement made by fact 7.4 for columns with null values in the database state.

The first difference is an effort to reduce the redundancy in the OWL knowledge base. In Section 5, we remarked that transformation ψ creates redundant information by associating to every uniqueness constraint a property which is independent of the properties associated to the columns concerned by that constraint. This is useful for multi-column constraints, because the axioms 6.13 guaranteeing the uniqueness can only apply to a *single* property. On the other hand, for constraints spanning a single column, there is no need for an additional property: the property associated to the column can represent the uniqueness constraint as well, and axiom 6.13 can be applied directly to the column property. This is what the implementation does, and it does the same for properties representing foreign keys. That difference makes definitions 6 and 7 and the proof of theorem 1 a little more complex (they require to treat single-column constraints differently from multi-columns constraints) but not significantly different.

The second difference is that, for the sake of completeness, the implemented transformation includes an axiom similar to axiom 7.7, i.e. forcing foreign keys to point to an existing value. We already explained in the discussion following the proof (Section 5) that this is not sufficient to strengthen the theorem. However it does not weaken it either, because that axiom adds no real constraint to the knowledge box: it demands the existence of an individual that no other axiom generated by our approach prevents from existing. So if the knowledge base without that axiom has a model, then it also has a model with the axiom. The axiom may nevertheless prove useful in the reasoning tasks described in Section 6.3, making explicit a constraint that is actually satisfied by legal database states.

The third difference is about the representation of data. While the transformation presented in Section 5 straightforwardly creates an individual per row and an individual per data value, Cross introduces an intermediate layer of individuals, as illustrated on Figure 2. While individuals of the rightmost layer represent raw data values (in the figure: the number 1, the number 2), individuals of the new intermediate layer represent values in the *context* of a given column. We call them *semantic values*, in the manner of [17]. Indeed, the number 1 must be treated differently when it represents, e.g., a length in meters or a price in euro. In a sense, semantic values can be viewed as reifications of the arcs from the straightforward transformation: they do not provide additional information, but only express the same information in a more detailed fashion (which will prove useful in Section 6.3). As a consequence, theorem 1 still holds for the transformation with semantic values.

6.2 Dealing with Semantic Values

As we saw, Cross creates for each column C two OWL object properties. The first one, noted $\phi_s(C)$, links the individual representing the row (row individual) to the semantic value, while the second one, noted $\phi_d(C)$, links the semantic value to its data value. In the straightforward transformation, $\psi(C)$ captures all the semantics of the column, while that semantics is somewhat split into $\phi_s(C)$ and $\phi_d(C)$. For example, consider column *Scholarship.amount*; values for that

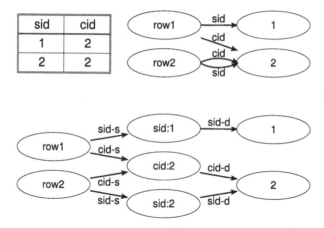

Fig. 2. An extract of table *Attends* (up-left), the straightforward transformation (up-right), and the Cross transformation (down) with semantic values

column represent the yearly amount of money, in Euro, received by the holder of the scholarship. In Cross, we can decide that the semantic value represents the yearly amount of money, independently of the currency; hence $\phi_s(amount)$ links a scholarship to the income it provides yearly, while $\phi_d(amount)$ links an amount of money to its value in Euro (but another property could link the same semantic value to its amount in US Dollars).

Note that our approach, though not incompatible, is different from the one proposed by [17]. The latter is to attach attributes[5] to columns and values in order to make their semantics explicit. According to their model, all values for *Scholarship.amount* would have the attributes (*Periodicity* = 'yearly', *Currency* = 'Euro'). Such elicitation requires of course a precise ontology of column attributes, which is not at all trivial. On the other hand, our approach assumes *a priori* that all columns have a distinct semantics (each column has its own "semantic value space"), and relies on human intervention to state differently, if deemed relevant. With the appropriate OWL axiom, one can indeed state that two columns happen to have the *same* semantics (e.g. two columns representing a yearly amount of money). We believe that this approach is more robust (because it assumes difference by default) and scalable (because it does not require an ontology of column attributes). Of course, should such an ontology be available, it could be used to formally document properties generated by Cross: using OWL annotations, it would be possible with an appropriate vocabulary to state that $\phi_s(amount)$ links to a yearly income as a semantic value, while $\phi_d(amount)$ links to a value in Euro as an integer. We see that the two approaches are actually complementary.

Given two columns C_1 and C_2, stating an equivalence between $\phi_s(C_1)$ and $\phi_s(C_2)$ means that values for the two columns are *commensurable*, i.e. that they

---

[5] The authors call them *properties*; we use the term "attribute" to avoid confusion with OWL properties.

have a common semantics (e.g. an amount of money), but that their values are not necessarily comparable (e.g. in different currencies). On the other hand, stating an equivalence between $\phi_d(C_1)$ and $\phi_d(C_2)$ means that the values are *comparable*, but not necessarily that they have the same semantics (e.g. an income and a price). Let us note that the boundary between ϕ_s and ϕ_d is not as objective as it may seem. For example, we decided above that semantic values for *Scholarship.amount* represent a *yearly* income, and that $\phi_d(amount)$ links it to its value in Euro. But we could as well have decided that the semantic value represents a *periodic* income, and that $\phi_d(amount)$ links it to its yearly value in Euro. That would make semantic values of *amount* commensurable with any other periodic income, whatever its periodicity.

6.3   Use Cases

In this section, we revisit the goals stated in Section 2 and show how Cross contributes to their achievement.

Schema reasoning and enriching. The first interest of our approach is to be able to express additional constraints on the ODBC schema and to reason about them. OWL expressiveness goes beyond the one of SQL, for example, with respect to relationships between classes: specialization, disjointness, or equivalence can easily be expressed in OWL. While some patterns in an ODBC schema can be used to simulate specialization (e.g. the primary key of *PracticalCourse* being a foreign key to *Course*), those patterns can not always be interpreted that way (see as a counterexample *Scholarship* and *Student*). Such specialization can be made explicit either directly ($\psi(PracticalCourse) \sqsubseteq \psi(Course)$) or by using columns ($\phi_s(pid) \sqsubseteq \phi_s(cid)$); the latter is preferable, because it also allows to properly identify the instances of the class[6].

Querying the data. While RDBMSs are usually capable of checking the legality of a database state, the use of an OWL inference engine to check the consistency of the corresponding knowledge base could in theory take into account additional constraints that are not known to the RDBMS. However, we already stressed the fact that it is only feasible for databases of a limited size.

Cross may however prove useful, if not to query the data, to reason about the queries themselves. It has been proved in [18] that some conjunctive queries on an OWL knowledge base can be reduced to a class expression. For that kind of queries, class satisfiability can be checked before executing, to ensure that the query can actually hold results. Furthermore, class subsumption can be used to test query containment, hence to help optimize queries by reusing cached results of containing queries [19]. The originality of using OWL reasoning for this purpose is its ability to take into account additional constraints expressed

---

[6] Provided also that $\phi_d(pid) \sqsubseteq \phi_d(cid)$, i.e. stating that *PracticalCourse* identifiers are special cases of *Course* identifiers. Any practical course with $pid = x$ will be recognized as having $cid = x$ as well. Since *cid* is functional, it will be identified as the course with $cid = x$.

in OWL, that would otherwise have been buried in triggers, CHECK constraints, or application code.

Interoperability. Interoperability has been a primary goal in the development of Cross. We argued that semantic values and the splitting of columns in two OWL properties allow fine grain comparison of column semantics (commensurable, comparable). Hence we believe that they provide a high flexibility for aligning the generated ontology with other ones. Considering an ontology about students and scholarship where US Dollar would be used instead of Euro. Without semantic values, we could only align classes representing scholarships, but not their properties. With semantic values, we can nevertheless state that the OWL property $\phi_s(amount)$ is equivalent to the corresponding property in the other ontology: they indeed bear the same general meaning. On the other hand, the fact that their numeric values can not be compared will be conveyed by the fact that $\phi_d(amount)$ would *not* be aligned.

7   Conclusion and Perspectives

In this paper, we have proposed the ODBC model, a formalization of relational databases focusing on their logic model. We have then presented a transformation of that model into OWL, a DL-based language designed for the Semantic Web. This transformation is implemented by the Cross open-source prototype, which effectively introduces the interesting notion of semantic values. We proved that the knowledge based produced by this transformation is consistent if and only if the source database state is weakly legal (i.e. legal but regarding foreign key constraints). Taking advantage of that result, we have shown how that transformation can prove useful for the purpose of analysing legacy RDBs, enhancing existing RDBs with additional constraints, and integrating them in the SW.

A first direction for further work would be to try and strengthen the theorem, to have an equivalence of OWL consistency with *full* legality, i.e. taking into account foreign keys. This could actually be done by using an expressive feature of OWL (the *oneOf* constructor, not mentioned in this paper), but would possibly make the reasoning intractable. Another solution would be to propose, in a similar way to *finite model* reasoning [3], an algorithm of *closed world* reasoning which would not be allowed to create individuals.

We also want to get more experimental results for the Cross implementation. Preliminary results[7] are encouraging: the transformation of the schema of real database (127 tables, 869 columns, 132 unicity constraints, no foreign key) took around 1.5s; the resulting ontology was loaded in Pellet in about 9s, while reasoning took about 3s. Those results seem reasonable for a quite big schema. We now plan to experiment on the use cases presented in Section 6.3 with that database and a sample of other real databases.

---

[7] On an Intel Core 2, 2.33GHz, with 2GB of memory.

References

1. Hainaut, J., Henrard, J., Hick, J., Roland, D., Englebert, V.: Database Design Recovery. In: Constantopoulos, P., Vassiliou, Y., Mylopoulos, J. (eds.) CAiSE 1996. LNCS, vol. 1080, pp. 272–300. Springer, Heidelberg (1996)
2. Halevy, A.Y., Ives, Z.G., Mork, P., Tatarinov, I.: Piazza: data management infrastructure for semantic web applications. In: WWW'03, pp. 556–567. ACM Press, New York (2003)
3. Calvanese, D., Lenzerini, M., Nardi, D.: Unifying Class-Based Representation Formalisms. J. Artif. Intell. Res (JAIR) 11, 199–240 (1999)
4. Levy, A.Y., Rousset, M.C.: Combining horn rules and description logics in carin. Artif. Intell. 104(1-2), 165–209 (1998)
5. Bizer, C.: D2R MAP - A Database to RDF Mapping Language. In: WWW 2003 (Posters) (2003)
6. de Laborda, C.P., Conrad, S.: Relational.OWL - A Data and Schema Representation Format Based on OWL. In: Hartmann, S., Stumptner, M. (eds.) APCCM 2005, vol. 43 of CRPIT, pp. 89–96. Australian Computer Society (2005)
7. Dean, M., Schreiber, G.: OWL Web Ontology Language. W3C Recommendation (2004), http://www.w3.org/TR/owl-ref/
8. Prud'hommeaux, E., Seaborne, A.: SPARQL Query Language for RDF. W3C Working Draft (2007), http://www.w3.org/TR/rdf-sparql-query/
9. Grau, B.C., Parsia, B., Sirin, E.: Combining OWL ontologies using ϵ-Connections. Web Semantics: Science, Services and Agents on the WWW 4(1), 40–59 (2006)
10. Wache, H., Vögele, T., Visser, U., Stuckenschmidt, H., Schuster, G., Neumann, H., Hübner, S.: Ontology-based integration of information — a survey of existing approaches. In: Stuckenschmidt, H. (ed.) IJCAI–01 Workshop: Ontologies and Information Sharing, pp. 108–117 (2001)
11. Euzenat, J.: An API for ontology alignment. In: McIlraith, S.A., Plexousakis, D., van Harmelen, F. (eds.) ISWC 2004. LNCS, vol. 3298, pp. 698–712. Springer, Heidelberg (2004)
12. The Description Logic Handbook: Theory, Implementation, and Applications. In: Baader, F., et al. (eds.) Description Logic Handbook. Cambridge University Press, Cambridge (2003)
13. Sirin, E., Parsia, B., Grau, B.C., Kalyanpur, A., Katz, Y.: Pellet: A practical owl-dl reasoner. Journal of Web Semantics (to appear)
14. Borgida, A., Lenzerini, M., Rosati, R.: Description Logics for Databases. DLHandbook [12], 462–484
15. Champin, P.A.: Representing data as resources in rdf and owl. In: Arenas, M., Hidders, J. (eds.) EROW 2007. CEUR Workshop Proceedings (January 2007), http://ceur-ws.org/Vol-229/
16. Champin, P.A., Houben, G.J., Thiran, P.: Wrapping relational databases on the semantic web. Technical Report RR-LIRIS- 2007-012 (2007), http://liris.cnrs.fr/publis/?id=2797
17. Sciore, E., Siegel, M., Rosenthal, A.: Using semantic values to facilitate interoperability among heterogeneous information systems. ACM Transaction on Database Systems 19(2), 254–290 (1994)
18. Glimm, B., Horrocks, I., Lutz, C., Sattler, U.: Conjunctive query answering for the description logic $\mathcal{SHIQ}$. In: IJCAI 2007 (2007)
19. Stuckenschmidt, H.: Similarity-based query caching. In: Christiansen, H., Hacid, M.-S., Andreasen, T., Larsen, H.L. (eds.) FQAS 2004. LNCS (LNAI), vol. 3055, pp. 295–306. Springer, Heidelberg (2004)

Augmenting Traditional Conceptual Models to Accommodate XML Structural Constructs

Reema Al-Kamha, David W. Embley, and Stephen W. Liddle

Brigham Young University, Provo, Utah 84602, USA

Abstract. Current graphical notations for XML Schema do not raise the level of abstraction for XML schemata in the same way traditional conceptual models raise the level of abstraction for data schemata. Traditional conceptual models, on the other hand, do not accommodate several XML Schema structures. Thus, there is a need to enrich traditional conceptual models with new XML Schema features. After establishing criteria for XML conceptual modeling, we propose an enrichment to represent the XML features missing in traditional models. We argue that our solution can be adapted generally for traditional conceptual models and show how it can be adapted for two popular conceptual models.

1 Introduction

Many organizations are now storing their data using XML, and XML Schema has become the predominant mechanism for describing valid XML document structures. Moreover, the number of applications that use XML as their native data model have increased. This increases the need for well-designed XML data models and the need for a conceptual model for designing XML schemas.

Commercial tools such as Visual Studio .NET [11], Stylus Studio [16], and XML Spy [15] each support proprietary graphical representations for XML structures. These tools include graphical XML Schema editors that use connected rectangular blocks to present the schema. Although these products provide visual XML Schema editing tools, they do not raise the level of abstraction because they only provide a direct view of an XML Schema document. Thus, these graphical representations do not serve the objective of conceptualizing XML Schema for modeling and design.

In systems modeling and design, traditional conceptual models have proven to be quite successful for graphically representing data at a higher level of abstraction. Conceptual models represent components and their relationships to other components in the system under study in a graphical way, at a conceptual level of understanding. Popular conceptual models that achieve these objectives are ER [4], extended ER models [17], and UML [3,18].

XML Schema, however, introduces a few features that are not explicitly supported in these and similar conceptual models. The most important of these features include the ability to (1) order lists of concepts, (2) choose alternative concepts from among several, (3) declare nested hierarchies of information, (4) specify mixed content, and (5) use content from another data model.

C. Parent et al. (Eds.): ER 2007, LNCS 4801, pp. 518–533, 2007.

This paper makes the following contributions. First, it proposes conceptual representation for XML content structures that are not explicitly present in traditional conceptual models. Second, based on the underlying idea of the proposed representation, it suggests ways to represent missing XML content structures in two of the most popular conceptual models, ER and UML.

We present the details of our contributions as follows. Section 2 lists criteria an XML conceptual model should satisfy. Section 3 describes the structural constructs in XML Schema that are missing in traditional conceptual models. Section 4 explains how we model these features of XML Schema in a modeling language we call Conceptual XML (C-XML). Section 5 compares our proposal with other proposals for ways to extend some traditional conceptual models to represent some XML features and shows how to adapt C-XML representations for traditional conceptual models. Section 6 summarizes and draws conclusions.

2   XML Modeling Criteria

Requirements for XML conceptual models have been presented in [19], [14], and [10]. Some of these requirements cover general goals of conceptual modeling, while others are specific to XML. General requirements include the following:

- *Graphical notation.* Notation should be graphical, user-friendly [10,14,19].
- *Formal foundation.* The model should be defined formally [10,14,19].
- *Structure independence.* The notation should ensure that the basics of the conceptual model are not influenced by the underlying structure, but reflect only the conceptual components of the data [10,14,19].
- *Reflection of the mental model.* The conceptual model must be consistent with a designer's mental conceptualization of objects and their interrelationships [14]. For example, there should be no distinction between element and attribute on the conceptual level, and hierarchies should not be required.
- *N-ary relationship sets.* The conceptual model should be able to represent *n*-ary relationship sets at the conceptual level [10].
- *Views.* It should be possible to transform the model to present multiple user views [10].
- *Logical level mapping.* There should be algorithms for mapping the conceptual modeling constructs to XML Schema [10,19].
- *Constraints.* The conceptual model should support common data constraints such as cardinality and uniqueness constraints [14].
- *Cardinality for all participants.* The hierarchical structure of XML data restricts the specification of cardinality constraints only to nested participants; however, it should be possible to specify cardinality constraints for all participants at the conceptual level [10].
- *Ordering.* The model should be able to order a list of concepts [10,14].
- *Irregular and heterogeneous structure.* The conceptual model should introduce constructs for modeling irregular and heterogeneous structure [10].
- *Document-centric data.* The conceptual model should be able to represent the mixed content and open content that XML Schema provides [10,14,19].

```
1   <?xml version="1.0" encoding="UTF-8"?>
2   <xs:schema xmlns:xs="http://www.w3.org/2001/XMLSchema">
3    <xs:element name="StudentInfo">
4     <xs:complexType>
5      <xs:sequence>
6       <xs:choice>
7        <xs:element name="Name" type="xs:string"/>
8        <xs:sequence>
9         <xs:element name="FirstName" type="xs:string"/>
10        <xs:element name="MiddleName"
             type="xs:string" minOccurs="0" maxOccurs="2"/>
11        <xs:element name="LastName" type="xs:string"/>
12       </xs:sequence>
13      </xs:choice>
14      <xs:sequence maxOccurs="5">
15       <xs:element name="School">
16        <xs:complexType>
17         <xs:sequence>
18          <xs:element name="SchoolName" type="xs:string"/>
19          <xs:element name="SchoolAddress" type="xs:string"/>
20          <xs:element name="SchoolID" type="xs:string"/>
21          <xs:element name="SchoolMascot"
               type="xs:string" minOccurs="0"/>
22         </xs:sequence>
23        </xs:complexType>
24        <xs:key name="schoolKey">
25         <xs:selector xpath=".//School"/>
26         <xs:field xpath="SchoolName"/>
27         <xs:field xpath="SchoolAddress"/>
28        </xs:key>
29        <xs:key name="schoolIDKey">
30         <xs:selector xpath=".//School"/>
31         <xs:field xpath="SchoolID"/>
32        </xs:key>
33       </xs:element>
34       <xs:element name="GraduationDate" minOccurs="0">
35        <xs:complexType>
36         <xs:sequence>
37          <xs:element name="Month" type="xs:string"/>
38          <xs:element name="Year" type="xs:string"/>
39         </xs:sequence>
40        </xs:complexType>
41       </xs:element>
42      </xs:sequence>
43      <xs:element name="RecommendationLetter"
             minOccurs="0" maxOccurs="3">
44       <xs:complexType mixed="true">
45        <xs:all>
46         <xs:element name="ProfessorName"
              type="xs:string"/>
47         <xs:element name="ContactInfo">
48          <xs:complexType>
49           <xs:choice maxOccurs="2">
50            <xs:element name="PhoneNumber"
                 type="xs:string"/>
51            <xs:element name="Email"
                 type="xs:string"/>
52            <xs:element name="Fax"
                 type="xs:string"/>
53           </xs:choice>
54          </xs:complexType>
55         </xs:element>
56        </xs:all>
57       </xs:complexType>
58      </xs:element>
59      <xs:any namespace="##other" minOccurs="0"/>
60     </xs:sequence>
61     <xs:attribute name="StudentNumber"
            type="xs:ID" use="required"/>
62     <xs:anyAttribute namespace="##any"/>
63    </xs:complexType>
64   </xs:element>
65  </xs:schema>
```

Fig. 1. Example of Choice/Sequence Structures in XML Schema

3   Missing Modeling Constructs

We now give an overview of the structural constructs in XML Schema that are missing in traditional conceptual models.

The *sequence* structure specifies that the child concepts declared inside it must appear in an XML document in the order declared. Each ordered child concept can occur zero or more times constrained by *minOccurs* and *maxOccurs* attributes. Likewise, the entire *sequence* itself can occur zero or more times. The default value for both *minOccurs* and *maxOccurs* is always *1*. The *sequence* construct may include several types of child constructs: *element, group, choice, sequence,* and *any*. Lines 15–23 in Figure 1 specify that in a complying XML document an element *School* contains a sequence of required *SchoolName*, *SchoolAddress*, and *SchoolID* elements, and an optional *SchoolMascot* element.

The *choice* structure specifies that for each choice only one of the child concepts declared within it can appear in an XML document. Each child concept in the *choice* can occur zero or more times within the choice constrained by *minOccurs* and *maxOccurs* attributes. Likewise, the entire *choice* itself can occur zero or more times. The default value for *minOccurs* and *maxOccurs* for both the entire choice and the component children is *1*. The *choice* construct may include several types of child constructs: *element, group, choice, sequence,* and *any*. In Figure 1, lines 47–55 specify that in a complying XML document an element *ContactInfo* contains one or two choices, and each choice contains either one *PhoneNumber*, one *Email*, or one *Fax*.

By default, structural constructs in XML Schema can contain child elements, but not text. To allow mixed content (child elements and text), XML Schema provides a *mixed* attribute that can be set to true. In Figure 1, lines 43–58 show an example of mixed content for a complex type. Setting *mixed* to true enables character data to appear between the child elements of *RecommendationLetter* in a complying XML document. Thus, the content of *RecommendationLetter* (abbreviated as RL) may, for example, be "<RL> <ProfessorName> Dr. Jones </ProfessorName> recommends this student. Email <ContactInfo><Email> jones@univ.edu </Email> </ContactInfo> with questions.</RL>".

The *any* and *anyAttribute* structures of XML Schema let designers reuse components from foreign schemata or namespaces. The *any* structure allows the insertion of any element belonging to a list of namespaces, and it can have *minOccurs* and *maxOccurs* attributes to define the number of occurrences of the *any* construct. The *anyAttribute* structure allows the insertion of any attribute belonging to a list of namespaces. Both *any* and *anyAttribute* can have *namespace* and *processContents* as attributes. The attribute *namespace* specifies the namespaces that an XML validator examines to determine the validity of an element in an XML document. The attribute *processContents* specifies how the XML processor should handle validation against the elements specified by the *any* or *anyAttribute*. In Figure 1, the *any* element in line 59 specifies that zero or more elements from any other namespace can appear after the *Recommendation-Letter* element. Further, the *anyAttribute* specification in line 62 indicates that the *StudentInfo* element can have additional attributes from any namespace.

In XML Schema, it is possible to nest structural constructs, thus forming a hierarchy of nested constructs. In Figure 1, for example, *StudentInfo* has the attributes *StudentNumber* and *anyAttribute*, and it also contains the following structures in order: first, either a *Name* or a sequence of one *FirstName*, zero to two *MiddleName*'s, and one *LastName*; second, one to five sequences such that each sequence includes one *SchoolName*, one *SchoolAddress*, and an optional *GraduationDate* (the *GraduationDate* itself contains a *Month* followed by a *Year*); third, an element *RecommendationLetter* that has two elements, *ProfessorName* and *ContactInfo* (*ContactInfo* in turn contains one to two choices such that in each choice either *PhoneNumber* or *Email* or *Fax* is specified); and fourth, an optional *any* element.

4   C-XML

In this section we propose an enrichment to represent XML Schema content structures that are usually missing in traditional conceptual models. Since hypergraphs provide a general representation for conceptual models, we begin with an augmented hypergraph whose vertices and edges are respectively object sets and relationship sets, and whose augmentations consist of decorations that represent constraints. A hypergraph foundation is amenable to the requirements of XML Schema, and thus this choice simplifies the correspondence between conceptual models and XML Schema. We call our representation Conceptual XML (C-XML).

We derive C-XML from OSM [6], a hypergraph-based conceptual model that defines structure in terms of *object sets* (or *concepts*), *relationship sets*, and *constraints* over these object and relationship sets. Figure 2 shows a C-XML model instance that corresponds to the XML schema of Figure 1. An object set with a solid border indicates a nonlexical concept, a dashed border indicates a lexical concept, and a double solid/dashed border indicates a *mixed* concept.[1] A shaded object set indicates a high-level object set that groups other object and relationship sets into a single object set. Lines connecting object sets are *relationship sets*. A *participation constraint* specifies how many times an object in a connected relationship may participate in a relationship set. For the most common participation constraints (*0:1*, *1:1*, *0:**, and *1:**), C-XML uses graphical notation as a shorthand: (1) an "o" on a connecting relationship-set line designates *optional participation*, while the absence of an "o" designates *mandatory*, and (2) an arrowhead specifies a *functional constraint*, limiting participation of objects on the tail side of the arrow to be at most one.

The *sequence* structure representation must be able to specify concepts in a sequence in a particular order. Also, the representation must be able to specify the minimum and maximum numbers of occurrence of the whole sequence and of each child element within the sequence. For C-XML we let a bounded half circle with a directional arrow represent a sequence. The sequenced child concepts connect to the curved side, and the parent concept that contains the sequenced child concepts connects to the flat side. We place participation constraints for the entire sequence near the connection to the parent. We place participation constraints for each child near the curved side of the sequence symbol. Note that C-XML has participation constraints that represent the minimum and maximum number of occurrences of the sequence in the relationship set between the parent and the sequence. C-XML also allows participation constraints that represent the minimum and maximum allowed occurrences of the sequence in the relationship set between the sequence and each sequenced child concept.

The representation for *choice* is similar in appearance to the representation for *sequence*, but instead of an arrow we use a vertical bar to indicate choice.

For *any* and *anyAttribute* we use a high-level object set to indicate that it contains some content from another schema. XML Schema is not specific enough to designate which concept, and thus we cannot specify which concept. We therefore name these concepts "any". Conceptually, in C-XML whether the concept is an attribute or an element does not matter, and we do not distinguish between these cases.

We now evaluate C-XML with respect to the criteria for XML conceptual models in Section 2.

---

[1] In an XML document, the content string for a mixed concept might be interspersed among a number of child nodes. However, in C-XML the *mixed* concept does not explicitly specify how text and child elements can be interleaved. If the pattern for interspersing chunks of the string among child nodes matters, then the user must model text nodes explicitly (in combination with a sequence structure) rather than use the generic *mixed* construct.

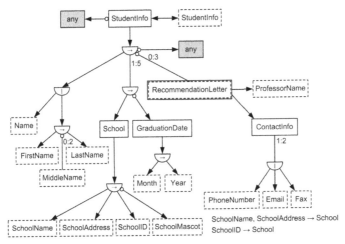

Fig. 2. Sequence/Choice Structures for Figure 1

- *Graphical notation.* We have presented a sufficient graphical notation, but this is just one possibility among many.
- *Formal foundation.* OSM has a solid formal foundation in terms of predicate calculus (see Appendix A of [6]). In OSM, each object set maps to a one-place predicate, and each n-ary relationship set ($n \geq 2$) relationship set maps to an n-place predicate. Each constraint (e.g. a participation constraint) maps to a closed predicate-calculus formula. The appendix describes formal representations for the added features for C-XML: sequence, choice, mixed content, and general co-occurrence constraints.
- *Structure independence.* XML in general, and XML Schema in particular, are strongly hierarchical in nature. C-XML is capable of representing the hierarchical aspect of XML Schema, but C-XML is more general, flexible, and conceptual. For example, C-XML allows multiple sequence and choice structures to be associated directly with a single concept (XML Schema allows only one sequence or choice structure for the content of an element). Also, C-XML supports the intermixing of ordinary relationship sets with sequence and choice structures. From this conceptual structure, we can derive many possible hierarchical representations. Similarly, C-XML defines generalized versions of the concepts of sequence, choice, and mixed content. C-XML provides a conceptual perspective that is structurally independent of XML Schema.
- *Reflection of the mental model.* Given its structure independence and generality, C-XML is well suited to reflect the mental model (design) of a modeler. C-XML can represent hierarchical and non-hierarchical structure. Conceptually, whether a concept is an attribute or an element does not matter, and C-XML does not distinguish between them. C-XML is also able to represent both sequences among related entities and non-sequences among related entities. Choices among alternative related entities are also possible, and choice

is distinct from generalization/specialization so that neither is overloaded. C-XML supports mixed content and open content. Finally, C-XML provides for all XML cardinality constraints; indeed it provides for a very large spectrum of cardinality constraints [9] encompassing and going beyond those provided by XML.

- *N-ary relationship sets.* C-XML supports *n*-ary relationship sets, ($n \geq 2$).
- *Views.* High-level object sets constitute a formal view mechanism, as do high-level relationship sets [6]. As described above, C-XML also can represent both hierarchical and non-hierarchical views.
- *Logical level mapping.* We have implemented automatic conversions from XML Schema to C-XML and vice versa.
- *Constraints.* C-XML supports several kinds of constraints: set, referential-integrity, cardinality, and general constraints.
- *Cardinality for all participants.* C-XML goes further than XML Schema, even allowing cardinality constraints for children of a sequence or choice.
- *Ordering.* C-XML explicitly supports ordering with its sequence construct.
- *Irregular and heterogeneous structure.* The features that give C-XML its structure independence (described above) provide for the modeling of irregular and heterogeneous structure.
- *Document-centric data.* C-XML can represent both mixed and open content.

5   Augmenting ER and UML

A number of conceptual modeling languages for XML Schema have been described in the literature. Sengupta and Mohan [12] and Necasky [10] present fairly recent surveys. As we explain in this section, however, most of these efforts do not support the full generality of XML Schema.

5.1   ER

Sengupta et al. [13] propose XER as an extension to the ER model for XML. Figure 3 shows an example of XER; in fact, it shows the best that can be done

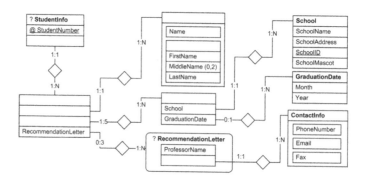

Fig. 3. Best Representation of Figure 1 using XER Notation

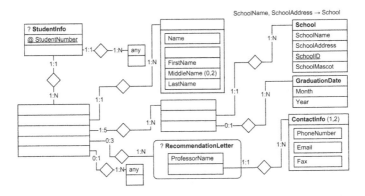

Fig. 4. Possible Way to Represent XML Schema Document in Figure 1 in ER-XML

to represent the XML schema in Figure 1. As we will see, it does not capture all the concepts and constraints in the XML schema in Figure 1.

XER represents an entity such as *StudentInfo* or *GraduationDate* using a rectangle with a title area giving the name of the entity and the body giving the attributes. For example, in Figure 1, *Month* and *Year* are sequenced elements nested under the element *GraduationDate*, so in Figure 3 *Month* and *Year* are represented as attributes for the *GraduationDate* entity. Multi-valued attributes are also allowed; their multiplicity constraints are in parentheses. *MiddleName*, for example, is a multi-valued attribute with a multiplicity *(0,2)*. XML attributes in an XER entity are prefixed with @, and key attributes are underlined. The attribute *StudentNumber* is a key in Figure 1, so in Figure 3 it appears as an underlined attribute with a prefix of @.

An XER entity can be ordered or unordered. Additionally, an XER entity can be mixed.

- Ordered Entity. XER entities are ordered by default from top to bottom. The ordered entity *GraduationDate* in Figure 3 indicates that its attributes are ordered first *Month*, then *Year*.
- Unordered Entity. An unordered entity is represented by placing a question mark (?) in front of the entity name. *StudentInfo* in Figure 3 is an unordered entity.
- Mixed Entity. A mixed entity is represented in XER using a rounded rectangle. *RecommendationLetter* in Figure 3 is a mixed entity.

XER relationships denote a connection between two or more entities, but in XER they can also denote that a complex entity contains a complex element as one of its sub-elements. When an entity E in XER has an attribute A and this attribute A by itself is an entity that contains other attributes, then A appears in the XER diagram twice, once as an attribute inside the entity E, and once as an entity A. In addition, there is a connection between the attribute A inside the entity E and the entity A. If $minA:maxA$ is the participation constraint on A

within E and $minE{:}maxE$ is the participation constraint on E for A, $minA{:}maxA$ appears on the side of the attribute A within E, and $minE{:}maxE$ appears on the side of the entity A. For example, *RecommendationLetter* has two attributes *ProfessorName* and *ContactInfo*, but *ContactInfo* by itself is an entity. Thus, a relationship set appears between the attribute *ContactInfo* inside *RecommendationLetter* and the entity *ContactInfo*. A participation constraint of *1:1* appears on the side of the attribute *ContactInfo* inside *RecommendationLetter* to denote that *RecommendationLetter* has one *ContactInfo*, and a participation constraint of *1:N* appears on the *ContactInfo* entity side to denote that *ContactInfo* is for one or more *RecommendationLetters*.[2]

XER represents the choice concept in XML Schema as a generalization/specialization. *Generalization* in XER refers to the concept of an entity that can have different specialization entities in an ISA relationship. XER represents a generalization using a covering rectangle containing the specialized XER entities. This, the authors claim in [13], is equivalent to using the "xs:choice" tag in XML Schema. In Figure 3 the rectangle representing the entity *ContactInfo* contains the rectangles of entities of choice elements *PhoneNumber*, *Email*, and *Fax*.

Comparing the conceptual components for C-XML (e.g. Figure 2) and XER (e.g. Figure 3), we see that several constructs and constraints are missing in XER. First, XER lacks the ability to represent the minimum and maximum occurrence of the whole sequence or choice within a containing entity when either of their values is more than *1*. For example, XER cannot represent the minimum and maximum occurrence of *1* to *2* for the *choice* within the entity *ContactInfo*. Second, XER has no representation for *any* and *anyAttribute* structures. For example, in Figure 3 the entity *StudentInfo* is missing the *anyAttribute*, and the sequence contained inside the *StudentInfo* entity does not have *any*. Third, XER has no representation for composite keys. For example, in Figure 3 the representation that *SchoolName* and *SchoolAddress* together constitute a key for the entity *School* is missing. Fourth, although XER has a representation for a single key, this representation only applies when the key for an entity is an attribute of that entity. The representation cannot specify a key constraint for an entity within the context of another entity.

Beyond these omissions, we have several concerns:

- Representing *choice* by generalization/specialization is problematic; the formal definition of *choice* differs from the formal definition of generalization/specialization. First, *choice* contains different types of alternative concepts, but all the specialized concepts in generalization/specialization hierarchies typically must have the same type. Second, in generalization/specialization hierarchies any specialized concept inherits relationship sets from its generalization concepts, while in *choice*, alternative concepts do not inherit relationship sets. Third, the participation constraints for *choice* allow alternative concepts to appear more than once, while in generalization/specialization hierarchies specialized concepts can appear at most once.

---

[2] Although ER more commonly uses look-across cardinality constraints, the designers of XER have chosen to use participation constraints [13].

- In XER it is not clear from [13] whether it is possible to represent an entity without having a name for the entity. For Figure 3 we assume that we are able to represent an entity in XER with a null name. Also, in XER it is not clear whether it is possible to have an empty slot in an entity to indicate that an attribute by itself is an entity without a name. We also assume for Figure 3 that we are able to do so in XER. From [13] it is not clear whether it is possible to have hierarchies of *choice* and *sequence* structures, but we assume that this is possible as Figure 3 shows.
- In XER when an entity has an attribute and this attribute is also an entity, the model instance in XER has an attribute and an entity with the same name. This redundancy might cause problems if XER developers are able to write the two names independently.

In light of these omissions and concerns, we extend XER, augmenting it with constructs and constraints that are missing and resolving our concerns. Figure 4 shows our suggested way of representing the schema in Figure 1 in ER-XML, our ER augmentation for XML. We add *any* and *anyAttribute* concepts to XER. We have chosen to add a representation of *any* and *anyAttribute* as entities with the name *any*. We also add minimum and maximum occurrence to *sequence* and *choice*, placing this minimum and maximum in parentheses in the name slot, following the name, if any, of the entity that declares the *sequence* or *choice*. We have chosen to add a representation for key constraints by allowing functional dependencies that must hold within entity sets or along paths of relationship sets. Thus, for example, as Figure 4 shows, we can specify the composite key *School-Name, SchoolAddress* by the functional dependency *SchoolName, SchoolAddress* ⟶ *School*. Although we use the same notation for *choice*, we do not consider the representation of *choice* in ER-XML to be a generalization concept. Finally, we do not repeat attribute names, writing the name only in the entity that represents the attribute.

5.2 UML

Conrad et al. [5] add features to UML to enable mappings from class diagrams to XML DTDs. Figure 5 shows an example; in fact, it shows the best that can be done to represent the XML schema in Figure 1. Unfortunately, it does not capture all the concepts and constraints in the XML schema in Figure 1.

As described in [5], Conrad et al. augment UML aggregation so that it can be transformed into a *sequence* construct or a *choice* construct. The designation {*sequence*} specifies a left-to-right ordering of elements, and the designation {*choice*} specifies a choice among elements. For a sequence the first constituent element is marked as *1*, the second as *2*, and so forth. A *sequence* or *choice* construct may have cardinality to represent the minimum and maximum occurrence of the entire sequence or choice. For example, the class *ContactInfo* in Figure 5 has one to two choices {*choice* : 1..2} of the classes *PhoneNumber*, *Email*, and *Fax*. For an *any* structure, the notation in [5] uses the « *content* » stereotype.

Comparing the conceptual components for C-XML (e.g. Figure 1) and extended UML presented in [5] (e.g. Figure 5), we see that several constructs are

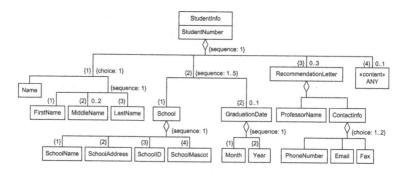

Fig. 5. Best Representation of Figure 1 Using Conrad Notation

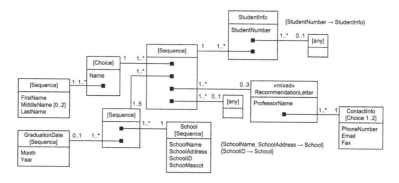

Fig. 6. Possible Way to Represent XML Schema Document in Figure 1 in UML-XML

missing. First, the extended UML in [5] does not support *anyAttribute*. For example, in Figure 5 the class *StudentInfo* is missing the *anyAttribute*. Second, the extended UML in [5] cannot represent mixed content. In Figure 5 the class *RecommendationLetter* does not appear as having mixed content. Third, the extended UML in [5] lacks key constraints, although, in principle, we could specify key constraints using OCL (the constraint language of UML).

Besides these omissions, we have concerns about the suggested representation of sequence and choice in [5]. The suggested representations can only be applied between classes, not between attributes. This is because Conrad et al. augment UML aggregation for *sequence* and *choice*. Since the aggregation in UML applies to classes, the notation forces attributes to be represented as classes. For example, to represent the *GraduationDate* class as a sequence of *Month* and *Year*, would-be attributes *Month* and *Year* must each become a class first.

To overcome these difficulties, we need to extend and adjust the representations in [5]. Figure 6 shows our suggested extensions and adjustments by rendering Figure 1 in UML-XML, our UML augmentation for XML.

– We have chosen to represent the *anyAttribute* as an associated class with the *any* content type rather than as a stereotype. For mixed content we use the «*mixed*» stereotype. *RecommendationLetter* in Figure 6 is an example.

- We suggest representing *sequence* and *choice* in a different way so that we do not force attributes to be represented as classes. When attributes in a class are ordered, we add the designation [*Sequence*] under the class name to specify a top-to-bottom ordering of the attributes. We also add *minOccurs..maxOccurs*, if needed, to express participation different from the default. For example, in Figure 6, the designation [*Sequence*] is added under *GraduationDate*. Similarly, we allow designating a choice construct by adding [*Choice minOccurs..maxOccurs*], allowing *minOccurs .. maxOccurs* to be omitted when it is *1..1*, the default. For example, in Figure 6, the designation [*Choice 1..2*] is added under *ContactInfo*.

- We add notation to denote that a class contains an attribute and that this attribute is a class that contains other attributes. A connection appears that connects an empty slot indicating the presence of an attribute inside the class with the class containing other attributes. For example, we indicate that *ContactInfo* is an attribute inside the class *RecommendationLetter* by the connection inside *RecommendationLetter* that extends to *ContactInfo*. Note also that *ContactInfo* by itself is a class that contains attributes. A multiplicity of *1* is added to the *ContactInfo* class side and a multiplicity of *1..** is added to the *ContactInfo* attribute side in the *RecommendationLetter* class to denote that *ContactInfo* is for *1* or more *RecommendationLetter*s and each *RecommendationLetter* has one *ContactInfo*.

- For the case when a sequence or choice is a complex attribute inside a class *C*, the *sequence* or *choice* is represented as a class with no name but has the designation [*Sequence*] or [*Choice*], and we connect the empty slot inside the class *C* with the class that represents the *sequence* or *choice*. For example, the class *StudentInfo* has a complex sequence attribute. Further, this sequence by itself is a class that contains other attributes including another complex choice attribute and a complex sequence attribute.

- We can specify key constraints in UML by using OCL. But, since this is a common task, we have an alternative representation that we can add to a diagram. We have chosen to add a representation for key constraints by allowing functional dependencies which must hold within classes or along paths of associations. Thus, for example, as Figure 6 shows, we can specify the composite key *SchoolName, SchoolAddress* by the functional dependency {*SchoolName, SchoolAddress* $\longrightarrow$ *School*}.

5.3   ER-XML, UML-XML, and C-XML

Comparing ER-XML, UML-XML, and C-XML, we make the following observations according to the criteria for XML conceptual modeling we described in Section 2. Criteria from Section 2 not listed here have equal validity among the three models (e.g. all three have a *graphical notation*).

- *Formal foundation.* C-XML has a solid formal foundation in terms of predicate calculus. ER-XML and UML-XML are respectively derived from XER as described in [13] and UML as described in [5]. There is no formal foundation for XER [10], and the underlying formalism of UML is not fully developed [7]. In principle both could have complete formal foundations.

- *Reflection of the mental model.* ER-XML distinguishes attributes from entities and UML-XML distinguishes attributes from classes. C-XML represents all concepts as object-set nodes in hypergraphs. Forcing attributes to be embedded within an entity/class has the disadvantage that a user of UML-XML or ER-XML has to decide before representing any concept whether it should be an attribute or entity/class. Distinguishing between an attribute and an entity/class is not necessary and may even be harmful as a mental-model conceptualization. Goldstein and Storey [8] showed that this can be a major source of errors in conceptual modeling.
- *Views.* Hypergraphs are typically more amenable to translations to various views and even alternate XML schemas such as normalized XML schemas. Further, although not discussed here, C-XML supports both high-level object sets and high-level relationship sets as first class concepts [6]. Neither ER-XML nor UML-XML supports high-level view constructs.
- *Logical level mapping.* We have implemented both a mapping from XML Schema to C-XML and vice versa [1,2]. In principle mappings to and from XML Schema and ER-XML as well as UML-XML are possible.
- *Cardinality for all participants.* The nesting representation for ER-XML and UML-XML restricts the specification of cardinality constraints to only the nesting participants. C-XML specifies cardinality constraints for all participants, beyond even those supported by XML Schema.

6   Conclusion

We have discussed the structural constructs in XML Schema that are missing in traditional conceptual models. Our proposed solution is to enrich conceptual models with the ability to order a list of concepts, choose alternative concepts from among several, specify mixed content, and use content from another data model. We presented our solution using C-XML, and we showed that our solution can be adapted and used for the ER and UML languages.

We also presented requirements for conceptual modeling for XML. We based these requirements on those presented in [10], [14], and [19]. We evaluated C-XML against these requirements and showed that C-XML satisfies all of them, which makes C-XML a good candidate for a conceptual modeling language for XML. We also argued that ER-XML and UML-XML, our adaptations for ER and UML, also largely satisfy these requirements, but do not satisfy them as well as does C-XML.

We have implemented a modeling tool for C-XML, and we have implemented conversions from XML Schema to C-XML and vice versa. Currently, we are working on a formal proof that our conversions to and from C-XML and XML Schema preserve information and constraints.

Acknowledgments

This work is supported in part by the National Science Foundation under grant number IIS-0083127 and by the Kevin and Debra Rollins Center for eBusiness under grant number EB-05046.

References

1. AL-Kamha, R.: Translating XML Schema to Conceptual XML. Technical Report, Computer Science Department, Brigham Young University (November 2006)
2. AL-Kamha, R.: Translating Conceptual XML to XML Schema. Technical Report, Computer Science Department, Brigham Young University (in progress)
3. Booch, G., Rumbaugh, J., Jacobson, I.: The Unified Modeling Language User Guide. Addison-Wesley, Massachusetts (1999)
4. Chen, P.P.: The entity-relationship model—toward a unified view of data. ACM Transactions on Database Systems 1(1), 9–36 (1976)
5. Conrad, R., Scheffner, D., Freytag, J.C.: XML conceptual modeling using UML. In: Laender, A.H.F., Liddle, S.W., Storey, V.C. (eds.) ER 2000. LNCS, vol. 1920, pp. 558–571. Springer, Heidelberg (2000)
6. Embley, D.W., Kurtz, B.D., Woodfield, S.N.: Object-oriented Systems Analysis: A Model-Driven Approach. Prentice Hall, Englewood Cliffs, New Jersey (1992)
7. A Formal Semantics for UML Workshop (October 2006), http://www.cs.queensu. ca/~stl/internal/uml2/MoDELS2006/
8. Goldstein, R.C., Storey, V.C.: Some findings on the intuitiveness of entity-relationship constructs. In: Proceedings of the Eighth International Conference on Entity-Relationship Approach (ER 1989),Toronto, Canada, pp. 9–23, North-Holland (October 1989)
9. Liddle, S.W., Embley, D.W., Woodfield, S.N.: Cardinality constraints in semantic data models. Data & Knowledge Engineering 11(3), 235–270 (1993)
10. Necasky, M.: Conceptual modeling for XML: A survey. In: Proceedings of the DATESO 2006 Annual International Workshop on Databases, Texts, Specifications and Objects (DATESO 2006), Desna, Czech Republic, pp. 40–53 (April 2006)
11. Visual Studio.NET, Microsoft. http://www.msdn.microsoft.com/vstudio
12. Sengupta, A., Mohan, S.: Formal and Conceptual Models for XML Structures—The Past, Present, and Future. Technical Report 137–1, Indiana University, Information Systems Department, Bloomington, Indiana (April 2003)
13. Sengupta, A., Mohan, S., Doshi, R.: XER — extensible entity relationship modeling. In: Proceedings of XML 2003, Philadelphia, Pennsylvania (December 2003)
14. Sengupta, A., Wilde, E.: The Case for Conceptual Modeling for XML. Technical Report No. 242, Computer Engineering and Networks Laboratory, ETH Zurich (February 2006)
15. XMLSpy, Altova, http://www.xmlspy.com
16. Stylus Studio, http://www.stylusstudio.com/xml_schema_editor.html
17. Teorey, T.J., Yang, D., Fry, J.P.: A logical design methodology for relational databases using the extended entity-relationship model. ACM Computing Surveys 18(2), 197–222 (1986)
18. UML 2.0 superstructure specification (August 2005)
19. Wilde, E.: Towards conceptual modeling for XML. In: Proceedings of the Berliner XML Tage 2005 (BXML2005), Berlin, Germany, pp. 213–224 (September 2005)

Appendix

Sequence

Figure 7 shows the schematic structure of a sequence. Exactly one parent object set connects to a sequence of n children, $n \geq 0$, with participation constraints on the several connections as Figure 7 shows. A sequenced child may be either an object set or a nested sequence or choice structure. In general, there may be many sequences in a model instance, and since we do not explicitly name sequence structures, we denote a particular sequence, the kth sequence, by $Sequence_k$. Let P be the name of the parent object set for $Sequence_k$, and let C_1, ..., C_n be the names of the n child object sets or nested sequences or choices that are sequenced within $Sequence_k$. To impose order, we introduce the unary predicate $Order$, which we can think of as an object set containing as many ordinal numbers as we need 1, 2, ... We denote the minimum and maximum cardinalities of $Sequence_k$ according to Figure 7. Let min and max be, respectively, the minimum and maximum number of occurrences of $Sequence_k$ allowed for an object in P. Let min_{C_i} and max_{C_i}, $1 \leq i \leq n$, be, respectively, the minimum and maximum number of allowed occurrences of C_i objects within $Sequence_k$. Let min' and max' be, respectively, the minimum and maximum number of occurrences of $Sequence_k$ sequences in the relationship set between P and $Sequence_k$. Finally, let min_{Seq_i} and max_{Seq_i}, $1 \leq i \leq n$, be, respectively, the minimum and maximum allowed occurrences of $Sequence_k$ in the relationship set between $Sequence_k$ sequences and C_i (i.e. the number of C_i objects that can be associated with $Sequence_k$ for a given order position). For $Sequence_k$, we have the following object sets, relationship sets, and constraints.

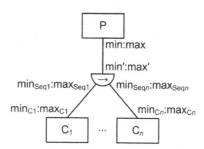

Fig. 7. Sequence Structure in C-XML

Object Sets:
    $P(x)$, $Sequence_k(x)$, $Order(x)$, and $C_1(x)$, ..., $C_n(x)$

Relationship Sets:
    $P(x)$ contains $Sequence_k(y)$, $C_1(x)$ has $Order(1)$ in $Sequence_k(y)$, ..., $C_n(x)$ has $Order(n)$ in $Sequence_k(y)$

Referential Integrity:

- $\forall x \forall y (P(x)$ *contains* $Sequence_k(y) \Rightarrow P(x) \wedge Sequence_k(y))$
- $\forall x \forall y (C_1(x)$ *has* $Order(1)$ *in* $Sequence_k(y) \Rightarrow C_1(x) \wedge Order(1) \wedge$ $Sequence_k(y))$
- ...
- $\forall x \forall y (C_n(x)$ *has* $Order(n)$ *in* $Sequence_k(y) \Rightarrow C_n(x) \wedge Order(n) \wedge$ $Sequence_k(y))$

Participation Constraints:

- $\forall x (P(x) \Rightarrow \exists^{\geq min} y(P(x)$ *contains* $Sequence_k(y))) \wedge \forall x (P(x) \Rightarrow \exists^{\leq max} y(P(x)$ *contains* $Sequence_k(y)))$
- $\forall x (Sequence_k(x) \Rightarrow \exists^{\geq min'} y(P(y)$ *contains* $Sequence_k(x))) \wedge$ $\forall x (Sequence_k(x) \Rightarrow \exists^{\leq max'} y(P(y)$ *contains* $Sequence_k(x)))$
- $\forall x (Sequence_k(x) \Rightarrow \exists^{\geq min_{Seq1}} y_1 \ldots \exists^{\geq min_{Seqn}} y_n ($ $C_1(y_1)$ *has* $Order(1)$ *in* $Sequence_k(x) \wedge \ldots \wedge$ $C_n(y_n)$ *has* $Order(n)$ *in* $Sequence_k(x))) \wedge$ $\forall x (Sequence_k(x) \Rightarrow \exists^{\leq max_{Seq1}} y_1 \ldots \exists^{\leq max_{Seqn}} y_n ($ $C_1(y_1)$ *has* $Order(1)$ *in* $Sequence_k(x) \wedge \ldots \wedge$ $C_n(y_n)$ *has* $Order(n)$ *in* $Sequence_k(x)))$
- $\forall x (C_1(x) \Rightarrow \exists^{\geq min_{C_1}} y(C_1(x)$ *has* $Order(1)$ *in* $Sequence_k(y))) \wedge$ $\forall x (C_1(x) \Rightarrow \exists^{\leq max_{C_1}} y(C_1(x)$ *has* $Order(1)$ *in* $Sequence_k(y))) \wedge \ldots \wedge$ $\forall x (C_n(x) \Rightarrow \exists^{\geq min_{C_n}} y(C_n(x)$ *has* $Order(n)$ *in* $Sequence_k(y))) \wedge$ $\forall x (C_n(x) \Rightarrow \exists^{\leq max_{C_n}} y(C_n(x)$ *has* $Order(n)$ *in* $Sequence_k(y)))$

Choice
The formalism for choice, which has a schematic structure similar to sequence, is omitted due to space constraints.

Mixed Content
Formally, marking an object set P as *mixed* is a template for creating a relationship set to a lexical object set $Text$ of type string: $P[1]$ *contains* $[1{:}*]Text$. The string associated with an object in a mixed object set may be interspersed among direct child elements.

Generalized Co-occurrence:
A generalized co-occurrence constraint $A_1, \ldots, A_n \rightarrow B_1, \ldots, B_m$ is shorthand for an ordinary co-occurrence constraint written over a high-level relationship set connecting the object sets $A_1, \ldots, A_n, B_1, \ldots, B_m$. If the subgraph that connects these object sets is unique, we can derive the corresponding high-level relationship set automatically. Otherwise, in addition to specifying the co-occurrence constraint, the user must also specify the derived relationship set using Prolog-like syntax (e.g., $r(A, B)$:- $r_1(A, X), r_2(X, B)$). The formal definition of co-occurrence constraints appears in Appendix A of [6].

VERT: A Semantic Approach for Content Search and Content Extraction in XML Query Processing

Huayu Wu, Tok Wang Ling, and Bo Chen

School of Computing, National University of Singapore
3 Science Drive 2, Singapore 117543
{wuhuayu,lingtw,chenbo}@comp.nus.edu.sg

Abstract. Processing a twig pattern query in XML document includes structural search and content search. Most existing algorithms only focus on structural search. They treat content nodes the same as element nodes during query processing with structural joins. Due to the high variety of contents, to mix content search and structural search suffers from management problem of contents and low performance. Another disadvantage is to find the actual values asked by a query, they have to rely on the original document. In this paper, we propose a novel algorithm *Value Extraction with Relational Table (VERT)* to overcome these limitations. The main technique of *VERT* is introducing relational tables to store document contents instead of treating them as nodes and labeling them. Tables in our algorithm are created based on semantic information of documents. As more semantics is captured, we can further optimize tables and queries to significantly enhance efficiency. Last, we show by experiments that besides solving different content problems, *VERT* also has superiority in performance of twig pattern query processing compared with existing algorithms.

1 Introduction

XML plays an important role in information exchange nowadays. As a result, how to process queries over XML documents efficiently attracts lots of research interests. In most XML query languages (see, e.g. [2][3]), the queries are expressed as *twig* patterns. Finding all appearances of a twig pattern in an XML document is a most significant operation in XML query processing.

Normally an XML query includes structural search and content search. E.g. in a query

$$book[author = "Jack"]/title$$

book[author]/title is a structural search and *author = "Jack"* is a content search. Most of existing works only focus on processing structural search efficiently and very few of them pay high attentions on contents. Content problems include how to properly manage contents, how to efficiently process content

C. Parent et al. (Eds.): ER 2007, LNCS 4801, pp. 534–549, 2007.

```
<book_store>
  <book>
    <ISBN>0-07-123057-2</ISBN>
    <title>Database Management Systems</title>
    <author>Ramakrishnan</author>
    <author>Gehrke</author>
    <price>33</price>
    <amount>20</amount>
  </book>
  <book>
    <ISBN>0-07-124650-9</ISBN>
    <title>Introduction to Database Systems</title>
    <author>Bressan</author>
    <author>Catania</author>
    <price>17</price>
    <amount>12</amount>
  </book>
    ......
</book_store>
```

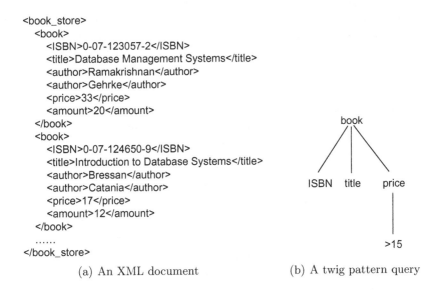

(a) An XML document   (b) A twig pattern query

Fig. 1. An example of XML document and twig pattern query

search during query processing and how to extract contents to answer the queries. E.g. *TwigStack* [4] and its subsequent algorithm *TwigStackList* [9] are optimal for processing path and twig pattern queries, but they all suffer from content problems when they process queries with content predicates, because they treat contents the same as other element nodes and perform structural search for the whole query. Although some algorithms like [12] and [11] use subsequence matchings to avoid problems on content search , they still suffer from other problems such as cost for content result fetching in XML databases.

In this paper, we propose a new algorithm to solve different kinds of content problems in twig pattern query processing. Our contribution can be summarized as follows:

- We propose a new algorithm, namely *Value Extraction with Relational Table (VERT)*. Our approach combines value contents to related element or attribute nodes and only assigns label to the element or attribute. Instead of organizing tremendous number of streams for different contents, e.g. streams for value content '33', 'Gehrke' and so on for document in Fig. 1(a), we adopt relational tables to store value contents together with their associated elements or attributes. In this point of view, we can reduce the number of labeled nodes and also we can solve the management problem of contents raised in previous algorithms.
- Content search can be accomplished efficiently by *SQL* queries on corresponding relational tables with proper indexes. Furthermore, after finding the appearances of a twig pattern we can easily get the desired value contents from tables. As a result, our approach need not consider the document storage for final results.

- Relational tables are created based on semantic information captured in documents. As more semantics is captured, we can further optimize the tables and queries to achieve better performance, as shown in Section 5.
- Besides solving content problems, we also present experimental results to show the superiority of $VERT$ and subsequent optimizations over previous algorithms in performance of twig pattern query processing.

The rest of the paper is organized as follows. We first describe some related works in Section 2. After that we discuss background knowledge and motivation for our work in Section 3. The $VERT$ algorithm with two semantics based optimizations is presented in Section 4. We present the experimental results in Section 5 and conclude our work in Section 6.

2   Related Work

In early work, Zhang et al. [14] proposed a $multi-predicate merge join$ algorithm based on (DocId, Start, End, Level) containment labeling of a XML document. Later an improved stack-based structural join algorithm is proposed by Al-Khalifa et al. [1]. These two algorithms, as well as most of prior works decomposed a twig pattern into a set of binary relationships, e.g. parent-child and ancestor-descendant relationships. Then twig pattern matching could be done by matching each binary relationship and combining these basic binary matches. The main problem of such approaches is that intermediate result size may be very large, even when the input and final result sizes are more manageable. To overcome this limitation, Bruno et al. [4] proposed a holistic twig join algorithm, $TwigStack$, which could avoid producing a large size of intermediate result. However, this algorithm is only optimal for a twig pattern with only ancestor-descendent relationships. There are many subsequent works [9] [8] [5] [10] [7] [13] to optimize $TwigStack$ in terms of I/O, or extend $TwigStack$ for different kinds of problems. In particular, Lu et al. [9] introduced a $list$ structure to make it optimal for queries containing parent-child relationships. However, all these existing works only focus on structural search. For content search they either treat content node the same as element node, or consider how contents are stored and perform a separate operation on content search. $ViST$ [12] and $PRIX$ [11] transform twig pattern queries into sequences and perform subsequence matchings for query processing. They can solve problems on content search, but they still do not pay attention to fetching content results of twig pattern queries, and are not efficient in structural search comparing with $TwigStack$.

3   Background and Motivations

3.1   Data Model and Twig Pattern

XML documents are commonly modelled as ordered trees, in which tree nodes represent tags, attributes or text values, and edges represent element-subelement,

element-attribute, element-content or attribute-value pairs. We call these binary relationships parent-child relationships (denoted by "/"). Queries normally appear to be twig patterns. A twig pattern is a small tree whose nodes stand for tags, attributes or contents in a document. Different from the parent-child relationship in XML tree, edges in twig query can also be ancestor-descendent relationships (denoted by "//") which stand for that some other nodes may appear on the path between the two nodes connected by "//".

Given a twig pattern query Q, finding all the occurrences in an XML tree T is the main operation for query processing. A match of Q in T is identified by a mapping of nodes and edges from Q to T such that query node predicates are satisfied by corresponding nodes in the document and the relationships between query nodes are satisfied by corresponding relationships between nodes in the document.

3.2 Motivations

TwigStack and its supplementary works are optimal for twig query processing in many cases. In this section, we take *TwigStack* as an example and discuss some drawbacks of existing algorithms regarding to contents, which motivate our research.

Similar as most existing algorithms, *TwigStack* processes content search in the same way as structural search. The problems regarding to contents in *TwigStack* can be summarized as follows:

1. In *TwigStack*, all the nodes including elements, attributes and contents in an XML tree are labeled and the labels are organized in streams. When we build streams for contents, stream management is a problem. Consider a bookstore document shown in Fig. 1(a). There are a large number of books and each of them has a unique ISBN number. For each ISBN number there is a stream, e.g. a stream for '0-07-123057-2', another stream for '0-07-124650-9' and so forth. The problem is how to manage the tremendous number of streams. When a query in Fig. 1(b) is issued, it is time consuming to get all the streams with numeric names which are greater than 15. Although we can organize streams using B^+ tree, after finding all the corresponding streams, to combine labels in them by document order is also time consuming.

2. Streams for contents do not have semantic meanings. This may cause additional checking. When the query is interested in books with price of 20, structural search scans the stream T_{20}. Since in T_{20} we do not differentiate *price* and *quantity*, we need check all the labels in this stream though many of them stand for *quantity* and definitely do not contribute to final answer.

3. When we issue a query over an XML document, what we need is not all the twig pattern appearances represented as tuples of labels, but the content results of that query. Like in the query example above, after finding a certain number of twig pattern appearances which contain element *ISBN* and *title*, we need to find their actual values. Since value contents are stored as stream names and it is not practical to get them using labels, they have to move

into the document again. That is relevant to how to store and manage XML document and is not negligible.

Our motivation is to avoid all these content problems raised in existing algorithms. After that, twig pattern queries can be processed more efficiently not only in content search, but also in entire execution.

4   VERT Algorithm

Some elements or attributes in XML documents describe certain properties of their parent elements, e.g. *title*, *price* are properties of *book* in the bookstore document. We use term *property* for such element or attribute, and term *object* for the element described by *property*. In this section, we first present *VERT* algorithm to handle content problems and improve efficiency on content search. Tables in *VERT* store relationships between properties and their values. Then in Section 4.4 we present another two approaches to optimize *VERT* using semantic information. Tables in these optimizations store relationships between objects and their properties with values.

4.1   XML Document Parsing in VERT

In our first approach, we use tables to store labels of properties and their values. When we parse an XML document, we only label elements and attributes, and put these labels into corresponding streams in document order. Contents in document are not labeled, instead we put them in relational tables together with labels of their *property* nodes. We adopt interval encoding labeling scheme in our approach (see [6]). The detailed algorithm *Parser* is presented as follows.

There are three major steps when we parse an XML document: labeling the elements, constructing streams for different types of elements or attributes, and inserting each pair of property and value content into relational tables. *SAX* reads the documents to transform each tag and content into event and line 3 captures the next event if there are more events in SAX stream. Based on different types of events, different operations are performed accordingly. Line 4-16 are executed if the event e is a starting element. In this case, the first 2 steps are processed. The system first constructs an object for this element and assigns a label to it. It then puts the label into the stream for that tag. A stack S is used to temporarily store the object so that when an ending tag is reached, the system can easily know on which object the operation will be executed. At line 9-14, the system analyzes the attributes for this element if any. Based on the same operating steps, it labels the attributes and puts labels into streams. The attribute values are treated in the same way as element contents. Line 17-18 is the case that the event is a content type. Then the content is simply bound to the top object in S for further insertion used. When the event is an ending element in line 19-25, last step is processed, which is popping the top object from the S and inserting the label together with contents into the table for that

Algorithm 1. Parser

```
 1: initialize Stack S
 2: while there are more events in SAX stream do
 3:    let e = next event
 4:    if e is a start tag then
 5:       //step 1: label elements
 6:       create object o for e
 7:       assign label to o
 8:       push o onto S
 9:       for all attributes attr of e do
10:          //we parse attributes in the same way as elements.
11:          assign label to attr
12:          put label of attr into stream T_attr
13:          insert the label of attr and the value of attr into table R_attr
14:       end for
15:       //step 2: put labels of elements into streams
16:       put label of o into stream T_e
17:    else if e is a content value then
18:       set e to be the child content of the top object in S
19:    else if e is an end tag then
20:       // step 3: Insert contents with their parent element into tables
21:       pop o from S
22:       if o contains child contents then
23:          insert label of o together with its child contents into table R_e
24:       end if
25:    end if
26: end while
```

---

object. A set of example tables are shown in Fig. 2(c). They are property-value
tables. The name of the tables are the property names and each table contains
two fields, the label of the property node and value content.

Example 1. Consider the XML data shown in Fig. 1(a), *Parser* assigns labels
to tags and the resulting labeled tree is shown in Fig. 2(a). Then all the labels
belonging to the same type of element in XML tree will be passed to the same
stream by document order as shown in 2(b). The contents in document together
with their parent elements will be stored in corresponding relational tables according to the type of parent elements. Fig. 2(c) shows the resulting tables in
this example.

4.2   Query Processing with *VERT*

Twig pattern query processing involving contents is composed of two parts. First
we analyze and rewrite the query. During this part, for each leaf node which is
a value content, a new stream for its parent property node is constructed using
the table of that property. In the second part, we process the new query using
existing efficient algorithms, e.g. *TwigStack* in new searching space.

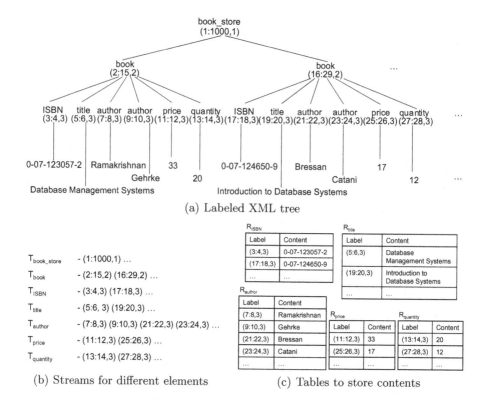

(a) Labeled XML tree

(b) Streams for different elements   (c) Tables to store contents

Fig. 2. An example of labeled XML tree with resulting streams and tables by Parser

In the main algorithm $VERT$, we first check for the validity of a given query in line 2-4. Validity of a query Q is defined as whether Q is meaningful for processing. Intuitively this validation can be accomplished by checking whether all the content comparisons in query predicates have parent element. If there is some content comparison in Q appearing in ancestor-descendance relationship ('//') with an element, we consider Q is not meaningful and our algorithm rejects such Q. Example 2 shows an invalid query. Line 6-12 recursively handle all the content comparisons in two phases: creating new streams and rewriting the predicates. In detail, Line 7-10 execute SQL selection on corresponding tables based on the content comparison, and then put all the selected labels, which are satisfied with the content comparison, into the new streams. Line 11 rewrites the query in such a way that the content and their respective parent elements or attributes are replaced by a new element which has an identical name as the corresponding new stream. At the end of the algorithm, we use $TwigStack$ or other efficient algorithm to process the new query with new streams.

Example 2. Consider the twig pattern query in Fig. 3(a). The value node with content comparison '>15' only has an ancestor instead of a parent. In this case we are not sure whether the query wants to get the books with price greater than

---

Algorithm 2. VERT

1: //check the validity of queries
2: **if** The query Q is not valid **then**
3:     reject Q
4: **end if**
5: //step 1: construct new streams and new queries
6: **while** there are more content comparisons in predicates of Q **do**
7:     let c be the next content comparison, and p be its parent element or attribute
8:     create a new stream $X_{p'}$ for p
9:     select the labels based on content c from the table T_p for p
10:     put the selected labels into $X_{p'}$
11:     rewrite the predicates such that replace sub-structure p/c by p'
12: **end while**
13: //step 2: process new queries in new streams
14: process the rewritten Q using existing efficient algorithms like $TwigStack$

15, or with the quantity greater than 15. As a result, this twig pattern query is considered invalid and by the line 2-4, $VERT$ rejects this query.

Example 3. The twig pattern query in Fig. 3(b) is valid. By $VERT$ we first find the predicate with content comparison, $price > 15$ in this case. In line 7-10, we execute SQL in table R_{price} to get all the labels of element $price$ having value content greater than '15'. Since all the records in database are inserted in document order, we can directly add resulting labels into a new stream $T_{price'}$, which contains all the labels for $price$ with value greater than 15. Then we rewrite the twig pattern query where the substructure with node $price$ and its child node '>15' is replaced by $price'$. To clearly explain $price'$ in the new query, we use $price_{>15}$ in Fig. 3(c). Finally we process $TwigStack$ on the new query using $T_{price'}$ for node $price_{>15}$.

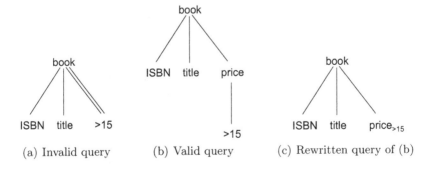

(a) Invalid query   (b) Valid query   (c) Rewritten query of (b)

Fig. 3. Invalid and valid twig pattern queries

4.3 Analysis of VERT

In this section, we will analyze our algorithm in four points of view: the management of data including labeled nodes and streams, content extraction for both predicates and final results, the size of streams to be searched and the number of structural joins during query processing.

Data management: $VERT$ combines contents and their parent elements together, and avoids labeling content nodes separately. Suppose an XML document is a full tree with height of h and each element has k children on average. Then the number of labeled elements is $(k^{h-1}-1)/(k-1)$ and the number of contents is k^{h-2}. When the document is large, the proportion of contents to the sum of elements and contents is around $(k-1)/(2k-1)$. In our algorithm, since contents are not labeled, the number of labeled nodes in memory will be reduced nearly by half for large documents and then the size of each stream will also be significantly narrowed down. Furthermore, since large variety of contents are ignored, the number of streams for different types of labeled nodes is limited to the number of element types. So the management of tremendous number of streams in previous work as mentioned in Section 3 can be solved.

Value extraction: Consider the XML document in Fig. 1(a) and a query in Fig. 3(b). When we extract the content '15' to answer this query, in previous approaches we need to move into the stream for content '15'. However, the stream for '15' contains different semantic labels like the *price* of a book and the *quantity* of a book. To mix them together will cause unnecessary search. Instead of searching in streams, $VERT$ handles contents in semantic tables. In this case, we just move into the table for *price* and avoid searching for content '15' under *quantity*. Furthermore, after getting all the appearances of $ISBN$ and *title* tags which satisfy the constraint, we aim to find the value contents under these tags. Previous approaches have to move into document again to fetch them because the streams for such contents cannot contribute to final result extraction. This depends how XML documents are stored and is not negligible. $VERT$ can be very efficient to get the desired content results without considering document storage because all the contents are stored in tables instead of streams and we can directly get these contents through SQL operations on tables. As a result, relational tables are not only helpful in content search, but also usable to get desired contents based on the labels found.

Stream searching reduction: Pre-processing contents is essential to reduce the size of streams. Consider the query that we want to find the quantity for a book with '$ISBN = 0 - 07 - 123057 - 2$' on the bookstore document. If the number of different books is b, the size of stream for element $ISBN$ is also b in previous approaches, as shown in Fig. 4(a). Then we need $O(b)$ to scan all the labels in $ISBN$ stream. $VERT$ processes selection in advance, such that the new stream for $ISBN$ is created based on content '0-07-123057-2'. That means the new stream has only 1 label inside since $ISBN$ is the key for books. Fig. 4(b) shows the rewritten query and size of new stream. $T_{ISBN'}$ is the new stream for element $ISBN$, and in Fig. 4(b) we use $ISBN_{0-07-123057-2}$ to explain $ISBN'$. So when the selectivity of an element is high, like in this example, $VERT$ also has high superiority to previous algorithms because it significantly reduces the searching in stream.

Structural joins reduction: There are two factors driving the high performance of $VERT$. One is searching space reduction as mentioned above and the other factor is number of structural joins reduction. Still consider the example in Fig. 4. The rewritten query has only two parent-child relationships need structural joins, while the original query has three. As we know structural join is an expensive operation, the reduction of structural joins leads a higher performance. Optimizations to further reduce size of streams and number of structural joins will be discussed in next section.

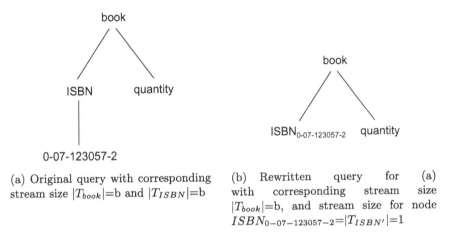

(a) Original query with corresponding stream size $|T_{book}|$=b and $|T_{ISBN}|$=b

(b) Rewritten query for (a) with corresponding stream size $|T_{book}|$=b, and stream size for node $ISBN_{0-07-123057-2}$=$|T_{ISBN'}|$=1

Fig. 4. Original and rewritten query examples in VERT

4.4   Optimizations for VERT

Tables in $VERT$ store label of each property and its value content. This approach differentiates contents by properties. However, there are still more semantics can be captured. With more semantic information, we can improve the performance by further reducing size of streams and number of structural joins in most documents. This motivates two approaches of optimizations for $VERT$.

Observation 1: Generally, after knowing the value on a certain property of an object, most queries want to find that object and then get some other properties of that object. For the query in Fig. 4, with the $ISBN$ value we need to find corresponding *book* and get the *quantity* of that book. After $VERT$ rewriting the query, the size of stream for $ISBN$ is significantly reduced. However the size of stream for *book* is still b, which means we need to search all the b labels in *book* stream although we know there is only one matches with the label in

ISBN stream. As a result, we can further rewrite the query to get the object *book* directly from property *ISBN* value.

Optimization 1: Instead of storing labels of property nodes and their value contents, we can put the labels of objects with property values into tables. E.g. in the bookstore document we put value contents for *ISBN*, *title* and so forth with labels of corresponding *book* in *object/property* tables as shown in Fig. 5(a). The 'Label' field of each table stores the label of object *book* and the following 'Content' corresponds the value contents of different properties in different tables, e.g. in $R_{book/ISBN}$ 'Content' in each tuple is the *ISBN* value of the book with 'Label' in the same tuple. The query in Fig. 4(a) is rewritten accordingly, as shown in Fig. 5(b), where $T_{book'}$ is the new stream for element *book* and $book_{ISBN=0-07-123057-2}$ is to explain *book'*. In new tables, we can directly select the label for book based on ISBN number in $R_{book/ISBN}$ without considering tags for element *ISBN*. Now we not only reduce the size of T_{book}, but also reduce the number of structural joins to be 1. So we can get a higher performance when we execute the new query.

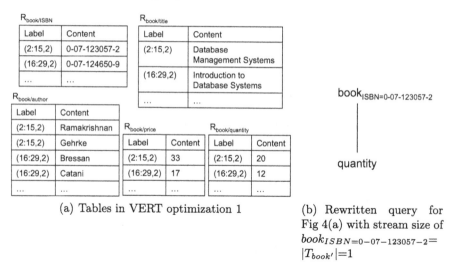

(a) Tables in VERT optimization 1

(b) Rewritten query for Fig 4(a) with stream size of $book_{ISBN=0-07-123057-2}=$ $|T_{book'}|=1$

Fig. 5. Tables and queries in VERT optimization 1

However, this optimization may lose order information in some cases. If we want to get all the authors' names of a certain book, since we ignore the element *author* and get all the name contents from $R_{book/author}$, we cannot differentiate the order in document. This limitation can be solved by adding ordinal number to different contents if the order is important.

Observation 2: There are some queries with multiple predicates on a certain element. E.g. a query on the bookstore document: find the ISBN number of the book with title 'Database Management Systems' and price of 33. To answer this query, *VERT* with optimization 1 needs to find the books with title 'Database

Management Systems' and books with price of 33 separately and join them to get results. With semantic information, we know *title* and *price* are properties of object *book*. If we have a table for this object which contains both of the properties, books satisfying these two constraints can be found directly and intermediate results can be avoided.

Optimization 2: A simple idea is to pre-merge tables in optimization 1 based on the same objects. But for multi-value properties, like *author* in our example, it is not practical to merge it with other properties. The information on multi-value properties can be found in document schema. After knowing this, we can merge all the single-value properties of an object into one table and keep tables for multi-value properties remain as what they are in optimization 1. The resulting tables for bookstore document is shown in Fig. 6. In R_{book}, each label of book is stored with all the single-value property contents of that book. When we process queries with multiple predicates on a certain object, we can do selection in that object table using these predicate constraints in one time. In this way, we can even simplify the query and prune intermediate results.

R_{book}

Label	ISBN	Title	Price	Quantity
(2:15,2)	0-07-123057-2	Database Management Systems	33	20
(16:29,2)	0-07-124650-9	Introduction to Database Systems	17	12
...	...	...	...	...

$R_{book/author}$

Label	Author
(2:15,2)	Ramakrishnan
(2:15,2)	Gehrke
(16:29,2)	Bressan
(16:29,2)	Catani
...	...

Fig. 6. Tables in VERT optimization 2

Declarations: Optimizations of $VERT$ are based on semantics captured from schema or document, or even declared by document owners. Generally, the more semantic information known, the further our algorithm can be optimized and the better performance can be achieved.

5   Experiments

In this section, we present experimental results on the performance of twig pattern search under $VERT$ algorithms with and without optimizations, which are introduced in section 4, and $TwigStack$. Final result extraction for each query can be done simply by selection in corresponding tables in our approach, however, in other algorithms it depends on the database implementation. The comparison for final result extraction is not included in our experiments.

5.1   Experimental Settings

Implementation and Hardware: We implemented all algorithms in Java. The experiments were performed on a 3.0GHz Pentium 4 processor with 1G RAM under OS of Windows XP.

XML Data Sets: We used three real-world and synthetic data sets for our experiments: NASA, DBLP and XMark. NASA is a 25 MB document with complex DTD schema. DBLP data set is a 127MB fragment of DBLP database. The characteristic of this data set is simple DTD schema and large data sources. We also used XMark benchmark data with size of 110MB.

Queries: We selected three meaningful queries for each data set. All the queries chosen contain predicates with content comparison, since content predicates appear in most practical queries. Generally, there are three types of queries: queries with predicates on equality comparison, queries with predicates on range comparison and queries with multiple predicates on different comparisons. The queries are shown in Table 1.

Table 1. Experimental queries

Query	Data Set	XPath Expression
Q1	NASA	//dataset//source/other[/date/year>'1919' and year<'2000']/author /lastName
Q2	NASA	//dataset/tableHead[//field/name='rah']//tableLinks //title
Q3	NASA	//dataset/history/ingest[/date[/year>'1949' and year<'2000'] [/month='Nov'][/day>'14' and day<'21']]/creator /lastName
Q4	DBLP	/dblp/article[/author='Jim Gray']/title
Q5	DBLP	//proceedings[/year>'1999']/isbn
Q6	DBLP	//inproceedings[/title='A Flexible Modelling Approach for Software Reliability Growth'][/year='1987'][/author='Sergio Bittanti'] /booktitle
Q7	XMark	//regions/africa/item[/mailbox/mail/from='Libero Rive'] /description
Q8	XMark	//item[//mail/date>'Sep']/location
Q9	XMark	//item[/location='United State'][/mailbox/mail[/date= '02/11/1999'][/to='Aamer Krolokowski']]/description

5.2   Experimental Results and Analysis

Our experiments mainly compare the stream management and total execution time between *TwigStack* and our approaches. The implementation of *TwigStack* adopts B^+ tree to organize streams, which ensures high performance of content stream management. The number of labeled nodes and number of streams to be managed for the three data sets under the two approaches are shown in Table 2. This result validates the analysis about the data management in last section.

The experimental results of execution time for the three data sets are shown in Fig. 7. From the results, we can see the execution time reduction is significant

Table 2. Number of labeled nodes and streams using *TwigStack* and *VERT*

Data Set	Number of Labeled Nodes		Number of Streams	
	TwigStack	VERT	TwigStack	VERT
NASA	997,987	532,963	121,833	68
DBLP	6,771,148	3,736,406	388,630	37
XMark	5,215,282	2,048,193	353,476	75

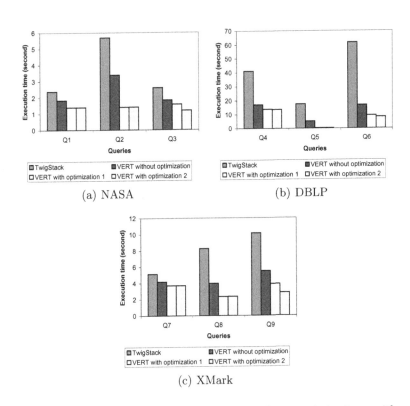

(a) NASA

(b) DBLP

(c) XMark

Fig. 7. Execution time by TwigStack and VERT without optimizations, with optimization 1 and with optimization 2 in three XML documents

for all the queries in DBLP document. This is in accord with our analysis in section 4.3, that is our approach works quite well for such XML document that has simple schema but large data sources. In DBLP document, there are only several types of data like proceedings, thesis, articles and so forth. There are large quantity of works under each type. The properties of each work type that appear as sub-elements in document are mostly the same and depth of the data tree is 3. As a result, for DBLP data, when we rewrite the query to reduce the query depth, we prune tremendous number of unnecessary tag checkings. Q2 in NASA data set is another example for the reason why *VERT* has higher performance than other approaches. The tag 'name' appears quite frequently in document with different semantic meanings, however, in Q2 what we are interested is only the field name. Instead of scanning all the 'name', our approach can move into field names directly using semantic tables. In this way, the execution time can be significantly reduced.

Comparing with optimization 1 and optimization 2 of $VERT$, we can see from the experimental result that for single-predicate queries there is no obvious difference. However, for multi-predicate queries, optimization 2 has a better performance as shown in Q3, Q6 and Q9. This again proves our analysis in Section 4.4.

6   Conclusion and Future Work

In this paper, we propose a novel algorithm $VERT$ to solve different content problems raised in existing algorithms. Unlike $TwigStack$ and its subsequent algorithms, our approach uses semantic tables to do content search, and then avoids the management of tremendous number data streams. Besides, $VERT$ can efficiently extract contents for predicate comparisons during query processing. Experimental results show that our method is much more efficient than $TwigStack$ for queries with content comparison as predicates. To answer the query, our method need not consider how the document stored in database. Instead, we can directly get the content results from tables.

One direction for future research to improve our algorithm is to discover more semantics in XML document and combine the semantic information into relational tables. Queries can be processed more efficient based on semantic tables and query rewriting by reducing unnecessary searches, number of structural joins and intermediate results. Also, our relational approach gives a new scheme to relate XML query processing algorithms to XML databases.

References

1. Al-Khalifa, S., Jagadish, H.V., Patel, J.M., Wu, Y., Koudas, N., Srivastava, D.: Structural joins: A primitive for efficient XML query pattern matching. In: Proc. of ICDE (2002)
2. Berglund, A., Chamberlin, D., Fernandez, M.F., Kay, M., Robie, J., Simeon, J.: XML Path Language (XPath) 2.0. W3C Working Draft (2003)
3. Boag, S., Chamberlin, D., Fernandez, M.F., Florescu, D., Robie, J., Simeon, J.: XQuery 1.0: An XML Query. W3C Working Draft (2003)
4. Bruno, N., Koudas, N., Srivastava, D.: Holistic twig joins: Optimal XML pattern matching. In: Proc. of ACM SIGMOD, ACM Press, New York (2002)
5. Chen, T., Lu, J., Ling, T.W.: On boosting holism in XML twig pattern matching using structural indexing techniques. In: Proc. of SIGMOD Conference (2005)
6. Grust, T.: Accelerating XPath location steps. In: Proc. of SIGMOD Conference (2002)
7. Jiang, H., Lu, H., Wang, W.: Efficient processing of XML twig queries with OR-predicates. In: Proc. of SIGMOD Conference (2004)

8. Jiang, H., Wang, W., Lu, H., Yu, J.: Holistic twig joins on indexed XML documents. In: Proc. of VLDB Conference (2003)

9. Lu, J., Chen, T., Ling, T.W.: Efficient processing of XML twig patterns with parent child edges: a look-ahead approach. In: Proc. of CIKM (2004)

10. Lu, J., Ling, T.W., Chan, C., Chen, T.: From region encoding to extended dewey: On efficient processing of XML twig pattern matching. In: Proc. of VLDB Conference (2005)

11. Rao, P.R., Moon, B.: PRIX: Indexing and Querying XML Using Prufer Sequences. In: Proc. of ICDE (2004)

12. Wang, H., Park, S., Fan, W., Yu, P.S.: ViST: A Dynamic index method for querying XML data by tree structures. In: Proc. of SIGMOD Conference (2003)

13. Yu, T., Ling, T.W., Lu, J.: Twigstacklistnot: A holistic twig join algorithm for twig query with NOT-predicates on XML data. In: Lee, M.L., Tan, K.-L., Wuwongse, V. (eds.) DASFAA 2006. LNCS, vol. 3882, Springer, Heidelberg (2006)

14. Zhang, C., Naughton, J., Dewitt, D., Luo, Q., Lohman, G.: On supporting containment queries in relational database management systems. In: Proc. of ACM SIGMOD, ACM Press, New York (2001)

A Conceptual Model for Multidimensional Analysis of Documents

Franck Ravat[2], Olivier Teste[1], Ronan Tournier[1], and Gilles Zurlfluh[2]

[1] IRIT, Université Toulouse 3, 118 route de Narbonne
F-31062 Toulouse Cedex 9, France
[2] IRIT, Université Toulouse 1, 2 rue du doyen G. Marty
F-31042 Toulouse Cedex 9, France
{ravat,teste,tournier,zurlfluh}@irit.fr

Abstract. Data warehousing and OLAP are mainly used for the analysis of transactional data. Nowadays, with the evolution of Internet, and the development of semi-structured data exchange format (such as XML), it is possible to consider entire fragments of data such as documents as analysis sources. As a consequence, an adapted multidimensional analysis framework needs to be provided. In this paper, we introduce an OLAP multidimensional conceptual model without facts. This model is based on the unique concept of dimensions and is adapted for multidimensional document analysis. We also provide a set of manipulation operations.

Keywords: Conceptual modelling, OLAP, Data warehouse, Document warehouse, Multidimensional analysis.

1 Introduction

OLAP (On-Line Analytical Processing) systems allow analysts to improve decision-making process by consulting and analysing aggregated historical business or scientific data. Such analyses are based on a centralized data resource management system, called a data warehouse [11].

1.1 Context and Motivation

The use of Multidimensional Databases (MDB) provides a global view of corporate data warehouse, and allows decision makers to gain insight into an enterprise performance through fast and interactive access to data. Within these databases, multidimensional modelling [11] represent data as points in a multidimensional space. To design MDBs, structures have been defined. These structures model data through the concepts of subjects of analysis, named *facts*, linked to the concept of analysis axes, named *dimensions* [11]. They compose a *star schema* [11]. Facts are groupings of analysis indicators or *measures*. Dimensions are composed of hierarchically ordered *parameters* which model the different detail levels or data granularities [11].

Transactional data may easily be processed because multidimensional analysis is robust and it is a well-mastered technique on numeric-centric data warehouses [24].

C. Parent et al. (Eds.): ER 2007, LNCS 4801, pp. 550–565, 2007.

But decision support systems have only excavated the surface layers of the task. Only 20% of corporate information system data is transactional, i.e. numeric [27]. The remaining 80%, namely "digital paperwork," stays out of reach of OLAP technology due to the lack of tools and resource management for non-numeric data such as text-rich documents. In order to provide increased analysis capacities, decision support systems should provide the use of 100% of all available data from corporate information systems. Analysts should be able to integrate text-rich documents or web data directly into the analysis process along with business data. Not taking into account these data sources would inevitably lead to the omission of relevant information during an important decision-making process or the inclusion of irrelevant information and thus producing inaccurate analyses [27].

OLAP provides powerful tools and methods but within a rigid framework. Unfortunately text is not as structured as data warehouse systems would tolerate. Recently, XML technology has provided a wide framework for sharing and working with documents within corporate networks or over the web. Thus, documents stored as semi-structured data were slowly integrated within data warehouses and repositories. Document warehousing slowly emerged [24], e.g. Xyleme[1]. On-line text and documents are now becoming conceivable data sources for multidimensional analysis.

By *multidimensional document analysis* throughout this paper we mean to analyse in an OLAP environment text-rich document data sources. To cope with the rigid framework inherited from the context, i.e. the data warehouse environment, we shall only consider structured or semi-structured sources (e.g. XML documents). For example, conference proceedings, patient files from a hospital information system, quality control reports…

In text-rich documents, internal data is almost exclusively text. As this data type is non-additive and non-numeric, traditional aggregation operations (sum, average…) will not work, thus there is a necessity for adapted aggregation operations. [18] lists a few ones inspired from text mining techniques and we defined in [21] an aggregation function for keywords. Within this paper, as an illustration, we shall use: TOP_KEYWORDS [18]. This aggregation function selects the major keywords of a text.

1.2 Motivating Example

In the following example, an analyst wishes to analyse the citations of some works of a research institute. The analysis task would be counting each time an author is cited in conference proceedings and display the results by author and by conference. For example, in the following table (Table 1a), author *A1* has been cited three times by *ER* authors. The analyst may then wish to determine the range of the researcher's works and analyse the subjects of the publications where the researcher's works are cited. As this analysis does not rest on traditional numerical data, but on factual data, the analyst will use the TOP_KEYWORDS function in order to display the two main keywords of the documents. These keywords will be aggregated per conference, hence giving a list of subjects instead of a number of publications. For example, in Table 1b, the three citations of the works of the author *A1* in *ER* conferences are related to *XML* and *Documents* topics. Author *A3* has always been cited in the same context (data mining), A3's works have a narrower range than works of A1 and A2.

---

[1] Xyleme Server from http://www.xyleme.com

Table 1. The number of times an author has been cited in a particular conference and the same analysis with the major keywords of the publications that cite the authors

a)

Conference	Institute Author	Inst1		
		A1	A2	A3
ER		3	2	1
SSDBM		2	-	-
DaWaK		1	1	2

b)

Conference	Institute Author	Inst1		
		A1	A2	A3
ER		XML, Docments	XML, Data Warehouse	Data Mining, Clustering
SSDBM		XML, Temporal DB	-	-
DaWaK		Data mining	Data mining	Data Mining, Clustering

The combination of these analyses would be very complex to model using traditional multidimensional modelling. Firstly, the analysis of textual data is not taken into account. Secondly, the analyst would need more than one data mart [11]. And thirdly, multidimensional modelling approaches explode the document structure into many separate elements requiring complex and tedious tasks from the data warehouse administrator. The two following subsections present the related works, the objectives and contributions of the paper.

1.3 Related Works

According to [5], two types of semi-structured documents may be found:

- *Data-centric documents* are raw data documents, mainly used by applications to exchange data (as in e-business application strategies). In this category, one may find lists and logs such as: invoices, orders, spreadsheets, or even "dumps" of databases.
- *Document-centric documents* also known as text-rich documents are the traditional paper documents, e.g. scientific articles, e-books, website pages.

The analysis of data-centric documents has been introduced in several propositions such as [9]. See [29,28,17] for a more complete list of these works. Although all these works consider textual data through the use of XML documents, these propositions do no take into consideration the more complex document-centric documents. As a consequence, this paper focuses on the analysis of document-centric documents.

We divide related works into two categories. The first category concerns multidimensional modelling and may be divided into two approaches:

1. Traditional conceptual multidimensional modelling: lists of works may be found in [25,22] and current issues are highlighted in [23]. Multidimensional modelling is based on the concepts of facts and dimensions. These models, conceptually or logically oriented, have been conceived for numeric data analysis and do not deal with documents where non-numeric data must be integrated. Extending these models is possible but would require dimensions using abnormal hierarchies and complex logical implementations.
2. Multidimensional modelling allowing complex data analysis: in [17] the authors defines an xFACT, a complex hierarchical structure containing structured and unstructured data (such as documents), where measures, called contexts, can be seen as complex object data. In [3], the authors present a complete XML approach for

modelling complex data analysis. Although this proposition takes into account complex data, the authors only use data-centric documents.

Current multidimensional modelling propositions are incomplete as they address only numeric analysis. To our knowledge there are no propositions taking into account document-centric document properties.

The second category concerns the addition of document-centric documents into multidimensional analysis. Within this category there are three approaches:

1. To assist multidimensional analysis by providing complementary documents: in [19] the authors combine traditional numeric analysis and information retrieval techniques to assist an analysis by providing documents relevant to the ongoing analysis context. The user must then read all retrieved documents.
2. To provide multidimensional OLAP analysis of documents: in [15,16,10,27], the authors present applications of document-centric document multidimensional analysis using a star schema. The authors propose the use of traditional OLAP framework to count documents according to keywords or topics organised into dimensions. These dimensions allow the user to analyse the number of documents represented by each keyword according to several analysis axes. Using a keyword dimension is limitative as no text analysis may be performed. In [27] the authors classify dimensions according to categories, but exclusively work on document meta-data (except for the keyword dimension). They neither take into account document structures nor document contents. Although limited, some commercial solutions start to appear, such as Text OLAP[2].
3. To analyse textual data directly: in [12] the authors describe a document warehouse where documents are grouped by structure families. Users can perform multidimensional analysis on documents or on structures, but limited to numeric analysis (numbers of documents or structure types). Finally, in [18], the authors describe a logical model based on the xFACT and specific aggregation functions inspired by text mining techniques for the multidimensional analysis of document-centric documents. More complete than [26], the authors provide adapted aggregation functions but do not detail them. The model lacks high level concepts that may easily be manipulated by decision makers. Moreover, apart from the informal description of aggregation functions, no adapted manipulation operations are presented.

These advanced propositions clearly show the limit of traditional models for analysing documents: 1) the suggested implementations never preserve document structure; 2) these structures remain unexploited; 3) non-numeric indicators cannot be handled easily; and as a consequence, 4) no flexibility is provided to the user in changing the focus of analysis.

So far, to our knowledge, there is no proposal for an adapted conceptual model for document-centric document analysis. Up to now, apart from [18], research works are based on quantitative analysis, e.g. the number of publications that contain a specific keyword. Textual data is provided for analysis through dimensions modelling analysis axes and not subjects of analysis. Analysis indicators (measures) are always numeric.

---

[2] Text OLAP, Megaputer, Polyanalyst Suite from http://www.megaputer/com/products/pa

1.4 Aims and Contributions

In this paper, as a first step to a more global framework for integrating documents in an OLAP system, we define a conceptual model adapted to the multidimensional analysis of documents. The aim of this model is to provide the analyst with a simple and adapted conceptual view [6], withdrawing all logical and physical constraints. In order to manipulate the concepts of the model, OLAP operations are revised.

The model has been designed to be used for scientific data sets, like the IASI[3] archive of the UMARF[4] facility. Although the facility holds numeric data, it mainly holds complex factual data (e.g. spectral data). Atmospheric research requires several complex analyses with many facts and dimensions. This would lead to the design of several data marts with a high redundancy between factual and dimensional data. Moreover, in a traditional model, an extensive use of complex operations to convert dimensions into facts and vice-versa would have been necessary [20]. Due to space limitation, we shall use throughout this paper an example of analysis of scientific publications and conference proceedings to monitor research activities.

The conceptual model has to ease the analyst's tasks and take into account document-centric documents characteristics. Firstly, these documents are composed of tree-like hierarchically structured data. Secondly, a document might refer to itself or to other documents (*e.g. hypertext links*). These links should be explicitly shown in order to ease understanding and navigation through data during analyses. For example, when analysing the references of a publication, the analyst has to clearly see (and not to guess) that a reference is nothing else than another publication. And thirdly and most important of all, when analysing documents, textual computer assisted analysis does not necessarily make sense. That is, when analysing a particular subject, the analyst may find himself in front of something lacking sense. Thus, the analyst must be able to easily change the subject and not be restrained by predefined subjects of analysis. In conclusion, the model needs to be: 1) able to represent document-centric data specificities; 2) ease the representation avoiding to provide the analyst with predefined and limited analysis solutions; and 3) ease manipulations of the concepts through a set of operations. To answer these objectives, we define a Galaxy model associated to a set of manipulation operations.

The rest of the paper is organized as follows: section 2 defines an adapted multidimensional model; section 3 presents a set of multidimensional operations. Finally section 4 concludes the paper and states future works.

2 Multidimensional Model

The model defined in the following section is based on a "factless multi-dimension" representation of a constellation schema. In this model, there are only analysis axes, named dimensions. These dimensions are gathered into groups to indicate compatible dimensions for a common analysis.

---

[3] **IASI:** Infrared Atmospheric Sounding Interferometer (http://smsc.cnes.fr/IASI/).
[4] **UMARF:** Unified Meteorological Archive and Retrieval Facility of EuMetSat (European Meteorology).

2.1 Grouping Dimensions in "Galaxies"

A dimensional scheme is conceptual grouping of dimensions. It is a generalisation of a constellation [11], and is nicknamed a "Galaxy" schema. Dimensions are grouped around nodes that model the dimensions that may be used together in a same analysis.

Definition: A *Galaxy* $G = (D^G, Star^G, Lk^G)$ where

- $D^G = \{D_1, \ldots, D_n\}$ is a set of *dimensions*,
- $Star^G : D_i \rightarrow 2^{D_i}$ is a function that associates each dimension D_i to its linked dimensions $D_j \in D^G$ ($D_j \neq D_i$). This expression models nodes c_z that may be expressed through: $\{D_{c1}, \ldots, D_{cn}\} \subseteq D^G \mid \forall i,j \in [c_1..c_n], i \neq j, \exists D_i \rightarrow 2^{Dj} \in Star^G$. This represents dimensions compatible within a same analysis.[5]
- $Lk^G = \{g_1, g_2, \ldots\}$ is a set of functions associating some attribute instances together through links, where $g^G : a_u^{D_i}\left(i_x^{D_i}\right) \rightarrow a_v^{D_j}\left(i_y^{D_j}\right)$ is the association of the instance i_x^{Di} of a_u^{Di} with the instance i_y^{Dj} of a_v^{Dj}, where ($D_i = D_j$) or ($D_i, D_j) \in D^G \mid D_j \in Star^G(D_i)$.

Links (Lk^G) represent "corresponds to" relationships between the values of the two attributes of the link. They are used within expressions of manipulation operations.

Notations. We note $D_j \in Star^G(D_i)$, the fact that D_i and D_j are linked together.

2.2 Dimension Concept

A dimension models an analysis axis along which data may be analysed. A dimension is characterized by hierarchically organised attributes, each attribute being a graduation of the analysis axis, i.e. detail levels or granularity levels.

Definition: A *dimension* $D=(A^D, H^D, I^D, IStar^D)$ where:

- $A^D = \{a_1^D, \ldots, a_r^D\}$ is a set of *attributes*,
- $H^D = \{H_1^D, \ldots, H_s^D\}$ is a set of *hierarchies*,
- $I^D = \{i_1^D, \ldots, i_t^D\}$ is a set of *dimension instances*. Each attribute has a value for each instance $a_u^{Di}(i_x^{Di})$, called an *attribute instance*.
- $IStar^D : I^D \rightarrow \left(I^{D_1}\right)^* \times \ldots \times \left(I^{D_n}\right)^*$ is a function that associates the instances of the D dimension to the instances of other linked dimensions through $Star^G$ ($\forall k \in [1..n], D_k \in D^G, D_k \neq D$ and $D_k \in Star^G(D)$, i.e. D_k is associated/linked to D).[6]

A hierarchy represents an analysis perspective within a dimension. It models the organisation of the different granularity levels, i.e. a particular view of the analysis axis graduations. A hierarchy H_i^D of D is an ordered list of attributes called parameters. It is an acyclic elementary path starting with the parameter of finest granularity and ending with one of coarsest granularity. Each parameter may be associated to weak attributes which represent complementary information.

---

[5] The notation 2^E represents the powerset of E.
[6] The notation $(I)^*$ represents a finite set of elements of I.

Definition: A *hierarchy* noted H^D_i or $H=(Param^H, Weak^H)$ where:
- $Param^H = <p^H_1,..., p^H_{np}>$ is an ordered set of attributes, called *parameters*, which represent the levels of granularity of the dimension, $\forall k \in [1..n_p]$, $p^H_k \in A^D$ and $p^H_1 = a^D_1$;
- $Weak^H : Param^H \rightarrow 2^{A^D - Param^H}$ is an application possibly associating *weak attributes* to parameters, completing the parameter semantic.

Attributes are of two types: a parameter is the data of a particular level of detail, e.g. a *research institute* or the *country* of a research institute; a weak attribute is complementary data of a parameter, such as the *name* or the *address* of a *research institute*. All hierarchies of a dimension start with a common root parameter ($\forall H_i \in H^D$, $p^{Hi}_1 = a^D_1$) and end by a parameter representing the coarser granularity (p^{Hi}_{np}).

To answer to document structure specificity, hierarchies are semantically richer than traditional hierarchies. This provides the analyst with a conceptual view as close as possible as document representation. Thus, dimensions modelling documents may use non-strict hierarchies [13].

Notations. $p_i \in H$ is a simplified notation for $p_i \in Param^H$. Whenever possible, if the context is obvious, notations H^D, $p^{Hi}_i (...)$ will be simplified by $H, p_i (...)$.

2.3   Example

In order to analyse the activity of research institutes, a decision-maker analyses scientific publications as well as reports produced by these institutes. To answer these requirements, the galaxy G_1 is created (see Fig. 1). It represents on the top part: articles published in a conference at a certain date and written by authors; and on the

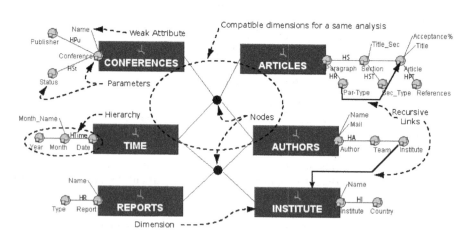

Fig. 1. Example of a Galaxy scheme (G_1): analysis of scientific publications and reports

bottom part: scientific reports. Within this example, two recursive links may be used to navigate through 1) the references of articles and 2) the institutes of authors.

Galaxy G_1 example: $D^{Gl} = \{D^{Conferences}, D^{Articles}, D^{Time}, D^{Authors}, \ldots\}$
$Star^{Gl} = \{D^{Conferences} \rightarrow (D^{Article}, D^{Time}, D^{Authors}), \ldots\}$
$Lk^{Gl} = \{g_{References}: a^{Articles}_{References} \rightarrow a^{Articles}_{Article}, \ldots\}$
Dimension example: $D^{Conferences} = \{A^{Conferences}, H^{Conferences}, I^{Conferences}, IStar^{Conferences}\}$
$A^{Conferences} = \{a_{Conference}, a_{Name}, a_{Publisher}, a_{Status}\}$; $H^{Conferences} = \{HPu, HSt\}$;
$I^{Conferences} = \{i^{Conference}_1, \ldots i^{Conference}_q\}$
$IStar^{Conferences} = \{i^{Conference}_k \rightarrow \{(i^{Articles}_{rk})^*, (i^{Time}_{sk})^*, (i^{Authors}_{tk})^*\} \mid \forall k \in [1..q],$
  $i^{Conference}_k \in I^{Conferences} \wedge \exists i^{Articles}_{rk} \in I^{Articles} \wedge \exists i^{Time}_{sk} \in I^{Time} \wedge \exists i^{Authors}_{tk} \in I^{Authors}\}$
Hierarchy example: $HPu = \{Param^{HPu}, Weak^{HPu}\}$
$Param^{HPu} = <a^{Conference}, a^{Publisher}>$ and $Weak^{HPu} = \{a^{Conference} \rightarrow \{a^{Name}\}\}$

Dimensions are used to define multidimensional analyses with a set of manipulation operations described in the following section. Links ease analysis expressions.

3 Multidimensional Operations

In order to manipulate concepts represented by the galaxy model, analysts need four operations that slightly differ from traditional OLAP operations [20]. The operations are based on the following needs:

- A focussing operation is necessary to select the subject of analysis projecting the subject data on several analysis axes.
- To narrow the analysis spectrum the user needs an operation to select a particular subset of data, thus reducing the whole quantity of analysed data.
- To take advantage of hierarchically ordered parameters, the user will need drilling operations to change the level of detail of the analysed data. The user will need two drilling operations: One to zoom into the details of the analysed data and the other for reversing the process, zooming out of the data.
- To change the analysis criteria, an operation is necessary either to rotate the analysed subject around other analysis axes or to rotate the analysis axes around different subjects.

In some models, authors pointed out the necessity of symmetric treatment of parameters and measures to ease definition and conception of algebras or calculus [2,4,8]. But some specific operations such as drilling did not operate symmetrically between all attributes. This problem put aside with our model.

Notations. $dom(D_i)$ is the domain of the dimension D_i, i.e. all $i_x \in I^{Di}$. We note $(dom(D_i))^*$ a finite set of elements of $dom(D_i)$. The instances of a galaxy G, composed of n dimensions, are represented by (1). All the instances of the attributes $a_j \in A^{Di}$ of dimension D_i are represented by (2). We define an aggregation function f_{AGG} (3) where $dom(f_{AGG}(dom(D_i)))$ corresponds to the domain of the aggregated values of the domain of the dimension D_i. In order to compare levels between parameters within a hierarchy H, we introduce the function $level$ (4).

$$dom(D_1) \times \ldots \times dom(D_n) = \prod_{i=1}^{n} dom(D_i) = dom(G) \tag{1}$$

$$dom(D_i.a_1) \times \ldots \times dom(D_i.a_n) = \prod_{j=1}^{\|A^{D_i}\|} dom(D_i.a_j) = dom(D_i) \tag{2}^7$$

$$f_{AGG} : (dom(D_i.p_j))^* \rightarrow dom(f_{AGG}(dom(D_i.p_j)))$$
$$(x_1,\ldots,x_m) \mapsto f_{AGG}(x_1,\ldots,x_m) \tag{3}$$

$$\text{Given } Param^H =< p_1,\ldots,p_{np} >, \ level^H(p_1) = 1,\ldots,level^H(p_{np}) = n_p$$
$$\text{and } \forall j \in [1..n], \ level^H(p_j) \le level^H(p_{np}) \tag{4}$$

All operations produce compatible outputs. The focus operation generates as output a subset of the galaxy, named s^G, and this subset is used as input for all other operations. In their turn these operations produce a subset, that allows chaining operations one after the other. The operation syntax is as follows:

$OPERATION\_NAME(input, operation\_parameters) = output$.

3.1 Focussing and Selection Operations

These two major manipulation operations allow the specification of analysis datasets.

Focussing is used to define an analysis subject and to project subject data on several analysis axes. Concretely, this operation allows the specification of a subject of analysis (DS) aggregating the analysis data through an aggregation function (f_{AGG}) for each selected measure according to the detail levels selected in the analysis axes.

Syntax: $FOCUS(G, S, P)=s^G$ where G is the input (a galaxy), $S=(f_{AGG}(DS.HS.p_i))$ is the focused subject of analysis with the parameter p_i of the hierarchy HS of dimension DS aggregated through the function f_{AGG} and $P=((D_x.H_x, Param_x),(D_y.H_y, Param_y),\ldots)$ is the set of projection axes with D_x being the dimension selected as the first analysis axis, D_y the second,... H_x is the current hierarchy of the axis represented by D_x, H_y is the current hierarchy of D_y,... $Param_x=<p_{x\_min},\ldots,p_{x\_max}>$ is an ordered set of parameters of H_x, where given $Param^{Hx}=<p_1,\ldots,p_{np}>$, $level^{Hx}(p_{x\_min}) \ge level^{Hx}(p_1)$ and $level^{Hx}(p_{x\_max}) \le level^{Hx}(p_{np})$. $Param_x$ represents the selected parameters of D_x (it is a subset of $Param^{Hx}$). In the same way $Param_y$ is a subset of $Param^{Hy}$.

Conditions: $\forall\ D_i \in P, D_i \in Star^G(DS)$, i.e. the dimensions selected as analysis axes are linked to the dimension selected as subject (DS). The aggregation function f_{AGG} must be compatible with the parameter instances of p_i that are to be aggregated.

Mathematically: $Focus$ (7) $= Aggregation$ (6) $\circ Projection$ (5) where:

$$\prod_{i=1}^{n} dom(D_i) \xrightarrow{\ PROJECT\ } (dom(DS.p_i))^* \times \prod_{j=1}^{\|P\|} \left(\prod_{k=\min}^{\max} dom(D_j.p_k) \right) \tag{5}$$

---

[7] We recall that $\|A^{Di}\|$ is the cardinality of A^{Di}. Here, the number of attributes within A^{Di}, i.e. r.

$$\left(dom(DS.p_i)\right)^* \times \prod_{j=1}^{\|P\|}\left(\prod_{k=j\_min}^{j\_max} dom\left(D_j.p_k\right)\right) \xrightarrow{\quad AGGREGATE \quad}$$

$$dom\left(f_{AGG}\left(dom(DS.p_i)\right)\right) \times \prod_{j=1}^{\|P\|}\left(\prod_{k=j\_min}^{j\_max} dom\left(D_j.p_k\right)\right) \quad (6)$$

$$\prod_{i=1}^{n} dom(D_i) \xrightarrow{\quad FOCUS \quad} dom\left(f_{AGG}\left(dom(DS.p_i)\right)\right) \times \prod_{j=1}^{\|P\|}\left(\prod_{k=j\_min}^{j\_max} dom\left(D_j.p_k\right)\right) \quad (7)$$

We also define a simplified notation (8), where s^G represents a subpart of the galaxy with a dimension designated as subject (S_{AGG}) analysed (projected and aggregated) according to the dimensions of the projection set (P).

$$dom(G) \xrightarrow{\quad FOCUS \quad} dom\left(s^G\right) \text{ with } dom\left(s^G\right) = dom\left(S_{AGG}\right) \times dom(P) \quad (8)$$

Example. Within the galaxy presented in figure 1 (G_1), the analyst may use any dimension as a subject of analysis. Here, the analyst focuses his analysis on major keywords of articles displayed by author and by year. We will suppose that the user uses a bi-dimensional table to produce the output, [8,22]. The user will thus focus on a dimension (DS) and project its data onto two analysis axes: a line dimension and the column dimension. The aggregation function TOP_KEYWORDS returns the two major keywords. The following instruction produces the table displayed in the following figure.

FOCUS (G₁, TOP_KEYWORDS(ARTICLES.HS.Section),
((TIME.HTime, <Year>), (AUTHORS.HA, <Author>))) = s^{G1}₁

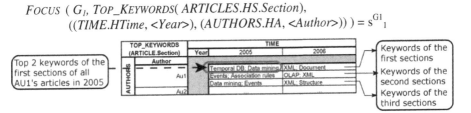

Fig. 2. Example of manipulations: focus instruction projecting analysis subject data onto two analysis axes (years and authors)

Selection is used to restrict the analysis data. By specifying a restrictive predicate, the user may restrict analysis data on an analysis axis or on the analysis subject. All instances selected by a predicate p are maintained in the current data selection. All other instances are removed. Notice that if this operation is applied directly on the galaxy, this allows the removal of instances before aggregation process.

Syntax: $SELECT(G, p) = s^G$ or $SELECT(s^G, p) = s^G$ where G (or s^G) is the input and p is a restrictive predicate on an attribute a_j of a dimension D_i.

Conditions: $a_j \in D_i$ and $D_i \in Star^G(DS)$.

Mathematically:

$$dom(G) \xrightarrow{\quad SELECT \quad} dom(G) - dom(\neg p) \text{ or } dom\left(s^G\right) \xrightarrow{\quad SELECT \quad} dom\left(s^G\right) - dom(\neg p) \quad (9)$$

The notation $dom(\neg p)$ is the subset of the domain that does not satisfy the predicate p. The reverse operation, $UNSELECT(s^G) = s^G$, removes all restrictive predicates.

Example. In order to narrow the analysis spectrum, the analyst decides to reduce the analysis to only *Au1*'s articles and to analyse major keywords only in introductions. Using the previously defined subset of data (s^G), the following instructions produce the table (b) displayed in the following figure:

$$SELECT(\ SELECT(s^{G1}{}_1, ARTICLE.Sec\_Type=`Introduction'),$$
$$AUTHORS.Author=`Au1') = s^{G1}{}_2$$

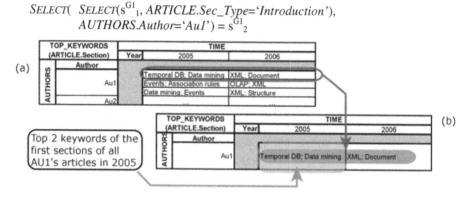

Fig. 3. Example of manipulations: application of two restrictions

3.2 Drilling Operations

Once an analysis has been specified, i.e. s^G has been defined, the user may wish to change the level of detail at which analysis data is being projected.

Using a drill-down operation, the analyst may zoom into more detailed data. This operation consists in adding to the parameter list of a projection axis ($Param_i$) a new parameter p_{new}, from the current hierarchy, whose level is inferior to the lowest currently selected parameter (p_{min}).

Syntax: $DRILLDOWN(s^G, D_i, p_{new})=s^G{}_1$ where s^G is the input, D_i is a dimension of the projection set P of s^G, i.e. $\exists(D_i.H_i, Param_i) \in P$ and $p_{new} \in H_i$.

Condition: The parameter must be of a lower level than the lowest one already selected: $level^{Hi}(p_{new}) < level^{Hi}(p_{min})$

Mathematically:

$$DrillDown: dom(s^G) \xrightarrow{DRILLDOWN} dom(S_{AGG}) \times dom(P) \times dom(D_i.p_{new})$$

$$\text{where} \quad dom(P) = \prod_{\substack{j=1 \\ j \neq i}}^{|P|} \left(\prod_{k=j\_min}^{j\_max} dom(D_j.p_k) \right) \times \prod_{k'=i\_min}^{i\_max} dom(D_i.p_{k'}) \tag{10}$$

Note that, $dom(P)$ represents the domains of the selected parameters of the dimensions not taking part in the drilling operations ($\forall D_j \mid \exists(D_j.H_j, Param_j) \in P$ and $j \neq i$) as well as the domains of the selected parameters of the dimensions taking part in the drilling operation (D_i). We recall that $Param_j=<p_{j\_min},...,p_{j\_max}>$.

The opposite operation, roll-up, is used to gain a more global view of the analysis data. This operation is used to zoom out of the analysis data. This operation consists in removing all parameters from the selected parameter list ($Param_i$) whose levels are lower than a selected parameter. The operation will eventually add the parameter had it not been in the list.

Syntax: $ROLLUP(s^G, D_i, p_{sup}) = s^G_1$ where s^G is the input, D_i is a dimension of the projection set P of s^G, i.e. $\exists (D_i.H_i, Param_i) \in P$ and $p_{sup} \in H_i$.

Condition: The parameter must be of a higher level than the lowest one already selected: $level^{Hi}(p_{sup}) > level^{Hi}(p_{min})$.

Mathematically: In the following, we express $level^{Hi}(p_{sup}) = sup$

$$RollUp: dom(s^G) \xrightarrow{\;ROLLUP\;}$$

$$dom(S_{AGG}) \times \prod_{\substack{j=1 \\ j \neq i}}^{|P|} \left(\prod_{k=j\_min}^{j\_max} dom(D_j.p_k) \right) \times \prod_{k'=sup}^{i\_max} dom(D_i.p_{k'}) \tag{11}$$

Here, $\prod_{k'=sup}^{i\_max} dom(D_i.p_{k'})$ is the domain of the parameters of the dimension taking part in the drilling operation (D_i). The domains of the parameters whose levels are inferior to p_{sup} are removed (thus k' minimal bound is $level^{Hi}(p_{sup}) = sup$).

Example. As in traditional models, the drill-down operation could be used to display the keywords by months rather than by year. But in our model, this operation may also be applied on the current hierarchy of the focused dimension. This is critical when textual aggregation functions produce results lacking sense as it enables users to gain insight within the aggregation process. In the following example, rather than analyzing keywords by section, the analyst decides to analyse then by subsections. The following instruction produces the table displayed in the following figure:

$$DRILLDOWN(s^{G1}_2, ARTICLE, Subsection) = s^{G1}_3$$

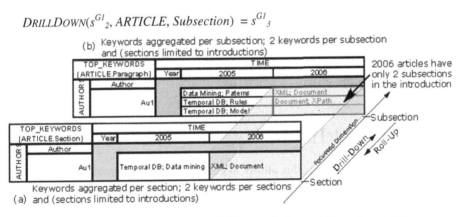

Fig. 4. Example of manipulations: drilling on the focused dimension: *Article*

Drilling on the focused hierarchy allows powerful combination of 1) the usage of the hierarchical model provided by the hierarchical structure of the dimension data; and 2) the usage of the aggregation process allowing the summarisation of selected data. Drilling on the focussed hierarchy may be seen as adding in the manipulation a "third" analysis axis.

This operation allows the user to gain insight within the aggregation process. This is due to the fact that textual aggregation functions do not operate like numeric aggregation functions. Indeed, extracting the major keywords of an article does not necessarily correspond to the extraction of the major keywords of each section. This is a common problem of 1) holistic functions [7] which may not be computed from lower results (e.g. median function); and 2) component ranking such as pointed out in [14] where in an information retrieval framework different granularities tend to mess up statistics. Physically, when drilling on textual data and using a holistic aggregation function, aggregates are recomputed with the newly designated granularity of the dataset. Thus the analyst may get a better understanding by seeing these different aggregates.

3.3 Analysis Reorganisation Operation

In some cases, the user might wish to reorganise the analysed dataset. To do this, he uses an operation that will change structural elements of the subpart of the galaxy s^G.

The rotation operation replaces by a new dimension one of the dimensions of s^G: the analysis subject (DS), or one of the analysis axes, i.e. a dimension from the projection set ($D_i \in P$).

Syntax: $Rotate(s^G, D_{old}, D_{new}.H_{new}, A) = s^G_1$ where s^G is the input, D_{old} is the dimension to be replaced, D_{new} is the new dimension, H_{new} its currently selected hierarchy and A depends on D_{old}. If $D_{old} = DS$ then $A = f'_{AGG}(p_{new})$, else if $D_{old} \in P$ then $A = Param_{new} = <p_{new\_min}, \ldots, p_{new\_max}>$ is a subset of $Param^{Hnew}$.

Condition: If $D_{old} = DS$ then $\forall D_k \in P$, $D_k \in Star^G(D_{new})$ and $p_{new} \in H_{new}$. If $D_{old} \in P$ then $D_{new} \in Star^G(DS)$ $Param_{new} \subseteq Param^{Hnew}$ and $level^{Hnew}(p_{new\_min}) < \ldots < level^{Hnew}(p_{new\_min})$

Mathematically: If $D_{old} = DS$ then the operation corresponds to (12), else if $D_{old} \in P$, the operation corresponds to (13).

$$Rotate : dom(s^G) \xrightarrow{ROTATE} dom(f'_{AGG}(dom(D_{new}.p_{new}))) \times dom(P) \tag{12}$$

$$Rotate : dom(s^G) \xrightarrow{ROTATE}$$
$$dom(S_{AGG}) \times \prod_{\substack{j=1 \\ j \neq old}}^{\|P\|} \left(\prod_{k=j\_min}^{j\_max} dom(D_j.p_k) \right) \times \prod_{k'=new\_min}^{new\_max} dom(D_{new}.p_{k'}) \tag{13}$$

Notice that if $D_{old} = D_{new}$, this allows to change one of the current selected hierarchy (HS, H_x, H_y...). Notice also that when rotating the subject of analysis, this is the equivalent of *FRotate* [22] or *DrillAcross* operations [1].

3.4 The Use of Recursive Links

Links within the Galaxy may be used as paths to access particular data. They allow flexibility when designating subparts of documents and simplify query specifications. For example, the following operation sequence uses the link between *Reference* and *ARTICLE* (see figure 1). It focuses on the major keywords of each section of articles that are cited by *Au1*, i.e. the articles in reference sections of all *Au1*'s publications.

SELECT (SELECT (FOCUS (TOP_KEYWORDS (ARTICLES.HR.Reference.Section),
((TIME.HTime, <Year>), (ARTICLE.Reference.AUTHORS.HA, <IdA>))), AUTHORS.IdA='Au1'),
ARTICLE.Reference.TIME.Year > 2005)

Where *ARTICLE.Reference.AUTHORS* are the authors of the articles referenced by *Au1*'s publications, *ARTICLE.Reference.TIME.Year* are years of publication of the referenced articles whereas *TIME.Year* are the years of publication of *Au1*'s articles.

As another example, the query that provides the table displayed in Table 1 is:

SELECT(FOCUS(TOP_KEYWORDS(ARTICLES.HS.Article),((ARTICLES.Reference.AUTHORS.HA,<Author,Institute>),(CONFERENCES.HConf,<Name>))),ARTICLES.References.AUTHORS.Institute='Inst1')

Where *ARTICLES.References.AUTHORS* are the authors of the articles cited in the conferences *CONFERENCES.Name* in the articles whose content is specified by *ARTICLES.Article*. Notice that hierarchies are specified only in the focus operation to allow drilling operations that follow the hierarchical structure of the parameters.

The links allow more flexibility when querying data sources that are interconnected together, as the links may be used to thoroughly explore and analyse datasets.

4   Conclusion and Future Works

In this paper we have defined an adapted multidimensional conceptual model for the analysis of text-rich documents. The model is based on a unique conceptual element: a dimension. It is associated to a set of manipulation operations to allow multidimensional OLAP analysis.

Contrarily to previous multidimensional models, this proposition has the advantage of preserving the document structure as well as the links within these structures. The usage of links allows thorough analysis of documents interconnected together such as articles that reference other articles. Moreover, these links simplify the expression of queries that would be very complex in other environments. The absence of factual entity does not restrain the analyst with predefined subjects of analysis that might produce analyses lacking sense on text-rich data sources. The associated manipulation operations allow easy switching of the focus of the analysis subject. Hence, the user may compensate the lack of accuracy in textual analysis by an increased flexibility within this OLAP framework. The preservation of the document structure allows analysts to use this structure in order to refine their analyses and perform fine tuning. Notice that facts may still be represented within this model by very simple dimensions, where each measure is a hierarchy with a unique parameter.

Due to lack of space we apologize for not having presented the logical level of this framework. We are currently extending a prototype: GraphicOLAPSQL [22]. This prototype is based on an Oracle 10g database, XML files for documents and a Java interface. In our implementation, in order to maintain performance, each dimension is linked to all other dimension instances allowing quick rotation around different subjects, i.e. in the Oracle R-OLAP environment this is physically implemented through VArrays and Nested Tables, depending on index sizes.

This conceptual model is the first step for a more complete framework. Throughout this paper, we have suggested the use of a simple aggregation function (TOP_KEYWORDS). As future works, we consider the specification of a set of adapted aggregation functions such as AVG_KW [21] for document-centric document analysis.

In parallel, as the goal of the conceptual model is to ease the process of analysis, we also intend to adapt and implement a graphical OLAP query language [22].

References

1. Abelló, A., Samos, J., Saltor, F.: Implementing operations to navigate semantic star schemas. In: 6th ACM int. workshop on Data Warehousing and OLAP (DOLAP), pp. 56–62. ACM, New York (2003)
2. Agrawal, R., Gupta, A., Sarawagi, S.: Modeling Multidimensional Databases. In: ICDE. Int. Conf. on Data Engineering, pp. 232–243 (1997)
3. Boussaid, O., Messaoud, R.B., Choquet, R., Anthoard, S.: X-Warehousing: An XML-Based Approach for Warehousing Complex Data. In: Manolopoulos, Y., Pokorný, J., Sellis, T. (eds.) ADBIS 2006. LNCS, vol. 4152, pp. 39–54. Springer, Heidelberg (2006)
4. Cabibbo, L., Torlone, R.: A Systematic Approach to Multidimensional Databases. In: SEBD. 5th Italian Symposium on Advanced Database Systems, pp. 361–377 (1997)
5. Fuhr, N., Großjohann, K.: A Query Language for Information Retrieval in XML Documents. In: 24th int. ACM SIGIR conf. on Research and development in information retrieval, pp. 172–180. ACM Press, New York (2001)
6. Golfarelli, M., Rizzi, S., Saltarelli, E.: WAND: A CASE Tool for Workload-Based Design of a Data Mart. In: SEBD. 10th Italian Symposium on Advanced Database Systems, pp. 422–426 (2002)
7. Gray, J., Bosworth, A., Layman, A., Pirahesh, H.: Data Cube: A Relational Aggregation Operator Generalizing Group-By, Cross-Tab, and Sub-Total. In: ICDE. 12th Int. Conf. on Data Engineering, pp. 152–159 (1996)
8. Gyssen, M., Lakshmanan, L.V.S.: A Foundation for Multi-Dimensional Databases. In: VLDB. 23rd Int. Conf. on Very Large Data Bases, pp. 106–115 (1997)
9. Jensen, M.R., Møller, T.H., Pedersen, T.B.: Specifying OLAP Cubes On XML Data. In: SSDBM. 13th Int. Conf. on Scientific and Statistical Database Management, pp. 101–112. IEEE Computer Society Press, Los Alamitos (2001)
10. Keith, S., Kaser, O., Lemire, D.: Analyzing Large Collections of Electronic Text Using OLAP. In: APICS 29th Conf. in Mathematics, Statistics and Computer Science, pp. 17–26 (2005)
11. Kimball, R.: The data warehouse toolkit, 2nd edn. John Wiley and Sons, Chichester (2003)
12. Khrouf, K., Soulé-Dupuy, C.: A Textual Warehouse Approach: A Web Data Repository. In: Mohammadian, M. (ed.) Intelligent Agents for Data Mining and Information Retrieval, pp. 101–124. Idea Publishing Group (2004)
13. Malinowski, E., Zimányi, E.: Hierarchies in a multidimensional model: From conceptual modeling to logical representation. J. of Data & Knowledge Engineering (DKE) 59(2), 348–377 (2006)
14. Mass, Y., Mandelbrod, M.: Component Ranking and Automatic Query Refinement for XML Retrieval. In: Fuhr, N., Lalmas, M., Malik, S., Szlávik, Z. (eds.) INEX 2004. LNCS, vol. 3493, pp. 73–84. Springer, Heidelberg (2005)
15. McCabe, C., Lee, J., Chowdhury, A., Grossman, D.A., Frieder, O.: On the design and evaluation of a multi-dimensional approach to information retrieval. In: 23rd Int. ACM SIGIR Conf. on Research and Development in Information Retrieval, pp. 363–365. ACM, New York (2000)

16. Mothe, J., Chrisment, C., Dousset, B., Alau, J.: DocCube: Multi-dimensional visualisation and exploration of large document sets. J. of the American Society for Information Science and Technology (JASIST) 54(7), 650–659 (2003)
17. Nassis, V., Rajugan, R., Dillon, T.S., Wenny Rahayu, J.: Conceptual Design of XML Document Warehouses. In: Kambayashi, Y., Mohania, M.K., Wöß, W. (eds.) DaWaK 2004. LNCS, vol. 3181, pp. 1–14. Springer, Heidelberg (2004)
18. Park, B.K., Han, H., Song, I.Y.: XML-OLAP: A Multidimensional Analysis Framework for XML Warehouses. In: Tjoa, A.M., Trujillo, J. (eds.) DaWaK 2005. LNCS, vol. 3589, pp. 32–42. Springer, Heidelberg (2005)
19. Pérez, J.M., Berlanga-Llavori, R., Aramburu-Cabo, M.J., Pedersen, T.B.: Contextualizing data warehouses with documents. In: Decision Support Systems (DSS), Elsevier, Amsterdam (in press, 2007), doi:10.1016/j.dss.2006.12.005
20. Rafanelli, M.: Operators for Multidimensional Aggregate Data. In: Rafanelli, M. (ed.) Multidimensional Databases: Problems and Solutions, ch.5, pp. 116–165. Idea Group Inc (2003)
21. Ravat, F., Teste, O., Tournier, R.: OLAP Aggregation Function for Textual Data Warehouse. In: ICEIS. 9th Int. Conf. on Enterprise Information Systems, pp. 151–156. INSTICC Press (June 2007)
22. Ravat, F., Teste, O., Tournier, R., Zurfluh, G.: Algebraic and graphic languages for OLAP manipulations. Int. j. of Data Warehousing and Mining (DWM) (to appear, 2007)
23. Rizzi, S., Abelló, A., Lechtenbörger, J., Trujillo, J.: Research in data warehouse modeling and design: dead or alive? In: DOLAP. 9th ACM Int. Workshop on Data Warehousing and OLAP, pp. 3–10. ACM, New York (2006)
24. Sullivan, D.: Document Warehousing and Text Mining. Wiley John & Sons, Chichester (2001)
25. Torlone, R.: Conceptual Multidimensional Models. In: Rafanelli, M. (ed.) Multidimensional Databases: Problems and Solutions, ch.3, pp. 69–90. Idea Group Inc, USA (2003)
26. Tseng, F.S.C.: Design of a multi-dimensional query expression for document warehouses. Information Sciences 174(1-2), 55–79 (2005)
27. Tseng, F.S.C., Chou, A.Y.H.: The concept of document warehousing for multi-dimensional modeling of textual-based business intelligence. J. of Decision Support Systems (DSS) 42(2), 727–744 (2006)
28. Vrdoljak, B., Banek, M., Skočir, Z.: Integrating XML Sources into a Data Warehouse. In: Lee, J., Shim, J., Lee, S.-g., Bussler, C., Shim, S. (eds.) DEECS 2006. LNCS, vol. 4055, pp. 133–142. Springer, Heidelberg (2006)
29. Yin, X., Pedersen, T.B.: Evaluating XML-extended OLAP queries based on a physical algebra. In: DOLAP. 7th Int. Workshop on Data Warehousing and OLAP, pp. 73–82. ACM, New York (2004)

Automatic Hidden-Web Table Interpretation by Sibling Page Comparison*

Cui Tao and David W. Embley

Brigham Young University, Provo, Utah 84602, USA

Abstract. The longstanding problem of automatic table interpretation still illudes us. Its solution would not only be an aid to table processing applications such as large volume table conversion, but would also be an aid in solving related problems such as information extraction and semi-structured data management. In this paper, we offer a conceptual modeling solution for the common special case in which so-called sibling pages are available. The sibling pages we consider are pages on the hidden web, commonly generated from underlying databases. We compare them to identify and connect nonvarying components (category labels) and varying components (data values). We tested our solution using more than 2,000 tables in source pages from three different domains—car advertisements, molecular biology, and geopolitical information. Experimental results show that the system can successfully identify sibling tables, generate structure patterns, interpret tables using the generated patterns, and automatically adjust the structure patterns, if necessary, as it processes a sequence of hidden-web pages. For these activities, the system was able to achieve an overall F-measure of 94.5%.

1 Introduction

The World Wide Web serves as a powerful resource for every community. Much of this online information, indeed, the vast majority, is stored in databases on the so-called hidden web.[1] Hidden-web information is usually only accessible to users through search forms and is typically presented to them in tables. Automatically understanding hidden-web pages is a challenging task. In this paper, we introduce a domain independent, web-site independent, unsupervised way to automatically interpret tables from hidden-web pages.

Tables present information in a simplified and compact way in rows and columns. Data in one row/column usually belongs to the same category or provides values for the same concept. The labels of a row/column describe this category or concept.

Although a table with a simple row and column structure is common, tables can be much more complex. Figure 1 shows an example. Tables may be nested

---

* Supported in part by the National Science Foundation under Grant #0414644.
[1] There are more than 500 billion hidden-web pages. The surface web, which is indexed by common search engines only constitutes less than 1% of the World Wide Web. The hidden web is several orders of magnitude larger than the surface web [10].

C. Parent et al. (Eds.): ER 2007, LNCS 4801, pp. 566–581, 2007.

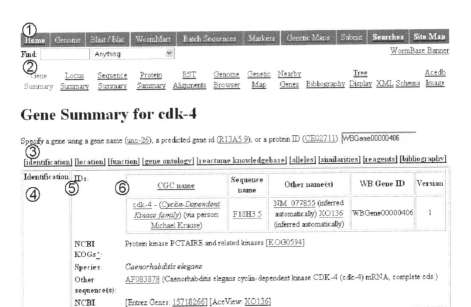

Fig. 1. A Sample Table from WormBase (http://www.wormbase.org)

or conjoined as are the tables in Figure 1. Labels may span across several cells to give a general description as do *Identification* and *Location* in Table 4 of Figure 1. Although labels commonly appear on the top or left, table designers occasionally place labels on the right side of a table. In long tables, labels sometimes appear at the end of a table or in the middle of a table, every few rows, in order to help a reader find the correspondence between labels and data. Sometimes tables are rearranged to fit the space available. Label-value pairs may appear in multiple columns across a page or in multiple rows placed below one another down a page. These complexities make automatic table interpretation challenging.

In this paper, we introduce a conceptual-modeling-based table interpretation system. We use a conceptual-modeling language to model both the input

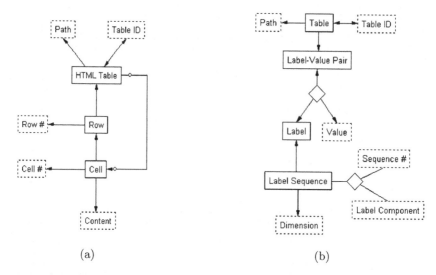

(a)   (b)

Fig. 2. Conceptual Model Instances for (a) An Input HTML Table and (b) An Output Interpretation

tables and the output interpretations as suggested in [5]. When we do, the table-interpretation problem becomes a problem of transforming one populated conceptual-model instance to another.

Figure 2(a) shows the model instance for an HTML page containing one or more tables. Each HTML table has a unique *Table ID* (e.g. the table numbers in Figure 1), and a unique *Path* in terms of the page's DOM tree (e.g. /html/table[4]/tbody/tr[1]/td[2]/table[1]/tbody/tr[6]/td[2][2]). The tags <table> and </table> delimit HTML tables in a web document. An *HTML Table* has one or more *Rows* (delimited by <tr> tags); each *Row* has a *Row#*. A *Row* has one or more *Cells* (delimited by <td> or <th> tags); each *Cell* has a *Cell#*. Each *Cell* contains *Content* and may contain other *HTML Tables*. The *Content* is the content of a cell, not between <table> and </table> tags. The *Content* may consist of HTML tags, images, and strings. Using Figure 1 as an example, Table 4 has three *Rows*, starting with *Identification*, *Location*, and *Function*. In the first *Row* are two *Cells*. The *Content* of the first *Cell* is the string "*Identification*", and the content of the second *Cell* is an *HTML Table*, Table 5, which has seven *Rows* and fourteen *Cells*, two of which contain tables, Table 6 and Table 7.

As Figure 2(b) shows, to interpret an HTML table is to properly associate table category labels with table data values, as the set of label-value pairs of the table. The *Path* for a table's interpretation is its path in an HTML page. We model the label-value pairs according to Wang notation [14]. The Wang Notation for a table is a set of *Label-Value Pairs*. Each *Label-Value Pair* contains one *Label* and one *Value*. Each *Label* has one or more *Label Sequences*, one to describe

---

[2] Each table has a unique path; each path does not necessary lead to an HTML table.

Home	Genome	Blast / Blat	WormMart	Batch Sequences	Markers	Genetic Maps	Submit	Searches	Site Map

Find: [   ] [Anything ▼]   WormBase Banner

| Gene Summary | Locus Summary | Sequence Summary | Protein Summary | EST Alignments | Genome Browser | Genetic Map | Nearby Genes | Bibliography | Tree Display | Acedb XML Schema | Image |

Gene Summary for dyb-1

Specify a gene using a gene name (unc-26), a predicted gene id (R13A5.9), or a protein ID (CE02711): [dyb-1]

[identification] [location] [function] [gene ontology] [reactome knowledgebase] [alleles] [similarities] [reagents] [bibliography]

<table>
<tr><td rowspan="9">Identification</td><td>IDs:</td><td colspan="6">

CGC name	Sequence name	Other name(s)	WB Gene ID	Version
dyb-1 - (DYstroBrevin homolog) (via person: Laurent Segalat)	F47G6.1	NM_058459 (inferred automatically) 1B963 (inferred automatically)	WBGene00001115	1

</td></tr>
<tr><td>Concise Description:</td><td colspan="6">The dyb-1 gene encodes a homolog of mammalian alpha-dystrobrevin (DTNA; OMIM:601239), mutation of which can lead to left ventricular noncompaction with congenital heart defects. [details]</td></tr>
<tr><td>NCBI KOGs*:</td><td colspan="6">Beta-dystrobrevin [KOG4301]</td></tr>
<tr><td>Species:</td><td colspan="6">Caenorhabditis elegans</td></tr>
<tr><td>NCBI:</td><td colspan="6">[Entrez Genes: 14670171] [AceView: 1B963]</td></tr>
<tr><td>Gene model(s):</td><td colspan="6">

Gene Model	Status	Nucleotides (coding/transcript)	Protein	Swissprot	Amino Acids
F47G6.1 1, 2	confirmed by cDNA(s)	1773/7391 bp	WP:CE26812	DTN1_CAEEL	590 aa

</td></tr>
<tr><td>Putative ortholog(s):</td><td colspan="6">Caenorhabditis briggsae: CBG22285 [syntenic alignment] (Stein LD et al ; best reciprocal blastp match-seg-off)</td></tr>
</table>

Location	Genetic Position: I:-15.38 +/- 0.361 cM [mapping data]
	Genomic Position: I:1483084..1490474 bp

Function	Mutant Phenotype: Definitions of abbreviations used in the text.
	RNAi: WT [For details see: Ahringer JA 16 Nov 2000]
	Phenotype(s): WT [For details see: Rual JF 01 Sep 2004]

Fig. 3. A Second Sample Table from WormBase

each *Dimension*. A *Label Sequence* is a sequence of *Label Components* ordered by their *Sequence #*'s. As an example, consider the value, *342 aa*, that appears in Table 7 of Figure 1. Table 7 is two-dimensional, as are many, if not most HTML tables. The first dimension has the label sequence *Identification.Gene model(s).Amino Acids* where the sequence #'s of the label sequence designate identification as the first label component, *Gene model(s)* as the second, and *Amino Acids* as the third. The second dimension has the label sequence *Identification.Gene model(s).1*[3].

Although automatic table interpretation can be complex, if we have another page, such as the one in Figure 3, that has essentially the same structure, the

---

[3] If a table has multiple records (usually multiple rows) and if the records do not have labels, we add record numbers. The table under *Identification.Gene model(s)*, for example, has two records (two rows), but no row labels. We therefore label the first record *1* and the second record *2*.

system might be able to obtain enough information about the structure to make automatic interpretation possible. We call pages that are from the same web site and have similar structures *sibling pages*.[4] The two pages in Figures 1 and 3 are sibling pages. They have the same basic structure, with the same top banners that appear in all the pages from this web site, with the same table title (*Gene Summary for* some particular gene), and a table that contains information about the gene. Corresponding tables in sibling pages are called *sibling tables*. If we compare the two large tables in the main part of the sibling pages, we can see that the first columns of each table are exactly the same. If we look at the cells under the *Identification* label in the two tables, both contain another table with two columns. In both cases, the first column contains identical labels *IDs, NCBI KOGs, ..., Putative ortholog(s)*. Further, the tables under *Identification.IDs* also have identical header rows. The data rows, however, vary considerably. Generally speaking, we can look for commonalities in sibling tables to find labels and look for variations to find data values.

Given that we can find most of the label and data cells in this way, our next task is to infer the general structure pattern of the web site and of the individual tables embedded within pages of the web site. With respect to identified labels, we look below or to the right for value associations; we may also need to look above or to the left. In Figure 1, the values for *Identification.Gene model(s).Amino Acids* are below, and the values for *Identification.Species* are to the right.

In addition to discovering the structure pattern for a web site, we can also dynamically adjust the pattern as we interpret the tables on each retrieved pages. If the system encounters a table that varies from the pattern by having an additional or missing label, the system can change the pattern by either adding the new label and marking it optional or marking the missing label optional. For example, if we had not seen the extra *Swissprot* column in the sibling table of Table 7 in Figure 3 in our initial pair of sibling pages, the system can add *Swissprot* as a new label and mark it as optional. The basic label-value association pattern is still the same.

By way of comparison with related work, we note that recent surveys [5,17] describe the vast amount of research that has been done in table processing and illustrate the challenges of the table interpretation problem. We focus in this paper, however, only HTML tables. A number of HTML table extraction systems use machine learning to recognize tables in web pages (e.g. [3,15]). Drawbacks of machine learning approaches, however, are that they need training data, and they need to be retrained for tables from different web sites. Other table interpretation systems work based on some simple assumptions and heuristics (e.g. [2,6]). These simple assumptions (labels are either the first row or the first column) are easily broken in complex tables. More sophisticated table interpretation techniques have appeared in recent papers [8,9,11]. None of this research makes use of

---

[4] Hidden-web pages are usually generated dynamically from a pre-defined templates in response to submitted queries. Therefore hidden-web pages usually have sibling pages.

sibling tables, but is complementary to our work and could potentially be used in conjunction with our work in future efforts to improve results for certain cases.

Other researchers have also tried to take advantage of sibling pages to determine page structure. RoadRunner [4] compares two HTML pages from one web site and analyzes the similarities and dissimilarities between them in order to generate extraction wrappers. It discovers data fields by string mismatches and discovers iterators and optionals by tag mismatches. EXALG [1] uses equivalence classes (sets of items that occur with the same frequency in sibling pages) and differentiating roles to generate extraction templates for the sibling pages. DEPTA [18] compares different records in a page instead of sibling pages and tries to find the extraction template for the record. Our system fundamentally differs from these approaches. These approaches focus on finding data fields. They do not discover labels or try to associate data and labels. Our system focuses on table interpretation. It looks for a table pattern in addition to data fields. Furthermore, Our system also tries to find the general structure pattern for the entire web site. It dynamically adjusts the structure pattern as it encounters new, yet-unseen structures.

We call our system *TISP* (*Table Interpretation with Sibling Pages*). We present the details of TISP and our contribution to table interpretation by sibling page comparison in the remainder of the paper as follows. Section 2 provides the details about how TISP analyzes a source page to find tables and match them with tables in sibling pages. Section 3 explains how TISP infers the general structure patterns of a web site and therefore how it interprets the tables from the site. In Section 4, we report the results of experiments we conducted involving sites for car advertisements, molecular biology, and geopolitical information, which we found on the hidden web. In Section 5, we make concluding remarks.

2   Sibling Table Recognition

After obtaining a source document, TISP first parses the source code and locates all HTML components enclosed by <table> and </table> tags (tagged tables). When tagged tables are nested inside of one another, TISP finds them and unnests them. In Figure 1, there are several levels of nesting in the large rectangular table. The first level is a table with two columns. The first column contains *Identification*, *Location*, and *Function*, and the second column contains some complex structures. Figure 1 shows only the first three rows of this table— one row for *Identification*, one for *Location*, and one for *Function*. (For the purpose of being explicit in this paper, we assume that these three rows are the only rows in this table.) The second column of the large rectangular table in Figure 1 contains three second-level nested tables, the first starting with *IDs*, the second with *Genetic Position*, and the third with *Mutant Phenotype*. In the right most cell of the first row is another table. There are also two third level nested tables.

We treat each tagged table as an individual table and assign a *Table ID* to it. If the table is nested, we replace the table in the upper level with its ID number.

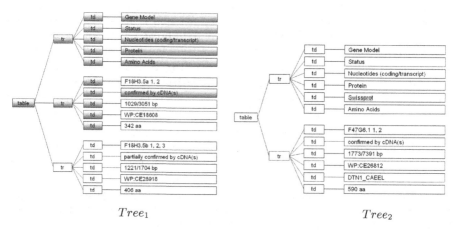

$Tree_1$ $Tree_2$

Fig. 4. DOM Trees for Table 7 in Figure 1 and its Sibling Table in Figure 3

By so doing, we are able to remove nested tables from upper level tables. As a result, TISP decomposes the page in Figure 1 into a set of tables, each with an ID and a path.

To compare and match tables, we first transform each HTML table into a DOM tree. It is easy to transform our input in Figure 2(a) to a DOM tree, indeed the conceptual-model instance abstractly models a DOM tree for the tables within an HTML page. $Tree_1$ in Figure 4 shows the DOM tree for Table 7 in Figure 1, and $Tree_2$ in Figure 4 shows the DOM tree for its corresponding table in Figure 3.

Tai [12] gives a well acknowledged formal definition of the concept of a tree mapping for labeled ordered rooted trees. Let T be a labeled ordered rooted tree and let $T[i]$ be the ith node in level order of tree T. A *mapping* from tree T to tree T' is defined as a triple (M, T, T'), where M is a set of ordered pairs (i, j), where i is from T and j is from T', satisfying the following conditions for all (i_1, j_1), $(i_2, j_2) \in$ M, where i_1 and i_2 are two nodes from T and j_1 and j_2 are two nodes from T':

(1) $i_1 = i_2$ iff $j_1 = j_2$;
(2) $T[i_1]$ comes before $T[i_2]$ iff $T'[j_1]$ comes before $T'[j_2]$ in level order;
(3) $T[i_1]$ is an ancestor of $T[i_2]$ iff $T'[j_1]$ is an ancestor of $T'[j_2]$.

According to this definition, each node appears at most once in a mapping and the order between sibling nodes and the hierarchical relation between nodes are preserved. The best match between two trees is a mapping with the maximum number of ordered pairs.

We use a simple tree matching algorithm introduced in [16] which was first proposed to compare two computer programs in software engineering. It calculates the similarity of two trees by finding the best match through dynamic programming with complexity $O(n_1 n_2)$, where n_1 is the size (number of nodes) of T and n_2 is the size of T'. This algorithm counts the matches of all possible combination pairs of nodes from the same level, one from each tree, and finds the pairs with maximum matches. The simple tree match algorithm returns the number of these maximum matched pairs. The highlighted part in $Tree_1$ in Figure 4 shows the matched nodes for $Tree_1$ with respect to $Tree_2$ in Figure 4. The highlighted nodes indicate a match.

In our research, we use the results of the simple tree matching algorithm for three tasks: (1) we filter out those HTML tables that are only for layout; (2) we identify the corresponding tables (sibling tables) from sibling pages; and (3) we match nodes in a sibling-table pair.

We call the maximum number of matched nodes among the two trees the *match score*. For each table in one source page, we obtain match scores and thus a ranking for all tables in a sibling page. Sibling tables should have a one to one correspondence. Based on the match score, we use the Gale-Shapley stable marriage algorithm [7] to pair potential sibling tables one to one.

For a pair of potential sibling tables, we calculate the *sibling table match percentage*, 100 times the match score divided by the number of nodes of the smaller tree. The match percentage between the two trees in Figure 4, for example, is 19 (match score) divided by 27 (tree size of $Tree_2$), which, expressed as a percentage, is 70.4%.

We classify potential sibling tables into three categories: (1) exact match or near exact match; (2) false match; and (3) sibling-table match. We use two threshold boundaries to classify potential sibling tables: a higher threshold between exact or near exact match and sibling-table match, and a lower threshold between sibling-table match and false match. Usually a large gap exists between the range of exact or near exact match percentages and the range of sibling-table match percentages, as well as between the range of sibling-table match percentages and the range of false match percentages. Using active learning with boostrap selective sampling [13], we first set initial thresholds by empirical observation (90% for the higher threshold and 20% for the lower threshold); then TISP dynamically adjusts the two thresholds as needed during the classification process as more sibling pages are considered.

In our example, Tables 1, 2, and 3 have match percentages of 100% with their sibling tables. The match percentages for Tables 4, 5, 6 and 7, and their corresponding sibling tables, are 66.7%, 58.8%, 69.2%, and 70.4% respectively. Our example has no false matches. A false match usually happens when a table does not have a corresponding table in the sibling page. In this case, we save the table. When more sibling pages are compared, we might find a matching table for this saved table.

3   Structure Patterns

The structure pattern of a table tells us how to transform the information contained in the model instances in Figure 2(a) to the model instance in Figure 2(b), and thus how to interpret a table.

Pattern 1:

<table>(<tbody>)?

$$\boxed{\text{<tr>}(< (td|th) > \{L\})^n}$$

$$\left(\boxed{\text{(<tr>}(< (td|th) > \{V\})^n}\right)^+$$

Pattern 2:

<table>(<tbody>)?

$$\left(\boxed{< tr >< (td|th) > \{L\}(< (td|th) > \{V\})^n}\right)^+$$

Pattern 3:

<table>(<tbody>)?

$$\boxed{\text{<tr>}(< (td|th) > \{L\})^n}$$

$$\left(\boxed{< tr >< (td|th) > \{L\}(< (td|th) > \{V\})^{(n-1)}}\right)^+$$

Fig. 5. Some Basic Pre-defined Pattern Templates

3.1   Pattern Templates

We use regular expression to describe table structure pattern templates. If we traverse a DOM tree, which is ordered and labeled, in a preorder traversal, we can layout the tree labels textually and linearly. We can then use regular-expression like notation to represent the table structure patterns (see Figure 5). In both templates and generated patterns we use standard notation: ? (optional), + (one or more repetitions), and | (alternative). In templates, we augment the notation as follows. A variable (e.g. n) or an expression (e.g. n-1) can replace a symbol to designate a specific number of repetitions, which is unknown but fixed for the expression as it is applied. A pair of braces { } indicates a leaf node. A capital letter L is a position holder for a label and a capital letter V is a position holder for value. The part in a box is an *atomic pattern* which we use for combinational structural patterns in Section 3.4.

Figure 5 shows three basic pre-defined pattern templates. Pattern 1 is for tables with n labels in the first row and with n values in each of the rest of the rows. The association between labels and values is column-wise; the label at the top of the column is the label for all the values in each column.

Pattern 2 is for tables with labels in the left-most column and values in the rest of the columns. Each row has a label followed by n values. The label-value association is row-wise; each label labels all values in the row.

Pattern 3 is for two-dimensional tables with labels on both the top and the left. Each value in this kind of table associates with both the row header label and the column header label.

3.2   Pattern Generation

To check whether a table matches any pre-defined pattern template, TISP tests each template until it finds a match. When we search for a matching template, we only consider leaf nodes and seek matches for labels and mismatches for

$<table>$
$<tr>$ $<td>$Gene Model $<td>$Status $<td>$Nucleotides(coding/transcript)
    $<td>$Protein $<td>$Amino Acids
$(<tr><td>V_{Gene\ Model}<td>V_{Status}$ $<td>V_{Nucleotides(coding/transcript)}$
    $<td>V_{Protein}$ $<td>V_{Amino\ Acids})^+$

Fig. 6. Structure Pattern for Table 7 in Figure 1

values. Variations, however, exist and we must allow for them. In tables, labels or values are usually grouped. We are seeking for a structure pattern instead of classifying individual cells. Sometimes we find a matched node, but all other nodes in the group are mismatched nodes and agree with a certain pattern (e.g. the highlighted record node in the second subtree in $Tree_1$ in Figure 4.), TISP should ignore the disagreement and assume the mismatched node is a node of value too. Specifically, we calculate a *template match percentage* between a pre-defined pattern template and a matched result, 100 times the number of leaf nodes that agree with a pattern template divided by total number of leaf nodes in the tree. We calculate the template match percentage between a table and each pre-defined structure template. A match must satisfy two conditions: (1) it must be the highest match percentage, and (2) the match percentage must be greater than a threshold. Similar to the way we determine thresholds for sibling table matches, we determine this template match percentage threshold using active learning with boostrap selective sampling, with an initial threshold of 80%.

Consider the mapped result in Figure 4 as an example. The highlighted nodes are matched nodes in $Tree_1$. Comparing the template match percentage for this mapped result for the three pattern templates in Figure 5, we obtain 93.3%, 53.3%, and 80% respectively. Pattern 1 has the highest match percentage, and it is greater than the threshold. Therefore we choose Pattern 1.

We now impose the chosen pattern, ignoring matches and mismatches. Note that for the $Tree_1$ in Figure 4, the first branch matches the part in Pattern 1 in the first box and the second and the third branch, each match the part in the second box, where n is 5. For Pattern 1, when $n=1$, we have a one-dimensional table; and when $n>1$, we have a two-dimensional table for which we must generate record numbers.

After TISP matches a table with a pre-defined pattern template, it generates a specific structure pattern for the table by substituting the actual labels for each L and by substituting a placeholder V_L for each value. The subscript L for a value V designates the label-value pair for each record in a table. Figure 6 shows the specific structure pattern for Table 7 in Figure 1.

3.3 Pattern Usage

With a structure pattern for a specific table, we can interpret the table and all its sibling tables. The path gives the location of the table, and the generated pattern gives the label-value pairs. The pattern must match exactly in the sense that each label string encountered must be identical to the pattern's corresponding label string. Any failure is reported to TISP. (In Section 3.5, we explain how TISP reacts to a failure notification).

When the pattern matches exactly, TISP can generate the label sequence and value for each label-value pair and thus can provide an interpretation for the table. For our example, the chosen pattern is Pattern 1 with + (which allows for multiple rows of values in the table). Thus, TISP needs to add another dimension and add row numbers. Since the table is inside of other tables, TISP recursively searches for the tables in the upper levels of nesting and collects all needed labels.

3.4   Pattern Combinations

It is possible that TISP cannot match any pre-defined template. In this case, it looks for pattern combinations. Using Figure 7 as an example, assume that TISP matches all the cells in the first and third column, but none in the second and forth column. Comparing the template match percentage for this mapped result for the three pattern templates in Figure 5, we obtain 50%, 75%, and 68.8% respectively. None of them is greater than the threshold, 80%. The first two columns, however, match Pattern 2 perfectly, as do the last two columns.

Location	chr8	Strand	+
Sequence Length	5095	Total Exon Length	2161
Number of Exons	4	Number of SNPs	0
Max Exon Length	1044	Min Exon Length	93

Fig. 7. An Example for Pattern Combination from MutDB

In many cases, tables can be more complicated. Most complex tables do not match to only one pre-defined pattern template, but do match to a combination of several of them. Patterns can be combined row-wise or column-wise. In a row-wise combination, one pattern template can appear after another, but only the first pattern template has the header: $< table > (< tbody >)?$. Therefore, a row-wise combined structure pattern has a few rows matching one template and other rows matching another template. In a column-wise combination, we combine different atomic patterns. If a pattern template has two atomic patterns, both patterns must appear in the combined pattern, in the same order, but they can be interleaved with other atomic patterns. If one atomic pattern appears after another atomic pattern from a different pattern template, the $< tr >$ tag at the beginning is removed. Figure 8 shows two examples of pattern combinations. Example 1 combines Pattern 2 and Pattern 1 row-wise. Example 2 combines Pattern 2 with itself column-wise. This second pattern matches the table in Figure 7, where $n = m = 1$, and the plus (+) is 4.

Example 1:
    $< table > (< tbody >)?$
$(< tr >< (td|th) >\{L\}(< (td|th) > \{V\})^n)^+$
$< tr > (< (td|th) > \{L\})^m (< tr > (< (td|th) > \{V\})^m)^+$
Example 2:
    $< table > (< tbody >)?$
$(< tr >< (td|th) >\{L\}(< (td|th) > \{V\})^n < (td|th) >\{L\}(< (td|th) > \{V\})^m)^+$

Fig. 8. Two Examples of Pattern Combinations

The initial search for combinations is similar to the search for single patterns. TISP checks patterns until it finds mismatches, it then checks to see whether the mismatched part matches with some other pattern. TISP first searches row-wise for rows of labels and then uses these rows as delimiters to divide the table into several groups. If it cannot find any row of labels, it repeats the same process column-wise. TISP then tries to match each sub group with a pre-defined template. This process repeats recursively until all sub-groups match with a template.

For the example in Figure 7, TISP is unable to find any rows of labels, but finds two columns of labels, the first and third column. It then divides the table into two groups using these two columns and tries to match each group with a pre-defined template. It matches each group with Pattern 2. Therefore, this table matches column-wise with two combinations of Pattern 2.

3.5 Dynamic Pattern Adjustment

Given a structure pattern for a table, we know where the table is in the source document (its path), the location of the labels and values, and the association between labels and values. When TISP encounters a new sibling page, it tries to locate each sibling table following the path, and then to interpret it by matching it with the sibling table structure pattern. If the new table matches the structure pattern regular expression perfectly, we successfully interpret this table. Otherwise, we might need to do some pattern adjustment. There are two ways to adjust a structure pattern: (1) adjust the path to locate a table, and (2) adjust the generated structure pattern regular expression.

Although sibling pages usually have the same base structure, some variations might exist. Some sibling pages might have additional or missing tables. Thus, sometimes, following the path, we cannot locate the sibling table for which we are looking. In this case, TISP searches for tables at the same level of nesting, looking for one that matches the pattern. If TISP finds one, it obtains the path and adds it as an alternative. Thus, for future sibling pages, TISP can (in fact, always does) check all alternative paths before searching for another alternative path. If TISP finds no matching table, it simply continues its processing with the next table.

We adjust a table pattern when we encounter a variation of an existing table. There might be additional or missing labels in the encountered variation. In this

$<table>$
$<tr>$ $<td>$Gene Model $<td>$Status $<td>$Nucleotides(coding/transcript)
     $<td>$Protein ($<td>$Swissprot)? $<td>$Amino Acids
$(<tr><td>V_{Gene\ Model}<td>V_{Status} <td>V_{Nucleotides(coding/transcript)}$
     $<td>V_{Protein} (<td>V_{Swissprot})? <td>V_{Amino\ Acids})^+$

Fig. 9. Structure Pattern for the Table in Figure 3

case, we need to adjust the structure pattern regular expression, to add the new optional label or to mark the missing label as optional. Consider the table that starts with *Gene Model* in Figure 3 (the sibling table of Table 7 in Figure 1) as an example. The table matches the pattern in Figure 6 until we encounter the label *Swissprot*. If we skip *Swissprot*, the next label *Amino Acids* matches the structure pattern. In this case, we treat *Swissprot* as an additional label, and we add it as an optional label as Figure 9 shows.

4   Experimental Results

We tested TISP for three different fields: car advertisements for commercial data, molecular biology for scientific data, and interesting information about U.S. states and about countries for geopolitical data. Most of the source pages were collected from popular and well-known web sites such as cars.com, NCBI database, Wormbase, MTB database, the CIA World Factbook, and the U.S. Geological Survey. We tested more than 2,000 tables found in 275 sibling pages in 35 web sites. For each web site, we randomly chose two sibling pages for initial pattern generation. For the initial two sibling pages, we tested (1) whether TISP was able to recognize HTML data tables and discard HTML tables used only for layout, (2) whether it was able to pair all sibling tables correctly, and (3) whether it was able to recognize the correct pattern template or pattern combination. For the rest of sibling pages from the same web site, we tested (1) whether TISP was able to interpret tables using the recognized structure patterns, (2) whether it correctly detected the need for dynamic adjustment, and (3) whether it recognized new structure patterns correctly.

We collected 75 sibling pages from 15 different web sites in the car-advertisements domain for a total of 780 HTML tables.[5] TISP correctly discarded all uses of tables for layout and successfully paired all sibling tables. There were no nested tables in this domain. Most of the web sites contained only one table pattern, except for one site that had three different patterns. Two web sites contained tables with structure combinations. TISP successfully interpreted all tables from the generated patterns. No adjustment were needed, neither for any path nor for any label.

---

[5] The sibling pages in this domain are usually very regular. Indeed, we found no table variations in any of the sites we considered. We, therefore, only tested five pages per site.

We collected 100 sibling pages from 10 different web sites in the molecular biology domain for a total of 862 HTML tables. Among these tables, TISP falsely classified three pairs of layout tables as data tables. TISP, however, successfully eliminated these false sibling pairs during pattern generation because it was unable to find a matching pattern. No false patterns were generated. TISP was able to recognize 28 of 29 structure patterns. TISP missed one pattern because the table contained too many empty cells. If it had considered empty cells as mismatches, TISP would have correctly recognize this pattern. As TISP processed additional sibling pages, it found 5 additional sibling tables and correctly interpreted all but one of them. The failure was caused by labels that varied across sibling tables causing them, in some cases, to look like values. There were 5 path adjustments and 12 label adjustments—all of them correct. One table was interpreted only partially correctly because TISP considered the irrelevant information *To Top* as a header.

For the geopolitical information domain, we tested 100 sibling pages from 10 different web sites with 884 HTML tables. TISP correctly paired 100% of all data tables and correctly discarded all layout tables. For initial pattern generation, TISP was able to recognize all 22 structure patterns. As TISP processed additional sibling pages, it found one additional sibling table and correctly interpreted it. There were no path adjustments, but there were 22 label adjustments— all of them correct. For two sets of sibling tables, TISP recognized the correct patterns, but failed to recognize some implicit information that affects the meaning of the tables. Therefore it interpreted the tables only partially correctly (i.e its label components were only partially correct).

For measuring the overall accuracy of TISP, we computed precision (P), recall (R), and an F-measure ($F = 2PR/(P+R)$). In its table recognition step, TISP correctly discarded 155 of 158 layout tables and discarded no data tables. It therefore achieved an F-measure of 99.0% (98.1% recall and 100% precision). TISP later discarded these three layout tables in its pattern generation step, but it also rejected two data tables, being unable to find any pattern for them. It thus achieved an F-measure of 99.4% (100% recall and 98.8% precision). For table interpretation, TISP correctly recognized 69 of 74 structure patterns. It therefore achieved a recall of 93.2%. Of the 72 structure patterns it detected, 69 were correct. It therefore achieved a precision of 95.8%. Overall the F-measure for table interpretation was 94.5% for the sites we tested.

We discuss the time performance of TISP in two phases: (1) initial pattern generation from a pair of sibling pages and (2) interpretation of the tables in the rest of the sibling pages. The time for pattern generation given a pair of sibling pages consists of: (1) the time to read and parse the two pages and locate all the HTML tables, (2) the time for sibling table comparisons, and (3) the time to select from pre-defined structure templates and generate a pattern. The complexity of parsing and locating HTML tables is O(n), where n is the number of HTML tags. The simple tree matching algorithm has time complexity O($m_1 m_2$), where m_1 and m_2 are the numbers of nodes of the two sibling trees. To find the best match for each HTML table, we need to compare each table with all the HTML tables in its sibling page. The time complexity is $O(km_1m_2)$, where k is the number of HTML tables in the sibling page. The time complexity for finding the correct pattern for each matched sibling table is $O(pl)$, where p is the number of pattern templates and l is the number of leaf nodes in the HTML table. If pattern combinations are involved, the complexity of template discovery increases multiplicatively since for each subgroup we must consider every template and find the best match. We conducted the experiment on a Pentium 4 computer running at 3.2 GHz. The typical actual time needed for the pattern generation for a pair of sibling pages was below or about one second. The actual time reached a maximum of 15 seconds for a complicated web site where pages had more than 20 tables.

The time for table interpretation for a single sibling web page when no adjustment is necessary consists of: (1) the time for locating each table and (2) the time for processing the table with a pattern. The complexity of locating a table is $O(p)$, where p is the number of path possibilities leading to the table. Each path possibility is itself logarithmic with respect to the number of nodes in the DOM tree for the pages. The complexity of matching a located table with the corresponding pattern is $O(el)$, where e is the number of pattern entries (an entry could be either a pattern label or a pattern value) of the pattern and l is the number of leaf nodes in the HTML table's DOM tree. The time to do adjustments ranges from the time to do a simple label adjustment, which is constant, to the time required to re-evaluate all sibling tables, which is the same as the time for initial pattern generation. Overall, the typical actual time needed for interpreting tables in one page was below one second. The actual time reached a maximum of 19 seconds for a complicated web page with several tables and several adjustments.

5   Concluding Remarks

In this paper we introduced TISP, which provides a way to automatically interpret tables in hidden-web pages—pages which are almost always sibling pages. By comparing data tables in sibling pages, TISP is able to find the location of table labels and data entries, and pair them to infer the general pattern for all sibling tables from the same site. Our experiments using source pages from three different domains—car advertisements, molecular biology, and geopolitical information—indicate that TISP can succeed in properly interpreting tables in sibling pages. TISP achieved an F-measure for sibling table interpretation of 94.5%.

References

1. Arasu, A., Garcia-Molina, H.: Extracting structured data from web pages. In: SIG-MOD 2003. Proceedings of the 2003 ACM SIGMOD International Conference on Management of Data, pp. 337–348. ACM Press, New York (2003)

2. Chen, H., Tsai, S., Tsai, J.: Mining tables from large scale HTML texts. In: Proceedings of the 18th International Conference on Computational Linguistics (COLING 2000), Saarbrücken, German, pp. 166–172 (July-August 2000)
3. Cohen, W.W., Hurst, M., Jensen, L.S.: A flexible learning system for wrapping tables and lists in HTML documents. In: Proceedings of the International World Wide Web Conference (WWW 2002), Honolulu, Hawaii, pp. 232–241 (May 2002)
4. Crescenzi, V., Mecca, G., Merialdo, P.: RoadRunner: Towards automatic data extraction from large web sites. In: Proceedings of the 27th International Conference on Very Large Data Bases (VLDB 2001), Rome, Italy, pp. 109–118 (September 2001)
5. Embley, D.W., Hurst, M., Lopresti, D., Nagy, G.: Table processing paradigms: A research survey. International Journal of Document Analysis and Recognition 8(2-3), 66–86 (2006)
6. Embley, D.W., Tao, C., Liddle, S.W.: Automating the extraction of data from HTML tables with unknown structure. Data & Knowledge Engineering 54(1), 3–28 (2005)
7. Gale, D., Shapley, L.S.: College admissions and the stability of marriage. American Mathematics Monthly 69, 9–14 (1962)
8. Gatterbauer, W., Bohunsky, P.: Table extraction using spatial reasoning on the CSS2 visual box model. In: Proceedings of the 21st National Conference on Artificial Intelligence (AAAI 2006), Boston, Massachusetts, pp. 1313–1318 (July 2006)
9. Gatterbauer, W., Bohunsky, P., Herzog, M., Krupl, B., Pollak, B.: Towards domain-independent information extraction from web tables. In: Proceedings of the 16th International World Wide Web Conference (WWW 2007), Banff, Canada (in press, 2007)
10. Ipeirotis, P.G., Gravano, L., Sahami, M.: Probe, count, and classify: categorizing hidden web databases. In: Proceedings of the 2001 ACM SIGMOD International Conference on Management of Data (SIGMOD 2001), Santa Barbara, California, pp. 67–78 (May 2001)
11. Pivk, A., Cimiano, P., Sure, Y.: From tables to frames. In: McIlraith, S.A., Plexousakis, D., van Harmelen, F. (eds.) ISWC 2004. LNCS, vol. 3298, pp. 166–181. Springer, Heidelberg (2004)
12. Tai, K.-C.: The tree-to-tree correction problem. Journal of the ACM 26(3), 422–433 (1979)
13. Thompson, C.A., Califf, M.E., Mooney, R.J.: Active learning for natural language parsing and information extraction. In: Proceedings of 16th International Conference on Machine Learning, Bled, Slovenia, pp. 406–414 (June 1999)
14. Wang, X.: Tabular Abstraction, Editing, and Formatting. PhD thesis, Univeristy of Waterloo (1996)
15. Wang, Y., Hu, J.: A machine learning based approach for table detection on the web. In: Proceedings of the 11th International Conference on World Wide Web (WWW 2002), Honolulu, Hawaii, pp. 242–250 (May 2002)
16. Yang, W.: Identifying syntactic differences between two programs. Software Practice and Experience 21(7), 739–755 (1991)
17. Zanibbi, R., Blostein, D., Cordy, J.R.: A survey of table recognition. International Journal of Document Analysis and Recognition 7(1), 1–16 (2004)
18. Zhai, Y., Liu, B.: Web data extraction based on partial tree alignment. In: Proceedings of the 14th International Conference on World Wide Web (WWW 2005), Chiba, Japan, pp. 76–85 (May 2005)

A Fine-Grained XML Structural Comparison Approach

Joe Tekli, Richard Chbeir, and Kokou Yetongnon

LE2I Laboratory UMR-CNRS, University of Bourgogne
21078 Dijon Cedex France
{joe.tekli,richard.chbeir,kokou.yetongnon}@u-bourgogne.fr

Abstract. As the Web continues to grow and evolve, more and more information is being placed in structurally rich documents, XML documents in particular, so as to improve the efficiency of similarity clustering, information retrieval and data management applications. Various algorithms for comparing hierarchically structured data, e.g., XML documents, have been proposed in the literature. Most of them make use of techniques for finding the edit distance between tree structures, XML documents being modeled as ordered labeled trees. Nevertheless, a thorough investigation of current approaches led us to identify several structural similarity aspects, i.e. sub-tree related similarities, which are not sufficiently addressed while comparing XML documents. In this paper, we provide an improved comparison method to deal with fine-grained sub-trees and leaf node repetitions, without increasing overall complexity with respect to current XML comparison methods. Our approach consists of two main algorithms for discovering the structural commonality between sub-trees and computing tree-based edit operations costs. A prototype has been developed to evaluate the optimality and performance of our method. Experimental results, on both real and synthetic XML data, demonstrate better performance with respect to alternative XML comparison methods.

Keywords: XML, Semi-structured data, Structural similarity, Tree edit distance.

1 Introduction

W3C's XML (eXtensible Mark-up Language) has recently gained unparalleled importance as a fundamental standard for efficient data management and exchange. Information destined to be broadcasted over the web is henceforth represented using XML, in order to guarantee its interoperability. The use of XML covers data representation and storage (e.g., complex multimedia objects), database information interchange, data filtering, as well as web services interaction. Owing to the unprecedented web exploitation of XML, XML-based comparison, especially for heterogeneous[1] documents, becomes a central issue in the information retrieval and database communities. The applications of XML comparison are numerous and range over: version control, change management and data warehousing (finding, scoring and browsing changes between different versions of a document, support of temporal queries and index maintenance) [4, 5, 6], XML retrieval (finding and ranking results

---

[1] We denote by *heterogeneous XML document* one that does not conform to a given grammar (DTD/XML Schema), which is the case of a lot of XML documents found on the web [13].

C. Parent et al. (Eds.): ER 2007, LNCS 4801, pp. 582–598, 2007.

according to their similarity in order to retrieve the best results possible) [16, 22] as well as the classification/clustering of XML documents gathered from the web against a set of DTDs declared in an XML database (just as schemas are necessary in traditional DBMS for the provision of efficient storage, retrieval, protection and indexing facilities, the same is true for DTDs and XML repositories) [2, 6, 13].

A range of algorithms for comparing semi-structured data, e.g., XML-based documents, have been proposed in the literature. Most of them make use of techniques for finding the edit distance between tree structures, XML documents being treated as Ordered Labeled Trees (OLT). Nonetheless, a thorough investigation of the most recent and efficient XML structural similarity approaches [4, 6, 13] led us to pinpoint certain cases where the edit distance outcome is inaccurate. These inaccuracies correspond to undetected sub-tree structural resemblances, as we will see in the motivating examples. The goal of our study here is to provide a fine-grained XML comparison method able to efficiently detect XML structural similarity without decreasing system performance. In short, we aim to build on existing approaches, mainly those provided in [4, 13], in order to consider the various sub-tree structural commonalities while comparing XML trees.

The remainder of this paper is organized as follows. Section 2 presents some motivating examples. In Section 3, we review background and related work in XML structural similarity. Section 4 develops our XML structural similarity approach. Section 5 is devoted to present our prototype and experimental tests. Conclusions and ongoing work are covered in Section 6.

2 Motivation

XML documents tend to have many optional and repeated elements. Such elements induce recurring sub-trees of similar or identical structures. As a result, algorithms for comparing XML document trees should be aware of such repetitions/resemblances so as to efficiently assess structural similarity.

2.1 Undetected Sub-tree Similarities

Consider, for example, dummy XML trees A, B and C in Fig. 1. One can realize that tree A is structurally more similar to B, than to C, the sub-tree A_1, made up of nodes b, c and d, appearing twice in B (B_1 and B_2) and only once in C (C_1). Nonetheless, such (sub-tree) structural similarities are left unaddressed by most existing approaches. For instance, Chawathe's[2] edit distance process [4] permits applying changes to only one node at a time (using node *insert*, *delete* and *update* operations, with unit costs), thus yielding the same structural similarity value while comparing trees A/B and A/C.

- $Dist(A, B) = Dist(A, C) = 3$, which is the cost of three consecutive insert operations introducing nodes b, c and d (e, f and g) in tree A transforming it into B (C).
- Therefore, $Sim(A, B) = Sim(A, C) = 0.25$ where $Sim = 1 / (1+Dist)$.

In theory, structural resemblances such as those between trees A/B and A/C could be taken into consideration by applying generalizations of Chawathe's approach [4],

---

[2] Considered as a reference point for the latest tree edit distance algorithms [6, 13].

developed by Nierman and Jagadish [13] and Dalamagas *et al.* [6] (introducing edit operations allowing the insertion and deletion of whole sub-trees). Yet, our examination of the approaches provided in [6, 13] led us to identify certain cases where sub-tree structural similarities are disregarded:

- Similarity between trees *A/D* (sub-trees A_1 and D_2) in comparison with *A/E*.
- Similarity between trees *F/G* (sub-trees F_1 and G_2) relatively to *F/H*.
- Similarity between trees *F/I* (sub-tree F_1 and tree *I*) in comparison with *F/J*.

In essence, the authors in [13] make use of the *contained in* relation between trees (cf. Definition 2) so as to capture sub-tree similarities. Following [13], a tree *A* may be inserted in *T* only if *A* is already *contained in* the source tree *T*. Similarly, a tree *A* may be deleted only if *A* is already *contained in* the destination tree *T*. Therefore, the approach in [13] captures the sub-tree structural similarities between XML trees *A/B* in Fig. 1, transforming *A* to *B* in a single edit operation: (inserting sub-tree B_2 in *A*, B_2 occurring in *A* as A_1), whereas transforming *A* to *C* would always need three consecutive insert operations (inserting nodes *e*, *f* and *g*).

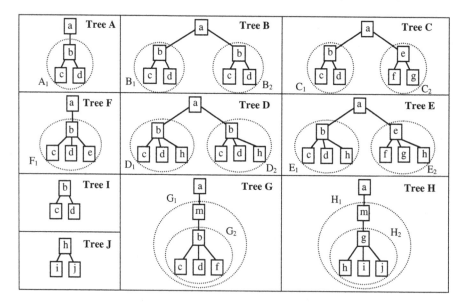

Fig. 1. Sample XML trees

Nonetheless, when the containment relation is not fulfilled, certain structural similarities are ignored. Consider, for instance, trees *A* and *D* in Fig. 1. Since D_2 is not contained in *A*, it is inserted *via* four edit operations instead of one (insert tree), while transforming *A* to *D*, ignoring the fact that part of D_2 (sub-tree of nodes *b*, *c*, *d*) is identical to A_1. Therefore, equal distances are obtained when comparing trees *A/D* and *A/E*, disregarding *A/D*'s structural resemblances:

- $\text{Dist}(A, D) = \text{Cost}_{\text{Ins}}(h) + \text{Cost}_{\text{Ins}}(b) + \text{Cost}_{\text{Ins}}(c) + \text{Cost}_{\text{Ins}}(d) + \text{Cost}_{\text{Ins}}(h) = 1+4 = 5$
- $\text{Dist}(A, E) = \text{Cost}_{\text{Ins}}(h) + \text{Cost}_{\text{Ins}}(e) + \text{Cost}_{\text{Ins}}(f) + \text{Cost}_{\text{Ins}}(g) + \text{Cost}_{\text{Ins}}(h) = 1+4 = 5$

Likewise for the D to A transformation (tree D_2 will not be deleted via a single delete tree operation since it is not contained in the destination tree A), achieving $Dist(D, A) = Dist(E, A) = 5$. Other types of sub-tree structural similarities that are missed by [13]'s approach (and likewise missed by [4, 6]) can be identified when comparing trees F/G and F/H, as well as F/I and F/J. The F, G, H case is different than its predecessor (the A, D, F case) in that the sub-trees sharing structural similarities (F_1 and G_2) occur at different depths (whereas with A/D, A_1 and D_2 are at the same depth). On the other hand, the F, I, J case differs from the previous ones since structural similarities occur, not only among sub-trees, but also at the sub-tree/tree level (e.g., between sub-tree F_1 and tree I).

Note that in [6], the authors complement their edit distance algorithm (which can be viewed as a specialized version of [13]'s algorithm) with a repetition/nesting reduction process, summarizing the XML documents prior to the comparison phase. Such a reduction pre-processing transforms, for instance, tree B to A, thus yielding $Dist(A, B) = 0$ which is not accurate (tree A is obviously different than B). While it might be useful for structural clustering tasks, the reduction process yields inaccurate comparison results in the general case, which is why it is disregarded in our discussion. Therefore, we only consider [6]'s edit distance algorithm in our analysis.

2.2 The Special Case of Single Leaf Node Sub-trees

In addition, none of the approaches mentioned above is able to effectively compare documents made of repeating leaf node sub-trees. For example, following [4, 6, 13], the same structural similarity value is obtained when comparing document K, of Fig. 2, to documents L and M, $Sim(K, L) = Sim(K, M) = 0.5$, having $Dist(K, L) = Dist(K, M) = 1$.

- $Dist(K, L) = Cost_{Ins}(b) = 1$
- $Dist(K, M) = Cost_{Ins}(c) = 1$

However, one can realize that document trees K and L are more similar than K and M, node b of tree K appearing twice in tree L, and only once in XML tree M. Likewise for K/N with respect to K/O and K/P. Identical distances are attained when comparing document trees K/N, K/O and K/P, $Dist(K, N)=Dist(K, O)= Dist(K, P)=2$, despite the fact that the node b is repeated three times in tree N, twice in tree O and only appears once in P.

- $Dist(K, N) = Cost_{Ins}(b) + Cost_{Ins}(b) = 2$
- $Dist(K, O) = Cost_{Ins}(b) + Cost_{Ins}(c) = 2$
- $Dist(K, P) = Cost_{Ins}(c) + Cost_{Ins}(d) = 2$

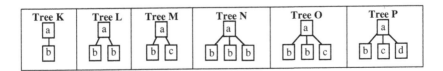

Fig. 2. XML documents consisting of leaf node sub-trees

In this paper, we explicitly mention the case of leaf node repetitions since:

- Leaf nodes are a special kind of sub-trees: *single node sub-trees*. Therefore, the study of sub-tree resemblances and repetitions should logically cover leaf nodes, so as to attain a more complete XML similarity approach.
- Leaf node repetitions are usually as frequent as substructure repetitions (i.e. non-leaf node sub-tree repetitions) in XML documents.
- Detecting leaf node repetitions is spontaneous in the XML context, and would help increase the discriminative power of XML comparison methods, as shown in the examples of Fig. 2 (which will be subsequently conferred in detail).

3   Related Work and Background

3.1   XML Data Model

XML documents represent hierarchically structured information and can be modeled as Ordered Labeled Trees (OLTs)[3] [20]. Nodes in a traditional DOM (Document Object Model) ordered labeled tree represent XML elements and are labeled with corresponding element tag names. Attributes mark the nodes of their containing elements. However, to incorporate attributes in their similarity computations, some approaches [13, 22] have considered OLTs with distinct attribute nodes, labeled with corresponding attribute names. Attribute nodes appear as children of their encompassing element nodes, sorted by attribute name, and appearing before all sub-element siblings [13]. The authors in [7, 13] agree on disregarding element/attribute values while studying the structural properties of heterogeneous XML documents.

3.2   Sate of the Art

Various methods, for determining structural similarities between hierarchically structured data, particularly XML documents, have been proposed. Most of them derive, in one way or another, the dynamic programming techniques for finding edit distance between strings [11, 18, 19]. In essence, all these approaches aim at finding the cheapest sequence of edit operations that can transform one tree into another. Nevertheless, tree edit distance algorithms can be distinguished by the set of edit operations that are allowed as well as overall complexity and performance levels. Early approaches in [17, 21] allow insertion, deletion and relabeling of nodes anywhere in the tree. Yet, they are relatively complex. For instance, the approach in [17] has a time complexity $O(|A||B|\ depth(A)\ depth(B))$ (where $|A|$ and $|B|$ denote tree cardinalities while $depth(A)$ and $depth(B)$ are the depths of the trees). The authors in [3, 5] restrict insertion and deletion operations to leaf nodes and add a move operator that can relocate a sub-tree, as a single edit operation, from one parent to another. However, corresponding algorithms do not guarantee optimal results. Recent work by Chawathe [4] restricts insertion and deletion operations to leaf nodes, and allows the relabeling of nodes anywhere in the tree, while disregarding the move operation. The overall complexity of [4]'s algorithm is of $O(N^2)$. Nierman and Jagadish [13] extend the approach of [4] by adding two new operations: insert tree and delete tree to allow insertion and deletion of whole sub-trees within in an OLT. This approach's

---

[3] In the following, *tree* designates *ordered labeled tree*.

overall complexity simplifies to $O(N^2)$ despite being conceptually more complex than its predecessor. A specialized version of [13]'s algorithm is provided in [6]. Following [6], tree insertion/deletion operations costs are computed as the sum of the costs of inserting/deleting all individual nodes in the considered sub-trees, whereas in [13], certain sub-tree similarities are considered (via the containment relation, cf. Definition 2) while assigning operations costs. On the other hand, an original structural similarity approach is presented in [7]. It disregards OLTs and utilizes the Fast Fourier Transform to compute similarity between XML documents. Yet, the authors did not compare their algorithm's optimality to existing edit distance approaches. Another approach, disregarding edit distance computations was introduced by Sanz *et al.* in [15]. It utilizes specific indexing structures rather than tree edit distance. Experimental results in [15] confirm that the approach is of linear complexity. Nonetheless, the authors in [15] do not compare their algorithm's optimality to existing approaches.

4 Proposal

Our XML structural similarity approach consists of two algorithms: i) an algorithm for identifying the *Commonality Between two Sub-trees (CBS)*[4], ii) and an algorithm for computing the *Tree edit distance Operations Costs (TOC)*. The *TOC* algorithm makes use of *CBS*, its results being exploited via [13]'s main edit distance algorithm (cf. Appendix), so as to identify the structural similarity between two XML documents (cf. Fig. 3). In the following, we start by presenting some basic definitions required to develop each of our algorithms.

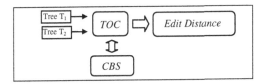

Fig. 3. Simplified activity diagram of our XML structural similarity approach

4.1 Preliminary Definitions

Def. 1 - Ordered Labeled Tree: it is a rooted tree in which the nodes are ordered and labeled. We denote by $\lambda(T)$ the label of the root node of tree T. In the rest of this paper, the term *tree* means *rooted ordered labeled tree*.

Def. 2 - Tree *"Contained in"* relationship: a tree A is said to be *contained in* a tree T if all nodes of A occur in T, with the same parent/child edge relationship and node order. Additional nodes may occur in T between nodes in the embedding of A (e.g., tree K in Fig. 2 is *contained in* tree A of Fig. 1).

Def. 3 - Sub-tree: given two trees T and T', T' is a sub-tree of T if all nodes of T' occur in T, with the same parent/child edge relationship and node order, such as no

---

[4] *CBS* can be applied to whole trees. However, in our study, its use is coupled with sub-trees.

additional nodes occur in the embedding of T' (e.g., A_1 in Fig. 1 is a sub-tree of A, whereas tree K does not qualify as a sub-tree of A since nodes c and d occur in its embedding in A).

Def. 4 - First level sub-tree: given a tree T with root p of degree k, the first level sub-trees, $T_1, ..., T_k$ of T are the sub-trees rooted at the children nodes of p: $p_1, ..., p_k$.

Def. 5 - Ld-pair representation of a node: it is defined as the pair (l, d) where l and d are respectively the node's label and depth in the tree. We use $p.l$ and $p.d$ to refer to the label and the depth of an ld-$pair$ node p respectively.

Def. 6 - Ld-pair representation of a tree: it is the list, in preorder, of the ld-$pairs$ of its nodes (cf. Fig. 4). Given a tree in ld-$pair$ representation $T = (t_1, t_2, ..., t_n)$, $T[i]$ refers to the ith node t_i of T. Consequently, $T[i].l$ and $T[i].d$ denote, respectively, the label and the depth of the ith node of T, i designating the preorder traversal rank of node $T[i]$ in T.

Def. 7 - Structural commonality between sub-trees: given two sub-trees $A = (a_1, ..., a_m)$ and $B = (b_1, ..., b_n)$, the structural commonality between A and B, designated by $ComSubTree(A, B)$, is a set of nodes $N = \{n_1, ..., n_p\}$ such that $\forall n_i \in N$, n_i occurs in A and B with the same label, depth and relative node order (in preorder traversal ranking) as in A and B. For $1 \le i \le p$; $1 \le r \le m$; $1 \le u \le n$:

    (1) $n_i.l = a_r.l = b_u.l$
    (2) $n_i.d = a_r.d = b_u.d$
    (3) For any $n_j \in N / i \le j$, $\exists$ $a_s \in A$ and $b_v \in B$ such as:
       • $n_j.l = a_s.l = b_v.l$
       • $n_j.d = a_s.d = b_v.d$
       • $r \le s, u \le v$
    (4) There is no set of nodes N' that satisfies conditions *1*, *2* and *3* and is of larger cardinality than N.

$A_1 = ((b, 0), (c, 1), (d, 1))$	$D_1 = ((b, 0), (c, 1), (d, 1), (h, 1))$	$F_1 = ((b, 0), (c, 1), (d, 1), (e, 1))$
$\quad A_{11} = (c, 0)$	$\quad D_{11} = (c, 0)$	$\quad F_{11} = (c, 0)$
$\quad A_{12} = (d, 1)$	$\quad D_{12} = (d, 0)$	$\quad F_{12} = (d, 0)$
$B_1 = ((b, 0), (c, 1), (d, 1))$	$\quad D_{13} = (h, 0)$	$\quad F_{13} = (e, 0)$
$\quad B_{11} = (c, 0)$	$D_2 = ((b, 0), (c, 1), (d, 1), (h, 1))$	$G_1 = ((m, 0), (b, 1), (c, 2), (d, 2), (e, 2))$
$\quad B_{12} = (d, 0)$	$\quad D_{21} = (c, 0)$	$G_2 = ((b, 0), (c, 1), (d, 1), (e, 1))$
$B_2 = ((b, 0), (c, 1), (d, 1))$	$\quad D_{22} = (d, 0)$	$\quad G_{21} = (c, 0)$
$\quad B_{21} = (c, 0)$	$\quad D_{23} = (h, 0)$	$\quad G_{22} = (d, 0)$
$\quad B_{22} = (d, 0)$	$E_1 = ((b, 0), (c, 1), (d, 1), (h, 1))$	$\quad G_{23} = (e, 0)$
$C_1 = ((b, 0), (c, 1), (d, 1))$	$\quad E_{11} = (c, 0)$	$H_1 = ((m, 0), (g, 1), (h, 2), (i, 2), (j, 2))$
$\quad C_{11} = (c, 0)$	$\quad E_{12} = (d, 0)$	$H_2 = ((g, 0), (h, 1), (i, 1), (j, 1))$
$\quad C_{12} = (d, 0)$	$\quad E_{13} = (h, 0)$	$\quad H_{21} = (h, 0)$
$C_2 = ((e, 0), (f, 1), (g, 1))$	$E_2 = ((e, 0), (f, 1), (g, 1), (h, 1))$	$\quad H_{22} = (i, 0)$
$\quad C_{21} = (f, 0)$	$\quad E_{21} = (f, 0)$	$\quad H_{23} = (j, 0)$
$\quad C_{22} = (g, 0)$	$\quad E_{22} = (g, 0)$	$I_1 = (c, 0) \qquad I_2 = (d, 0)$
	$\quad E_{23} = (h, 0)$	$J_1 = (i, 0) \qquad J_2 = (j, 0)$

Fig. 4. Ld-pair representations of all sub-trees in Fig. 1, including single leaf node sub-trees

In other words, *ComSubTree(A, B)*[5] identifies the set of matching nodes between sub-trees *A* and *B*, node matching being undertaken with respect to the node label, depth and relative preorder ranking. Please note that in the rest of the paper, the term *commonality* always designates the structural commonality.

Def. 8 - Insert node: given a node *x* of degree 0 (leaf node) and a tree *T* with root node *p* having first level sub-trees T_1, ..., T_m, *Ins(x, i, p, l)* is a node insertion applied to *T*, inserting *x* as the ith child of *p*, thus yielding *T'* with first level sub-trees T_1, ... , T_{i-1}, *x*, T_{i+1}, ... , T_{m+1}, where *l* is the label of *x*.

Def. 9 - Delete node: given a leaf node *x* and a tree *T* with root node *p*, *x* being the ith child of *p*, *Del(x, p)* is a node deletion operation applied to *T* that yields *T'* with first level sub-trees T_1, ... , T_{i-1}, T_{i+1}, ... , T_m.

Def. 10 - Update node: given a node *x* in tree *T*, and a label *l*, *Upd(x, l)* is a node update operation applied to *x* resulting in *T'* which is identical to *T* except that in *T'*, *x* bears *l* as its label. The update operation could be also formulated as follows: *Upd(x, y)* where *y.l* denotes the new label to be assumed by *x*.

Def. 11 - Insert tree: given a tree *A* and a tree *T* with root node *p* having first level sub-trees T_1, ..., T_m, *InsTree(A, i, p)* is a tree insertion applied to *T*, inserting *A* as the ith sub-tree of *p*, thus yielding *T'* with first level sub-trees T_1, ..., T_{i-1}, *A*, T_{i+1}, ..., T_{m+1}.

Def. 12 - Delete tree: given a tree *A* and a tree *T* with root node *p*, *A* being the ith sub-tree of *p*, *DelTree(A, p)* is a tree deletion operation applied to *T* that yields *T'* with first level sub-trees T_1, ... , T_{i-1}, T_{i+1}, ... , T_m.

4.2   Commonality Between Sub-trees *(CBS)*

In order to capture the sub-tree structural similarities not well addressed by current approaches, we identify the need to replace the tree *contained in* relation making up a necessary condition for executing tree insertion and deletion operations in [13], by introducing the notion of *commonality* between two sub-trees. Following Definition 7, the problem of finding the structural commonality between two sub-trees SbT_i and SbT_j is equivalent to finding the maximum number of matching nodes in SbT_i and SbT_j (|*ComSubTree(SbT_i, SbT_j)*|). However, the problem of finding the shortest edit distance between SbT_i and SbT_j comes down to identifying the minimal number of edit operations that can transform SbT_i to SbT_j. Those are dual problems since identifying the shortest edit distance between two sub-trees (trees) underscores, in a roundabout way, their maximum number of matching nodes.

Therefore, we introduce in Fig. 5 our CBS algorithm, based on the edit distance concept, to identify the structural commonality between sub-trees (similarly to the approach provided in [12] in which Myers develops an edit distance based approach for computing the longest common sub-sequence between two strings). Note that in CBS, sub-trees are treated in their *ld-pair* representations (cf. Fig. 4). Using the *ld-pair* tree representations, sub-trees are transformed into *modified* sequences (*ld-pairs*), making them suitable for *standard* edit distance computations.

---

[5] Our sub-tree structural commonality definition can be equally applied to whole trees (a sub-tree being basically a tree). However, in this study, it is mostly utilized with sub-trees.

Afterward, the maximum number of matching nodes between SbT_i and SbT_j, $|ComSubTree(SbT_i, SbT_j)|$, is identified with respect to the minimum edit distance:

- Total number of deletions - we delete all nodes of SbT_i except those having matching nodes in SbT_j: $\sum_{\text{Deletions}} = |SbT_i| - |ComSubTree(SbT_i, SbT_j)|$

- Total number of insertions - we insert into SbT_i all nodes of SbT_j except those having matching nodes in SbT_i: $\sum_{\text{Insertions}} = |SbT_j| - |ComSubTree(SbT_i, SbT_j)|$

- Following CBS, using constant unit costs (=1) for node insertion and deletion operations, the edit distance between sub-trees SbT_i and SbT_j becomes as follows: $Dist[|SbT_i|][|SbT_j|] = \sum_{\text{Deletions}} \times 1 + \sum_{\text{Insertions}} \times 1 = |SbT_i| + |SbT_j| - 2 |ComSubTree(SbT_i, SbT_j)|$

- Therefore, $|ComSubTree(SbT_i, SbT_j)| = \dfrac{|SbT_i| + |SbT_j| - Dist[|SbT_i|][|SbT_j|]}{2}$

For instance, $|ComSubTree(A_1, D_1)| = 3$ (nodes b, c, d), $|ComSubTree(E_2, G_2)| = 1$ (node f). Note that applying CBS to leaf node sub-trees comes down to comparing two labels: those of the leaf nodes at hand. For example:

- $|ComSubTree(A_{11}, B_{11})| = 1$, A_{11} and B_{11} consisting of leaf node c,
- $|ComSubTree(A_{11}, B_{12})| = 0$, A_{11} and B_{12} having different labels ($\lambda(A_{11}) = A_{11}[0].l = c$ whereas $\lambda(B_{12}) = B_{12}[0].l = d$).

Similarly, when computing the commonality between a leaf node sub-tree (e.g., A_{11}) and a non-leaf node sub-tree (e.g., B_1), CBS comes down to comparing the label of the former (e.g., $\lambda(A_{11})$) to the label of the root node of the latter (e.g., $\lambda(B_1)$). For example, $|ComSubTree(A_{11}, B_1)| = 0$, A_{11} and the root of B_{11} having different labels ($\lambda(A_{11}) = A_{11}[0].l = c$ whereas $\lambda(B_1) = B_1[0].l = b$).

4.3 Tree Edition Operations Costs (TOC)

Our CBS algorithm, for the identification of the *commonality* between sub-trees, is to be utilized in TOC: an algorithm dedicated to computing the tree edit distance operations costs (insert tree and delete tree, cf. definitions 11 and 12). Consequently, those costs will be exploited via [13]'s main edit distance approach (cf. Fig. 5) providing an improved and more accurate XML structural similarity measure. TOC is developed in Fig. 5 and consists of three main steps:

- Step 1 (lines 2-15) identifies the structural commonalities between each pair of sub-trees in the source and destination trees respectively (T_1 and T_2), assigning tree insert/delete operation costs accordingly.
- Step 2 (lines 16-20) identifies the structural commonalities between each sub-tree in the source tree (T_1) and the destination tree (T_2) as a whole, updating delete tree operation costs correspondingly.
- Step 3 (lines 21-25) identifies the structural commonalities between each sub-tree in the destination tree (T_2) and the source tree (T_1) as a whole, modifying insert tree operation costs accordingly.

Algorithm TOC()

Input: Trees T_1 and T_2
Output: Insert tree and delete tree operations costs

Begin   1

  For each sub-tree SbT_i in T_1 // Going through
  {   // all sub-trees in T_1

    $Cost_{DelTree}(SbT_i) = \sum\limits_{All\ nodes\ x\ of\ SbT_i} Cost_{Del}(x)$ // sub-trees in T_1. 5

  For each sub-tree SbT_j in T_2 // Going through
  {   // all sub-trees in T_2

    $Cost_{InsTree}(SbT_j) = \sum\limits_{All\ nodes\ x\ of\ SbT_j} Cost_{Ins}(x)$

    $Cost_{DelTree}(SbT_i) = Min\{ Cost_{DelTree}(SbT_i),$ 10

$$\sum\limits_{All\ nodes\ x\ of\ SbT_i} Cost_{Del}(x) \times \cfrac{1}{1 + \cfrac{CBS(SbT_i, SbT_j)}{Max(|SbT_i|, |SbT_j|)}} \}$$

    $Cost_{InsTree}(SbT_j) = Min\{ Cost_{InsTree}(SbT_j),$

$$\sum\limits_{All\ nodes\ x\ of\ SbT_j} Cost_{Ins}(x) \times \cfrac{1}{1 + \cfrac{CBS(SbT_i, SbT_j)}{Max(|SbT_i|, |SbT_j|)}} \}$$

  }
  }   15

  For each sub-tree SbT_i in T_1 // Comparing sub-trees in T_1
  {   // to whole tree T_2.
    $Cost_{DelTree}(SbT_i) = Min\{ Cost_{DelTree}(SbT_i),$

$$\sum\limits_{All\ nodes\ x\ of\ SbT_i} Cost_{Del}(x) \times \cfrac{1}{1 + \cfrac{CBS(SbT_i, T_2)}{Max(|SbT_i|, |T_2|)}} \}$$

  }   20

  For each sub-tree SbT_j in T_2 // Comparing sub-trees in T_2
  {   // to whole tree T_1.
    $Cost_{InsTree}(SbT_j) = Min\{ Cost_{InsTree}(SbT_j),$

$$\sum\limits_{All\ nodes\ x\ of\ SbT_j} Cost_{Ins}(x) \times \cfrac{1}{1 + \cfrac{CBS(T_1, SbT_j)}{Max(|T_1|, |SbT_j|)}} \}$$

  }   25
End

Algorithm CBS()

Input: Sub-trees SbT_i and SbT_j (in Id-pair)
Output: $|ComSubTree(SbT_i, SbT_j)|$

Begin   1
  Dist [][] = new $[0...|SbT_i|][0...|SbT_j|]$
  Dist[0][0] = 0

  For (n = 1 ; n ≤ $|SbT_i|$; n++)   5
  {Dist[n][0] = Dist[n-1][0] + $Cost_{Del}(SbT_i[n])$}
  For (m = 1 ; m ≤ $|SbT_j|$; m++)
  {Dist[0][m] = Dist[0][m-1] + $Cost_{Ins}(SbT_j[m])$}

  For (n = 1 ; n ≤ $|SbT_i|$; n++)   10
  {
    For (m = 1 ; m ≤ $|SbT_j|$; m++)
    {
      Dist[n][m] = min{
      If ($SbT_i[n].d = SbT_j[m].d$ &
        $SbT_i[n].l = SbT_j[m].l$)   15
      { Dist[n-1][m-1] },
      Dist[n-1][m] + $Cost_{Del}(SbT_i[n])$,
      Dist[n][m-1] + $Cost_{Ins}(SbT_j[m])$ }
    }
  }   20

  Return $\cfrac{|SbT_i| + |SbT_j| - Dist[|SbT_i|][|SbT_j|]}{2}$
End   // $|CBS(SbT_i, SbT_j)|$

Algorithm EditDistance()

Input: Trees A and B
Output: Edit distance between A and B

Begin   1
  M = Degree(A) // Number of 1st level sub-trees in A
  N = Degree(B) // Number of 1st level sub-trees in B

  Dist [][] = new [0...M][0...N]   5
  Dist[0][0] = $Cost_{Upd}(\lambda(A), \lambda(B))$

  For (i = 1 ; i ≤ M ; i++)
  { Dist[i][0] = Dist[i-1][0] + $Cost_{DelTree}(A_i)$ }

  For (j = 1 ; j ≤ N ; j++)
  { Dist[0][j] = Dist[0][j-1] + $Cost_{InsTree}(B_j)$ }   10

  For (i = 1 ; i ≤ M ; i++)
  {
    For (j = 1 ; j ≤ N ; j++)
    {
      Dist[i][j] = min{   15
      Dist[i-1][j-1] + EditDistance(A_i, B_j),
      Dist[i-1][j] + $Cost_{DelTree}(A_i)$,
      Dist[i][j-1] + $Cost_{InsTree}(B_j)$ }
    }
  }   20
  Return Dist[M][N]
End

Fig. 5. Our *TOC* and *CBS* algorithms, along with [13]'s *Edit Distance* algorithm

Steps 2 and 3 are introduced to capture, not only the structural similarities between sub-trees, but also the similarities between the sub-trees and the overall structures of the trees being compared. The relevance of steps 2 and 3 becomes obvious when one of the trees involved in the comparison process shares structural similarities with one (or more) of the sub-trees encompassed in the other XML document tree (e.g., the F, I, J case in Fig. 1, where tree I is structurally similar to sub-tree F_I of tree F).

Using *CBS*, *TOC* identifies the structural *commonality* between each and every pair of sub-trees (SbT_i, SbT_j) in the two trees A and B being compared (step 1), as well as their commonalities with the whole trees A and B, respectively (steps 2 and 3). Consequently, those values are normalized via corresponding tree/sub-tree cardinalities $Max(|SbT_i|, |SbT_j|)$ to be comprised between 0 and 1:

$$- \quad \frac{CBS(SbT_i, SbT_j)}{Max(|SbT_i|, |SbT_j|)} = 0 \qquad \begin{array}{l}\text{When there is no structural commonality}\\ \text{between } SbT_i \text{ and } SbT_j : CBS(SbT_i, SbT_j) = 0\end{array}$$

$$- \quad \frac{CBS(SbT_i, SbT_j)}{Max(|SbT_i|, |SbT_j|)} = 1 \qquad \begin{array}{l}\text{When the sub-trees are identical:}\\ CBS(SbT_i, SbT_j) = |SbT_i| = |SbT_j|\end{array}$$

For instance, $\dfrac{CBS(A_1, D_1)}{Max(|A_1|, |D_1|)} = \dfrac{3}{4} = 0.75$, $\dfrac{CBS(E_2, G_2)}{Max(|E_2|, |G_2|)} = \dfrac{1}{4} = 0.25$ (cf. Fig. 1).

Thus, using the normalized commonality, tree operations costs would vary as follows:

Maximum insert/delete tree cost for sub-tree Sb_i:

Minimum insert/delete tree cost for sub-tree Sb_i:

$$\text{Cost}_{\text{InsTree/DelTree}}(Sb_i) = \sum_{\substack{\text{All nodes } x \text{ of } SbT_i}} \text{Cost}_{\text{Ins/Del}}(x) \times 1$$

$$\text{Cost}_{\text{InsTree/DelTree}}(Sb_i) = \sum_{\substack{\text{All nodes } x \text{ of } SbT_i}} \text{Cost}_{\text{Ins/Del}}(x) \times \frac{1}{2}$$

Lemma 1. Following *TOC*, the maximal insert/delete tree operation cost for a given sub-tree SbT_i (attained when no sub-tree structural similarities with SbT_i are identified in the source/destination tree respectively) is the sum of the costs (unit costs, $=1)^6$ of inserting/deleting every individual node of SbT_i (the proof is evident).

Lemma 2. Following *TOC*, the minimal insert/delete tree operation cost for SbT_i (attained when a sub-tree structurally identical to SbT_i is identified in the source/destination tree respectively) is equal to half its corresponding insert/delete tree maximum cost.

Proof: The smallest sub-tree that can be treated via a tree operation is a sub-tree consisting of two nodes. For such a tree, the minimum insert/delete tree operation cost would be equal to 1 (its maximum cost being equal to 2), equivalent to the cost of inserting/deleting a single node, which is the lowest tree operation cost attainable following TOC.

The minimal tree operation cost is defined in such a way in order to guarantee that the cost of inserting/deleting a non-leaf node sub-tree will never be less than the cost of inserting/deleting a single node (single node operations having unit costs). In fact, *TOC* is based on the intuition that tree operations are more costly than node

---

[6] An intuitive and natural way has been usually used to assign single node operation costs and consists of considering identical unit costs for *insertion* and *deletion* operations [4, 15].

operations. Consequently, for leaf node sub-trees, the maximum insert/delete tree operation cost is equal to 1, the cost of inserting/deleting the single node at hand:

− $\text{Cost}_{\text{InsTree/DelTree}}(\text{SbT}_i) = \text{Cost}_{\text{Ins/Del}}(x) \times 1 = 1$, that is when SbT_i is made of single node x

Likewise, the minimum cost for inserting/deleting a single node sub-tree is equal to 0.5, half its insert/delete maximum cost:

− $\text{Cost}_{\text{InsTree/DelTree}}(\text{SbT}_i) = \text{Cost}_{\text{Ins/Del}}(x) \times 1/2 = 0.5$, SbT_i consisting of single node x

Note that in our approach, single node insertions/deletions are undertaken via tree insert/delete operations (cf. definitions 11 and 12) applied on leaf node sub-trees. On the other hand, insert/delete node operations (cf. definitions 8 and 9, which are assigned unit costs as with traditional edit distance approaches) are only utilized to compute tree insertion/deletion operations costs (cf. *CBS* and *TOC* in Fig. 5). They do not however contribute to the dynamic programming procedure adopted in our edit distance approach (similarly to [6, 13], cf. *Edit Distance* algorithm in Fig. 5).

Using *TOC*, we compute the costs of tree insertion and deletion operations based on their corresponding trees' maximum normalized commonality values (a maximum commonality value inducing a minimum tree operation cost).

Therefore, instead of utilizing the *contained in* relation introduced in [13] (cf. Definition 2) in order to permit or deny tree insertion/deletion operations (thus disregarding certain sub-tree structural similarities while comparing two XML trees as shown in Section 3), we permit the insertion and deletion of any/all sub-trees by varying their corresponding tree insertion/deletion operation costs with respect to their structural similarities with the source/destination trees/sub-trees respectively (cf. similarity results in Table 1). Note that inserting/deleting the whole destination/source trees is not allowed in our approach. In fact, by rejecting such operations, one could not delete the entire source tree in one step and insert the entire destination tree in a second step, completely ignoring the purpose of the insert/delete tree operations.

Table 1. Distance/similarity values attained using our comparison approach for the various XML comparison examples treated throughout the paper

	Our Approach		N. & J. [13]	Dalamagas *et al.* [6]	Chawathe [4]
	Distance	*Similarity*			
A/B	1.5	0.4	*Detected*	*Not detected*	*Not detected*
A/C	3	0.25			
A/D	3.2856	0.2333	*Not detected*	*Not detected*	*Not detected*
A/E	5	0.1667			
F/G	5.4106	0.1560	*Not detected*	*Not detected*	*Not detected*
F/H	7	0.125			
F/I	4.2857	0.1892	*Not detected*	*Not detected*	*Not detected*
F/J	6	0.1429			
K/L	0.5	0.6667	*Not detected*	*Not detected*	*Not detected*
K/M	1	0.5			
K/N	1	0.5	*Not detected*	*Not detected*	*Not detected*
K/O	1.5	0.4			
K/P	2	0.3333			

4.4 Efficiency w.r.t. Existing Approaches

In the previous paragraphs, the comparison of our method with existing tree XML structural similarity approaches is done via examples. Here, we formalize the comparison and show that existing methods are lower bounds of our approach.

Theorem. Let T_1 and T_2 be XML trees, and $Sim(T_1, T_2) = 1 / 1 + Dist(T_1, T_2)$, then:

- $Sim_{Chawathe}(T_1, T_2) \leq Sim_{Our\ Approach}(T_1, T_2)$
- $Sim_{Dalamagas\ et\ al.}(T_1, T_2) \leq Sim_{Our\ Approach}(T_1, T_2)$
- $Sim_{N.\&J}(T_1, T_2) \leq Sim_{Our\ Approach}(T_1, T_2)$

Proof:

- *Proving that Chawathe's algorithm [4] is a lower bound of our XML comparison method is straight forward. When computing the distance between two trees using Chawathe's approach [4], all sub-trees are inserted/deleted via single node insertion/deletion operations regardless of the sub-tree similarities at hand. The costs of these insertions/deletions are equivalent to the maximum tree insertion/deletion operations' costs following our TOC algorithm (cf. Section 4.3), which yield a maximum edit distance, thus a minimum similarity value between the trees being compared. In other words, Chawathe's algorithm [4] always yields similarity values lesser or equal to those computed via our approach.*

- *Proving that Dalamagas et al.'s algorithm [6] is a lower bound of our XML comparison method is also trivial. Indeed, the costs of tree insertion/deletion operations in [6] are computed as the sum of the costs of inserting/deleting all individual nodes in the considered sub-trees. These costs come down to the maximum tree operations costs computed following our method. Consequently, Dalamagas et al.'s algorithm [6] always yields similarity values that are lesser or equal to those computed via our method. Recall that we do not consider [6]'s repetition/nesting reduction process in our analysis (cf. Section 2.1).*

- *As for Nierman and Jagadish [13], tree insertion/deletion operations costs are affected by the tree containment relation (cf. Definition 2). Maximum costs (i.e. the costs of inserting/deleting all single nodes in the considered sub-trees) are attained when the containment relation is not verified. Otherwise, tree operations costs are minimal (the minimum tree operation cost is not formally defined in [13]. Thus, for a given sub-tree, we consider that it is equal to half its maximum tree operation cost so as to respect the intuition that tree operations costs are always higher or equal than single node operations costs). In other words, Nierman and Jagadish's algorithm [13] only considers the containment relation between sub-trees while varying tree operations costs. However, our algorithm detects fined-grained structural similarities (i.e. sub-tree commonalities) between sub-trees, among which the containment relation, and varies tree operations accordingly. Thus, our approach is able to detect a wider set or structural similarities and consequently yields higher similarity values. In other words, when comparing two XML trees, Nierman and Jagadish's algorithm [13] yields similarity values that are lesser or equal to those obtained via our XML structural comparison method.*

4.5 Complexity Analysis

The overall complexity of our approach simplifies to $O(|T_1||T_2|)$, where $|T_1|$ and $|T_2|$ denote the cardinalities of the compared trees, and is computed as follows:

- *CBS* algorithm for the identification of the commonality between two sub-trees is of complexity: $O(|SbT_i||SbT_j|)$ where $|SbT_i|$ and $|SbT_j|$ denote the cardinalities of the compared sub-trees.
- *TOC* algorithm for computing the costs of tree insert/delete operations, which makes use of *CBS*, is time complexity: $\sum_{i=1}^{|T_1|}\sum_{j=1}^{|T_2|} O(|SbT_i|\,|SbT_j|) + \sum_{i=1}^{|T_1|} O(|SbT_i|\,|T_2|)$

$+ \sum_{j=1}^{|T_2|} O(|SbT_j|\,|T_1|)$.

Lemma 3. Let T_1 and T_2 be two ordered labeled trees, where n_{T_1} and n_{T_2} represent the number of leafs in T_1 and T_2, SbT_i and SbT_j the sub-trees of T_1 and T_2 respectively. Then TOC's complexity: $\sum_{i=1}^{|T_1|}\sum_{j=1}^{|T_2|}O(|SbT_i|\,|SbT_j|) + \sum_{i=1}^{|T_1|}O(|SbT_i|\,|T_2|) + \sum_{j=1}^{|T_2|}O(|SbT_j|\,|T_1|)$, simplifies to $O(|T_1||T_2|)$.

Proof:

- *Step 1 of TOC – Identifying the structural commonalities between each pair of sub-trees in the source and destination trees:*

$$\sum_{i=1}^{|T_1|}\sum_{j=1}^{|T_2|}O(|SbT_i|\,|SbT_j|) \leq O(|T_1||T_2|) \quad (demonstrated\ in\ [9])$$

- *Step 2 of TOC – Identifying the structural commonalities between each sub-tree in the source tree (T_1) and the whole destination tree (T_2):*

$$\sum_{i=1}^{|T_1|}O(|SbT_i|\,|T_2|) = |T_2|\sum_{i=1}^{|T_1|}O(|SbT_i|) < O(|T_1||T_2|)$$

- *Step 3 of TOC – Identifying the structural commonalities between the source tree as a whole (T_1) and each sub-tree in the destination tree (T_2):*

$$\sum_{j=1}^{|T_2|}O(|SbT_j|\,|T_1|) = |T_1|\sum_{j=1}^{|T_2|}O(|SbT_j|) < O(|T_1||T_2|)$$

Note that the edit distance algorithm adopted from [13], which utilizes the results attained by *TOC* (tree operations costs), is of complexity $O(|T_1||T_2|)$.

5 Experimental Evaluation

In order to validate our structural similarity approach and compare its optimality with alternative methods, we make use of structural clustering. In our experiments, we adopt the well known single link hierarchical clustering techniques [8, 10] although any form of clustering could be utilized. In order to evaluate clustering quality, we make use of *precision* and *recall* metrics commonly used in information retrieval. Having an a priori knowledge of which documents should be members of the appropriate cluster (mapping between original DTD clusters and the extracted clusters), Dalamagas *et al.* [6] define precision PR and recall R as:

$$PR = \frac{\sum_{i=1}^{n} a_i}{\sum_{i=1}^{n} a_i + \sum_{i=1}^{n} b_i} \quad \text{and} \quad R = \frac{\sum_{i=1}^{n} a_i}{\sum_{i=1}^{n} a_i + \sum_{i=1}^{n} c_i} \quad \text{where:}$$

- n is the total number of clusters in the clustering set considered,
- a_i is the number of XML documents in C_i that indeed correspond to DTD_i
- b_i is the number of documents in C_i that do not correspond to DTD_i (misclustered)
- c_i is the number of XML documents not in C_i, although they correspond to DTD_i (documents that should have been clustered in C_i).

Nonetheless, in addition to comparing one approach's precision improvement to another's recall improvement, it is a common practice to compare F-values, *F-value = $2 \times PR \times R / (PR+R)$*. Therefore, as in traditional information retrieval evaluation, high *precision* and *recall*, and thus high *F-value* (indicating in our case excellent clustering quality) characterize a good similarity method.

5.1 Experimental Results

We conducted a battery of experiments on real and synthetic XML documents. Two sets of 600 documents were generated from 20 real-case[7] and synthetic DTDs, using an adaptation of the IBM XML documents generator[8]. We varied the *MaxRepeats* parameter to determine the number of times a node will appear as a child of its parent node. For a real dataset, we considered the online version of the ACM SIGMOD Record[9]. Overall *precision, recall* and *F-value* results are reported in Table 2.

Table 2. Average *PR, R* and *F-values* obtained by varying the clustering level between [0, 1]

	SIGMOD			Set 1 (MaxRepeats=5)			Set 2 (MaxRepeats =10)		
	PR	R	F-value	PR	R	F-value	PR	R	F-value
Chawathe [4]	0.8782	0.3910	0.6346	0.2502	0.4737	0.3619	0.2602	0.3809	0.3031
DCWS [6]	0.8782	0.3931	0.6356	0.2581	0.4838	0.3709	0.2779	0.3821	0.3061
N & J [13]	0.8637	0.4615	0.6626	0.2334	0.6162	0.4248	0.2234	0.4177	0.3271
Our approach	0.9086	0.4866	0.6706	0.2341	0.6262	0.4302	0.2203	0.4656	0.3458

Results, with respect to all three data sets, indicate that our approach yields improved clustering quality (i.e. structural comparison quality) vis-à-vis current alternative approaches. Note that the complete *precision vs. recall* curves, describing the detailed behavior of each comparison method while varying the clustering level (and which clearly reveal that our method achieves better combinations of *precision* and *recall*, and thus higher clustering quality) are disregarded due to lack of space.

---

[7] From http://www.xmlfiles.com and http://www.w3schools.com
[8] http://www.alphaworks.ibm.com
[9] Available at http://www.acm.org/sigmod/xml

5.2 Timing Results

Following the complexity analysis developed in Section 4.4, our XML structural similarity method is linear in the number of nodes of each tree, and polynomial (quadratic) in the size of the two trees being compared: $O(|T_1||T_2|)$ (which can be simplified to $O(N^2)$, N being the maximum number of nodes in trees T_1 and T_2). This linear dependency on the size of each tree is experimentally verified, timing results being presented in Fig. 6. Timing experiments were carried out on a PC with an Intel Xeon 2.66 GHz processor (1GB RAM), running at 533 MHz. Fig. 6 shows that the time to identify the structural similarity between two XML trees of various sizes grows in an almost perfect linear fashion with tree size. Therefore, despite appearing theoretically more complex, timing results demonstrate that our method's complexity is the same as the approaches by Nierman & Jagadish [13], Dalamagas et al. [6] as well as Chawathe [4].

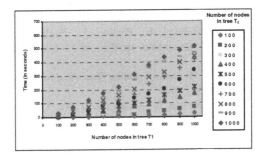

Fig. 6. Timing results obtained using our comparison method

6 Conclusion

In this paper, we proposed a structure-based similarity approach for comparing XML documents. Based on a tree edit distance technique, our approach captures fine-grained structural similarities while comparing XML documents not fully addressed in current approaches. Our theoretical study as well as our experimental evaluation showed that the proposed method yields improved structural similarity results with respect to existing alternatives, while having the same time complexity $(O(N^2))$.

As continuing work, we are exploring the use of our approach in order to compare, not only the structure of XML documents (element/attribute labels) but also their information content (element/attribute values). In such a framework, XML schemas might have to be integrated in the comparison process, schemas underlining element/attribute data types which are required to compare corresponding element/attribute values. We are also working on extending our approach to encompass semantic similarity assessment between element/attribute node labels while comparing XML documents (taking into account synonyms, antonyms, acronyms, etc. in the edit distance process). In addition, we plan on releasing a public web service version of our prototype.

References

1. Aho, A., Hirschberg, D., Ullman, J.: Bounds on the Complexity of the Longest Common Subsequence Problem. Association for Computing Machinery 23(1), 1–12 (1976)
2. Bertino, E., Guerrini, G., Mesiti, M.: A Matching Algorithm for Measuring the Structural Similarity between an XML Documents and a DTD and its Applications. Elsevier Computer Science 29, 23–46 (2004)
3. Chawathe, S., Rajaraman, A., Garcia-Molina, H., Widom, J.: Change Detection in Hierarchically Structured Information. In: Proc. of the ACM SIGMOD 1996, ACM Press, New York (1996)
4. Chawathe, S.: Comparing Hierarchical Data in External Memory. In: VLDB 1999, pp. 90–101 (1999)
5. Cobéna, G., Abiteboul, S., Marian, A.: Detecting Changes in XML Documents. In: Proc. of the IEEE Int. Conf. on Data Engineering, pp. 41–52. IEEE Computer Society Press, Los Alamitos (2002)
6. Dalamagas, T., Cheng, T., Winkel, K., Sellis, T.: A methodology for clustering XML documents by structure. Information Systems 31(3), 187–228 (2006)
7. Flesca, S., Manco, G., Masciari, E., Pontieri, L., Pugliese, A.: Detecting Structural Similarities Between XML Documents. In: Proc. of 5th SIGMOD Workshop on The Web and Databases (2002)
8. Gower, J.C., Ross, G.J.S.: Minimum Spanning Trees and Single Linkage Cluster Analysis. Applied Statistics 18, 54–64 (1969)
9. Guha, S., Jagadish, H.V., Koudas, N., Srivastava, D., Yu, T.: Approximate XML Joins. In: Proceedings of ACM SIGMOD 2002, pp. 287–298 (2002)
10. Halkidi, M., Batistakis, Y., Vazirgiannis, M.: Clustering Algorithms and Validity Measures. In: SSDBM Conference, Virginia, USA (2001)
11. Levenshtein, V.: Binary Codes Capable of Correcting Deletions, Insertions and Reversals. Sov. Phys. Dokl. 6, 707–710 (1966)
12. Myers, E.: An O(ND) Difference Algorithm and Its Variations. Algorithmica 1, 251–266 (1986)
13. Nierman, A., Jagadish, H.V.: Evaluating structural similarity in XML documents. In: Proceedings of the 5th SIGMOD Workshop on The Web and Databases (2002)
14. van Rijsbergen, C.J.: Information Retrieval. Butterworths, London (1979)
15. Sanz, I., Mesiti, M., Guerrini, G., Berlanga Lavori, R.: Approximate Subtree Identification in Heterogeneous XML Documents Collections. In: Bressan, S., Ceri, S., Hunt, E., Ives, Z.G., Bellahsène, Z., Rys, M., Unland, R. (eds.) XSym 2005. LNCS, vol. 3671, pp. 192–206. Springer, Heidelberg (2005)
16. Schlieder, T.: Similarity Search in XML Data Using Cost-based Query Transformations. In: Proceedings of 4th SIGMOD Workshop on The Web and Databases (2001)
17. Shasha, D., Zhang, K.: Approximate Tree Pattern Matching. In: Pattern Matching in Strings, Trees and Arrays, ch. 14, Oxford University Press, Oxford (1995)
18. Wagner, J., Fisher, M.: The String-to-String correction problem. ACM J. 21, 168–173 (1974)
19. Wong, C., Chandra, A.: Bounds for the String Editing Problem. ACM J. 23(1), 13–16 (1976)
20. WWW Consortium, The Document Object Model, http://www.w3.org/DOM
21. Zhang, K., Shasha, D.: Simple Fast Algorithms for the Editing Distance Between Trees and Related Problems. SIAM J. of Computing 18(6), 1245–1262 (1989)
22. Zhang, Z., Li, R., Cao, S., Zhu, Y.: Similarity Metric in XML Documents. In: Knowledge Management and Experience Management Workshop (2003)

Fine-Grained Compatibility and Replaceability Analysis of Timed Web Service Protocols

Julien Ponge[1,2], Boualem Benatallah[2], Fabio Casati[3], and Farouk Toumani[1]

[1] Univ. Clermont-Ferrand 2, France
{ponge,ftoumani}@isima.fr
[2] UNSW, Sydney, Australia
boualem@cse.unsw.edu.au
[3] Univ. of Trento, Italy
casati@dit.unitn.it

Abstract. We deal with the problem of automated analysis of web service protocol compatibility and replaceability in presence of timing abstractions. We first present a timed protocol model for services and identify different levels of compatibility and replaceability that are useful to support service development and evolution. Next, we present operators that can perform such analysis. Finally, we present operators properties by showing that timed protocols form a new class of timed automata, and we briefly present our implementation.

1 Introduction

Service-oriented architectures (SOAs) and web service technologies are emerging computing paradigm for the development and integration of distributed applications [1]. They are based on the notion of *services*, which are loosely-coupled applications interfaces accessible via a programmatic API relying on open standards (e.g., XML, HTTP or SOAP). The idea behind loose coupling is that services can be made generally accessible to a community of users and clients, as opposed to being specifically developed for certain clients, as it was the case in conventional, CORBA-style integration where clients and services were often developed concurrently and by the same team. This capability comes at a price: the need of providing fairly detailed service descriptions, so that (i) at design time, developers know how to write applications that can correctly interact with the service, and (ii) at deployment or run time, it is possible to identify if a client can correctly interact with a service.

Today, service descriptions typically include the interface definition, the transport-level properties (both specified in WSDL), and *business protocol* definitions, that is, the specification of possible message exchange sequences (conversations) that are supported by the service [2]. Protocols can be specified using WS-BPEL (*Web Services Business Process Execution Language*) or any of the many other formalisms developed for this purpose (e.g., [2,3]). Providing such descriptions only solves part of the problem. To facilitate service development and interoperability there is the need for formal methods and software tools that allow the automated analysis of service descriptions to (i) identify which conversations can be carried out between two services, understand mismatches between protocols and, if possible, create adapters to allow interactions

C. Parent et al. (Eds.): ER 2007, LNCS 4801, pp. 599–614, 2007.

between incompatible services (called *compatibility analysis*), and (ii) manage service evolution, that is, understand if a new version of a service protocol is compatible with the intended clients (called *replaceability analysis*).

Such a need is widely recognized and many approaches have been developed, including some by the authors. In particular, in our previous work we developed a simple but expressive business protocol model based on state machines, an algebra for business protocol analysis, and a set of operators to compare and manipulate protocols and that form the basis for compatibility and replaceability analysis [4]. The operators have been implemented within *ServiceMosaic* [5], a CASE tool environment that enables the model-based design, development and management of Web services.

While previous approaches provide significant contributions to protocol analysis (and, in general, to service specification analysis), little work has been done in the context of *timed protocols*, that is, protocols that include time-related properties. This limitation is significant: time is an essential ingredient of any real-life protocol specification. There are countless examples of behaviors that involve timing issues in any kind of protocol [2], from business protocol for web services (e.g., see the RosettaNet PIPs), to interactions between traditional web-based services and users (see e-commerce web sites such as Travelocity or Amazon), to lower level protocols such as TCP. Time-related behaviors range from session timeouts to "logical" deadlines with different kinds of behaviors (e.g., seats reserved on a flight needs to be paid within n hours otherwise they are released). In [2], we have identified extensions to protocol models suitable for representing timing aspects. The extensions are based on an analysis of existing protocols so that we could identify a modeling framework that is simple but expressive. More specifically, we identified the need for representing two kinds of temporal constraints in protocol descriptions: (i) time intervals during which an operation can be invoked and (ii) deadline expirations. Such kinds of constraints can also model timing properties of languages such as WS-BPEL and RosettaNet. The introduction of time aspects adds significant complexity to the protocol analysis problem. Indeed, many formal models enabling explicit representation of time exist (e.g., timed automata, timed petri-nets), all showing extreme difficulties to handle algorithmic analysis of timed models. For example, timed automata, which are today considered as a standard modeling formalism to deal with timing constraints, suffer from undecidability of many problems such as language inclusion and complementation that are fundamental to system analysis and verification tasks [6]. Such problems have been shown to be very sensitive to several criteria (e.g., density of the time axis, type of constraints, presence of silent transitions) This paper extends our previous work in the following directions and makes the following contributions:

1. We formally define *timed protocols*, an extension of business protocols that is suitable to represent both time intervals and deadline expirations constraints.
2. We define a framework for timed protocol analysis, introducing fine-grained classes to study different degrees of compatibility and replaceability among protocols.
3. We define an algebra for protocol analysis and management by defining operators that can manipulate and analyze timed protocols and that can be used to characterize the various compatibility and replaceability classes. We see this work as being inspired, at least conceptually, by work done over the last 30 years in databases,

leading to generic abstraction techniques such as relational algebras that eventually generated the widespread adoption of the relational model. We argue that an algebra for protocol analysis can bring to service-oriented computing similar benefits to what relational algebra brought to relational databases.

4. We establish a semantic-preserving mapping from timed protocols to a new class of timed automata [7] with a restricted form of ε transitions (i.e., "unobservable" or silent transitions). Based on this mapping, we reuse and extend existing results in timed automata theory to derive decidability results for our timed protocol operators. The obtained result is interesting by itself because timed protocols lead to an innovative class of timed automata that includes ε transitions that strictly increase the expressiveness of the automata (i.e., they cannot be removed without a loss of expressiveness) and despite this fact, this class still exhibits a *deterministic behavior*. Especially, the *complementation problem* is decidable for this class. To the best of our knowledge, this is the first identified class of timed automata displaying such a feature.

Due to a lack of space, proofs and additional technical details regarding this work are omitted from this paper but are given in [8] which contains them in its appendix.

2   Timed Protocol Modeling

This section introduces first informally and then formally the model of *timed business protocols* which extends *business protocols* [4] with timing-related abstractions.

2.1   Extending Business Protocols with Temporal Abstractions

We built our model upon the traditional state-machine formalism, which is commonly used to model protocols and, more generally, to model the external behaviors of systems, due to the fact that they are simple and intuitive. In the model, states represent the different phases that a service may go through during its interaction with a requester. Transitions can be associated with a message and/or a constraint. Transitions associated with a message must also indicate the message *polarity*, that denotes whether the message is incoming (plus sign) or outgoing (minus sign). They are triggered when the associated message is sent (or received, depending on the polarity). A message corresponds to the invocation of a service operation or to its reply. Hence, each state identifies a set of outgoing transitions, and therefore a set of possible messages that can be sent or received when the conversation with a client is in that state. For instance, the protocol depicted in Figure 1, inspired from the *Ford Credit web portal*, specifies that a financing service is initially in the $Start$ state, and that clients begin using the service by sending a login message, upon which the service moves to the $Logged$ state (transition $(login(+))$. In the figure, the initial state is indicated by an unlabeled entering arrow without source while final (accepting) states are double-circled. Furthermore, the figure shows that the sequence of message $login(+) \cdot selectVehicle(+) \cdot estimatePayment(+)$ is a conversation supported by the protocol, while the conversation $fullCredit(+) \cdot selectVehicle(+)$ is not. By defining constraints on the ordering of the messages that a web service accepts, a protocol makes explicit to clients how they can *correctly* interact with a service without generating errors due to incorrect sequencing of messages.

Constraints can also be associated to transitions. In this paper we focus on timing abstractions, as we have identified two kinds of constraints that are often needed in practice:

– **C-Invoke** constraints specify a time window within which a given transition can be fired. Outside the window, the transition is disabled (exchanging the message results in an error).
– **M-Invoke** constraints specify when a transition is automatically fired.

M-Invoke constraints can only be associated with *implicit* (as opposed to explicit) transitions, which are used to model transitions that can occur without an explicit invocation by requesters. Implicit transitions are analogous to the so-called silent or ε transitions in automata theory [9]. We assume that implicit transitions are associated with an empty message noted ε.

We use the term *timed protocol* to denote a business protocol whose definition contains such temporal abstractions. Timed protocols must be deterministic, as the client always needs to be able to determine in which state the service is, else much of the purpose of the protocol specification is lost.

Continuing with the example, the financing service may need to specify that a full credit application is accepted only if it is received 24 hours after a payment estimation has been made. This behavior is specified by tagging the transition $T_{14} : fullCredit(+)$ with a time constraint C-Invoke($T_{13} \leq 24h$). This constraint indicates that transition

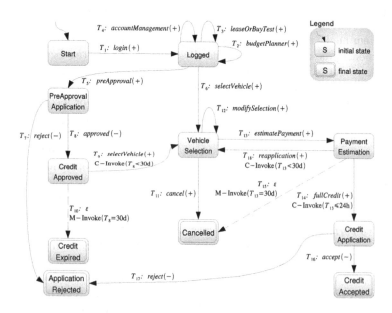

Fig. 1. A timed protocol of an online financing services

T_{14} can only be fired within a time window $[0h, 24h]$ after the execution of the transition T_{13}. The implicit transition T_{10}, depicted in the figure using a dotted arrow, is associated with constraint M-Invoke($T_8 = 30d$) to specify that once a pre-approval application is approved (i.e., after transition $T_8 : approved(-)$ is fired which makes a service entering state $CreditApproved$, a client has 30 days to use the credit, after that the credit decision expires. Note that, the presence of an implicit transition at a given state affects the timing constraints of the other explicit transitions that can be fired from this state. In our example, the presence of the implicit transition T_{10} implies that transition $T_9 : selectVehicle(+)$ can only be executed within a time window $[0d, 30d]$ after the service has entered state $CreditApproved$.

2.2 Formalization

To formally define timed protocols, we first introduce the types of constraints used in this paper. Let $\mathcal{X}$ be a set of variables referring to transition identifiers, i.e., if r is a transition then $x_r \in \mathcal{X}$ is variable referring to this transition. We consider the following two kinds of time constraints defined over a set of variables $\mathcal{X}$:

- C-Invoke(c) with c defined as follows: $c ::= x \ op \ k \mid c \wedge c \mid c \vee c$ with $op \in \{=, \neq, <, >, \leq, \geq\}$, $x \in \mathcal{X}$ and $k \in \mathbb{Q}^{\geq 0}$, where $\mathbb{Q}^{\geq 0}$ denotes the set of nonnegative rational numbers.
- M-Invoke(c) is also defined with $x \in \mathcal{X}$ and $k \in \mathbb{Q}^{\geq 0}$ as above but with the restriction that $c ::= x = k \ [\wedge(x \neq k \mid c \wedge c)]$ (it is an equality with an optional conjunction of equalities and inequalities).

We can now introduce a formal definition of timed protocols.

Syntax:

- $\mathcal{S}$ is a finite set of states, with $s_0 \in \mathcal{S}$ being the initial state.
- $\mathcal{F} \subseteq \mathcal{S}$ is the set of final states. If $\mathcal{F} = \emptyset$, then $\mathcal{P}$ is said to be an empty protocol.
- $M = M_e \cup \{\varepsilon\}$ is a finite set of messages M_e augmented with the empty message ε. For each message $m \in M_e$, we define a function Polarity($\mathcal{P}, m$) which will be positive $(+)$ if m is an input message in $\mathcal{P}$, and negative $(-)$ if m is an output message in $\mathcal{P}$.
- $\mathcal{X} = \{x_r \mid \exists r \in \mathcal{R}\}$ is a set of variables defined over the set of transitions $\mathcal{R}$.
- $\mathcal{C}$ is a set of time constraints defined over a set of variables $\mathcal{X}$. The absence of a constraint is interpreted as a constraint with the value of true.
- $\mathcal{R} \subseteq \mathcal{S}^2 \times M \times \mathcal{C}$ is a finite set of transitions. Each transition (s, s', m, c) identifies a source state s, a target state s', a message m and a constraint c. We say that the message m is enabled from a state s. When $m = \varepsilon$, c must be a M-Invoke constraint. Otherwise c must be either a C-Invoke constraint or true.

In the sequel, we use the notation $\mathcal{R}(s, s', m, c)$ to denote the fact that $(s, s', m, c) \in \mathcal{R}$. To enforce determinism, we require that a protocol has only one initial state, and that for every state s and every two transitions (s, s_1, m_1, c_1) and (s, s_2, m_2, c_2) enabled from s, we have either $m_1 \neq m_2$ or $c_1 \wedge c_2 \equiv$ false. To enforce preemption of M-Invoke constraints over C-Invoke constraints, it is assumed that for each state that offers implicit transitions, the explicit transitions satisfy C-Invoke constraints as follows. They must satisfy the conjunction of all the $T_i < k_i$ constraints where $T_i = k_i$ appears in a M-Invoke constraint. Otherwise, an explicit transition could still be fired after all the implicit transitions have expired. Finally, we do not allow cycles only made of implicit transitions as the system would enter an infinite loop.

Variable interpretation. To formally define the semantics of timed protocols we introduce the notion of variable valuation. We consider as a time domain the set of non-negative reals $\mathbb{R}^{\geq 0}$. Let $\mathcal{X}$ be a set of variables with values in $\mathbb{R}^{\geq 0}$. A (variable) valuation $\mathcal{V} : \mathcal{X} \rightarrow \mathbb{R}^{\geq 0}$ is a mappings that assigns to each variable $x \in \mathcal{X}$ a time value $\mathcal{V}(x)$. We note by $\mathcal{V}_t$ the variable valuation at an instant t. At the beginning (i.e., instant $t_0 = 0$) we assume that all the variables are set to zero, i.e., $\mathcal{V}_{t_0}(x_r) = 0, \forall x_r \in \mathcal{X}$. Then, a variable valuation at a time t_j, is completely determined by a protocol execution. Consider for example an execution $\sigma = s_0 \cdot (m_0, t_0) \cdot s_1 \ldots s_{n-1} \cdot (m_{n-1}, t_{n-1}) \cdot s_n$ of a protocol $\mathcal{P}$ and let r be a transition in $\mathcal{R}$. The valuation of a variable x_r at time t_j, with $0 < j \leq n$, is defined as follows:

$$\mathcal{V}_{t_j}(x_r) = \begin{cases} 0, \text{ if } r = (s_{j-1}, s_j, m_{j-1}, c_{j-1}) \\ \mathcal{V}_{t_{j-1}}(x_r) + t_j - t_{j-1}, \text{ otherwise} \end{cases}$$

Given a variable valuation $\mathcal{V}$ and a constraint C-Invoke(c) (respectively, M-Invoke(c)), we note by $c(\mathcal{V})$, the constraint obtained by substituting each variable x in c by its value $\mathcal{V}(x)$. A variable valuation $\mathcal{V}$ satisfies a constraint C-Invoke(c) (respectively, M-Invoke(c)) iff $c(\mathcal{V}) \equiv \texttt{true}$. In this case, we write $\mathcal{V} \models$ C-Invoke(c) (respectively, $\mathcal{V} \models$ M-Invoke(c)).

Protocol semantics. We define the semantics of timed protocols using the notion of *timed conversation* (this is inspired from *timed words* in [7]).

Let $\mathcal{P} = (\mathcal{S}, s_0, \mathcal{F}, \mathsf{M}, \mathcal{R}, \mathcal{C})$ be a timed protocol. A correct execution (or simply, an execution) of $\mathcal{P}$ is a sequence $\sigma = s_0 \cdot (m_0, t_0) \cdot s_1 \ldots s_{n-1} \cdot (m_{n-1}, t_{n-1}) \cdot s_n$ such that: (i) $t_0 \leq t_1 \leq \ldots \leq t_n$ (i.e., the occurrence of times increase monotonically), (ii) s_0 is the initial state and s_n is a final state of $\mathcal{P}$, and (iii) $\forall j \in [1, n]$, we have: $\mathcal{R}(s_{j-1}, s_j, m_{j-1}, c_{j-1})$ and $\mathcal{V}_{j-1} \models c_{j-1}$.

As an example, the sequence $\sigma' = Start \cdot (login(+), 0) \cdot Logged \cdot (preApproval(+), 1)$ $\cdot PreApprovalApplication \cdot (approved(-), 3) \cdot CreditApproved \cdot (\varepsilon, 33) \cdot CreditExpired$ is a correct execution of the financing service protocol depicted at figure 1. If $\sigma = s_0 \cdot (m_0, t_0) \cdot s_1 \ldots s_{n-1} \cdot (m_{n-1}, t_{n-1}) \cdot s_n$ is a correct execution of protocol $\mathcal{P}$, then the sequence $tr(\sigma) = (m_0, t_0) \ldots (m_{n-1}, t_{n-1})$ forms a timed trace which is compliant with $\mathcal{P}$. Continuing with the example, the execution σ' of the financing service protocol leads to the timed trace $tr(\sigma') = (login(+), 0) \cdot (preApproval(+), 1) \cdot (approved(-), 3) \cdot (\varepsilon, 33)$. During an execution σ of a protocol $\mathcal{P}$, the externally timed observable behavior of $\mathcal{P}$, hereafter called *timed conversation* of $\mathcal{P}$ and noted $conv(\sigma)$, is obtained by removing from the corresponding timed trace $tr(\sigma)$ all the non observable events (i.e., all the pairs (m_i, t_i) with $m_i = \varepsilon$). For example, during the previous execution σ', the observable behavior of the financing service is described by the timed conversation $conv(\sigma') = (login(+), 0) \cdot (preApproval(+), 1) \cdot (approved(-), 3)$. In the following, given a protocol $\mathcal{P}$, we denote by $Tr(\mathcal{P})$ the (possibly infinite) set of timed conversations of (or compliant with) $\mathcal{P}$.

Protocol interaction semantics. Timed conversations describe the externally observable behavior of timed protocols and, as it will be shown below, are essential to analyze the ability of two services to interact correctly. Let us consider the protocol $\mathcal{P}$ depicted on Figure 1 and its reversed protocol $\mathcal{P}'$ obtained from $\mathcal{P}$ by reversing the polarity of the messages (i.e., input messages becomes outputs and vice versa). We can observe that when $\mathcal{P}'$ interacts with $\mathcal{P}$ following a given timed conversation τ, $\mathcal{P}$ follows exactly a similar conversation but with reversed polarities on the messages. If during such an interaction the timed conversation of $\mathcal{P}'$ is $(login(+), 0) \cdot (selectVehicle(+), 1)$ $\cdot (estimatePayment(+), 10) \cdot (fullCredit(+), 30) \cdot (accept(-), 100)$, then the timed conversation of $\mathcal{P}'$ will be $(login(-), 0) \cdot (selectVehicle(-), 1) \cdot (estimatePayment(-),$ $10) \cdot (fullCredit(-), 30) \cdot (accept(+), 100)$. In this case, we call the path $(login, 0) \cdot$ $(selectVehicle, 1) \cdot (estimatePayment, 10) \cdot (fullCredit, 30) \cdot (accept, 100)$ a *timed interaction trace* of $\mathcal{P}$ and $\mathcal{P}'$. Please note that the polarity of the messages that appear in interaction traces is not defined, as in such traces each input message m of one protocol coincides with an output message m of the other protocol. More precisely, let $\mathcal{P}$ and $\mathcal{P}'$ be two timed protocols and let $\tau = (a_0, t_0), \dots (a_n, t_n)$ be a sequence of events for which the messages polarities are not defined. Then τ is a timed interaction trace of $\mathcal{P}$ and $\mathcal{P}'$ if and only if there exist two timed conversation σ_1 and σ_2 such that: (i) $\sigma_1 \in Tr(\mathcal{P})$ and $\sigma_2 \in Tr(\mathcal{P}')$, and (ii) σ_1 is the reverse conversation of σ_2 (i.e., the conversation obtained from σ_2 by inverting polarity of messages), and (iii) $\tau = Unp(\sigma_1) = Unp(\sigma_2)$, where $Unp(\sigma)$ denotes the trace obtained from σ by removing the messages polarities.

3   Timed Protocol Analysis

We target two types of protocol analysis, namely *compatibility* and *replaceability* analysis. Compatibility analysis consists in checking whether two services can interact correctly based on their protocol definitions (i.e., whether a conversation can take place between the considered services), while replaceability analysis is concerned with the verification of whether two protocols can support the same set of conversations (e.g., a service can replace another in general or when interacting with specific clients). These two kinds of analysis are useful for lifecycle management of web services as, for example, to provide support for static and dynamic binding as well as in protocol evolution. For both compatibility and replaceability, we have defined several *classes* to identify different levels of compatibility and replaceability, as well as *operators* that can be applied to protocol definition to asses the level of compatibility and replaceability.

3.1   Compatibility Analysis

Compatibility analysis aims at characterizing whether two protocols (which typically depict a service provider and service requester) can interact. It also defines to which extent the compatibility is possible, as some conversations that a protocol supports may not be supported by the other protocol. More specifically, the following compatibility classes can be identified.

- *Partial compatibility* (or simply, compatibility): A timed protocol $\mathcal{P}_1$ is partially compatible with another timed protocol $\mathcal{P}_2$ if there are some executions of $\mathcal{P}_1$ that

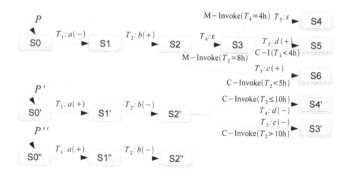

Fig. 2. Three protocols to illustrate protocols analysis

can interoperate with $\mathcal{P}_2$. In other words, partial compatibility implies that there is at least one timed conversation σ of $\mathcal{P}_1$ which is *"understood"* by $\mathcal{P}_2$ (i.e., the reversed conversation of σ is compliant with $\mathcal{P}_2$).

- *Full compatibility*: a protocol $\mathcal{P}_1$ is fully compatible with another protocol $\mathcal{P}_2$ if all the executions of $\mathcal{P}_1$ can interoperate with $\mathcal{P}_2$, i.e., any conversation that can be generated by $\mathcal{P}_1$ is understood by $\mathcal{P}_2$.

We illustrate compatibility analysis and its challenges on the examples below. Let us consider the protocols $\mathcal{P}$ and $\mathcal{P}'$ depicted at figure 2. Abstracting from the timing constraints, we can observe that $\mathcal{P}$ is fully compatible with $\mathcal{P}'$ (i.e., $a \cdot b \cdot c$ and $a \cdot b \cdot d$ are valid interaction traces of the untimed versions of $\mathcal{P}$ and $\mathcal{P}'$). However, due to the C-Invoke constraints specified on the transitions T_3 of each protocol, $\mathcal{P}$ and $\mathcal{P}'$ cannot interact correctly. Indeed, $\mathcal{P}$ supports timed conversations of the form $(a(-), 0) \cdot (b(+), t) \cdot (c(+), t')$, with $t' < t + 5$ while $\mathcal{P}'$ supports timed conversations of the form $(a(+), 0) \cdot (b(-), t) \cdot (c(-), t')$, with $t' > t + 10$. Hence, these two protocols cannot interact correctly since $\mathcal{P}'$ will always send message c too late. Therefore, to be able to interact correctly, two protocols must agree on the ordering of the messages to be exchanged as well as on the corresponding timing constraints.

Let us now consider the protocols $\mathcal{P}$ and $\mathcal{P}''$ of Figure 2. We can observe that when interacting according to the timed interaction trace $(a, 0) \cdot (b, t)$, $\mathcal{P}$ moves to a non-final state s_2 while $\mathcal{P}''$ moves to a final state s_2'' ending its conversation. However, due the presence of the implicit transitions T_4 and T_5, $\mathcal{P}$ is able to terminate correctly its execution by moving automatically to the final state s_4 (i.e., it waits at state s_2 for 8 hours and then moves automatically to state s_3 where it waits for 4 hours before finally moving automatically to the final state s_4). Therefore, the two protocols $\mathcal{P}$ and $\mathcal{P}''$ can interact correctly following the interaction trace $(a, 0) \cdot (b, t)$.

The next example shows that implicit transitions can influence the identification of final states and this naturally impacts compatibility analysis. We consider again protocols $\mathcal{P}$ and $\mathcal{P}'$ of figure 2. After exchanging messages a and b, the two protocols move to states s_2 and s_2' respectively. If we consider the operations that are defined explicitly at these two states, we can observe that s_2' provides an operation $d(-)$ while state s_2 does not enable any invocation of a d operation. Consequently, focusing compatibility checking only on these two states is not enough. Indeed, the presence of the implicit transition T_4 in $\mathcal{P}$ changes the service state automatically to the state s_3 after 8 hours from which $d(+)$ can be fired. Consequently, $\mathcal{P}$ and $\mathcal{P}'$ can interact correctly following timed interactions traces of the form $(a, 0) \cdot (b, t) \cdot (c, t')$, with $t + 8 < t' \leq t + 10$ (i.e., if a message d is sent between 8 and 10 hours after a message b).

3.2 Replaceability Analysis

Replaceability analysis aims at characterizing whether, and to which extent, a given service can be replaced by another one. In such a situation, the substitute service can be transparently used by clients of the original service without the need to change them beyond binding details such as the service URL. Like in the case of compatibility analysis, replaceability analysis aims at supporting flexible schemes as one cannot realistically expect to find services that are completely replaceable. We have identified the following replaceability classes.

- *Protocol equivalence w.r.t. replaceability*: two business protocols $\mathcal{P}_1$ and $\mathcal{P}_2$ are equivalently replaceable if they can be interchangeably used in any context and the change is transparent to clients.
- *Protocol subsumption w.r.t. replaceability*: a protocol $\mathcal{P}_2$ is subsumed by another protocol $\mathcal{P}_1$ w.r.t. replaceability if $\mathcal{P}_1$ supports at least all the conversations that $\mathcal{P}_2$ supports. In this case, protocol $\mathcal{P}_1$ can be transparently used instead of $\mathcal{P}_2$ but the opposite is not necessarily true.
- *Protocol replaceability w.r.t. a client protocol*: A protocol $\mathcal{P}_1$ can replace another protocol $\mathcal{P}_2$ with respect to a client protocol $\mathcal{P}_C$ if $\mathcal{P}_1$ behaves as $\mathcal{P}_2$ when interacting with a specific client protocol $\mathcal{P}_C$. This class is important in those cases where we expect the service to predominantly interact with certain types of clients.
- *Protocol replaceability w.r.t. an interaction role*: Let $\mathcal{P}_R$ be a business protocol. A protocol $\mathcal{P}_1$ can replace another protocol $\mathcal{P}_2$ with respect to a role $\mathcal{P}_R$ if $\mathcal{P}_1$ behaves as $\mathcal{P}_2$ when $\mathcal{P}_2$ behaves as $\mathcal{P}_R$. This replace-ability class allows to identify executions of a protocol $\mathcal{P}_2$ that can be replaced by protocol $\mathcal{P}_1$ even when $\mathcal{P}_1$ and $\mathcal{P}_2$ are not comparable with respect to any of the previous replace-ability classes. This class is important when we want to assess replaceability when considering only certain functionality of the service, e.g., the purchasing part of a supply chain management service.

For all of the above classes, we can distinguish between full and partial replaceability. Full replaceability is as defined above. Partial replaceability is when there is replaceability but only for some conversations and not others. For example, we have partial replaceability with respect to a client protocol when protocol $\mathcal{P}_1$ can replace another protocol $\mathcal{P}_2$ in at least some of the conversations that can occur with $\mathcal{P}_c$.

As an example, consider a protocol $\mathcal{P}_1$ obtained from $\mathcal{P}''$ of Figure 2 by reversing the messages polarities. Such a protocol can be replaced by $\mathcal{P}$ of Figure 2. Indeed, the only timed conversations supported by $\mathcal{P}_1$ are of the form $(a(-), 0) \cdot (b(-), t)$, with $t > 0$. Such conversations are also supported by $\mathcal{P}$. The opposite is however not true. Indeed, $\mathcal{P}$ may support some conversations that contain the messages c or d while $\mathcal{P}_1$ does not.

However, we can observe that $\mathcal{P}_1$ can replace $\mathcal{P}$ when interacting with $\mathcal{P}''$: the only timed conversations of $\mathcal{P}$ that are understood by $\mathcal{P}''$ are of the form $(a(-), 0) \cdot (b(-), t)$, with $t > 0$. Such conversations are also supported by $\mathcal{P}_1$.

4   Protocol Operators

The discussion above concerning the compatibility and replaceability classes emphasized the need for operators to analyze and compare timed protocols. There is also a need for understanding (when two timed protocols are neither equivalent nor compatible) which conversations can take place and which ones cannot. This motivates the development of a protocol algebra that enables the manipulation and analysis of timed protocols.

We split the set of protocol operators in two categories: *manipulation* and *comparison* operators. The former category allows to compute protocols that captures a property regarding a pair of protocols, for example to compute a protocol that captures all of the common timed conversations of two protocols. The later category allows to compare two protocols, for example to assess if they are equivalent or not. We define these operators below.

Manipulation operators are applied to protocols and result in protocols. We describe their formal semantics in Table 1. The introduction of time does not change the definition compared to the case (untimed) business protocols of [4].

To illustrate these operators, Figure 3 shows three simple timed protocols $\mathcal{P}_1$, $\mathcal{P}_2$ and $\mathcal{P}_3$ as well as the results when applying operators on them. For example, the protocol $\mathcal{P}_1 \parallel^{\text{TI}} \mathcal{P}_3$ captures the timed conversations that are commonly supported by both $\mathcal{P}_1$ and $\mathcal{P}_3$: $\mathcal{P}_1$ does not support receiving a message c, hence it does not appear in $\mathcal{P}_1 \parallel^{\text{TI}} \mathcal{P}_3$. Similarly $\mathcal{P}_1$ can only receive a b message within the 10 seconds that follow the reception of a a message. Another example is the protocol $\mathcal{P}_3 \parallel^{\text{TD}} \mathcal{P}_1$ that captures all the conversations that $\mathcal{P}_3$ supports, but that $\mathcal{P}_1$ doesn't. This is why the C-Invoke constraint of T_2 in $\mathcal{P}_3 \parallel^{\text{TD}} \mathcal{P}_1$ is the negation of the one of T_2 in $\mathcal{P}_1$ as $\mathcal{P}_3$ does not carry a C-Invoke constraint on its transition T_2. Similarly, $\mathcal{P}_3$ supports receiving c messages while $\mathcal{P}_1$ does not.

Table 1. Protocol manipulation operators semantics

Operator name	Symbol	Semantics
Compatible Composition	$\parallel^{\text{TC}}$	$\mathcal{P} = \mathcal{P}_1 \parallel^{\text{TC}} \mathcal{P}_2$ is a protocol $\mathcal{P}$ such that $T \in Tr(\mathcal{P})$ iff T is an interaction trace of $\mathcal{P}_1$ and $\mathcal{P}_2$
Intersection	$\parallel^{\text{TI}}$	$\mathcal{P} = \mathcal{P}_1 \parallel^{\text{TI}} \mathcal{P}_2$ is a protocol $\mathcal{P}$ such that $Tr(\mathcal{P}) = Tr(\mathcal{P}_1) \cap Tr(\mathcal{P}_2)$
Difference	$\parallel^{\text{TD}}$	$\mathcal{P} = \mathcal{P}_1 \parallel^{\text{TD}} \mathcal{P}_2$ is a protocol $\mathcal{P}$ that satisfies the following condition: $Tr(\mathcal{P}) = Tr(\mathcal{P}_1) \setminus Tr(\mathcal{P}_2)$
Projection	$[\parallel^{\text{TC}}]$	Let $\mathcal{P} = \mathcal{P}_1 \parallel^{\text{TC}} \mathcal{P}_2$. $[\mathcal{P}_1 \parallel^{\text{TC}} \mathcal{P}_2]_{\mathcal{P}_i}$, with $i \in \{1, 2\}$, is the protocol obtained from $\mathcal{P}_1 \parallel^{\text{TC}} \mathcal{P}_2$ by defining the polarity function of the messages as follows: $Polarity([\mathcal{P}_1 \parallel^{\text{TC}} \mathcal{P}_2]_{\mathcal{P}_i}, m) = Polarity(\mathcal{P}_i, m), \forall m \in \text{M}$

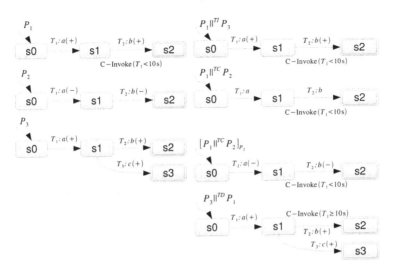

Fig. 3. Three timed protocols $\mathcal{P}_1, \mathcal{P}_2$ and $\mathcal{P}_3$ and some resulting protocols when using protocol manipulation operators

Table 2. Characterization of the compatibility and replaceability classes

Class	Characterization
Partial compatibility of $\mathcal{P}_1$ and $\mathcal{P}_2$	$\mathcal{P}_1 \parallel^{TC} \mathcal{P}_2$ is not *empty*
Full compatibility of $\mathcal{P}_1$ and $\mathcal{P}_2$	$\left[\mathcal{P}_1 \parallel^{TC} \mathcal{P}_2 \right]_{\mathcal{P}_1} \equiv \mathcal{P}_1$
Replaceability of $\mathcal{P}_1$ by $\mathcal{P}_2$	$\mathcal{P}_2 \sqsubseteq \mathcal{P}_1$
Equivalence of $\mathcal{P}_1$ and $\mathcal{P}_2$ w.r.t. replaceability	$\mathcal{P}_1 \equiv \mathcal{P}_2$
Replaceability of $\mathcal{P}_2$ by $\mathcal{P}_1$ w.r.t. a client protocol $\mathcal{P}_C$	$\left[\mathcal{P}_C \parallel^{TC} \mathcal{P}_2 \right]_{\mathcal{P}_2} \sqsubseteq \mathcal{P}_1$ or equivalently $\mathcal{P}_C \parallel^{TC} (\mathcal{P}_2 \parallel^{TD} \mathcal{P}_1)$ is *empty*
Replaceability of $\mathcal{P}_2$ by $\mathcal{P}_1$ w.r.t. a role $\mathcal{P}_R$	$(\mathcal{P}_R \parallel^{TI} \mathcal{P}_2) \sqsubseteq \mathcal{P}_1$

We define two comparison operators, namely *subsumption* and *equivalence*. They enable to compare timed protocols w.r.t. their timed conversations. The subsumption, noted $\sqsubseteq$, assesses whether one protocol supports all of the timed conversations of another protocol (i.e., $\mathcal{P} \sqsubseteq \mathcal{P}'$ iff $Tr(\mathcal{P}) \subseteq Tr(\mathcal{P}')$). The equivalence, noted $\equiv$, checks whether two protocols support exactly the same set of conversations (i.e., $\mathcal{P} \equiv \mathcal{P}'$ iff $Tr(\mathcal{P}) = Tr(\mathcal{P}')$).

The characterization of the protocol compatibility and replaceability analysis classes using the protocol manipulation and comparison operators is given in Table 2. The introduction of time does not change the characterization that had been defined for (untimed) business protocols in [4].

5   Protocol Operators Properties

This section investigates the decidability and complexity properties underlying our protocol operators. We show that there is a semantic-preserving mapping from protocols into a new class of timed automata [7] with ε-transitions (i.e., ε-transitions). We illustrate such a mapping on an example and then we discuss how existing results in timed automata theory can be reused/extended to deal with our specific problems. More technical details can be found in [8].

5.1 Mapping Protocols into Timed Automata

Briefly, a timed automaton [7] is a finite automaton augmented with a finite set of real-valued clocks. Clock constraints can be associated with transitions and can also be reset to zero simultaneously with any transition. Figure 4 shows a timed protocol and its corresponding timed automaton. The obtained automaton uses two clock variables, x_1 and x_2, to implement the timing constraints described in the corresponding timed protocol. For example, the constraint C-Invoke($T_1 < 5h$) of transition T_1 is captured in the timed automaton by the constraint $x_1 < 5$ associated with the arc $b(+)$ between states s_1 and s_2. Indeed, this constraint is defined over variable x_1 which is reset to zero when the automaton switches from state s_0 to s_1 on symbol $a(-)$. Then, while the automaton is at state s_1, the value of variable x_1 shows the time elapsed since the occurrence of the last transition $s_0 \cdot a(-) \cdot s_1$. The transition from state s_1 to s_2 on symbol $b(+)$ is enabled only if the value of variable x_1 is less than 5. Thus, the timing constraint expressed by this automaton is that the symbol $b(+)$ must occur less than 5 units of time after the occurrence of the symbol $a(-)$ (and this is exactly what the constraint C-Invoke($T_1 < 5h$) on transition T_1 prescribes). Also, note that the implicit transition T_4 in the timed protocol is described using an ε-transition between states s_2 and s_4 in the corresponding timed automaton. The associated M-Invoke($T_2 = 10h$) constraint is modeled in the timed automaton using two clock constraints $x = 10$, associated with the ε transition, and $x < 10$ associated with the remaining transition that is enabled from state s_2 on symbol $c(+)$. In the remainder, we assume that timed protocols have been *normalized* by making explicit all the temporal constraints as described above.

Timed automata are in general more expressive than timed protocols and hence not any timed automaton can be mapped into a protocol. However, the restricted class of timed automata that are obtained by a mapping from a timed protocol can be translated back into timed protocols without loss of semantics. We call this class *PTA* for *Protocol Timed Automata*. The procedure that we propose translates a protocol into a timed automaton, as briefly explained below. To do that, and to make sure that the mapping is effectively bijective, we give three conditions that identify timed automata that can be mapped back into timed protocols.

Let $\mathcal{P} = (\mathcal{S}, s_0, \mathcal{F}, \mathsf{M}, \mathcal{X}, \mathcal{C}, \mathcal{R})$ be a timed protocol. An associated timed automaton $A_\mathcal{P} = (L, L^0, L^f, X_\mathcal{P}, E)$ over alphabet $\Sigma_\mathcal{P} = \mathsf{M}$ is built as follows: $L = \mathcal{S}$, $L^0 = \{s_0\}$, $L^f = \mathcal{F}$, $X_\mathcal{P} = \mathcal{X}$ and $\forall r = (s, s', m, c) \in \mathcal{R}$, a new switch $(s, a, \varphi, \lambda, s')$ is added to E such that: $a = m$, $\varphi = \alpha$ if $c =$ C-Invoke(α) or $c =$ M-Invoke(α), and $\lambda = \{x_r\}$. Figure 4 depicts a timed protocol and its associated timed automaton.

Let $A = (L, L^0, L^f, X, E)$ be a timed automaton verifying the following conditions:

(C_1) $\forall e = (l, a, \varphi, \lambda, l') \in E$, $|\lambda| = 1$ (i.e., exactly one clock is reset), and the clock in λ is only reset on e: for every two distinct switches $(l_1, a_1, \varphi_1, \lambda_1, l'_1)$ and $(l_2, a_2, \varphi_2, \lambda_2, l'_2)$ of E, we have $\lambda_1 \cap \lambda_2 = \emptyset$,

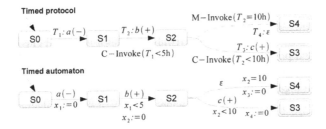

Fig. 4. A timed protocol and its associated timed automaton

($\mathbf{C_2}$) A is deterministic, i.e., for every two switches $(l, a, \varphi_1, \lambda_1, l'_1)$ and $(l, a, \varphi_2, \lambda_2, l'_2)$ from E recognizing the same event a from the same location l, then $\varphi_1 \wedge \varphi_2 \equiv \mathtt{false}$,

($\mathbf{C_3}$) The allowed guards of the ε-transitions are conjunctions of atomic equality and inequality constraints such that each guard has at least 1 equality constraint,

($\mathbf{C_4}$) Given the set $\{(l, \varepsilon, \varphi_1, \lambda_1, l'_1), \cdots, (l, \varepsilon, \varphi_n, \lambda_1, l'_n)\}$ of ε-transitions starting from a location l, the guard φ_j of each switch $(l, m, \varphi_j, \lambda_j, l'_j)$ (with $m \in \Sigma \cup \{\varepsilon\}$) satisfies $\bigwedge_{i \neq j} (x_i < k_i)$ such that $(x_i = k_i)$ appears in φ_k with $k \in \{1, \cdots, n\}$.

Condition (C_1) enforces that every switch resets only one clock. Indeed, a timed automaton switch is allowed to reset an arbitrary number of clocks, while in the case of the mappings of timed protocols we need to reset only one clock: the one that is associated with the transition. This defines a bijection between the set of clocks and the set of switches. Condition (C_2) ensures determinism the guards of 2 switches that recognize the same event from the same location must be disjoint. Condition (C_3) enforces the definition of guards on the ε-labeled switches. Finally, condition (C_4) enforces the semantics of the M-Invoke constraints (determinism and preemption).

Every timed automaton that verifies the conditions (C_1), (C_2), (C_3) and (C_4) above can be mapped into a timed protocol, and hence is a *timed protocol automaton*. This mapping can be performed by reversing the procedure described above. The following theorem says that a timed protocol and its associated timed automaton are semantically equivalent.

Theorem 1. *Let $\mathcal{P}$ be a timed protocol and $A_\mathcal{P}$ its associated protocol timed automata. Then: $Tr(\mathcal{P}) = \mathcal{L}(A_\mathcal{P})$, where $\mathcal{L}(A_\mathcal{P})$ denotes the timed language recognized by the automaton $A_\mathcal{P}$.*

The proof derives from the definition of both the PTA class and the mapping from timed protocols to PTA.

5.2 Closure Property of Protocol Manipulation Operators

Through the aforementioned mapping, we derive results regarding intersection and compatible composition operators. Indeed, it is well known that timed automata are closed under intersection [6]. Such a property is established by extending the classical automata product construction to timed automata. In [8] we extend the product construction to show that the closure property also holds for the PTA class (e.g., intersection of two timed protocol automata is a timed protocol automaton). This leads to an algorithm to compute timed intersection or composition of protocols.

The situation regarding the difference and subsumption operators is however more complex. The main problem lies in the undecidability of the complementation in timed automata with ε-transitions. Since the difference and the language inclusion problem (or subsumption) depend on the complementation (e.g., $A \backslash B \equiv A \sqcap \overline{B}$ and $L(A) \subseteq L(B)$ iff $L(A) \cap L(\overline{B}) = \emptyset$), the decidability of these operators requires a proper investigation of the characteristics of protocol timed automata. The main difficulty lies in the presence of the ε-transitions, which unlike in the case of classical (untimed) automata, strictly increase the expressiveness level of timed automata. [9] investigates the expressive power of ε-transitions and identifies cases where ε-transitions can be removed without a loss of expressiveness (e.g., case of ε-transitions that do not reset clocks). Unfortunately, this result is of no use in our case as the ε-transitions that we deal with do not belong to the identified cases. Indeed, in the PTA class, ε-transitions strictly increase the expressiveness of protocol timed automata as they reset clocks, and hence they cannot be removed [10]. However, we have shown that the class PTA is closed under complementation, which allows claiming that timed protocols are closed under difference. Moreover, since PTA are closed under intersection, and given that the emptiness checking problem is decidable for timed automata [6], the protocol subsumption and equivalence problems are decidable. The proof of closure under complementation is based on the observation that although PTA automata contain ε-transitions with clocks resets, they still exhibit a *deterministic behavior* which ensures that at each step of an execution, all clock values are solely determined by the input word. Therefore, closure under complementation can be proved by extending the usual construction to PTA. The main result of this section is given below.

Theorem 2. *Timed protocols are closed under intersection, compatible composition and difference.*

Performing a subsumption or equivalence test between two protocols is thus decidable, as described by the theorem hereafter. We also give a complexity result which is derived from existing work on the *timed language inclusion* problem for timed automata [7].

Theorem 3. *The subsumption and equivalence operators on timed protocols are decidable, and their decision problems are* PSPACE-COMPLETE.

With the two theorems above, we have proved that our full set of operators can be implemented by reusing the already-known constructs on timed automata [7]. Those results directly come from the novel class of timed automata that we have identified. This makes it possible to conduct automated analysis for all of the compatibility and replaceability classes on timed protocols.

6   Implementation and Discussion

We have developed a prototype as part of the larger *ServiceMosaic* project [5]. Briefly, *ServiceMosaic* (see http://servicemosaic.isima.fr/) is a CASE-toolset model-driven prototype platform for modeling, analyzing, and managing web service models including business protocols, orchestration, and adapters. The *ServiceMosaic* projects are developed for the Java™ platform version 5. We created libraries that provide the functionalities of our contributions, then we integrate them into the Eclipse platform as plug-ins. Regarding the work presented in this paper, we have designed a model for timed protocols and implemented the operators (the subsumption and equivalence operators rely on the *UPPAAL* model checker). We have also created a graphical editor for protocols as well as component that can extract the protocols of the services that are used in a BPEL orchestration. In our experimentations, we have also worked on protocols (manually) extracted from RosettaNet PIPs.

The approach that we have described in this paper can be used in several practical contexts. We briefly outline one of them where we have used our prototype to facilitate service composition development [8]. Given a BPEL orchestration, we have used it to check if the selected services where fully or partially compatible with the BPEL process behavior. By identifying which conversations can or cannot be carried out, we have been able to support the development of protocol adapters in a similar fashion as in [11] which tackles adaptation in the case of untimed business protocols.

We now provide a brief outlook of related work. Several ongoing efforts in the area of Web services recognize the importance of high level modeling and analysis of services protocols (e.g., [4,12,3,13]). Similar approaches for protocols compatibility and replaceability exist in the area of component-based systems [14, 15]. In terms of protocol description, the existing models do not explicitly take timing constraints into account. In terms of protocols analysis, mechanisms have been proposed to verify protocols compatibility and replaceability. However, the verifications are still *"black or white"* whereas our approach targets a fine-grained analysis for the cases where *partial* results are desirable. Standardization efforts recognize the need for supporting the explicit description of web services functional and non-functional properties [16]. Of most interest in the case of making explicit business protocols are the Business Process Execution Language for Web Services (BPEL), the Web Services Conversation Language (WSCL) and the Web Service Choreography Interface (WSCI). Documents complying to those specifications can be derived from protocols and vice-versa as our approach is complementary to them.

In our work, we used a states machine-based model for describing protocols. However, the formal foundations could have been also based on another model such as Petri nets. In this case, the protocol operators would have to be ported to this formalism to be able to perform compatibility and replaceability analysis. In fact, timed protocols can be viewed as a syntactic variant of timed automata. In this paper we have also significantly extended our initial work on service protocols [17] by proposing: (i) a model for service business protocols that supports rich timing constraints, (ii) a set of fine-grained protocol compatibility and replaceability classes, and (iii) a set of operators with formal foundations that can be combined for performing those types of analysis. The results we have achieved is a framework and a tool that can support development and binding of services with timing properties. We believe that this is a significant contribution as the number of available services increases and as the need of automated support for service lifecycle management becomes a necessity. Interestingly, this work has also lead to the discovery of an innovative class of timed automata. In future work, we aim at extending the approach for analyzing web services compositions in presence of timing abstractions.

References

1. Alonso, G., Casati, F., Kuno, H., Machiraju, V.: Web Services: Concepts, Architectures, and Applications. Springer, Heidelberg (2004)
2. Benatallah, B., Casati, F., Toumani, F.: Web services conversation modeling: The Cornerstone for E-Business Automation. IEEE Internet Computing 8(1) (January 2004)
3. Bultan, T., Fu, X., Hull, R., Su, J.: Conversation specification: a new approach to design and analysis of e-service composition. In: WWW 2003, pp. 403–410. ACM Press, New York (2003)
4. Toumani, F., Benatallah, B., Casati, F.: Analysis and Management of Web Services Protocols. ER 2004 (2004)
5. Benatallah, B., Casati, F., Toumani, F., Ponge, J., Nezhad, H.R.M.: Service mosaic: A model-driven framework for web services life-cycle management. IEEE Internet Computing 10(4), 55–63 (2006)
6. Alur, R., Madhusudan, P.: Decision problems for timed automata: A survey. In: 4th Intl. School on Formal Methods for Computer, Communication, and Software Systems (2004)
7. Alur, R., Dill, D.L.: A theory of timed automata. Theoretical Computer Science 126, 183–235 (1994)
8. Ponge, J., Benatallah, B., Casati, F., Toumani, F.: Fine-grained Compatibility and Replaceability Analysis of Timed Web Service Protocols (extended version) (2007), http://www.isima.fr/~ponge/publications/tr/er07-extended.pdf
9. Berard, B., Diekert, V., Gastin, P., Petit, A.: Characterization of the expressive power of silent transitions in timed automata. Technical report, LIAFA Jussieu (1999)
10. Diekert, V., Gastin, P., Petit, A.: Removing ε-transitions in timed automata. In: Reischuk, R., Morvan, M. (eds.) STACS 1997. LNCS, vol. 1200, Springer, Heidelberg (1997)
11. Benatallah, B., Casati, F., Grigori, D., Nezhad, H.R.M., Toumani, F.: Developing Adapters for Web Services Integration. In: Pastor, Ó., Falcão e Cunha, J. (eds.) CAiSE 2005. LNCS, vol. 3520, Springer, Heidelberg (2005)
12. Bordeaux, L., Salaun, G., Berardi, D., Marcella, M.: When are two Web Services Compatible? In: VLDB TES'04, Toronto, Canada (2004)
13. Beyer, D., Chakrabarti, A., Henzinger, T.A.: Web service interfaces. In: WWW 2005, pp. 148–159. ACM Press, New York (2005)
14. Yellin, D., Storm, R.: Protocol Specifications and Component Adaptors. ACM Trans. Program. Lang. Syst. 19(2), 292–333 (1997)
15. Canal, C., Fuentes, L., Pimentel, E., Troya, J.M., Vallecillo, A.: Adding roles to corba objects. IEEE Trans. Softw. Eng. 29(3), 242–260 (2003)
16. Nezhad, H.R.M., Benatallah, B., Casati, F., Toumani, F.: Web services interoperability specifications. Computer 39(5), 24–32 (2006)
17. Benatallah, B., Casati, F., Ponge, J., Toumani, F.: Compatibility and replaceability analysis for timed web service protocols. In: BDA (October 2005)

Author Index

Lecture Notes in Computer Science

Sublibrary 3: Information Systems and Application, incl. Internet/Web and HCI

For information about Vols. 1– 4328
please contact your bookseller or Springer